PostScript® Language Reference Manual

SECOND EDITION

Adobe Systems Incorporated

Addison-Wesley Publishing Company

Reading, Massachusetts • Menlo Park, California • New York
Don Mills, Ontario • Wokingham, England • Amsterdam
Bonn • Sydney • Singapore • Tokyo • Madrid • San Juan
Paris • Seoul • Milan • Mexico City • Taipei

Library of Congress Cataloging-in-Publication Data

PostScript language reference manual / Adobe Systems. — 2nd ed.
    p.   cm.
Includes index.
ISBN 0-201-18127-4
1. PostScript (Computer program language) I. Adobe Systems.
QA76.73.P67P67 1990
005.13'3—dc20   90-43535

8 9 10 11 12–AL–96959493
Eighth printing, July 1993

Contents

Preface

It has been only five years since the first *PostScript Language Reference Manual* was published and the first products based on the PostScript language were introduced. In 1985, we had no reason to anticipate the far-reaching effects that the PostScript language would have on the printing and publishing industry. At that time, there were no effective page-description standards, popular typefaces were used only with specific typesetting equipment, producing high-quality visual materials was restricted to specialists, and the cost of producing most corporate communication pieces was prohibitive.

In its brief history, the PostScript language and the many corporations and individuals working with PostScript products have changed all that. Today all major computer, printer, and imagesetter vendors support the PostScript language as a standard. The major type libraries are becoming available in PostScript-compatible formats. The cost of producing high-quality, printed material has dropped substantially. As a result, the PostScript language is becoming a part of the basic fabric of the printing, publishing, and computing industries.

We at Adobe not only take great pride in this success, but more importantly, we feel a significant responsibility to those who have placed their trust in us and in this technology. We are committed to enhancing the PostScript language standard so that we can continue to earn that trust.

In developing this language, we have tried to remember that PostScript is only one advancement in the rich 500-year history of printing and typography. We are constantly sensitive to the fact that we are working with a delicate combination of art, tradition, and technology. Not only must the technological effectiveness of the PostScript language be improved, but our aspiration to provide the highest-quality printed results must be preserved and enhanced in each implementation of a PostScript product.

Any standard, if it is to continue to serve the community in the face of technological change, must grow and adapt; the PostScript language is no exception. We hope that you, the users, will find that this second edition of the *PostScript Language Reference Manual* incorporates many of the ideas you have given us. We have tried to use good taste, sound judgment, and some restraint in extending an already effective and useful standard.

None of the success of the PostScript language would be possible without the efforts of the many individuals and corporations that have supported PostScript. Successful standards are never the result of one individual or group. We take this opportunity to thank all of the organizations and individuals who have lent their support in the past, and hope we can continue working together to enjoy the benefits of an effective standard for communicating visual information.

John Warnock & Chuck Geschke
December 1990

CHAPTER 1

Introduction

The PostScript® language is a simple interpretive programming language with powerful graphics capabilities. Its primary application is to describe the appearance of text, graphical shapes, and sampled images on printed or displayed pages. A program in this language can communicate a description of a document from a composition system to a printing system or control the appearance of text and graphics on a display. The description is high level and device independent.

The page description and interactive graphics capabilities of the PostScript language include the following features, which can be used in any combination:

- Arbitrary shapes made of straight lines, arcs, rectangles, and cubic curves. Such shapes may self-intersect and have disconnected sections and holes.

- Painting operators that permit a shape to be outlined with lines of any thickness, filled with any color, or used as a clipping path to crop any other graphic. Colors can be specified in a variety of ways: gray-level, RGB, CMYK, and CIE based. Certain other features are also modelled as special kinds of colors: repeating patterns, color mapping, and separations.

- Text fully integrated with graphics. In the PostScript language's graphics model, text characters in both standard and user-defined fonts are treated as graphical shapes that may be operated on by any of the normal graphics operators.

- Sampled images derived from natural sources (such as scanned photographs) or generated synthetically. The PostScript language can describe images sampled at any resolution and according to a variety of color models. It provides a number of ways to reproduce images on an output device.

- A general coordinate system that supports all combinations of linear transformations, including translation, scaling, rotation, reflection, and skewing. These transformations apply uniformly to all elements of a page, including text, graphical shapes, and sampled images.

A PostScript language page description can be rendered on a printer, display, or other output device by presenting it to a PostScript interpreter controlling that device. As the interpreter executes commands to paint characters, graphical shapes, and sampled images, it converts the high-level PostScript language description into the low-level raster data format for that particular device.

Normally, application programs such as document composition systems, illustrators, and computer-aided design systems generate Post-Script language page descriptions automatically. Programmers generally write PostScript language programs only when creating new applications. However, in special situations a programmer can write PostScript language programs to take advantage of capabilities of the PostScript language that are not accessible through an application program.

The extensive graphical capabilities of the PostScript language are embedded in the framework of a general-purpose programming language. The language includes a conventional set of data types, such as numbers, arrays, and strings; control primitives, such as conditionals, loops, and procedures; and some unusual features, such as dictionaries. These features enable application programmers to define higher-level operations that closely match the needs of the application and then to generate commands that invoke those higher-level operations. Such a description is more compact and easier to generate than one written entirely in terms of a fixed set of basic operations.

PostScript language programs can be created, transmitted, and interpreted in the form of ASCII source text as defined in this manual. The entire language can be described in terms of printable characters and white space. This representation is convenient for programmers to create, manipulate, and understand. It also facilitates storage and transmission of files among diverse computers and operating systems, enhancing machine independence.

There are also binary encoded forms of the language for use in suitably controlled environments—for example, when the program is assured of a fully transparent communications path such as in the Display Post-Script® system. Adobe recommends strict adherence to the ASCII representation of PostScript language programs for document interchange or archival storage.

1.1 About This Manual

This is the programmer's reference manual for the PostScript language. It is the definitive documentation for the syntax and semantics of the language, the imaging model, and the effects of the graphical operators. Here is what the manual contains:

Chapter 2, "Basic Ideas," is an informal presentation of some basic ideas underlying the more formal descriptions and definitions in the manual. These include the properties and capabilities of raster output devices, requirements for a language that effectively uses those capabilities, and some pragmatic information about the environments in which the PostScript interpreter operates and the kinds of PostScript language programs it typically executes.

Chapter 3, "Language," introduces the fundamentals of the PostScript language: its syntax, semantics, data types, execution model, and interactions with application programs. This chapter concentrates on the conventional programming aspects of the language, ignoring its graphical capabilities and use as a page-description language.

Chapter 4, "Graphics," introduces the PostScript language imaging model at a device-independent level. It describes how to define and manipulate graphical entities—lines, curves, filled areas, sampled images, and higher-level structures such as patterns and forms. It includes complete information on the color models that the PostScript language supports. Finally, it describes how a page description communicates its document processing requirements to the output device.

Chapter 5, "Fonts," describes how the PostScript language deals with text. Characters are defined as graphical shapes, whose behavior conforms to the graphical model presented in Chapter 4. Because of the importance of text in most applications, the PostScript language provides special capabilities for organizing sets of characters as fonts and for painting characters efficiently.

Chapter 6, "Rendering," details the device-dependent aspects of rendering PostScript language page descriptions on printers and displays. These include color rendering, transfer functions, halftoning, and scan conversion, each of which is device dependent in some way.

Chapter 7, "Display PostScript," explains the concepts and PostScript language operators specific to interactive display applications.

Chapter 8, "Operators," describes all PostScript language operators and procedures. The chapter begins by categorizing operators into functional groups. Then the operators appear in alphabetical order, with complete descriptions of their operands, results, side effects, and possible errors.

The manual concludes with several appendices containing useful information that is not a formal part of the PostScript language.

Appendix A, "Changes to Language and Implementation," lists the changes that have been made to the PostScript language since the first edition of this manual.

Appendix B, "Implementation Limits," describes typical limits imposed by implementations of the PostScript interpreter—for example, maximum integer value and maximum stack depth.

Appendix C, "Interpreter Parameters," specifies various parameters to control the operation and behavior of the PostScript interpreter. Most of these parameters have to do with allocation of memory and other resources for specific purposes.

Appendix D, "Compatibility Strategies," helps PostScript language programmers take advantage of PostScript Level 2 features while maintaining compatibility with the installed base of Level 1 interpreter products.

Appendix E, "Standard Character Sets and Encoding Vectors," describes the organization of most common fonts that are built into interpreters or are available as separate software products.

Appendix F, "System Name Encodings," assigns numeric codes to standard names, for use in binary-encoded PostScript language programs.

Appendix G, "Document Structuring Conventions—Version 3.0," describes a convention for structuring PostScript language page descriptions to facilitate their handling and processing by other programs.

Appendix H, "Encapsulated PostScript File Format—Version 3.0," describes a format that enables applications to treat each others' output as included illustrations.

Appendix I, "Guidelines for Specific Operators," provides guidelines for PostScript language operators whose use can cause unintended side effects, make a document device dependent, or inhibit post-processing of a document by other programs.

"Bibliography" is a list of sources for many of the concepts in the Post-Script language.

Since this is a reference manual and not a tutorial, it provides relatively few guidelines on how to use the PostScript language effectively. As with any programming language, certain techniques yield the best solutions to particular programming problems; there are issues of style that influence the performance, quality, and consistency of the results. These matters are the main topics of two companion books.

- *PostScript Language Tutorial and Cookbook* introduces the PostScript language at a basic level. It includes a large number of techniques and recipes for obtaining results from the mundane to the exotic. This book emphasizes examples, not efficient programming strategies, to illustrate in a clear way many of the capabilities of the Post-Script language.

- *PostScript Language Program Design* is for programmers interested in the effective and efficient design of PostScript language programs and printer drivers. It includes many programming examples that are recommended for direct use in applications.

An additional book, *Adobe Type 1 Font Format*, specifies the internal organization of a Type 1 font program. That specification is logically part of the PostScript language, but it is published separately because it is highly specialized and is of interest to a different user community.

A great deal of additional technical documentation is available through the Adobe Systems Developers' Association. Registered software developers receive regular mailings of technical papers, telephone support, and discounts on PostScript hardware and software products. For information about the Developers' Association, please write to this address:

PostScript Developer Support
Adobe Systems Incorporated
1585 Charleston Road
P.O. Box 7900
Mountain View, CA 94039-7900

1.2 Evolution of the PostScript Language

Since its introduction in 1985, the PostScript language has been considerably extended for greater programming power, efficiency, and flexibility. Typically, these language extensions have been designed to adapt the PostScript language to new imaging technologies or system environments. While these extensions have introduced significant new functionality and flexibility to the language, the basic imaging model remains unchanged. The principal extensions are:

- *Color.* The color extensions provide a cyan-magenta-yellow-black (CMYK) color model for specifying colors and a **colorimage** operator for painting color sampled images. They also include additional rendering controls for color output devices.

- *Composite fonts.* The composite font extensions enhance the basic font facility to support character sets that are very large or have complex requirements for encoding or character positioning.

- *Display PostScript.* The Display PostScript system enables workstation applications to use the PostScript language and imaging model for managing the appearance of the display. Some of the extensions are specialized to interactive display applications, such as concurrent execution and support for windowing systems. Other extensions are more general and are intended to improve performance or programming convenience.

In addition to the language extensions above, there have been other minor additions to the language, such as file system extensions to support products that include disks or cartridges. See Appendix A for complete details.

This manual documents the entire PostScript language, which consists of three distinct groups of operators: Level 1, Level 2, and Display PostScript operators. Level 1 operators are the ones documented in the first edition of the *PostScript Language Reference Manual*. Level 2 operators include all operators from the language extensions described above and new operators introduced into the language for PostScript Level 2. Display PostScript operators are those operators present only in Display PostScript systems. Chapter 8 clearly identifies Level 2 and Display PostScript operators with the following icons:

> LEVEL 2   Level 2 operator

> DPS   Display PostScript operator

While the Postscript language is a well-defined standard, not all Post-Script interpreters include all language features. Products that contain PostScript software from Adobe Systems can be categorized as follows:

- Level 1 implementations include all Level 1 operators. Some Level 1 implementations include one or more language extensions. For example, PostScript color printers support Level 1 operators plus the color extensions.

- Level 2 implementations include *all* Level 1 and Level 2 operators.

- Display PostScript systems include the Display PostScript operators and can be based on either Level 1 or Level 2 implementations. Display PostScript systems based on Level 1 include the Display Post-Script and color extensions mentioned above and sometimes other extensions as well. Display PostScript systems based on Level 2 include all Level 2 operators.

Appendix D describes strategies for writing PostScript language programs that can run compatibly on interpreters based on either Level 1 or Level 2 implementations of the language.

1.3 PostScript Level 2 Overview

In addition to unifying all previous language extensions, PostScript Level 2 introduces a number of new language features. This section summarizes both new language features and ones from previous language extensions, which are now part of PostScript Level 2.

- *Dictionaries*. Many Level 2 operators expect a dictionary operand that contains key-value pairs specifying parameters to the operator. Language features controlled in this way include halftones, images, forms, patterns, and device setup. This organization allows for optional parameters and future extensibility. For convenience in using such operators, the PostScript language syntax includes new tokens, << and >>, to construct a dictionary containing the bracketed key-value pairs.

- *Memory management*. It is now possible to remove individual entries from dictionaries and to remove font definitions in an order unrelated to the order in which they were created. Virtual memory (VM) is reclaimed automatically for composite objects that are no longer accessible. In general, memory is more efficiently shared among different uses and arbitrary memory restrictions have been eliminated

- *Resources.* A resource is a collection of named objects that either reside in VM or can be located and brought into VM on demand. There are separate categories of resources with independent name spaces—for example, fonts and forms are distinct resource categories. The language includes convenient facilities for locating and managing resources.

- *Filters.* A filter transforms data as it is being read from or written to a file. The language supports filters for ASCII encoding of binary data, compression and decompression, and embedded subfiles. Properly used, these filters reduce the storage and transmission costs of page descriptions, especially ones containing sampled images.

- *Binary encoding.* In addition to the standard ASCII encoding, the language syntax includes two binary-encoded representations. These binary encodings improve efficiency of generation, representation, and interpretation. However, they are less portable than the ASCII encoding and are suitable for use only in controlled environments.

- *User paths.* A user path is a self-contained procedure that consists entirely of path construction operators and their coordinate operands. User path operators perform path construction and painting as a single operation; this is both convenient and efficient. There is a user path cache to optimize interpretation of user paths that are invoked repeatedly. There are also some convenience operators for painting rectangles.

- *Forms.* A form is a self-contained description of any arbitrary graphics, text, and sampled images that are to be painted multiple times—on each of several pages or several times at different locations on a single page. There is a form cache to optimize repeated uses of the same form.

- *Color spaces.* Colors can be specified according to a variety of color systems, including gray-scale, RGB, CMYK, and CIE based. Patterns, color mapping, and separations are also modelled as color spaces. The color space is now an explicit parameter of the graphics state.

- *CIE-based color spaces.* The language supports several device-independent color spaces based on the CIE 1931 (XYZ)-space, a system for specifying color values in a way that is related to human visual perception. A given CIE-based color specification can be expected to produce consistent results on different color output devices, independent of variations in marking technology, ink colorants, or screen phosphors.

- *Patterns*. It is possible to paint with patterns as well as with solid colors. When the current color is a pattern, painting operators apply "paint" that is produced by replicating (or tiling) a small graphical figure, called a pattern cell, at fixed intervals in x and y to cover the areas being painted. The appearance of a pattern cell is defined by an arbitrary PostScript language procedure, which can include graphics, text, and sampled images. There is a pattern cache to optimize repeated uses of the same pattern.

- *Images*. There are several enhancements to the facilities for painting sampled images: use of any color space, 12-bit component values, direct use of files as data sources, and additional decoding and rendering options.

- *Other text and graphics operators*. There are several other new operators optimized for performance. Graphics state objects allow fast switching among arbitrary graphics states. Automatic stroke adjustment efficiently compensates for rasterization effects to produce strokes of uniform thickness when rendering thin lines at low resolutions. New variants of **show** provide a natural way for applications to deal with individual character positioning and enable simultaneous pair kerning, track kerning, and justification. The **selectfont** operator optimizes switching among fonts.

- *Device setup*. The **setpagedevice** operator provides a device-independent framework for specifying the requirements of a page description and for controlling both standard features, such as the number of copies, and optional features of a device, such as duplex printing.

- *Interpreter parameters*. Administrative operations, such as system configuration and changing input-output device parameters, are now organized in a more systematic way. Allocation of memory and other resources for specific purposes is under software control. For example, there are parameters controlling the maximum amount of memory to be used for VM, font cache, form cache, pattern cache, and halftone screens.

1.4 Copyrights and Trademarks

The general *idea* of utilizing a page-description language is in the public domain. Anyone is free to devise his own set of unique commands that constitute a page-description language. However, Adobe Systems Incorporated owns the copyright in the list of operators and the written specification for Adobe's PostScript language. Thus, these elements of the

PostScript language may not be copied without Adobe's permission. Additionally, Adobe owns the trademark "PostScript," which is used to identify both the PostScript language and Adobe's PostScript software.

Adobe will enforce its copyright and trademark rights. Adobe's intentions are to:

- Maintain the integrity of the PostScript language standard. This enables the public to distinguish between the PostScript language and other page-description languages.

- Maintain the integrity of "PostScript" as a trademark. This enables the public to distinguish between Adobe's PostScript interpreter and other interpreters that can execute PostScript language programs.

However, Adobe desires to promote use of the PostScript language for information interchange among diverse products and applications. Accordingly, Adobe gives permission to anyone to:

- Write programs in the PostScript language.

- Write drivers to generate output consisting of PostScript language commands.

- Write software to interpret programs written in the PostScript language.

- Copy Adobe's copyrighted list of commands to the extent necessary to use the PostScript language for the above purposes.

The only condition of such permission is that anyone who uses the copyrighted list of commands in this way must include an appropriate copyright notice.

This limited right to use the copyrighted list of commands does not include a right to copy the *PostScript Language Reference Manual*, other copyrighted publications from Adobe, or the software in Adobe's PostScript interpreter, in whole or in part. The trademark "PostScript" may not be used to identify any product not originating from or licensed by Adobe.

CHAPTER 2

Basic Ideas

To obtain a complete understanding of the PostScript language, one must consider it from several points of view:

- As a general-purpose programming language with powerful built-in graphics primitives.

- As a page-description language that includes programming features.

- As an interactive system for controlling raster output devices (displays and printers).

- As an interchange format.

This chapter contains some basic ideas that are essential to understanding the problems the PostScript language is designed to solve and the environments in which it is designed to operate. Terminology introduced here appears throughout the manual.

2.1 Raster Output Devices

Much of the power of the PostScript language derives from its ability to deal with the general class of *raster output devices*. This class encompasses such technology as laser, dot-matrix, and ink-jet printers, digital phototypesetters, and raster scan displays.

The defining property of a raster output device is that a printed or displayed image consists of a rectangular array of dots, called *pixels* (picture elements), that can be addressed individually. On a typical black and white output device, each pixel can be made either black or white. On certain devices, each pixel can be set to an intermediate shade of gray or to some color. By individually setting the colors of many pixels, one can generate printed or displayed output that includes text, arbitrary graphical shapes, and reproductions of sampled images.

The *resolution* of a raster output device is a measure of the number of pixels per unit of distance along the two linear dimensions. Resolution is typically—but not necessarily—the same horizontally and vertically.

Manufacturers' decisions on device technology and price/performance trade-offs create characteristic ranges of resolution:

- Displays in computer terminals have relatively low resolution, typically 50 to 110 pixels per inch.

- Dot-matrix printers generally range from 100 to 250 pixels per inch.

- Laser scanning coupled to xerographic printing technology is capable of medium resolution output of 300 to 600 pixels per inch.

- Photographic technology permits high resolutions of 1,000 pixels per inch or more.

Higher resolution yields better quality and fidelity of the resulting output, but is achieved at greater cost.

2.2   Scan Conversion

An abstract graphical entity (for example, a line, a circle, a text character, or a sampled image) is rendered on a raster output device by a process known as *scan conversion*. Given a PostScript language description of the graphical entity, this process determines which pixels to adjust and what values to assign those pixels to achieve the most faithful rendition possible at the device resolution.

The pixels on the page can be represented by a two-dimensional array of pixel values in computer memory. For an output device whose pixels can be only black or white, a single bit suffices to represent each pixel. For a device whose pixels can reproduce gray shades or colors, multiple bits per pixel are required.

Note   *Although the ultimate representation of a printed or displayed page is logically a complete array of pixels, its actual representation in computer memory need not consist of one memory cell per pixel. Some implementations use other representations, such as display lists. The PostScript language's imaging model has been carefully designed so as not to depend on any particular representation of raster memory.*

For each graphical entity that is to appear on the page, the scan converter sets the values of the corresponding pixels. When the interpretation of the page description is complete, the pixel values in memory represent the appearance of the page. At this point, a raster output process can make this representation visible on a printed page or a display.

Scan converting a graphical shape, such as a rectangle or a circle, involves determining which device pixels lie "inside" the shape and setting their values appropriately (for example, by setting them to black). Because the edges of a shape do not always fall precisely on the boundaries between pixels, some policy is required for deciding which pixels along the edges are considered to be "inside." Scan converting a text character is conceptually the same as scan converting an arbitrary graphical shape; however, characters are much more sensitive to legibility requirements, and must meet more rigid objective and subjective measures of quality.

Rendering gray-scale images on a device whose pixels can be only black or white is accomplished by a technique known as *halftoning*. The array of pixels is divided into small clusters according to some pattern (called the *halftone screen*). Within each cluster, some pixels are set to black and some to white in proportion to the level of gray desired at that point in the image. When viewed from a sufficient distance, the individual dots become unnoticeable and the result is a shade of gray. This enables a black-and-white raster output device to reproduce shades of gray and to approximate natural images, such as photographs. Some color devices use a similar technique.

2.3 Page-Description Languages

Theoretically, an application program could describe any page as a full-page pixel array. But this would be unsatisfactory because the description would be bulky, the pixel array would be device dependent, and memory requirements would be beyond the capacity of many personal computers.

A page-description language should produce files that are relatively compact for storage and transmission, and independent of any one output device.

2.3.1 Levels of Description

In today's computer printing industry, raster output devices with different properties are proliferating, as are the applications that generate output for those devices. Meanwhile, expectations are also rising; typewriter emulation (text-only output in a single typeface) is no longer adequate. Users want to create, display, and print documents that combine sophisticated typography and graphics.

A high-level, device-independent page-description language that can take advantage of the capabilities of different output devices answers the need for high-quality output on many different printers and displays. Ideally, such a language should be able to describe the appearance of pages containing text and graphics in terms of high-level, abstract graphical entities rather than in terms of device pixels. Such a description is economical and *device independent*.

Producing printed output from an application program then becomes a two-stage process:

1. The application generates a device-independent description of the desired output in the page-description language.

2. A program controlling a specific raster output device interprets the description and renders it on that device.

The two stages may be executed in different places and at different times; the page-description language serves as an *interchange standard* for transmission and storage of printable or displayable documents.

2.3.2 Static versus Dynamic Formats

Today's page-description languages may be considered on the basis of their *intrinsic* capabilities and on whether they are *static* or *dynamic*. Intrinsic capabilities include the built-in operations of the language, such as the ability to deal with various sorts of text and graphics. Also, the degree to which the built-in operations interact harmoniously is important. A page-description language that treats text, graphical shapes, and sampled images consistently facilitates applications that must combine elements of all three on a single page.

- A *static format* provides some fixed set of operations (sometimes called "control codes") and a syntax for specifying the operations and their arguments. Static formats have been in existence since computers first used printers; classic examples are format control codes for line printers and "format effector" codes in standard character sets. Historically, static formats have been designed to capture the capabilities of a specific class of printing device and have evolved to include new features as needed.

- A *dynamic format* allows much more flexibility than a static format. The operator set may be extensible and the exact meaning of an operator may not be known until it is actually encountered. A page described in a dynamic format is a program to be executed rather than data to be consumed. Dynamic page-description languages contain elements of programming languages, such as procedures, variables, and control constructs.

A print or display format that is primarily static but that purports to cover a lot of graphic and text capabilities tends to have many special-purpose operators. A dynamic format that allows primitive operations to be combined according to the needs of the application will always be superior to a static format that tries to anticipate all possible needs.

The PostScript language design is dynamic. The language includes a set of primitive graphic operators that can be combined to describe the appearance of any printed or displayed page. It has variables and allows arbitrary computations while interpreting the page description. It has a rich set of programming language control structures for combining its elements.

For very complicated page layouts, there may be times when a page description must depend on information about the specific output device in use. This information may be known only when the page description is executed, not when it is composed. It is essential for a page description to be able to read information from its execution environment and to perform arbitrary computations based on that information while generating the desired output.

These considerations have led to the design of the PostScript language, a dynamic format whose page descriptions are programs to be executed by an interpreter. PostScript language programs can be simplified to a form that resembles a static format—in other words, an uninterrupted sequence of basic commands to image text or graphics. Page descriptions generated by applications with simple needs will often have this simple nature. However, when the need arises, the power is there for the knowledgeable application designer to exploit.

2.4   Using the PostScript Language

It is important to understand the PostScript interpreter and how it interacts with applications using it.

A *page description* is a self-contained PostScript language description of a document, which is generated at one time for execution at some arbitrarily later time. To facilitate document interchange, a page description should conform to the structuring conventions discussed below.

An *interactive session* is a two-way interaction between an application program and a PostScript interpreter. There is no notion that the information being communicated represents a document to be preserved for later execution. A session has no obvious overall structure; the structuring conventions do not apply.

2.4.1   The Interpreter

The PostScript *interpreter* controls the actions of the output device according to the instructions provided in the PostScript program generated by an application.

The interpreter executes the page description and produces output on a printer, display, or other raster device. The PostScript interpreter and the output device are bundled together and treated essentially as a black box by the application; the interpreter has little or no direct interaction with the application's end user.

There are three ways the PostScript interpreter and the application interact (Figure 2.1 on page 17 illustrates these scenarios):

- In the traditional PostScript printer model, the application creates a page description. The page description can be sent to the PostScript interpreter immediately or stored for transmission at some other time. The interpreter consumes a sequence of page descriptions as "print jobs" and produces the requested output. The output device is typically a printer, but it can be a preview window on a workstation's display. The PostScript interpreter is often implemented on a dedicated processor that has direct control over the raster output device.

- In the display model, an application interacts with the PostScript interpreter controlling a display or windowing system. The interaction consists of a *session* instead of a one-way transmission of a page description. In response to user actions, the application issues commands to the PostScript interpreter and sometimes reads information back from it. This form of interaction is supported by the Display PostScript system, described in Chapter 7.

- In the interactive programming language model, a programmer interacts with the PostScript interpreter directly, issuing PostScript language commands for immediate execution. Many PostScript interpreters (for both printers and displays) have a rudimentary interactive executive to support this mode of use; see section 2.4.4, "Using the Interpreter Interactively."

Figure 2.1 *How the PostScript interpreter and an application interact*

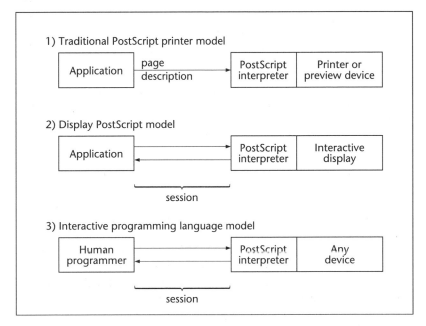

Even when a PostScript interpreter is being used non-interactively to execute page descriptions prepared previously, there may be some dynamic interactions between the print manager or spooler and the PostScript interpreter. For example, the sender may ask the PostScript interpreter if certain fonts referenced by a document are available. This is accomplished by sending the interpreter a short program to read and return the information. The PostScript interpreter makes no distinction between a page description and a program that makes environmental queries or performs other arbitrary computations. To ensure consistent and reliable behavior in a variety of system environments, queries should conform to the conventions described in Appendix G.

2.4.2 Program Structure

A well-structured PostScript language page description generally consists of two parts: a prolog followed by a script. There is nothing in the PostScript language that formally distinguishes the prolog from the script or imposes any overall document structure. Such structuring is merely a convention, but one that is quite useful and is recommended for most applications.

- The *prolog* is a set of application-specific procedure definitions that an application may use in the execution of its script. It is included as the first part of every PostScript language file generated by the application. It contains definitions that match the output functions of the application with the capabilities supported by the PostScript language.

- The *script* is generated automatically by the application program to describe the specific elements of the pages being produced. It consists of references to PostScript operators and to procedure definitions in the prolog, together with operands and data. The script, unlike the prolog, is usually very stylized, repetitive, and simple.

Dividing a PostScript language program into a prolog and a script reduces the size of each page description and minimizes data communication and disk storage. An example may help explain the purpose of a separate prolog and script. One of the most common tasks in a PostScript language program is placing text at a particular location on the current page. This is really *two* operations: "moving" the current point to a specific location and "showing" the text. A program is likely to do this often, so it's useful for the prolog to define a procedure that combines the operations:

```
/ms {moveto show} bind def
```

Later, the script can call the "ms" procedure instead of restating the individual operations:

```
(some text) 100 200 ms
```

The script portion of a printable document ordinarily consists of a sequence of separate pages. The description of an individual page should stand by itself, depending only on the definitions in the prolog and not on anything in previous pages of the script. The language includes facilities (described in section 3.7, "Memory Management") that may be used to guarantee page independence.

Adobe has established conventions to make document structure explicit. These document structuring conventions appear in Appendix G. Document structure is expressed as PostScript language comments; the interpreter pays no attention to them. However, there are good reasons to adhere to the conventions:

- Utility programs can operate on structured documents in various ways: change the order of pages, extract subsets of pages, embed individual pages within other pages, and so on.

- Print managers and spoolers can obtain useful information from a properly structured document to determine how the document should be handled.

- The structuring conventions serve as a good basis for organizing printing from an application.

An application has its own model of the appearance of printable output that it generates. Some parts of this model are fixed for an entire document or for all documents; the application should incorporate their descriptions into the prolog. Other parts vary from one page to another; the application should produce the necessary descriptions of these as they appear. At page boundaries, the application should generate commands to restore the standard environment defined by the prolog and then explicitly re-establish non-standard portions of the environment for the next page. This technique ensures that each page is independent of any other.

2.4.3 Translating From Other Print Formats

Many existing applications generate printable documents in some other print file format or in some intermediate representation. It is possible to print such documents by translating them into PostScript language page descriptions. For example, Adobe's TranScript® software package translates documents from a number of widely-used representations in the UNIX® environment into the PostScript language.

Implementing a translator is often the least expensive way to interface an existing application to a PostScript printer. Unfortunately, while such translation is usually straightforward, a translator may not be able to generate page descriptions that make the best use of the descriptive capabilities of the PostScript language. This is because the print file being translated often describes the desired results at a level that is too low; any higher-level information maintained by the original application has been lost and is not available to the translator.

While direct PostScript language output from applications is most desirable, translation from another print format may be the only choice available for some applications. A translator should do the best it can to produce output that conforms to the document structuring conventions (see Appendix G). This ensures that such output is compatible with the tools for manipulating PostScript page descriptions.

Once again, these guidelines for program structure are not part of the PostScript language and are not enforced by the PostScript interpreter. In some cases, a program may require an organization that is incompatible with the structuring conventions; this is most likely to be true of programs composed directly by a programmer. However, for page descriptions generated automatically by applications, adherence to the structuring conventions is strongly recommended.

2.4.4 Using the Interpreter Interactively

Normally, the interpreter executes PostScript language programs generated by application programs; a user does not interact with the PostScript interpreter directly. However, many PostScript interpreters provide an *interactive executive* that enables a user to control the interpreter directly. That is, from a terminal or terminal emulator connected directly to the PostScript interpreter, you can issue commands for immediate execution and control the operation of the interpreter in limited ways. This is useful for experimentation and debugging.

To use the interpreter this way, you must first connect your terminal directly to the standard input and output channels of the PostScript interpreter, so characters that you type are sent directly to the interpreter and characters that the interpreter sends appear on your terminal's screen. How to accomplish this depends on the product. A typical method is to connect an ordinary character terminal (or personal computer running terminal emulation software) to a PostScript printer via the printer's serial connector.

Then, invoke the interactive executive by typing:

    executive

(all lower case) followed by the return or line-feed key. The interpreter responds with a herald, such as:

PostScript(r) Version 2001.3
Copyright (c) 1984-1990 Adobe Systems Incorporated.
All Rights Reserved.
PS>

The PS> prompt is an indication that the PostScript interpreter is waiting for you to issue a command.

Each time you type a complete PostScript language statement followed by return or line-feed, the interpreter executes that statement, then sends another PS> prompt. If the statement causes the interpreter to send back any output (produced by execution of the **print** or = operators, for example), that output appears before the PS> prompt. If the statement causes an error to occur, an error message appears before the PS> prompt; control remains in the interactive executive whereas errors normally cause a job to terminate.

The interactive executive provides a few simple amenities. While you are typing, the interpreter ordinarily "echoes" the typed characters—it sends them back to your terminal so you can see them. You can use the control characters in Table 2.1 to make corrections while entering a statement.

Table 2.1 *Control characters for the interactive executive*

Character	Function
Backspace (BS)	Backs up and erases one character.
Delete (DEL)	Same as backspace.
Control-U	Erases the current line.
Control-R	Redisplays the current line.
Control-C	Aborts the entire statement and starts over. Control-C can also abort a statement that is executing and force the executive to revert to a PS> prompt.

The interactive executive remains in operation until you invoke the **quit** operator or enter a channel-dependent end-of-file indication (for example, Control-D for a serial connection).

There are several important things you should understand about the interactive executive:

- It is intended solely for direct interaction with the user; an application that is generating PostScript language programs should never invoke **executive**. In general, a program behaves differently when sent through the interactive executive than when executed directly by the PostScript interpreter. For example, the executive produces extraneous output such as echoes of the input characters and PS> prompts. Furthermore, a program that explicitly reads data embedded in the program file malfunctions if invoked via the executive, since the executive itself is interpreting the file.

- The user amenities are intentionally minimal. The executive is not a full-scale programming environment; it lacks a text editor and other tools required for program development and it does not keep a record of your interactive session. The executive is useful mainly for experimenting and debugging.

- **executive** is not necessarily available in all PostScript interpreters. Its behavior may vary among different products.

CHAPTER 3

Language

Syntax, data types, and execution semantics are essential aspects of any PostScript language program. Later chapters document the graphics and font capabilities that specialize PostScript language software to the task of controlling the appearance of a printed page or controlling an interactive session on the screen. This chapter is concerned with explaining the PostScript language as a *programming* language.

As with all programming languages, the PostScript language builds on elements and ideas from several of the great programming languages. The syntax most closely resembles that of the programming language FORTH. It incorporates a *postfix* notation in which operators are preceded by their operands. The number of special characters is small and there are no reserved words.

Note   *Although the number of built-in operators is large, the names that represent operators are not reserved by the language. A PostScript language program may change the meanings of operator names.*

The data model includes elements, such as numbers, strings, and arrays, that are found in many modern programming languages. It also includes the ability to treat programs as data and to monitor and control many aspects of the language's execution state; these notions are derived from programming languages such as LISP.

PostScript is a relatively simple language. It derives its power from the ability to combine these features in unlimited ways without arbitrary restrictions. Though you may seldom fully exploit this power, you can design sophisticated graphical applications that would otherwise be difficult or impossible.

Because this is a reference manual and not a tutorial, this chapter describes each aspect of the language systematically and thoroughly before moving on to the next. It begins with a brief overview of the

PostScript interpreter. The following sections detail the syntax, data types, execution semantics, memory organization, and general-purpose operators of the PostScript language—excluding those that deal with graphics and fonts. The final sections cover file input and output, named resources, errors, how the interpreter evaluates name objects, and details on binary encodings and filtered files.

3.1 Interpreter

The PostScript interpreter executes the PostScript language according to the rules in this chapter. These rules determine the order in which operations are carried out and how the pieces of a PostScript language program fit together to produce the desired results.

The interpreter manipulates entities called PostScript *objects*. Some objects are data, such as numbers, booleans, strings, and arrays. Other objects are elements of programs to be executed, such as names, operators, and procedures. However, there is not a distinction between data and programs; any PostScript object may be treated as data or be executed as part of a program.

The interpreter operates by executing a sequence of objects. The effect of executing a particular object depends on that object's *type*, *attributes*, and *value*. For example, executing a number object causes the interpreter to push a copy of that object on the operand stack (to be described shortly). Executing a name object causes the interpreter to look up the name in a dictionary, fetch, and execute the associated value. Executing an operator object causes the interpreter to perform a built-in action, such as adding two numbers or painting characters in raster memory.

The objects to be executed by the interpreter come from two principal sources:

- A character stream may be scanned according to the syntax rules of the PostScript language, producing a sequence of new objects. As each object is scanned, it is immediately executed. The character stream may come from an external source, such as a file or a communication channel, or it may come from a string object previously stored in the PostScript interpreter's memory.

- Objects previously stored in an array in memory may be executed in sequence. Such an array is known as a *procedure*.

The interpreter can switch back and forth between executing a procedure and scanning a character stream. For example, if the interpreter encounters a name in a character stream, it executes that name by looking it up in a dictionary and retrieving the associated value. If that value is a procedure object, the interpreter suspends scanning the character stream and begins executing the objects in the procedure. When it reaches the end of the procedure, it resumes scanning the character stream where it left off. The interpreter maintains an *execution stack* for remembering all of its suspended execution contexts.

3.2 Syntax

As the interpreter scans the text of a PostScript language program, it creates various types of PostScript objects, such as numbers, strings, and procedures. This section discusses only the *syntactic* representation of such objects. Their internal representation and behavior are covered in section 3.3, "Data Types and Objects."

There are three encodings for the PostScript language: *ASCII*, *binary token*, and *binary object sequence*. The ASCII encoding is preferred for expository purposes (such as this manual), for archiving documents, and for transmission via communications facilities because it is easy to read and does not rely on any special characters that might be reserved for communications use. The two binary encodings are usable in controlled environments to improve efficiency of representation or execution; they are intended exclusively for machine generation. There is detailed information on the binary encodings in section 3.12, "Binary Encoding Details," at the end of this chapter.

3.2.1 Scanner

The PostScript language differs from most other programming languages in that it does not have any syntactic entity for a "program," nor is it necessary for an entire "program" to exist in one place at one time. PostScript has no notion of "reading in" a program before executing it. Instead, the PostScript interpreter *consumes* a program by reading and executing one syntactic entity at a time. From the interpreter's point of view, the program has no permanent existence. Execution of the program may have side effects in the interpreter's memory or elsewhere. These side effects may include the creation of procedure objects in memory that are intended to be invoked later in the program; their execution is *deferred*.

It is not correct to think the PostScript interpreter "executes" the character stream directly. Rather, a scanner groups characters into *tokens* according to the PostScript language syntax rules. It then assembles one or more tokens to create a PostScript *object*—in other words, a data value in the interpreter's memory. Finally, the interpreter executes the object.

For example, when the scanner encounters a group of consecutive digits surrounded by spaces or other separators, it assembles the digits into a token and then converts the token into a number object represented internally as a binary integer. The interpreter then executes this number object; in this case, it pushes a copy of the number object on the operand stack.

3.2.2 ASCII Encoding

The standard character set for ASCII-encoded PostScript language programs is the printable subset of the ASCII character set, plus the characters *space*, *tab*, and *newline* (return or line-feed). ASCII is the American Standard Code for Information Interchange, a widely used convention for encoding characters as binary numbers. ASCII encoding does not prohibit the use of characters outside this set, but such use is not recommended because it impairs portability and may make transmission and storage of PostScript language programs more difficult.

Note   *Control characters are often usurped by communications functions. Control codes are device dependent—not part of the PostScript language. For example, the serial communications protocol supported by many products uses the Control-D character as an end-of-file indication. In such cases, Control-D is a communications function and should not be part of a PostScript language program.*

Table 3.1 *Characters treated as white space*

Octal	Hex	Decimal	Name
000	00	0	Null (nul)
011	09	9	Tab (tab)
012	0A	10	Line-feed (LF)
014	0C	12	Form-feed (FF)
015	0D	13	Carriage-return (CR)
040	20	32	Space (SP)

White-space characters separate other syntactic constructs such as names and numbers from each other. The interpreter treats any number of consecutive white space characters as if there were just one. All white-space characters are equivalent, except in comments and strings.

The characters carriage-return (CR) and line-feed (LF) are also called *newline* characters. A CR followed immediately by an LF are treated together as one newline.

The characters (,), <, >, [,], {, }, /, and % are special. They delimit syntactic entities such as strings, procedure bodies, name literals, and comments. Any of these characters terminates the entity preceding it and is not included in the entity.

All characters besides the white-space characters and delimiters are referred to as *regular* characters. These include non-printing characters that are outside the recommended PostScript ASCII character set.

Comments

Any occurrence of the character % outside a string introduces a *comment*. The comment consists of all characters between the % and the next newline or form-feed, including regular, delimiter, space, and tab characters.

The scanner ignores comments, treating each one as if it were a single white-space character. That is, a comment separates the token preceding it from the one following. Thus, the ASCII-encoded program fragment

```
abc% comment {/%) blah blah blah
123
```

is treated by the scanner as just two tokens: abc and 123.

Numbers

Numbers in the PostScript language include signed integers, such as

```
123 –98 43445 0 +17
```

reals, such as

```
–.002 34.5 –3.62 123.6e10 1E–5 –1. 0.0
```

and radix numbers, such as

```
8#1777 16#FFFE 2#1000
```

An integer consists of an optional sign followed by one or more decimal digits. The number is interpreted as a signed decimal integer and is converted to an integer object. If it exceeds the implementation's limit for integers, it is converted to a real object (see Appendix B).

A real consists of an optional sign and one or more decimal digits, with an embedded period (decimal point), a trailing exponent, or both. The exponent, if present, consists of E or e followed by an optional sign and one or more decimal digits. For example, the following numbers are legal reals:

```
1E6 1.0E6 1.0E–6
```

The number is interpreted as a real and is converted to a real (floating point) object. If it exceeds the implementation limit for reals, a **limitcheck** error occurs.

A radix number takes the form *base#number*, where *base* is a decimal integer in the range 2 through 36. The *number* is then interpreted in this base; it must consist of digits ranging from 0 to *base* – 1. Digits greater than 9 are represented by the letters A through Z (or a through z). The number is treated as an unsigned integer and is converted to an integer object. This notation is intended for specifying integers in a non-decimal radix, such as binary, octal, or hexadecimal. If the number exceeds the implementations limit for integers, a **limitcheck** error occurs.

Strings

There are three conventions for quoting a literal string object:

• As literal text enclosed in (and).

• As hexadecimal encoded data enclosed in < and >.

• As ASCII base-85 encoded data enclosed in <~ and ~> (*Level 2 only*).

A literal text string consists of an arbitrary number of characters enclosed in (and). Any characters may appear in the string other than (,), and \, which must be treated specially. Balanced pairs of parentheses in the string require no special treatment.

The following lines show several valid strings:

```
(This is a string)
(Strings may contain newlines
and such.)
(Strings may contain special characters *–&}^% and
balanced parentheses ( ) (and so on).)
(The following is an "empty" string.)
( )
(It has 0 (zero) length.)
```

Within a text string, the \ (backslash) character is treated as an "escape" for various purposes, such as including unbalanced parentheses, nonprinting characters, and the \ character itself. The character immediately following the \ determines its precise interpretation.

\n	line-feed (LF or newline)
\r	carriage return (CR)
\t	horizontal tab
\b	backspace
\f	form-feed
\\	backslash
\(	left parenthesis
\)	right parenthesis
\ddd	character code ddd (octal)

If the character following the \ is not in the preceding list, the scanner ignores the \. If the \ is followed immediately by a newline (CR, LF, or CR LF pair), the scanner ignores both the initial \ and the newline. But if a newline appears without a preceding \, the result is equivalent to \n. For more information about end-of-line conventions, see section 3.8, "File Input and Output."

The \ newline combination breaks a string into multiple lines but without including the newline characters as part of the string, as in the following examples:

```
(These\
two strings\
are the same.)
(These two strings are the same.)

(This string has a newline at the end of it.
)
(So does this one.\n)
```

The *ddd* form may be used to include any 8-bit character constant in a string. One, two, or three octal digits may be specified with high-order overflow ignored. This notation is preferred for specifying a character outside the recommended ASCII character set for the PostScript language, since the notation itself stays within the standard set and thereby avoids possible difficulties in transmitting or storing the text of the program.

There are two other conventions for representing arbitrary data as ASCII text: the hexadecimal (base 16) encoding and the ASCII base-85 encoding.

A hexadecimal string consists of a sequence of hex characters (the digits 0 through 9 and the letters A through F or a through f) enclosed within < and >. Each pair of hex digits defines one character of the string. If the final digit of a given string is missing—in other words, if there is an odd number of digits—the final digit is assumed to be zero. White-space characters are ignored. For example,

    <901fa3>

is a three-character string containing the characters whose hex codes are 90, 1f, and a3. But

    <901fa>

is a three-character string containing the characters whose hex codes are 90, 1f, and a0. Hexadecimal strings are useful for including arbitrary binary data as literal text.

An ASCII base-85 encoded string (*Level 2 only*) consists of a sequence of printable ASCII characters enclosed in <~ and ~>. This represents arbitrary binary data using an encoding technique that produces a 4:5 expansion as opposed to the 1:2 expansion for hexadecimal. If a hexadecimal or ASCII base-85 string is malformed, a **syntaxerror** occurs. The ASCII base-85 encoding algorithm is described under **ASCII85Encode** in section 3.13, "Filtered Files Details."

Names

Any token that consists entirely of regular characters and cannot be interpreted as a number is treated as a *name* object (more precisely, an *executable* name). All characters except delimiters and white space can appear in names, including characters ordinarily considered to be punctuation.

The following are examples of valid names:

```
abc  Offset  $$  23A  13-456  a.b  $MyDict  @pattern
```

Use care when choosing names that begin with digits. For example, while 23A is a valid name, 23E1 is a real number, and 23#1 is a radix number token that represents an integer.

A / (slash—*not* backslash) introduces a *literal* name. The slash is not part of the name itself, but is a prefix indicating that the following name is a literal. There can be no white space between the / and the name. The characters // (two slashes) introduce an *immediately evaluated name*. The important properties and uses of names, and the distinction between executable and literal names are described in section 3.3, "Data Types and Objects"; immediately evaluated names are discussed in section 3.11.2, "Immediately Evaluated Names."

Arrays

The characters [and] are self-delimiting tokens that specify the construction of an array. The program fragment

```
[ 123 /abc (xyz) ]
```

results in the construction of an array object containing the integer object 123, the literal name object abc, and the string object xyz. Each token within [ ] is executed in turn.

[and] are special syntax for names that, when executed, invoke PostScript language operators that collect objects and construct an array containing them. Thus, the example

```
[ 123 /abc (xyz) ]
```

really contains the five tokens described below:

- The name object [.

- The integer object 123.

- The literal name object abc.

- The string object xyz.

- The name object].

When the example is executed, a sixth object (the array) results from executing the [and] name objects.

Procedures

The special characters { and } delimit an *executable array*, otherwise known as a *procedure*. The syntax is superficially similar to that for the array construction operators [and]; however, the semantics are entirely different and arise as a result of *scanning* the procedure rather than *executing* it.

Scanning the program fragment

{add 2 div}

produces a single procedure object that contains the name object **add**, the integer object 2, and the name object **div**. When the scanner encounters the initial {, it continues scanning and creating objects, but the interpreter does not execute them. When the scanner encounters the matching }, it puts all of the objects created since the initial { into a new executable array (procedure) object.

The interpreter does not execute a procedure immediately, but treats it as data; it pushes the procedure on the operand stack. Only when the procedure is explicitly invoked (by means yet to be described) will it be executed. Execution of the procedure—and of all objects within the procedure, including any embedded procedures—has been *deferred*. The matter of immediate versus deferred execution is discussed in section 3.5, "Execution."

The procedure object created by { and } is either an array or a packed array, according to the current setting of a mode switch. The distinction between these types of arrays is discussed in section 3.3, "Data Types and Objects."

Dictionaries

The special character sequences << and >> (*Level 2 only*) are self-delimiting tokens that denote the construction of a dictionary, much the same as [and] denote the construction of an array. They are intended to be used as follows:

<< key_1 $value_1$ key_2 $value_2$ ... key_n $value_n$ >>

This creates a dictionary containing the bracketed key-value pairs, and pushes the dictionary on the operand stack. Dictionaries are introduced in section 3.3, "Data Types and Objects."

<< and >> are merely special names for operators that, when executed, cause a dictionary to be constructed. This is like the [and] array constructor operators, but unlike the { and } delimiters for procedure literals.

The << and >> tokens are self-delimiting, so they need not be surrounded by white space or other delimiters. Do not confuse these tokens with < and >, which delimit a hexadecimal string literal, or <~ and ~>, which delimit an ASCII base-85 string literal. The << and >> tokens are objects in their own right (specifically, name objects); the < ... > and <~ ... ~> are merely punctuation for the enclosed literal string objects.

3.3 Data Types and Objects

All data accessible to PostScript language programs, including procedures that are part of the programs themselves, exist in the form of *objects*. Objects are produced, manipulated, and consumed by the PostScript operators. They are also created by the scanner and executed by the interpreter.

Each object has a *type,* some *attributes,* and a *value.* Objects contain their own dynamic types; that is, an object's type is a property of the object itself, not of where it is stored or what it is called. Table 3.2 lists all the object types supported by the PostScript language. Extensions to the language may introduce additional object types. The distinction between simple and composite objects is explained below.

Table 3.2 *Types of objects*

Simple objects	Composite objects
boolean	array
fontID	condition (*Display PostScript*)
integer	dictionary
mark	file
name	gstate (*Level 2*)
null	lock (*Display PostScript*)
operator	packedarray (*Level 2*)
real	string
save	

3.3.1 Simple and Composite Objects

Objects of most types are simple, atomic entities. An atomic object is always constant—a 2 is always 2. There is no visible substructure in the object; the type, attributes, and value are irrevocably bound together and cannot be changed.

However, objects of certain types indicated in Table 3.2 are *composite*. Their values have internal substructure that is visible and can sometimes be modified selectively. The details of the substructures are presented later in the descriptions of these individual types.

An important distinction between simple and composite objects is the behavior of operations that *copy* objects. *Copy* refers to any operation that transfers the contents of an object from one place to another in the memory of the PostScript interpreter. "Fetching" and "storing" objects are copying operations. It is possible to derive a new object by copying an existing one, perhaps with modifications.

When a simple object is copied, all of its parts (type, attributes, and value) are copied together. When a composite object is copied, the value is not copied; instead, the original and copy objects *share* the same value. Consequently, any changes made to the substructure of one object's value also appear as part of the other object's value.

The sharing of composite objects' values in the PostScript language corresponds to the use of *pointers* in system-programming languages such as C and Pascal. Indeed, the PostScript interpreter uses pointers to implement shared values: a composite object contains a pointer to its value. However, the PostScript language does not have any explicit notion of a pointer. It is better to think in terms of the copying and sharing notions presented here.

The values of simple objects are contained in the objects themselves. The values of composite objects reside in a special region of memory called *virtual memory* or *VM*. Section 3.7, "Memory Management," describes the behavior of VM.

3.3.2 Attributes of Objects

In addition to type and value, each object has one or more *attributes*. These attributes affect the behavior of the object when it is executed or when certain operations are performed on it. They do not affect its behavior when it is treated strictly as data; so, for example, two integers with the same value are considered "equal" even if their attributes differ.

Literal and Executable

Every object is either *literal* or *executable*. This distinction comes into play when the interpreter attempts to execute the object.

- If the object is *literal*, the interpreter treats it strictly as data and pushes it on the operand stack for use as an operand of some subsequent operator.

- If the object is *executable*, the interpreter executes it.

What it means to execute an object depends on the object's type. This is described in section 3.5, "Execution." For some types of objects, such as integers, execution consists of pushing the object on the operand stack; the distinction between literal and executable integers is meaningless. But for other types, such as names, operators, and arrays, execution consists of performing a different action.

- Executing an *executable name* causes it to be looked up in the current dictionary context and the associated value to be executed.

- Executing an *executable operator* causes some built-in action to be performed.

- Executing an *executable array* (otherwise known as a procedure) causes the elements of the array to be executed in turn.

As described in section 3.2, "Syntax," some tokens produce literal objects and some produce executable ones.

- Integer, real, and string constants are always literal objects.

- Names are literal if they are preceded by / and executable if they are not.

- The [and] operators, when executed, produce a literal array object with the enclosed objects as elements. Likewise, << and >> (*Level 2 only*) produce a literal dictionary object.

- { and } enclose an executable array or procedure.

As mentioned above, it doesn't matter whether an object is literal or executable when it is accessed as data, only when it is executed. However, referring to an executable object by name often causes that object to be executed automatically; see section 3.5.5, "Execution of Specific Types." To avoid unintended behavior, it's best to use the executable attribute only for objects that are meant to be executed, such as procedures.

Access

The other attribute of an object is its *access*. Only composite objects have access attributes, which restrict the set of operations that can be performed on the value of an object.

There are four values of access. In increasing order of restriction, they are:

1. *Unlimited.* Normally, objects have unlimited access: all operations defined for that object are allowed. However, packed array objects always have read-only (or even more restricted) access.

2. *Read-only.* An object with read-only access may not have its value written, but may still be read or executed.

3. *Execute-only.* An object with execute-only access may not have its value either read or written, but may still be executed by the Post-Script interpreter.

4. *None.* An object with no access may not be operated on in any way by a PostScript language program. Such objects are not of any direct use to PostScript language programs, but serve internal purposes that are not documented in this manual.

The literal/executable distinction and the access attribute are entirely independent, although there are combinations that are not of any practical use (for example, a literal array that is execute-only).

With one exception, attributes are properties of an *object* itself and not of its *value*. Two composite objects can share the same value but have different literal/executable or access attributes. The exception is the dictionary type: A dictionary's access attribute is a property of the value, so multiple dictionary objects sharing the value have the same access attribute.

3.3.3 Integer and Real

The PostScript language provides two types of numeric objects: *integer* and *real*. Integer objects represent mathematical integers within a certain interval centered at zero. Real objects approximate mathematical real numbers within a much larger interval but with limited precision. They are implemented as floating-point numbers.

Most PostScript arithmetic and mathematical operators can be applied to numbers of both types. The interpreter performs automatic type conversion when necessary. Some operators expect only integers or a subrange of the integers as operands. There are operators to convert from one data type to another explicitly. Throughout this manual, *number* means an object whose type is either integer or real.

The range and precision of numbers is limited by the internal representations used in the machine on which the PostScript interpreter is running. Appendix B gives these limits for typical implementations of the PostScript interpreter.

Note　*The machine representation of integers is accessible to a PostScript language program through the bitwise operators. However, the representation of integers may depend on the CPU architecture of the implementation. The machine representation of reals is not accessible to PostScript language programs.*

3.3.4 Boolean

The PostScript language provides boolean objects with values *true* and *false* for use in conditional and logical expressions. Booleans are the results of the relational (comparison) and logical operators. Various other operators also return them as status information. Booleans mainly are used as operands for the control operators **if** and **ifelse**. The names **true** and **false** are associated with the two values of this type.

3.3.5 Array

An array is a one-dimensional collection of objects accessed by a numeric index. Unlike arrays in many other computer languages, PostScript language arrays may be heterogeneous; that is, an array's elements may be any combination of numbers, strings, dictionaries, other arrays, or any other objects. A *procedure* is an array that may be executed by the PostScript interpreter.

All arrays are indexed from zero, so an array of *n* elements has indices from 0 through *n* – 1. All accesses to arrays are bounds-checked, and a reference with an out-of-bounds index results in a **rangecheck** error.

The PostScript language directly supports only one-dimensional arrays. Arrays of higher dimension may be constructed by using arrays as elements of arrays, nested to any arbitrary depth.

As discussed earlier, an array is a composite object. When an array object is copied, the value is *not* copied. Instead, the old and new objects share the same value. Additionally, there is an operator (**getinterval**) that creates a new array object whose value is a subinterval of an existing array; the old and new objects share the array elements in that subinterval.

3.3.6   Packed Array

A packed array is a more compact representation of an ordinary array, intended primarily for use as a procedure. A packed array object is distinct from an ordinary array object, but in most respects it behaves the same as an ordinary array. Its principal distinguishing feature is that it occupies much less space in memory (see section B.2, "Virtual Memory Use").

Throughout this manual, any mention of a procedure may refer to either an executable array or an executable packed array. The two types of arrays are not distinguishable when they are executed, only when they are treated as data. See the introduction to the array operators in section 3.6, "Overview of Basic Operators."

3.3.7   String

A string is similar to an array, but its elements must be integers in the range 0 to 255. The string elements are not integer objects, but are stored in a more compact format. However, the operators that access string elements accept or return ordinary integer objects with values in the range 0 to 255.

String objects are conventionally used to hold text, one character per string element. However, the PostScript language does not have a distinct "character" syntax or data type and does not require that the integer elements of a string encode any particular character set. String objects may also be used to hold arbitrary binary data.

To enhance program portability, strings appearing literally as part of a PostScript language program should be limited to characters from the printable ASCII character set, with other characters inserted by means of the \ddd escape convention (see section 3.2, "Syntax"). ASCII text strings are fully portable; ASCII base-85 text strings are fully portable among Level 2 implementations.

Like an array, a string is a composite object. Copying a string object or creating a subinterval (substring) results in sharing the string's value.

3.3.8 Name

A *name* is an atomic symbol uniquely defined by a sequence of characters. Names serve the same purpose as "identifiers" in other programming languages: as tags for variables, procedures, and so on. However, PostScript language names are not just language artifacts, but are first-class data objects, similar to "atoms" in LISP.

A name object is ordinarily created when the scanner encounters a PostScript token consisting entirely of regular characters, perhaps preceded by /, as described in section 3.2, "Syntax." However, a name may also be created by explicit conversion from a string; so there is no restriction on the set of characters that can be included in names.

Unlike a string, a name is a *simple* object not made up of other objects. Although a name is defined by a sequence of characters, those characters are not "elements" of the name. A name object, although logically simple, does have an invisible "value" that occupies space in VM.

A name is *unique*. Any two name objects defined by the same sequence of characters are identical copies of each other. Name equality is based on an exact match between the corresponding characters defining each name. This includes the case of letters, so the names A and a are different. Literal and executable objects can be equal, however.

The interpreter can inexpensively determine whether two existing name objects are equal or unequal without comparing the characters that define the names. This makes names useful as keys in dictionaries.

Names do not *have* values, unlike variable or procedure names in other programming languages. However, names can be *associated* with values in dictionaries.

3.3.9 Dictionary

A *dictionary* is an associative table whose elements are pairs of PostScript objects. The first element of a pair is the *key* and the second element is the *value*. The PostScript language includes operators that insert a key-value pair into a dictionary, look up a key and fetch the associated value, and perform various other operations.

Keys are normally name objects; the PostScript language syntax and the interpreter are optimized for this most common case. However, a key may be any PostScript language object except **null** (defined later). If you attempt to use a string as a key, the PostScript interpreter will first convert the string to a name object; thus, *strings and names are interchangeable when used as keys in dictionaries.*

A dictionary has the capacity to hold a certain maximum number of key-value pairs; the capacity is specified when the dictionary is created. Level 1 and Level 2 implementations of the PostScript language differ in their behavior when a program attempts to insert an entry into a dictionary that is full. In Level 1, a **dictfull** error occurs. In Level 2, the interpreter enlarges the dictionary automatically.

Dictionaries ordinarily associate the names and values of a program's components, such as variables and procedures. This corresponds to the conventional use of identifiers in other programming languages. But there are many other uses for dictionaries. For example, a PostScript language font program contains a dictionary that associates the names of characters with the procedures for drawing those characters' shapes (see Chapter 5).

There are three primary methods for accessing dictionaries:

- Operators exist to access a specific dictionary supplied as an operand.

- There is a *current dictionary* and a set of operators to access it implicitly.

- The interpreter automatically looks up executable names it encounters in the program being executed.

The interpreter maintains a *dictionary stack* defining the current dynamic name space. Dictionaries may be pushed on and popped off the dictionary stack at will. The topmost dictionary on the stack is the *current dictionary.*

When the interpreter looks up a key implicitly—for example, when it executes a name object—it searches for the key in the dictionaries on the dictionary stack. It searches first in the topmost dictionary, then in successively lower dictionaries on the dictionary stack, until it either finds the key or exhausts the dictionary stack.

In Level 1 implementations of the PostScript language, there are two built-in dictionaries permanently on the dictionary stack; they are called **systemdict** and **userdict**. In Level 2 implementations, there are three dictionaries: **systemdict**, **globaldict**, and **userdict**.

- **systemdict** is a read-only dictionary that associates the names of all the PostScript operators (those defined in this manual) with their values (the built-in actions that implement them).

- **globaldict** (*Level 2*) is a writable dictionary in *global VM*. This is explained in section 3.7.2, "Local and Global VM."

- **userdict** is a writable dictionary in *local VM*. It is the default modifiable naming environment normally used by PostScript language programs.

userdict is the topmost of the permanent dictionaries on the dictionary stack. The **def** operator puts definitions there unless the program has pushed some other dictionary on the dictionary stack. Applications can and should create their own dictionaries rather than put things in **userdict**.

A dictionary is a composite object. Copying a dictionary object does not copy the dictionary's contents. Instead, the contents are shared.

3.3.10 Operator

An *operator* object represents one of the PostScript language's built-in actions. When the object is executed, its built-in action is invoked. Most of this manual is devoted to describing the semantics of the various operators.

Operators have names. Most operators are associated with names in **systemdict**: The names are the keys and the values are the operators. When the interpreter executes one of these names, it looks up the name in the context of the dictionary stack. Unless the name has been defined in some dictionary higher on the dictionary stack, the interpreter finds its definition in **systemdict**, fetches the associated value (the operator object itself), and executes it.

All standard operators are defined in **systemdict**. However, an application that tests if an operator is defined should not do a **known** in **systemdict**; it should use **where** to check all dictionaries on the dictionary stack. This enables proper handling of operator emulations (see Appendix D).

Note   *There are some special internal PostScript operators whose names begin with* **@**. *These operators are not officially part of the PostScript language and are not defined in* **systemdict**. *They may appear as the "offending command" in error messages.*

There is nothing special about an operator name, such as **add**, that distinguishes it as an operator. Rather, the name **add** is associated in **systemdict** with the operator for performing addition, and execution of the operator causes the addition to occur. Thus the name **add** is not a "reserved word," as it might be in other programming languages. Its meaning can be changed by a PostScript language program.

Throughout this manual, the notation **add** means "the operator object associated with the name **add** in **systemdict**" or, occasionally, in some other dictionary.

3.3.11   File

A *file* is a readable or writable stream of characters transferred between the PostScript interpreter and its environment. The characters in a file may be stored permanently—in a disk file, for instance—or may be generated dynamically and transferred via a communication channel.

A *file object* represents a file. There are operators to open a file and create a file object for it. Other operators access an open file to read, write, and process characters in various ways—as strings, as PostScript language tokens, as binary data represented in hexadecimal, and so on.

Standard input and output files are always available to a PostScript language program. The standard input file is the usual source of programs to be interpreted; the standard output file is the usual destination of such things as error and status messages.

Although a file object does not have components visible at the PostScript language level, it is composite in the sense that all copies of a file object share the same value, namely the underlying file. If a file operator has a side effect on the underlying file, such as closing it or changing the current position in the stream, all file objects sharing the file are affected.

The properties of files and the operations on them are described in more detail in section 3.8, "File Input and Output."

3.3.12 Mark

A *mark* is a special object used to denote a position on the operand stack. This use is described in the presentation of stack and array operators in section 3.6, "Overview of Basic Operators." There is only one value of type mark, created by invoking the operator **mark**, [, or <<. Mark objects are not legal operands for most operators. Mark objects *are* legal operands for], >>, **counttomark**, **cleartomark**, and a few generic operators such as **pop** and **type**.

3.3.13 Null

The PostScript interpreter uses *null* objects to fill empty or uninitialized positions in composite objects when they are created. There is only one value of type null; the name **null** is associated with a null object in **systemdict**. Null objects are not legal operands for most operators.

3.3.14 Save

Save objects represent snapshots of the state of the PostScript interpreter's memory. They are created and manipulated by the **save** and **restore** operators, introduced in section 3.7.3, "Save and Restore."

3.3.15 Other Object Types

FontIDs are special objects used in the construction of fonts; see section 5.2, "Font Dictionaries."

A *gstate* object represents an entire *graphics state*; see section 4.2, "Graphics State." Gstate objects are a Level 2 feature.

Locks and conditions are special objects used to synchronize multiple execution contexts in a Display PostScript system; see section 7.1, "Multiple Execution Contexts."

3.4 Stacks

The PostScript interpreter manages four stacks representing the execution state of a PostScript language program. Three of them—the operand, dictionary, and execution stacks—are described here; the fourth—

the graphics state stack—is presented in Chapter 4. Stacks are "last-in-first-out" (LIFO) data structures. In this manual, "the stack" with no qualifier means the operand stack.

- The *operand stack* holds arbitrary PostScript objects that are the operands and results of PostScript operators being executed. When an operator requires one or more operands, it obtains them by popping them off the top of the operand stack. When an operator returns one or more results, it does so by pushing them on the operand stack. The interpreter pushes objects on the operand stack when it encounters them as literal data in a program being executed.

- The *dictionary stack* holds only dictionary objects. The current set of dictionaries on the dictionary stack defines the environment for all implicit name searches, such as those that occur when the interpreter encounters an executable name. The role of the dictionary stack is introduced in section 3.3, "Data Types and Objects," and is further explained in section 3.5, "Execution."

- The *execution stack* holds executable objects (mainly procedures and files) that are in stages of execution. At any point in the execution of a PostScript language program, this stack represents the *call stack* of the program. Whenever the interpreter suspends execution of an object to execute some other object, it pushes the *new* object on the execution stack. When the interpreter finishes executing an object, it pops that object off the execution stack and resumes executing the suspended object beneath it.

The three stacks are independent and there are different ways to access each of them:

- The operand stack is directly under control of the PostScript language program being executed. Objects may be pushed and popped arbitrarily by various operators.

- The dictionary stack is also under control of the PostScript language program being executed. But it can hold only dictionaries, and the bottom three dictionaries (two dictionaries in Level 1 implementations) on this stack—**systemdict**, **globaldict**, and **userdict**—cannot be popped off. The operators **begin**, **end**, and **cleardictstack** are the only operators that can alter the dictionary stack.

- The execution stack is under the control of the interpreter. It can be read but not modified by a PostScript language program.

When an object is pushed on a stack, the *object* is copied onto the stack from wherever it was obtained; however, in the case of a composite object (array, string, or dictionary), the object's *value* is not copied on the stack, but rather is shared with the original object. Similarly, when a composite object is popped off a stack and put somewhere, only the object itself is moved, not its value. See section 3.3, "Data Types and Objects," for more details.

The maximum capacity of stacks may be limited. See Appendices B and C.

3.5 Execution

Execution semantics are different for each of the various object types. Also, execution can be either *immediate*, occurring as soon as the object is created by the scanner, or *deferred* to some later time.

3.5.1 Immediate Execution

Several PostScript language program fragments will help clarify the concept of execution. Example 3.1 illustrates immediate execution of a few operators and operands to perform some simple arithmetic.

Example 3.1

    40 60 add 2 div

The interpreter first encounters the literal integer object 40 and pushes it on the operand stack. Then it pushes the integer object 60 on the operand stack.

Now it encounters the executable name object **add**, which it looks up in the environment of the current dictionary stack. Unless **add** has been redefined elsewhere, the interpreter finds it associated with an operator object, which it executes. This invokes a built-in function that pops the two integer objects off the operand stack, adds them together, and pushes the result (a new integer object whose value is 100) back on the operand stack.

The rest of the program fragment is similarly executed. The interpreter pushes the integer 2 on the operand stack, then it executes the name **div**. The **div** operator pops two operands off the stack (the integers whose values are 2 and 100), divides the second-to-top one by the top one (100 divided by 2, in this case), and pushes the integer result 50 on the stack.

The source of the objects being executed by the PostScript interpreter does not matter. They may have been contained within an array or scanned in from a character stream. Executing a sequence of objects produces the same result regardless of where the objects come from.

3.5.2 Operand Order

In Example 3.1, 40 is the first and 60 is the second operand of the **add** operator. That is, objects are referred to according to *the order in which they are pushed on the operand stack*. This is the reverse of the order in which they are popped off by the **add** operator. Similarly, the result pushed by the **add** operator is the first operand of the **div** operator, and the 2 is its second operand.

The same terminology applies to the results of an operator. If an operator pushes more than one object on the operand stack, the first object pushed is the first result. This order corresponds to the usual left-to-right order of appearance of operands in a PostScript language program.

3.5.3 Deferred Execution

The first line of Example 3.2 defines a procedure named average that computes the average of two numbers. The second line applies that procedure to the integers 40 and 60, producing the same result as Example 3.1.

Example 3.2

```
/average {add 2 div} def
40 60 average
```

The interpreter first encounters the literal name average. Recall from section 3.2, "Syntax," that / introduces a literal name. The interpreter pushes this object on the operand stack, as it would any object having the literal attribute.

Next the interpreter encounters the executable array {add 2 div}. Recall that { and } enclose a *procedure* (an executable array, or packed array object) that is produced by the scanner. This procedure contains three elements: the executable name **add**, the literal integer 2, and the executable name **div**. The interpreter has not encountered these elements yet.

Here is what the interpreter does:

1. Upon encountering this procedure object, the interpreter pushes it on the operand stack, even though the object has the executable attribute. This is explained soon.

2. The interpreter then encounters the executable name **def**. Looking up this name in the current dictionary stack, it finds **def** to be associated in **systemdict** with an operator object, which it invokes.

3. The **def** operator pops two objects off the operand stack (the procedure {add 2 div} and the name average). It enters this pair into the current dictionary (most likely **userdict**), creating a new association having the name average as its key and the procedure {add 2 div} as its value.

4. The interpreter pushes the integer objects 40 and 60 on the operand stack, then encounters the executable name average.

5. It looks up average in the current dictionary stack, finds it to be associated with the procedure {add 2 div}, and *executes* that procedure. In this case, execution of the array object consists of executing the elements of the array in sequence, namely the objects **add**, 2, and **div**. This has the same effect as executing those objects directly. It produces the same result: the integer object 50.

Why did the interpreter treat the procedure as data in the first line of the example but execute it in the second, despite the procedure having the executable attribute in both cases? There is a special rule that determines this behavior: An executable array or packed array encountered *directly* by the interpreter is treated as data (pushed onto the operand stack). But an executable array or packed array encountered *indirectly*—as a result of executing some other object, such as a name or an operator—is invoked as a procedure.

This rule reflects how procedures are ordinarily used. Procedures appearing directly (either as part of a program being read from a file or as part of some larger procedure in memory) are usually part of a definition or of a construct, such as a conditional, that operates on the procedure explicitly. But procedures obtained indirectly—for example, as a result of looking up a name—are usually intended to be executed. A PostScript language program can override these semantics when necessary.

3.5.4 Control Constructs

In the PostScript language, control constructs such as conditionals and iterations are specified by means of operators that take procedures as operands. Example 3.3 computes the maximum of the values associated with the names a and b, as in the steps that follow.

Example 3.3

    a b gt {a} {b} ifelse

1. The interpreter encounters the executable names a and b in turn and looks them up. Assume both names are associated with numbers. Executing the numbers causes them to be pushed onto the operand stack.

2. The **gt** (greater than) operator removes two operands from the stack and compares them. If the first operand is greater than the second, it pushes the boolean value *true*. Otherwise, it pushes *false*.

3. The interpreter now encounters the procedure objects {a} and {b}, which it pushes onto the operand stack.

4. The **ifelse** operator takes three operands: a boolean and two procedures. If the boolean's value is *true*, **ifelse** causes the first procedure to be executed. Otherwise, it causes the second procedure to be executed. All three operands are removed from the operand stack before the selected procedure is executed.

In this example, each procedure consists of a single element that is an executable name (either a or b). The interpreter looks up this name and, since it is associated with a number, pushes that number on the operand stack. So the result of executing the entire program fragment is to push on the operand stack the maximum of the values associated with a and b.

3.5.5 Execution of Specific Types

An object with the literal attribute is *always* treated as data—pushed on the operand stack by the interpreter—regardless of its type. Even operator objects are treated this way if they have the literal attribute.

For many objects, executing them has the same effect as treating them as data. This is true of integer, real, boolean, dictionary, mark, save, gstate, and fontID objects. So the distinction between literal and executable objects of these types is meaningless. The following descriptions apply *only* to objects having the executable attribute.

- An *executable array* or *executable packed array* (procedure) object is pushed on the operand stack if it is encountered directly by the interpreter. If it is invoked *indirectly* as a result of executing some other object (a name or an operator), it is *called* instead. The interpreter calls a procedure by pushing it on the execution stack and then executing the array elements in turn. When the interpreter reaches the end of the procedure, it pops the procedure object off the execution stack. (Actually, it pops the procedure object when there is one element remaining and then pushes that element. This is to permit unlimited depth of "tail recursion" without overflowing the execution stack.)

- An *executable string* object is pushed onto the execution stack. The interpreter then uses the string as a source of characters to be converted to tokens and interpreted according to the PostScript language syntax rules. This continues until the interpreter reaches the end of the string, when it pops the string object from the execution stack.

- An *executable file* object is treated much the same as a string: The interpreter pushes it on the execution stack. It reads the characters of the file and interprets them as PostScript tokens until it encounters end-of-file. Then it closes the file and pops the file object from the execution stack. See section 3.8, "File Input and Output."

- An *executable name* object is looked up in the environment of the current dictionary stack and its associated value is executed. The interpreter looks first in the top dictionary on the dictionary stack and then in other dictionaries successively lower on the stack. If it finds the name as a key in some dictionary, it executes the associated value. To do that, it examines the value's type and executable attribute, and performs the appropriate action described in this section. Note that if the value is a procedure, the interpreter executes it. If the interpreter fails to find the name in any dictionary on the dictionary stack, an **undefined** error occurs.

- An *executable operator* object causes the interpreter to perform one of the built-in operations described in this manual.

- An *executable null* object causes the interpreter to perform no action (in particular, it does *not* push the object on the operand stack).

3.6 Overview of Basic Operators

This is an overview of the general-purpose PostScript language operators, excluding all operators that deal with graphics and fonts, which are described in later chapters. The organization of this section roughly parallels that of the operator summary at the beginning of Chapter 8. The information here is insufficient for actual programming; it is intended only to acquaint you with the available facilities. For complete information about any particular operator, you should refer to the operator's detailed description in Chapter 8.

3.6.1 Stack Operators

The operand stack is the PostScript interpreter's mechanism for passing arguments to operators and for gathering results from operators. It was introduced in section 3.4, "Stacks."

There are various operators that rearrange or manipulate the objects on the operand stack. Such rearrangement is often required when the results of some operators are to be used as arguments to other operators that require their operands in a different order. These operators manipulate only the objects themselves; they do not copy the values of composite objects.

- **dup** duplicates an object.

- **exch** exchanges the top two elements of the stack.

- **pop** removes the top element from the stack.

- **copy** duplicates portions of the operand stack.

- **roll** treats a portion of the stack as a circular queue.

- **index** accesses the stack as if it were an indexable array.

- **mark** marks a position on the stack.

- **clear** clears the stack.

- **count** counts the number of elements in the stack.

- **counttomark** counts the elements above the highest mark. This is used primarily for array construction (described later), but has other applications as well.

3.6.2 Arithmetic and Mathematical Operators

The PostScript language includes a conventional complement of arithmetic and mathematical operators. In general, these operators accept either integer or real number objects as operands. They produce either integer or real numbers as results, depending on the types of the operands and the magnitude of the results. If the result of an operation is mathematically meaningless or cannot be represented as a real, an **undefinedresult** error occurs.

- **add**, **sub**, **mul**, **div**, **idiv**, and **mod** are arithmetic operators of two arguments.

- **abs**, **neg**, **ceiling**, **floor**, **round**, and **truncate** are arithmetic operators of one argument.

- **sqrt**, **exp**, **ln**, **log**, **sin**, **cos**, and **atan** are mathematical and trigonometric functions.

- **rand**, **srand**, and **rrand** access a pseudo-random number generator.

3.6.3 Array, Packed Array, Dictionary, and String Operators

A number of operators are *polymorphic*—they may be applied to operands of several different types and their precise functions depend on the types of the operands. In particular, there are various operators that perform similar operations on the values of several types of composite objects—arrays, packed arrays, dictionaries, and strings.

- **get** takes a composite object and an index (or key, in the case of a dictionary) and returns a single element of the object.

- **put** stores a single element in a composite object. (**put** does not apply to packed array objects because they are read-only.)

- **copy** copies the *value* of a composite object to another composite object of the same type, replacing the second object's former value. This is different from merely copying the object. See the discussion of simple versus composite objects in section 3.3, "Data Types and Objects."

- **length** returns the number of elements in a composite object.

- **forall** accesses all of the elements of a composite object in sequence, calling a procedure for each one.

- **getinterval** creates a new object that shares a subinterval of an array, packed array, or string. This does not apply to dictionary objects.

- **putinterval** overwrites a subinterval of one array or string with the contents of another. **putinterval** does not apply to dictionary or packed array objects.

In addition to the polymorphic operators, there are operators that apply to only one of the array, packed array, dictionary, and string types. For each type, there is an operator (**array**, **packedarray**, **dict**, **string**) that creates a new object of that type and a specified length. These four operators explicitly create new composite object values, consuming virtual memory (VM) resources (see section 3.7.1, "Virtual Memory"). Most other operators read and write the values of composite objects, but do not create new ones. Operators that return composite results usually require an operand that is the composite object into which the result values are to be stored. The operators are organized this way to give programmers maximum control over consumption of VM.

Array, packed array, and string objects have a fixed length that is specified when the objects are created. In Level 1, dictionary objects also have this property. In Level 2, a dictionary's capacity can grow beyond its initial allocation.

The following operators apply only to arrays and (sometimes) packed arrays:

- **aload** and **astore** transfer all the elements of an array to or from the operand stack in a single operation. **aload** may also be applied to a packed array.

- The array construction operators [and] combine to produce a new array object whose elements are the objects appearing between the brackets in a PostScript language program. The [operator, which is a synonym for **mark**, pushes a mark object on the operand stack. Execution of the program fragment between the [and the] causes zero or more objects to be pushed on the operand stack. Finally, the] operator counts the number of objects above the mark on the stack, creates an array of that length, stores the elements from the stack in the array, removes the mark from the stack, and pushes the array on the stack.

- **setpacking** and **currentpacking** (*both Level 2*) control a mode setting that determines the type of procedure objects the scanner generates when it encounters a sequence of tokens enclosed in { and }. If the array packing mode is *true*, the scanner produces packed arrays; if the mode is *false*, it produces ordinary arrays. The default value is *false*.

- Packed array objects are always read-only, so the **put**, **putinterval**, and **astore** operations are not allowed on them. Accessing arbitrary elements of a packed array object can be quite slow; however, accessing the elements sequentially, as the PostScript interpreter and the **forall** operator do, is efficient.

The following operators apply only to dictionaries:

- **begin** and **end** push new dictionaries on the dictionary stack and pop them off.

- **def** and **store** associate keys with values in dictionaries on the dictionary stack; **load** and **where** search for keys there.

- **countdictstack**, **cleardictstack**, and **dictstack** operate on the dictionary stack.

- **known** queries whether a key is present in a specific dictionary.

- **maxlength** obtains a dictionary's maximum capacity.

- **undef** (*Level 2*) removes individual keys from a dictionary.

- **<<** and **>>** (*Level 2*) construct a dictionary consisting of the bracketed objects interpreted as key-value pairs.

The following operators apply only to strings:

- **search** and **anchorsearch** perform textual string searching and matching.

- **token** scans the characters of a string according to the PostScript language syntax rules, without executing the resulting objects.

There are many additional operators that use array, dictionary, or string operands for special purposes—for instance, as transformation matrices, font dictionaries, or text to be shown.

3.6.4 Relational, Boolean, and Bitwise Operators

The relational operators compare two operands and produce a boolean result indicating if the relation holds. Any two objects may be compared for equality (**eq** and **ne**—*equal* and *not equal*); numbers and strings may be compared by the inequality operators (**gt**, **ge**, **le**, and **lt**—*greater than*, *greater than or equal to*, *less than or equal to*, and *less than*).

The boolean and bitwise operators (**and**, **or**, **xor**, **true**, **false**, and **not**) compute logical combinations of boolean operands or bitwise combinations of integer operands. The bitwise shift operator **bitshift** applies only to integers.

3.6.5 Control Operators

The control operators modify the interpreter's usual sequential execution of objects. Most of them take a procedure operand that they execute conditionally or repeatedly.

- **if** and **ifelse** execute a procedure conditionally depending on the value of a boolean operand. (**ifelse** is introduced in section 3.5, "Execution.")

- **exec** executes an arbitrary object unconditionally.

- **for**, **repeat**, **loop**, and **forall** execute a procedure repeatedly. Several specialized graphics and font operators, such as **pathforall** and **kshow**, behave similarly.

- **exit** transfers control out of the scope of any of these looping operators.

- **countexecstack** and **execstack** are used to read the execution stack.

A PostScript language program may terminate prematurely by executing the **stop** operator. This occurs most commonly as a result of an error; the default error handlers (in **errordict**) all execute **stop**.

The **stopped** operator establishes an execution environment that encapsulates the effect of a **stop**. That is, **stopped** executes a procedure given as an operand, just the same as **exec**. If the interpreter executes **stop** during that procedure, it terminates the procedure and resumes execution at the object immediately after the **stopped** operator.

3.6.6 Type, Attribute, and Conversion Operators

These operators deal with the details of PostScript types, attributes, and values, introduced in section 3.3, "Data Types and Objects."

- **type** returns the type of any operand as a name object (integertype, realtype, and so on).

- **xcheck**, **rcheck**, and **wcheck** query the literal/executable and access attributes of an object.

- **cvlit** and **cvx** change the literal/executable attribute of an object.

- **readonly**, **executeonly**, and **noaccess** reduce an object's access attribute. Access can only be reduced, never increased.

- **cvi** and **cvr** convert between integer and real types, and interpret a numeric string as an integer or real number.

- **cvn** converts a string to a name object defined by the characters of the string.

- **cvs** and **cvrs** convert objects of several types to a printable string representation.

3.7 Memory Management

A PostScript language program executes in an environment with these major components: stacks, virtual memory, standard input and output files, and the graphics state.

- The *operand stack* is working storage for objects that are the operands and results of operators. The *dictionary stack* contains dictionary objects that define the current name space. The *execution stack* contains objects that are in partial stages of execution by the PostScript interpreter. See section 3.4, "Stacks."

- The *virtual memory* (VM) is a storage pool for the values of all composite objects. The adjective "virtual" emphasizes the behavior of this memory visible at the PostScript language level, not its implementation in computer storage.

- The *standard input file* is the normal source of program text to be executed by the PostScript interpreter. The *standard output file* is the normal destination of output from the **print** operator and of error messages. Other files can exist as well. See section 3.8, "File Input and Output."

- The *graphics state* is a collection of parameters that control the production of text and graphics on a raster output device. See section 4.2, "Graphics State."

This section describes the behavior of VM and its interactions with other components of the PostScript execution environment. It describes facilities for controlling the environment as a whole. The PostScript interpreter can execute a sequence of self-contained PostScript programs as independent "jobs"; similarly, each job can have internal structure whose components are independent of each other.

3.7.1 Virtual Memory

As described in section 3.3, "Data Types and Objects," there are two classes of objects: simple and composite. A simple object's value is contained in the object itself. A composite object's value is stored separately; the object contains a reference to it. The virtual memory (VM) is the storage in which the values of composite objects reside.

For example, the program fragment

    234 (Here is a string)

pushes two objects, an integer and a string, on the operand stack. The integer, which is a simple object, contains the value 234 as part of the object itself. The string, which is a composite object, contains a reference to the value (Here is a string), which is a text string that resides in VM. The elements of the text string are characters (actually, integers in the range 0 to 255) that can be individually selected or replaced.

Here is another example:

    {234 (Here is a string)}

This pushes a single object, a two-element executable array, on the operand stack. The array is a composite object whose value resides in VM. The value in turn consists of two objects, an integer and a string. Those objects are elements of the array, which can be individually selected or replaced.

Several composite objects can share the same value. For example, in

{234 (Here is a string)} dup

the **dup** operator pushes a second copy of the array object on the operand stack. The two objects share the same value—that is, the same storage in VM. So, replacing an element of one array will affect the other. Other types of composite objects, including strings and dictionaries, behave similarly.

Creating a new composite object consumes VM storage for its value. This occurs in two principal ways:

- The scanner allocates storage for each composite literal object that it encounters. Composite literals are delimited by (...), <...>, <~...~>, and {...}. The first three produce strings; the fourth produces an executable array. There also are binary encodings for composite objects.

- Some operators explicitly create new composite objects and allocate storage for them. The **array**, **packedarray**, **dict**, **string**, and **gstate** operators create new array, packed array, dictionary, string, and gstate objects, respectively. Also, the bracketing constructs [...] and <<...>> create new array and dictionary objects, respectively. The brackets are just special names for operators; the closing bracket operators allocate the storage.

For the most part, consumption and management of VM storage are under the control of the PostScript language program. Aside from the operators mentioned above and a few others that are clearly documented, most operators do not create new composite objects or allocate storage in VM. Some operators place their results in existing objects supplied by the caller. For example, the **cvs** (convert to string) operator overwrites the value of a supplied string operand and returns a string object that shares a substring of the supplied string's storage.

3.7.2   Local and Global VM

There are two divisions of VM containing the values of composite objects: *local* and *global*. Only composite objects occupy VM. An "object in VM" means a "composite object whose *value* occupies VM"; the location of the object (for example, on a stack or stored as an element of some other object) is immaterial.

Note   *Global VM exists only in Level 2 and Display PostScript implementations of the PostScript language. In Level 1 implementations, all of VM is local.*

Local VM is a storage pool that obeys a stack-like discipline. Allocations in local VM and modifications to existing objects in local VM are subject to a feature called **save** and **restore**, named after the operators that invoke it. **save** and **restore** bracket a section of a PostScript language program whose local VM activity is to be encapsulated. **restore** deallocates new objects and undoes modifications to existing objects that were made since the matching **save**. **save** and **restore** are described in section 3.7.3, "Save and Restore."

Global VM is a storage pool for objects that don't obey a fixed discipline. Objects in global VM can come into existence and disappear in an arbitrary order during execution of a program. Modifications to existing objects in global VM are not affected by occurrences of **save** and **restore** within the program. However, an entire job's VM activity can be encapsulated, enabling separate jobs to be executed independently. This is described in section 3.7.7, "Job Execution Environment."

In a hierarchically structured program, such as a page description, local VM is used to hold information whose lifetime conforms to the structure; that is, it persists to the end of a structural division, such as a single page. Global VM may be used to hold information whose lifetime is independent of the structure, such as definitions of fonts and other resources that are loaded dynamically during execution of a program.

Control over allocation of objects in local versus global VM is provided by the **setglobal** operator (a Level 2 feature). This operator establishes a *VM allocation mode*, a boolean value that determines where subsequent allocations are to occur (*false* means local, *true* means global). It affects objects created implicitly by the scanner and objects created explicitly by operators. The default VM allocation mode is local; a program can switch to global VM allocation mode when it needs to.

The following example illustrates creation of objects in local and global VM:

```
/lstr (string1) def
/ldict 10 dict def
true setglobal
/gstr (string2) def
/gdict 5 dict def
false setglobal
```

In the first line, when the scanner encounters (string1), it allocates the string object in local VM. In the second line, the **dict** operator allocates a new dictionary in local VM. The third line switches to global VM allocation mode. The fourth and fifth lines allocate a string object and a dictionary object in global VM. The sixth line switches back to local VM allocation mode. The program associates the four newly created objects with the names lstr, ldict, gstr, and gdict in the current dictionary, presumably **userdict**.

It is illegal for an object in global VM to contain a reference to an object in local VM. An attempt to store a local object as an element of a global object will result in an **invalidaccess** error. The reason for this restriction is that subsequent execution of the **restore** operator might deallocate the local object, leaving the global object with a reference to a non-existent object.

This restriction applies only to storing a *composite* object in local VM as an element of a *composite* object in global VM. All other combinations are allowed. The following example illustrates this, using the objects that were created in the preceding example:

```
ldict /a lstr put    % Legal—a local object into a local dict
gdict /b gstr put    % Legal—a global object into a global dict
ldict /c gstr put    % Legal—a global object into a local dict
gdict /d lstr put    % Illegal (invalidaccess error)—a local object into a global dict
gdict /e 7 put       % Legal—a simple object into any dict
```

There are no restrictions on storing simple objects, such as integers and names, as elements of either local or global composite objects. The **gcheck** operator inquires whether an object can be stored as an element of a global composite object. It returns *true* for a simple object or for a composite object in global VM, *false* for a composite object in local VM.

3.7.3   Save and Restore

The **save** operator takes a snapshot of the state of local VM; it returns a *save object* that represents the snapshot. The **restore** operator causes local VM to revert to a snapshot generated by a preceding **save**. Specifically:

- **restore** discards all objects in local VM that were created since the corresponding **save**, and reclaims the memory they occupied.

- **restore** resets the values of all composite objects in local VM, except strings, to their state at the time of the **save**.

- **restore** performs an implicit **grestoreall**, which resets the graphics state to its value at the time of the **save** (see section 4.2, "Graphics State.")

- **restore** closes files that were opened since the corresponding **save**, so long as those files were opened while local VM allocation mode was in effect (see section 3.8, "File Input and Output").

The effects of **restore** are limited to the ones described above.

- **restore** does not affect the contents of the operand, dictionary, and execution stacks. If a stack contains a reference to a composite object in local VM that would be discarded by the **restore**, the **restore** is not allowed. An **invalidrestore** error occurs.

- It does not affect any objects that reside in global VM, except as described in section 3.7.7, "Job Execution Environment."

- It does not undo side effects outside VM, such as writing data to files or rendering graphics on the raster output device. (However, the implicit **grestoreall** may deactivate the current device, thereby erasing the current page. See section 4.11, "Device Setup," for details.)

save and **restore** can be nested to a limited depth (see Appendix B for implementation limits). A PostScript language program can use **save** and **restore** to encapsulate the execution of an embedded program that also uses **save** and **restore**.

save and **restore** are intended for use in structured programs, such as page descriptions. The conventions for structuring programs are introduced in section 2.4.2, "Program Structure," and detailed in Appendix G. In such programs, **save** and **restore** serve the following functions:

- A document consists of a prolog and a script. The prolog contains definitions that are used throughout the document. The script consists of a sequence of independent pages. Each page has a **save** at the beginning and a **restore** at the end, immediately before the **showpage** operator. Each page begins execution with the initial conditions established in local VM by the prolog. There are no unwanted legacies from previous pages.

- A page sometimes contains additional substructure, such as embedded illustrations, whose execution needs to be encapsulated. The encapsulated program can make wholesale changes to the contents of local VM to serve its own purposes. By bracketing the program with **save** and **restore**, the enclosing program can isolate the effects of the embedded program.

- As a PostScript language program executes, new composite objects accumulate in local VM. These include objects created by the scanner, such as literal string tokens, and objects allocated explicitly by operators. The **restore** operator reclaims all local VM storage allocated since the corresponding **save**; executing **save** and **restore** periodically ensures that unreclaimed objects will not exhaust available VM resources. In Level 1 implementations, **save** and **restore** are the *only* way to reclaim VM storage. Even in Level 2, explicit reclamation by **save** and **restore** is much more efficient than automatic reclamation, described in section 3.7.4, "Garbage Collection."

- The PostScript interpreter uses **save** and **restore** to encapsulate the execution of individual jobs, as described in section 3.7.7, "Job Execution Environment."

3.7.4 Garbage Collection

In addition to the **save** and **restore** operators for explicit VM reclamation, Level 2 implementations and Display PostScript systems include a facility for automatic reclamation, popularly known as a *garbage collector*. The garbage collector reclaims the memory occupied by composite objects that are no longer accessible to the PostScript language program.

For example, after the following program is executed,

```
/a (string 1) def
/a (string 2) def
(Here is some text) show
```

the string object (string 1) is no longer accessible, since the dictionary entry that referred to it has been replaced by a different object, (string 2). Similarly, the string (Here is some text) is no longer accessible, since the **show** operator consumes its operand, but does not store it anywhere. The inaccessible strings are candidates for garbage collection.

Garbage collection normally takes place without explicit action by the PostScript language program. It has no effects that are visible to the program. However, the presence of a garbage collector strongly influences the style of programming that is permissible. If no garbage collector is present, a program that consumes VM endlessly and never executes **save** and **restore** will eventually exhaust available memory and cause a **VMerror**.

Creating and destroying composite objects in VM have a cost. The most common case is that of literal objects—particularly strings, user paths, and binary object sequences—that are immediately consumed by operators such as **show** and **ufill**, and never used again. The garbage collector is engineered to deal with this case inexpensively, so application programs should not hesitate to take advantage of it. However, the cost of garbage collection is greater for objects that have longer lifetimes or are allocated explicitly. Programs that frequently require temporary objects are encouraged to create them once and reuse them instead of creating new ones—for example, allocate a string object *before* an image data acquisition procedure, rather than within it (see section 4.10.7, "Using Images").

Even with garbage collection, the **save** and **restore** operators still have their standard behavior. That is, **restore** resets all accessible objects in local VM to their state at the time of the matching **save**. It reclaims all composite objects created in local VM since the **save**, and does so very cheaply. On the other hand, garbage collection is the only way to reclaim storage in global VM, since **save** and **restore** normally do not affect global VM.

With garbage collection comes the ability to explicitly discard composite objects that are no longer needed. This can be done in an order unrelated to the time of creation of those objects, as opposed to the stack-like order imposed by **save** and **restore**. This is particularly desirable for very large objects, such as font definitions.

If the only reference to a particular composite object is an element of some array or dictionary, replacing that element with something else (say, using **put**) renders the object inaccessible. Alternatively, the **undef** operator removes a dictionary entry entirely; that is, it removes both the key and the value of a key-value pair, as opposed to replacing the value with some other value. In either case, the removed object becomes a candidate for garbage collection.

Regardless of the means used to remove a reference to a composite object, if the object containing the reference is in local VM, the action can be undone by a subsequent **restore**. This is true even for **undef**. Consider the following example:

```
/a (string 1) def
save
currentdict /a undef
restore
```

Execution of **undef** removes the key a and its value from the current dictionary, seemingly causing the object (string 1) to become inaccessible. However, assuming that the current dictionary is **userdict**, or some other dictionary in local VM, **restore** reinstates the deleted entry, since it existed at the time of the corresponding **save**. The value is still accessible and cannot be garbage collected.

As a practical matter, this means that the technique of discarding objects explicitly (in expectation of their being garbage collected) is useful mainly for objects in global VM, where **save** and **restore** have no effect, and for objects in local VM that were created at the current level of **save** nesting.

3.7.5 Standard and User-Defined Dictionaries

A job begins execution with three standard dictionaries on the dictionary stack: **systemdict**, **globaldict**, and **userdict**, with **userdict** on top.

- **systemdict** is a global dictionary that is permanently read-only. It contains mainly operators.

- **globaldict** is a global dictionary that is writable (*Level 2*).

- **userdict** is a local dictionary that is writable.

There are other standard dictionaries that are the values of permanent named entries in **systemdict**. Some of these are in local VM, some in global VM, as shown in Table 3.3 and Table 3.4. A PostScript language program can also create new dictionaries in either local or global VM, then push them on the dictionary stack or store them as entries in **userdict** or **globaldict**.

Table 3.3 *Standard local dictionaries*

Dictionary	Definition
userdict	Standard writable local dictionary. Initially, it is the top dictionary on the dictionary stack, making it the current dictionary.
errordict	Error dictionary. See section 3.10, "Errors."
$error	Dictionary accessed by the built-in error-handling procedures to store stack snapshots and other information. See section 3.10, "Errors."
statusdict	Dictionary for product-specific operators and other definitions. See Chapter 8.
FontDirectory	Dictionary for font definitions. It is normally read-only, but is updated by **definefont** and consulted by **findfont**. See section 3.9, "Named Resources," and section 5.2, "Font Dictionaries."

Table 3.4 *Standard global dictionaries*

Dictionary	Definition
systemdict	Read-only system dictionary containing all operators and other definitions that are standard parts of the PostScript language. It is the bottom dictionary on the dictionary stack.
globaldict	(*Level 2*) Standard writable global dictionary. It is on the dictionary stack between **systemdict** and **userdict**.
GlobalFontDirectory	(*Level 2*) Dictionary for font definitions in global VM. It is normally read-only, but is updated by **definefont** and consulted by **findfont**. See section 3.9, "Named Resources," and section 5.2, "Font Dictionaries."

The dictionaries **userdict** and **globaldict** are intended to be the principal repositories for application-defined dictionaries and other objects. When a PostScript language program creates a dictionary in local VM, it then typically associates that dictionary with a name in **userdict**. Similarly, when the program creates a dictionary in global VM, it typically associates the dictionary with a name in **globaldict**. Note that the latter step requires explicit action on the part of the program. Entering global VM allocation does *not* alter the dictionary stack (say, to put **globaldict** on top).

The principal intended use of global VM is to hold font definitions and other resources that are loaded dynamically during execution of a Post-Script language program. The **findfont** operator loads fonts into global VM automatically when necessary. However, any program can take advantage of global VM when its properties are useful. The following guidelines are suggested:

- Objects that are created during the prolog can be in either local or global VM; in either case, they will exist throughout the job, since they are defined outside the **save** and **restore** that enclose individual pages of the script. A dictionary in local VM reverts to the initial state defined by the prolog at the end of each page. This is usually the desirable behavior. A dictionary in global VM accumulates changes indefinitely and never reverts to an earlier state. This is useful when there is a need to communicate information from one page to another (strongly discouraged in a page description).

- When using a writable dictionary in global VM, you must be careful about what objects you store in it. Attempting to store a local composite object in a global dictionary will cause an **invalidaccess** error. So, it is advisable to segregate local and global data and to use global VM only for those objects that must persist through executions of **save** and **restore**.

- In general, the prologs for most existing PostScript language programs do not work correctly if they are simply loaded into global VM. The same is true of some user-defined (Type 3) fonts. These programs must be altered to define global and local information separately. Typically, global VM should be used to hold procedure definitions and constant data; local VM should be used to hold temporary data needed during execution of the procedures. There is no advantage to putting prologs in global VM except to share them among multiple contexts in a Display PostScript system (see below).

- Creating gstate (graphics state) objects in global VM is particularly risky. This is because the graphics state almost always contains one or more local objects, which cannot be stored in a global gstate (see **currentgstate** operator in Chapter 8).

In a Display PostScript system, which supports multiple execution contexts operating simultaneously, global VM serves an additional purpose. Two or more contexts can share the same global VM, enabling them to communicate with each other dynamically. This is described in section 7.1, "Multiple Execution Contexts."

3.7.6 User Objects

Some applications require a convenient and efficient way to refer to PostScript language objects previously constructed in VM. The conventional way to accomplish this is to store such objects as named entries in dictionaries and later to refer to them by name. In a PostScript language program written by a programmer, this approach is natural and straightforward. When the program is generated mechanically by another program, however, it is more convenient to number the objects with small integers and later to refer to them by the numbers. This simplifies the bookkeeping the application program must do.

The PostScript language provides built-in support for a single space of numbered objects, called *user objects*. There are three operators, **defineuserobject**, **undefineuserobject**, and **execuserobject**, which manipulate an array named **UserObjects**. These operators don't introduce any fundamental capability. They merely provide convenient and efficient notation for accessing the elements of a special array.

Note   *User objects exist only in Level 2 and Display PostScript implementations. The user object facility is entirely separate from the encoded user name feature of the binary encoding of the PostScript language. The latter is a Display PostScript extension that is described in Chapter 7.*

Example 3.4 illustrates the intended use of user objects:

Example 3.4

```
17 {ucache 132 402 316 554 setbbox ... } cvlit defineuserobject
17 execuserobject ufill
```

The first line of the example constructs an interesting object that is to be used repeatedly (in this case, a user path; see section 4.6, "User Paths") and associates the user object index 17 with this object.

The second line pushes the user object onto the operand stack, from which **ufill** takes it. **execuserobject** *executes* the user object associated with index 17. However, because the object in this example is not executable, the result of the execution is to push the object onto the operand stack.

Note *The pswrap translator, an adjunct to the Display PostScript system, enables an application program to refer to user objects conveniently (see Chapter 7).*

defineuserobject manages the **UserObjects** array automatically; there is no reason for a PostScript language program to refer to **UserObjects** explicitly. The array is allocated in local VM and defined in **userdict**. This means that the effect of **defineuserobject** is subject to **save** and **restore**. The values of user objects given to **defineuserobject** can be in either local or global VM.

3.7.7 Job Execution Environment

As indicated in section 2.4, "Using the PostScript Language," the conventional model of a PostScript interpreter is a "print server"—a single-threaded process that consumes and executes a sequence of "print jobs," each of which is a complete, independent PostScript language program. This model is also appropriate for certain other environments, such as a document previewer built on top of a Display PostScript system.

This model *does not* apply when an application uses the Display Post-Script system to manage the display screen interactively. That is described in Chapter 7. The following material applies *only* to a Post-Script interpreter that is being operated as a job server.

The notion of a "print job" is not formally a part of the PostScript language, because it involves not only the PostScript interpreter but also some description of the environment in which the interpreter operates. Still, it is useful to describe a general *job* model that is accurate for most PostScript printers, though perhaps lacking in some details. Information about communication protocols, job control, system management, and so on, does not appear here, but in documentation for specific products.

A job begins execution in an initial environment that consists of an empty operand stack, a dictionary stack containing the three standard dictionaries (**systemdict**, **globaldict** (*Level 2*), and **userdict**), many other objects accessible via those dictionaries, and miscellaneous interpreter parameters.

During execution, the job may alter its environment. Ordinarily, when a job finishes, the environment reverts to its initial state to prepare for the next job. That is, the job is *encapsulated*. The server accomplishes this encapsulation by executing **save** and **restore** and by explicitly resetting stacks and parameters between jobs.

With suitable authorization, a job can make persistent alterations to objects in VM. That is, the job is not encapsulated. Instead, its alterations appear as part of the initial state of the next and all subsequent jobs. This is accomplished by means of the **startjob** and **exitserver** facilities described below.

Server Operation

A job server is presented a sequence of files via one or more communication channels. For each file, the server performs the following sequence of steps:

1. Establish standard input and output file objects for the channel from which the file is to be obtained.

2. Execute **save**. This is the outermost **save**, which unlike a normal **save** obtains a snapshot of the initial state of objects in both local and global VM.

3. Establish default initial state for the interpreter: empty operand stack, local VM allocation mode, default user space for the raster output device, and so on.

4. Execute the standard input file until it reaches end-of-file or an error occurs. If an error occurs, report it and flush input to end-of-file.

5. Execute **restore**, causing objects in VM (both local and global) to revert to the state saved in step 2.

6. Close the standard input and output files, transmitting an end-of-file indication over the communication channel.

Ordinarily, the server executes all six steps once for each file that it receives. Each file is treated as a separate job, and each job is encapsulated.

Altering Initial VM

A program can circumvent job encapsulation and alter the initial VM for subsequent jobs. To do so, it can use either **startjob**, a Level 2 feature, or **exitserver**, a feature available in all implementations that include a job server. This capability is controlled by a password. The system administrator can choose not to make the capability available to ordinary users. Applications and drivers must be prepared to deal with the possibility that altering the initial VM is not allowed.

Note *startjob and exitserver should be invoked only by a print manager, spooler, or system administration program. They should never be used by an application program composing a page description. Appendix I gives more guidelines for using startjob and exitserver.*

startjob is invoked as follows:

 true *password* startjob

where *password* is a password—a string or integer; see section C.3.1, "Passwords." If this is successful, **startjob** causes the server to execute steps 5, 3, and 4 in the above sequence. In other words, it logically ends the current job, undoing all modifications it has made so far, and starts a new job. However, it does not precede the new job with a **save**, so its execution is not encapsulated. Furthermore, it does not disturb the standard input and output files; the interpreter resumes consuming the remainder of the same input file.

Having started an unencapsulated job, the PostScript language program can alter the VM in arbitrary ways. Those alterations are persistent. If the job simply runs to completion, ending step 4 in the above sequence, the server skips step 5 (since there is no saved VM snapshot to restore), continues with step 6, and processes the next job normally starting at step 1.

Alternatively, a program can explicitly terminate its alterations to initial VM:

 false *password* startjob

This has the effect of executing steps 2, 3, and 4, logically starting yet another job that is encapsulated in the normal way, but still continuing to read from the same file.

If **startjob** executes successfully, it always starts a new job in the sense described above. It clears all the stacks and then pushes the result *true* on the operand stack. But if **startjob** is unsuccessful, it has no effect other than to push *false* on the operand stack. In the latter case, the effect is as if the program text before and after the occurrence of **startjob** were a single combined job.

A typical sequence is:

```
true password startjob pop
...application prolog here...
false password startjob pop
...application script here...
```

This installs the application prolog in initial VM if it is allowed to do so. However, the script executes successfully, regardless of whether the attempt to alter initial VM was successful. The program can determine the outcome by testing the result returned by **startjob**.

Although the above sequence is typical, there is no restriction on the sequence of encapsulated and unencapsulated jobs. If the password is correct and the boolean operand to **startjob** is *true*, the job that follows it is unencapsulated; if *false*, the job is encapsulated. But if the password is incorrect, **startjob** does not start a new job; the current job simply continues.

startjob also fails to start a new job if, at the time it is executed, the current **save** nesting is more than one level deep. In other words, **startjob** works only when the current **save** level is equal to the level at which the current job started. This permits a file that executes **startjob** to be encapsulated as part of another job simply by bracketing it with **save** and **restore**.

Note   *If an unencapsulated job uses **save** and **restore**, the **save** and **restore** affect global as well as local VM, since they are at the outermost **save** level. Also, if the job ends with one or more **save**s pending, a **restore** to the outermost saved VM is performed automatically.*

exitserver

exitserver is an unofficial Level 1 feature that is retained in Level 2 implementations for compatibility. Although **exitserver** has never been a formal part of the PostScript language, it exists in nearly every Adobe

PostScript product. Some applications have come to depend on it. The **startjob** feature, described above, is more flexible and is preferred for new Level 2 applications.

The canonical method of invoking **exitserver** is:

    serverdict begin *password* exitserver

This has the same effect as:

    true *password* startjob not
    {/exitserver errordict /invalidaccess get exec} if

In other words, if successful, **exitserver** initiates an unencapsulated job that can alter initial VM; if unsuccessful, it generates an **invalidaccess** error. Like **startjob**, a successful **exitserver** clears the stacks—it removes **serverdict** from the dictionary stack. The program that follows (terminated by end-of-file) is executed as an unencapsulated job.

In many implementations, successful execution of **exitserver** sends the message %%[exitserver: permanent state may be changed]%% to the standard output file. This message is not generated by **startjob**. It is suppressed if **binary** is *true* in the **$error** dictionary. See section 3.10.2, "Error Handling."

Note   *Aside from **exitserver**, the other contents of **serverdict** are not specified as part of the language. In Level 2, the effect of executing **exitserver** more than once in the same file is the same as that of executing the equivalent **startjob** sequence multiple times. In Level 1, the effect of executing the **exitserver** operator multiple times is undefined and unpredictable.*

3.8 File Input and Output

A file is a finite sequence of characters bounded by an end-of-file indication. These characters may be stored permanently in some place (for instance, a disk file) or they may be generated on the fly and transmitted over some communication channel. Files are the means by which the PostScript interpreter receives executable programs and exchanges data with the external environment.

There are two kinds of files: *input* and *output*. An input file is a source from which a PostScript language program can read a sequence of characters. An output file is a destination to which a PostScript language program can write characters. Some files in permanent storage media can be read and written.

3.8.1 Basic File Operators

A PostScript *file object* represents a file. The file operators take a file object as an operand to read or write characters. Ignoring for a moment *how* a file object comes into existence, the file operators include:

- **read** reads the next character from an input file.

- **write** appends a character to an output file.

- **readstring**, **readline**, and **writestring** transfer the contents of strings to and from files.

- **readhexstring** and **writehexstring** read and write binary data represented in the file by hexadecimal notation.

- **token** scans characters from an input file according to the PostScript language syntax rules.

- **exec**, applied to an input file, causes the PostScript interpreter to execute a PostScript language program from that file.

The operators that write to a file do not necessarily deliver the characters to their destination immediately. They may leave some characters in buffers for reasons of implementation or efficiency. The **flush** and **flushfile** operators deliver these buffered characters immediately. These operators are useful in certain situations, such as during two-way interactions with another computer or with a human user, when such data must be transmitted immediately.

Standard Input and Output Files

All PostScript interpreters provide *standard input* and *standard output* files, which usually represent a real-time communication channel to and from another computer or user terminal. The standard input and output files always exist; it is not necessary for a program to create or close them.

The PostScript interpreter reads and interprets the standard input file as PostScript language program text. It sends error and status messages to the standard output file. Also, a PostScript language program may execute the **print** operator to send arbitrary data to the standard output file. Note that **print** is a *file* operator; it has nothing to do with placing text on a page or causing pages to emerge from a printer.

It seldom is necessary for a PostScript language program to deal explicitly with file objects for the standard files, because the PostScript interpreter reads the standard input file by default and the **print** operator references the standard output file implicitly. Additionally, the file currently being read by the PostScript interpreter is available via the **currentfile** operator. This file need not be the standard input file. However, when necessary, a program may apply the **file** operator to the identifying strings %stdin or %stdout to obtain file objects for the standard input and output files.

End-of-Line Conventions

The PostScript language scanner and the **readline** operator recognize all three external forms of end-of-line (EOL)—LF alone, CR alone, and the CR LF pair—and treat them uniformly. The PostScript interpreter does not translate data read by other means or written by any means.

End-of-line sequences are recognized and treated specially in the following situations:

- Any of the three forms of EOL appearing in a literal string are converted to a single *newline* (LF character) in the resulting string object.

  (any text$^{(CR)}$some more text)
  (any text$^{(LF)}$some more text)
  (any text$^{(CR)(LF)}$some more text)

  These three examples produce identical string objects, each of which has a single newline (LF) separating "text" and "some."

- Any of the three forms of EOL appearing immediately after \ in a string are treated as a line continuation; both the \ and the EOL are discarded.

  (any text\$^{(CR)}$some more text)
  (any text\$^{(LF)}$some more text)
  (any text\$^{(CR)(LF)}$some more text)
  (any textsome more text)

  These four examples produce identical string objects.

- Any of the three forms of EOL appearing outside a string are treated as a single white-space character. Since the language treats multiple white-space characters as a single white-space character, the treatment of EOL is interesting only when a PostScript language token is followed by data to be read explicitly by one of the file operators.

```
currentfile read(CR)x
currentfile read(LF)x
currentfile read(CR)(LF)x
```

The above three examples produce identical results: the operator reads the character x from the current input file and leaves its character code (the integer 120) on the stack.

- The **readline** operator treats any of the three forms of EOL as the termination condition.

- Data read by **read** and **readstring** do not undergo EOL translation. The PostScript interpreter reads whatever characters were received from the channel. However, the channel itself may perform some EOL translation, as discussed below.

- Data written by **write** and **writestring** do not undergo EOL translation. Whatever characters the PostScript interpreter provides are sent to the channel. However, the channel itself may perform some EOL translation, as discussed below.

Communication Channel Behavior

Communications functions often usurp control characters. Control codes are device dependent and not part of the PostScript language. For example, the serial communication protocol supported by many products uses the Control-D character as an end-of-file indication. In this case, Control-D is a communications function and not logically part of a PostScript language program. This specifically applies to the serial channel; other channels, such as LocalTalk™ and Ethernet, have different conventions for end-of-file and other control functions. *In all cases, communication channel behavior is independent of the actions of the Post-Script interpreter.*

There are two levels of PostScript EOL translation: one in the PostScript interpreter and one in the serial communication channel. The previous description applies *only* to the EOL conventions at the level of the Post-Script interpreter. The purpose of the seemingly redundant communication level EOL translation is to maintain compatibility with diverse host operating system and communications environments.

As discussed in section 3.2, "Syntax," the ASCII encoding of the language is designed for maximum portability. It avoids using control characters that might be pre-empted by operating systems or communication channels. However, there are situations in which transmission of arbitrary binary data is desirable. For example, sampled images are represented by large quantities of binary data. The PostScript language has an alternative binary encoding that is advantageous in certain situations. There are two main ways to deal with PostScript language programs that contain binary information:

- Communicate with the interpreter via binary channels exclusively. Some channels, such as LocalTalk and Ethernet, are binary by nature. They do not pre-empt any character codes, but instead communicate control information separately from the data. Other channels, such as serial channels, may support a binary communication protocol that allows control characters to be quoted. This approach presupposes a well-controlled environment. PostScript language programs produced in that environment may not be portable to other environments.

- Take advantage of filters for encoding binary data as ASCII text. Filters are a Level 2 feature, described in section 3.8.4, "Filters." Programs represented in this way do not include any control codes and are therefore portable to any Level 2 interpreter in any environment.

3.8.2 Named Files

The PostScript language provides access to named files in secondary storage. The file access capabilities are part of the integration of the language with an underlying operating system; there are variations from one such integration to another. Not all the file system capabilities of the underlying operating system are necessarily made available at the PostScript language level.

The PostScript language provides a standard set of operators for accessing named files. These operators are supported in all Level 2 implementations and also in certain Level 1 implementations that have access to file systems. The operators are **deletefile**, **renamefile**, **filenameforall**, **setfileposition**, and **fileposition**. Although the language defines a standard framework for dealing with files, the detailed semantics of the file system operators, particularly file-naming conventions, are operating system dependent.

Files are in one or more "secondary storage devices," hereafter referred to simply as *devices*. (These are not to be confused with the "current device," which is a raster output device identified in the graphics state.) The PostScript language defines a uniform convention for naming devices, but it says nothing about how files in a given device are named. Different devices have different properties, and not all devices support all operations.

A complete file name is in the form %*device*%*file*, where *device* identifies the secondary storage device and *file* is the name of the file within the device. When a complete file name is presented to a file system operator, the *device* portion selects the device; the *file* portion is in turn presented to the implementation of that device, which is operating system and environment dependent.

When a file name is presented without a %*device*% prefix, a search rule determines which device is selected. The available storage devices are consulted in order; the requested operation is attempted on each device until the operation succeeds. The number of available devices, their names, and the order in which they are searched is environment dependent. Not all devices necessarily participate in such searches; some devices can be accessed only by explicitly naming them.

In an interpreter that runs on top of an operating system (OS), such as the Display PostScript system in a workstation, there is a device that represents the complete file system provided by the OS. If so, by convention that device's name is os; thus, complete file names are in the form %os%*file*, where *file* conforms to underlying file system conventions. This device always participates in searches, as described above; a program can access ordinary files without specifying the %os% prefix. There may be more than one device that behaves in this way; the names of such devices are product dependent.

Note   *The os device may impose some restrictions on the set of files that can be accessed. Restrictions are necessary when the PostScript interpreter executes with a user identity different from that of the user running the application program.*

In an interpreter that controls a dedicated product, such as a typical printer product, there can be one or more devices that represent file systems on disks and cartridges. Files on these devices have names such as %disk0%*file*, %disk1%*file*, and %cartridge0%*file*. Once again, these devices participate in searches when the device name is not specified.

For the operators **file**, **deletefile**, **renamefile**, **status**, and **filenameforall**, a *filename* is a string object that identifies a file. The name of the file can be in one of three forms.

- %*device*%*file* identifies a named file on a specific *device*, as described above.

- *file* (first character not %) identifies a named file on an unspecified device, which is selected by an environment-specific search rule, as described above.

- %*device* or %*device*% identifies an unnamed file on the device. Certain devices, such as cartridges, support a single unnamed file as opposed to a collection of named files. Other devices represent communication channels rather than permanent storage media. There are also special files named %stdin, %stdout, %lineedit, and %statementedit, described below. The **deletefile**, **renamefile**, and **filenameforall** operators do not apply to file names of this form.

"Wildcard" file names are handled by the **filenameforall** operator. See **filenameforall** in Chapter 8 for more information on wildcards.

Creating and Closing a File Object

File objects are created by the **file** operator. This operator takes two strings: the first identifies the file and the second specifies access. **file** returns a new file object associated with that file.

An *access* is a string object that specifies how a file is to be accessed. File access conventions are operating system specific. The following access specifications are typical of the UNIX operating system and are supported by many others. The access string always begins with r, w, or a, possibly followed by +; any additional characters supply operating system specific information. Table 3.5 lists access strings and their meanings.

Table 3.5 *Access strings*

Access string	Meaning
r	Open for reading only. Error if file doesn't already exist.
w	Open for writing only. Create file if it doesn't already exist. Truncate and overwrite it if it does exist.
a	Open for writing only. Create file if it doesn't already exist. Append to it if it does.

r+	Open for reading and writing. Error if file doesn't already exist.
w+	Open for reading and writing. Create file if it doesn't already exist. Truncate and overwrite it if it does.
a+	Open for reading and writing. Create file if it doesn't already exist. Append to it if it does.

Like other composite objects, such as strings and arrays, file objects have access attributes. The access attribute of a file object is based on the access string used to create it. Attempting to access a file object in a way that would violate its access causes an **invalidaccess** error.

Certain files—in particular, named files on disk—are *positionable*, meaning that one can access the data in the file in an arbitrary order rather than only sequentially from the beginning. The **setfileposition** operator adjusts a file object so it refers to a specified position in the underlying file; subsequent reads or writes access the file at that new position. One can open a positionable file for reading and writing by specifying + in the access string, as shown in Table 3.5. To ensure predictable results, it is necessary to execute **setfileposition** when switching between reading and writing.

At the end of reading or writing a file, a program should *close* the file to break the association between the PostScript file object and the actual file. The file operators close a file automatically if end-of-file is encountered during reading (see below). The **closefile** operator closes a file explicitly. **restore** closes a file if the file object was created since the corresponding **save** while in local VM allocation mode. Garbage collection closes a file if the object is no longer accessible.

All operators that access files treat end-of-file and exception conditions the same. During reading, if an end-of-file indication is encountered before the requested item can be read, the file is closed and the operation returns an explicit end-of-file result. This also occurs if the file has already been closed when the operator is executed. All other exceptions during reading and any exceptions during writing result in execution of the errors **ioerror**, **invalidfileaccess**, or **invalidaccess**.

3.8.3 Special Files

The **file** operator can also return special files that are identified by the *filename* string. These special files are:

• %stdin, the standard input file.

- %stdout, the standard output file.

- %stderr, the standard error file. This is for reporting low-level errors. In many configurations, it is the same as the standard output file.

- %statementedit, the statement editor filter file, described below.

- %lineedit, the line editor filter file, described below.

For example, the statements

```
(%stdin) (r) file
(%stdout) (w) file
```

push copies of the standard input and output file objects on the operand stack. These are duplicates of existing file objects, not new objects.

Some PostScript interpreters support an *interactive executive,* invoked by **executive**; this is described in section 2.4.4, "Using the Interpreter Interactively." **executive** obtains commands from the user by means of a special file named %statementedit. Applying the **file** operator to the file name string %statementedit causes the following:

- The **file** operator begins reading characters from the standard input file and storing them in a temporary buffer. While doing so, it echoes the characters to the standard output file. It also interprets certain control characters as editing functions for making corrections, as described in section 2.4.4, "Using the Interpreter Interactively."

- When a complete statement has been entered, the **file** operator returns. A statement consists of one or more lines terminated by newline that together form one or more complete PostScript language tokens, with no opening brackets ({, (, <, or <~) left unmatched.

- The returned file object represents a temporary file containing the statement that was entered. Reading from that file obtains the characters of the statement in turn; end-of-file is reported when the end of the statement is reached. Normally, this file is used as an operand to **exec**, causing the statement to be executed as a PostScript language program.

The %lineedit special file is similar to %statementedit. However, the file operator returns after a single line has been entered, regardless of whether it constitutes a complete statement. If the standard input file reaches end-of-file before any characters have been entered, the **file** operator issues an **undefinedfilename** error.

It is important to understand that the file object returned by **file** for the %statementedit and %lineedit special files is not the same as the standard input file. It represents a temporary file containing a single buffered statement. When the end of that statement is reached, the file is closed and the file object is no longer of any use. Successive executions of **file** for %statementedit and %lineedit return different file objects.

The %statementedit and %lineedit special files are not available in PostScript interpreters that do not support an interactive executive. PostScript language programs that are page descriptions should never refer to these files.

3.8.4   Filters

A *filter* is a special kind of file object that can be layered on top of some other file to transform data being read from or written to that file. When a PostScript language program reads characters from an input filter, the filter reads characters from its underlying file and transforms the data in some way, depending on the filter. Similarly, when a program writes characters to an output filter, the filter transforms the data and writes the results to its underlying file. Filters are a Level 2 feature.

There are two main classes of filters:

- An *encoding filter* is an output file that takes the data written to it, converts them to some encoded representation depending on the filter, and writes the encoded data to the underlying file. For example, the **ASCIIHexEncode** filter transforms binary data to an ASCII hexadecimal encoded representation, which it writes to its underlying file. All encoding filters have "Encode" as part of their names.

- A *decoding filter* is an input file that reads encoded data from its underlying file and decodes them. The program reading from the filter receives the decoded data. For example, the **ASCIIHexDecode** filter reads ASCII hexadecimal encoded data from its underlying file and transforms them to binary. All decoding filters have "Decode" as part of their names.

Decoding filters are most likely to be used in page descriptions. An application program generating a page description can encode certain information (for example, data for sampled images) to compress it or to convert it to a portable ASCII representation. Then, within the page description itself, it invokes the corresponding decoding filter to convert the information back to its original form.

Encoding filters are unlikely to be used in most page descriptions. However, a PostScript language program can use them to encode data to be sent back to the application or written to a disk file. In the interest of symmetry, the PostScript language supports both encoding and decoding filters for all of its standard data transformation algorithms.

Creating Filters

Filter files are created by the **filter** operator, which is a Level 2 feature. The **filter** operator expects the following operands in the order given:

1. A *data source* or *data target*. This is ordinarily a file object that represents the underlying file the filter is to read or write. However, it can also be a string or a procedure. This is described in section 3.13, "Filtered Files Details."

2. *Filter parameters*. Some filters require additional parameters to control how they operate. This information must be given as one or more operands following the data source or target. Most filters require no additional parameters.

3. *Filter name*. This is a name object, such as **ASCIIHexDecode**, that specifies the data transformation the filter is to perform. It also determines how many parameters there are and how they are to be interpreted.

The **filter** operator returns a new file object that represents the filtered file. For an encoding filter, this is an output file, and for a decoding filter, an input file. The direction of the underlying file—that is, its read/write attribute—must match that of the filter. Filtered files can be used just the same as other files; they are valid as operands to file operators such as **read**, **write**, **readstring**, and **writestring**. Input filters are also valid as data sources for operators such as **exec** or **image**.

Since a filter is itself a file, it can be used as the underlying file for yet another filter. One can cascade filters to form a *pipeline* that passes the data stream through two or more encoding or decoding transformations in sequence. Example 3.5 illustrates the construction of an input pipeline for decoding sampled image data that is embedded in the program. The application has encoded the image data twice: once using the **RunLengthEncode** method to compress the data and then using the **ASCII85Encode** method to represent the binary compressed data as ASCII text.

Example 3.5

```
256 256 8 [256 0 0 –256 0 256]    % Other operands of image operator
currentfile
/ASCII85Decode filter
/RunLengthDecode filter
image
...Encoded image data...
~>                                % ASCII85 end-of-data marker
```

The **currentfile** operator returns the file object from which the Post-Script interpreter is currently executing. The first execution of **filter** creates an **ASCII85Decode** filter whose underlying file is the one returned by **currentfile**. It pushes the filter file object on the stack. The second execution of **filter** creates a **RunLengthDecode** filter whose underlying file is the first filter file; it pushes the new filter file object on the stack. Finally, the **image** operator uses the second filter file as its data source. As **image** reads from its data source, the data are drawn from the underlying file and transformed by the two filters in sequence.

Standard Filters

The PostScript language supports a standard set of filters. These filters fall into three main categories. Each category includes encoding and decoding filters.

- *ASCII encoding filters* enable arbitrary 8-bit binary data to be represented in the printable subset of the ASCII character set. This improves the portability of the resulting data, since it avoids the problem of interference by operating systems or communication channels that pre-empt use of control characters, represent text as 7-bit bytes, or impose line-length restrictions.

- *Compression and decompression filters* enable data to be represented in a compressed form. This is particularly valuable for large sampled images. Compressing the image data reduces storage requirements and transmission time. There are several compression filters, each of which is best suited for particular kinds of image data. Note that the compressed data is in 8-bit binary form. For maximum portability of the encoded data, these filters should be used with ASCII encoding filters, as illustrated in Example 3.5.

- *Subfile filters* pass data through without modification. These filters permit the creation of file objects that access arbitrary user-defined data sources or data targets. Input filters also can read data from an underlying file up to a specified end-of-data marker.

Table 3.6 summarizes the available filters. A program can determine the complete list of filters that the PostScript interpreter supports by applying the **resourceforall** operator to the **Filter** category; see section 3.9, "Named Resources."

Table 3.6 *Standard filters*

Filter name	Parameters	Semantics
ASCIIHexEncode	(none)	Encodes binary data in an ASCII hexadecimal representation. Each binary data byte is converted to two hexadecimal digits, resulting in an expansion factor of 1:2 in the size of the encoded data.
ASCIIHexDecode	(none)	Decodes ASCII hexadecimal encoded data, producing the original binary data.
ASCII85Encode	(none)	Encodes binary data in an ASCII base-85 representation. This encoding uses nearly all of the printable ASCII character set. The resulting expansion factor is 4:5, making this encoding much more efficient than hexadecimal.
ASCII85Decode	(none)	Decodes ASCII base-85 encoded data, producing the original binary data.
LZWEncode	(none)	Compresses text or binary data using the LZW (Lempel-Ziv-Welch) adaptive compression method. This is a good general-purpose encoding that is especially well-suited for English language and PostScript language text.
LZWDecode	(none)	Decompresses LZW encoded data, producing the original text or binary data.
RunLengthEncode	recordsize	Compresses binary data using a simple byte-oriented run-length encoding algorithm. This encoding is best suited to monochrome image data, or any data that contain frequent long runs of a single byte value.
RunLengthDecode	(none)	Decompresses run-length encoded data, producing the original binary data.
CCITTFaxEncode	dictionary	Compresses binary data using a bit-oriented encoding algorithm (the CCITT facsimile standard). This encoding is specialized to monochrome image data at 1 bit per pixel.
CCITTFaxDecode	dictionary	Decompresses facsimile encoded data, producing the original binary data.
DCTEncode	dictionary	Compresses continuous-tone (gray-scale or color) sampled image data using a DCT (discrete cosine transform) technique based on the proposed JPEG standard. This encoding is specialized to image data. It is "lossy," meaning that the encoding algorithm can lose some information.

DCTDecode	dictionary	Decompresses DCT encoded data, producing image sample data that approximate the original data.
NullEncode	(none)	Passes all data through, without any modification. This permits an arbitrary data target (procedure or string) to be treated as an output file.
SubFileDecode	count, string	Passes all data through, without any modification. This permits an arbitrary data source (procedure or string) to be treated as an input file. Optionally, this filter detects an end-of-data marker in the source data stream, treating the preceding data as a subfile.

Section 3.13, "Filtered Files Details," has complete information about individual filters, including specifications of the encoding algorithms for some of them. The section also describes the semantics of data sources and data targets in more detail.

3.8.5 Additional File Operators

There are other miscellaneous file operators:

- **status** and **bytesavailable** return status information about a file.

- **currentfile** returns the file object from which the interpreter is currently reading.

- **run** is a convenience operator that combines the functions of **file** and **exec**.

Several built-in procedures print the values of objects on the operand stack, sending a readable representation of those values to the standard output file:

- = pops one object from the operand stack and writes a text representation of its value to the standard output file, followed by a newline.

- == is similar to =, but produces results closer to full PostScript language syntax and expands the values of arrays.

- **stack** prints the entire contents of the operand stack with =, but leaves the stack unchanged.

- **pstack** performs a similar operation to **stack**, but uses ==.

Input/output and storage devices can be manipulated individually by Level 2 operators. In particular:

- **setdevparams** and **currentdevparams** access device-dependent parameters (see Appendix C).

- **resourceforall**, applied to the **IODevice** category, enumerates all available devices (see section 3.9, "Named Resources").

3.9 Named Resources

The PostScript language has various features involving the use of open-ended collections of objects to control what the features do. For example, the font machinery uses font dictionaries that describe the appearance of characters. The number of possible font dictionaries is unlimited. For Level 2 implementations this same idea applies to forms, patterns, color rendering dictionaries, and many other categories of objects.

It is often convenient to associate these objects with names in some central registry. This is particularly true for fonts, which are assigned standard names, such as Times-Roman or Palatino-BoldItalic, when they are created. Other categories of objects also can benefit from a central naming convention.

If all available objects in a particular category (for example, all possible fonts) were *permanently* resident in VM, they could simply be stored in some dictionary. Accessing a named object would be a matter of performing **get** from the dictionary; checking if a named object is available would be accomplished by performing a **known** on the dictionary.

There are many more fonts and objects of other categories than can possibly reside in VM at any given time. These objects originate from a source external to the PostScript interpreter. They are introduced into VM in two ways:

1. The application or spooler embeds the objects' definitions directly in the job stream.

2. During execution, the PostScript language program requests the objects by name. The interpreter loads them into VM automatically from an external source, such as a disk file, a ROM cartridge, or a network file server.

The notion of "named resources" supports the second method. A resource is a collection of named objects that either reside in VM or can be located and brought into VM on demand. There are separate categories of resources with independent name spaces. For example, fonts and forms are distinct resource categories. Within each category, there is a collection of named resource instances. Some instances are objects that reside in VM, while others exist in some external form that can be brought into VM on demand. Each category can have its own policy for locating instances that are not in VM and for managing the instances that are in VM.

3.9.1   Resource Operators

There are five operators that apply to resources: **findresource**, **resourcestatus**, **resourceforall**, **defineresource**, and **undefineresource**. These operators and the general concept of named resources are Level 2 features. A more limited facility applicable only to fonts—the **findfont** and **definefont** operators—is available in Level 1.

The **findresource** operator is the key feature of the resource facility. Given a resource category name and an instance name, **findresource** returns an object. If the requested resource instance does not already exist as an object in VM, **findresource** gets it from an external source and loads it into VM. A PostScript language program can access named resources without knowing if they are already in VM or how they are obtained from external storage.

Other important features include **resourcestatus**, which returns information about a resource instance, and **resourceforall**, which enumerates all available resource instances in a particular category. These operators apply to all resource instances, whether or not they reside in VM; the operators do not cause the resource instances to be brought into VM. **resourceforall** should be used with care and only when absolutely necessary, since the set of available resource instances is potentially extremely large.

A program can explicitly define a named resource instance in VM. That is, it can create an object in VM, then execute **defineresource** to associate the object with a name in a particular resource category. This resource instance will be visible in subsequent executions of **findresource**, **resourcestatus**, and **resourceforall**. A program can also execute **undefineresource** to reverse the effect of a prior **defineresource**. The **findresource** operator automatically executes **defineresource** and **undefineresource** to manage the VM for resource instances that it obtains from external storage.

Resource instances can be defined in either local or global VM. The lifetime of the definition depends on the VM allocation mode in effect at the time the definition is made (see section 3.7.2, "Local and Global VM"). Normally, both local and global resource instances are visible and available to a program. However, when the current VM allocation mode is global, only global instances are visible; this ensures correct behavior of resource instances that are defined in terms of other resource instances.

When a program executes **defineresource** to define a resource instance explicitly, it has complete control over whether to use local or global VM. However, when execution of **findresource** causes a resource instance to be brought into VM automatically, the decision whether to use local or global VM is independent of the VM allocation mode at the time **findresource** is executed. Usually, resource instances are loaded into global VM; this enables them to be managed independently of the **save** and **restore** activity of the executing program. However, certain resource instances do not function correctly when they reside in global VM; they are loaded into local VM instead.

The language does not specify a standard method for installing resources in external storage. Installation typically consists of writing a named file in a file system. However, details of how resource names are mapped to file names and how the files are managed are environment dependent. In some environments, resources may be installed using facilities entirely separate from the PostScript interpreter.

Resource instances are identified by keys that ordinarily are name or string objects; the resource operators treat names and strings equivalently. Use of other types of keys is permitted but not recommended. The **defineresource** operator can define a resource instance with a key that is not a name or string; the other resource operators can access the instance using that key. However, such a key can never match any resource instance in external storage.

3.9.2 Resource Categories

Resource categories are identified by name. The standard resource categories are in the following tables. Within a given category, every resource instance that resides in VM is of a particular type and has a particular intended interpretation or use.

Table 3.7 *Regular resources*

Category name	Object type	Interpretation
Font	dictionary	Font dictionary
Encoding	array	Encoding vector
Form	dictionary	Form definition
Pattern	dictionary	Pattern definition (prototype)
ProcSet	dictionary	Procedure set
ColorSpace	array	Parameterized color space
Halftone	dictionary	Halftone dictionary
ColorRendering	dictionary	Color rendering dictionary

Table 3.8 *Resources whose instances are implicit*

Category name	Object type	Interpretation
Filter	name	Filter algorithm
ColorSpaceFamily	name	Color space family
Emulator	name	Language interpreter
IODevice	string	Input/output or storage device
ColorRenderingType	integer	Color rendering dictionary type
FMapType	integer	Composite font mapping algorithm
FontType	integer	Font dictionary type
FormType	integer	Form dictionary type
HalftoneType	integer	Halftone dictionary type
ImageType	integer	Image dictionary type
PatternType	integer	Pattern dictionary type

Table 3.9 *Resources used in defining new resource categories*

Category name	Object type	Interpretation
Category	dictionary	Resource category (recursive)
Generic	any	Prototype for new categories

Regular resources are those whose instances are ordinary useful objects, such as font or halftone dictionaries. For example, a program typically uses the result returned by **findresource** as an operand of some other operator, such as **scalefont** or **sethalftone**.

Implicit resources are those whose instances are not objects, but which represent some built-in capability of the PostScript interpreter. For example, the instances of the **Filter** category are filter names, such as **ASCII85Decode** and **CCITTFaxDecode**, that are passed directly to the **filter** operator. For such resources, the **findresource** operator returns only its name operand. However, **resourceforall** and **resourcestatus** are useful for inquiring about the availability of capabilities, such as specific filter algorithms.

The **Category** and **Generic** resources are used in defining new categories of resources. This is described in section 3.9.3, "Creating Resource Categories."

The resource operators—**findresource**, **resourcestatus**, **resourceforall**, **defineresource**, and **undefineresource**—have standard behavior that is uniform across all resource categories. This behavior is specified in the operator descriptions in Chapter 8. For some categories, the operators have additional semantics that are category specific. The following sections describe the semantics of each resource category.

Font

Instance names of the **Font** resource category are font names, such as Times-Roman. The instances are prototype font dictionaries. Those instances are suitable for use as operands to **scalefont** or **makefont**, producing a transformed font dictionary that can be used to paint characters on the page.

There are several special-purpose operators that apply only to fonts, but are otherwise equivalent to the resource operators:

- **findfont** is equivalent to /Font findresource

- **definefont** is equivalent to /Font defineresource

- **undefinefont** is equivalent to /Font undefineresource

The **definefont** and **undefinefont** operators have additional font-specific semantics, which are described under those operators. Those semantics also apply to **defineresource** and **undefineresource** when applied to the **Font** category. **findfont** and **definefont** are available in Level 1 implementations, even though the general facility for named resources exists only in Level 2.

The font operators also maintain dictionaries of font names and instances that are defined in VM. Those dictionaries are **FontDirectory** (all fonts in VM) and **GlobalFontDirectory** (only fonts in global VM). They are provided solely for compatibility with existing applications, which use them to enumerate the defined fonts; they are obsolete. The preferred method of enumerating all available fonts is:

(*) *proc scratch* /Font resourceforall

where *proc* is a procedure and *scratch* is a string used repeatedly to hold font names. This method works for all available fonts, whether or not they are in VM. Normally, it's preferable to use **resourcestatus** to determine the availability of specific resources rather than enumerate all resources and check whether those of interest are in the list.

Encoding

Instances of the **Encoding** resource category are array objects, suitable for use as the **Encoding** entry of font dictionaries (see section 5.3, "Character Encoding"). An encoding array usually contains 256 names, permitting it to be indexed by any 8-bit character code. An encoding array for use with composite fonts contains integers instead of names, and can be of any length.

There are two standard encodings that are permanently defined in VM and available by name in **systemdict**. If any other encodings exist, they are available only through **findresource**. There are three special-purpose operators that apply only to encodings, but are otherwise equivalent to the resource operators:

- **StandardEncoding** is equivalent to /StandardEncoding /Encoding findresource

- **ISOLatin1Encoding** is equivalent to /ISOLatin1Encoding /Encoding findresource

- **findencoding** is equivalent to /Encoding findresource

Form

Instances of the **Form** resource category are form dictionaries, described in section 4.7, "Forms." A form dictionary is suitable as the operand to **execform** to render the form on the page. There are no standard instances of this resource category.

Pattern

Instances of the **Pattern** resource category are prototype pattern dictionaries, described in section 4.9, "Patterns." A prototype pattern dictionary is suitable as the operand to **makepattern**, producing a transformed pattern dictionary describing a tiling that is locked to device space. This pattern can then be used in painting operations by establishing a **Pattern** color space or by invoking the **setpattern** operator. There are no standard instances of this resource category.

ProcSet

Instances of the **ProcSet** resource category are *procedure sets* or procsets. A procset is a dictionary containing named procedures. Application prologs can be organized as one or more procsets that are available from a library instead of being included in-line in every document that uses them. The **ProcSet** resource category is a way to organize such a library. There are no standard instances of this resource category.

Color Space

Instances of the **ColorSpace** resource category are array objects that represent fully parameterized color spaces. The first element of a color space array is a color space family name; the remaining elements are parameters to the color space. See section 4.8, "Color Spaces." There are no standard instances of this resource category.

Note   *The **ColorSpace** resource category is distinct from the **ColorSpaceFamily** category, described below.*

Halftone

Instances of the **Halftone** resource category are halftone dictionaries, suitable as operands to the **sethalftone** operator (see section 6.4, "Halftones"). There are no standard instances of this resource category.

ColorRendering

Instances of the **ColorRendering** resource category are color rendering dictionaries, suitable as operands to the **setcolorrendering** operator (see section 6.1, "CIE-Based Color to Device Color"). There are no standard instances of this resource category.

Implicit Resources

For all implicit resources, the **findresource** operator returns the instance's key if the instance is defined. The **resourcestatus** and **resourceforall** operators have their normal behavior, although the *status* and *size* values returned by **resourcestatus** are meaningless. The **defineresource** operator is ordinarily not allowed, but the ability to define new instances of implicit resources may exist in some implementations. The mechanisms are implementation dependent.

The instances of the **Filter** category are filter names, such as **ASCII85Decode** and **RunLengthEncode**, which are used as an operand of the **filter** operator to determine its behavior. Filters are described in section 3.8.4, "Filters."

The instances of the **ColorSpaceFamily** category are color space family names, which appear as the first element of a color space array object. Some color spaces, such as **DeviceRGB**, are determined by their family name; others, such as **CIEBasedABC**, require additional parameters to describe them. Color spaces are described in section 4.8, "Color Spaces."

The instances of the **Emulator** category are names of emulators for languages other than PostScript that may be built into a particular implementation. Those emulators are not a standard part of the PostScript language, but one or more of them may be present in some products.

The instances of the **IODevice** category are names of input/output and storage devices, expressed as strings of the form %*device*%. See section 3.8.2, "Named Files," and section C.4, "Device Parameters."

The instances of the **ColorRenderingType**, **FMapType**, **FontType**, **FormType**, **HalftoneType**, **ImageType**, and **PatternType** categories are integers that are the acceptable values for the correspondingly named entries in various classes of special dictionaries. For example, the

FontType category always includes the integers 0, 1, and 3 as keys. If an interpreter supports additional **FontType** values, the **FontType** category will also include those values as instances.

3.9.3   Creating Resource Categories

The language support for named resources is quite general. Most of it is independent of the semantics of specific resource categories. It's occasionally useful to create new resource categories, each containing an independent collection of named instances. This is accomplished through a level of recursion in the resource machinery itself.

The resource category named **Category** contains all of the resource categories as instances. The instance names are resource category names, such as **Font, Form**, and **Halftone**. The instance values are dictionary objects, each containing information about how the resource category is implemented.

A new resource category is created by defining a new instance of the **Category** category. Example 3.6 creates a Widget category.

Example 3.6

```
    true setglobal
    /Widget catdict /Category defineresource pop
    false setglobal
```

In this example, *catdict* is a dictionary describing the implementation of the Widget category. Once defined, one can manipulate instances of the Widget category like other categories:

```
    /Frob1 w /Widget defineresource        % Returns w
    /Frob1 /Widget findresource            % Returns w
    /Frob1 /Widget resourcestatus          % Returns status size true
    (*) proc scratch /Widget resourceforall % Pushes (Frob1) on stack,
                                            % then calls proc
```

In this example, *w* is an instance of the Widget category whose type is whatever is appropriate for widgets. /Frob1 is the name of that instance.

It is possible to redefine existing resource categories this way. Make sure the new definition correctly implements any special semantics of the category.

Category Implementation Dictionary

The behavior of all the resource operators, such as **defineresource**, is determined by entries in the resource category's implementation dictionary. This was supplied as an operand to **defineresource** when the category was created. In the example

/Frob1 *w* /Widget defineresource

the **defineresource** operator:

1. Obtains *catdict*, the implementation dictionary for the Widget category.

2. Executes **begin** on the implementation dictionary.

3. Executes the **DefineResource** entry in the dictionary, which is ordinarily a procedure, but might be an operator. When the procedure corresponding to the **DefineResource** entry is called, the operand stack contains the operands that were passed to **defineresource**, except the category name (Widget in this example) has been removed. **DefineResource** is expected to consume the remaining operands, perform whatever action is appropriate for this resource category, and return the appropriate result.

4. Executes the **end** operator. If an error occurred during step 3, it also restores the operand and dictionary stacks to their initial state.

The other resource operators—**undefineresource**, **findresource**, **resourcestatus**, and **resourceforall**—behave the same way, with the exception that **resourceforall** does not restore the stacks upon error. Aside from the steps described above, all of the behavior of the resource operators is implemented by the corresponding procedures in the dictionary.

A category implementation dictionary contains the following entries:

Table 3.10 *Entries in a category implementation dictionary*

Key	Type	Semantics
DefineResource	procedure	(*Required*) Implements **defineresource** behavior.
UndefineResource	procedure	(*Required*) Implements **undefineresource** behavior.
FindResource	procedure	(*Required*) Implements **findresource** behavior.
ResourceStatus	procedure	(*Required*) Implements **resourcestatus** behavior.

ResourceForAll	procedure	(*Required*) Implements **resourceforall** behavior.
Category	name	(*Required*) The category name. Inserted by **defineresource** when the category is defined.
InstanceType	name	(*Optional*) The expected type of instances of this category. If this entry is present, **defineresource** checks that the instance's type, as returned by the **type** operator, matches it.
ResourceFileName	procedure	(*Optional*) Translates a resource instance name to a file name (see below).

The dictionary may also contain other information useful to the procedures in the dictionary. Since the dictionary is on the dictionary stack at the time those procedures are called, the procedures can access the information conveniently.

A single dictionary provides the implementation for both local and global instances of a category. The implementation must maintain the local and global instances separately and must respect the VM allocation mode in effect at the time each resource operator is executed. The category implementation dictionary must be in global VM; the **defineresource** that installs it in the **Category** category must be executed while in global VM allocation mode.

Generic Category

The preceding section describes a way to define a new resource category, but it does not provide guidance about how the individual procedures in the category's dictionary should be implemented. In principle, every resource category has complete freedom over how to organize and manage resource instances, both in VM and in external storage.

Since different implementations have different conventions for organizing resource instances, especially in external storage, a program that seeks to create a new resource category might need implementation-dependent information. To overcome this problem, it is useful to have a generic resource implementation that can be copied and used to define new resource categories. The **Category** category contains an instance named **Generic,** whose value is a dictionary containing a generic resource implementation.

The following example of defining the Widget resource category is similar to Example 3.6 on page 93. However, Example 3.7 generates the category implementation dictionary by copying the one belonging to the **Generic** category. This avoids the need to know anything about how resource categories actually work.

Example 3.7

```
true setglobal
/Generic /Category findresource
dup length 1 add dict copy
dup /InstanceType /dicttype put
/Widget exch /Category defineresource pop
false setglobal
```

The **Generic** resource category's implementation dictionary does not have an **InstanceType** entry; instances need not be of any particular type. In the above example, the third line makes a copy of the dictionary with space for one additional entry. The fourth line inserts an **InstanceType** entry with value dicttype. As a result, **defineresource** requires that instances of the Widget category be dictionaries.

3.9.4 Resources as Files

The PostScript language does not specify how external resources are installed, how they are loaded, or what correspondence, if any, exists between resource names and file names. In general, all knowledge of such things is in the category implementation dictionary and in environment-dependent installation software.

Typically, resource instances are installed as named files, which can also be accessed by ordinary PostScript file operators such as **file** and **run**. There is a straightforward mapping from resource names to file names, though the details of this mapping vary because of restrictions on file name syntax imposed by the underlying file system.

In some implementations, including many dedicated printers, the only access to the file system is through the PostScript interpreter. In such environments, it is important for PostScript language programs to be able to access the underlying resource files directly to install or remove them. Only resource installation or other system management software should do this. Page descriptions should never attempt to access resources as files; they should use only resource operators, such as **findresource**.

The implementation dictionary for a category can contain an optional entry, **ResourceFileName**, which is a procedure that translates from a resource name to a file name. If the procedure exists, a program can call it as follows:

1. Push the category implementation dictionary on the dictionary stack. The **ResourceFileName** procedure requires this to obtain category-specific information, such as **Category**.

2. Push the instance name and a scratch string on the operand stack. The scratch string must be long enough to accept the complete file name for the resource.

3. Execute **ResourceFileName**.

4. Pop the dictionary stack.

ResourceFileName builds a complete file name in the scratch string and returns the substring that was used on the operand stack. This string can then be used as the *filename* operand of file operators, such as **file**, **deletefile**, **status**, and so on. For example, the following program fragment obtains the file name for the Times-Roman font:

```
/Font /Category findresource
begin
/Times-Roman scratch ResourceFileName
end
```

If this is successful, it leaves a string on the operand stack, such as %font%Times-Roman or %os%C:\FONT\TIMESRMN.PS, that can be used as the name of the font file. This file name uniquely identifies the file containing the resource definition for the specified category and instance names. It also conforms to all restrictions imposed by the underlying file system.

There may be a limit on the length of a resource file name, which in turn imposes a length limit on the instance name. The inherent limit on resource instance names is the same as that on name objects in general (see Appendix B). By convention, font names are restricted to fewer than 40 characters. This convention is recommended for other resource categories as well. Note that the resource file name may be longer or shorter than the resource instance name, depending on details of the name-mapping algorithm. When calling **ResourceFileName**, it is prudent to provide a scratch string at least 100 characters long.

A resource file contains a PostScript language program that can be executed to load the resource instance into VM. The last action the program should do is execute **defineresource** or an equivalent operator, such as **definefont**, to associate the resource instance with a category and a name. In other words, each resource file must be self-identifying and self-defining. The resource file must be well-behaved: it must leave the stacks in their original state and it must not execute any operators (graphics operators, for instance) not directly related to creating the resource instance.

For most resource categories, the implementation of **findresource** executes true setglobal prior to executing the resource file. As a result, the resource instance is loaded into global VM and **defineresource** defines the resource instance globally. Unfortunately, certain resource instances behave incorrectly if they reside in global VM. Some means are required to force such resources to be loaded into local VM instead. Two methods are currently used.

- The implementation of **findresource** for the **Font** category makes the decision based on the **FontType** of the font being loaded. If the **FontType** is 1, **findresource** executes true setglobal prior to executing the font file; otherwise, it leaves the VM allocation mode unchanged. This is based on the assumption that Type 1 fonts always behave correctly in global VM but the behavior of Type 3 fonts is unpredictable.

- For other resource categories, the implementation of **findresource** always executes true setglobal. This is based on the assumption that resource instances normally behave correctly in global VM. If a particular instance is known not to work in global VM, the resource file should begin with an explicit false setglobal. See the explanation of the %%VMlocation convention in section G.6, "Requirement Conventions."

A resource file can contain header comments, as specified in Appendix G. If there is a header comment of the form

    %%VMusage: *int int*

then the **resourcestatus** operator returns the larger of the two integers as its *size* result. If the %%VMusage comment is not present, **resourcestatus** may not be able to determine the VM consumption for the resource instance; it will return a size of −1.

The definition of an entire resource category—that is, an instance of the **Category** category—can come from a resource file in the normal way. If any resource operator is presented with an unknown category name, it automatically executes

category /Category findresource

in an attempt to cause the resource category to become defined. Only if that fails will the resource operator generate an **undefined** error to report that the resource category is unknown.

3.10 Errors

Various sorts of errors can occur during execution of a PostScript language program. Some errors are detected by the interpreter, such as overflow of one of the PostScript interpreter's stacks. Others are detected during execution of the built-in operators, such as occurrence of the wrong type of operand.

Errors are handled in a uniform fashion that is under the control of the PostScript language program. Each error is associated with a name, such as **stackoverflow** or **typecheck**. Each error name appears as a key in a special dictionary called **errordict** and is associated with a value that is the handler for that error. The complete set of error names appears in section 8.1, "Operator Summary."

3.10.1 Error Initiation

When an error occurs, the interpreter

1. Restores the operand stack to the state it was when it began executing the current object.

2. Pushes that object onto the operand stack.

3. Looks up the error's name in **errordict** and executes the associated value, which is the *error handler* for that error.

This is everything the interpreter itself does in response to an error. The error handler in **errordict** is responsible for all other actions. A PostScript language program can modify error behavior by defining its own error-handling procedures and associating them with the names in **errordict**.

The **interrupt** and **timeout** errors, which are initiated by events external to the PostScript interpreter, are treated specially. The interpreter merely executes **interrupt** or **timeout** from **errordict**, sandwiched between execution of two objects being interpreted in normal sequence. It does not push the object being executed, nor does it alter the operand stack in any other way. In other words, it omits steps 1 and 2 above.

3.10.2 Error Handling

The **errordict** present in the initial state of VM provides standard handlers for all errors. However, **errordict** is a writable dictionary; a program can replace individual error handlers selectively. **errordict** is in local VM, so changes obey **save** and **restore**; see section 3.7, "Memory Management."

The default error handler procedures all operate in a standard way. They record information about the error in a special dictionary named **$error**, set the VM allocation mode to local, and execute **stop**. They do not print anything.

Execution of **stop** exits the innermost enclosing context established by **stopped**. Assuming the user program has not invoked **stopped**, interpretation continues in the job server, which invoked the user program with **stopped**. In a Display PostScript execution context that is not under the control of a job server, interpretation continues in the context's outer-level **start** or **resyncstart** procedure.

As part of error recovery, the job server executes the name **handleerror** from **errordict**. The default **handleerror** procedure accesses the error information in the **$error** dictionary and reports the error in an installation-dependent fashion. In some environments, **handleerror** simply writes a text message to the standard output file. In other environments, it invokes more elaborate error-reporting mechanisms. In a Display PostScript system, **handleerror** normally transmits a binary object sequence back to the application (see section 3.12.6, "Structured Output").

After an error occurs, **$error** contains the key-value entries as shown in Table 3.11.

Table 3.11 *Entries in the $error dictionary*

Key	Type	Value
newerror	boolean	Set to *true* to indicate that an error has occurred. **handleerror** sets it to *false*.
errorname	name	The name of the error that was invoked.

command	any	The operator or other object being executed by the interpreter at the time the error occurred.
errorinfo	array	If the error was a **configurationerror** caused by **setpagedevice** or **setdevparams**, this array contains the key and value of the request that could not be satisfied.
ostack	array	A snapshot of the entire operand stack immediately before the error, stored as if by the **astore** operator.
estack	array	A snapshot of the execution stack, stored as if by the **execstack** operator.
dstack	array	A snapshot of the dictionary stack, stored as if by the **dictstack** operator.
recordstacks	boolean	(*Level 2*) Controls whether the standard error handlers record the **ostack**, **estack**, and **dstack** snapshots. Default value: *true* in a printer, *false* in a Display PostScript system.
binary	boolean	(*Level 2*) Controls the format of error reports produced by the standard **handleerror** procedure. *false* produces a text message; *true* produces a binary object sequence. Default value: *false* in a printer, *true* in a Display PostScript system.

A program that wishes to modify the behavior of error handling can do so in one of two ways. First, it can change the way errors are *reported* simply by redefining **handleerror** in **errordict**. For example, a revised error handler might report more information about the context of the error, or it might produce a printed page containing the error information instead of reporting it to the standard output file.

Second, a program can change the way errors are *invoked* by redefining the individual error names in **errordict**. There is no restriction on what an error-handling procedure can do. For example, in an interactive environment, an error handler might invoke a debugging facility that would enable the user to examine or alter the execution environment and perhaps resume execution.

3.11 Early Name Binding

Normally, when the PostScript language scanner encounters an executable name in the program being scanned, it simply produces an executable name object; it does not look up the value of the name. It looks up the name only when the name object is *executed* by the interpreter. The lookup occurs in the dictionaries on the dictionary stack at the time of *execution*.

A name object contained in a procedure is looked up each time the procedure is executed. For example, given the definition

/average {add 2 div} def

the names **add** and **div** are looked up, yielding operators to be executed, every time the **average** procedure is invoked.

This so-called *late binding* of names is an important feature of the PostScript language. However, there are situations in which *early binding* is advantageous. There are two facilities for looking up the values of names before execution: the **bind** operator and the *immediately evaluated name*.

3.11.1   bind Operator

bind performs early name binding on entire procedures. **bind** looks up all the executable names in a procedure. For each name whose value is an *operator* (not an array, procedure, or other type), it replaces the name with the operator object. This lookup occurs in the dictionaries on the dictionary stack at the time **bind** is executed. The effect of **bind** applies not only to the procedure, but to all subsidiary procedures (executable arrays) nested to arbitrary depth.

When the interpreter executes this procedure, it encounters the *operator objects*, not the *names* of operators. For example, if the **average** procedure has been defined this way:

/average {add 2 div} bind def

then during execution of **average**, the interpreter executes the **add** and **div** operators directly, without looking up the names **add** and **div**.

There are two main benefits of using **bind**:

• A procedure that has been bound will execute the sequence of operators that were intended when the procedure was defined, even if one or more of the operator names have been redefined in the meantime.

• A bound procedure executes somewhat faster than one that has not been bound, since the interpreter need not look up the operator names each time, but can execute the operators directly.

The first benefit is mainly of interest in procedures that are part of the PostScript implementation, such as **findfont** and =. Those procedures are expected to behave correctly and uniformly, regardless of how a user program has altered its name environment.

The second benefit is of interest in most PostScript language programs, particularly in the prologs of page descriptions. It is worthwhile to apply **bind** to any procedure that will be executed more than a few times.

It is important to understand that **bind** replaces only those names whose values are *operators* at the time **bind** is executed. Names whose values are of other types, particularly procedures, are not disturbed. If an operator name has been redefined in some dictionary above **systemdict** on the dictionary stack *before* execution of **bind**, occurrences of that name in the procedure will not be replaced.

Note   *Certain standard language features, such as **findfont**, are implemented as built-in procedures instead of as operators. Also, certain names, such as **true**, **false**, and **null**, are associated directly with literal values in **systemdict**. Occurrences of such names in a procedure are not altered by **bind**.*

3.11.2   Immediately Evaluated Names

Level 2 implementations and many Level 1 implementations (see Appendix A) include a syntax feature called the *immediately evaluated name*. When the PostScript language scanner encounters a token of the form //*name* (a name preceded by two slashes with no intervening spaces), it immediately looks up the name and substitutes the corresponding value for the name. This lookup occurs in the dictionaries on the dictionary stack at the time the scanner encounters the token. If it can't find the name, an **undefined** error occurs.

The substitution occurs *immediately*, even inside an executable array delimited by { and }, where execution is deferred. Note that this process is a *substitution* and not an *execution*; that is, the name's value is not executed, but rather is substituted for the name itself, just as if the **load** operator were applied to the name.

The most common use of immediately evaluated names is to perform early binding of objects (other than operators) in procedure definitions. The **bind** operator, described in section 3.11.1, "bind Operator," performs early binding of operators; to bind objects of other types, explicit use of immediately evaluated names is required.

Example 3.8 illustrates using an immediately evaluated name to bind a reference to a dictionary.

Example 3.8

```
/mydict << ... >> def
/proc {
 //mydict begin
 ...
 end
} bind def
```

In the definition of proc, //mydict is an immediately evaluated name. At the moment the scanner encounters the name, it substitutes the name's current value, which is the dictionary defined earlier in the example. The first element of the proc executable array is a dictionary object, not a name object. When proc is executed, it will access that dictionary, even if in the meantime mydict has been redefined or the definition has been removed.

Another use of immediately evaluated names is to refer directly to permanent objects: standard dictionaries, such as **systemdict**, and constant literal objects, such as the values of **true**, **false**, and **null**. On the other hand, it does not make sense to treat the names of variables as immediately evaluated names. Doing so would cause a procedure to be irrevocably bound to particular values of those variables.

A word of caution is in order. Indiscriminate use of immediately evaluated names may change the semantics of a program. As discussed in section 3.5, "Execution," the behavior of a procedure differs depending on whether the interpreter encounters it directly or as the result of executing some other object (a name or operator). Execution of the program fragments

```
{... b ...}
{... //b ...}
```

will have different effects if the value of the name b is a procedure. So, it is inadvisable to treat the names of operators as immediately evaluated names. A program that does so will malfunction in an environment in which some operators have been redefined as procedures. This is why **bind** applies only to names whose values are operators, not procedures or other types.

3.12 Binary Encoding Details

In Level 2 and the Display PostScript system, the scanner recognizes two encoded forms of the PostScript language in addition to ASCII. These are *binary token* encoding and *binary object sequence* encoding. All three encoding formats can be mixed in any program.

The binary encodings are intended for machine generation. Display PostScript system applications are further encouraged to make use of the *Client Library* and *pswrap* facilities, available from vendors of systems that support the Display PostScript system.

The *binary token* encoding represents elements of the PostScript language as individual syntactic entities. This encoding emphasizes compactness over efficiency of generation or interpretation. Still, the binary token encoding is usually more efficient than using ASCII. Most elements of the language, such as integers, reals, and operator names, are represented by fewer characters in the binary encoding than in the ASCII encoding. Binary encoding is most suitable for environments in which communication bandwidth or storage space is the scarce resource.

The *binary object sequence* encoding represents a sequence of one or more PostScript objects as a single syntactic entity. This encoding is not compact, but it can be generated and interpreted very efficiently. In this encoding, most elements of the language are in a natural machine representation or something very close to one. Also, this encoding is oriented toward sending fully or partially precompiled sequences of objects, as opposed to sequences generated "on the fly." This organization matches that of the *Client Library*, which is the principal interface between Display PostScript applications and the PostScript interpreter. Binary object sequence encoding is most suitable for environments in which execution costs dominate communication costs.

Use of the binary encodings requires that the communication channel between the application and the PostScript interpreter be fully transparent. That is, the channel must be able to carry an arbitrary sequence of arbitrary 8-bit character codes, with no characters reserved for communication functions, no "line" or "record" length restrictions, and so on. If the communication channel is not transparent, an application must use the ASCII encoding. Alternatively, it can make use of the filters that encode binary data as ASCII text. See section 3.13, "Filtered Files Details."

The various language encodings apply only to characters the PostScript language scanner consumes. Applying **exec** to an executable file or string object invokes the scanner, as does the **token** operator. File operators such as **read** and **readstring**, however, read the incoming sequence of characters as data, not as encoded PostScript language programs.

The first character of each token determines what encoding is to be used for that token. If the character code is in the range 128 to 159 inclusive (that is, one of the first 32 codes with the high-order bit set), one of the binary encodings is used. For binary encodings, the character code is treated as a *token type*: it determines which encoding is used and sometimes also specifies the type and representation of the token.

Note   *The codes 128 to 159 are control characters in most standard character sets, such as ISO and JIS; they do not have glyphs assigned to them and are unlikely to be used to construct names in PostScript language programs. Interpretation of binary encodings can be disabled. See the **setobjectformat** operator.*

Following the token type character, subsequent characters are interpreted according to the same encoding until the end of the token is reached, regardless of character codes. A character code outside the range 128 to 159 can appear within a multiple-byte binary encoding. A character code in the range 128 to 159 can appear within an ASCII string literal or a comment. However, a binary token type character terminates a preceding ASCII name or number token.

In the following descriptions, the term *byte* is synonymous with *character* but emphasizes that the information represents binary data instead of ASCII text.

3.12.1   Binary Tokens

Binary tokens are variable-length binary encodings of certain types of PostScript objects. A binary token represents an object that can also be represented in the ASCII encoding, but it can usually represent the object with fewer characters. The binary token encoding is usually the most compact representation of a program.

Semantically, a binary token is equivalent to some corresponding ASCII token. When the scanner encounters the binary encoding for the integer 123, it produces the same result as when it encounters an ASCII token consisting of the characters 1, 2, and 3. That is, it produces an integer object whose value is 123; the object is the same and occupies the same amount of space if stored in VM whether it came from a binary or an ASCII token.

Unlike the ASCII and binary object sequence encodings, the binary token encoding is incomplete; not everything in the language can be expressed as a binary token. For example, it doesn't make sense to have binary token encodings of { and }, because their ASCII encodings are already compact. It also doesn't make sense to have binary encodings for the names of operators that are rarely used, because their contribution to the overall length of a PostScript language program is negligible. The incompleteness of the binary token encoding is not a problem, because ASCII and binary tokens can be mixed.

The binary token encoding is summarized in Table 3.12. A binary token begins with a token type byte. A majority of the token types (132 to 149) are used for binary tokens; the remainder are used for binary object sequences or are unassigned. The token type determines how many additional bytes constitute the token and how the token is interpreted.

Table 3.12 *Binary token interpretation*

Token type(s)	Additional bytes	Interpretation
128–131	—	Binary object sequence (see section 3.12.2, "Binary Object Sequences").
132	4	32-bit integer, high-order byte first.
133	4	32-bit integer, low-order byte first.
134	2	16-bit integer, high-order byte first.
135	2	16-bit integer, low-order byte first.
136	1	8-bit integer, treating the byte after the token type as a signed number n; $-128 \leq n \leq 127$.
137	3 or 5	16- or 32-bit, fixed-point number. The number representation (*size*, *byte order*, and *scale*) is encoded in the byte immediately following the token type; the remaining two or four bytes constitute the number itself. The representation parameter is treated as an unsigned integer r in the range 0 to 255:
		$0 \leq r \leq 31$ 32-bit fixed point number, high-order byte first. The *scale* parameter (number of bits of fraction) is equal to r.
		$32 \leq r \leq 47$ 16-bit fixed point number, high-order byte first; *scale* = $r - 32$.
		$r \geq 128$ Same as $r - 128$, except all numbers are given low-order byte first.
138	4	32-bit IEEE standard real, high-order byte first.

139	4	32-bit IEEE standard real, low-order byte first.
140	4	32-bit native real.
141	1	Boolean. The byte following the token type gives the value 0 for *false*, 1 for *true*.
142	1 + *n*	String of length *n*. The parameter *n* is in the byte following the token type; $0 \leq n \leq 255$. The *n* characters of the string follow the parameter.
143	2 + *n*	Long string of length *n*. The 16-bit parameter *n* is contained in the two bytes following the token type, represented high-order byte first; $0 \leq n \leq 65535$. The *n* bytes of the string follow the parameter.
144	2 + *n*	Long string of length *n*. The 16-bit parameter *n* is contained in the two bytes following the token type, represented low-order byte first; $0 \leq n \leq 65535$. The *n* bytes of the string follow the parameter.
145	1	Literal name from the system name table indexed by *index*. The *index* parameter is contained in the byte following the token type; $0 \leq index \leq 255$.
146	1	Executable name from the system name table indexed by *index*. The *index* parameter is contained in the byte following the token type; $0 \leq index \leq 255$.
147	1	(*Display PostScript only*) Literal name from the user name table indexed by *index*. The *index* parameter is contained in the byte following the token type; $0 \leq index \leq 255$.
148	1	(*Display PostScript only*) Executable name from the user name table indexed by *index*. The *index* parameter is contained in the byte following the token type; $0 \leq index \leq 255$.
149	3 + *data*	Homogeneous number array, which consists of a four-byte header, including the token type, followed by a variable length array of numbers whose size and representation are specified in the header. The header is described in detail below.
150–159	—	Unassigned. Occurrence of a token with these types will cause a **syntaxerror**.

The encodings for integers, reals, and booleans are straightforward. They are explained in section 3.12.4, "Number Representations." The other token types require additional discussion.

A *fixed point number* is a binary number having integer and fractional parts. The position of the binary point is specified by a separate *scale* value. In a fixed point number of *n* bits, the high-order bit is the sign, the next *n* – *scale* – 1 bits are the integer part, and the low-order *scale* bits are the fractional part. For example, if the number is 16 bits wide and *scale* is 5, it is interpreted as a sign, a 10-bit integer part, and a 5-bit fractional part. A negative number is represented in two's complement form.

There are both 16- and 32-bit fixed point numbers, enabling an application to make a trade-off between compactness and precision. Regardless of the token's length, the object produced by the scanner for a fixed point number is an integer if *scale* is zero; otherwise it is a real. A 32-bit fixed point number takes more bytes to represent than a 32-bit real. It is useful only if the application already represents numbers that way. Using this representation makes somewhat more sense in homogeneous number arrays, described below.

A *string token* specifies the string's length as a one- or two-byte, unsigned integer. The specified number of characters of the string follow immediately. All characters are treated literally. There is no special treatment of \ (backslash) or other characters.

The name encodings specify a *system name index* or a *user name index* that selects a name object from the system or user name table (see Appendix F) and uses it as either a literal or an executable name. This mechanism is described in section 3.12.3, "Encoded System Names."

A *homogeneous number array* is a single binary token that represents a literal array object whose elements are all numbers. Figure 3.1 on page 110 illustrates the organization of the homogeneous number array. The token consists of a four-byte header, including the token type, followed by an arbitrarily long sequence of numbers. All of the numbers are represented in the same way, which is specified in the header. The header consists of the token type byte (149, denoting a homogeneous number array), a byte that describes the number representation, and two bytes that specify the array length (number of elements). The number representation is treated as an unsigned integer r in the range 0 to 255 and is interpreted as shown in Table 3.13.

Table 3.13 *Number representation in the header for a homogeneous number array*

Representation	Interpretation
$0 \leq r \leq 31$	32-bit fixed point number, high-order byte first. The *scale* parameter (number of bits of fraction) is equal to r.
$32 \leq r \leq 47$	16-bit fixed point number, high-order byte first. *scale* = $r - 32$.
48	32-bit IEEE standard real, high-order byte first.
49	32-bit native real.
$128 \leq r \leq 177$	Same as $r - 128$, except all numbers are given low-order byte first.

This interpretation is similar to that of the representation parameter r in individual fixed point number tokens.

Figure 3.1 *Homogeneous number array*

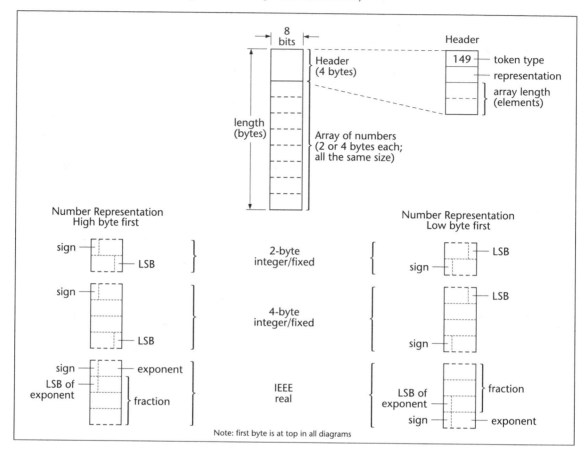

The array's *length* is given by the last two bytes of the header, treated as an unsigned 16-bit number. The byte order in this field is specified by the number representation. $r < 128$ indicates high-order byte first; $r \geq 128$ indicates low-order byte first.

Following the header are $2 \times length$ or $4 \times length$ bytes, depending on representation, that encode successive numbers of the array.

When the homogeneous number array is consumed by the PostScript language scanner, the scanner produces a *literal array object*. The elements of this array are all integers if the representation parameter r is 0, 32, 128, or 160, specifying fixed point numbers with a *scale* of zero. Otherwise, they are all reals. Once scanned, such an array is indistinguishable from an array produced by other means and occupies the same amount of space.

Although the homogeneous number array representation is useful in its own right, it is particularly useful with operators that take an encoded number string as an operand. This is described in section 3.12.5, "Encoded Number Strings."

3.12.2 Binary Object Sequences

A *binary object sequence* is a single token that describes an executable array of objects, each of which may be a simple object, a string, or another array nested to arbitrary depth. The entire sequence can be constructed, transmitted, and scanned as a single, self-contained, syntactic entity.

Semantically, a binary object sequence is an ordinary executable array, as if the objects in the sequence were surrounded by { and }, but with one important difference: Its execution is immediate instead of deferred. That is, when the PostScript interpreter encounters a binary object sequence in a file being executed directly, the interpreter performs an implicit **exec** instead of pushing the array on the operand stack, as it ordinarily would do. This special treatment does not apply when a binary object sequence appears in a context where execution is already deferred—for example, nested in ASCII-encoded { and } or consumed by the **token** operator.

Because a binary object sequence is syntactically a single token, the scanner processes it completely before the interpreter executes it. The VM allocation mode in effect at the time the binary object sequence is scanned determines whether the entire array and all of its composite objects are allocated in local or global VM.

The encoding emphasizes ease of construction and interpretation over compactness. Each object is represented by eight successive bytes. In the case of simple objects, these eight bytes describe the entire object— type, attributes, and value. In the case of composite objects, the eight bytes include a reference to some other part of the binary object sequence where the value of the object resides. The entire structure is easy to describe using the data type definition facilities of implementation languages, such as C and Pascal. Figure 3.2 on page 112 shows the organization of the binary object sequence.

Figure 3.2 *Binary object sequence*

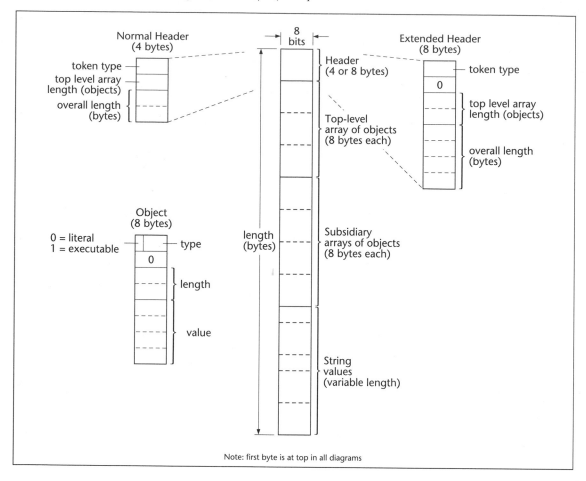

Note: first byte is at top in all diagrams

A binary object sequence consists of four parts, in the following order:

- Header—four or eight bytes of information about the binary object sequence as a whole.

- Top-level array—a sequence of objects, eight bytes each, which constitute the value of the main array object.

- Subsidiary arrays—more eight-byte objects, which constitute the values of nested array objects.

- String values—an unstructured sequence of bytes, which constitute the values of string objects and the text of name objects.

The first byte of the header is the token type, mentioned earlier. Four token types denote a binary object sequence and select a number representation for all integers and reals embedded within it (see section 3.12.4, "Number Representations"). They are:

128   high-order byte first, IEEE standard real format
129   low-order byte first, IEEE standard real format
130   high-order byte first, native real format
131   low-order byte first, native real format

There are two forms of header, *normal* and *extended*, as shown in Figure 3.2. The normal header can describe a binary object sequence that has no more than 255 top-level objects and 65,535 bytes overall. The extended header is required for sequences that exceed these limits.

Following the header is an uninterrupted sequence of eight-byte objects that constitute the top-level array and subsidiary arrays. The length of this sequence is not explicit. It continues until the earliest string value referenced from an object in the sequence, or until the end of the entire token.

The first byte of each object in the sequence gives the object's literal/executable attribute in the high-order bit and its type in the low-order 7 bits. The attribute values are:

0   literal
1   executable

The meaning of the object type field is given in Table 3.14.

Table 3.14 *Object types; length and value fields interpretation*

Object	Type	Length field	Value field
0	null	Unused	Unused
1	integer	Unused	Signed, 32-bit integer
2	real	Selects representation	Real or fixed point number
3	name	(See below)	Offset or index
4	boolean	Unused	0 for *false*, 1 for *true*
5	string	Number of elements	Offset of first element
6	immediately evaluated name	(See below)	Offset or index
9	array	Number of elements	Offset of first element
10	mark	Unused	Unused

The second byte of an object is unused; its value must be zero. The third and fourth bytes constitute the *length*; the fifth through eighth bytes constitute the *value*. The bytes interpretation of the *length* and *value* fields depends on the object's type and are given in Table 3.14. Once again, the byte order within these fields is according to the number representation for the binary object sequence overall.

Number representations are explained in section 3.12.4, "Number Representations." For a real, if *length* is zero, *value* is a floating point number. If *length* is non-zero, *value* is a fixed point number, using *length* as its scale factor (see section 3.12.1, "Binary Tokens").

For types *string* and *array*, the *length* field specifies the number of elements (characters in a string or objects in an array). It is treated as an unsigned 16-bit integer. The *value* field specifies the offset, in bytes, of the start of the object's value relative to the first byte of the first object in the top-level array. An array offset must refer somewhere within the top-level or subsidiary arrays; it must be a multiple of 8. A string offset must refer somewhere within the string values. The strings have no alignment requirement and need not be null-terminated or otherwise delimited. If the length of a string or array object is zero, its value is disregarded.

For the *name* type, the length field is treated as a signed, 16-bit integer that selects one of three interpretations of the value field:

$n > 0$ Value is an offset to the text of the name, just as with a string. n is the name's length, which must be within the implementation limit for names.

$n = 0$ Value is a *user name index*. This is a Display PostScript feature, not a standard part of Level 2 implementations.

$n = -1$ Value is a *system name index* (see 3.12.3, "Encoded System Names").

An *immediately evaluated name* object corresponds to the //*name* syntax of the ASCII encoding. See section 3.11.2, "Immediately Evaluated Names." Aside from the type code, its representation is the same as a name. However, with an immediately evaluated name object, the scanner immediately looks up the name in the environment of the current dictionary stack and substitutes the corresponding value for that name. If the name is not found, an **undefined** error occurs.

For the composite objects, there are no enforced restrictions against multiple references to the same value or to recursive or self-referential arrays. However, such structures cannot be expressed directly in the ASCII or binary token encodings of the language; their use violates the interchangeability of the encodings. The recommended structure of a binary object sequence is for each composite object to refer to a distinct value. There is one exception: References from multiple name objects to the same string value are encouraged, because name objects are unique by definition.

The scanner generates a **syntaxerror** when it encounters a binary object sequence that is malformed in any way. Possible causes include:

- An object type that is undefined.

- An "unused" field that is not zero.

- Lengths and offsets that, combined, would refer outside the bounds of the binary object sequence.

- An array offset that is not a multiple of 8 or that refers beyond the earliest string offset.

When a **syntaxerror** occurs, the PostScript interpreter pushes onto the operand stack the object that caused the error. For an error detected by the scanner, however, there is not such an object, because the error occurs before the scanner has finished creating one. Instead, the scanner fabricates a string object consisting of the characters encountered so far in the current token. If a binary token or binary object sequence was being scanned, the string object produced is a description of the token rather than the literal characters, which would be gibberish if printed as part of an error message.

An example of such as error string is:

(bin obj seq, type=128, elements=23, size=234, array out of bounds)

3.12.3 Encoded System Names

Both the binary token and binary object sequence encodings provide optional means for representing certain names as small integers instead of as full text strings. Such an integer is referred to as a *system name index* or a *user name index*. Careful use of encoded names can save substantial space and improve execution performance.

Encoded system names are a Level 2 feature; they are described below. Encoded user names are supported only in the Display PostScript system; they are documented in Chapter 7.

A name index is a reference to an element of a name table already known to the PostScript interpreter. When the scanner encounters a name token that specifies a name index, rather than a text name, it immediately substitutes the corresponding element of the table. This substitution occurs at scan time, not at execution time. The result of the substitution is an ordinary PostScript name object.

The system name table contains standard operator names, single-letter names, and miscellaneous other useful names. The contents of this table are documented in Appendix F. They are also available as a machine-readable file for use by drivers, translators, and other programs that deal with binary encodings; contact the Adobe Systems Developers' Association.

If there is no name associated with a specified system name index, the scanner generates an **undefined** error. The offending command is system*n*, where *n* is the decimal representation of the index.

An encoded binary name specifies, as part of the encoding, whether the name is to be literal or executable. A given element of the system name table can be treated as either literal or executable when referenced from a binary token or object sequence. In the binary object sequence encoding, one can also specify an immediately evaluated name object analogous to //name. When such an object specifies a name index, there are *two* substitutions: the first obtains a name object from the table, the second looks up that name object in the current dictionary stack.

A program can depend on a given system name index representing a particular name object. Applications that generate binary encoded PostScript language programs are encouraged to take advantage of system name index encodings, because they save both space and time.

Note   *The binary token encoding can reference only the first 256 elements of the system name table. Therefore, this table is organized such that the most commonly used names are in the first 256 elements. The binary object sequence encoding does not have this limitation.*

3.12.4 Number Representations

Binary tokens and binary object sequences use various representations for numbers. Some numbers are the values of number objects (integers and reals). Others provide structural information, such as lengths and offsets within binary object sequences.

Different machine architectures use different representations for numbers. The two most common variations are the byte order within multiple-byte integers and the format of real (floating point) numbers.

Rather than specify a single convention for representing numbers, the language provides a choice of representations. The application program chooses whichever convention is most appropriate for the machine on which it is running. The PostScript language scanner accepts numbers conforming to any of the conventions, translating to its own internal representation when necessary. This translation is needed only when the application and the PostScript interpreter are running on machines with different architectures.

The number representation to be used is specified as part of the token type—the initial character of the binary token or binary object sequence. There are two independent choices, one for byte order and one for real format.

The byte order choices are:

- High-order byte first in a multiple-byte integer or fixed point number. The high-order byte comes first, followed by successively lower-order bytes.

- Low-order byte first in a multiple-byte integer or fixed point number. The low-order byte comes first, followed by successively higher-order bytes.

The real format choices are:

- IEEE standard—a real number is represented in IEEE 32-bit, floating point format (see the bibliography). The order of the bytes is the same as the integer byte order. For example, if the high-order byte of an integer comes first, then the byte containing the sign and first 7 exponent bits of an IEEE standard real comes first.

- Native—a real number is represented in the native format for the machine on which the PostScript interpreter is running. This may be a standard format or something completely different. The choice of byte order is not relevant. The application program is responsible for finding out what the correct format is. In general, this is useful only in environments where the application and the PostScript interpreter are running on the same machine or on machines with compatible architectures. PostScript language programs that use this real-number representation are not portable.

Because each binary token and binary object sequence specifies its own number representation, binary encoded programs with different number representations can be mixed. This is a convenience for applications that obtain portions of PostScript language programs from different sources.

The **ByteOrder** and **RealFormat** system parameters indicate the native byte order and real number representation of the machine on which the PostScript interpreter is running (see Appendix C). A Display PostScript application can query **RealFormat** to determine whether the interpreter's native real number format is the same as the application's. If so, translation to and from IEEE format can be avoided.

3.12.5   Encoded Number Strings

Several operators require as operands an indefinitely long sequence of numbers to be used as coordinate values, either absolute or relative. The operators include those dealing with user paths, rectangles, and explicitly positioned text. In the most common use of these operators, all of the numbers are provided as literal values by the applications rather than being computed by the PostScript language program.

In order to facilitate this common use and to streamline generation and interpretation of numeric operand sequences, these operators permit their operands to be presented in either of two ways:

- As an array object whose elements are numbers to be used successively.

- As a string object to be interpreted as an *encoded number string.*

An encoded number string is a string that contains a single *homogeneous number array* according to the binary token encoding. That is, the first four bytes are treated as a header. The remaining bytes are treated as a sequence of numbers encoded as described in the header. (See Figure 3.1 on page 110.)

An encoded number string is a compact representation of a number sequence both in its external form *and in VM*. Syntactically, it is simply a string object. It remains in that form after being scanned and placed in VM. It is interpreted as a sequence of numbers only when it is used as an operand of an operator that is expecting a number array. Furthermore, even then it is neither processed by the scanner nor expanded into an array object; instead, the numbers are consumed directly by the operator. This arrangement is compact and efficient, particularly for large number sequences.

Example 3.9 shows equivalent ways of invoking **rectfill**, which is one of the Level 2 operators that expect number sequences as operands.

Example 3.9

```
[100 200 40 50] rectfill
<95200004 0064 00c8 0028 0032> rectfill
```

The first line constructs an ordinary PostScript array object containing the numbers and passes it to **rectfill**. This is the most general form, because the [and] could enclose an arbitrary computation that produces the numbers and pushes them on the stack.

On the second line, a string object appears in the program. When **rectfill** notices that it has been given a string object, it interprets the value of the string, expecting to find the binary token encoding of a homogeneous number array.

Example 3.9 does not use encoded number strings to best advantage. In this example, it is an ASCII-encoded hexadecimal string enclosed in < and >. In a real application, one would use a more efficient encoding, such as a binary string token or an ASCII base-85 string literal. An ordinary ASCII string enclosed in (and) is unsuitable because of the need to quote special characters.

The operators that use encoded number strings include **rectfill**, **rectstroke**, **rectclip**, **rectviewclip**, **xshow**, **yshow**, and **xyshow**. An encoded user path can represent its numeric operands as an encoded number string. The relevant operators are **ufill**, **ueofill**, **ustroke**, **uappend**, **inufill**, **inueofill**, and **inustroke**.

3.12.6   Structured Output

In some environments, a PostScript language program can transmit information back to the application program that generated it. This is particularly true in the Display PostScript system, where the application program and the PostScript interpreter communicate interactively via the Client Library (see Chapter 7). This information includes the values of objects produced by queries, error messages, and unstructured text generated by **print**.

A PostScript language program writes all of this data to its standard output file. The Client Library or application requires a way to distinguish among these different kinds of information received from the PostScript interpreter. To serve this need, the language includes operators to write output in a *structured output format*. This format is basically the same as the binary object sequence representation for input, described in section 3.12.2, "Binary Object Sequences."

A program that writes structured output should take care when using unstructured output operators, such as **print** and =. Because the start of a binary object sequence is indicated by a character whose code is in the range 128 to 159 inclusive, unstructured output should consist only of character codes outside that range. Otherwise, confusion will ensue in the Client Library or the application. Of course, this is only a convention. By prior arrangement, a program can send arbitrary unstructured data to the application.

The operator **printobject** writes an object as a binary object sequence to the standard output file. A similar operator, **writeobject**, writes to any file. The binary object sequence contains a top-level array consisting of one element that is the object being written (see section 3.12.2, "Binary Object Sequences"). That object, however, can be composite, so the binary object sequence may include subsidiary arrays and strings.

In the binary object sequences produced by **printobject** and **writeobject**, the number representation is controlled by the **setobjectformat** operator. The binary object sequence has a token type that identifies the representation used.

Accompanying the top-level object in the object sequence is a one-byte *tag*, which is specified as an operand of **printobject** and **writeobject**. This tag is carried in the second byte of the object, which is otherwise unused (see Figure 3.2 on page 112). Only the top-level object receives a tag; the second byte of subsidiary objects is zero. Despite its physical position, the tag is logically associated with the object sequence as a whole.

The purpose of the tag is to enable the PostScript language program to specify the intended disposition of the object sequence. A few tag values are reserved for reporting errors (see below). The remaining tag values may be used arbitrarily. For example, the Display PostScript Client Library uses tags when it issues queries to the PostScript interpreter. A query consists of a PostScript language program that includes one or more instances of **printobject** to send responses back to the Client Library. A different tag is specified for each **printobject** so the Client Library can distinguish among the responses as they arrive.

Tag values 0 through 249 are available for general use. Tag values 250 through 255 are reserved for identifying object sequences that have special significance. Of these, only tag value 250 is presently defined; it is used to report errors.

Errors are initiated as described in section 3.10, "Errors." Normally, when an error occurs, control automatically passes from the PostScript language program to a built-in procedure that catches errors. That procedure invokes **handleerror**. Subsequent behavior depends on the definition of **handleerror**. The following description applies to the standard definition of **handleerror**.

If the value of **binary** in the **$error** dictionary is *true* and binary encoding is enabled, **handleerror** writes a binary object sequence with a tag value of 250. But if **binary** is *false* or binary encoding is disabled, **handleerror** writes a human-readable text message whose format is product-dependent.

The binary object sequence that reports an error contains a four-element array as its top-level object. The array elements, ordered as they appear, are:

- The name Error, which indicates an ordinary error detected by the PostScript interpreter. A different name could indicate another class of errors, in which case the meanings of the other array elements might be different.

- The name that identifies the specific error—for example, **typecheck**.

- The object that was being executed when the error occurred. If the object that raised the error is not printable, some suitable substitute is provided—for example, an operator name in place of an operator object.

- An error-handler flag—a boolean object whose value is *true* if the program expects to resynchronize with the client, and *false* otherwise. The normal value is *false*, but certain Display PostScript applications set it to *true* (see the section on handling errors in *The Display PostScript Reference Manual*, available from the Adobe Systems Developers' Association).

3.13   Filtered Files Details

Level 2 implementations of the PostScript language support a special kind of file called a *filter*, which reads or writes an underlying file and transforms the data in some way. Filters are introduced in 3.8.4, "Filters." This section describes the semantics of filters in more detail. It includes information about:

- Use of files, procedures, and strings as data sources and targets.

- End-of-data conventions.

- Details of individual filters.

- Specifications of encoding algorithms for some filters.

3.13.1   Data Sources and Targets

As stated in section 3.8.4, "Filters," there are two kinds of filters, *decoding* filters and *encoding* filters. A decoding filter is an input file that reads from an underlying *data source* and produces transformed data as it is read. An encoding filter is an output file that takes the data written to it and writes transformed data to an underlying *data target*. Data sources and data targets may be files, procedures, or strings.

Files

A file is the most common data source or target for a filter. A file used as a data source must be an input file; one used as a data target must be an output file. Otherwise, an **invalidaccess** error occurs.

If a file is a data source for a decoding filter, the filter reads from it as necessary to satisfy demands on the filter, until either the filter reaches its end-of-data (EOD) condition or the data source reaches end-of-file. If a file is a data target for an encoding filter, the filter writes to it as necessary to dispose of data that have been written to the filter and transformed.

Closing a filter file does not close the underlying file. A program typically creates a decoding filter to process data embedded in the program file itself—the one designated by **currentfile**. When the filter reaches EOD, execution of the underlying file resumes. Similarly, a program can embed the output of an encoding filter in the middle of an arbitrary data stream being written to the underlying output file.

Once a program has begun reading from or writing to a filter, it should not attempt to access the underlying file in any way until the filter has been closed. Doing so could interfere with the operation of the filter and leave the underlying file in an unpredictable state. However, it is safe to access the underlying file after execution of **filter** but before the first read or write of the filter file. The procedure for establishing a filter pipeline in Example 3.5 on page 82 depends on this.

Procedures

The data source or target can be a procedure. When the filter file is read or written, it calls the procedure to obtain input data to be decoded or to dispose of output data that have been encoded. This enables the data to be supplied or consumed by an arbitrary program.

If a procedure is a data source, the filter calls it whenever it needs to obtain input data. The procedure must return (on the operand stack) a readable string containing any number of bytes of data. The filter pops this string from the stack and uses its contents as input to the filter. This process repeats until the filter encounters end-of-data (EOD). Any left-over data in the final string are discarded. The procedure can return a string of length zero to indicate that no more data are available.

If a procedure is a data target, the filter calls it whenever it needs to dispose of output data. Before calling the procedure, it pushes two operands on the stack: a string and a boolean flag. It expects the procedure to consume those operands and to return a string. The filter calls the procedure in the following three situations:

- Upon the first write to the filter after the **filter** operator creates it, the filter calls the data target procedure with an empty string and the boolean *true*. The procedure must return a writable string of non-zero length, into which the filter may write filtered data.

- Whenever the filter needs to dispose of accumulated output data, it calls the procedure again, passing it a string containing the data and the boolean *true*. This string is either the same string that was returned from the previous call or a substring of that string. The procedure must now do whatever is appropriate with the data, then return another string or the same string into which the filter can write additional filtered data.

- When the filter file is closed, it calls the procedure a final time, passing it a string or substring containing the remaining output data, if any, and the boolean *false*. The procedure must now do whatever is appropriate with the data and perform any required end-of-data actions, then return a string. Any string (for example, one of length zero) is acceptable. The filter does not use this string, but merely pops it off the stack.

It is normal for the data source or target procedure to return the same string each time. The string is allocated once at the beginning and serves simply as a buffer that is used repeatedly. Each time a data source procedure is called, it fills the string with one buffer's worth of data and returns it. Similarly, each time a data target procedure is called, it first disposes of any buffered data passed to it, then returns the original string for reuse.

Between successive calls to the data source or target procedure, a program should not do anything that would alter the contents of the string returned by that procedure. The filter reads or writes the string at unpredictable times, so altering it could disrupt the operation of the filter. If the string returned by the procedure is reclaimed by a **restore** before the filter becomes closed, the results are unpredictable. Typically, an **ioerror** occurs.

One use of procedures as data sources or targets is to run filters "backward." Filters are organized such that decoding filters are input files and encoding filters are output files. Normally, a PostScript language program obtains encoded data from some external source, decodes them, and uses the decoded data; or it generates some data, encodes them, and sends them to some external destination. The organization of filters supports this model. However, if a program must provide the input to a decoding filter or consume the output of an encoding filter, it can do so by using procedures as data sources or targets.

Strings

If a string is a data source, the filter simply uses its contents as data to be decoded. If the filter encounters EOD, it ignores the remainder of the string. Otherwise, it continues until it has exhausted the string data.

If a string is a data target, the filter writes encoded data into it. This continues until the filter is closed. The contents of the string are not dependable until that time. If the filter exhausts the capacity of the string, an **ioerror** occurs. There is no way to determine how much data the filter has written into the string. If a program needs to know, it should use a procedure as the data target.

3.13.2 End-of-Data and End-of-File

A filter can reach a state in which it cannot continue filtering data. This is called the *end-of-data* (EOD) condition. Most decoding (input) filters can detect an EOD marker encoded in the data that they are reading. The nature of this marker depends on the filter. Most encoding (output) filters append an EOD marker to the data that they are writing. This generally occurs automatically when the filter file is closed. In a few instances, the EOD condition is based on predetermined information, such as a byte count or a scan line count, instead of on an explicit marker in the encoded data.

A file object, including a filter, can be closed at an arbitrary time, and a readable file can run out of data. This is called the *end-of-file* (EOF) condition. When a decoding filter detects EOD and all the decoded data have been read, the filter reaches the EOF condition. The underlying data source or target for a filter can itself reach EOF. This usually results in the filter reaching EOF, perhaps after some delay.

For efficient operation, filters must be buffered. The PostScript interpreter automatically provides buffering as part of the filter file object. Due to the effects of buffering, the filter reads from its data source or writes to its data target at irregular times, not at times when the filter file itself is read or written. Also, many filtering algorithms require an unpredictable amount of state to be held within the filter object.

Decoding Filters

Before encountering EOD, a decoding filter reads an unpredictable amount of data from its data source. However, when it encounters EOD, it stops reading from its data source. If the data source is a file, encoded data that are properly terminated by EOD can be followed by additional unencoded data, which a program can then read directly from that file.

When a filter reaches EOD and all the decoded data have been read from it, the filter file reaches EOF and is closed automatically. Automatic closing of input files at EOF is a standard feature of *all* file objects, not just of filters. Unlike other file objects, a filter reaches EOF and is closed immediately after the *last* data character is read from it instead of at the following attempt to read a character. A filter also reaches EOF if its data source runs out of data by reaching EOF.

Applying **flushfile** to a decoding filter causes data to be drawn from the data source until the filter reaches EOD or the source runs out of data, whichever occurs first. This can be used to flush the remainder of the encoded data from the underlying file when reading of filtered data must be terminated prematurely. After **flushfile**, the underlying file is positioned so the next read from that file will begin immediately following the EOD of the encoded data. If a program closes a decoding filter prematurely before it reaches EOD and *without* explicitly flushing it, the data source will be in an indeterminate state. Because of buffering, there is no dependable way to predict how much data will have been consumed from the data source.

Encoding Filters

As stated earlier, writing to an encoding (output) filter causes it to write encoded data to its data target. However, due to the effects of buffering, the writes to the data target occur at unpredictable times. The only way to ensure that all encoded data have been written is to close the filter.

Most encoding filters can accept an indefinite amount of data to be encoded. The amount usually is not specified in advance. Closing the filter causes an EOD marker to be written to the data target at the end of the encoded data. The nature of the EOD marker depends on the filter being used; it is sometimes under the control of parameters specified when the filter is created.

The standard filter **DCTEncode** requires the amount of data to be specified in advance. This information is supplied when the filter is created. When that amount of data has been encoded, the filter reaches the EOD condition automatically. Attempting to write additional data to the filter causes an **ioerror**, possibly after some delay.

Some data targets can become unable to accept further data. For instance, if the data target is a string, that string may become full. If the data target is a file, that file may become closed. Attempting to write to a filter whose data target cannot accept data causes an **ioerror**.

Applying **flushfile** to an encoding filter file causes the filter to flush buffered data to its data target to the extent possible. If the data target is a file, **flushfile** is also invoked for it. The effect of **flushfile** will propagate all the way down a filter pipeline. However, due to the nature of filter algorithms, it is not possible to guarantee that all data stored as part of a filter's internal state will be flushed.

On the other hand, applying **closefile** to an encoding filter flushes both the buffered data and the filter's internal state. This causes all encoded data to be written to the data target, followed by an EOD marker, if appropriate.

When closing a pipeline consisting of two or more encoding filters, one must close each component filter file in sequence, starting with the one that was created last (in other words, the one farthest upstream). This ensures that all buffered data and all appropriate EOD markers are written in the proper order.

3.13.3 Details of Individual Filters

As stated in 3.8.4, "Filters," the PostScript language supports three categories of standard filters: ASCII encoding filters, compression and decompression filters, and subfile filters. The following sections document the individual filters.

Some of the encoded formats these filters support are the same as or similar to those supported by applications or utility programs on many computer systems. It should be straightforward to make those programs compatible with the filters. Also, C language implementations of some filters are available from the Adobe Systems Developers' Association.

ASCIIHexDecode Filter

The syntax for using the **ASCIIHexDecode** filter is:

source /ASCIIHexDecode filter

This filter decodes data encoded as ASCII hexadecimal and produces binary data. For each pair of ASCII hexadecimal digits (0–9 and A–F or a–f), it produces one byte of binary data. All white-space characters—space, tab, carriage return, line-feed, form-feed, and null—are ignored. The character > indicates EOD. Any other characters will cause an **ioerror**.

If the filter encounters EOD when it has read an odd number of hexadecimal digits, it will behave as if it had read an additional zero digit.

ASCIIHexEncode Filter

The syntax for using the **ASCIIHexEncode** filter is:

target /ASCIIHexEncode filter

This filter encodes binary data as ASCII hexadecimal. For each byte of binary data, it produces two ASCII hexadecimal digits (0–9 and A–F or a–f). It inserts a newline (line-feed) character in the encoded output at least once every 80 characters, thereby limiting the lengths of lines.

When the **ASCIIHexEncode** filter is closed, it writes a > character as an EOD marker.

ASCII85Decode Filter

The syntax for using the **ASCII85Decode** filter is:

source /ASCII85Decode filter

This filter decodes data encoded in the ASCII base-85 encoding and produces binary data. See the description of the **ASCII85Encode** filter for a definition of the ASCII base-85 encoding.

The ASCII base-85 encoded data format uses the characters ! through u and the character z. All white-space characters—space, tab, carriage-return, line-feed, form-feed, and null—are ignored. If the filter encounters the character ~ in its input, the next character must be > and the filter will reach EOD. Any other characters will cause the filter to issue an **ioerror**. Also, any character sequences that represent impossible combinations in the ASCII base-85 encoding will cause an **ioerror**.

ASCII85Encode Filter

The syntax for using the **ASCII85Encode** filter is:

target /ASCII85Encode filter

This filter encodes binary data in the ASCII base-85 encoding. Generally, for every 4 bytes of binary data it produces 5 ASCII printing characters in the range ! through u. It inserts a newline (line-feed) character in the encoded output at least once every 80 characters, thereby limiting the lengths of lines.

When the **ASCII85Encode** filter is closed, it writes the two-character sequence ~> as an EOD marker.

Binary data bytes are encoded in 4-tuples (groups of 4). Each 4-tuple is used to produce a 5-tuple of ASCII characters. If the binary 4-tuple is (b_1 b_2 b_3 b_4) and the encoded 5-tuple is (c_1 c_2 c_3 c_4 c_5), then the relation between them is:

$$(b_1 \times 256^3) + (b_2 \times 256^2) + (b_3 \times 256^1) + b_4 =$$

$$(c_1 \times 85^4) + (c_2 \times 85^3) + (c_3 \times 85^2) + (c_4 \times 85^1) + c_5$$

In other words, four bytes of binary data are interpreted as a base-256 number and then converted into a base-85 number. The five "digits" of this number, (c_1 c_2 c_3 c_4 c_5), are then converted into ASCII characters by adding 33, which is the ASCII code for !, to each. ASCII characters in the range ! to u are used, where ! represents the value 0 and u represents the value 84. As a special case, if all five digits are zero, they are represented by a single character z instead of by !!!!!.

If the **ASCII85Encode** filter is closed when the number of characters written to it is not a multiple of 4, it uses the characters of the last, partial 4-tuple to produce a last, partial 5-tuple of output. Given n (1, 2, or 3) bytes of binary data, it first appends $4 - n$ zero bytes to make a complete 4-tuple. Then, it encodes the 4-tuple in the usual way, but without applying the z special case. Finally, it writes the first $n + 1$ bytes of the resulting 5-tuple. Those bytes are followed immediately by the ~> EOD marker. This information is sufficient to correctly encode the number of final bytes and the values of those bytes.

The following conditions constitute encoding violations:

- The value represented by a 5-tuple is greater than $2^{32} - 1$.

- A z character occurs in the middle of a 5-tuple.

- A final partial 5-tuple contains only one character.

These conditions never occur in the output produced by the **ASCII85Encode** filter. Their occurrence in the input to the **ASCII85Decode** filter causes an **ioerror**.

The ASCII base-85 encoding is similar to one used by the public domain utilities *btoa* and *atob*, which are widely available on workstations. However, it is not exactly the same; in particular, it omits the begin-data and end-data marker lines, and it uses a different convention for marking end-of-data.

LZWDecode Filter

The syntax for using the **LZWDecode** filter is:

  source /LZWDecode filter

The **LZWDecode** filter decodes data that are encoded in a Lempel-Ziv-Welch compressed format. See the description of the **LZWEncode** filter for details of the format. A code of 257 indicates EOD.

LZWEncode Filter

The syntax for using the **LZWEncode** filter is:

  target /LZWEncode filter

The **LZWEncode** filter encodes ASCII or binary data according to the basic LZW (Lempel-Ziv-Welch) data compression method, which is a variable-length, adaptive compression method. The output produced by the **LZWEncode** filter is always binary, even if the input is ASCII text.

LZW compression can discover and exploit many patterns in its input data, whether that input is text or image data. It is especially well-suited to English language and PostScript language text.

The encoded data consist of a sequence of codes that can be from 9 to 12 bits long. Each code denotes a single character of input data (0 to 255), a clear-table marker (256), an EOD marker (257), or a table entry representing a multi-character sequence that has been encountered previously in the input (258 and greater).

Initially, the code length is 9 bits and the table contains only entries for the 258 fixed codes. As encoding proceeds, entries are appended to the table associating new codes with longer and longer input character sequences. The encoding and decoding filters maintain identical copies of this table.

Whenever both encoder and decoder independently (but synchronously) realize that the current code length is no longer sufficient to represent the number of entries in the table, they increase the number of bits per code by one. The first output code that is 10 bits long is the one following the creation of table entry 511, and so on for 11 (1023) and 12 (2047) bits. Codes are never longer than 12 bits, so entry 4095 is the last entry of the LZW table.

The encoder executes the following sequence of steps to generate each output code.

1. Accumulate a sequence of one or more input characters matching some sequence already present in the table. For maximum compression, the encoder should find the longest such sequence.

2. Output the code corresponding to that sequence.

3. Create a new table entry for the first unused code. Its value is the sequence found in step 1 followed by the *next* input character.

For example, suppose the input begins with the following sequence of ASCII character codes:

    45 45 45 45 45 65 45 45 45 66 ...

Starting with an empty table, the encoder proceeds as shown in Table 3.15.

Table 3.15 *Typical LZW encoding sequence*

Input sequence	Output code	Code added to table	Sequence represented by new code
–	256 (clear-table)		
45	45	258	45 45
45 45	258	259	45 45 45
45 45	258	260	45 45 65
65	65	261	65 45
45 45 45	259	262	45 45 45 66

Codes are packed into a continuous bit stream, high-order bit first. This stream is then divided into 8-bit bytes, high-order bit first. Thus, codes can straddle byte boundaries arbitrarily. After the EOD marker (code value of 257), any leftover bits in the final byte are set to 0.

In the above example, all the output codes are nine bits long; they would pack into bytes like this (represented in hexadecimal):

80 0B 60 50 22 0C 0 ...

To adapt to changing input sequences, the encoder may at any point issue a clear-table code, which causes both encoder and decoder to restart with initial tables and 9-bit codes. By convention, the encoder begins by issuing a clear-table code. It must issue a clear-table code when the table becomes full; it may do so sooner.

LZW has been adopted as one of the standard compression methods in the *tag image file format* (TIFF) 5.0 standard. The PostScript language **LZWEncode** and **LZWDecode** filters use the same coding as is used by other popular implementations of LZW; this coding differs slightly from the one described in the TIFF 5.0 specification. Variants of LZW are used in the UNIX *compress* and personal computer *ARC* utilities.

The LZW compression method is said to be the subject of United States patent number 4,558,302 and corresponding foreign patents owned by the Unisys Corporation. Adobe Systems has licensed this patent for use in its products. Independent software vendors (ISVs) may be required to license this patent to develop software using the LZW method to compress PostScript language programs or data for use with Adobe products. Unisys has agreed that ISVs may obtain such a license for a modest one-time fee. Further information can be obtained from: Welch Licensing Department, Law Department, M/SC2SW1, Unisys Corporation, Blue Bell, Pennsylvania, 19424.

RunLengthDecode Filter

The syntax for using the **RunLengthDecode** filter is:

source /RunLengthDecode filter

This filter decodes data in run-length encoded format. The encoded data consist of pairs of run-length bytes and data. See the description of the **RunLengthEncode** filter for details of the format. A run length of 128 indicates EOD.

RunLengthEncode Filter

The syntax for using the **RunLengthEncode** filter is:

target recordsize /RunLengthEncode filter

The **RunLengthEncode** filter encodes data in a simple byte-oriented, run-length encoded format. The compressed data format is a sequence of runs, where each run consists of a *length* byte followed by 1 to 128 bytes of data. If the *length* byte is in the range 0 to 127, the following *length* + 1 bytes (1 to 128 bytes) are to be copied literally upon decompression. If *length* is in the range 129 to 255, the following single byte is to be replicated 257 − *length* times (2 to 128 times) upon decompression.

When the **RunLengthEncode** filter is closed, it writes a final byte, with value 128 as an EOD marker.

recordsize is a positive integer specifying the number of bytes in a "record" of source data. The **RunLengthEncode** filter will not create a run that contains data from more than one source record. If *recordsize* is zero, the filter does not treat its source data as records. The notion of a "record" is irrelevant in the context of the PostScript interpreter (in particular, the **image** operator does not require its data to be divided into records). A non-zero *recordsize* is useful only if the encoded data is to be sent to some application program that requires it.

This encoding is very similar to that used by the Apple® Macintosh®
PackBits routine and by TIFF Data Compression scheme #32773. Output from PackBits is acceptable as input to the **RunLengthDecode** filter
if an EOD marker (byte value 128) is appended to it. Output from the
RunLengthEncode filter is acceptable to UnPackBits if the *recordsize*
parameter is equal to the length of one scan line for the image being
encoded.

CCITTFaxDecode Filter

The syntax for using the **CCITTFaxDecode** filter is:

> *source dictionary* /CCITTFaxDecode filter

This filter decodes image data that have been encoded according to the
CCITT facsimile standard. See **CCITTFaxEncode** for a description of the
filter parameters.

If the **CCITTFaxDecode** filter encounters improperly encoded source
data, it will issue an **ioerror**. It will not perform any error correction or
resynchronization.

CCITTFaxEncode Filter

The syntax for using the **CCITTFaxEncode** filter is:

> *target dictionary* /CCITTFaxEncode filter

This filter encodes image data according to the CCITT facsimile (*fax*)
standard. This encoding is defined by an international standards organization named CCITT, the *International Coordinating Committee for Tele-
phony and Telegraphy*. The encoding is designed to achieve efficient
compression of monochrome (1 bit per pixel) image data at relatively
low resolutions. The encoding algorithm is not described in this manual but in the CCITT standard (see the bibliography).

Note   *PostScript language support for the CCITT standard is limited to encoding
and decoding of image data. It does not include initial connection and
handshaking protocols that would be required to communicate with a fax
machine. The purpose of these filters is to enable efficient interchange of bi-
level sampled images between an application program and a PostScript
interpreter.*

The **CCITTFaxDecode** and **CCITTFaxEncode** filters support two encoding schemes, Group 3 and Group 4, and various optional features of the CCITT standard. Parameters for these filters are provided in the form of a dictionary object whose entries define the parameters. Table 3.16 describes the contents of this dictionary. All of its entries are optional and have default values.

Table 3.16 *Entries in CCITTFaxEncode and CCITTFaxDecode dictionaries*

Key	Type	Semantics
Uncompressed	boolean	(*Optional*) If *true*, the **CCITTFaxEncode** filter is permitted to use uncompressed encoding when advantageous. If *false*, it never uses uncompressed encoding. The **CCITTFaxDecode** filter always accepts uncompressed encoding. Default value: *false*.
		Uncompressed encoding is an optional part of the CCITT fax encoding standard. Its use can prevent significant data expansion when encoding certain image data, but many fax machine manufacturers and software vendors do not support it.
K	integer	(*Optional*) Selects the encoding scheme to be used. A negative value indicates pure two-dimensional (Group 4) encoding. Zero indicates pure one-dimensional encoding (Group 3, 1-D). A positive value indicates mixed one- and two-dimensional encoding (Group 3, 2-D), in which a line encoded one-dimensionally can be followed by at most **K** − 1 lines encoded two-dimensionally. Default value: 0.
		The **CCITTFaxEncode** filter uses the value of **K** to determine how to encode the data. The **CCITTFaxDecode** filter distinguishes among negative, zero, and positive values of **K** to determine how to interpret the encoded data. However, it does not distinguish between different positive **K** values.
EndOfLine	boolean	(*Optional*) If *true*, the **CCITTFaxEncode** filter prefixes an end-of-line bit pattern to each line of encoded data. The **CCITTFaxDecode** filter always accepts end-of-line bit patterns, but requires them to be present only if **EndOfLine** is *true*. Default value: *false*.
EncodedByteAlign	boolean	(*Optional*) If *true*, the **CCITTFaxEncode** filter inserts extra zero bits before each encoded line so that the line begins on a byte boundary; the **CCITTFaxDecode** filter skips over encoded bits to begin decoding each line at a byte boundary. If *false*, the filters neither generate nor expect extra bits in the encoded representation. Default value: *false*.
Columns	integer	(*Optional*) Specifies the width of the image in pixels. If **Columns** is not a multiple of 8, the filters adjust the width of the unencoded image to the next multiple of 8. This is for consistency with the **image** operator, which requires that each line of source data start on a byte boundary. Default value: 1728.
Rows	integer	(*Optional*) Affects **CCITTFaxDecode** only. Specifies the height of the image in scan lines. If this parameter is zero or absent, the image's height is not predetermined. The encoded data must be terminated by an end-of-block bit pattern or by the end of the filter's data source. Default value: 0.

EndOfBlock	boolean	(*Optional*) If *true*, the **CCITTFaxEncode** filter appends an end-of-block pattern to the encoded data; the **CCITTFaxDecode** filter expects the encoded data to be terminated by end-of-block, overriding the **Rows** parameter. If *false*, **CCITTFaxEncode** does not append an end-of-block pattern. **CCITTFaxDecode** stops when it has decoded **Rows** lines or when its data source is exhausted, whichever happens first. The end-of-block pattern is the CCITT end-of-facsimile-block (EOFB) or return-to-control (RTC) appropriate for the **K** parameter. Default value: *true*.
BlackIs1	boolean	(*Optional*) If *true*, causes 1 bits to be interpreted as black pixels and 0 bits as white pixels, the reverse of the normal PostScript language convention for image data. Default value: *false*.
DamagedRowsBeforeError		
	integer	(*Optional*) Affects **CCITTFaxDecode** only. If **DamagedRowsBeforeError** is positive **EndOfLine** is *true*, and **K** is non-negative, then up to **DamagedRowsBeforeError** rows of data will be tolerated before an **IOError** is generated. Tolerating a damaged row means locating its end in the encoded data by searching for an **EndOfLine** pattern, then substituting decoded data from the previous row if the previous row was not damaged, or a white scan line if the previous row was also damaged. Default value: 0.

The CCITT fax standard specifies a bi-level picture encoding in terms of black and white pixels. It does not define a representation for the unencoded image data in terms of 0 and 1 bits in memory. However, the PostScript language (specifically, the **image** operator) does impose a convention: Normally, 0 means black and 1 means white. Therefore, the **CCITTFaxEncode** filter normally encodes 0 bits as black pixels and 1 bits as white pixels. Similarly, the **CCITTFaxDecode** filter normally produces 0 bits for black pixels and 1 bits for white pixels. The **BlackIs1** parameter can be used to reverse this convention if necessary.

The fax encoding method is bit-oriented, not byte-oriented. This means that, in principle, encoded or decoded data might not end at a byte boundary. The **CCITTFaxEncode** and **CCITTFaxDecode** filters deal with this problem in the following ways:

- Unencoded data are treated as complete scan lines, with unused bits inserted at the end of each scan line to fill out the last byte. This is compatible with the convention the **image** operator uses.

- Encoded data are ordinarily treated as a continuous, unbroken bit stream. However, the **EncodedByteAlign** parameter can be used to cause each encoded scan line to be filled to a byte boundary. This is not prescribed by the CCITT standard, and fax machines never do this. But some software packages find it convenient to encode data this way.

- When a filter reaches EOD, it always skips to the next byte boundary following the encoded data.

DCTDecode Filter

The syntax for using the **DCTDecode** filter is:

source dictionary /DCTDecode filter

This filter decodes gray-scale or color image data in JPEG baseline encoded format (see the **DCTEncode** filter). Usually, no parameters are required—that is, the *dictionary* operand can be an empty dictionary. This is because all information required for decoding an image is usually contained in the JPEG signalling parameters, which accompany the encoded data in the compressed data stream. The only parameter that is likely to be needed is **ColorTransform** (see Table 3.17 on page 138).

The decoded data are a stream of image samples, each of which consists of 1, 2, 3, or 4 color components, interleaved on a per-sample basis. Each component value occupies one 8-bit byte. The dimensions of the image and the number of components per sample depend on parameters that were specified when the image was encoded. Given suitable parameters, the **image** operator can consume data directly from a **DCTDecode** filter.

Note   *An image consisting of 2 components per sample is not directly useful as a source for the **image** operator, because the PostScript language does not define any color spaces that have 2 color components (only 1, 3, and 4). Also, an image whose components are sent as separate scans instead of interleaved is not useful, because **image** requires that components from separate sources be read in parallel.*

DCTEncode Filter

The proper syntax for using the **DCTEncode** filter is:

target dictionary /DCTEncode filter

This filter encodes gray-scale or color image data in JPEG baseline format. JPEG is the ISO/CCITT *Joint Photographic Experts Group*, an organization responsible for developing an international standard for compression of color image data. The **DCTEncode** filter conforms to the JPEG-proposed standard at the time of publication of this manual (see the bibliography). DCT refers to the primary technique (discrete cosine transform) used in the encoding and decoding algorithms. The algorithm can achieve very impressive compression of color images. For example, at a compression ratio of 10 to 1, there is little or no perceptible degradation in quality.

Note *The compression algorithm is "lossy," meaning the data produced by the* **DCTDecode** *filter are not exactly the same as the data originally encoded by the* **DCTEncode** *filter. These filters are designed specifically for compression of sampled continuous-tone images, not for general data compression.*

Input to the **DCTEncode** filter is a stream of image samples, each of which consists of 1, 2, 3, or 4 color components, interleaved on a per-sample basis. Each component value occupies one 8-bit byte. The dimensions of the image and the number of components per sample must be specified in a dictionary provided as an operand to the **filter** operator. This dictionary can also contain other optional parameters that control the operation of the encoding algorithm. Table 3.17 describes the contents of this dictionary.

To specify the optional parameters properly requires understanding details of the encoding algorithm. That algorithm is not described here, but in the JPEG-proposed standard. The **DCTDecode** and **DCTEncode** filters do not support certain features of the standard that are irrelevant to images following PostScript language conventions. Additionally, Adobe has made certain choices regarding reserved marker codes and other optional features of the standard. Contact the Adobe Systems Developers' Association for futher information.

Table 3.17 *Entries in a* **DCTEncode** *dictionary*

Key	Type	Semantics
Columns	integer	(*Required*) Width of the image—in other words, samples per scan line.
Rows	integer	(*Required*) Height of the image—in other words, the number of scan lines.
Colors	integer	(*Required*) Number of color components in the image. It must be 1, 2, 3, or 4.
HSamples	array	(*Optional*) Array of **Colors** integers specifying horizontal sampling factors. The ith element of the array specifies the sampling factor for the ith color component. The allowed sampling factors are 1, 2, 3, and 4. Default value: an array containing 1 for all components, meaning that all components are to be sampled at the same rate.
		When the sampling factors are not all the same, **DCTEncode** sub-samples the image for those components whose sampling factors are less than the largest one. For example, if **HSamples** is [4 3 2 1] for a four-color image, then for every 4 horizontal samples of the first component, **DCTEncode** sends only 3 samples of the second component, 2 of the third, and 1 of the fourth. However, **DCTDecode** inverts this sampling process so that **DCTDecode** produces the same amount of data as was presented to **DCTEncode**. In other words, this parameter affects only the encoded representation, not the unencoded or decoded representation. The filters deal correctly with the situation in which the width or height of the image is not a multiple of the corresponding sampling factor.

VSamples	array	(*Optional*) Array of **Colors** integers specifying vertical sampling factors. Interpretation and default value are the same as for **HSamples**.

The JPEG-proposed standard imposes a restriction on the values in the **HSamples** and **VSamples** arrays, taken together. For each color component, multiply its **HSamples** value by its **VSamples** value, then add all of the products together. The result must not exceed 10.

QuantTables	array	(*Optional*) Array of **Colors** quantization tables. The ith entry in **QuantTables** is the table to be used, after scaling by **QFactor**, for quantization of the ith component. As many as four unique quantization tables can be specified, but several elements of the **QuantTables** array can refer to the same table.

Each table must be either an array or a string. If it is an array, the elements must be numbers; if it is a string, the elements are interpreted as integers in the range 0 to 255. In either case, each table must contain 64 numbers organized according to the zigzag pattern defined by the JPEG-proposed standard. After scaling by **QFactor**, every element is rounded to the nearest integer in the range 1 to 255. Default value: quantization tables chosen by Adobe.

QFactor	number	(*Optional*) Scale factor applied to the elements of **QuantTables**. This enables straightforward adjustment of the tradeoff between image compression and image quality without respecifying the quantization tables. **QFactor** must be positive. A value less than 1 improves image quality but decreases compression. A value greater than 1 increases compression but degrades image quality. Default value: 1.0.

HuffTables	array	(*Optional*) Array of $2 \times$ **Colors** encoding tables. The pair of tables at indices $2 \times i$ and $2 \times i + 1$ in **HuffTables** are used to construct Huffman tables for coding of the ith color component. The first table in each pair is used for the DC coefficients, the second for the AC coefficients. At most two DC tables and two AC tables can be specified, but several elements of the **HuffTables** array can refer to the same tables. Default value: chosen by Adobe.

Each table must be either an array or a string. If it is an array, the elements must be numbers; if it is a string, the elements are interpreted as integers in the range 0 to 255. The first 16 values specify the number of codes of each length from 1 to 16 bits. The remaining values are the symbols corresponding to each code; they are given in order of increasing code length. This information is sufficient to construct a Huffman coding table according to an algorithm given in the JPEG proposed standard. A **QFactor** value other than 1.0 may alter this computation.

ColorTransform	integer	(*Optional*) Specifies a transformation to be performed on the sample values:

0   No transformation.

1   If **Colors** is 3, transform RGB values to YUV before encoding and from YUV to RGB after decoding. If **Colors** is 4, transform CMYK values to YUVK before encoding and from YUVK to CMYK after decoding. This option is ignored if **Colors** is 1 or 2.

If performed, these transformations occur entirely within the **DCTEncode** and **DCTDecode** filters. The RGB and YUV used here have nothing to do with the color spaces defined as part of the PostScript language's imaging model. The purpose of converting from RGB to YUV is to separate luminance and chrominance information (see below).

The default value of **ColorTransform** is 1 if **Colors** is 3 and 0 otherwise. In other words, conversion between RGB and YUV is performed for all 3-component images unless explicitly disabled by setting **ColorTransform** to 0. Additionally, the **DCTEncode** filter inserts an Adobe-defined marker code in the encoded data indicating the **ColorTransform** value used. If present, this marker code overrides the **ColorTransform** value given to **DCTDecode**. Thus, it's necessary to specify **ColorTransform** only when decoding data that does not contain the Adobe-defined marker code.

The default values for **QuantTables** and **HuffTables** are chosen without reference to the image color space and without specifying any particular trade-off between image quality and compression. Although they will work, they will not produce optimal results for most applications. For superior compression, applications should provide custom **QuantTables** and **HuffTables** arrays rather then relying on the default values.

Better compression is often possible for color spaces that treat luminance and chrominance separately than for those that do not. The RGB to YUV conversion provided by the filters is one attempt to separate luminance and chrominance. Other color spaces, such as the CIE 1976 (L*a*b*)-space, may also achieve this objective. The chrominance components can then be compressed more than the luminance by using coarser sampling or quantization, with no degradation in quality.

Unlike other encoding filters, the **DCTEncode** filter requires that a specific amount of data be written to it: **Columns** $\times$ **Rows** samples of **Colors** bytes each. The filter reaches EOD at that point. It cannot accept further data, so attempting to write to it will cause an **ioerror**. The program must now close the filter file to cause the buffered data and EOD marker to be flushed to the data target.

SubFileDecode Filter

The syntax for using the **SubFileDecode** filter is:

> *source EODcount EODstring* /SubFileDecode filter

This filter does not perform data transformation, but it can detect an EOD condition. Its output is always identical to its input, up to the point where EOD occurs. The data preceding the EOD are called a *sub-file* of the underlying data source.

The **SubFileDecode** filter can be used in a variety of ways:

- A subfile can contain data that should be read or executed conditionally, depending on information that is not known until execution. If a program decides to ignore the information in a subfile, it can easily skip to the end of the subfile by invoking **flushfile** on the filter file.

- Subfiles can help recover from errors that occur in encapsulated programs. If the encapsulated program is treated as a subfile, the enclosing program can regain control if an error occurs, flush to the end of the subfile, and resume execution from the underlying data source. The application, not the PostScript interpreter, must provide such error handling; it is not the default error handling provided by the PostScript interpreter.

- The **SubFileDecode** filter enables an arbitrary data source (procedure or string) to be treated as an input file. This use of subfiles does not require detection of an EOD marker.

The **SubFileDecode** filter requires two parameters, *EODcount* and *EODstring*, which specify the condition under which the filter is to recognize EOD. The filter will allow data to pass through the filter until it has encountered exactly *EODcount* instances of the *EODstring*; then it will reach EOD.

EODcount must be a non-negative integer. If *EODcount* is greater than zero, all input data up to and including that many occurrences of the *EODstring* will be passed through the filter and made available for reading. If *EODcount* is zero, the first occurrence of the *EODstring* will be consumed by the filter, but it will *not* be passed through the filter.

EODstring is ordinarily a string of non-zero length. It is compared with successive subsequences of the data read from the data source. This comparison is based on equality of 8-bit character codes so matching is case-sensitive. Each occurrence of *EODstring* in the data is counted once. Overlapping instances of the *EODstring* will not be recognized. For example, an *EODstring* of "eee" will be recognized only once in the input "XeeeeX".

The *EODstring* may also be of length zero, in which case the **SubFileDecode** filter will simply pass *EODcount* bytes of arbitrary data. This is dependable only for binary data, when suitable precautions have been taken to protect the data from any modification by communication channels or operating systems. Ordinary ASCII text is subject to modifications such as translation between different end-of-line conventions, which can change the byte count in unpredictable ways.

A recommended value for *EODstring* is a document structuring comment, such as %%EndBinary. *EODstring*s containing newline (\n) characters are *not* recommended. Translating the data between different end-of-line conventions could subvert the string comparisons.

If *EODcount* is zero and *EODstring* is of zero length, detection of EOD markers is disabled; the filter will not reach EOD. This is useful primarily when using procedures or strings as data sources. It is illegal for *EODcount* to be negative.

NullEncode Filter

The syntax for using the **NullEncode** filter is:

> *target* /NullEncode filter

This is an encoding filter that does not perform data transformation, and its output is always identical to its input. The purpose of this filter is to allow an arbitrary data target (procedure or string) to be treated as an output file.

CHAPTER 4

Graphics

The PostScript language graphics operators describe the appearance of pages that are to be reproduced on a raster output device. The facilities described here are intended for both display and printer applications.

The graphics operators form six major groups:

- *Graphics state operators*. This group contains operators that manipulate the data structure called the *graphics state*, which is the global framework in which the other graphics operators execute.

- *Coordinate system and matrix operators*. The graphics state includes the current transformation matrix (CTM) that maps coordinates specified by the PostScript language program into output device coordinates. The operators in this group manipulate the CTM to achieve any combination of translation, scaling, rotation, reflection, and skewing of user coordinates onto device coordinates.

- *Path construction operators*. The graphics state includes the current path that defines shapes and line trajectories. The operators in this group begin a new path, add line segments and curves to the current path, and close the current path. All of these operators implicitly reference the CTM parameter in the graphics state.

- *Painting operators*. These operators paint graphical elements, such as lines, filled areas, and sampled images into the raster memory of the output device. The painting operators are controlled by the current path, current color, and many other parameters in the graphics state.

- *Character and font operators*. These operators select and paint characters from fonts, or descriptions of typefaces. Because the PostScript language treats characters as general graphical shapes, many of the font operators should be grouped with the path construction or painting operators. However, the data structures and mechanisms for dealing with character and font descriptions are sufficiently specialized that Chapter 5 focuses on them.

- *Device setup and output operators.* Device setup operators establish the association between raster memory and a physical output device, such as a printer or a display. Once a page has been completely described, executing an output operator transmits the page to the device.

This chapter presents general information about device-independent graphics in the PostScript language: how a program describes the abstract appearance of a page. Rendering—the device dependent part of graphics—is covered in Chapter 6.

4.1 Imaging Model

The PostScript language's imaging model is a simple and unified view of two-dimensional graphics borrowed from the graphic arts. A PostScript language program builds an image by placing "paint" on a "page" in selected areas.

- The painted figures may be in the form of letter shapes, general filled shapes, lines, or digitally sampled representations of photographs.

- The paint may be in color or in black, white, or any shade of gray.

- The paint may take the form of a repeating pattern (*Level 2*).

- Any of these elements may be clipped to appear within other shapes as they are placed onto the page.

- Once a page has been built up to the desired form, it may be transmitted to an output device.

The PostScript interpreter maintains an implicit *current page* that accumulates the marks made by the *painting operators*. When a program begins, the current page is completely white. As each painting operator executes, it places marks on the current page. Each new mark completely obscures any marks it may overlay. This method is known as a *painting model*: No matter what color a mark has—white, black, gray, or color—it is put onto the current page as if it were applied with opaque paint. Once the page has been completely composed, invoking the **showpage** operator renders the accumulated marks on the output media and then clears the current page to white again.

The imaging model applies to raster display devices and printers. However, there usually is not a separate operation for transmitting the page to a display device; instead, marks placed on the current page appear on the display immediately. There are some extensions to the imaging model to serve the special needs of interactive display applications. Those extensions are supported by the Display PostScript system and are documented in Chapter 7.

The principal painting operators, among many others, are as follows:

- **fill** paints an area.

- **stroke** paints lines.

- **image** paints a sampled image.

- **show** paints character shapes.

The painting operators require various parameters, some explicit and others implicit. Chief among the implicit parameters is the *current path* used by **fill**, **stroke**, and **show**. A path consists of a sequence of connected and disconnected points, lines, and curves that together describe shapes and their positions. It is built up through the sequential application of the *path construction operators*, each of which modifies the current path in some way, usually by appending one new element.

Path construction operators include **newpath**, **lineto**, **curveto**, **arc**, and **closepath**. None of the path construction operators places marks on the current page; the painting operators do that. Path construction operators create the shapes that the painting operators paint. Some operators, such as **ufill** and **ustroke**, combine path construction and painting in a single operation for efficiency.

Implicit parameters to the painting operators include the current color, current line thickness, current font (typeface-size combination), and many others. There are operators that examine and set each implicit parameter in the graphics state. The values used for implicit parameters are those in effect at the time an operator is invoked.

PostScript language programs contain many instances of the following typical sequence of steps:

1. Build a path using path-construction operators.

2. Set any implicit parameters if their values need to change.

3. Perform a painting operation.

There is one additional implicit element in the PostScript imaging model that modifies this description: The *current clipping path* outlines the area of the current page on which paint may be placed. Initially, this clipping path outlines the entire imageable area of the current page. By using the **clip** operator, a PostScript language program can shrink the current clipping path to any shape desired. It is possible for a painting operator to attempt to place marks outside the current clipping path. Marks falling within the clipping area will affect the current page; marks falling outside will not.

4.2 Graphics State

The PostScript interpreter maintains a data structure called the *graphics state* that holds current graphics control parameters. These parameters define the global framework in which the graphics operators execute. For example, the **show** operator implicitly uses the *current font* parameter as set in the graphics state, and the **fill** operator implicitly uses the *current color* parameter.

The graphics state is not itself an object. However, it contains many objects, nearly all of which can be read and altered by special graphics state operators. For example, the operator **setfont** changes the current font parameter in the graphics state, and **currentfont** reads that parameter from the graphics state.

There are two mechanisms for saving and later restoring the entire graphics state. One is a *graphics state stack*. The **gsave** operator pushes a copy of the entire graphics state onto the graphics state stack. The **grestore** operator restores the entire graphics state to its former value by popping it from the graphics state stack.

The second mechanism uses *gstate objects* in VM that contain saved copies of the graphics state. This is a Level 2 feature. The **gstate** operator creates a new gstate object. The **currentgstate** operator copies the entire graphics state into a gstate object given as an operand. The **setgstate** operator replaces the entire graphics state by the value of the supplied gstate object.

The graphics state stack, with its LIFO (last in, first out) organization, serves the needs of PostScript programs that are page descriptions. A well-structured document typically contains many graphical elements that are essentially independent of each other and sometimes nested to multiple levels. The **gsave** and **grestore** operators can be used to encapsulate these elements so they can make local changes to the graphics state without disturbing the graphics state of the surrounding environment.

In some interactive applications, however, a program must switch its attention among multiple, more-or-less independent imaging contexts in an unpredictable order. This is most conveniently done by creating a separate gstate object for each one and using **setgstate** to switch among them as needed.

Saving a graphics state captures *every* parameter, including such things as the current path and current clipping path. For example, if a nonempty current path exists at the time that **gsave**, **gstate**, or **currentgstate** is executed, that path will be reinstated by the corresponding **grestore** or **setgstate**. Unless this effect is specifically desired, it's best to save a graphics state only when the current path is empty and the current clipping path is in its default state to minimize storage demands.

Most graphics state parameters are ordinary PostScript language objects. The operators that set them simply store them, unchanged, for later use by other graphics operators. However, certain parameters have special properties or behavior:

- The current path, clipping path, and device parameters are internal objects that are not directly accessible to a PostScript language program.

- Most parameters must be of the correct type or have values that fall into a certain range.

- Parameters that are numbers, such as color, line width, and miter limit, are forced into legal range, if necessary, and stored as reals. If they are later read out, they are always reals, regardless of how they were originally specified. However, they are *not* adjusted to reflect capabilities of the raster output device, such as resolution or number of distinguishable colors. Such adjustments are performed by graphics rendering operators, but the adjusted values are not stored back in the graphics state.

- Certain parameters are composite objects, such as arrays or dictionaries. In general, graphics operators consult the values of those objects at unpredictable times, so altering them can have unpredictable results. A PostScript language program should treat the values of graphics state parameters as if they were read-only.

Table 4.1 lists the set of graphics state parameters that are device *independent* and are appropriate to specify in page descriptions. Table 4.2 lists the set of graphics state parameters that are device *dependent*. Device-dependent parameters control details of the rendering (scan-conversion) process. A page description that is intended to be device *independent* should not alter these parameters.

Table 4.1 *Device-independent parameters of the graphics state*

Parameter	Type	Definition
CTM	array	Current transformation matrix, which maps positions from user coordinates to device coordinates. This matrix is modified by each application of the coordinate system operators. Initial value: a matrix that transforms default user coordinates to device coordinates.
color	(various)	The color to use during painting operations. This is interpreted according to any of several different color spaces. For most color spaces, a color value consists of one to four numbers. Initial value: black.
color space	array	(*Level 2*) Determines how color values are to be interpreted. Initial value: **DeviceGray**.
position	2 numbers	Location of the *current point* in user space: the coordinates of the last element of the current path. Initial value: undefined.
path	(internal)	The current path as built up by the path construction operators. The current path is an implicit argument to operators, such as **fill**, **stroke**, and **clip**. Initial value: empty.
clipping path	(internal)	A path defining the current boundary against which all output is cropped. Initial value: the boundary of the entire imageable portion of the output page.
font	dictionary	The set of graphic shapes (characters) that define the current typeface. Initial value: an invalid font dictionary.
line width	number	The thickness (in user coordinate units) of lines to be drawn by the **stroke** operator. Initial value: 1.
line cap	integer	A code that specifies the shape of the endpoints of any open path that is stroked. Initial value: 0 for a square butt end.

line join	integer	A code that specifies the shape of joints between connected segments of a stroked line. Initial value: 0 for mitered joins.
miter limit	number	The maximum length of mitered line joins for the **stroke** operator. This limits the length of "spikes" produced when line segments join at sharp angles. Initial value: 10 for a miter cutoff below 11 degrees.
dash pattern	(several)	A description of the dash pattern to be used when lines are painted by the **stroke** operator. Initial value: a normal solid line.
stroke adjust	boolean	(*Level 2*) Specifies whether to compensate for resolution effects that may be noticeable when line thickness is a small number of device pixels. Initial value: installation dependent (typically *false* for printers, *true* for displays).

Table 4.2 *Device-dependent parameters of the graphics state*

Parameter	Type	Definition
color rendering	dictionary	(*Level 2*) Describes how to transform CIE-based color specifications to device color values. Initial value: installation dependent.
overprint	boolean	(*Level 2*) When generating color separations, specifies whether painting on one separation causes the corresponding areas of other separations to be erased (*false*) or left unchanged (*true*). Initial value: *false*.
black generation	proc	(*Level 2*) Calculates the amount of black to use when converting RGB colors to CMYK. Initial value: installation dependent.
undercolor removal	proc	(*Level 2*) Calculates the reduction in the amount of cyan, magenta, and yellow components to compensate for the amount of black added by black generation. Initial value: installation dependent.
transfer	proc	Transfer function that adjusts device gray or color component values to correct for non-linear response in a particular device. Support for four transfer functions is a Level 2 feature. Initial value: installation dependent.
halftone	(various)	Halftone screen for gray and color rendering, specified either as frequency, angle, and spot function or as a halftone dictionary. Support for four halftone screens is a Level 2 feature. Initial value: installation dependent.
halftone phase	2 integers	(*Display PostScript*) A shift in the alignment of halftone and pattern cells in device space to compensate for window system operations that involve scrolling. Initial values: 0, 0.
flatness	number	The accuracy (or smoothness) with which curves are to be rendered on the output device. This number gives the maximum error tolerance, measured in output device pixels. Smaller numbers give smoother curves at the expense of more computation and memory use. Initial value: 1.0.
device	(internal)	An internal data structure representing the current output device. Initial value: installation dependent.

4.3 Coordinate Systems and Transformations

Paths and shapes are defined in terms of pairs of points on the Cartesian plane specified as *coordinates*. A coordinate pair is a pair of real numbers x and y that locate a point within a Cartesian (two-axis) coordinate system superimposed on the *current page*. The PostScript language defines a default coordinate system that PostScript language programs can use to locate any point on the current page.

4.3.1 User Space and Device Space

Coordinates specified in a PostScript language program refer to locations within a coordinate system that always bears the same relationship to the current page regardless of the output device on which printing or displaying will be done. This coordinate system is called *user space*.

Output devices vary greatly in the built-in coordinate systems they use to address pixels within their imageable areas. A particular device's coordinate system is a *device space*. A device space *origin* can be anywhere on the output page. This is because the paper moves through different printers and typesetters in different directions. On displays, the origin can vary depending on the window system. Different devices have different resolutions. Some devices even have resolutions that are different in the x and y directions.

The operands of the path operators are user space coordinates. The PostScript interpreter automatically transforms user space coordinates into device space. For the most part, this transformation is hidden from the PostScript language program. A program must consider device space only rarely for certain special effects. This independence of user space from device space is key to the device independent nature of PostScript language page descriptions.

One can define a coordinate system with respect to the current page by stating:

- The location of the origin.

- The orientation of the x and y axes.

- The lengths of the units along each axis.

Initially, the user space origin is located at the lower-left corner of the output page or display window, with the positive *x* axis extending horizontally to the right and the positive *y* axis extending vertically upward, as in standard mathematical practice. The length of a unit along both the *x* and *y* axes is 1/72 of an inch. This coordinate system is the *default user space*. In default user space, all points within the current page have positive *x* and *y* coordinate values.

Note   *The default unit size (1/72 of an inch) is approximately the same as a "point," a unit used widely in the printing industry. It is not exactly the same as a point, however; there is no universal definition of a point.*

The default user space origin coincides with the lower-left corner of the *physical* page. Portions of the physical page may not be imageable on certain output devices. For example, many laser printers cannot place marks at the extreme edges of their physical page areas. It may not be possible to place marks at or near the default user space origin. The physical correspondence of page corner to default origin ensures that marks within the imageable portion of the output page will be consistently positioned with respect to the edges of the page.

Coordinates in user space may be specified as either integers or reals. Therefore, *the unit size in default user space does not constrain locations to any arbitrary grid*. The resolution of coordinates in user space is not related in any way to the resolution of pixels in device space.

The default user space provides a consistent, dependable starting place for PostScript language programs regardless of the output device used. If necessary, the PostScript language program may then modify user space to be more suitable to its needs by applying *coordinate transformation operators*, such as **translate**, **rotate**, and **scale**.

What may appear to be absolute coordinates in a PostScript language program are not absolute with respect to the current page, because they are described in a coordinate system that may slide around and shrink or expand. Coordinate system transformation not only enhances device independence, but is a useful tool in its own right. For example, a page description originally composed to occupy an entire page may be incorporated without change into another page description as just one element of the page by shrinking the coordinate system in which it is drawn.

Conceptually, user space is an infinite plane. Only a small portion of this plane corresponds to the imageable area of the output device: a rectangular area above and to the right of the origin in default user space.

The actual size and position of the area is device and media dependent. An application can request a particular page size or other media properties using the Level 2 operator **setpagedevice**, described in section 4.11, "Device Setup."

4.3.2 Transformations

A *transformation matrix* specifies how to transform the coordinate pairs of one coordinate space into another coordinate space. The graphics state includes the *current transformation matrix* (CTM) that describes the transformation from user space to device space.

The elements of a matrix specify the coefficients of a pair of linear equations in x and y that generate a transformed x and y. However, in graphical applications, matrices are not often thought of in this abstract mathematical way. Instead, a matrix is considered to capture some sequence of geometric manipulations: translation, rotation, scaling, reflection, and so on. Most of the PostScript language matrix operators are organized according to this latter model.

The most commonly used matrix operators are those that *modify* the current transformation matrix in the graphics state. These operators *do not* create a new transformation matrix from nothing; instead, they change the existing transformation matrix in some specific way. Operators that modify user space include the following:

- **translate** moves the user space origin to a new position with respect to the current page while leaving the orientation of the axes and the unit lengths unchanged.

- **rotate** turns the user space axes about the current user space origin by some angle, leaving the origin location and unit lengths unchanged.

- **scale** modifies the unit lengths independently along the current x and y axes, leaving the origin location and the orientation of the axes unchanged.

- **concat** applies an arbitrary linear transformation to the user coordinate system.

Such modifications have a variety of uses:

- *Changing the user coordinate system conventions for an entire page.* For example, in some applications it might be convenient to express user coordinates in centimeters rather than in 72nds of an inch, or it might be convenient to have the origin in the center of the page rather than in the lower left corner.

- *Defining each graphical element of a page in its own coordinate system,* independent of any other element. The program can then position, orient, and scale each element to the desired location on the page by temporarily modifying the user coordinate system. This permits decoupling the description of an element from the description of its placement on the page.

Example 4.1 may aid in understanding the second type of modification. Comments explain what each operator does.

Example 4.1

```
/box {newpath        % Define a procedure to construct a unit square
0 0 moveto           % path in the current user coordinate system,
0 1 lineto           % with its lower-left corner at the origin.
1 1 lineto
1 0 lineto
closepath
} def

gsave                % Save the current graphics state and create a
                     % new one that we shall then modify.

72 72 scale          % Modify the current transformation matrix so
                     % everything subsequently drawn will be 72 times
                     % larger; that is, each unit will represent an inch
                     % instead of 1/72nd of an inch.

box fill             % Draw a unit square with its lower-left corner at
                     % the origin and fill it with black. Because the unit
                     % size is now one inch, this box is one inch on a side.

2 2 translate        % Change the transformation matrix again so
                     % the origin is at 2", 2" (displaced two inches
                     % in from the left and bottom edges of the page).

box fill             % Draw the box again. This box has its lower-
                     % left corner two inches up from and two inches
                     % to the right of the lower-left corner of the page.

grestore             % Restore the saved graphics state.
                     % Now we are back to default user space.
```

Figure 4.1 *Two squares produced by Example 4.1*

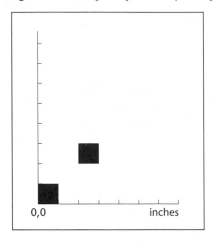

Figure 4.1 is a reduction of the entire page containing the two squares painted by Example 4.1, along with scales indicating *x* and *y* positions in inches. This shows how coordinates, such as the ones given to the **moveto** and **lineto** graphics operators, are transformed by the current transformation matrix. By combining translation, scaling, and rotation, one may use very simple prototype graphics procedures—such as box in the example—to generate an infinite variety of instances.

4.3.3   Matrix Representation and Manipulation

The descriptions of the coordinate system and matrix operators in Chapter 8 are easier to understand with some knowledge of the representation and manipulation of matrices. What follows is a brief introduction to this topic. It is not essential that you understand the details of matrix arithmetic on first reading, only that you obtain a clear geometrical model of the effects of the various transformations.

A two-dimensional transformation is described mathematically by a 3×3 matrix:

$$\begin{bmatrix} a & b & 0 \\ c & d & 0 \\ t_x & t_y & 1 \end{bmatrix}$$

In the PostScript language, this matrix is represented as a six-element array object

$$[a \ b \ c \ d \ t_x \ t_y]$$

omitting the matrix elements in the third column, which always have constant values.

This matrix transforms a coordinate pair (x, y) into another coordinate pair (x', y') according to the linear equations:

$$x' = ax + cy + t_x$$
$$y' = bx + dy + t_y$$

The common transformations are easily described in this matrix notation. Translation by a specified displacement (t_x, t_y) is described by the matrix:

$$\begin{bmatrix} 1 & 0 & 0 \\ 0 & 1 & 0 \\ t_x & t_y & 1 \end{bmatrix}$$

Scaling by the factor s_x in the x dimension and s_y in the y dimension is accomplished by the matrix:

$$\begin{bmatrix} s_x & 0 & 0 \\ 0 & s_y & 0 \\ 0 & 0 & 1 \end{bmatrix}$$

Rotation counterclockwise about the origin by an angle θ is described by the matrix:

$$\begin{bmatrix} \cos\theta & \sin\theta & 0 \\ -\sin\theta & \cos\theta & 0 \\ 0 & 0 & 1 \end{bmatrix}$$

Figure 4.2 *Effects of coordinate transformations*

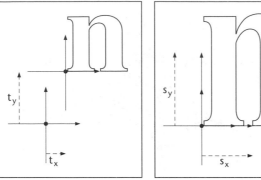

| Translation | Scaling | Rotation |

A PostScript language program can describe any desired transformation as a sequence of these operations performed in some order. An important property of the matrix notation is that a program can *concatenate* a sequence of operations to form a single matrix that embodies *all* of those operations in combination. That is, transforming any coordinate by the single concatenated matrix produces the same result as transforming it by all the original matrices in sequence. Any linear transformation from user space to device space can be described by a single transformation matrix, the CTM.

Note *Concatenation is performed by matrix multiplication. The order in which transformations are concatenated is important (technically, matrix operations are associative, but not commutative). The requirement that matrices conform during multiplication is what leads to the use of 3×3 matrices. Otherwise, 2×3 matrices would suffice to describe transformations.*

The operators **translate**, **scale**, and **rotate** each concatenate the CTM with a matrix describing the desired transformation, thus producing a new matrix that describes the combination of the original and additional transformations. This matrix is then established as the new CTM:

new CTM = transformation × original CTM

It is sometimes necessary to perform the *inverse* of a transformation—that is, to find the user space coordinate that corresponds to a specific device space coordinate. PostScript language programs explicitly do this only occasionally, but it occurs commonly in the implementation.

Not all transformations are invertible in the way just described. For example, if a matrix contains *a*, *b*, *c*, and *d* elements that are all zero, all user coordinates map to the same device coordinate and there is no unique inverse transformation. This condition produces the error **undefinedresult**. Non-invertible transformations aren't very useful and generally arise from unintentional operations, such as scaling by zero.

4.4 Path Construction

In the PostScript language, a *path* defines shapes, trajectories, and regions of all sorts. Programs use paths to draw lines, specify boundaries of filled areas, and define templates for clipping other graphics.

A path is composed of straight and curved line segments. These segments may connect to one another or they may be disconnected. The topology of a path is unrestricted: It may be concave or convex; it may contain multiple closed *subpaths*, representing several areas; and it may intersect itself in arbitrary ways.

Paths are represented by data structures internal to the interpreter. Although a path is not directly accessible as an object, a PostScript language program directly controls its construction and use. A path is constructed by sequential application of one or more *path construction operators*. At any time, the path may be read out, or more commonly, be used to control the application of one of the painting operators described in section 4.5, "Painting."

The *current path* is part of the graphics state. The path construction operators *modify* the current path, usually by appending to it, and the painting operators implicitly *refer* to the current path. The **gsave** and **grestore** operators respectively save and restore the current path, as they do all components of the graphics state.

The order of the segments that define a path is significant. A pair of line segments is said to "connect" *only* if they are defined consecutively, with the second segment starting where the first one ends. Non-consecutive segments that meet or intersect fortuitously are not considered to connect.

A *subpath* of a path is a sequence of connected segments. A path is made up of one or more disconnected subpaths. There is an operator, **closepath**, that explicitly connects the end of a subpath back to its starting point; such a subpath is said to be *closed*. A subpath that has not been closed explicitly is *open*.

A program may begin a path by executing the **newpath** operator. This initializes the current path to be empty. Some of the painting operators also initialize the path at the *end* of their execution. The program builds up the path by executing one or more of the operators that add segments to the current path. A program may execute them in any sequence, but a **moveto** must come first.

All the points used to describe the path are coordinates in user space. Each coordinate is transformed by the CTM into device space at the time the program enters the point into the current path. Changing the CTM does not cause existing points to move in device space.

The trailing endpoint of the segment most recently entered is referred to as the *current point*. If the current path is empty, the current point is undefined. Most operators that add a segment to the current path start at the current point. If the current point is undefined, they execute the error **nocurrentpoint**.

Following is a list of the most common path operators. There are several other path construction operators. Complete details are presented in Chapter 8.

- **moveto** establishes a new current point without adding a segment to the path. This begins a new subpath of the current path.

- **lineto** adds a straight line segment to the path, connecting the previous current point to the new one.

- **arc**, **arcn**, **arct**, and **arcto** add an arc of a circle to the current path.

- **curveto** adds a section of a Bézier cubic curve to the current path.

- **rmoveto**, **rlineto**, and **rcurveto** perform the **moveto**, **lineto**, and **curveto** operations, but specify new points as displacements in user space relative to the current point.

- **closepath** adds a straight line segment connecting the current point to the starting point of the current subpath (usually the point most recently specified by **moveto**), thereby *closing* the current subpath.

The graphics state also contains a *clipping path* that defines the regions of the page that may be affected by the painting operators. Marks falling inside the area defined by the closed subpaths of this path will be applied to the page; marks falling outside will not. (Precisely what is considered to be "inside" a path is discussed in section 4.5, "Painting.") The **clip** operator computes a new clipping path from the intersection of the current path with the existing clipping path.

Note *Remember that the path construction operators do not place any marks on the page. Only the painting operators do that. The usual procedure for painting a graphic element on the page is to define that element as a path and then invoke one of the painting operators. This is repeated for each element on the page.*

A path that is to be used more than once in a page description can be defined by a PostScript language procedure that invokes the operators for constructing the path. Each instance of the path may then be constructed and painted on the page by a three-step sequence:

1. Modify the CTM, if necessary, by invoking coordinate transformation operators to properly locate, orient, and scale the path to the desired place on the page.

2. Call the procedure to construct the path.

3. Execute a painting operator to mark the path on the page in the desired manner.

In the common situation that the path description is constant, you may invoke the user path operators (described in section 4.6, "User Paths") to combine steps 2 and 3. User paths are a Level 2 feature.

You may encapsulate the entire sequence by surrounding it with **gsave** and **grestore**. A simple illustration of this use appears in the "box" example of section 4.3, "Coordinate Systems and Transformations."

A path is unrestricted in its topology. However, because the entire set of points defining a path must exist as data simultaneously, there is a limit to the number of segments a path may have. Because several paths may also exist simultaneously (current path, clipping path, and paths saved by **gsave** and **currentgstate**), this limit applies to the *total* amount of storage occupied by *all* paths. If a path exhausts available storage, a **limitcheck** error occurs. The value of the limit is implementation dependent; see Appendix B.

As a practical matter, the limits on path storage are sufficiently large that they do not impose an unreasonable restriction. It is important, however, that separate elements of a page be constructed as separate paths with each one painted *and then discarded*. An attempt to describe an entire page as a single path is likely to exceed the path storage limit.

4.5 Painting

The painting operators mark graphical shapes on the current page. The principal, general-purpose painting operators are **stroke** and **fill**, described in this section. More specialized operators include **image**, described in section 4.10, "Images," and the character and font operators, described in Chapter 5.

The operators and graphics state parameters described here control the abstract appearance of graphical shapes; they are device independent. Additional facilities to control graphics rendering in raster memory are described in Chapter 6. Those facilities are device dependent.

4.5.1 Stroking

The **stroke** operator draws a line of some thickness along the current path. For each straight or curved segment in the path, **stroke** draws a line that is *centered* on the segment with sides *parallel* to the segment.

The settings of graphics state parameters control the results of the **stroke** operator. These parameters include CTM, color, line width, line cap, line join, miter limit, dash, and stroke adjustment (a Level 2 feature). Graphics state parameters are summarized in section 4.2, "Graphics State." Details on each of the operators appear in Chapter 8.

stroke treats each subpath of a path separately.

- Wherever two consecutive segments are connected, the joint between them is treated with the current *line join*, which may be mitered, rounded, or beveled (see the description of the **setlinejoin** operator).

- If the subpath is open, the unconnected ends are treated with the current *line cap*, which may be butt, rounded, or square (see **setlinecap**).

- Points at which unconnected segments happen to meet or intersect receive no special treatment. In particular, "closing" a subpath with an explicit **lineto** rather than with **closepath** may result in a messy corner, because line caps rather than a line join are applied in that case.

A stroke can be made either with a solid line or with a user-specified dash pattern (see **setdash**). The color of the line is determined by the current color or pattern in the graphics state (see **setgray**, **setrgbcolor**, **sethsbcolor**, **setcmykcolor**, **setcolor**, and **setpattern**; the last three are Level 2 operators).

A program can request that coordinates and line widths be adjusted automatically to produce strokes of uniform thickness despite rasterization effects. This is a Level 2 feature, controlled by the stroke adjustment parameter (see **setstrokeadjust**; section 6.5.2, "Automatic Stroke Adjustment," gives details of the effects produced).

4.5.2 Filling

The **fill** operator uses the current color or pattern to paint the entire region enclosed by the current path. If the path consists of several disconnected subpaths, **fill** paints the insides of all subpaths, considered together. Any subpaths of the path that are open are implicitly closed before being filled.

For a simple path, it is intuitively clear what region lies "inside." However, for a more complex path—for example, a path that intersects itself or has one subpath that encloses another—the interpretation of "inside" is not so obvious. The path machinery uses one of two rules for determining which points lie inside a path.

The *non-zero winding number rule* determines whether a given point is inside a path by conceptually drawing a ray from that point to infinity in any direction and then examining the places where a segment of the path crosses the ray. Here's how it works:

Starting with a count of zero, add one each time a path segment crosses the ray from left to right and subtract one each time a path segment crosses the ray from right to left. After counting all the crossings, if the result is zero then the point is *outside* the path. Otherwise it is *inside*.

Note   *The rule does not specify what to do if a path segment coincides with or is tangent to the ray. Since any ray will do, one may simply choose a different ray that does not encounter such problem intersections.*

With the non-zero winding number rule, a simple convex path yields inside and outside as you would expect. Now consider a five-pointed star, drawn with five connected straight line segments intersecting each other. The entire area enclosed by the star, including the pentagon in the center, is considered *inside* by the non-zero winding number rule. For a path composed of two concentric circles, *if they are both drawn in the same direction*, the areas enclosed by both circles are inside, according to the rule. If they are drawn in opposite directions, only the "doughnut" shape between the two circles is inside, according to the rule; the "doughnut hole" is outside. Figure 4.3 shows the effects of applying this rule.

Figure 4.3 *Non-zero winding number rule*

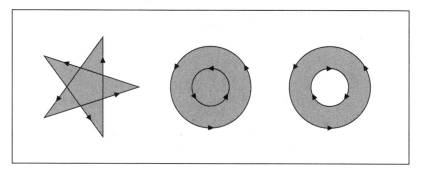

An alternative to the non-zero winding number rule is the *even-odd rule*. This rule determines the "insideness" of a point by drawing a ray from that point in any direction and counting the number of path segments that the ray crosses. If this number is odd, the point is inside; if even, the point is outside. Figure 4.4 shows the effects of applying this rule.

Figure 4.4 *Even-odd rule*

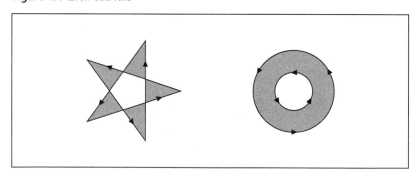

The even-odd rule yields the same results as the non-zero winding number rule for paths with simple shapes, but yields different results for more complex shapes. For the five-pointed star drawn with five intersecting lines, the even-odd rule considers the triangular points to be inside, but the pentagon in the center to be outside. For the two concentric circles, only the "doughnut" shape between the two circles is inside, according to the even-odd rule, regardless of whether the circles are drawn in the same or opposite directions.

The non-zero winding number rule is more versatile than the even-odd rule and is the standard rule the **fill** operator uses. The even-odd rule is occasionally useful for special effects or for compatibility with other graphics systems. The **eofill** operator invokes this rule.

The **clip** operator uses the same rule as the **fill** operator to determine the inside of the current clipping path. The **eoclip** operator uses the same rule as **eofill**.

4.5.3 Insideness Testing

It is sometimes useful for a program to test whether a point lies inside a path or a path intersects another path, without actually painting anything. The Level 2 "insideness" operators can be used for this purpose. They are useful mainly for interactive applications using the Display PostScript system, where they can assist in hit detection (see section 7.3.2, "Hit Detection"). However, they have other uses as well.

There are several insideness testing operators that vary according to how the paths to be tested are specified. All of the operators return a single boolean result. What it means for a given point to be "inside" a path is that painting the path (by **fill** or **stroke**) would cause the device pixel lying under the point to be painted. These tests disregard the current clipping path.

- **infill** tests the current path in the graphics state. There are two forms of **infill**. One returns *true* if the device pixel corresponding to a specific point in user space would be painted by **fill** with the current path. The second tests whether any pixels in some *aperture* would be painted by **fill**. The aperture is specified by a *user path* given as a separate operand. See section 4.6, "User Paths."

- **instroke** is similar to **infill**, but it tests pixels that would be painted by **stroke** with the current path, using the current stroke-related parameters in the graphics state (line width, dash pattern, and so on).

- **inufill** and **inustroke** are similar to **infill** and **instroke**, but they test a path given as a separate user path operand instead of testing the current path in the graphics state.

- **ineofill** and **inueofill** are similar to **infill** and **inufill**, but their "insideness" test is based on the even-odd rule instead of the non-zero winding number rule. See section 4.5.2, "Filling."

4.6   User Paths

A *user path* is a procedure that consists entirely of path construction operators and their coordinate operands expressed as literal numbers. In other words, it is a completely self-contained description of a path in user space. Several operators *combine* the execution of a user path description with painting the resulting path, using it for filling or stroking. User paths are a Level 2 feature.

Example 4.2 illustrates the construction and use of a user path. It defines a path and paints its interior with the current color.

Example 4.2

```
{
    ucache                              % This is optional
    100 200 400 500 setbbox             % This is required
    150 200 moveto
    250 200 400 390 400 460 curveto
    400 480 350 500 250 500 curveto
    100 400 lineto
    closepath
} ufill
```

The tokens enclosed in { and } constitute a user path definition. **ucache** must appear first if it is used. The **setbbox** operator, with its four numeric operands (integers or reals), must appear after the optional **ucache**. The remainder of the user path consists of path construction operators and their operands in any sensible order. The path is assumed to begin empty, so the first operator after the **setbbox** must be an absolute positioning operator (**moveto**, **arc**, or **arcn**).

ufill is a combined path construction and painting operator. It interprets the user path as if it were an ordinary PostScript language procedure being executed with **systemdict** as the current dictionary; it then performs a **fill**. Moreover, it automatically performs a **newpath** prior to interpreting the user path and it encloses the entire operation with **gsave** and **grestore**. The overall effect of the preceding example is to define a path and to paint its interior with the current color. It leaves no side effects in the graphics state or anywhere else, except in raster memory.

The user path painting operators can be fully described in terms of other path construction and painting operators. The combined operators offer several advantages in efficiency and convenience:

- They closely match the needs of many application programs.

- A user path consists of path construction operators and numeric operands, not arbitrary computations. The user path is self-contained; its semantics are guaranteed not to depend on an unpredictable execution environment. Also, the information provided by **setbbox** assures that the coordinates of the path will be within predictable bounds. As a result, interpretation of a user path may be much more efficient than execution of an arbitrary PostScript language procedure.

- Most of the user path painting operators have no effect on the graphics state. The absence of side effects is a significant reason for the efficiency of the operations. There is no need to build up an explicit current path only to discard it after one use. Although the behavior of the operators can be described as if the path were built up, painted, and discarded in the usual way, the actual implementation of the operators is optimized to avoid unnecessary work.

- Because a user path is represented as a procedure object and is self-contained, the PostScript interpreter can save its output in a cache. This eliminates redundant interpretation of a path that is used repeatedly.

4.6.1 User Path Construction

A user path is an array or packed array object consisting of a sequence of the following operators and their operands:

	ucache
ll_x ll_y ur_x ur_y	**setbbox**
x y	**moveto**
dx dy	**rmoveto**
x y	**lineto**
dx dy	**rlineto**
x_1 y_1 x_2 y_2 x_3 y_3	**curveto**
dx_1 dy_1 dx_2 dy_2 dx_3 dy_3	**rcurveto**

$$x \; y \; r \; ang_1 \; ang_2 \quad \textbf{arc}$$
$$x \; y \; r \; ang_1 \; ang_2 \quad \textbf{arcn}$$
$$x_1 \; y_1 \; x_2 \; y_2 \; r \quad \textbf{arct}$$
$$\textbf{closepath}$$

The permitted operators are all the standard PostScript operators that append to the current path, with the exception of **arcto** and **charpath**, which are not allowed. There are two special user path construction operators, **ucache** and **setbbox**.

Note   *arcto is not allowed because it would push results onto the operand stack.* ***arct*** *is the same as* ***arcto****, except for this effect.* ***charpath*** *is not allowed because the resulting user path would not be self-contained, but would depend on the current font.*

The permitted operands are literal numbers: integers and reals. The correct number of operands must be supplied to each operator. The user path must be structured as follows (any deviation from these rules will result in a **typecheck** error when the user path is interpreted):

1. The optional **ucache** places the user path in a special cache. It speeds up execution for paths that a program uses frequently. If **ucache** is present, it must come first. See section 4.6.3, "User Path Cache."

2. Next must be a **setbbox**, which establishes a bounding box in user space enclosing the entire path.

3. The remainder of the user path must be path construction operators and their operands. All coordinates must fall within the bounds specified by **setbbox**. If they don't, a **rangecheck** error will occur when the user path is interpreted.

The path construction operators in a user path may appear either as executable name objects, such as **moveto**, or as operator objects, such as the value of **moveto** in **systemdict**. An application program constructing a user path specifies name objects. However, the program might happen to apply **bind** to the user path or to a procedure containing it, causing the names to be replaced by the operator objects. No advantage is gained by binding a user path.

The user path painting operators interpret a user path as if **systemdict** were the current dictionary (see the definition of **uappend**). The path construction operators contained in the user path are guaranteed to have their standard meanings.

Note It is illegal for a user path to contain names other than the standard path construction operator names. Aliases are prohibited to ensure that the user path definition is self-contained and its meaning entirely independent of its execution environment.

4.6.2 Encoded User Paths

An *encoded user path* is a very compact representation of a user path. It is an array consisting of two string objects, or an array and a string. The strings effectively encode the operands and operators of an equivalent user path procedure, using a compact binary encoding.

The encoded user path representation is accepted and understood by the user path painting operators, such as **ufill**. Those operators interpret the data structure and perform the encoded operations. It does not make sense to think of "executing" the encoded user path directly.

Note Operator encoding is specialized to user path definitions; it has nothing to do with the alternative external encodings of the PostScript language, which are described in section 3.12, "Binary Encoding Details."

The elements of an encoded user path are:

- A *data string* or *data array* containing numeric operands.

- An *operator string* containing encoded operators.

This two-part organization is for the convenience of application programs that generate encoded user paths. In particular, operands always fall on natural addressing boundaries. All the characters in both strings are interpreted as binary numbers, not as ASCII character codes.

If the first element is a string, it is interpreted as an encoded number string, whose representation is described in section 3.12.5, "Encoded Number Strings." If it is an array, its elements are simply used in sequence. All elements must be numbers.

The operator string is interpreted as a sequence of encoded path construction operators, one operation code (opcode) per character. Table 4.3 shows the allowed opcode values.

Table 4.3 *Opcodes for encoded user paths*

Opcode	Operator	Opcode	Operator
0	**setbbox**	6	**rcurveto**
1	**moveto**	7	**arc**
2	**rmoveto**	8	**arcn**
3	**lineto**	9	**arct**
4	**rlineto**	10	**closepath**
5	**curveto**	11	**ucache**
$32 < n \leq 255$	repetition count: repeat next code $n - 32$ times.		

Associated with each opcode in the operator string are zero or more operands in the data string or data array. The order of the operands is the same as in an ordinary user path. For example, execution of a **lineto** (opcode 3) consumes an x operand and a y operand from the data sequence.

Note   *If the encoded user path does not conform to the rules described above, a **typecheck** error will occur when the path is interpreted. Possible errors include invalid opcodes in the operator string or premature end of the data sequence.*

Example 4.3 shows an encoded version of the user path from Example 4.2 on page 164. It specifies its operand list as an ordinary data array encoded in ASCII. Example 4.4 shows the same user path with the operands given as an encoded number string.

Example 4.3

```
{
 {100 200 400 500
  150 200
  250 200 400 390 400 460
  400 480 350 500 250 500
  100 400 }
 <0B 00 01 22 05 03 0A>
} ufill
```

Example 4.4

```
{
<95200014
 0064 00C8 0190 01F4
 0096 00C8
```

```
        00FA 00C8 0190 0186 0190 01CC
        0190 01E0 015E 01F4 00FA 01F4
        0064 0190>
      <0B 00 01 22 05 03 0A>
    } ufill
```

The second example illustrates how encoded user paths are likely to be used. Although it does not appear to be more compact than the first example in its ASCII representation, it occupies less space in VM and executes considerably faster. The example shows the operand as a hexadecimal literal string for clarity of exposition. An ASCII base-85 string literal or a binary string token would be more compact.

4.6.3 User Path Cache

Some applications define paths that must be redisplayed frequently or that are repeated many times. To optimize interpretation of such paths, the PostScript language provides a facility called the *user path cache*. This cache, analogous to the font cache, retains the results from having interpreted the user path definitions. When the PostScript interpreter encounters a user path that is already in the cache, it substitutes the cached results instead of reinterpreting the path definition.

There is a non-trivial cost associated with placing a user path in the cache: Extra computation is required and existing paths may be displaced from the cache. Because most user paths are used once and immediately thrown away, it does not make sense to place every user path in the cache. Instead, the application program must explicitly identify the user paths that are to be cached. It does so by including the **ucache** operator as the first element of the user path definition before the **setbbox** sequence, as shown in Example 4.5.

Example 4.5

```
/Circle1 {ucache –1–1 1 1 setbbox 0 0 1 0 360 arc} cvlit def
Circle1 ufill
```

The **ucache** operator notifies the PostScript interpreter that the enclosing user path should be placed in the cache if it is not already there, or obtained from the cache if it is. This cache management is not performed directly by **ucache**; instead, it is performed by the painting operator applied to the user path (**ufill** in this example). This is because the results retained in the cache differ according to what painting operation is performed. User path painting operators produce the same effects on the current page whether or not the cache is accessed.

Note   Invoking **ucache** *outside a user path has no effect.*

Caching is based on the *value* of a user path object. That is, two user paths are considered the same for caching purposes if all elements of one are equal to the corresponding elements of the other, *even if the objects themselves are not equal.* A user path placed in the cache need not be explicitly retained in VM. An equivalent user path appearing literally later in the program can take advantage of the cached information. Of course, if it is known that a given user path will be used many times, defining it explicitly in VM avoids creating it multiple times.

User path caching, like font caching, is effective across translations of the user coordinate system, but not across other transformations, such as scaling or rotation. In other words, multiple instances of a given user path painted at different places on the page take advantage of the user path cache when the CTM has been altered only by **translate**. If the CTM has been altered by **scale** or **rotate**, the instances will be treated as if they were described by different user paths.

Two other features of Example 4.5 are important to note:

- The user path object is explicitly saved for later use (as the value of Circle1 in this example). This is done in anticipation of painting the same path multiple times.

- The **cvlit** operator is applied to the user path object to remove its executable attribute. This ensures that the subsequent reference to Circle1 pushes the object on the operand stack rather than inappropriately executing it as a procedure. It is unnecessary to do this if the user path is to be consumed immediately by a user path painting operator, not saved for later use.

Note   It is necessary to build the user path as an executable array with { and } rather than as a literal array with [and] so that the user path construction operators are not executed while building the array. Executable arrays have deferred execution.

4.6.4   User Path Operators

There are three categories of user path operators:

- User path painting operators, combining interpretation of a user path with a painting operation (**fill** or **stroke**)—for example, **ufill**, **ueofill**, **ustroke**.

- Some of the insideness testing operators. See section 4.5.3, "Insideness Testing."

- Miscellaneous operators that involve user paths—for example, **uappend**, **upath**, **ustrokepath**.

The *userpath* operand of any of those operators is one of the following:

- *Ordinary user path:* an array, which need not be executable, whose length is at least 5.

- *Encoded user path:* an array of two elements. The first element is either an array whose elements are all numbers or a string that can be interpreted as an encoded number string. See section 3.12.5, "Encoded Number Strings." The second element is a string that encodes a sequence of operators, as described in Table 4.3 on page 168.

In either case, the value of the object must conform to the rules for constructing user paths, as detailed in preceding sections. That is, the operands and operators must appear in the correct sequence. If the user path is malformed, a **typecheck** error occurs.

Several of the operators take an optional matrix as their top-most operand. This is a six-element array of numbers that describe a transformation matrix. A matrix is distinguished from a user path, which is also an array, by the number and types of its elements.

There is no user path clipping operator. Because the whole purpose of the clipping operation is to alter the current clipping path, there is no way to avoid building the path. The best way to clip with a user path is

newpath *userpath* uappend clip newpath

This operation can still take advantage of information in the user path cache under favorable conditions.

Note *The **uappend** operator and the user path painting operators perform a temporary adjustment to the current transformation matrix as part of their execution. This adjustment consists of rounding the t_x and t_y components of the CTM to the nearest integer values. This ensures that scan conversion of the user path produces uniform results when it is placed at different positions on the page through translation. This is especially important if the user path is cached. This adjustment is not ordinarily visible to a PostScript language program and is not mentioned in the descriptions of the individual operators.*

4.6.5 Rectangles

Rectangles are used very frequently, so it is useful to have a few operators to paint rectangles directly. This is a convenience to application programs. Also, knowing that the figure will be a rectangle results in significantly optimized execution. The rectangle operators are similar to the user path operators in that they combine path construction with painting. However, their operands are in a considerably simpler form.

A rectangle is defined in the user coordinate system, just as if it were constructed as an ordinary path. The Level 2 rectangle operators **rectfill**, **rectstroke**, and **rectclip** accept three different forms of operands:

- Four numbers: *x*, *y*, *width*, and *height*, which describe a single rectangle. The rectangle's sides are parallel to the user space axes. It has corners located at coordinates (*x*, *y*), (*x* + *width*, *y*), (*x* + *width*, *y* + *height*), and *(x, y + height)*. Note that *width* and *height* can be negative.

- An arbitrarily long sequence of numbers represented as an array.

- An arbitrarily long sequence of numbers represented as an encoded number string, described in section 3.12.5, "Encoded Number Strings."

The sequence in the latter two operand forms must contain a multiple of four numbers. Each group of four consecutive numbers is interpreted as the *x*, *y*, *width*, and *height* values defining a single rectangle. The effect produced is equivalent to specifying all the rectangles as separate subpaths of a single combined path that is then operated on by a single **fill**, **stroke**, or **clip** operator.

The PostScript interpreter draws all rectangles in a counterclockwise direction in user space, regardless of the signs of the *width* and *height* operands. This ensures that when multiple rectangles overlap, all of their interiors are treated as "inside" the path according to the non-zero winding number rule.

4.7   Forms

A *form* is a self-contained description of any arbitrary graphics, text, or sampled images that are to be painted multiple times—on each of several pages or several times at different locations on a single page. The appearance of a form is described by a PostScript language procedure that executes graphical operators. Language support for forms is a Level 2 feature.

What distinguishes a form from an ordinary procedure is that it is self-contained and behaves according to certain rules. By defining a form, a program declares that each execution of the form will produce the same output. The output depends only on the graphics state at the time the form is executed. The form's definition does not refer to variable information in dictionaries or elsewhere in VM, and its execution has no side effects in VM.

These rules permit the PostScript interpreter to save the graphical output of the form in a cache. Later, when the same form is used again, the interpreter substitutes the saved output instead of re-executing the form's definition. This can significantly improve performance when the form is used many times.

There are various uses for forms:

- As suggested by its name, a form can serve as the template for an entire page. For example, a program that prints filled-in tax forms can first paint the fixed template as a form, then paint the variable information on top of it.

- A form can also be any graphic element that is to be used repeatedly. For example, in output from computer-aided design systems, it is common for certain standard components to appear many times. A company's logo can be treated as a form.

4.7.1 Using Forms

Two steps are required to use forms:

1. *Describe the appearance of the form.* This is done by creating a dictionary, called a *form dictionary*, that contains information about the form. A crucial element of the dictionary is the **PaintProc**, a PostScript language procedure that can be executed to paint the form.

2. *Invoke the form.* This is accomplished simply by executing the **execform** operator with the form dictionary as the operand. Before doing so, a program should set appropriate parameters in the graphics state; in particular, it should alter the CTM to control the position, size, and orientation of the form in user space.

Table 4.4 lists the entries in a form dictionary.

Table 4.4 *Entries in a form dictionary*

Key	Type	Semantics
FormType	integer	(*Required*) Must be 1.
XUID	array	(*Optional*) An *extended unique ID* that uniquely identifies the form; see section 5.8.2, "Extended Unique ID Numbers." Presence of an **XUID** in a form dictionary enables the PostScript interpreter to save cached output from the form for later use, even when the form dictionary is loaded into VM multiple times (by different jobs, for instance). To ensure correct behavior, **XUID** values must be assigned from a central registry. This is particularly appropriate for forms treated as named resources. Forms that are created dynamically by an application program should *not* contain **XUID** entries.
BBox	array	(*Required*) Array of four numbers in the form coordinate system giving lower-left *x*, lower-left *y*, upper-right *x*, and upper-right *y* of the form's bounding box. This bounding box is used to clip the output of the form and to determine its size for caching.
Matrix	matrix	(*Required*) A transformation matrix that maps from the form's coordinate space into user space. This matrix is concatenated with the CTM before the **PaintProc** is called.
PaintProc	procedure	(*Required*) A PostScript language procedure for painting the form (see below).
Implementation	any	Added by **execform**. This entry contains data used by the implementation to support form caching. The type and value of this entry are implementation dependent.

The form dictionary can contain other constant information that is required by the **PaintProc**.

The form is defined in its own coordinate system, the *form coordinate system*, which is defined by concatenating **Matrix** with the CTM each time **execform** is executed. The **BBox** parameter is interpreted in the form coordinate system; the **PaintProc** is executed in that coordinate system.

The **execform** operator first checks if the form dictionary has previously been used as an operand to **execform**. If not, it verifies that the dictionary contains the required elements and it makes the dictionary read-only. It then paints the form, either by invoking the form's **PaintProc** or by substituting cached output produced by a previous execution of the same form.

Whenever **execform** needs to execute the form definition, it:

1. Executes **gsave**.

2. Concatenates the **Matrix** entry with the CTM.

3. Clips according to the **BBox** entry.

4. Executes **newpath**.

5. Pushes the form dictionary on the operand stack.

6. Executes the form's **PaintProc**.

7. Executes **grestore**.

The **PaintProc** is expected to consume its dictionary operand and to use the information at hand to paint the form. It must obey certain guidelines to avoid disrupting the environment in which it is invoked.

- It should not execute any of the operators that are unsuitable for use in encapsulated PostScript files; these are listed in Appendix I.

- It should not execute **showpage**, **copypage**, or any device setup operator.

- Except for removing its dictionary operand, it should leave the stacks unchanged.

- It should have no side effects beyond painting the form. It should not alter objects in VM or anywhere else. Due to the effects of caching, the **PaintProc** is called at unpredictable times and in unpredictable environments. It should depend only on information in the form dictionary and should produce the same effect every time it is called.

Form caching is most effective when the graphics state does not change between successive executions of **execform** with a given form. Changes to the translation components of the CTM usually do not influence caching behavior. Other changes may require the interpreter to re-execute the **PaintProc**.

4.8 Color Spaces

The PostScript language includes powerful facilities for describing the colors of graphical objects to be marked on the current page. The color facilities are divided into two parts:

- *Color specification.* A PostScript language program can specify abstract colors in a device-independent way. Colors can be described in any of a variety of color systems or *color spaces*. Some color spaces are related to device color representation (gray scale, RGB, and CMYK); others are related to human visual perception (CIE based). Certain special features are also modelled as color spaces: patterns, separations, and color mapping.

- *Color rendering.* The PostScript interpreter reproduces colors on the raster output device by a multi-step process that includes color conversions, gamma correction, halftoning, and scan conversion. Certain aspects of this process are under PostScript language control. However, unlike the facilities for color specification, the color rendering facilities are device dependent and ordinarily should not be accessed from a page description.

This section introduces the color specification facilities and describes how they work. It covers everything that most PostScript language programs need to specify colors. Chapter 6 describes the facilities to control color rendering; a program should use those facilities only to configure new output devices or to achieve special device-dependent effects.

Figure 4.5 and Figure 4.6 on pages 178 and 179 illustrate the organization of the major language features for dealing with color. They show the division between color specification (device independent) and color rendering (device dependent).

4.8.1 Types of Color Spaces

As described in section 4.5, "Painting," marks placed on the page by operators such as **fill** and **stroke** have a color that is determined by the *current color* parameter of the graphics state. A color value consists of one or more *color components*, which are usually numbers. For example, a gray value can be specified by a single number, ranging from 0 (black) to 1 (white). A full color value can be specified in any of several ways. A common method uses three numbers to specify red, green, and blue components.

In Level 2, color values are interpreted according to the *current color space*, which is another parameter of the graphics state. A PostScript language program first selects a color space by executing the **setcolorspace** operator. It then selects color values in that color space by executing the **setcolor** operator. Also, there are convenience operators—**setgray, setrgbcolor, sethsbcolor, setcmykcolor,** and **setpattern**—that select both a color space and a color value in a single step.

In Level 1, this distinction between color spaces and color values is not explicit, and the set of color spaces is limited. Colors can be specified only by **setgray, setrgbcolor,** and **sethsbcolor** (**setcmykcolor** is also available in some implementations). However, in the color spaces that are supported, the semantics of the color values are consistent between Level 1 and Level 2.

The **image** and **colorimage** operators, introduced in section 4.10, "Images," enable sampled images to be painted on the current page. Each sample of an image is a color value consisting of one or more components that are to be interpreted in some color space. Since the color values come from the image itself, the current color in the graphics state is not used.

Regardless of whether color values originate from the graphics state or from a sampled image, all later stages of color processing treat them the same way. The following sections describe the semantics of color values that are specified as operands to the **setcolor** operator, but the same semantics apply to color values originating as image samples.

There are three categories of color spaces:

- *Device color spaces* collectively refer to several methods for directly specifying colors or gray levels that the output device is to produce. These methods include RGB (red-green-blue), HSB (hue-saturation-brightness), and CMYK (cyan-magenta-yellow-black).

- *CIE* (the *Commission Internationale de l'Éclairage*) has created an international standard for color specification. Colors can be specified in the CIE-based color spaces in a way that is independent of the characteristics of any particular output device.

- *Special color spaces* add special semantics to an underlying color space. They include facilities for patterns, color mapping, and separations.

Figure 4.5 *Color specification*

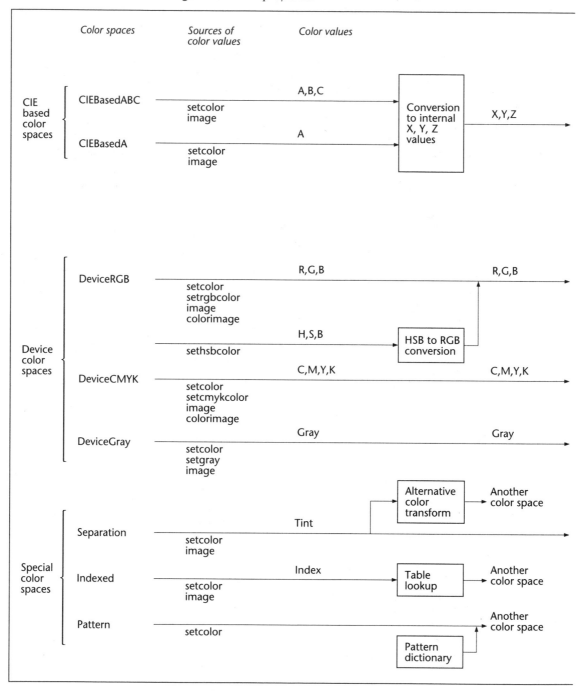

Figure 4.6 *Color rendering*

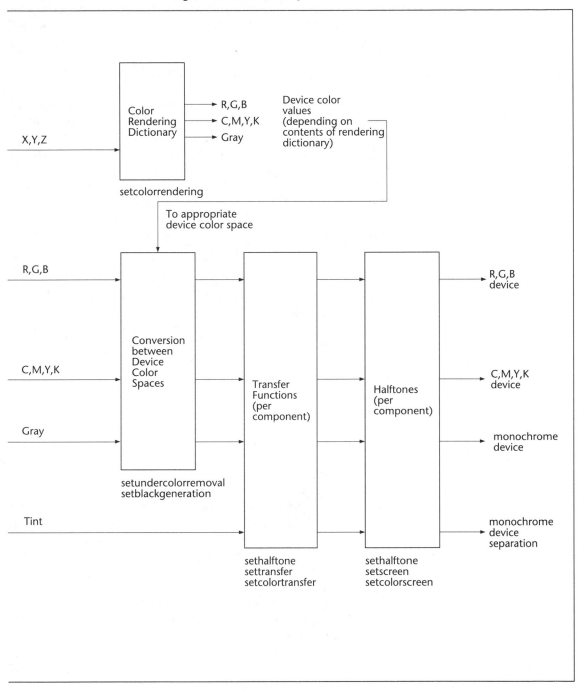

Regardless of which method a PostScript language program uses to *specify* a color (device, CIE-based, or special color space), *rendering* that color on a particular device is under separate control. Rendering is described in Chapter 6.

The following operators control color space and color value selection:

- **setcolorspace** sets the color space parameter in the graphics state. Its operand is an array object. The first element of the array is a name object that identifies the color space; the remaining elements, if any, are parameters that further describe the color space as a whole. The standard color space names are:

DeviceGray	**CIEBasedABC**	**Pattern**
DeviceRGB	**CIEBasedA**	**Indexed**
DeviceCMYK		**Separation**

  The number and types of the parameters vary according to the color space name. For color spaces that do not require parameters, the operand to **setcolorspace** can be the color space name instead of an array. **currentcolorspace** returns the current color space parameter (always as an array).

- **setcolor** sets the current color parameter in the graphics state to a value that is interpreted according to the current color space. **setcolor** requires one or more operands, depending on the color space; each operand specifies one component of the color value. **currentcolor** returns the current color parameter.

- **setgray**, **setrgbcolor**, **sethsbcolor**, **setcmykcolor**, and **setpattern** set the color space implicitly and the current color value as specified by the operands. **currentgray**, **currentrgbcolor**, **currenthsbcolor**, and **currentcmykcolor** return the current color according to an implicit color space. They perform conversions in certain limited cases if the current color space differs from the implicit one.

The **setcolorspace** and **setcolor** operators sometimes install composite objects, such as arrays or dictionaries, as parameters in the graphics state. To ensure predictable behavior, a PostScript language program should thereafter treat all such objects as if they were read-only.

In certain circumstances, it is illegal to execute operators that specify colors or other color-related parameters in the graphics state. This restriction occurs when defining graphical figures whose colors are to be specified separately each time they are used. The circumstances are:

- After execution of **setcachedevice** or **setcachedevice2** in the **BuildChar** or **BuildGlyph** procedure of a font dictionary (see section 5.7, "Type 3 Fonts").

- In the **PaintProc** procedure of a pattern whose **PaintType** is 2 (see section 4.9, "Patterns").

In those circumstances, execution of any of the following operators will cause an **undefined** error:

colorimage	setcolortransfer
image	setgray
setblackgeneration	sethsbcolor
setcmykcolor	setpattern
setcolor	setrgbcolor
setcolorrendering	setscreen
setcolorscreen	settransfer
setcolorspace	setundercolorremoval

Note that **imagemask** is not restricted, because it does not specify colors, but rather designates places where the current color is to be painted.

4.8.2 Device Color Spaces

The device color spaces enable a page description to specify color values that are *directly* related to their representation on an output device. The color values map directly—or via simple conversions—to the application of device colorants, such as quantities of ink or intensities of display phosphors. This enables a PostScript language program to control colors precisely for a *particular* device, but the results produced may not be consistent between *different* devices.

The device color spaces are as follows:

- **DeviceRGB** controls the intensities of red, green, and blue light, the three primary colors used in displays. Colors in this space can alternatively be specified as hue, saturation, and brightness values.

- **DeviceCMYK** controls the concentrations of cyan, magenta, yellow, and black inks, the four process colors used in printing.

- **DeviceGray** controls the intensity of achromatic light, on a scale from black to white.

Although the notion of explicit color spaces is a Level 2 feature, the operators for specifying colors in the **DeviceRGB** and **DeviceGray** color spaces—**setrgbcolor**, **sethsbcolor**, and **setgray**—are supported by Level 1. The **setcmykcolor** operator is also supported by some (but not all) Level 1 implementations.

DeviceRGB Color Space

Colors in the **DeviceRGB** color space can be specified according to two color models, called the *red-green-blue* (RGB) and *hue-saturation-brightness* (HSB) models. Each of these models can specify any reproducible color by three numeric parameters, but the numbers mean different things in the two models. Example 4.6 shows different ways to select the **DeviceRGB** color space and a color in that space.

Example 4.6

```
[/DeviceRGB] setcolorspace red green blue setcolor
/DeviceRGB setcolorspace red green blue setcolor
red green blue setrgbcolor
hue saturation brightness sethsbcolor
```

In the RGB model, a color is described as a combination of the three primary colors—red, green, and blue—in particular concentrations. The intensity of each primary color is specified by a number in the range 0 to 1, where 0 indicates no contribution at all and 1 indicates maximum intensity of that color.

If all three colors have equal intensity, the perceived result theoretically is a pure gray on the scale from black to white. If the intensities are not all equal, the result is some color that is a function of the relative intensities of the primary colors.

In the HSB model, a color is described as a combination of three parameters called *hue*, *saturation*, and *brightness*. HSB colors are often illustrated as arranged around a *color wheel*. The hue parameter specifies the angular position of a color on this wheel: 0 corresponds to pure red, 1/3 to pure green, 2/3 to pure blue, and 1 to red again. Intermediate values correspond to mixtures of the adjacent colors.

- Hue corresponds to the property that is intuitively meant by the term "color." Common hues have names such as "yellow" or "blue-green."

- Saturation indicates how pure the color is. A saturation of 0 indicates that none of the color's hue is visible; the result is a shade of gray. A saturation of 1 indicates that the color is pure—consists entirely of the color's hue. Intermediate values indicate a mixture between a pure hue and white light.

- Brightness determines how light the color determined by the hue and saturation will be. A brightness of 0 is always black. A brightness of 1 sets the lightness of the color to the maximum that the hue-saturation combination can allow. For example, pure red can never be as light as the brightest white because it is missing two components.

Note   *HSB is not a color space in its own right. It is simply a convention for specifying **DeviceRGB** color values in a different coordinate system.*

As shown in Example 4.6, **setcolorspace** and **setcolor** select the color space and color value separately; **setrgbcolor** and **sethsbcolor** set them in combination. Of these operators, only **setrgbcolor** and **sethsbcolor** are supported by Level 1 implementations. For **DeviceRGB**, **setcolorspace** sets the three components of the current color to 0.

When the current color space is **DeviceRGB**, both **currentcolor** and **currentrgbcolor** return the current color value as red, green, and blue, regardless of how it was specified. **currenthsbcolor** returns the current color value as hue, saturation, and brightness, converting among color models as necessary. Of these operators, only **currentrgbcolor** and **currenthsbcolor** are supported by Level 1 implementations.

When the current color space is one of the other device color spaces (**DeviceCMYK** or **DeviceGray**), **currentcolor** returns the current color value in that color space. **currentrgbcolor** and **currenthsbcolor** first convert the current color value into the **DeviceRGB** color space. The conversions are described in section 6.2, "Conversions Among Device Color Spaces." These operators cannot convert from CIE-based or special color spaces.

DeviceCMYK Color Space

Colors are formed either by adding light sources or by subtracting light from an illuminating source. Computer displays and film recorders typically add colors, while printing inks typically subtract colors. These two methods for forming colors give rise to two major complementary color specifications: the additive RGB specification and the subtractive CMYK specification. The **DeviceCMYK** color space allows specifying colors according to the CMYK model.

A color component in a **DeviceCMYK** color value specifies the amount of light that component *absorbs*. In theory, each one of three standard printing process colors—*cyan*, *magenta*, and *yellow*—absorbs one of the standard light components—*red*, *green*, and *blue*—respectively. *Black*, a fourth standard printing process color, absorbs all components of light in equal amounts. In this CMYK color specification, each of the four components is a number between 0 and 1, where 0 represents no ink (that is, absorbs no light) and 1 represents maximum ink (absorbs all the light it can). Note that the sense of these numbers is opposite to that of RGB color components.

Example 4.7 shows different ways to select the **DeviceCMYK** color space and a color in that space.

Example 4.7

```
[/DeviceCMYK] setcolorspace cyan magenta yellow black setcolor
/DeviceCMYK setcolorspace cyan magenta yellow black setcolor
cyan magenta yellow black setcmykcolor
```

setcolorspace and **setcolor** select the color space and color value separately; **setcmykcolor** sets them in combination. For **DeviceCMYK**, **setcolorspace** sets the four components of the current color to 0, 0, 0, and 1.

When the current color space is **DeviceCMYK**, both **currentcolor** and **currentcmykcolor** return the current color value as cyan, magenta, yellow, and black. When the current color space is one of the other device color spaces (**DeviceRGB** or **DeviceGray**), **currentcolor** returns the current color value in that color space. **currentcmykcolor** converts the current color value into the **DeviceCMYK** color space; the conversions are described in section 6.2, "Conversions Among Device Color Spaces." This operator cannot convert from CIE-based or special color spaces.

setcmykcolor and **currentcmykcolor** are supported by some, but not all, Level 1 implementations.

DeviceGray Color Space

Black, white, and intermediate shades of gray are special cases of full color. A gray-scale value is described by a single number in the range 0 to 1, where 0 corresponds to black, 1 to white, and intermediate values to different gray levels. Example 4.8 shows different ways to select the **DeviceGray** color space and a color in that space.

Example 4.8

```
[/DeviceGray] setcolorspace gray setcolor
/DeviceGray setcolorspace gray setcolor
gray setgray
```

setcolorspace and **setcolor** select the color space and color value separately; **setgray** sets them in combination. For **DeviceGray**, **setcolorspace** sets the current color to 0.

When the current color space is **DeviceGray**, both **currentcolor** and **currentgray** return the current color value as a single gray component. When the current color space is one of the other device color spaces (**DeviceRGB** or **DeviceCMYK**), **currentcolor** returns the current color value in that color space. **currentgray** converts the current color value into the **DeviceGray** color space; the conversions are described in section 6.2, "Conversions Among Device Color Spaces." This operator cannot convert from CIE-based or special color spaces.

setgray and **currentgray** are supported by all implementations.

4.8.3 CIE-Based Color Spaces

CIE-based color is defined relative to an international standard used in the graphic arts, television, and printing industries. It enables a page description to specify color values in a way that is related to human visual perception. The goal of this standard is for a given CIE-based color specification to produce consistent results on different output devices, up to the limitations of each device.

The detailed semantics of the CIE colorimetric system and the theory on which it is based are beyond the scope of this manual. The bibliography lists several books that should be consulted for further information.

The semantics of the CIE-based color spaces are defined in terms of the relationship between the space's components and the tristimulus values X, Y, and Z of the CIE 1931 (XYZ)-space. Level 2 implementations of the PostScript language support two CIE-based color spaces named **CIEBasedABC** and **CIEBasedA**. Both CIE-based color spaces are invoked by

[*name dictionary*] setcolorspace

where *name* is one of two CIE-based color space names and *dictionary* is a dictionary containing parameters that further characterize the color space. The key-value pairs in this dictionary have specific interpretations that vary among the color spaces; some key-value pairs are required and some are optional.

Having selected a color space, a PostScript language program can then specify color values using the **setcolor** operator. Color values in the **CIEBasedABC** color space consist of three components; those in the **CIEBasedA** color space consist of a single component. Interpretation of those values depends on the color space and its parameters.

Note   *To use any of the CIE-based color spaces with the **image** operator requires using the 1-operand (dictionary) form of that operator, which causes **image** to interpret sample values according to the current color space. See section 4.10.5, "Image Dictionaries."*

CIE-based color spaces are available only in Level 2 implementations. They are entirely separate from device color spaces. Operators that refer to device color spaces implicitly, such as **setrgbcolor** and **currentrgbcolor**, have no connection with CIE-based color spaces; they do not perform conversions between CIE-based and device color spaces. **setrgbcolor** changes the color space to **DeviceRGB**. When the current color space is a CIE-based or special color space, **currentrgbcolor** returns the initial value of the **DeviceRGB** color space, which has nothing to do with the current color in the graphics state.

CIEBasedABC Color Space

The **CIEBasedABC** color space is defined in terms of a two-stage, non-linear transformation of the CIE 1931 (XYZ)-space. The formulation of the **CIEBasedABC** color space models a simple *zone theory* of color vision, consisting of a non-linear trichromatic first stage combined with a non-linear opponent color second stage. This formulation allows colors to be digitized with minimum loss of fidelity; this is important in sampled images.

Special cases of **CIEBasedABC** include a variety of interesting and useful color spaces, such as the CIE 1931 (XYZ)-space, a class of calibrated RGB spaces, and a class of opponent color spaces such as the CIE 1976 (L*a*b*)-space and the NTSC, SECAM, and PAL television spaces.

Color values in **CIEBasedABC** have three components, arbitrarily named A, B, and C. They can represent a variety of independent color components, depending on how the space is parameterized. For example, A, B, and C may represent:

- X, Y, and Z in the CIE 1931 (XYZ)-space.

- R, G, and B in a calibrated RGB space.

- $L*$, $a*$, and $b*$ in the CIE 1976 (L*a*b*)-space.

- Y, I, and Q in the NTSC space.

- Y, U, and V in the SECAM and PAL spaces.

The initial values of A, B, and C are 0 unless the range of valid values for a color component does not include 0, in which case the nearest valid value is substituted.

The parameters for the **CIEBasedABC** color space must be provided in a dictionary that is the second element of the array operand to the **setcolorspace** operator. Table 4.5 describes the contents of this dictionary.

Table 4.5 *Entries in a **CIEBasedABC** color space dictionary*

Key	Type	Semantics
RangeABC	array	(*Optional*) Array of six numbers $[A_0\ A_1\ B_0\ B_1\ C_0\ C_1]$ that specify the range of valid values for the A, B, and C components of the color space—that is, $A_0 \leq A \leq A_1$, $B_0 \leq B \leq B_1$, and $C_0 \leq C \leq C_1$. Default value: [0 1 0 1 0 1].
DecodeABC	array	(*Optional*) Array of three PostScript language procedures $[D_A\ D_B\ D_C]$ that decode the A, B, and C components of the color space into values that are linear with respect to an intermediate LMN representation; this is explained below. Default value: the array of identity procedures [{} {} {}].
		Each of these procedures is called with an encoded A, B, or C component on the operand stack and must return the corresponding decoded value. The result must be a monotonic function of the operand. Because these procedures are called at unpredictable times and in unpredictable environments, they must operate as pure functions without side effects.

MatrixABC	array	(*Optional*) Array of nine numbers $[L_A\ M_A\ N_A\ L_B\ M_B\ N_B\ L_C\ M_C\ N_C]$ that specify the linear interpretation of the decoded A, B, and C components of the color space with respect to the intermediate LMN representation. Default value: the identity matrix $[1\ 0\ 0\ 0\ 1\ 0\ 0\ 0\ 1]$.

The transformation defined by the **DecodeABC** and **MatrixABC** entries is:

$$L = D_A(A) \times L_A + D_B(B) \times L_B + D_C(C) \times L_C$$
$$M = D_A(A) \times M_A + D_B(B) \times M_B + D_C(C) \times M_C$$
$$N = D_A(A) \times N_A + D_B(B) \times N_B + D_C(C) \times N_C$$

In other words, the A, B, and C components of the color space are first decoded individually by the **DecodeABC** procedures. The results are treated as a three element vector and multiplied by **MatrixABC** (a three by three matrix) to provide the L, M, and N components of the intermediate LMN representation.

RangeLMN	array	(*Optional*) Array of six numbers $[L_0\ L_1\ M_0\ M_1\ N_0\ N_1]$ that specify the range of valid values for the L, M, and N components of the intermediate LMN representation—that is, $L_0 \le L \le L_1$, $M_0 \le M \le M_1$, and $N_0 \le N \le N_1$. Default value: $[0\ 1\ 0\ 1\ 0\ 1]$.

DecodeLMN	array	(*Optional*) Array of three PostScript language procedures $[D_L\ D_M\ D_N]$ that decode the L, M, and N components of the intermediate LMN representation into values that are linear with respect to the CIE 1931 (XYZ)-space. This is explained below. Default value: the array of identity procedures $[\{\}\ \{\}\ \{\}]$.

Each of these procedures is called with an encoded L, M, or N component on the operand stack and must return the corresponding decoded value. The result must be a monotonic function of the operand. Because these procedures are called at unpredictable times and in unpredictable environments, they must operate as pure functions without side effects.

MatrixLMN	array	(*Optional*) Array of nine numbers $[X_L\ Y_L\ Z_L\ X_M\ Y_M\ Z_M\ X_N\ Y_N\ Z_N]$ that specify the linear interpretation of the decoded L, M, and N components of the intermediate LMN representation with respect to the CIE 1931 (XYZ)-space. Default value: the identity matrix $[1\ 0\ 0\ 0\ 1\ 0\ 0\ 0\ 1]$.

The transformation defined by the **DecodeLMN** and **MatrixLMN** entries is:

$$X = D_L(L) \times X_L + D_M(M) \times X_M + D_N(N) \times X_N$$
$$Y = D_L(L) \times Y_L + D_M(M) \times Y_M + D_N(N) \times Y_N$$
$$Z = D_L(L) \times Z_L + D_M(M) \times Z_M + D_N(N) \times Z_N$$

WhitePoint	array	(*Required*) Array of three numbers $[X_W\ Y_W\ Z_W]$ that specify the CIE 1931 (XYZ)-space tristimulus value of the diffuse white point. This is explained below. The numbers X_W and Z_W must be positive and Y_W must be equal to 1.
BlackPoint	array	(*Optional*) Array of three numbers $[X_B\ Y_B\ Z_B]$ that specify the CIE 1931 (XYZ)-space tristimulus value of the diffuse black point. These numbers must be non-negative. Default value: $[0\ 0\ 0]$.

The **WhitePoint** and **BlackPoint** entries control the overall effect of the CIE-based gamut mapping function described in section 6.1, "CIE-Based Color to Device Color." Typically, the colors specified by **WhitePoint** and **BlackPoint** are mapped nearly to the lightest and the darkest achromatic colors that the output device is capable of rendering in a way that preserves color appearance and visual contrast.

WhitePoint is assumed to represent the diffuse, achromatic highlight, and not a specular highlight. Specular highlights, achromatic or otherwise, are often reproduced lighter than the diffuse highlight. **BlackPoint** is assumed to represent the diffuse, achromatic shadow. Its value is typically limited by the dynamic range of the input device. In images produced by a photographic system, the values of **WhitePoint** and **BlackPoint** vary with exposure, system response, and artistic intent; hence, their values are image dependent.

The following PostScript language program fragments illustrate various interesting and useful special cases of **CIEBasedABC**.

Example 4.9 establishes the CIE 1931 (XYZ)-space with the CCIR XA/11 recommended white point.

Example 4.9

```
[/CIEBasedABC <<
    /RangeABC [0  0.9505  0  1  0  1.0890]
    /RangeLMN [0  0.9505  0  1  0  1.0890]
    /WhitePoint [0.9505  1  1.0890]
>>] setcolorspace
```

Example 4.10 establishes a calibrated RGB color space with the CCIR XA/11 recommended phosphor set, white point, and opto-electronic transfer function.

Example 4.10

```
[/CIEBasedABC <<
    /DecodeLMN [{1  0.45  div  exp} bind  dup  dup]
    /MatrixLMN [0.4124  0.2126  0.0193  0.3576  0.7152  0.1192
        0.1805  0.0722  0.9505]
    /WhitePoint [0.9505  1  1.0890]
>>] setcolorspace
```

In many cases, the parameters of calibrated RGB color spaces are specified in terms of the CIE 1931 chromaticity coordinates (x_R, y_R), (x_G, y_G), (x_B, y_B) of the red, green, and blue phosphors, respectively, and the chromaticity (x_W, y_W) of the diffuse white point corresponding to some linear RGB value (R, G, B), where usually $R = G = B = 1$. Note that standard CIE notation uses lower-case letters to specify chromaticity coordinates and upper-case letters to specify tristimulus values. Given this information, **MatrixLMN** and **WhitePoint** can be found as follows:

$$z = y_W \times ((x_G - x_B) \times y_R - (x_R - x_B) \times y_G + (x_R - x_G) \times y_B)$$

$$Y_L = \frac{y_R}{R} \times \frac{(x_G - x_B) \times y_W - (x_W - x_B) \times y_G + (x_W - x_G) \times y_B}{z}$$

$$X_L = Y_L \times \frac{x_R}{y_R} \qquad Z_L = Y_L \times \left(\frac{1 - x_R}{y_R} - 1\right)$$

$$Y_M = -\frac{y_G}{G} \times \frac{(x_R - x_B) \times y_W - (x_W - x_B) \times y_R + (x_W - x_R) \times y_B}{z}$$

$$X_M = Y_M \times \frac{x_G}{y_G} \qquad Z_M = Y_M \times \left(\frac{1 - x_G}{y_G} - 1\right)$$

$$Y_N = \frac{y_B}{B} \times \frac{(x_R - x_G) \times y_W - (x_W - x_G) \times y_R + (x_W - x_R) \times y_G}{z}$$

$$X_N = Y_N \times \frac{x_B}{y_B} \qquad Z_N = Y_N \times \left(\frac{1 - x_B}{y_B} - 1\right)$$

$$X_W = R \times X_L + G \times X_M + B \times X_N$$
$$Y_W = R \times Y_L + G \times Y_M + B \times Y_N$$
$$Z_W = R \times Z_L + G \times Z_M + B \times Z_N$$

Example 4.11 establishes the CIE 1976 (L*a*b*)-space with the CCIR XA/11 recommended white point. The $a*$ and $b*$ components, although theoretically unbounded, are defined to lie in the useful range −128 to +127. The transformation from $L*$, $a*$, and $b*$ component values to CIE 1931 (XYZ)-space tristimulus values X, Y, and Z is defined as:

$$X = X_W \times g\left(\frac{L* + 16}{116} + \frac{a*}{500}\right)$$

$$Y = Y_W \times g\left(\frac{L* + 16}{116}\right)$$

$$Z = Z_W \times g\left(\frac{L* + 16}{116} - \frac{b*}{200}\right)$$

where the function $g(x)$ is defined as:

$$g(x) = x^3 \qquad\qquad \text{if } x \geq \frac{6}{29}$$

$$g(x) = \frac{108}{841} \times (x - \frac{4}{29}) \qquad\qquad \text{otherwise}$$

Example 4.11

```
[/CIEBasedABC <<
    /RangeABC [0 100 -128 127 -128 127]
    /DecodeABC [{16 add 116 div} bind {500 div} bind {200 div} bind]
    /MatrixABC [1 1 1 1 0 0 0 0 -1]
    /DecodeLMN
        [{dup 6 29 div ge {dup dup mul mul}
            {4 29 div sub 108 841 div mul} ifelse 0.9505 mul} bind
        {dup 6 29 div ge {dup dup mul mul}
            {4 29 div sub 108 841 div mul} ifelse} bind
        {dup 6 29 div ge {dup dup mul mul}
            {4 29 div sub 108 841 div mul} ifelse 1.0890 mul} bind]
    /WhitePoint [0.9505 1 1.0890]
>>] setcolorspace
```

CIEBasedA Color Space

The **CIEBasedA** color space is the one-dimensional and usually achromatic analog of **CIEBasedABC**. Color values in **CIEBasedA** have a single component, arbitrarily named A. It can represent a variety of color components, depending on how the space is parameterized. For example, A may represent:

- The luminance Y component of the CIE 1931 (XYZ)-space.

- The gray component of a calibrated gray space.

- The CIE 1976 psychometric lightness $L*$ component of the CIE 1976 (L*a*b*)-space.

- The luminance Y component of the NTSC, SECAM, and PAL television spaces.

The initial value of A is 0 unless the range of valid values does not include 0, in which case the nearest valid value is substituted.

The parameters for the **CIEBasedA** color space must be provided in a dictionary that is the second element of the array operand to the **setcolorspace** operator. Table 4.6 describes the contents of this dictionary.

Table 4.6 *Entries in a CIEBasedA color space dictionary*

Key	Type	Semantics
RangeA	array	(*Optional*) Array of two numbers $[A_0 \ A_1]$ that specify the range of valid values for the A component of the color space—that is, $A_0 \leq A \leq A_1$. Default value: [0 1].
DecodeA	procedure	(*Optional*) PostScript language procedure D_A that decodes the A component of the color space into a value that is linear with respect to an intermediate LMN representation. See **DecodeABC** in Table 4.5. Default value: the identity procedure {}.
MatrixA	array	(*Optional*) Array of three numbers $[L_A \ M_A \ N_A]$ that specify the linear interpretation of the decoded A component of the color space with respect to the intermediate LMN representation. Default value: the matrix [1 1 1].
		The transformation defined by the **DecodeA** and **MatrixA** entries is:
		$$L = D_A(A) \times L_A$$ $$M = D_A(A) \times M_A$$ $$N = D_A(A) \times N_A$$
		See **MatrixABC** in Table 4.5.
RangeLMN	array	(*Optional*) Array of six numbers $[L_0 \ L_1 \ M_0 \ M_1 \ N_0 \ N_1]$ that specify the range of valid values for the L, M, and N components of the intermediate LMN representation—that is, $L_0 \leq L \leq L_1$, $M_0 \leq M \leq M_1$, and $N_0 \leq N \leq N_1$. Default value: [0 1 0 1 0 1].
DecodeLMN	array	(*Optional*) Array of three PostScript language procedures $[D_L \ D_M \ D_N]$ that decode the L, M, and N components of the intermediate LMN representation into values that are linear with respect to the CIE 1931 (XYZ)-space. See **DecodeLMN** in Table 4.5.
MatrixLMN	array	(*Optional*) Array of nine numbers $[X_L \ Y_L \ Z_L \ X_M \ Y_M \ Z_M \ X_N \ Y_N \ Z_N]$ that specify the linear interpretation of the decoded L, M, and N components of the intermediate LMN representation with respect to the CIE 1931 (XYZ)-space. See **MatrixLMN** in Table 4.5.
WhitePoint	array	(*Required*) Array of three numbers $[X_W \ Y_W \ Z_W]$ that specify the CIE 1931 (XYZ)-space tristimulus value of the diffuse white point. See **WhitePoint** in Table 4.5.
BlackPoint	array	(*Optional*) Array of three numbers $[X_B \ Y_B \ Z_B]$ that specify the CIE 1931 (XYZ)-space tristimulus value of the diffuse black point. See **BlackPoint** in Table 4.5.

The following PostScript language program fragments illustrate various interesting and useful special cases of **CIEBasedA**.

Example 4.12 establishes a space consisting of the *Y* dimension of the CIE 1931 (XYZ)-space with the CCIR XA/11 recommended white point.

Example 4.12

```
[/CIEBasedA <<
    /MatrixA [0.9505  1  1.0890]
    /RangeLMN [0  0.9505  0  1  0  1.0890]
    /WhitePoint [0.9505  1  1.0890]
>>] setcolorspace
```

Example 4.13 establishes a calibrated gray space with the CCIR XA/11 recommended white point and opto-electronic transfer function.

Example 4.13

```
[/CIEBasedA <<
    /DecodeA {1  0.45  div  exp} bind
    /MatrixA [0.9505  1  1.0890]
    /RangeLMN [0  0.9505  0  1  0  1.0890]
    /WhitePoint [0.9505  1  1.0890]
>>] setcolorspace
```

Example 4.14 establishes a space consisting of the L^* dimension of the CIE 1976 (L*a*b*)-space with the CCIR XA/11 recommended white point.

Example 4.14

```
[/CIEBasedA <<
    /RangeA [0  100]
    /DecodeA
        {16  add  116  div  dup  6  29  div  ge {dup  dup  mul  mul}
            {4  29  div  sub  108  841  div  mul} ifelse} bind
    /MatrixA [0.9505  1  1.0890]
    /RangeLMN [0  0.9505  0  1  0  1.0890]
    /WhitePoint [0.9505  1  1.0890]
>>] setcolorspace
```

4.8.4   Special Color Spaces

Special color spaces add special semantics to an underlying color space. There are three special color spaces: **Pattern**, **Indexed**, and **Separation**. All of the special color spaces are Level 2 features.

Pattern Color Space

The **Pattern** color space enables painting with a "color" defined as a *pattern*, a graphical figure used repeatedly to cover the areas that are to be painted. Section 4.9, "Patterns," describes how patterns are defined and used.

Indexed Color Space

The **Indexed** color space provides a *color map* or *color table* that allows a PostScript language program to use small integers to select from a table of arbitrary colors in some other color space. With the **Indexed** color space, a program can, for example, use image samples that are 8-bit index values rather than 24-bit RGB color values. For each sample, the PostScript interpreter uses the sample value to index into the color table and uses the color value it finds there. This technique can reduce considerably the amount of data required to represent a sampled image.

An **Indexed** color space is installed as follows:

> [/Indexed *base hival lookup*] setcolorspace

In other words, the operand to **setcolorspace** is a four-element array. The first element is the color space name **Indexed**; the remaining elements are the parameters *base*, *hival*, and *lookup*, which the **Indexed** color space requires. **setcolorspace** sets the current color to 0.

The *base* parameter is an array or name that identifies the *base color space*. This is the space in which the color values in the table are to be interpreted. It can be any device or CIE-based color space, but not a special color space (**Pattern**, **Indexed**, or **Separation**). For example, if the base color space is **DeviceRGB**, the values in the table are to be interpreted as *red*, *green*, and *blue* components. If the base color space is **CIEBasedABC**, the values are to be interpreted as *A*, *B*, and *C* components. The *base* parameter should be constructed just as if it were to be used as an operand to **setcolorspace**.

The *hival* parameter is an integer that specifies the maximum valid index value. In other words, the color table is to be indexed by integers in the range 0 to *hival*, inclusive. *hival* can be no greater than 4095, which is what would be required to index a table with 12-bit color sample values.

The color table is described by the *lookup* parameter, which can be either a procedure or a string. It provides the mapping between the values of *index* and the colors in the base color space.

If *lookup* is a procedure, the PostScript interpreter calls it to transform an *index* value into corresponding color component values in the *base* color space. The procedure is called with the index on the operand stack and must return the color component values in a form acceptable to the **setcolor** operator in the base color space. The number of components and interpretation of the component values depends on the base color space. Since the *lookup* procedure is called by the **setcolor** and **image** operators at unpredictable times, it must operate as a pure function, without side effects. It must be able to return color component values for any integer between 0 and *hival*, inclusive.

If *lookup* is a string object, it must be of length $m \times (hival + 1)$, where m is the number of color components in the base color space. Each byte in the string is interpreted as an integer. To look up an *index*, the PostScript interpreter multiplies *index* by m and uses the result to access the *lookup* string. The m bytes located starting at that position in the string are interpreted as coded values for the m color components of the base color space. Those bytes are treated as 8-bit integers in the range 0 to 255, which are then divided by 255, yielding component values in the range 0 to 1.

Example 4.15 illustrates specification of an **Indexed** color space that maps 8-bit index values to 3-component color values in the **DeviceRGB** color space.

Example 4.15

```
[/Indexed /DeviceRGB 255
  <000000 FF0000 00FF00 0000FF B57342 ... >
] setcolorspace
```

The example shows only the first five color values in the lookup string; there should be 256 color values and the string should be 768 characters long. Having established this color space, the program can now specify single-component color values in the range 0 to 255. For example, a color value of 4 selects an RGB color whose components are coded as the hexadecimal integers B5, 73, and 42. Dividing these by 255 yields a color whose red, green, and blue components are .710, .451, and .259, respectively.

Note   *To use the **Indexed** color space with the **image** operator requires using the 1-operand (dictionary) form of that operator, which causes **image** to interpret sample values according to the current color space. See section 4.10.5, "Image Dictionaries."*

Although the **Indexed** color space is mainly useful for images, you can use index values with the **setcolor** operator. For example,

    123 setcolor

selects the same color as does an image sample value of 123. An *index* component should be an integer in the range 0 to *hival*, inclusive. If *index* is a real number, it is truncated to an integer. If it is outside the range 0 to *hival*, it is clipped to the nearest bound.

Separation Color Space

Color output devices produce full color by combining *primary* or *process colors* in varying amounts. In a display, the primaries consist of red, green, and blue phosphors. In a printer, they consist of cyan, magenta, yellow, and sometimes black inks.

When the **showpage** or **copypage** operator is executed, most devices produce a single *composite* page on which all primary colors have been combined. However, some devices, such as typesetters, produce a collection of pages, one for each primary or process color. These pages are called *separations*. Each separation is a monochromatic rendition of the page for a single primary color. When the separations are later combined—on a printing press, for example—and the proper inks or other colorants are applied to them, a full-color page results.

There are situations in which it is desirable to produce additional separations to control the application of special colorants, often called *spot colors*. There are many colors and other effects that cannot be achieved by combining the primary colors. Examples include metallic and fluorescent colors and special textures.

The **Separation** color space provides a means for a PostScript language program to specify that additional separations are to be produced or special colors are to be applied. Those separations or colors are identified by name. When the current color space is a particular named separation, the current color is a single-component value, called a *tint*, that controls application of colorant for that separation only.

The effect of using the **Separation** color space depends on the nature and configuration of the device. Only a few devices, such as typesetters, support the production of arbitrary separations. Some other color printing devices support one or more special colorants that are to be applied to the composite page in addition to the primary colorants. In such devices, "separations" are not actually separate pages. Most devices do not support separations at all. The **Separation** color space provides predictable behavior when a program requests separations that the device can't produce.

A **Separation** color space is installed as follows:

[/Separation *name alternativeSpace tintTransform*] setcolorspace

In other words, the operand to **setcolorspace** is a four-element array. The first element is the color space name **Separation**. The remaining elements are the parameters *name*, *alternativeSpace*, and *tintTransform*, which the **Separation** color space requires.

A color value in a **Separation** color space consists of a single *tint* component in the range 0 to 1. The value 0 represents application of the minimum amount of colorant to the separation; 1 represents application of the maximum amount. Tints are treated as *subtractive* colors; this is the same as the convention for **DeviceCMYK** color components, but opposite the one for **DeviceRGB** and **DeviceGray**. The **setcolor** operator sets the current color in the graphics state to a tint value; the initial value is 1. A sampled image with single-component samples can also be treated as a source of tint values.

Note   *To use the **Separation** color space with the **image** operator requires using the 1-operand (dictionary) form of that operator, which causes **image** to interpret sample values according to the current color space. See section 4.10.5, "Image Dictionaries."*

The *name* parameter, a name or string object, specifies the name of the separation or colorant. The names of separations are arbitrary, and there can be an arbitrary number of separations, subject to implementation limits. Name and string objects can be used interchangeably. Some separation names contain spaces or other special characters, so strings may be more convenient.

At the moment **setcolorspace** is executed, the device determines if it can produce the named separation. If it can, **setcolorspace** ignores the *alternativeSpace* and *tintTransform* parameters. Subsequent painting operations apply colorant to the named separation according to the supplied tint values, as explained above.

If the device cannot produce the named separation, **setcolorspace** arranges instead for subsequent painting operations to be performed in an *alternative color space*. This enables the special colors to be approximated by colors in some device or CIE-based color space, which are then rendered using the usual primary or process colors. The way this works is as follows:

- The *alternativeSpace* parameter must be an array or name object that identifies the alternative color space. This can be any device or CIE-based color space, but not a special color space (**Pattern**, **Indexed**, or **Separation**). The *alternativeSpace* parameter should be constructed just as if it were to be used as an operand to **setcolorspace**.

- The *tintTransform* parameter must be a procedure. During subsequent painting operations, the PostScript interpreter calls this procedure to transform a tint value into color component values in the alternative color space. The procedure is called with *tint* on the operand stack and must return the color component values in a form acceptable to the **setcolor** operator in the alternative color space. The number of components and interpretation of the component values depends on the alternative color space. Since the *tintTransform* procedure is called by the **setcolor** and **image** operators at unpredictable times, it must operate as a pure function without side effects.

Example 4.16 illustrates specification of a **Separation** color space that is intended to produce a separation named AdobeGreen. If the device cannot produce an AdobeGreen separation, the program selects **DeviceCMYK** as the alternative color space, and it provides a *tintTransform* procedure that maps tint values linearly into shades of a CMYK color value that approximates the "Adobe green" color.

Example 4.16

```
[/Separation (AdobeGreen) /DeviceCMYK
  {dup .84 mul exch 0 exch dup .44 mul exch .21 mul}
] setcolorspace
```

For convenience, the separation names **Cyan**, **Magenta**, **Yellow**, and **Black** correspond to the conventional subtractive device's cyan, magenta, yellow, and black colorants, respectively. The names **Red**,

Green, and **Blue** correspond to the conventional additive device's red, green, and blue primaries, respectively. This enables a program to select one of the device's primary colors as if it were a separation.

Note   *Tint values are always subtractive, even if the device produces output for the named component by an additive method. The value 0 represents the lightest color; 1 represents the darkest color.*

The separation named **All** refers to all separations that are produced, including both process color separations and specific named separations that have been requested previously. When the current color space is the **All** separation, painting operators apply tint values to all separations instead of to only one. This is useful for purposes such as painting registration marks in the same place on every separation. Ordinarily, a program should do this as the last step of composing a page, immediately before executing **showpage**, when the set of separations the device will produce has been completely determined.

The separation named **None** will never be produced. If the device is producing separations, none of them will be marked. In other words, painting on the separation named **None** does not change the current page. All implementations support the separation named **None**, even if they do not support any other named separations. The *alternativeSpace* and *tintTransform* parameters are ignored, though dummy values must still be provided.

The graphics state contains an *overprint* parameter, controlled by the **setoverprint** operator. This parameter controls an aspect of color *rendering*, not of color *specification*. However, it applies only when separations are being produced, so it is described here.

When the device produces separations, the overprint parameter indicates if painting on one separation causes the corresponding areas of other separations—unrelated to the current color space—to be erased. To "erase" an area means to paint it with a tint value of 0.

If overprint is *false*, painting in a **Separation** color space causes corresponding areas of all other separations, including the ones for the primary colors, to be erased. Painting in any other color space, which is rendered onto the primary separations, causes the corresponding areas of all non-primary separations to be erased. If overprint is *true*, these erasing actions are not performed. Whatever was previously painted on the other separations is left undisturbed.

The effect of the overprint parameter becomes apparent when the separations are combined. If overprint is *false*, the color at any position on the page is whatever was painted there last. This is consistent with the normal opaque painting model of the PostScript language. If overprint is *true*, the color at some position may be a function of colors painted by several painting operations on different separations. The effect produced by such "overprinting" is device dependent and is not defined by the PostScript language. The default value of the overprint parameter is *false*.

When the device is not producing separations, the value of the overprint parameter has no effect on the current page.

4.9 Patterns

When operators such as **fill**, **stroke**, and **show** paint areas of the page with the current color, they ordinarily apply a single color that covers the areas uniformly. Sometimes it is desirable to apply "paint" that consists of a repeating figure instead of a simple color. Such a repeating figure is called a *pattern*.

The ability to paint with patterns is a Level 2 feature. With some effort, it is possible to achieve a limited form of patterns in Level 1 by defining them as characters in a special font and showing them repeatedly. Another technique—defining patterns as halftone screens—is *not* recommended, because the effect produced is device dependent.

"Painting with a pattern" means replicating a small graphical figure (called a *pattern cell*) at fixed intervals in x and y to cover the areas to be painted. The effect is as if one were to paint the figure on the surface of a clear glass tile, lay down copies of the tile in an array covering an area to be painted, and trim the tiles' edges to the boundaries of the area. Laying down copies of a pattern cell to fill an area is called *tiling*.

Patterns are quite general, and there are many uses for them. The appearance of a pattern cell is defined by an arbitrary PostScript language procedure. It can include graphical elements such as filled areas, text, and sampled images. The shape of a pattern cell need not be rectangular, and the spacing of tiles can differ from the size of the pattern cell. Patterns can be used to create various graphical textures, such as weaves, brick walls, and similar geometrical tilings.

4.9.1 Using Patterns

Painting with a pattern is a four-step procedure:

1. *Describe the prototype pattern.* This is done by creating a dictionary, called a *pattern dictionary*, that contains information about the pattern. A crucial element of the dictionary is the **PaintProc**, a PostScript language procedure that can be executed to paint a single pattern cell.

2. *Instantiate the pattern.* The **makepattern** operator copies a prototype pattern dictionary and produces an instance of the pattern that is locked to current user space. In other words, the size of a pattern cell and the phase of the tiling in device space are determined by the CTM at the time **makepattern** is executed. The pattern is unaffected by subsequent changes to the CTM or to other graphics state parameters.

3. *Select the pattern as the current color.* There is a special color space, named **Pattern**, whose color values are pattern dictionaries instead of the numeric color values used with other color spaces. The **setcolorspace** and **setcolor** operators set the color space and color value separately; the convenience operator **setpattern** installs a pattern as the current color in a single step.

4. *Invoke painting operators*, such as **fill**, **stroke**, **imagemask**, or **show**. All areas that normally would be painted with a uniform color are instead tiled with the pattern cell. To accomplish this, the PostScript interpreter calls the pattern dictionary's **PaintProc** (with the graphics state altered in certain ways) to obtain the pattern cell. It then paints this cell on the current page as many times as necessary. To optimize execution, the interpreter maintains a cache of recently used pattern cells.

4.9.2 Pattern Dictionaries

Table 4.7 lists the entries in a pattern dictionary. All entries except **Implementation** can appear in a prototype pattern dictionary (operand to **makepattern**). The pattern dictionary returned by **makepattern** contains an **Implementation** entry as well as the others.

Table 4.7 *Entries in a pattern dictionary*

Key	Type	Semantics
PatternType	integer	(*Required*) Must be 1.
XUID	array	(*Optional*) An *extended unique ID* that uniquely identifies the pattern; see section 5.8.2, "Extended Unique ID Numbers." Presence of an **XUID** in a pattern dictionary enables the PostScript interpreter to save cached instances of the pattern cell for later use, even when the pattern dictionary is loaded into VM multiple times—by different jobs, for instance. To ensure correct behavior, **XUID** values must be assigned from a central registry. This is particularly appropriate for patterns treated as named resources. Patterns that are created dynamically by an application program should *not* contain **XUID** entries.
PaintType	integer	(*Required*) Determines how the color of the pattern cell is to be specified. The choices are:

> 1   *Colored pattern*. The **PaintProc** itself specifies the colors used to paint the pattern cell.
>
> 2   *Uncolored pattern*. The **PaintProc** does not specify any color information. Instead, the entire pattern cell is painted with a separately specified color each time the pattern is used. Essentially, **PaintProc** describes a *stencil* through which the current color is to be poured. **PaintProc** must not execute operators that specify colors or other color-related parameters in the graphics state; otherwise, an **undefined** error will occur (see section 4.8.1, "Types of Color Spaces"). Use of the **imagemask** operator is permitted, however, because it does not specify any color information.

Key	Type	Semantics
TilingType	integer	(*Required*) Controls adjustments to the tiling to quantize it to the device pixel grid. The choices are:

> 1   *Constant spacing*. Pattern cells are spaced consistently—that is, by a multiple of a device pixel. To achieve this, **makepattern** may need to distort the pattern slightly by making small adjustments to **XStep**, **YStep**, and the transformation matrix. The amount of distortion does not exceed one device pixel.
>
> 2   *No distortion*. The pattern cell is not distorted, but the spacing between pattern cells may vary by as much as one device pixel in both *x* and *y* dimensions when the pattern is painted. This achieves the spacing requested by **XStep** and **YStep** on average, but not for individual pattern cells.
>
> 3   *Constant spacing and faster tiling*. Like **TilingType** 1, but with additional distortion of the pattern cell permitted to enable a more efficient implementation.

Key	Type	Semantics
BBox	array	(*Required*) An array of four numbers in the pattern cell coordinate system, giving lower-left *x*, lower-left *y*, upper-right *x*, and upper-right *y* of the pattern cell bounding box. This bounding box is used to clip the pattern cell and to determine its size for caching.

XStep	number	(*Required*) The desired horizontal spacing between pattern cells, measured in the pattern cell coordinate system. Note that **XStep** and **YStep** may differ from the dimensions of the pattern cell implied by the **BBox** entry. This enables tiling with irregularly shaped figures. **XStep** and **YStep** may be either positive or negative, but not zero.
YStep	number	(*Required*) The desired vertical spacing between pattern cells, measured in the pattern cell coordinate system.
PaintProc	procedure	(*Required*) A PostScript language procedure for painting the pattern cell (see below).
Implementation	any	This entry is inserted by **makepattern**. Its value consists of information used by the interpreter to achieve proper tiling of the pattern. The type and value of this entry are implementation dependent.

The pattern dictionary can contain other constant information that is required by the **PaintProc**.

The pattern cell is described in its own coordinate system, the *pattern coordinate system*, which is defined by concatenating the *matrix* operand of **makepattern** with the CTM at the time **makepattern** is executed. The **XStep**, **YStep**, and **BBox** parameters are interpreted in the pattern coordinate system; the **PaintProc** is executed in that coordinate system.

The placement of pattern cells in the tiling is based on the location of one *key pattern cell*, which is then displaced by multiples of **XStep** and **YStep** to replicate the pattern cell. The origin of the key pattern cell coincides with the origin of the coordinate system defined by concatenating *matrix* with CTM at the time **makepattern** is executed. The phase of the tiling can be controlled by the translation components of the *matrix* operand. This tiling is frozen; that is, whenever the pattern dictionary created by **makepattern** is used for painting, the same tiling is used, regardless of intervening changes to the CTM.

In Display PostScript systems, there is a *halftone phase* parameter that controls the placement of halftone cells relative to device space. This is to support operations such as scrolling (see section 7.3.3, "Halftone Phase"). Changing the halftone phase also alters the placement of patterns by the same amount. This applies only to patterns subsequently painted using *existing* pattern dictionaries—those created by **makepattern** before the halftone phase was changed. It does not affect the placement of newly created patterns.

To paint with a pattern, one must first establish the pattern dictionary as the current color in the graphics state; this is described in section 4.9.3, "Pattern Color Space." Subsequent painting operations will tile the painted areas with the pattern cell that is described in the dictionary. Whenever it needs to obtain the pattern cell, the interpreter:

1. Executes **gsave**.

2. Installs the graphics state that was in effect at the time **makepattern** was executed, with certain parameters altered as documented in the operator description for **makepattern**.

3. Pushes the pattern dictionary on the operand stack.

4. Executes the pattern's **PaintProc**.

5. Executes **grestore**.

The **PaintProc** is expected to consume its dictionary operand and to use the information at hand to paint the pattern cell. It must obey certain guidelines to avoid disrupting the environment in which it is invoked.

- It should not execute any of the operators that are unsuitable for use in encapsulated PostScript files; these are listed in Appendix I.

- It should not execute **showpage**, **copypage**, or any device setup operator.

- Except for removing its dictionary operand, it should leave the stacks unchanged.

- It should have no side effects beyond painting the pattern cell. It should not alter objects in VM or anywhere else. Due to the effects of caching, the **PaintProc** is called at unpredictable times and in unpredictable environments. It should depend only on information in the pattern dictionary and it should produce the same effect every time it is called.

4.9.3   Pattern Color Space

There is a special color space called **Pattern** whose "color values" are specified as pattern dictionaries. Selecting a pattern as the current color is a two-step process:

1. Execute **setcolorspace** to set the current color space to **Pattern**.

2. Execute **setcolor** with a pattern dictionary operand (and possibly other operands) to select that pattern as the current color.

Section 4.8, "Color Spaces," gives general information about color spaces and color values. Details of the **Pattern** color space and color value specifications appear below.

The initial color value in a pattern color space selected by **setcolorspace** is a *null* object, which is treated as if it were a pattern dictionary whose **PaintType** is 1 and whose **PaintProc** is an empty procedure. Painting with this pattern does not produce any marks on the current page.

A convenience operator, **setpattern**, combines the two steps for selecting a pattern. It takes a pattern dictionary as an operand, selects the **Pattern** color space, and sets the pattern as the current color. Details of its behavior depend on the value of the **PaintType** entry in the pattern dictionary. **setpattern** is the normal method for selecting patterns. For the purpose of exposition, the descriptions below specify the color space and color value separately, even though it is rarely necessary to do so.

Colored Patterns

A *colored pattern* is one whose color is self-contained. As part of painting the pattern cell, the **PaintProc** explicitly sets the colors of all graphical elements it paints. A single pattern cell can contain elements that are painted different colors. It can also contain sampled gray-scale or color images.

When used with colored patterns, the **Pattern** color space requires no additional parameters. The color space operand to **setcolorspace** can be either the name **Pattern** or a one-element array containing the name **Pattern**. The **Pattern** color space can also have a parameter, the *underlying color space*, as a second element of the array. This is required when using uncolored patterns, but is ignored when using colored patterns.

A color value operand to **setcolor** in this space has a single component, a pattern dictionary whose **PaintType** is 1. Example 4.17 establishes a colored pattern as the current color, where *pattern* is a type 1 pattern dictionary.

Example 4.17

```
[/Pattern] setcolorspace        % Alternatively, /Pattern setcolorspace
pattern setcolor
```

Subsequent executions of painting operators, such as **fill**, **stroke**, **show**, and **imagemask**, use the pattern to tile the areas to be painted.

Note   *The **image** operator in its 5-operand form and the **colorimage** operator use a predetermined color space (**DeviceGray**, **DeviceRGB**, or **DeviceCMYK**) for interpreting their color samples, regardless of the current color space. A pattern color space has no effect on those operators. The 1-operand (dictionary) form of **image** is not allowed, because numeric color components are not meaningful in a pattern color space. The **imagemask** operator is allowed, because the image samples do not represent colors, but rather designate places where the current color is to be painted.*

Example 4.18 defines a colored pattern and then uses it to paint a rectangle and a character.

Example 4.18

```
<<                              % Begin prototype pattern dictionary
   /PaintType 1                 % Colored pattern
   /PatternType 1 /TilingType 1
   /BBox [0 0 60 60]
   /XStep 60 /YStep 60
   /star {                      % Private procedure used by PaintProc
      gsave
      0 12 moveto 4 { 144 rotate 0 12 lineto } repeat closepath fill
      grestore
   }
   /PaintProc {
      begin                     % Push pattern on dictionary stack
      0.3 setgray               % Set color for dark gray stars
      15 15 translate star 30 30 translate star
      0.7 setgray               % Set color for light gray stars
      −30 0 translate star 30 −30 translate star
      end
   }
>>                              % End prototype pattern dictionary
matrix                          % Identity matrix
makepattern                     % Instantiate the pattern
/Star4 exch def

120 120 184 120 4 copy          % 2 copies of rectangle operands
/Pattern setcolorspace
Star4 setcolor rectfill         % Fill rectangle with stars
0 setgray rectstroke            % Stroke black outline
```

```
/Times-Roman 270 selectfont
160 100 translate
0.9 setgray 0 0 moveto (A) show          % Paint character with gray
Star4 setpattern 0 0 moveto (A) show     % Paint character with stars
```

Figure 4.7 *Output from Example 4.18*

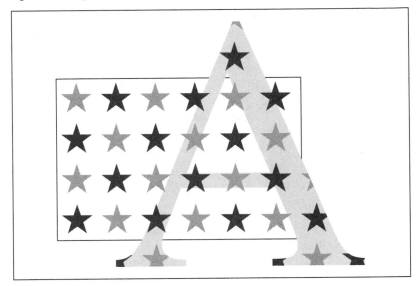

The pattern consists of four stars in two different colors. The **PaintProc** specifies the colors of the stars. There are several features of Example 4.18 that are noteworthy:

- After constructing the prototype pattern dictionary, the program immediately invokes **makepattern** on it. The value that it assigns to Star4 is the *instantiated* pattern returned by **makepattern**. There is no need to save the prototype pattern unless the program desires to instantiate it in multiple ways, perhaps with different sizes or orientations.

- The program illustrates both methods of selecting a pattern for painting. The first time, it invokes the **setcolorspace** and **setcolor** operators separately. The second time, it invokes the convenience operator **setpattern**. Note that the occurrences of **setgray** also change the color space to **DeviceGray**.

- The rectangle and the letter A are painted with the same pattern (the pattern dictionary returned by a single execution of **makepattern**). The patterns align even though the CTM is altered between the two uses of the pattern.

- The pattern cell does not completely cover the tile. There are areas of the tile (the spaces between the stars) that are not painted. When the pattern is used as a color, the stars are painted, but the background shows through the areas between the stars. The appearance of the letter A demonstrates this: It is painted once with gray and again with the star pattern. The gray shows between the stars.

Uncolored Patterns

An *uncolored pattern* is one that does not have any inherent color. Instead, the color must be specified separately whenever the pattern is used. This provides a way to tile different regions of the page with pattern cells having the same shape but different colors. The pattern's **PaintProc** does not explicitly specify any colors; it cannot use the **image** or **colorimage** operators, but it can use the **imagemask** operator.

When used with uncolored patterns, the **Pattern** color space requires a parameter: an array or name that identifies the *underlying color space* in which the actual color of the pattern is to be specified. A color value to be given to **setcolor** in this **Pattern** color space has at least two components: a color value in the underlying color space, given as one or more numbers, and a pattern dictionary whose **PaintType** is 2.

Example 4.19 establishes an uncolored pattern as the current color, using **DeviceRGB** as the underlying color space. The values *r*, *g*, and *b* specify a color in the underlying color space; *pattern* is a type 2 pattern dictionary.

Example 4.19

```
[/Pattern [/DeviceRGB]] setcolorspace
r g b pattern setcolor
```

Subsequent executions of painting operators, such as **fill**, **stroke**, **show**, and **imagemask**, use the pattern to tile the areas to be painted. They paint the pattern cells with the color value described by *r*, *g*, and *b*.

Note   *The underlying color space of a **Pattern** color space cannot itself be a **Pattern** color space.*

Example 4.20 defines an uncolored pattern and then uses it to paint a rectangle and a circle with different colors applied through the pattern.

Example 4.20

```
<<                                  % Begin prototype pattern dictionary
  /PaintType 2                      % Uncolored pattern
  /PatternType 1 /TilingType 1
  /BBox [–12 –12 12 12]
  /XStep 30 /YStep 30
  /PaintProc {
    pop                             % Pop pattern dictionary
    0 12 moveto 4 { 144 rotate 0 12 lineto } repeat closepath
    fill
  }
>>                                  % End prototype pattern dictionary
matrix                              % Identity matrix
makepattern                         % Instantiate the pattern
/Star exch def


140 110 170 100 4 copy              % 2 copies of rectangle operands
0.9 setgray rectfill                % Fill rectangle with gray
[/Pattern /DeviceGray] setcolorspace
1 Star setcolor rectfill            % Fill rectangle with white stars
225 185 60 0 360 arc                % Build circular path
0 Star setpattern gsave fill grestore   % Fill circle with black stars
0 setgray stroke                    % Stroke black outline
```

Figure 4.8 *Output from Example 4.20*

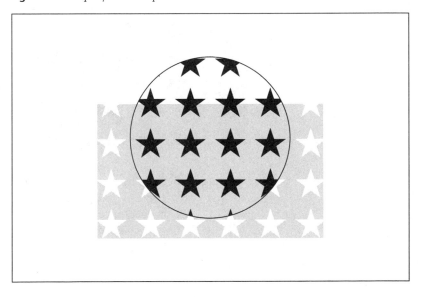

The pattern consists of a single star, which the **PaintProc** paints without first specifying a color. Most of the remarks after Example 4.18 on page 206 also apply to Example 4.20. Additionally:

- The program paints the rectangle twice, first with gray, then with the pattern. To paint with the pattern, it supplies two operands to **setcolor**: the number 1, designating white in the **DeviceGray** color space, and the pattern dictionary.

- The program paints the circle with the same pattern, but with the color set to 0 (black). Note the use of **setpattern** in this instance. It inherits parameters from the existing color space (see the **setpattern** operator description for details).

4.10 Images

The PostScript language's painting operators include general facilities for dealing with sampled images. A *sampled image* (or just "image" for short) is a rectangular array of sample values, each representing some color. This image may approximate the appearance of some natural scene obtained through a television camera or a color input scanner, or it may be generated synthetically.

Figure 4.9 *Typical sampled image*

An image is defined by a sequence of samples obtained by scanning the image rectangle in row or column order. Each sample in the array consists of 1, 3, or 4 components (for example, representing gray-scale, RGB, or CMYK color). Each component consists of a 1-, 2-, 4-, 8-, or 12-bit integer, permitting the representation of 2, 4, 16, 256, or 4096 different values for each component.

Level 1 and Level 2 implementations of the PostScript language differ in the facilities they offer for images:

- Most Level 1 implementations support only gray-scale images—that is, ones whose image samples consist of a single gray component. These can be painted by means of the 5-operand form of the **image** operator. Image samples must consist of 1, 2, 4, or 8 bits per component (12-bit components are not supported). The image source data must be provided by a procedure. Direct use of files or strings as data sources is not supported.

- A few Level 1 implementations have been extended to support color images containing 3 or 4 components per sample interpreted as RGB or CMYK. These can be painted by means of the **colorimage** operator. The Level 1 products containing this feature are primarily color printers. They also support the **setcmykcolor** operator and 4-color rendering features.

- Level 2 implementations support all the features of Level 1. Additionally, they support *image dictionaries*, which are a more general means for specifying parameters to the **image** operator. The **image** operator has a 1-operand form in which the operand is an image dictionary. Other features available only in Level 2 include interpretation of sample values in any color space (CIE-based, for instance), 12-bit component values, direct use of files or strings as data sources, and additional decoding and rendering options.

- All implementations support the **imagemask** operator, which paints the current color through a mask specified as a bitmap (see section 4.10.6, "Masks"). However, specification of its operands using an image dictionary is supported only in Level 2.

There are often several ways to paint a given image, depending on what level of language features are to be used. Fortunately, most of the semantics of images do not depend on how painting is invoked or how operands are represented. In the sections that follow, frequent reference is made to specific features, such as **colorimage** or image dictionaries. Refer to the above summary to determine which features are supported in a particular implementation.

4.10.1 Image Parameters

The properties of an image—resolution, orientation, scanning order, and so on—are entirely independent of the properties of the raster output device on which the image is to be rendered. The PostScript interpreter usually renders an image by a sampling and halftoning technique that attempts to approximate the color values of the source as accurately as possible. The accuracy depends on the resolution and other properties of the raster output device.

To paint an image, a PostScript language program must specify four interrelated items:

- The format of the source image: number of columns (width), number of rows (height), number of components, and number of bits per component.

- A data source capable of providing the image sample data, which consist of *height × width × components × bits/component* bits of information.

- The correspondence between coordinates in user space and coordinates in the source image space, defining the region of user space that will receive the image.

- The mapping from component values in the source image to component values in the current color space.

The PostScript language program entirely controls these four aspects of image specification.

4.10.2   Sample Data Representation

The source format for an image can be described by four parameters: *width, height, components,* and *bits/component*. A PostScript language program specifies *width, height,* and *bits/component* explicitly. The interpreter infers the *components* parameter, as follows:

- With the 5-operand form of the **image** operator and with **imagemask**, *components* is always 1.

- With the 1-operand (image dictionary) form of the **image** operator, *components* is the number of components in the current color space. See section 4.8, "Color Spaces."

- With the **colorimage** operator, *components* is specified explicitly as the *ncomp* operand.

Image data are represented as a stream of characters—specifically, 8-bit integers in the range 0 to 255, obtained from some data source (returned from a procedure or read from a file or string). These characters represent a continuous bit stream, with the high-order bit of each character first. This bit stream is in turn divided into units of *bits/component* bits each, ignoring character boundaries. 12-bit sample values straddle character boundaries; other sizes never do. Each unit encodes a color component value, given high-order bit first.

Each row of the source image begins on a character boundary. If the number of data bits per row is not a multiple of 8, the end of the row must be padded with extra bits to fill up the last character. The PostScript interpreter ignores these bits.

Each source sample component is an integer in the range 0 to $2^n - 1$, where n is the number of bits per component. The PostScript interpreter maps this to a color component value (equivalent to what could be used with operators such as **setgray** or **setcolor**) by one of two methods:

- With the 5-operand form of **image**, and with all forms of **colorimage**, the integer 0 maps to the number 0.0, the integer $2^n - 1$ maps to the number 1.0, and intermediate values map linearly to numbers between 0.0 to 1.0.

- With the 1-operand (dictionary) form of **image**, the mapping is specified explicitly by the **Decode** entry in the image dictionary.

- With **imagemask**, image samples do not represent color values, so mapping is not relevant. See section 4.10.6, "Masks."

The imaging operators (**image**, **colorimage**, and **imagemask**) can obtain source data from any of three types of objects:

- *Procedure*. Whenever the interpreter requires additional data, it calls the procedure, which is expected to return a string containing some more data. The amount of data returned by each call is arbitrary. However, returning one or more complete scan lines at a time simplifies programming, especially when reading image data that appear in-line in a PostScript language program. This is the only type of data source permitted by Level 1 implementations.

- *File*. The interpreter simply reads data from the file as necessary. Note that the file can be a *filtered file* that performs some form of decoding or decompression (see section 3.8.4, "Filters"). This type of data source is a Level 2 feature.

- *String*. The interpreter simply reads data from the string, reusing it as many times as is necessary to provide the amount of data that the imaging operation expects. This type of data source is a Level 2 feature, though equivalent behavior can be obtained with Level 1 by providing a procedure that simply returns the same string each time it is called.

Data sources for images are much the same as data sources for filters. For further elaboration on the semantics of data sources, see section 3.13.1, "Data Sources and Targets." When reading from a data source causes a PostScript language procedure to be invoked, that procedure must not do anything to disturb the ongoing imaging operation—for example, alter the graphics state or image dictionary, or initiate a new imaging operation.

A data source can end prematurely. This occurs if a procedure returns a string of length zero or a file encounters end-of-file. If a data source ends before all source samples have been read, the remainder of the image that would have been painted by the missing samples is left unpainted. If the last source row is incomplete—that is, the data source ends in mid-row—the partial source row may be discarded and not painted.

When there are multiple components per sample (*components* is greater than 1), the source data can be organized in one of two ways:

- *Single data source*. All components are obtained from the same source, interleaved on a per-sample basis. For example, in a 3-component RGB image, the red, green, and blue components for one sample are followed by the red, green, and blue components for the next sample.

- *Multiple data sources*. Each component is obtained from a separate source—for example, all red components from one source, all green components from a second, all blue components from a third. The three sources must be of the same type and must actually be independent—for example, three different files, or three procedures using different strings to buffer the data, because the interpreter reads from them in parallel. If the data sources are procedures, all of them must return strings of the same length on any given call.

A PostScript language program specifies which organization to use by means of the *multi* operand of **colorimage** or the **MultipleDataSources** entry in the image dictionary. Figure 4.10 illustrates some typical organizations for data sources. It also shows the image sample decode mapping operation.

Figure 4.10 *Image data organization and processing*

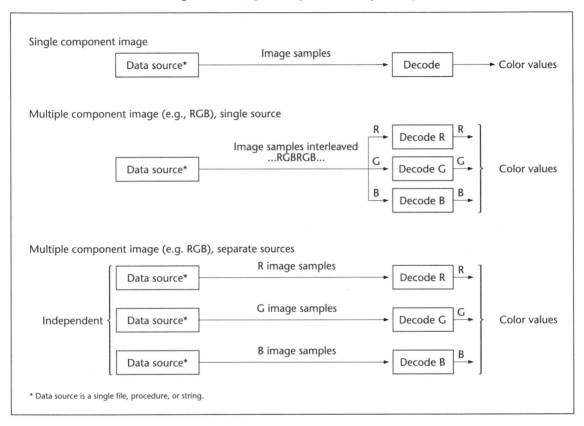

4.10.3   Source Coordinate System

The image operators impose a coordinate system on the source image. They consider the source image to be a rectangle that is *height* units high and *width* units wide. Each sample occupies one square unit. The origin (0, 0) is in the lower-left corner. *x* values range from 0 to *width* inclusive, and *y* values range from 0 to *height* inclusive.

The image operators assume that they receive sample data from their data source in *x*-axis major indexing order. The coordinate of the lower-left corner of the first sample is (0, 0), of the second (1, 0), and so on through the last sample of the first row, whose lower-left corner is at (*width* – 1, 0) and whose lower-right corner is at (*width*, 0). The next samples after that are at coordinates (0, 1), (1, 1), and so on, until the final sample of the image, whose lower-left corner is at (*width* – 1, *height* – 1) and whose upper-right corner is at (*width*, *height*).

Figure 4.11 illustrates the organization of the source coordinate system. The numbers inside the squares indicate the order of the samples, counting from 0.

Figure 4.11 *Source image coordinate system*

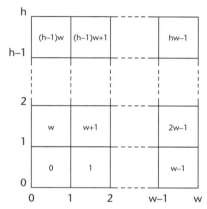

The source coordinate system and scanning order imposed by the image operators do not preclude using different conventions in the actual source image. Coordinate transformation can map other conventions into the PostScript language convention.

The correspondence between this source image coordinate system (or *image space*) and user space is specified by a special matrix. This matrix is provided in one of two ways:

- In the 5-operand forms of **image** and **imagemask** and in all forms of **colorimage**, there is a separate *matrix* operand.

- In image dictionaries, there is a required **ImageMatrix** entry.

This matrix defines a mapping from user space to image space. That is, a user space coordinate transformed by the matrix yields an image space coordinate. There are four points in user space that map to the coordinates of the four corners of the image in image space. This is a general linear transformation that can include translation, rotation, reflection, and shearing (see section 4.3, "Coordinate Systems and Transformations").

Figure 4.12 *Mapping the source image*

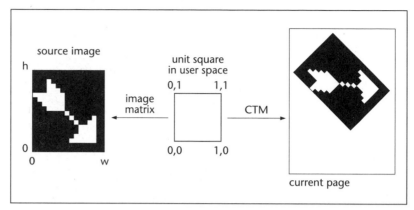

Although it's possible to map directly from current user space to image space by appropriate definition of the image matrix, it's easier to think about the transformation by dividing it into two steps:

1. The image matrix maps the *unit square* of user space, bounded by (0, 0) and (1, 1) in user space, to the boundary of the source image in image space.

2. The CTM maps the unit square of user space to the rectangle or parallelogram on the page that is to receive the image.

This is just a convention, but it is a useful one that is recommended (see Figure 4.12). With this convention, the image matrix is used solely to describe the image itself, independent of how it is to be positioned, oriented, and scaled on a particular page. It defines an idealized image space consisting of a unit square that corresponds to the PostScript language's conventions for coordinate system and scanning order. A program can then map this idealized image space into current user space by altering the CTM in straightforward ways.

An image that happens to use the PostScript language conventions (scanning left-to-right, bottom-to-top) can be described by the image matrix

[*width* 0 0 *height* 0 0]

An image that is scanned left-to-right, top-to-bottom (a commonly used order) is described by the image matrix

[*width* 0 0 −*height* 0 *height*]

Images scanned in other common orders can be described in similar ways.

An image that has been mapped into the unit square this way can then be placed on the output page in the desired position, orientation, and size by invoking the PostScript operators that transform user space: **translate**, **rotate**, and **scale**.

For example, to map such an image into a rectangle whose lower-left corner is at (100, 200), is rotated 45 degrees counterclockwise, and is 150 units wide and 80 high, a program can execute

100 200 translate 45 rotate 150 80 scale

before invoking the **image**, **colorimage**, or **imagemask** operator. This works for *any* image that has been mapped into the unit square by an appropriate image matrix. Of course, if the aspect ratio (ratio of width to height) of the source image in this example were different from the ratio 150:80, the result would be distorted.

Note   *Although images themselves are always rectangular, you can clip an image to any desired shape by establishing a clipping path using the **clip** operator before invoking **image**, **colorimage**, or **imagemask**.*

4.10.4   Images and Color Spaces

The color samples in an image are interpreted according to some color space (see section 4.8, "Color Spaces"). The color space to be used depends on how imaging is invoked:

- The 5-operand form of the **image** operator always interprets color samples according to the **DeviceGray** color space, regardless of the current color space. It does not alter the current color space parameter in the graphics state.

- The **colorimage** operator always interprets color samples according to the **DeviceGray**, **DeviceRGB**, or **DeviceCMYK** color space, depending on whether its *ncomp* operand is 1, 3, or 4. It neither reads nor alters the current color space parameter in the graphics state.

- The 1-operand (dictionary) form of the **image** operator interprets color samples according to the current color space. The number of components per sample and the interpretation of the component values depend on the color space. This form of **image** can be used with any color space except **Pattern**.

- The **imagemask** operator always interprets its source data as a *mask* for applying the current color in the current color space (see section 4.10.6, "Masks"). This works for *any* color space.

4.10.5 Image Dictionaries

In Level 2, the **image** and **imagemask** operators, but not **colorimage**, have a 1-operand form in which all imaging parameters are bundled together as an *image dictionary* operand. This arrangement provides more flexibility than the 5-operand form of **image** or any form of **colorimage**. The following features can be accessed only by means of image dictionaries:

- Use of arbitrary color spaces, such as **CIEBasedABC** or **Separation**.

- User-defined decoding of image sample values.

- Interpolation between samples.

An image dictionary contains various entries, some of which are required and some optional. Table 4.8 describes the semantics of each of the image dictionary entries. There are many relationships among these entries. The current color space may limit the choices for various entries in the image dictionary. Attempting to use an image dictionary in which required entries are missing or of the wrong type will cause a **typecheck** error. Attempting to use an image dictionary whose entries are inconsistent with each other or with the current color space will result in a **rangecheck** error.

Table 4.8 *Entries in an image dictionary*

Key	Type	Semantics
ImageType	integer	(*Required*) Must be 1.
Width	integer	(*Required*) Width of the source image in samples.
Height	integer	(*Required*) Height of the source image in samples.
ImageMatrix	array	(*Required*) An array of six numbers that define a transformation from current user space to image source space.

MultipleDataSources boolean   (*Optional*) The value *true* indicates that the image data are provided through multiple data sources, one per color component. The value *false* indicates that the image data for all color components are packed into one data stream, interleaved on a per-sample basis. **MultipleDataSources** must be *false* or absent in an image dictionary used with **imagemask**. Default value: *false*.

DataSource (various)   (*Required*) If **MultipleDataSources** is *false* or is not present, the value of **DataSource** must be a single data source (file, procedure, or string). If **MultipleDataSources** is *true*, **DataSource** must be an array of data sources; the length of the array must be the same as the number of components in the current color space.

BitsPerComponent integer   (*Required*) Specifies the number of bits used to represent each color component. The number must be 1, 2, 4, 8, or 12. Only a single number may be specified. The number of bits is the same for all color components. **BitsPerComponent** must be 1 in an image dictionary used with **imagemask**.

Decode array   (*Required*) An array of numbers. The length of the array must be twice the number of color components in the current color space. This describes how to map image sample values into the range of values appropriate for the current color space (see below).

Interpolate boolean   (*Optional*) If present with the value *true*, requests that image interpolation be performed (see below). Default value: *false*.

The following sections describe the semantics of some of these entries in more detail. All of this information applies to image dictionaries used with the **image** operator. Most of it also applies to image dictionaries used with the **imagemask** operator. See section 4.10.6, "Masks."

Decode

The bit stream of image data is initially decomposed into integers between 0 and $2^n - 1$, where n is the value of **BitsPerComponent**. There is one of these integers for each component of a given color sample. The number of components depends on the current color space.

The **Decode** array specifies a linear mapping of an integer component value to a number that would be appropriate as an operand to **setcolor** in the current color space. For each color component, **Decode** specifies a minimum and maximum output value for the mapping. The linear mapping is defined as:

$$o = D_{min} + i \times \frac{D_{max} - D_{min}}{2^n - 1}$$

where

> n is the value of **BitsPerComponent**;
> i is the input value, in the range 0 to $2^n - 1$;
> D_{min} and D_{max} are the parameters in the **Decode** array;
> o is the output value, to be interpreted as a color component.

In other words, an input value of zero will be mapped to D_{min}, an input value of $2^n - 1$ will be mapped to D_{max}, and intermediate input values will be linearly mapped to values between D_{min} and D_{max}.

The numbers in the **Decode** array are interpreted in pairs, with successive pairs applying to successive components of the current color space in their standard order. Table 4.9 lists recommended **Decode** arrays for use with the various color spaces.

Table 4.9 *Typical **Decode** arrays*

Color space	*Decode array*
DeviceGray	[0 1]
DeviceRGB	[0 1 0 1 0 1]
DeviceCMYK	[0 1 0 1 0 1 0 1]
CIEBasedABC	[0 1 0 1 0 1]
CIEBasedA	[0 1]
Separation	[0 1]
Indexed	[0 N] where $N = 2^n - 1$
Pattern	(**image** is not permitted)

For most color spaces, the **Decode** arrays listed above map into the full range of allowed component values. For the **CIEBasedABC** and **CIEBasedA** color spaces, the suggested **Decode** array maps to component values in the range 0.0 to 1.0. This is typical for the class of calibrated gray or RGB color spaces, but the appropriate values actually depend on how the color spaces have been parameterized. For the **Indexed** color space, the suggested **Decode** array ensures component values that index a color table are passed through unchanged.

It is possible to specify a mapping that *inverts* sample color intensities by specifying a D_{min} value which is greater than the D_{max}. For example, if the current color space is **DeviceGray** and the **Decode** array is [1 0], an input value of 0 will be mapped to 1.0 (white), while an input value of $2^n - 1$ will be mapped to 0.0 (black).

The D_{min} and D_{max} parameters for a color component are not required to fall within the range of values allowed for that component. For instance, if an application uses 6-bit numbers as its native image sample format, it can send those samples to the PostScript interpreter in 8-bit format, setting the two unused high-order bits of each sample to zero. When imaging that data, it should specify a **Decode** array of [0 4.04762], which maps the input values 0 to 63 into the range 0.0 to 1.0. If an output value falls outside the range allowed for a component, the value will be automatically adjusted to the nearest allowed value.

Interpolate

When the resolution of a source image is significantly lower than the resolution of the device, each source sample covers many device pixels. This can result in a "jaggy" appearance of binary images or a "blocky" appearance of continuous-tone images.

These visual artifacts can be reduced by applying an *image interpolation* algorithm during rendering. Instead of painting all of the pixels covered by a source sample with the same color, it attempts to make a smooth transition between adjacent sample values.

Setting the **Interpolate** entry to *true* in the image dictionary for either **image** or **imagemask** enables image interpolation. The default is not to interpolate. Enabling interpolation may increase the time required to render the image.

4.10.6 Masks

The **image** and **colorimage** operators are consistent with other painting operators in that all areas of a page affected by an image are marked as though by opaque paint (see section 4.1, "Imaging Model"). Any portion of an image, whether black, white, color, or gray, completely obscures any marks that previously existed in the same place on the page.

There is a special variant of a binary image, called a *mask*, whose properties are quite different. Whereas an image is opaque, a mask is partially transparent. The **imagemask** operator applies masks.

The samples of a mask do not represent colors; they designate places on the page that should be marked with the current color in the current color space or not marked at all. The places that are not marked retain their former color values. One should think of pouring paint "through" a mask, where a 1 sample permits the paint to reach the page, but a 0 blocks it, or vice versa.

Masks are most often useful for painting characters represented as bitmaps. Ordinarily, when painting such characters, one wants the "black" bits of the character to be transferred to the page, but the "white" bits, which are really just background, to be left alone.

Note   *For reasons discussed in section 5.5, "Font Cache,"* **imagemask** *rather than* **image** *should almost always be used to paint bitmap characters.*

A program invokes **imagemask** in much the same way as **image**; most of the parameters have equivalent meanings. As with **image**, there is a 5-operand form supported by all implementations and a 1-operand image dictionary form, which is a Level 2 feature. **imagemask** differs from **image** in the following significant ways:

- The number of components per sample is always 1, regardless of the current color space, because sample values for **imagemask** do not represent color values.

- The number of bits per component is always 1. When an image dictionary is used with **imagemask**, the **BitsPerComponent** entry must be 1.

- The 5-operand form of **imagemask** includes a *polarity* operand that determines how the source samples are to be interpreted. If *polarity* is *false*, 0 designates a painted sample and 1 designates an unpainted sample. If *polarity* is *true*, 1 designates a painted sample and 0 designates an unpainted sample. The 1-operand form of **imagemask** uses the **Decode** entry in the image dictionary for the same purpose. **Decode** arrays of [0 1] and [1 0] correspond to *polarity* values of *false* and *true*, respectively.

4.10.7 Using Images

This section contains some simple examples that demonstrate typical uses of images. The examples are incomplete; they cannot show the image data itself, since it is very bulky. For further information about the imaging operators themselves, see the operator descriptions in Chapter 8.

Monochrome Image

Example 4.21 uses the **image** operator to paint a gray-scale image, using facilities available in Level 1 implementations.

Example 4.21

```
/picstr 256 string def              % String to hold image data

45 140 translate                    % Locate lower-left corner of image
132 132 scale                       % Map image to 132 unit square

256 256 8                           % Dimensions of source image
[256 0 0 –256 0 256]                % Map unit square to source
{currentfile                        % Read image data from program file
  picstr readhexstring pop}
image

4c47494b4d4c524c4d50535051554c5152 ...
...Total of 131072 hex digits of image data, representing 65536 samples...
```

This program paints an image consisting of 256×256 samples at 8 bits per sample. It positions the image with its lower-left corner at (45, 140) in current user space and scales it to a width and height of 132 user space units. The image data are represented with the first sample in the upper-left corner, so the program uses the image matrix to match its coordinate system with the normal PostScript language convention. See section 4.10.3, "Source Coordinate System."

The image data appear in-line in the PostScript language program. This is the most common way to access image data in a document. Only occasionally will a program refer to image data stored elsewhere—in a file, for instance. The image data are represented in hexadecimal, not 8-bit binary, so as to maximize portability of the document.

The program specifies a data source which is a procedure. Each time the procedure is called by **image**, it executes **readhexstring** to read one row of image sample data into a string, which it then returns to **image**. It reuses this string during every call. It is not necessary to read one row at a time, but doing so simplifies programming. If the procedure reads multiple rows at a time, or an amount of data that is not a multiple of the image's width, it must take special care not to read past the end of the image data the last time it is called by **image**. Doing so would cause some program text following the image data to be lost.

With most images, it's very important to read the image data incrementally, as shown in this example. Attempting to read the entire image into a single string or to represent it as a PostScript language string literal would run the risk of exceeding implementation limits or exhausting available VM.

Color Image with Single Source

As indicated earlier, color images with multiple components per sample can be organized in two ways: interleaved components obtained from a single source, or separate components obtained from separate sources. The first organization is the only one that is useful for images whose data are provided in-line in a PostScript language program. The second organization is limited to situations in which the separate components are stored elsewhere, such as in separate files that can be read in parallel.

Example 4.22 illustrates use of the **colorimage** operator to paint an image consisting of interleaved RGB data from a single source. This example works in Level 2 implementations, and also in those Level 1 implementations that have the CMYK color extensions.

Example 4.22

```
/picstr 768 string def          % String to hold 256 RGB samples
45 140 translate                % Locate lower-left corner of image
132 132 scale                   % Map image to 132 unit square

256 256 8                       % Dimensions of source image
[256 0 0 –256 0 256]            % Map unit square to source
{currentfile                    % Read image data from program file
  picstr readhexstring pop}
false 3                         % Single data source, 3 colors
colorimage

94a1bec8c0b371a3a5c4d281...
...393216 hex digits of image data, representing 65536 samples...
```

This **colorimage** example is superficially similar to the **image** example given earlier. The major change is that two additional operands are supplied to **colorimage**, specifying that the image has a single data source and 3 components. The image data consists of 8-bit red, green, and blue color components for each sample in turn.

Image Dictionary

Example 4.23 is a program that produces the same output as Example 4.22, but uses an image dictionary and other features available only in Level 2.

Example 4.23

```
/DeviceRGB setcolorspace          % How color values will be interpreted
45 140 translate                  % Locate lower-left corner of image
132 132 scale                     % Map image to 132 unit square
<<                                % Start image dictionary
  /ImageType 1
  /Width 256 /Height 256          % Dimensions of source image
  /BitsPerComponent 8
  /Decode [0 1 0 1 0 1]           % Decode color values in normal way
  /ImageMatrix [256 0 0 –256 0 256] % Map unit square to source
  /DataSource currentfile /ASCIIHexDecode filter
                                  % Obtain in-line data through filter
>>                                % End image dictionary
image

94a1bec8c0b371a3a5c4d281...
...393216 hex digits of image data, representing 65536 samples...
```

In this program, the image data source is a file instead of a procedure. The file is a *filtered file* that converts the hexadecimal encoded data from **currentfile** to binary form. For an explanation of this and an example of how to obtain image data that has been compressed, see section 3.8.4, "Filters."

4.11 Device Setup

This section explains the PostScript language facilities for setting up a raster output device in order to fulfill the processing requirements of a page description. Setting up a raster output device (hereafter, simply *device*) includes:

• Selecting the proper input media.

- Establishing a default transformation matrix from user space to device space, along with other device dependent rendering parameters for producing output on the media.

- Selecting processing options, such as multiple copies, or special features of the output device, such as duplex printing (2-sided).

Once a device has been set up, a PostScript language program can describe a sequence of pages. For each page in turn, the program paints the current page in raster memory with everything that is to appear on it—text, graphics, and images. It then executes the **showpage** operator to cause the page to be produced. **showpage** transmits the contents of raster memory to the physical output device, then erases the current page and partially resets the graphics state in preparation for the next page.

This model is appropriate to PostScript language programs that are *page descriptions*. A page description is intended to produce a sequence of pages on a *page device*, usually causing the page images to appear on physical media, such as sheets of paper. On the other hand, this model is *not* appropriate for applications that use the PostScript language to control the appearance of a display interactively (see Chapter 7).

Level 1 and Level 2 implementations of the PostScript language differ in the facilities they offer for setting up a device to meet the requirements of a page description.

- Level 1 implementations provide a collection of device control operators, defined in a special dictionary named **statusdict**. The contents of **statusdict** are product dependent, although an attempt has been made to maintain a consistent specification for common features. **statusdict** features are not described in this manual, but in the documentation for each product. Application programs desiring to use **statusdict** features can extract information from *PostScript printer description* (PPD) files. Specifications for those files are available from Adobe Systems Developers' Association.

- Level 2 implementations support a page device setup operator named **setpagedevice**. This operator provides a standard framework for specifying the requirements of a page description and for controlling both standard and optional features of a device. Although the page device facilities are oriented toward devices that produce hard copy, such as printers or typesetters, the **setpagedevice** operator exists in all Level 2 implementations.

The remainder of this section describes the page device setup facilities supported by Level 2.

4.11.1 Using Page Devices

In the following discussion, the term *media* indicates the physical material on which the output appears (paper, transparency material, film, a virtual page on a display, or whatever). Most of the processing options are oriented toward printers that produce paper output, so "paper" is a good universal material to envision when you read "media."

Many products have special hardware features, such as multiple paper trays with different sizes of paper, duplex printing, collation, finishing options, and so on. The PostScript interpreter supports the special features of each product. It knows what features are currently available and ready for use. The **setpagedevice** operator is the way a page description specifies its processing requirements and selects optional features. Also, **setpagedevice** is the way a user or system administrator specifies default device setup or configuration parameters to be used when a page description doesn't specify them.

Not all features are available in all products. **setpagedevice** provides a uniform framework for specifying processing requirements and options. It uses a standard syntax to request features supported by all devices, such as selecting a page size, and features supported only by some devices, such as duplex printing. **setpagedevice** also provides a standard mechanism for determining what to do when a page description makes requests the device can't fulfill. A page description must contain the minimum required device setup information, because including such information limits the set of devices on which the document can be printed.

It is useful, at least in concept, to envision two separate tasks when printing from an application:

1. Generate the device-independent page description.

2. Request that the page description be printed on a particular device. At this point, the user should have an opportunity to add processing options, including device-dependent ones, to the page description.

Even if a single application provides both of these functions, it is best to maintain this distinction. Most applications have an option to store the generated page description in a file for later use. That file should not contain unnecessary device-dependent processing options. The distinction between document generation and document printing is essential when using PostScript language programs for document storage and interchange.

While there is no clear division between device-independent processing requests and device-dependent ones, you should keep in mind the important goal of producing device-independent page descriptions. One important criterion to apply is whether a particular feature is inherently a part of the document specification or only a processing option. For example, the page size—in particular, the aspect ratio between width and height—is an important part of the document specification, because the application generating the document must make formatting decisions based on the page size. On the other hand, the number of copies to be printed or the color of the paper to be used are *not* an inherent part of the document description, but rather are processing options.

4.11.2 Page Device Dictionary

The current internal state of a page device is modelled as a *dictionary* containing some number of key-value pairs. The keys in the dictionary represent particular device features or processing options; the values represent the current settings of those features or options. This dictionary is not directly accessible to a PostScript language program, but it can be altered and read by the **setpagedevice** and **currentpagedevice** operators.

The operand of **setpagedevice** is a dictionary supplying information in the form of key-value pairs that request particular device features or processing options. The dictionary is simply a container that can hold multiple key-value pairs to be supplied in a single call to **setpagedevice**. The interpreter uses the information in the dictionary to alter its internal device state, but it does not retain the dictionary. The **currentpagedevice** operator returns a dictionary describing the current state of the page device using the same key-value organization.

Executing **setpagedevice** alters the PostScript interpreter's internal device state. Its effects are *cumulative* over multiple executions. That is, **setpagedevice** merges new requests into the existing state of the device. The effect of specifying a particular key-value pair persists through subsequent calls to **setpagedevice** until overridden explicitly or until the device is restored to some previous state by **restore**, **grestore**, **grestoreall**, or **setgstate**. This cumulative behavior also applies recursively (to one level) to the contents of subsidiary dictionaries that are the values of the keys **Policies**, **InputAttributes**, and **OutputAttributes**. It does not apply to the contents of other entries whose values happen to be dictionaries.

Since the effects of **setpagedevice** are cumulative, a PostScript language program can make independent calls to **setpagedevice**, each requesting particular features or processing options, but leaving the settings for other features undisturbed. This allows different options to be specified at different times; in particular:

1. When an application generates a page description, it can include a call to **setpagedevice** specifying parameters, such as **PageSize** and **ImagingBBox**, that reflect assumptions the application has made in formatting the document.

2. When a user requests printing, an additional call to **setpagedevice** can be *prepended* to the page description to specify processing options, such as **NumCopies**, **Duplex**, or **MediaColor**.

3. The person who is operating the printer can invoke **setpagedevice**, as part of an unencapsulated job, to configure the available input media (**InputAttributes**), to establish policies for dealing with unsatisfied requests (**Policies**), and to establish default values for other device options.

For certain options, there is a "null" value that indicates absence of any request or preference for the value of that option. In all cases, the *null* object (value of **null** in **systemdict**) is used for this purpose. For example, a **MediaColor** value of *null* indicates that no specific paper color has been requested. Null values are permitted only for certain features; see the tables in section 4.11.3, "Semantics of Specific Entries."

Omitting a particular key in a dictionary passed to **setpagedevice** has an effect different from providing that key with a *null* value. The absence of the key allows the value to be inherited from the previous state of the device. The presence of the key with a *null* value causes the value in the device to be set to *null*, cancelling any previous request for that feature.

The dictionary returned by **currentpagedevice** always contains an entry for every feature supported by that specific device. For some features, the value might be *null*, indicating that the feature is supported, but no request has been made for that feature yet.

If the dictionary passed to **setpagedevice** includes any requests that the device cannot satisfy, the PostScript interpreter invokes a uniform policy for determining what to do. This policy is based on information in the **Policies** sub-dictionary of the page device dictionary. **Policies** can be altered by **setpagedevice**. For example, if a program requests duplex printing on a device that doesn't support it, the policy existing at that time may be either to ignore the request (print simplex) or to generate a **configurationerror** (reject the job).

If a device does not support a particular feature, **setpagedevice** does not recognize any request to specify a value for that feature. For example, if a device does not have a duplexing mechanism, **setpagedevice** does not recognize the key **Duplex**, even if the request is to set the value of **Duplex** to *false*, which indicates no duplexing. Instead, it consults **Policies** to determine what to do. This behavior might seem surprising, but it is necessitated by the fact that the set of device features is open-ended.

A *page device* is only one of several kinds of raster output devices. Other devices include the *cache device* to put characters into the font cache and the *null device* to discard output entirely. These are set, usually temporarily, by the **setcachedevice** and **nulldevice** operators. A Display PostScript system provides one or more *window devices* that allow painting onto various portions of a display. Ordinarily, a window device is not a page device; however, Display PostScript products often provide a *preview* capability that emulates a page device using a display window. If **setpagedevice** is executed when the current device is not a page device, the effect produced is device dependent.

Note   *The* ***setpagedevice*** *operator is a page-oriented operator used to control the output processing of one or more pages of a page description. Any call to* ***setpagedevice*** *implicitly performs* ***erasepage*** *and* ***initgraphics***; *thus, it must precede the descriptions of the pages to be affected.*

4.11.3   Semantics of Specific Entries

The following tables describe the entries in a page device dictionary that have been defined at the time of publication of this manual. In the future, other entries will be defined to satisfy requirements for new processing options or product features. Once defined in any product, a given key will always be used for the same feature in any subsequent products that support it.

Note   *Not all keys listed in the tables are recognized by all products. Consult each product's documentation to see exactly which keys it recognizes.*

The entries are divided into four categories. This classification is not rigid; entries in different categories can sometimes interact with each other. However, organizing the entries this way facilitates understanding their purpose.

- *Input media selection* entries (Table 4.10) provide information that can be used to select the appropriate type of paper or other media. The **PageSize** entry should be specified by the application generating the page description. Other entries should generally be specified only when printing is requested. There is a fairly elaborate interaction among these entries. See section 4.11.4, "Media Selection."

- *Processing and output* entries (Table 4.11) specify how pages are to be rendered onto the media and how the media are to be processed thereafter. The **ImagingBBox** entry should be specified by the application generating the page description. Other entries should generally be specified only when printing is requested.

- *Roll media* entries (Table 4.12) provide additional information that is usually relevant only to devices that feed media from a continuous roll, such as film in a typesetter.

- *Policy and special action* entries (Table 4.13) specify how requests for unsupported features are to be handled and define special actions to be performed when the device is installed and before and after each page is printed.

The PostScript language does not prescribe a default value for any entry. The usual default value for optional features is either *false* or *null*, but this is not invariably the case in all products. A PostScript language program can change the defaults by executing **setpagedevice** as part of an unencapsulated job.

Table 4.10 *Input media selection entries*

Key	Type	Semantics
PageSize	array	Defines the overall page size that was assumed during generation of the page description. **PageSize** is an array of two numbers, [*width height*], indicating the width and height of the assumed page, expressed in units of the default user coordinate system (1/72 inch). These are the overall dimensions of the page, including borders, if any. In other words, the lower-left corner and upper-right corner of the assumed physical page are at user space coordinates (0, 0) and (*width*, *height*), respectively.

setpagedevice uses **PageSize** with **MediaColor**, **MediaWeight**, **MediaType**, **InputAttributes**, **ManualFeed**, and **Policies** to select the appropriate medium. Section 4.11.4, "Media Selection," describes the matching rules that are used.

setpagedevice attempts to match the size requirements of the pages with the media sizes currently available. Each media size is considered to be available in either of two orientations. Whether the media size is expressed as [*width height*] or [*height width*] is immaterial insofar as matching is concerned. Likewise, the orientation of media in the printing mechanism is unspecified and varies from one device to another. The PostScript interpreter takes care of setting up the transformation from user space to device space so the long and short dimensions specified by **PageSize** are oriented with the long and short dimensions of the physical media.

If a **PageSize** of [*a b*] specifies a "portrait" orientation (that is, $a < b$), then a **PageSize** of [*b a*] specifies a "landscape" orientation of the same size page. **setpagedevice** follows a rule that allows the portrait and landscape orientations of a given size page to be related to each other. The default user space in the landscape orientation will be rotated 90 degrees counterclockwise with respect to the default user space in the portrait orientation. This relationship holds only between the two orientations of the same size media. No such relationship is guaranteed between different media.

The tolerance for matching **PageSize** with an available media size is 5 default user space units in either dimension. A match falling within this tolerance is considered to be exact. Failure to match *any* available media within this tolerance triggers the **PageSize** recovery policy specified in **Policies**.

MediaColor	string or null	Specifies the color of the media. If **MediaColor** is not *null*, **setpagedevice** compares it with the **MediaColor** values, if any, in the **InputAttributes** entries for all media that it considers. See section 4.11.4, "Media Selection."
MediaWeight	number or null	Specifies the weight of the media. If **MediaWeight** is not *null*, **setpagedevice** compares it with the **MediaWeight** values, if any, in the **InputAttributes** entries for all media that it considers. See section 4.11.4, "Media Selection." Weight is expressed in grams per square meter. "Basis weight" or "ream weight" in pounds can be converted to grams per square meter by multiplying by 3.76; 10-pound paper is approximately 37.6 grams per square meter.
MediaType	string or null	Specifies the type of the media. If **MediaType** is not *null*, **setpagedevice** compares it with the **MediaType** values, if any, in the **InputAttributes** entries for all media that it considers. See section 4.11.4, "Media Selection." The value of **MediaType** is an arbitrary string that can identify such things as preprinted forms or other media attributes not covered by size, color, or weight.
InputAttributes	dictionary	Contains an entry for each source of input media currently available for use by this device—for example, each input paper tray in a printer. The sources are arbitrarily numbered by integers. Those integers are the keys for entries in the **InputAttributes** dictionary.

The value of each entry is a dictionary describing the media currently available from that physical source. Keys used in these dictionaries include **PageSize**, **MediaColor**, **MediaWeight**, and **MediaType**, which have the same meanings as the corresponding keys described above. Two other entries, **Priority** and **MatchAll**, control details of the matching algorithm. See section 4.11.4, "Media Selection," for a complete description of how this matching is done.

Changes to the contents of the **InputAttributes** dictionary are cumulative. That is, the **InputAttributes** entries in a **setpagedevice** request are merged with the existing **InputAttributes** entries for the current device. However, the sub-dictionaries that are the values of **InputAttributes** entries are *not* merged.

ManualFeed	boolean	If *true*, input media are drawn from the manual feed position. If *false*, automatic feeding takes place. Setting **ManualFeed** to *true* is an assertion that the person operating the device *will* manually feed media that conform to the specified attributes—**PageSize**, **MediaColor**, **MediaWeight**, and **MediaType**. Thus, those attributes are *not* used to select from available media sources as is done normally. Their values may be presented to the user as an aid in selecting the correct media. In products that offer more than one manual feeding mechanism, the attributes may select among them.

Table 4.11 *Processing and output entries*

Key	Type	Semantics
ImagingBBox	array or null	Optional page bounding box. If not *null*, the value is an array of four numbers in the default user coordinate system stating lower-left x, lower-left y, upper-right x, and upper-right y of the page image bounding box. This defines a rectangle, which should lie within the boundaries of the page specified by **PageSize**. When a PostScript language program specifies an **ImagingBBox**, it asserts that it will not paint any marks outside this rectangle. Any marks that do fall outside the rectangle may or may not be painted.
		Although the information provided by **ImagingBBox** is optional, specifying it can improve performance by freeing raster memory for other purposes. If an application knows that unpainted borders appear on all pages, it should specify an appropriate value for **ImagingBBox**. The effect of specifying **ImagingBBox** is not necessarily the same as executing **clip**. **ImagingBBox** should not be used for purposefully clipping page content.
		An **ImagingBBox** value of *null* requests the largest bounding box that is possible for the given **PageSize**. This may not enclose the entire page; many devices are incapable of placing marks close to the edges of the media. If a program specifies **PageSize**, but chooses not to provide **ImagingBBox** information, it should explicitly set **ImagingBBox** to *null* to prevent an inappropriate value from being inherited from the previous device state.
OutputType	string or null	**OutputType** is analogous to the input **MediaType**, but for output. If not *null*, the value is an arbitrary string that requests special output treatment, such as placing the finished media into a selected output tray. This is used in conjunction with **OutputAttributes** to make such a selection.

OutputAttributes	dictionary	Contains an entry for each media destination currently available for use by this device—for example, each output paper tray in a printer. The destinations are arbitrarily numbered by integers. Those integers are the keys for entries in the **OutputAttributes** dictionary.

OutputAttributes has the same structure and analogous function as the **InputAttributes** dictionary. The matching is somewhat simpler because the only key considered in the match is **OutputType**. See section 4.11.4, "Media Selection."

NumCopies	integer or null	If **NumCopies** is not *null*, it specifies the number of copies to produce. This value applies to each page individually or to the entire document, depending on the setting of **Collate**. A *null* value indicates that **showpage** and **copypage** should consult the value of **#copies** in the current dictionary stack each time they are executed (this is compatible with the convention used by Level 1 implementations). See the **showpage** operator description.
Collate	boolean	Determines how the output is to be organized when multiple copies are requested (by **NumCopies** or **#copies**) for a multiple-page document. Output consists of "sets" of pages that are delivered together. If **Collate** is *true*, a set consists of one copy of all pages of the document. If **Collate** is *false*, a set consists of all copies of one page of the document. This concept of a "set" is also used by the **Jog**, **CutMedia**, and **AdvanceMedia** features.

How collation is performed is device-dependent. If the device has a physical sorter and the number of copies requested is no greater than the number of bins in the sorter, the sorter handles the collation. Otherwise, the interpreter may need to reorder the output in order to deliver all pages of a set together. In the latter case, a **Collate** value of *true* implies that the interpreter must store the results of executing the entire page description in order to deliver multiple copies correctly ordered. This use of **Collate** is supported by relatively few products and is subject to resource limits in products that do support it.

If **Collate** is *true*, a set can span multiple invocations of **setpagedevice** within a single job, so long as **NumCopies** doesn't change and the device is physically capable of delivering the output sorted that way. If that is not possible, multiple invocations of **setpagedevice** within a job will cause multiple documents to be produced.

Duplex	boolean	If *true*, the pages are printed duplex—that is, each pair of consecutive pages is printed on opposite sides of a single sheet of paper. If *false*, the pages are printed simplex—one side only.

When a duplex device is activated, it always prints the first page on a new sheet of paper. When the device is deactivated, it automatically delivers the last sheet if it has been printed on only one side. Device activation and deactivation are explained in section 4.11.6, "BeginPage and EndPage."

Tumble	boolean	When **Duplex** is *true*, **Tumble** specifies how the page images on opposite sides of a sheet are oriented with respect to each other. If **Tumble** is *false*, the default user spaces of the two pages are oriented such that the highest values of y in the two spaces lie along the same edge of the media. If **Tumble** is *true*, the default user spaces are oriented such that the highest values of y lie along opposite edges of

the media. Informally, a **Tumble** value of *false* produces output suitable for binding on the left or right; *true* produces output suitable for binding at the top or bottom.

Note that **Tumble** is defined in terms of *default user space*—the user space established by **setpagedevice**. The orientation of default user space with respect to the media is determined by the **PageSize** and **Orientation** entries, possibly altered by the **Install** procedure. Consistent results are obtained across all products that support duplexing, regardless of how the media move through the mechanism. However, if the page description alters user space by executing operators such as **rotate**, the visual orientation of the material printed on the page may differ from the orientation of default user space.

OutputFaceUp	boolean	If *true*, pages are stacked so the back side of page n is placed against the front side of page $n - 1$. If *false*, pages are stacked so the front side of page n is placed against the back side of page $n - 1$. These are the effects usually achieved by "face up" and "face down" stackers, respectively. Most products support only one stacking method; the value of **OutputFaceUp** indicates which method that is. Relatively few products allow both values of **OutputFaceUp** to be specified.
Jog	integer	Requests that output pages be "jogged"—physically shifted in the output tray—at specific times indicated by an integer code:

0   Don't jog pages at all.

1   Jog at device deactivation. The notion of "device deactivation" is explained in section 4.11.6, "BeginPage and EndPage."

2   Jog at the end of the job. The notion of a "job" is explained in section 3.7.7, "Job Execution Environment." Jogging between jobs is controlled by the value of **Jog** for the page device that is current between jobs. Thus, this feature can be turned on or off only by executing **setpagedevice** as part of an unencapsulated job.

3   Jog after each set. The notion of a "set" is explained in the description of the **Collate** entry.

Separations	boolean	If *true*, the device should produce each page by printing multiple color separations—one for each device colorant (primary or spot color). If *false*, the device should produce each page as a single composite page with all the colors, if any, combined on the same page. Color separations are explained in section 4.8, "Color Spaces."

The availability of this feature is product dependent. Most products cannot produce separations.

HWResolution	array	Array of two numbers, [$x\ y$], that indicates resolution of the physical device in pixels per inch along the x and y dimensions of device space. Most products support only a single resolution. The few products that permit the resolution to be varied usually support only certain specific resolutions, not arbitrary ones.
Margins	array	Array of two numbers, [$x\ y$], that relocates the page image on the media by x device units in the direction of the device x coordinate and by y device units in the direction of the device y coordinate. This positioning is usually accomplished by device-dependent means that are independent of the graphics state

(the CTM in particular). The range and precision of the parameter values may be restricted by the physical implementation. The purpose of **Margins** is to compensate for mechanical misadjustments in the device, not to perform purposeful positioning of output in a page description.

NegativePrint   boolean   If *true*, the device should produce a negative image of the page. This is accomplished by device-dependent means that are independent of the graphics state (the transfer functions in particular). **NegativePrint** inverts the *entire* page, perhaps including portions that lie outside the imageable area or that are generated by means independent of the PostScript interpreter. This feature is supported only by certain products, such as typesetters, that produce output intended for further photographic processing.

MirrorPrint   boolean   If *true*, the device should produce a page image that is reflected along one of the axes of device space. This is usually accomplished by device-dependent means that are independent of the graphics state (the CTM in particular). This feature is supported only by certain products, such as typesetters, that produce output intended for further photographic processing. For example, when output is produced on transparent film, **MirrorPrint** controls whether the page image should be viewed with the film emulsion face up or face down.

Table 4.12 *Roll media entries*

Key	Type	Semantics
Orientation	integer	For roll media, pages have no inherent orientation, so **PageSize** may not unambiguously select the orientation of the page image on the medium. The **Orientation** entry selects one of four orientations:

     0   Normal default orientation for the specified **PageSize**.

     1   Rotate the image on the medium 90 degrees counterclockwise with respect to the default orientation.

     2   Rotate the image 180 degrees counterclockwise.

     3   Rotate the image 270 degrees counterclockwise.

| **CutMedia** | integer | Indicates when to cut the medium. Valid codes are: |

     0   Don't cut the medium.

     1   Cut the medium at device deactivation.

     2   Cut the medium at the end of the job.

     3   Cut the medium after each set.

     4   Cut the medium after each **showpage** or **copypage**.

See **Jog** for an explanation of the terminology.

| **AdvanceMedia** | integer | Indicates when to advance the medium by an extra amount—that is, in addition to the amount occupied by the page images themselves. Valid codes are: |

     0   Don't advance the medium.

1		Advance the medium at device deactivation.
2		Advance the medium at the end of the job.
3		Advance the medium after each set.
4		Advance the medium after each **showpage** or **copypage**.

See **Jog** for an explanation of the terminology.

AdvanceDistance   integer   Indicates the distance, in default user space units, to advance the medium when it is advanced as controlled by **AdvanceMedia**.

Table 4.13 *Policy and special action entries*

Key	Type	Semantics
Policies	dictionary	Contains feature-policy pairs that specify what **setpagedevice** should do when a feature request cannot be satisfied. It contains an overall policy and can optionally contain individual policies for specific named features. A policy is an integer that specifies a choice of one of several ways to handle an unsatisfied request. See section 4.11.5, "Policies," for an explanation of how this dictionary is used. Changes to the contents of **Policies** are cumulative; **setpagedevice** adds new entries to the ones already present.
Install	procedure	Executed to install values in the graphics state during each invocation of **setpagedevice**. **setpagedevice** calls this procedure after setting up the device and installing it as the current device in the graphics state, but before executing the implicit **erasepage** and **initgraphics**. This procedure can execute graphics state operators to install device-dependent parameters, such as halftone, color rendering, flatness, and so on. It can also alter the CTM. The resulting CTM becomes the default device matrix used by **defaultmatrix**, **initmatrix**, and **initgraphics**. The procedure cannot usefully alter most of the device-independent parameters, such as current path or color, because **initgraphics** resets those parameters to standard values. The **Install** procedure should not do anything besides alter parameters in the graphics state.
BeginPage	procedure	Executed at the beginning of each page. This occurs at the end of **setpagedevice**, at the end of each **showpage** or **copypage**, and during any operation that activates a page device, such as a **grestore** that reinstates a page device different from the existing one. When **BeginPage** is called, the graphics state has been initialized and the current page has been erased, if appropriate. **BeginPage** is supplied an integer on the operand stack indicating how many times **showpage** has been invoked since the current device was activated. See section 4.11.6, "BeginPage and EndPage."
EndPage	procedure	Executed at the end of each page. This occurs at the beginning of each **showpage** or **copypage**, and also when the current page device is about to be deactivated (replaced by a different page device). **EndPage** is supplied two integers on the operand stack: a count of previous **showpage** executions for this device and a code indicating the condition under which this call is being made.

EndPage must return a boolean value specifying whether to transmit the page image to the physical output device. See section 4.11.6, "BeginPage and EndPage."

4.11.4 Media Selection

A page description specifies its processing requirements by including appropriate entries in the dictionary it passes to **setpagedevice**. Certain of these entries—**PageSize**, **MediaColor**, **MediaWeight**, and **Media-Type**—control the selection of input media. Another entry—**OutputType**—controls the disposition of the media after they have been printed. This section describes how **setpagedevice** uses this information to determine the physical media source and destination to be used in the device.

A given product supports one or more physical sources and one or more physical destinations for media. These sources and destinations are often called "trays" or "positions." They are arbitrarily numbered by small integers. A particular integer usually refers to a specific physical location in the hardware, though it might refer to some logical capability such as a pair of trays that contain the same media and are used alternately. The correspondence between numbers and positions is product dependent; it is not described in this manual but in product documentation.

The device includes two special dictionaries, **InputAttributes** and **OutputAttributes**, that describe the attributes of each of the sources and destinations, respectively. This information is discovered automatically by the implementation or is configured manually by a human operator or system administrator. **setpagedevice** matches the media requirements specified by the page description against the attributes described in **InputAttributes** and **OutputAttributes** to determine which media source and destination to select.

The keys in the **InputAttributes** dictionary are integers representing media sources. The value of each entry is a dictionary containing key-value pairs describing the attributes of the media currently available from that source. The keys used in this dictionary are **PageSize**, **Media-Color**, **MediaWeight**, and **MediaType**. These keys have the same meanings as the corresponding ones described in Table 4.10 on page 232, but they specify the actual attributes of the media instead of the requirements of the page description.

OutputAttributes is treated similarly, but its entries contain only the **OutputType** attribute. A page description can request a specific **OutputType**, which **setpagedevice** matches against the **OutputType** attributes of entries in **OutputAttributes** to determine which destination to select. **OutputAttributes** and **OutputType** are supported only in those products that provide choices for output handling.

A simple example illustrates the most common use of this approach for input media selection. (Output selection works analogously.) Suppose the current value of the **InputAttributes** dictionary for the device is:

```
<<
  0 << /PageSize [612 1008] >>
  1 << /PageSize [612 792] >>
>>
```

In other words, the product has two paper trays. Tray 0 contains legal-size $(8.5 \times 14$ inch) paper; tray 1 contains letter-size $(8.5 \times 11$ inch) paper. Now suppose a page description executes:

```
<< /PageSize [612 792] >> setpagedevice
```

The **PageSize** request to **setpagedevice** matches the **PageSize** attribute for media source 1, and there are no non-matching requests. Therefore, **setpagedevice** selects tray 1.

Matching Requests With Attributes

Each time **setpagedevice** is executed, it uses the following algorithm to match media requests with media attributes in order to select a source and destination.

1. Merge the entries in the **setpagedevice** operand dictionary with the ones in the existing state of the device, as described in section 4.11.2, "Page Device Dictionary." The resulting set of key-value pairs is considered together, without regard to which ones are specified in the **setpagedevice** operand dictionary and which ones are inherited from the existing state of the device.

2. Collect together those of the **PageSize**, **MediaColor**, **MediaWeight**, and **MediaType** entries whose values are not *null* and treat them as an "input media request." Ignore the entries whose values are *null*.

3. Enumerate the entries in the **InputAttributes** dictionary. Each entry's key is an integer identifying a media source; its value is a dictionary containing the attributes of the media. For each entry in the input media request (step 2), compare its value with the corresponding media attribute. If all the values are equal, we say that the media request matches the media source. (**PageSize** values are compared with a tolerance of 5 units in each dimension.)

4. If the result of step 3 is that the media request matches exactly one media source, select that source. If there is more than one match, select the source with the highest priority (see **Priority**, below). If there are no matches at all, consult **Policies** to determine what to do (see section 4.11.5, "Policies").

5. Similarly, perform steps 2 through 4 to select a media destination, using the **OutputType** entry as an "output media request" and the **OutputAttributes** dictionary as a description of the attributes of the available destinations.

For example, consider a product with two paper trays. Tray 0 contains white letter-size (8.5 × 11 inches) office paper and tray 1 contains a much less expensive letter-size paper (also 8.5 × 11 inches). The **InputAttributes** dictionary in the device state might be as follows:

```
<<
  0 << /PageSize [612 792] /MediaColor (white)  /MediaType (office) >>
  1 << /PageSize [612 792] >>
  /Priority [1 0]
>>
```

(How the **InputAttributes** dictionary got to be this way is discussed later, as is the meaning of the **Priority** entry.)

Note   *In each **InputAttributes** entry, **PageSize** is required, but other attributes are optional. A non-null media request will not match an **InputAttributes** entry in which the corresponding attribute is absent. In the example above, only **PageSize** is given for source 1 and **MediaWeight** is not given for either source.*

If a page description now executes

```
<< /PageSize [612 792] /MediaColor (white) >> setpagedevice
```

then **setpagedevice** will select input tray 0. This is because the **PageSize** and **MediaColor** entries in the **setpagedevice** request match only the attributes given in entry 0 of the **InputAttributes** dictionary. The values of **MediaType** and **MediaWeight** in the request are *null* (assuming that non-null values haven't been inherited from the existing state of the device). A *null* value in a request means "don't care."

Given the same **InputAttributes**, execution of

    << /PageSize [612 792] /MediaColor (red) >> setpagedevice

will not match either tray. The requested **MediaColor** does not match the **MediaColor** attribute for tray 0. The **MediaColor** for tray 1 is unknown and therefore does not satisfy a request for a specific color.

Now consider what happens during execution of

    << /PageSize [612 792] >> setpagedevice

This request matches both tray 0 and tray 1 (again, assuming that non-null values for **MediaColor**, **MediaType**, or **MediaWeight** haven't been inherited from the existing state of the device). In this situation, if a **Priority** entry exists in the **InputAttributes** dictionary, **setpagedevice** consults it to determine which tray to select. If **Priority** is not present, **setpagedevice** chooses one of the matching trays arbitrarily.

The value of **Priority** is an array of integers. The first integer in the array represents the highest-priority media source; subsequent integers represent media sources in decreasing priority. When a **setpagedevice** request matches two or more media sources, **setpagedevice** chooses the one whose number appears earliest in the **Priority** array. If none of the matching sources appears in the array, **setpagedevice** chooses among them arbitrarily.

The effect of the **InputAttributes** definition given in the example above is that a document requesting a **MediaColor** of white or a **MediaType** of office (or both) will be printed on paper from tray 0, but a document not requesting either of those attributes will be printed on the less expensive paper from tray 1.

Certain media are special-purpose, such as company letterhead or preprinted forms. Such media should be selected only if a page description specifically requests *all* the attributes of the media. For example, company letterhead should be selected only if a program requests company letterhead. If a program simply requests letter-size paper, it's inappropriate for **setpagedevice** to satisfy this request by selecting company letterhead, even if company letterhead happens to be the only available media of the correct size.

Suppose the available media consist of legal-size paper in tray 0 and company letterhead (letter-size) in tray 1. The **InputAttributes** dictionary for the device might be something like this:

```
<<
  0  << /PageSize [612 1008] >>
  1  << /PageSize [612 792]  /MediaType (letterhead)  /MatchAll true >>
>>
```

The special **MatchAll** attribute in entry 1 indicates that media source 1 can satisfy only requests for *all* the source's attributes. That is,

```
<< /PageSize [612 792]  /MediaType (letterhead) >> setpagedevice
```

will select media source 1, but

```
<< /PageSize [612 792] >> setpagedevice
```

will not select *either* media source. (Information in the **Policies** dictionary determines what to do when there is no match with any available media; see section 4.11.5, "Policies.")

The precise semantics of **MatchAll** are as follows. If **MatchAll** is present in an **InputAttributes** entry and its value is *true*, a **setpagedevice** request will match that entry only if it specifies matching (non-null) values for *all* the attributes present in the entry (except the **MatchAll** attribute itself). If **MatchAll** is *false* or absent, a **setpagedevice** request will match the entry if it specifies *any subset* of the entry's attributes and leaves the others *null* (indicating "don't care").

Note   *All implementations of **setpagedevice** support media selection by means of the **PageSize**, **MediaColor**, **MediaWeight**, and **MediaType** input attributes, whether or not the product can sense those media attributes automatically. In some products, other attributes also influence media selection. In such products, those attributes can appear in the **InputAttributes** dictionary as well.*

Managing InputAttributes and OutputAttributes

The **InputAttributes** and **OutputAttributes** dictionaries are part of the state of the device and can be altered by executing **setpagedevice**. However, a page description should never do this. These dictionaries are intended to describe the attributes of the available media sources and destinations. They should be changed only by a human operator or system management software in control of the physical device.

Some products can sense the attributes of the available media sources and destinations automatically. For example, many printers can sense the size of paper installed in an input paper tray. Some printers can sense other attributes as well, usually by reading coded tags attached to the trays.

When an implementation can sense media attributes, it automatically updates the contents of the **InputAttributes** and **OutputAttributes** dictionaries to reflect the physical state of the hardware. How and when this is done is product dependent, but the following conventions are typical.

• At the beginning of a job (see section 3.7.7, "Job Execution Environment"), the job server senses the attributes of all available media sources and destinations. It then executes **setpagedevice** to update the **InputAttributes** and **OutputAttributes** dictionaries.

• Additionally, the job server selects a default media source and destination. These defaults are used if a page description fails to specify its media requirements. (Non-null attributes of the default media will be inherited during a **setpagedevice** request that does not explicitly override those attributes.) How defaults are selected is product-dependent; a common method is to use the first element of the **Priority** array if one is present.

• Execution of **setpagedevice** at other times may also result in **InputAttributes** and **OutputAttributes** being updated to reflect the state of the hardware. In particular, this occurs if a **Policies** recovery policy specifies interaction with a human operator and the operator installs different media (see section 4.11.5, "Policies"). It can occur at other times as well.

Some products cannot sense media attributes automatically, or they can sense **PageSize** but not other attributes. For such products, explicit execution of **setpagedevice** is required to update **InputAttributes** and **OutputAttributes** whenever media are changed. This is usually done by a system management program submitted by a human operator and executed as an unencapsulated job. Some products provide a "front panel" user interface to accomplish this.

Changes to the contents of the **InputAttributes** and **OutputAttributes** dictionaries are cumulative. **setpagedevice** combines the key-value pairs supplied to it with those in the existing state of the device, replacing or adding entries as appropriate. However, this cumulative behavior does not extend to the contents of the sub-dictionaries that are the values of individual entries in **InputAttributes** and **OutputAttributes**. For example, suppose the contents of the device's **InputAttributes** dictionary are as follows:

```
<<
  0 << /PageSize [612 1008] >>
  1 << /PageSize [612 792]  /MediaType (letterhead)  /MatchAll true >>
>>
```

If a program executes

```
<< /InputAttributes <<
  1 << /PageSize [612 792] >>
  /Priority [1 0]
>> >> setpagedevice
```

then the device's **InputAttributes** dictionary becomes

```
<<
  0 << /PageSize [612 1008] >>
  1 << /PageSize [612 792] >>
  /Priority [1 0]
>>
```

In other words, entry 0 is left undisturbed, entry 1 is replaced by the one given to **setpagedevice**, and the new **Priority** entry is inserted. Note that the *value* of entry 1 is not merged but is simply replaced.

Note   *If an entry in **InputAttributes** or **OutputAttributes** has a null value instead of a dictionary, it indicates an input or output position that is unavailable for use—for example, no paper tray is installed. If a single execution of **setpagedevice** includes changes to **InputAttributes** or **OutputAttributes** as well as requests for other features, the merging of these dictionaries occurs before processing of other features.*

4.11.5 Policies

When a page description makes a request that the device cannot satisfy, **setpagedevice** consults the **Policies** dictionary to determine what to do. Inability to satisfy a request arises in two situations.

- The device does not support the requested feature at all—for example, duplex printing is requested but the device has no duplex capability. The key **Duplex** is not defined in the device dictionary; the implementation has no idea what **Duplex** means. If a request includes an entry with the key **Duplex**, **setpagedevice** treats it as a request for an unknown feature—even if the requested value is *false*.

- The device supports the requested feature but cannot achieve the requested value at the moment—for example, an A4-size page is requested when the A4 paper tray is not currently installed.

Policies is a dictionary that is part of the state of the device. For most entries in this dictionary, the key is the name of a feature; the value is an integer code specifying a policy for handling unsatisfied requests for that feature. For most features, there are three policy choices: generate an error (**configurationerror**), ignore the request, or interact with a human operator. For **PageSize** requests, there are additional policy choices. Table 4.14 describes the entries that can appear in the **Policies** dictionary.

Table 4.14 *Entries in the* **Policies** *dictionary*

Key	Type	Semantics
PolicyNotFound	integer	Specifies the policy to use when a requested feature (other than **PageSize**) cannot be satisfied and the feature's name is not present as a key in the **Policies** dictionary. The policy is an integer code with the following meanings.
		0 Generate a **configurationerror**—that is, do not attempt recovery but simply abandon execution of **setpagedevice**, leaving the current device undisturbed. **configurationerror** is a standard PostScript language error, much the same as **undefined** or **typecheck**. Before generating the error, **setpagedevice** inserts an **errorinfo** entry into the **$error** dictionary. Error handling in general and **errorinfo** in particular are described in section 3.10, "Errors."
		1 Ignore the feature request. This is the usual default policy in most products.
		2 Interact with a human operator or print manager to determine what to do. The semantics of this policy vary among different products and environments. Some products issue a message (on a front panel, for instance) indicating an operator action that is required, then wait for confirmation. Other products have no ability to interact with an operator and generate a **configurationerror** in this case. The details are product dependent.
any feature name	integer	Specifies the policy to use when a specific named feature (other than **PageSize**) cannot be satisfied. The policy is an integer code whose meaning is as specified above for **PolicyNotFound**.
		Any key that can appear in a dictionary supplied to **setpagedevice** may also be used as a key in the **Policies** dictionary. This is not limited to keys recognized by the implementation but may include any key. That is, **setpagedevice** consults **Policies** the same way for an unknown feature as it does for a known feature whose requested value cannot be achieved.

| **PageSize** | integer | Specifies the recovery policy to use when the **PageSize** cannot be matched (within a tolerance of 5 units) with any available media. The policy is an integer code with the following meanings. |

0   Generate a **configurationerror**, as described above for **PolicyNotFound**. This is the usual default policy in most products.

1   Ignore the requested **PageSize**.

2   Interact with a human operator or print manager, as described above for **PolicyNotFound**.

3   Select the nearest available medium and adjust the page to fit. This adjustment is described below.

4   Select the next larger available medium and adjust the page to fit.

5   Select the nearest available medium but do not adjust the page.

6   Select the next larger available medium but do not adjust the page.

| **PolicyReport** | procedure | Called upon successful completion of **setpagedevice** if it needed to consult **Policies** in order to handle one or more unsatisfied feature requests. This procedure can report the actions that were taken or perform alternative actions. **PolicyReport** is described below. The default value of **PolicyReport** is {pop}. |

The **Policies** dictionary is part of the state of the device and can be altered by executing **setpagedevice**. Ordinarily, a page description composed by an application program should not do this; policies should be changed only by a human operator or by system management software in control of the physical device. However, if a user requests special policies when submitting a print job, it's appropriate for print manager software to insert a **setpagedevice** command to change **Policies** at the beginning of the page description. For example, the user might consider it essential that a particular job use certain features; if the features aren't available, the job should be rejected instead of being executed with the feature requests ignored.

Changes to the contents of the **Policies** dictionary are cumulative. **setpagedevice** combines the key-value pairs supplied to it with those in the existing state of the device, replacing or adding entries as appropriate. If a single invocation of **setpagedevice** includes changes to **Policies** as well as requests for other features, the merging of **Policies** entries occurs before the processing of other features. Thus, the *revised* **Policies** dictionary is consulted to determine policy if one of the other feature requests can't be satisfied. For example,

```
<< /Duplex true
    /Policies << /Duplex 0 >>
>> setpagedevice
```

requests duplex printing and generates a **configurationerror** if the device doesn't support duplex printing.

Policies and Media Selection

If a media request fails to match any of the available media sources or destinations described in **InputAttributes** or **OutputAttributes**, **setpagedevice** consults **Policies** in an attempt to make an alternative media selection. For each relevant media request (**PageSize**, **Media-Color**, **MediaWeight**, and **MediaType** for a source; **OutputType** for a destination), if the value of the corresponding entry in **Policies** is 1 (ignore), **setpagedevice** replaces the media request with *null*. It then repeats the matching algorithm (steps 2 through 4 on page 240).

Note   *Ignoring media requests cannot result in selection of a media source or destination that has a* ***MatchAll*** *attribute of true.*

If this second attempt at media selection succeeds, the resulting device dictionary contains *null* values for all the media requests other than **PageSize** that were ignored. If **PageSize** was ignored, the resulting device dictionary contains the **PageSize** of the media source that was actually selected.

If the second attempt at media selection fails, the next action depends on whether any of the non-matching requests have a corresponding **Policies** entry of 2 (interact with a human operator or print manager). If so, **setpagedevice** performs such interaction, which may cause new media to be installed and **InputAttributes** or **OutputAttributes** to be updated. It then restarts the media selection process from the beginning. If no **Policies** entry specifies user interaction or if user interaction is not possible, **setpagedevice** terminates unsuccessfully and generates a **configurationerror**.

For **PageSize**, there are additional policy choices that permit compromises to be made in matching the requested page size to the set of available media. These include all four combinations of the following pair of choices:

- Select an alternative medium that is either nearest in size or the next larger size to the requested **PageSize**.

- Either adjust the page (by scaling and centering) to fit the alternative medium or perform no adjustment.

The *nearest size* is the one closest in area to the requested size. The *next larger size* is the one that is at least as large as the requested size in both width and height and is smallest in area. If the policy is to select the next larger size but no larger size is available, the nearest size is used.

Once an alternative medium has been selected, the adjustment option determines how the page image is to be placed on the medium—in other words, how the CTM defining the device's default user space is to be computed.

To *adjust* the page means to scale the page image (if necessary) to fit the medium, then center the image on the medium. In more detail, adjustment consists of the following two steps.

1. If the selected medium is smaller than the requested **PageSize** in either dimension, scale the page image to fit the medium in the most restrictive dimension. Scaling is the same in both dimensions so as to preserve the page's aspect ratio (height to width). No scaling is performed if the selected medium is at least as large as the requested **PageSize** in both dimensions.

2. Center the page image on the medium along both dimensions.

The effect of this adjustment is to set up a "virtual page" conforming to the requested **PageSize** (scaled down if necessary), centered on the physical medium. The origin of user space is the lower-left corner of the virtual page, not of the physical medium. The **PageSize** in the resulting device dictionary is the **PageSize** that was requested, not that of the physical medium.

In the case where the page is *not* adjusted, the default user space is not scaled and is aligned with its origin at the lower-left corner of the medium. The effect is precisely as if the medium's **PageSize** had been requested in the first place. If the actual **PageSize** is smaller than the requested one along either dimension, the page image will be clipped.

The limited set of built-in policies for handing unsatisfied requests can be augmented by judicious use of the **PolicyReport** procedure in the **Policies** dictionary (described below). Additional adjustments to the CTM can be implemented as part of the **Install** procedure in the device dictionary.

PolicyReport

The **Policies** dictionary contains an entry whose key is **PolicyReport** and whose value is a procedure. Upon successful completion, **setpagedevice** calls the **PolicyReport** procedure if it needed to consult **Policies** during its execution to determine how to handle one or more unsatisfied requests. **setpagedevice** does *not* call **PolicyReport** if it was able to satisfy all requests without consulting **Policies** or if it terminated unsuccessfully with a **configurationerror**.

Before calling **PolicyReport**, **setpagedevice** constructs a dictionary and pushes it on the operand stack. The dictionary contains one entry for each requested feature that was initially unsatisfied. The key is the name of the feature that was requested; the value is the integer policy code that was obtained from **Policies**. The **PolicyReport** procedure is expected to consume this dictionary from the stack.

For example, suppose a **setpagedevice** request includes:

- A request for **Duplex** that cannot be met, and the **Policies** entry for **Duplex** is 1 (ignore the request).

- A **PageSize** request that doesn't match any available media, and the **Policies** entry for **PageSize** is 5 (select the nearest available medium and don't adjust).

Then upon successful completion, **setpagedevice** calls the **PolicyReport** procedure with the operand stack containing:

    << /Duplex 1 /PageSize 5 >>

At the time **setpagedevice** calls **PolicyReport**, it has completed setting up the new page device and installing it as the current device in the graphics state. It has also called the device's **BeginPage** procedure (see section 4.11.6, "BeginPage and EndPage"). Thus, executing **currentpagedevice** within the **PolicyReport** procedure will return the newly installed device's dictionary. It is permissible for the **PolicyReport** procedure to execute **setpagedevice** recursively.

There are two main uses for a **PolicyReport** procedure.

- It can transmit a notification to the human operator or print manager, warning that one or more requests were unsatisfied and that substitute actions have been taken.

- It can inspect the resulting device dictionary and perhaps make additional alterations. This provides additional flexibility when the standard set of policy choices is found to be inadequate.

4.11.6 BeginPage and EndPage

The **BeginPage** and **EndPage** entries in the device dictionary are Post-Script language procedures that are called each time **showpage** and **copypage** are executed and also at certain other times. The interpreter calls **BeginPage** before beginning to execute the description of each page and **EndPage** after execution of each page has finished. With suitable definitions, these procedures can

- Cause multiple virtual pages within a document to be printed on a single physical page ("2-up" or "*n*-up" printing).

- Shift the positions of even- and odd-page images differently for binding.

- Add marks to each page that either underlay or overprint the material provided by the page description.

Note   *Use of **BeginPage** and **EndPage** to achieve effects spanning multiple pages sacrifices whatever page independence the document may have. In general, a page description should not include definitions of **BeginPage** or **EndPage** in its invocations of **setpagedevice**. Instead, a print manager should prepend such commands to the page description when printing is requested.*

The interpreter calls the current device's **BeginPage** procedure at the beginning of executing each page. Precisely,

- **setpagedevice** calls **BeginPage** as its last action before returning. (However, if it calls **PolicyReport**, it does so after calling **BeginPage**.) This indicates the beginning of the *first* page to be rendered on the device.

- **showpage** and **copypage** call **BeginPage** as their last action before returning. This indicates the beginning of the *next* page, following the one that **showpage** or **copypage** has just ended.

- Operators that reactivate an existing page device call **BeginPage** as their last action before returning. Device activation and deactivation are explained later.

When **BeginPage** is called, the graphics state has been initialized and the current page erased, if appropriate, in preparation for beginning execution of the PostScript language commands describing a page. The operand stack contains an integer stating the number of executions of **showpage** (but not **copypage**) that have occurred since the device was activated. That is, the operand is 0 at the first call to **BeginPage**, 1 at the call that occurs during the first **showpage**, and so on. The **BeginPage** procedure is expected to consume this operand. The procedure is permitted to alter the graphics state and to paint marks on the current page.

The interpreter calls the current device's **EndPage** procedure at the end of executing each page. Precisely,

- **showpage** and **copypage** call **EndPage** as their first action. This indicates the end of the preceding page.

- Operators that deactivate the device call **EndPage** as their first action. Device activation and deactivation are explained later.

When **EndPage** is called, the PostScript language commands describing the preceding page have been completely executed, but the contents of raster memory have not yet been transferred to the medium and the graphics state is undisturbed. The operand stack contains two integers:

- The number of executions of **showpage** (but not **copypage**) that have occurred since the device was activated, *not* including this one. That is, the operand is 0 at the call to **EndPage** during the first **showpage**, 1 during the second **showpage**, and so on.

- A code indicating the circumstance under which **EndPage** is being called: 0 during **showpage**, 1 during **copypage**, 2 during device deactivation (see below).

The **EndPage** procedure is expected to consume these operands. The procedure is permitted to alter the graphics state and to paint marks on the current page; such marks are added to the page just completed. **EndPage** must return a boolean result specifying the disposition of the current page:

- The value *true* means transfer the contents of raster memory to the medium. Then, if **showpage** is being executed, execute the equivalent of **initgraphics** and **erasepage** in preparation for the next page. (The latter actions are not performed during **copypage**.)

- The value *false* means do not transfer the contents of raster memory to the medium or erase the current page. (If **showpage** is being executed, **initgraphics** is still performed.)

The normal definition of **EndPage** returns *true* during **showpage** or **copypage** (code 0 or 1) but *false* during device deactivation (code 2). That is, normally every **showpage** and **copypage** causes a physical page to be produced, but an incomplete last page (not ended by **showpage** or **copypage**) produces no output. Other behavior can be obtained by defining **EndPage** differently.

The state of any device, including a page device, is represented as an internal object that is an element of the graphics state. Each execution of a device setup operator—**setpagedevice**, **nulldevice**, **setcachedevice**, and perhaps others in a Display PostScript system—creates a new instance of an internal device object (hereafter, simply "device"). Multiple devices can refer to the same physical resource, such as a print engine, perhaps with different values of device parameters such as **PageSize** or feature settings.

Only one device is active at any given time, namely the current device in the graphics state. However, there can be multiple inactive devices that belong to copies of the graphics state that have been saved by **save**, **gsave**, or **currentgstate**. An inactive device can be reactivated when a saved graphics state is reinstated by execution of **restore**, **grestore**, **grestoreall** or **setgstate**. When a device is reactivated, it brings its device parameters with it.

When **setpagedevice** is executed or when **restore**, **grestore**, **grestoreall** or **setgstate** causes a page device to be deactivated and a *different* page device to be activated, the interpreter

1. Calls the **EndPage** procedure of the device that is being deactivated, passing it a reason code of 2. At the time this call is made, the current device in the graphics state is still the old device. This enables any necessary cleanup actions to be performed, such as printing an incomplete "*n*-up" page.

2. Performs any actions that the **Jog**, **AdvanceMedia**, and **CutMedia** entries indicate are to be done upon device deactivation. Also, if **Duplex** is *true* and the last sheet has been printed on only one side, the sheet is delivered at this time.

3. Calls the **BeginPage** procedure of the device that is being activated. At the time this call is made, the current device in the graphics state is the new one. Its count of previous **showpage** executions is reset to zero.

The above actions occur only when switching from a *page device* to a *different page device* (however, **setpagedevice** always calls **BeginPage**). They do not occur when switching to or from other kinds of devices, such as the ones set up by the **nulldevice** and **setcachedevice** operators. Usually, those devices are installed temporarily. For example, **setcachedevice** and the operations for rendering a character into the font cache are bracketed by **gsave** and **grestore**, thereby reinstating the page device that was previously in effect. The page device's **BeginPage** and **EndPage** procedures are not called in such cases and the current page is not erased or otherwise disturbed.

A few examples illustrate this distinction. Example 4.24 switches between two page devices. All of the activations and deactivations cause the devices' **BeginPage** and **EndPage** procedures to be called, as described above.

Example 4.24

```
dict1 setpagedevice       % BeginPage for device 1
gsave
dict2 setpagedevice       % EndPage for device 1, BeginPage for device 2
grestore                  % EndPage for device 2, BeginPage for device 1
```

In Example 4.25, on the other hand, temporary activation of the null device does not cause the page device's **EndPage** procedure to be called, nor does reactivation of the page device cause its **BeginPage** procedure to be called. In fact, the state of the page device is not disturbed in any way, since the null device is not a page device.

Example 4.25

```
dict3 setpagedevice       % BeginPage for device 3
gsave
nulldevice
grestore
```

It is possible to switch devices in an order that prevents a page device's **EndPage** procedure from ever being called. Example 4.26 switches from a page device to a null device without saving a graphics state that refers to the page device. Thus, there is no possibility of reactivating the page device in order to call its **EndPage** procedure. This sequence of operations is *not recommended*.

Example 4.26

```
gsave
dict4 setpagedevice          % BeginPage for device 4
nulldevice
grestore
```

Example 4.27 shows the skeleton structure of a simple two-page document. For completeness, it includes the recommended document structuring conventions, which are explained in Appendix G. The comments to the right indicate the points at which the interpreter calls **BeginPage** and **EndPage** and the arguments it passes to each.

Example 4.27

```
%!PS-Adobe-3.0
...Document prolog...
%%BeginSetup
%%BeginFeature: *Duplex
<< /Duplex true >> setpagedevice          % 0 BeginPage
%%EndFeature
%%BeginFeature: *PageSize Letter
<< /PageSize [612 792]  /ImagingBBox null >> setpagedevice
                                          % 0 2 EndPage 0 BeginPage
%%EndFeature
%%EndSetup
%%Page: 1 1
save
...PostScript language description for page 1...
restore
showpage                                  % 0 0 EndPage 1 BeginPage
%%Page: 2 2
save
...PostScript language description for page 2...
restore
showpage                                  % 1 0 EndPage 2 BeginPage
%%EOF
...Job server executes restore, which deactivates the page device...
                                          % 2 2 EndPage
```

CHAPTER 5

Fonts

This chapter describes the special facilities in the PostScript language for dealing with text—more generally, with *characters* from *fonts*. A character is a general graphical shape and is subject to all graphical manipulations, such as coordinate transformation. Because of the importance of text in most page descriptions, the PostScript language provides higher-level facilities that permit a program to describe, select, and render characters conveniently and efficiently.

The first section is a general description of how fonts are organized and accessed. This description covers all normal uses of fonts that are already installed.

The information in subsequent sections is somewhat more complex, but it is required only by programs with sophisticated needs. It discusses the organization of font dictionaries, the encoding scheme that maps character codes to character names and descriptions, the metric information available for fonts, and the operation of the font cache. Finally, it describes how to construct new base and composite fonts.

Details of the individual PostScript operators are given in Chapter 8. All facilities are supported by Level 1 implementations except for the ones specifically documented as Level 2 features. Some of the Level 2 features are also available as part of composite font or Display PostScript extensions; for details, consult Appendix A.

5.1 Organization and Use of Fonts

Sets of characters are organized into *fonts*. A font for use with the Post-Script interpreter is prepared in the form of a program. When such a *font program* is introduced into a PostScript interpreter, its execution causes a *font dictionary* to come into existence and to be associated with a font name.

In the PostScript language, the term *font* refers to a font dictionary, through which the PostScript interpreter obtains definitions that generate character shapes. The interpreter uses a character's code to select the definition that represents the character. A character's *definition* is a procedure that executes graphics operations to produce the character's shape. The procedure is usually encoded in a special compact representation. To render a character, the PostScript interpreter executes this procedure.

If you have experience with scan conversion of general shapes, you may be concerned about the amount of computation that this description seems to imply. However, this is only the abstract behavior of character shapes and font programs, not how they are implemented. In fact, the PostScript font machinery works very efficiently.

5.1.1 Basic Text Setting

Example 5.1 illustrates the most straightforward use of a font. Suppose you wish to place the text ABC, 10 inches from the bottom of the page and 4 inches from the left edge, using 12-point Helvetica.

Example 5.1

```
/Helvetica findfont
12 scalefont setfont
288 720 moveto
(ABC) show
```

The four lines of this program perform the following steps:

1. Select the font to use.

2. Scale it to the desired size and install it as the current font in the graphics state.

3. Specify a starting position on the page.

4. Paint a string of characters there.

The following paragraphs explain these operations in more detail.

Each PostScript implementation includes a collection of fonts that are either built-in or can be obtained automatically from sources such as disks or cartridges. A user can download additional fonts, and a PostScript language program can define special fonts for its own use. The interpreter maintains a *font directory* associating the names of fonts, which are name objects, with their definitions, which are font dictionaries. The **findfont** operator takes the name of the font and returns on the operand stack a font dictionary containing all information the PostScript interpreter needs to render any of that font's characters.

A font specifies the shapes of its characters for one standard size. This standard is so arranged that the nominal height of tightly-spaced lines of text is 1 unit. In the default user coordinate system, this means the standard character size is one unit in user space, or 1/72 of an inch. The standard size font must then be scaled to be usable.

The **scalefont** operator scales the characters in a font without affecting the user coordinate system. **scalefont** takes two operands: the original font dictionary and the desired scale factor. It returns a new font dictionary that renders character shapes in the desired size. It is possible to scale the user coordinate system with the coordinate system operators, but it is usually more convenient to encapsulate the desired size in the font dictionary. Another operator, **makefont**, applies more complicated linear transformations to a font.

In Example 5.1, the **scalefont** operator scales the Helvetica font left on the stack by **findfont** to a 12-unit size and returns the scaled font on the operand stack. The **setfont** operator establishes the resulting font dictionary as the *current font* in the graphics state.

Once the font has been selected, scaled, and set, it can be used to paint characters. The **moveto** operator (described in section 4.4, "Path Construction") sets the current position to the specified *x* and *y* coordinates—in units of 1/72 inch—in the default user coordinate system. This determines the position on the page at which to begin painting characters.

The **show** operator takes a string from the operand stack and renders it using the current font. The **show** operator treats each element of the string (an integer in the range 0 to 255) as a character code. Each code selects a character description in the font dictionary; the character description is executed to paint the desired character on the page. This is the behavior of **show** for base fonts, such as ordinary Roman text fonts. Its behavior is more complex for composite fonts, described in section 5.9, "Composite Fonts."

What these steps produce on the page is not a 12-point character, but rather a 12-unit character, where the unit size is that of the user space at the time the characters are rendered on the page. If the user space is later scaled to make the unit size one centimeter, showing characters from the same 12-unit font will generate results that are 12 centimeters high.

5.1.2 Selecting Fonts

Example 5.1 used PostScript operators in a direct way. It is usually desirable to define procedures to help the application that is generating the text. To illustrate this point, assume that an application is setting many independently positioned text strings and requires switching frequently among three fonts: Helvetica, Helvetica-Oblique, and Helvetica-Bold, all in a 10-point size. Example 5.2 shows the programming to do this.

Example 5.2

```
/FSD {findfont exch scalefont def} bind def     % In the document prolog:  define
/SMS {setfont moveto show} bind def             % some useful procedures
/MS {moveto show} bind def

/F1 10 /Helvetica FSD                           % At the start of the script:  set up
/F2 10 /Helvetica-Oblique FSD                   % commonly used font dictionaries
/F3 10 /Helvetica-Bold FSD

(This is in Helvetica.) 10 78 F1 SMS            % In the body of the script:  show
(And more in Helvetica.) 10 66 MS               % some text
(This is in Helvetica-Oblique.) 10 54 F2 SMS
(This is in Helvetica-Bold.) 10 42 F3 SMS
(And more Helvetica-Bold.) 10 30 MS
```

Figure 5.1 *Results of Example 5.2*

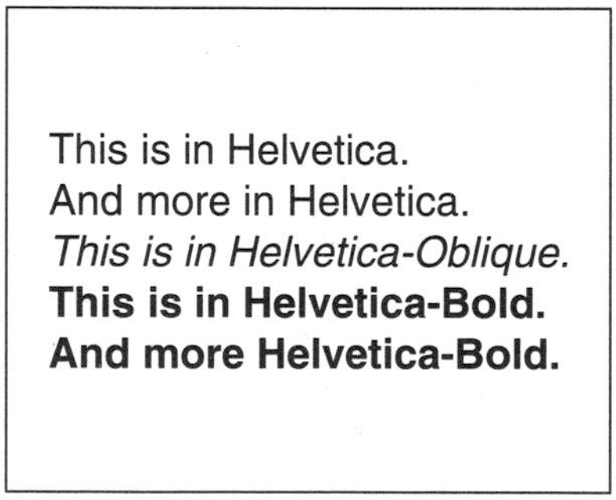

This is in Helvetica.
And more in Helvetica.
This is in Helvetica-Oblique.
This is in Helvetica-Bold.
And more Helvetica-Bold.

There are several features of Example 5.2 that are noteworthy. The document prolog defines three procedures:

- FSD takes a variable name, a scale factor, and a font name. It generates a font dictionary described by the font name and scale factor, then executes **def** to associate the font dictionary with the variable name. This assists in setting up fonts.

- SMS takes a string, a pair of coordinates, and a font dictionary; it shows the string starting at those coordinates, using the specified font.

- MS takes a string and a pair of coordinates. It shows the string at those coordinates, using the current font.

At the beginning of the document script, the program sets up font dictionaries and associates them with the names F1, F2, and F3. The body of the script sets text using the procedures and font dictionaries defined earlier. This example avoids switching fonts when it's unnecessary to do so; taking care in this respect is important for efficient execution.

Many applications must switch frequently among arbitrarily named fonts, where the names and sizes are not known in advance. To facilitate this, the Level 2 operator **selectfont** combines the actions of the **findfont**, **scalefont** (or **makefont**), and **setfont** operators. **selectfont** saves information from one call to the next to avoid calling **findfont** or performing the **scalefont** or **makefont** computations unnecessarily. In the common case of selecting a font and size combination that has been used recently, **selectfont** works with great efficiency.

5.1.3 Achieving Special Graphical Effects

Normal uses of **show** and other character painting operators cause black-filled characters to be painted. By combining font operators with general graphics operators, one can obtain other effects.

The color used for painting characters is determined by the current color in the graphics state. The default color is black, but other colors may be obtained by executing **setgray** or some other color-setting operator before painting characters. Example 5.3 paints characters in 50 percent gray.

Example 5.3

```
/Helvetica-Bold findfont 48 scalefont setfont
20 40 moveto
.5 setgray
(ABC) show
```

Figure 5.2 *Characters painted in 50 percent gray*

More general graphical manipulations can be performed by treating the character outline as a path instead of immediately painting it. **charpath** is a path construction operator that appends the outlines of one or more characters to the current path in the graphics state.

This is useful mainly with characters that are defined as outlines (as all Type 1 fonts are). Paths derived from characters defined as strokes can be used in limited ways. It is not possible to obtain paths for characters defined as images or bitmaps; **charpath** produces an empty path. Also, a path consisting of the outlines of more than a few characters is likely to exceed the limit on number of path elements (see Appendix B). If possible, it is best to deal with only one character's path at a time.

Example 5.4 uses character outlines as a path to be stroked. This program uses **charpath** to obtain the outlines for the string of characters ABC in the current font. The *false* operand to **charpath** is explained in the description of **charpath** in Chapter 8. The program then strokes this path with a line 2 points thick, rendering the characters' outlines on the page.

Example 5.4

```
/Helvetica findfont 48 scalefont setfont
20 38 moveto
(ABC) false charpath
2 setlinewidth stroke
```

Figure 5.3 *Character outlines treated as a path*

Example 5.5 obtains the characters' path as before, then establishes it as the current clipping path. All subsequent painting operations will mark the page only within this path. This state persists until some other clipping path is established—for example, by the **grestore** operator.

Example 5.5

```
/Helvetica findfont 48 scalefont setfont
newpath 20 40 moveto (ABC) false charpath clip
...Graphics operators to draw a starburst...
```

Figure 5.4 *Graphics clipped by a character path*

5.1.4   Character Positioning

A character's *width* is the amount of space the character occupies along the baseline of a line of text. In other words, it is the distance the current point moves when the character is shown. Note that the width is distinct from the dimensions of the character outline (see section 5.4, "Font Metric Information").

In some fonts, the width is constant; it does not vary from character to character. Such fonts are called *fixed-pitch* or *monospaced*. They are used mainly for typewriter-style printing. However, most fonts used for high-quality typography associate a different width with each character. Such fonts are called *proportional* fonts or *variable-pitch* fonts. In either case, the **show** operator positions consecutive characters of a string according to their widths.

The width information for each character is stored in the font dictionary. A PostScript language program can use any of several character painting operators—**show, xshow, yshow, xyshow, widthshow, ashow, awidthshow**—to obtain a variety of width modification effects. If necessary, it can execute **stringwidth** to obtain the width information itself.

The standard operators for setting text (**show** and its variants) are designed on the assumption that characters are ordinarily shown with their standard metrics. (See section 5.4, "Font Metric Information"). However, means are provided to vary the metrics in certain limited ways. For example, the **ashow** operator systematically adjusts the widths of all characters of a string during one **show** operation. The optional **Metrics** entry of a font dictionary can be added to adjust the widths of all instances of particular characters of a font.

Certain applications that set text require very precise control of the positioning of each character. There are three Level 2 operators to streamline the setting of individually positioned characters: **xyshow, xshow**, and **yshow**. Each operator is given a string of text to be shown, the same as **show**. Also, it expects a second operand, which is either an array of numbers or a string that can be interpreted as an encoded number string as described in section 3.12.5, "Encoded Number Strings." The numbers are used in sequence to control the widths of the characters being shown. *They completely override the standard widths of the characters.*

The **kshow** and **cshow** operators provide ways for an arbitrary PostScript language procedure to intervene in the positioning and painting of each character in a string. **cshow** is a Level 2 operator. These are the most general but least efficient text setting operations.

5.2 Font Dictionaries

Font dictionaries are ordinary dictionary objects, but with certain special key-value pairs. The PostScript language has several operators that deal with font dictionaries (see Chapter 8). Some of the contents of a font dictionary are optional and user-definable, while other key-value pairs *must* be present and have the correct semantics for the PostScript interpreter's font machinery to operate properly.

There are several kinds of fonts, each distinguished by the **FontType** entry in the font dictionary. Each type of font has its own conventions for organizing and representing the information within it. The font types defined at present are:

- Type 0 is a *composite font* composed of other fonts called *base fonts*, organized hierarchically. Composite fonts are a Level 2 feature. See section 5.9, "Composite Fonts."

- Type 1 is a base font that defines character shapes by using specially encoded procedures. That encoded format is described in a separate book, *Adobe Type 1 Font Format*.

- Type 3 is a *user-defined* base font that defines character shapes as ordinary PostScript language procedures, which are the values of entries named **BuildGlyph** or **BuildChar** in the font dictionary. See section 5.7, "Type 3 Fonts."

A PostScript language program creates a font dictionary by ordinary means (operators such as **dict**, **begin**, **end**, and **def**), then makes it known to the interpreter by executing the **definefont** operator. **definefont** takes a name and a dictionary, checks that the dictionary is a well-formed font dictionary, makes the dictionary's access read-only, and associates the font name with the dictionary in the font directory. It also inserts into the font dictionary an additional entry whose name is **FID** and whose value is an object of type fontID. This entry serves internal purposes in the font machinery. For this reason, a font dictionary presented to **definefont** must have room for at least one additional key-value pair.

The Level 2 operator **undefinefont** removes a named font from the font directory. A font dictionary that has been removed in this fashion is still a valid font assuming it is still accessible, but it can no longer be returned by **findfont**.

In Level 2 implementations, fonts are actually a special case of *named resources*: A font is an instance of the **Font** resource category. A font dictionary can reside in either local or global VM. See section 3.9, "Named Resources," and the description of the **defineresource** operator for complete information on how resource instances are named and are loaded into VM.

Table 5.1 lists the key-value pairs that have defined meanings in the font dictionaries of *all* types of fonts. Table 5.2 lists *additional* key-value pairs that are meaningful in all *base* fonts (types 1 and 3). Table 5.3 lists *additional* key-value pairs that are meaningful only in Type 1 fonts. Any font dictionary can have additional entries containing information that is useful to PostScript language procedures that are part of the font's definition. The interpreter pays no attention to those entries.

Table 5.1 *Entries in all types of font dictionaries*

Key	Type	Semantics
FontType	integer	(*Required*) Indicates where the information for the character descriptions is to be found and how it is represented.
FontMatrix	array	(*Required*) Transforms the *character coordinate system* into the user coordinate system (see section 5.4, "Font Metric Information"). For example, Type 1 font programs from Adobe are usually defined in terms of a 1000-unit character coordinate system, and their initial **FontMatrix** is [0.001 0 0 0.001 0 0]. When a font is derived by the **scalefont** or **makefont** operator, the new matrix is concatenated with the **FontMatrix** to yield a new copy of the font with a different **FontMatrix**.
FontName	name	(*Optional*) The font's name. This entry is for information only; it is not used by the PostScript interpreter. Ordinarily, it is the same as the key passed to **definefont**, but it is not required to be the same.
FontInfo	dictionary	(*Optional*) See Table 5.4 on page 268 for the entries that can be in this dictionary.
LanguageLevel	integer	(*Optional*) Minimum language level required for correct behavior of the font. Any font that uses Level 2 features for rendering characters (for example, a character definition uses **rectfill** or **glyphshow**) should specify a **LanguageLevel** of 2. On the other hand, presence of Level 2 information that a Level 1 interpreter can safely ignore (for example, an **XUID** entry in the font dictionary) does *not* require a **LanguageLevel** of 2. Default value: 1.
WMode	integer	(*Optional*) Indicates which of two sets of metrics will be used when characters are shown from the font. Level 1 implementations lacking composite font extensions ignore this entry. Default value: 0.

Table 5.2 *Additional entries in all base fonts (**FontType** not 0)*

Key	Type	Semantics
Encoding	array	(*Required*) Array of names that maps character codes (integers) to character names—the values in the array. This is described in section 5.3, "Character Encoding."
FontBBox	array	(*Required*) Array of four numbers in the character coordinate system giving lower-left x, lower-left y, upper-right x, and upper-right y of the font bounding box. The font bounding box is the smallest rectangle enclosing the shape that

would result if all of the characters of the font were placed with their origins coincident, and then painted. This information is used in making decisions about character caching and clipping. If all four values are zero, the PostScript interpreter makes no assumptions based on the font bounding box.

If any value is non-zero, it is essential that the font bounding box be accurate; if any character's marks fall outside this bounding box, incorrect behavior may result. For a Type 1 font, the **FontBBox** *must* be accurate (not all zeros) if the font uses the **seac** command for creating accented characters. See *Adobe Type 1 Font Format* for more information.

In many type 1 fonts, the **FontBBox** array is executable, though there is no good reason for this to be so. Programs that access the **FontBBox** should execute an explicit **get** or **load** to avoid unintended execution.

UniqueID	integer	(*Optional*) Integer in the range 0 to 16777215 ($2^{24} - 1$) that uniquely identifies this font. See section 5.8, "Unique ID Generation."
XUID	array	(*Optional*) Array of integers that uniquely identifies this font or any variant of it. See section 5.8, "Unique ID Generation." Level 1 implementations ignore this entry.

Table 5.3 *Additional entries specific to Type 1 fonts*

Key	Type	Semantics
PaintType	integer	(*Required*) A code indicating how the characters of the font are to be painted. 0 The character outlines are filled. 2 The character outlines (designed to be filled) are stroked. Type 1 fonts are ordinarily created with a **PaintType** of 0. A program desiring to convert it to a stroked outline font can copy the font dictionary, change the **PaintType** from 0 to 2, add a **StrokeWidth** entry, and define a new font using this dictionary. Note that the previously documented **PaintType** values of 1 and 3 are not supported.
StrokeWidth	number	(*Optional*) Stroke width (in units of the *character* coordinate system) for *stroked* outlined fonts (**PaintType** 2). This field is not initially present in filled font descriptions. It must be added when creating a stroked font from an existing filled font. Default value: 0.
Metrics	dictionary	(*Optional*) Width and sidebearing information for writing mode 0. This entry is not normally present in the original definition of a font. Adding a **Metrics** entry to a font overrides the widths and sidebearings encoded in the character descriptions. See sections 5.4, "Font Metric Information," and 5.6.2, "Changing Character Metrics."
Metrics2	dictionary	(*Optional*) Dictionary containing metric information for writing mode 1 (see section 5.6.2, "Changing Character Metrics"). Level 1 implementations lacking composite font extensions ignore this entry.

CDevProc	procedure	(*Optional*) Procedure that algorithmically derives global changes to a font's metrics. Level 1 implementations lacking composite font extensions ignore this entry.
CharStrings	dictionary	(*Required*) Associates character names (keys) with shape descriptions. Each entry's value is ordinarily a string that represents the character's description in a special encoded format; see *Adobe Type 1 Font Format* for details. The value can also be a PostScript language procedure; see section 5.6.3, "Replacing or Adding Individual Characters."
Private	dictionary	(*Required*) Contains other internal information about the font. See *Adobe Type 1 Font Format* for details.

Any font dictionary can contain a **FontInfo** entry whose value is a dictionary containing the information listed in Table 5.4. This information is *entirely* for the benefit of PostScript language programs using the font, or for documentation. It is not accessed by the PostScript interpreter.

Table 5.4 *Entries in a **FontInfo** dictionary*

Key	Type	Semantics
FamilyName	string	Human-readable name for a group of fonts that are stylistic variants of a single design. All fonts that are members of such a group should have exactly the same **FamilyName**.
FullName	string	Unique, human-readable name for an individual font.
Notice	string	Trademark or copyright notice, if applicable.
Weight	string	Human-readable name for the weight, or "boldness," attribute of a font.
version	string	Version number of the font program.
ItalicAngle	number	Angle in degrees counterclockwise from the vertical of the dominant vertical strokes of the font.
isFixedPitch	boolean	If *true*, indicates that the font is a fixed-pitch (monospaced) font.
UnderlinePosition	number	Recommended distance from the baseline for positioning underlining strokes. This number is the y coordinate (in character space) of the center of the stroke.
UnderlineThickness	number	Recommended stroke width for underlining, in units of the character coordinate system.

The PostScript language does not specify any formal rules for the names of fonts or for the entries in the **FontInfo** dictionary. However, there are various conventions for organizing fonts that facilitate their use by application programs.

- Some applications use **FamilyName** as part of a hierarchical font-selection user interface. This divides a very large set of individual fonts into a smaller, more manageable set of "font families." The **FamilyName** parameter should be suitable for use in a font selection menu.

- Typically, **FullName** begins with **FamilyName** and continues with various style descriptors separated by spaces—for example, Adobe Garamond Bold Italic. In some designs, a numbering system replaces or augments verbal descriptors—for example, Univers 55 Medium.

- **Weight** is derived from the **FullName** parameter by dropping everything from the **FullName** that does not explicitly relate to weight. For example, the **FullName** ITC Franklin Gothic Condensed Extra Bold Oblique reduces to a **Weight** of Extra Bold.

- The font dictionary's **FontName** parameter, which is also usually used as the key passed to **definefont**, is a condensation of the **FullName**. It is customary to remove spaces and to limit its length to less than 40 characters. The resulting name should be unique.

5.3 Character Encoding

Font definitions use a flexible *encoding* scheme by which character codes select character descriptions. The association between character codes and descriptions is not part of the character descriptions themselves, but instead is described by a separate *encoding vector*. A PostScript language program can change a font's encoding vector to match the requirements of the application generating the description.

This section describes the character encoding scheme used with most base fonts. Composite fonts (**FontType** 0) use a more complicated character mapping algorithm, defined in section 5.9, "Composite Fonts."

Note   *Use of this encoding scheme is required for Type 1 fonts and is strongly recommended for Type 3 fonts. Every base font must have an **Encoding** entry. A Type 3 font's **BuildChar** procedure should use it in the standard way.*

In a font dictionary, the descriptions of the individual characters are keyed by character *names*, not by character *codes*. Character names are ordinary PostScript language name objects. Descriptions of Roman alphabetic characters are normally associated with names consisting of single letters, such as A or a. Other characters are associated with names composed of words, such as three, ampersand, or parenleft.

The encoding vector is defined by the array object that is the value of **Encoding** in the font dictionary. The array is indexed by character code (an integer in the range 0 to 255). The elements of the array must be character names, and the array should be 256 elements long.

The operand to the **show** operator is a PostScript language string object. Each element of the string is treated as a character code. When **show** paints a character:

1. It uses the character code as an index into the current font's **Encoding** array to obtain a character name.

2. It invokes the character description by name. For a Type 1 font, it looks up the name in the font's **CharStrings** dictionary to obtain an encoded character description, which it executes. For a Type 3 font, it calls the font's **BuildGlyph** procedure (if present) with the name as operand. See section 5.7, "Type 3 Fonts."

For example, in the standard encoding vector used by Type 1 Roman text fonts such as Helvetica, the element at index 38 is the name object ampersand. When **show** encounters the value 38 (the ASCII character code for &) as an element of a string it is printing, it fetches the encoding vector entry at index 38, obtaining the name object ampersand. It then uses ampersand as a key in the current font dictionary's **CharStrings** subdictionary and executes the associated description that renders the & letterform.

Changing an existing font's encoding involves creating a new font dictionary that is a copy of the existing one except for its **Encoding** entry. The subsidiary dictionaries, such as **CharStrings** and **FontInfo**, continue to be shared with the original font. Of course, a new font may be created with any desired encoding vector.

This flexibility in character encoding is valuable for two reasons:

- It permits printing text encoded by methods other than ASCII (EBCDIC, for example).

- It allows applications to specify how characters outside a standard character set are to be encoded. Some fonts contain more than 256 characters, including ligatures, accented characters, and other symbols required for high-quality typography or non-Roman languages.

Roman text font programs produced by Adobe Systems use the "Adobe standard" encoding vector, which is associated with the name **StandardEncoding** in **systemdict**. An alternate encoding vector called ISO Latin-1 is associated with the name **ISOLatin1Encoding**. Complete details of these encodings and of the characters present in typical fonts appear in Appendix E.

All unused positions in an encoding vector must be filled with the name .notdef. The name .notdef is defined in **CharStrings**, just as is any other character. It is special in only one regard: If some encoding maps to a character name that does not exist in the font, .notdef is substituted. Every font must contain a definition of the .notdef character. The effect produced by showing the .notdef character is at the discretion of the font designer. In Adobe Type 1 font programs, it is the same as the space character.

The **glyphshow** operator, a Level 2 feature, shows a single character selected by name instead of by character code. This enables direct use of any character in the font regardless of the font's **Encoding**. The principal use of **glyphshow** is defining fonts whose character descriptions refer to other characters in the same or a different font. Referring to those characters by name ensures proper behavior if the font is subsequently re-encoded.

5.4 Font Metric Information

The *character coordinate system* is the space in which an individual character shape is defined. All path coordinates and metrics are interpreted in character space. Figure 5.5 shows a typical character outline and its metrics.

Figure 5.5 *Character metrics*

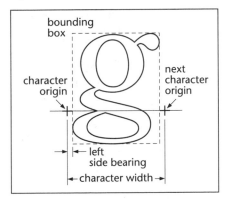

The *origin*, or *reference point*, of the character is the point (0, 0) in the character coordinate system. **show** and other character painting operators position the origin of the first character to be shown at the current point in user space. For example,

```
40 50 moveto (ABC) show
```

places the origin of the A at coordinate (40, 50) in the user coordinate system.

The *width* of a character is the distance from the character's origin to the point at which the origin of the *next* character should normally be placed when painting the consecutive characters of a word. This distance is a vector in the character coordinate system; it has x and y components. Most Indo-European alphabets, including Roman, have a positive x width and a zero y width. Semitic alphabets have a negative x width. Some Asian glyphs have a non-zero y width.

The *bounding box* of a character is the smallest rectangle (oriented with the character coordinate system axes) that will just enclose the entire character shape. The bounding box is expressed in terms of its lower-left corner and upper-right corner relative to the character origin in the character coordinate system.

The *left sidebearing* of a character is the position of the *left sidebearing point* in character space; this is usually the intersection of the left edge of the bounding box with the character's baseline (see *Adobe Type 1 Font Format*). Note that the x coordinate of the left sidebearing can be negative for characters that extend to the left of their origin. The y coordinate is almost always 0.

Type 1 fonts are defined in such a way that a character's left sidebearing and width can be adjusted; that is, the character bounding box and the position of the next character can be shifted around relative to the origin (see section 5.6, "Modifications to Existing Fonts").

In some writing systems, text is frequently aligned in two different directions. For example, it is common to write Japanese and Chinese characters either horizontally or vertically. To handle this, a font can optionally contain a second set of metrics for each character. This feature is available only in Level 2 or in Level 1 implementations with composite font extensions.

The metrics are accessed by **show** and other operators according to a writing mode, given by a **WMode** entry in the font dictionary or in some parent font dictionary in a composite font. By convention, writing mode 0 (the default) specifies horizontal writing; mode 1 specifies vertical writing. If a font contains only one set of metrics, the **WMode** parameter is ignored.

When a character has two sets of metrics, each set specifies a character origin and a width vector. Figure 5.6 illustrates the relationship between the two sets of metrics.

Figure 5.6 *Relationship between two sets of metrics*

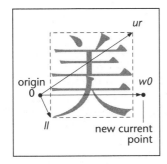 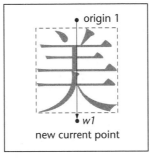 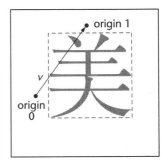

Writing mode 0   *Writing mode 1*   *Mode 1 relative to mode 0*

The left diagram illustrates the character metrics associated with writing mode 0. The coordinates *ll* and *ur* specify the bounding box of the character relative to origin 0. *w0* is the character width vector that specifies how the current point is changed after the character is shown in writing mode 0. The center diagram illustrates writing mode 1; *w1* is the character width vector for writing mode 1. In the right diagram, *v* is a vector defining the position of origin 1 relative to origin 0.

Character metric information can be accessed procedurally by a Post-Script language program. The **stringwidth** operator obtains character widths. The sequence

    charpath flattenpath pathbbox

computes character bounding boxes, though this is relatively inefficient. The bounding box for an entire font appears in the font dictionary as an array of four numbers associated with the key **FontBBox**.

Character metric information is also available separately in the form of Adobe font metrics (AFM) and Adobe composite font metrics (ACFM) files. These files are for use by application programs that generate PostScript language page descriptions and must make formatting decisions based on the widths and other metrics of characters. Kerning information is also available in the AFM and ACFM files. When possible, applications should use this information directly instead of generating PostScript language instructions to compute it.

Specifications for the AFM and ACFM file formats are available from the Adobe Systems Developers' Association.

5.5 Font Cache

The PostScript interpreter includes an internal data structure called the *font cache* whose purpose is to make the process of painting characters very efficient. For the most part, font cache operation is automatic. However, there are several operators that control the behavior of the font cache. Also, font definitions must adhere to certain conventions to take advantage of the font cache.

Rendering a character from an outline or other high-level description is a relatively costly operation, because it involves performing scan conversion of arbitrary shapes. This presents special problems for printing text, because it is common for several thousand characters to appear on a single page. However, a page description that includes large amounts of text normally has many repetitions of the same character in a given font, size, and orientation. The number of distinct characters thus is very much smaller than the total number of characters.

The font cache operates by saving the results of character scan conversions (including metric information and device pixel arrays) in temporary storage and using those saved results when the same character is requested again. The font cache is usually large enough to accommodate all of the distinct characters in a page description. Painting a character that is already in the font cache is typically hundreds of times faster than scan converting it from the character description in the font.

The font cache does not retain color information; it remembers only which pixels were painted and which pixels were left unchanged within the character's bounding box. For this reason, there are a few restrictions on the set of graphical operators that may be executed as part of character descriptions that are to be cached. In particular, the **image** operator is not permitted. However, **imagemask** may be used to define a character according to a bitmap representation; see section 4.10, "Images." Execution of operators that specify colors or other color-related parameters in the graphics state is also not permitted; see section 4.8, "Color Spaces."

The principal manifestation of the font cache visible to the PostScript language program is that showing a character does not necessarily result in the character's description being executed. This means that font definitions must interact with the font cache machinery so the results of their execution are properly saved. This is done by means of the **setcachedevice** or **setcachedevice2** operators, described in section 5.7, "Type 3 Fonts."

5.6   Modifications to Existing Fonts

This section applies to *base fonts*, whose **FontType** is any value other than 0. Composite fonts are described in section 5.9, "Composite Fonts."

A PostScript language program can create a font in two ways: by copying an existing font and modifying certain things in it, or by defining a new font from scratch. The programming examples given in this and the next section are compatible with Level 1 implementations. They can be significantly simplified by taking advantage of Level 2 features. Of course, doing so sacrifices Level 1 compatibility.

5.6.1   Changing the Encoding Vector

The most common modification to an existing font is installing a different encoding vector, discussed in section 5.3, "Character Encoding." Example 5.6 creates a copy of the Helvetica font in which the Adobe standard encoding for the Helvetica font is replaced by the ISO Latin-1 encoding, described in Appendix E.

Example 5.6

```
/Helvetica findfont
dup length dict begin
    {1 index /FID ne {def} {pop pop} ifelse} forall
    /Encoding ISOLatin1Encoding def
    currentdict
end
/Helvetica-ISOLatin1 exch definefont pop
```

This program performs the following steps:

1. Make a copy of the font dictionary including all entries, except the one whose name is **FID**.

2. Install the desired changes. This program replaces the font's **Encoding** with the value of **ISOLatin1Encoding**, which is a built-in, 256-element array of character names defined in **systemdict**.

3. Register this modified font under some new name—for example, Helvetica-ISOLatin1.

In Type 1 fonts, some accented characters are produced by combining two or more other characters (for example, a letter and an accent) defined in the same font. In Level 1 implementations, if an encoding vector includes the name of an accented character, it must also include the names of the components of that character.

Note   *If you create a new encoding for a Type 1 font, Adobe suggests that you place the accents in control character positions, which are typically unused. The built-in ISOLatin1Encoding uses this technique.*

5.6.2   Changing Character Metrics

To change a Type 1 font's metrics, add a **Metrics** entry to the font dictionary. The value of this entry should be another dictionary containing the new metric information.

Note   *It is possible to change a Type 1 font's metric information (character widths and sidebearings) on a per-character basis. However, determining a pleasing and correct character spacing is a difficult and laborious art that requires considerable skill. A font's character shapes have been designed with certain metrics in mind. Changing those metrics haphazardly will almost certainly produce poor results.*

The **Metrics** dictionary consists of entries in which the keys are character names, as they appear in the **CharStrings** dictionary and **Encoding** array. The values of these entries take various forms. Entries in the **Metrics** dictionary override the normal metrics for the corresponding characters. An entry's value may be:

• A single number, indicating a new x width only (the y value is zero).

• An array of two numbers, indicating the x components of a new left sidebearing and new width (the y values are zero).

- An array of four numbers, indicating x and y components of the left sidebearing followed by x and y components of the width.

These forms can be intermixed in one **Metrics** dictionary. All of the numeric values are in the character coordinate system of the font.

In a font that supports two writing modes (see section 5.4, "Font Metric Information"), the **Metrics** dictionary is used during writing mode 0. Another dictionary, **Metrics2**, is used during writing mode 1. The value of an entry in this dictionary must be an array of four numbers, which specify x and y components of *w1* followed by x and y components of *v* (see Figure 5.6 on page 273).

Whereas the **Metrics** and **Metrics2** dictionaries allow modifications of individual character metrics in a given font, a procedure named **CDevProc** allows global changes to a font's metrics to be algorithmically derived from the Type 1 metric data.

CDevProc, a Level 2 feature, is an optional entry in the font dictionary. If present, **CDevProc** is called after metrics information has been extracted from the character description and from the **Metrics** and **Metrics2** dictionaries, but immediately before the interpreter makes an internal call to **setcachedevice2**. Eleven operands are on the stack: the ten values that are to be passed to **setcachedevice2** followed by the character's name. On return, there should be ten values, which are then passed to **setcachedevice2**.

5.6.3 Replacing or Adding Individual Characters

It is also possible to add characters to existing Type 1 fonts. If the current font is a Type 1 font and an entry in the **CharStrings** dictionary is a PostScript language procedure instead of a Type 1 encrypted string, the PostScript interpreter executes the procedure to render the character.

This technique can be used to extend a Type 1 font that is already present in the VM of a PostScript interpreter. However, it should not be used to create a Type 1 font program for download purposes, as the font will *not* be compatible with any Type 1 font interpreter not containing a full PostScript language interpreter (for example, the Adobe Type Manager software).

The required behavior of such a "charstring procedure" is very similar to the **BuildGlyph** mechanism for Type 3 fonts, described in section 5.7, "Type 3 Fonts." The procedure must perform essentially the same functions as a Type 3 **BuildGlyph** procedure, including executing one of the

setcachedevice, **setcachedevice2**, or **setcharwidth** operators. Unlike the situation with **BuildGlyph**, there is potentially a different procedure for each character, although several characters can share one procedure.

The execution environment of a charstring procedure is slightly different from that of a Type 3 **BuildGlyph** procedure.

- Before executing a charstring procedure, the PostScript interpreter first pushes **systemdict** and then the font dictionary on the dictionary stack, and pushes either the character code or the character name on the operand stack. The operand is a character code if the interpreter is in the midst of an ordinary **show** or any **show** variant that takes a string operand. The operand is a character name if the interpreter is executing the **glyphshow** operator (a Level 2 feature).

- After executing the procedure, the PostScript interpreter pops the two dictionaries that it pushed on the dictionary stack. It expects the procedure to have consumed the character code or character name operand.

Because a charstring procedure must be able to accept either a character code or a character name as operand, it is strongly recommended that every charstring procedure begin as follows:

```
dup type /integertype eq {/Encoding load exch get} if
```

This ensures that the object on the stack is a name object, which the procedure can now use to look up the character description. If the character description is contained in the charstring procedure itself, the procedure can simply discard its operand.

The technique for extending a font, then, is to copy both the top-level dictionary and the **CharStrings** dictionary, add or replace entries in **CharStrings**, and define a new font. It is possible to replace .notdef the same as any other character.

5.7 Type 3 Fonts

This section describes how to construct a Type 3 font from scratch. A Type 3 font is one whose behavior is determined entirely by PostScript language procedures. Type 3 fonts must be carefully constructed. The PostScript interpreter assumes that such fonts will be reasonably well-behaved.

A Type 3 font *must:*

- Contain the required entries listed in Table 5.1 and Table 5.2.

- Have a **FontType** value of 3.

- Contain a procedure named **BuildChar**, and perhaps also one named **BuildGlyph**.

- Be able to render a character named .notdef.

Level 2 implementations support the **BuildGlyph** semantics, described in section 5.7.1, "BuildGlyph." Level 1 implementations support only the **BuildChar** semantics, described in section 5.7.2, "BuildChar."

5.7.1 BuildGlyph

When a PostScript language program tries to show a character from a Type 3 font, and the character is not already present in the font cache, the PostScript interpreter:

1. Uses the character code as an index into the current font's **Encoding** array, obtaining the corresponding character name. (This step is omitted during **glyphshow**.)

2. Pushes the current font dictionary and the character name on the operand stack.

3. Executes the font's **BuildGlyph** procedure. **BuildGlyph** must remove these two objects from the operand stack and use this information to construct the requested character. This typically involves determining the character definition needed, supplying character metric information, constructing the character shape, and painting it.

BuildGlyph is called within the confines of a **gsave** and a **grestore**, so any changes **BuildGlyph** makes to the graphics state do not persist after it finishes. Each call to **BuildGlyph** is independent of any other call. Because of the effects of font caching, no assumptions may be made about the order in which character descriptions will be executed. In particular, **BuildGlyph** should not depend on any non-constant information in VM, and it should not leave any side effects in VM or on stacks.

When **BuildGlyph** gets control, the current transformation matrix (CTM) is the concatenation of the font matrix (**FontMatrix** in the current font dictionary) and the CTM that was in effect at the time **show** was invoked. This means that shapes described in the character coordinate system will be transformed into the user coordinate system and will appear in the appropriate size and orientation on the page. **BuildGlyph** should describe the character in terms of absolute coordinates in the character coordinate system, placing the character origin at (0, 0) in this space. It should make no assumptions about the initial value of the current point parameter.

Aside from the CTM, the graphics state is inherited from the environment of the **show** operator (or **show** variant) that caused **BuildGlyph** to be invoked. To ensure predictable results despite font caching, **BuildGlyph** must initialize any graphics state parameters on which it depends. In particular, if **BuildGlyph** executes the **stroke** operator, **BuildGlyph** should explicitly set the line width, line join, line cap, and dash pattern to appropriate values. Normally, it is unnecessary and undesirable to initialize the current color parameter, because **show** is defined to paint characters with the current color.

Before executing the graphics operators that describe the character, **BuildGlyph** must execute one of the following operators to pass width and bounding box information to the PostScript interpreter:

- **setcachedevice** establishes a single set of metrics for both writing modes, and requests that the interpreter save the results in the font cache if possible.

- **setcachedevice2** establishes separate sets of metrics for writing modes 0 and 1, and requests that the interpreter save the results in the font cache. **setcachedevice2** is a Level 2 feature.

- **setcharwidth** passes just the character's width (to be used once only), and requests that the character *not* be cached. This is typically used only if the character description includes operators to set the color explicitly.

See the descriptions of **setcachedevice**, **setcachedevice2**, and **setcharwidth** in Chapter 8 for more information.

After executing one of these operators, **BuildGlyph** should execute a sequence of graphics operators to perform path construction and painting. The PostScript interpreter transfers the results into the font cache, if appropriate, and onto the page at the correct position. It also uses the width information to control the spacing between this character and the next. The final position of the current point in the character coordinate system does not influence character spacing.

5.7.2 BuildChar

In Level 2 implementations, if there is no **BuildGlyph** procedure for the font, the interpreter calls the **BuildChar** procedure instead. Level 1 implementations always call **BuildChar**, whether or not a **BuildGlyph** procedure is present.

The semantics of **BuildChar** are essentially the same as for **BuildGlyph**. The only difference is that **BuildChar** is called with the font dictionary and the *character code* on the operand stack, instead of the font dictionary and *character name*. The **BuildChar** procedure must then perform its own lookup to determine what character definition corresponds to the given character code.

For backward compatibility with the installed base of Level 1 interpreters, all new Type 3 fonts should contain the following **BuildChar** procedure:

```
/BuildChar {
    1 index /Encoding get exch get
    1 index /BuildGlyph get exec
}bind def
```

This defines **BuildChar** in terms of the same font's **BuildGlyph** procedure, which contains the actual commands for painting the character. This permits the font to be used with Level 2 features such as **glyphshow**, which requires **BuildGlyph** to be present, yet retains compatibility with Level 1 implementations.

5.7.3 Constructing a Type 3 Font

All Type 3 fonts must include a character named .notdef. The **BuildGlyph** procedure should be able to accept that character name regardless of whether such a character is encoded in the **Encoding** array. If the **BuildGlyph** procedure is given a character name that it does not recognize, it can handle that condition by painting the .notdef character instead.

Any Type 3 font that depends on Level 2 features to draw character shapes (for example, uses **glyphshow** or **rectfill**) should have an entry

```
/LanguageLevel 2 def
```

in the font dictionary. A file containing a font program should use appropriate document structuring comments (see Appendix G).

Example 5.7 shows the definition of a Type 3 font with only two characters—a filled square and a filled triangle—selected by the characters a and b. The character coordinate system is on a 1000-unit scale. This is not a realistic example, but it does illustrate all the elements of a Type 3 font, including a **BuildGlyph** procedure, an **Encoding** array, and a subsidiary dictionary for the individual character definitions.

Example 5.7

```
8 dict begin

/FontType 3 def                         % Required elements of font
/FontMatrix [.001 0 0 .001 0 0] def
/FontBBox [0 0 1000 1000] def

/Encoding 256 array def                 % Trivial encoding vector
0 1 255 {Encoding exch /.notdef put} for
Encoding 97 /square put                 % ASCII a = 97
Encoding 98 /triangle put               % ASCII b = 98
/CharProcs 3 dict def                   % Subsidiary dictionary for
CharProcs begin                         % individual character definitions
  /.notdef { } def
  /square
    {0 0 moveto 750 0 lineto 750 750 lineto
     0 750 lineto closepath fill} bind def
  /triangle
    {0 0 moveto 375 750 lineto 750 0 lineto
     closepath fill} bind def
end                                     % of CharProcs

/BuildGlyph {                           % Stack contains: font charname
  1000 0                                % Width
  0 0 750 750                           % Bounding box
  setcachedevice
  exch /CharProcs get exch              % Get CharProcs dictionary
  2 copy known not {pop /.notdef} if    % See if charname is known
  get exec                              % Execute character procedure
} bind def

/BuildChar {                            % Level 1 compatibility
  1 index /Encoding get exch get
```

```
    1 index /BuildGlyph get exec
} bind def

currentdict
end                                    % of font dictionary
/ExampleFont exch definefont pop

/ExampleFont findfont 12 scalefont setfont    % Now show some characters
36 52 moveto (ababab) show
```

Figure 5.7 *Output from Example 5.7*

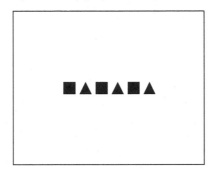

5.8 Unique ID Generation

A *unique ID* is an optional entry in a font dictionary that helps identify
the font to the interpreter. Its primary purpose is to identify cached
characters built from that font. The PostScript interpreter can retain
characters in the font cache even for a font that is not permanently in
VM. Some implementations can save cached characters on disk. This
can have a beneficial effect on performance when using fonts that are
loaded into VM dynamically either by explicit downloading or automatically via the resource facility.

If a font has a unique ID, the interpreter can recognize that the cached
characters belong to that font, even if the font dictionary itself is
removed from VM and is later reloaded (by a subsequent job, for
instance). If a font does not have a unique ID, the interpreter can recognize cached characters for that font only while it remains in VM. When
the font is removed, the cached characters must be discarded.

Correct management of unique IDs is essential to ensure predictable behavior. If two fonts have the same unique ID but produce characters with different appearances when executed, it is unpredictable which characters will appear when those fonts are used. Therefore, unique IDs must be assigned systematically from some central registry.

The reason that font caching is based on a special unique ID entry rather than on the font's name, or other identifying information, is that font names are not necessarily unique. A font with a particular name, such as Garamond-Bold, may be available from several sources, and there may be successive releases of a font from the same source.

For information about assigning unique IDs, consult *Adobe Type 1 Font Format*, or contact Adobe Systems Incorporated.

There are two kinds of unique ID entries that can appear in font dictionaries: **UniqueID** and **XUID**. Both kinds are described below. The **UniqueID** is supported by both Level 1 and Level 2 implementations; it applies only to fonts. The **XUID** is a Level 2 feature; it applies to fonts and also to certain other categories of resources. See section 4.7, "Forms," and section 4.9, "Patterns."

When you create a new font program that will be saved permanently and perhaps will be distributed widely, you should assign **UniqueID** and **XUID** values for that font and embed those values in the definition of the font dictionary. On the other hand, when an application program constructs a font as part of building a page description, it should not include a **UniqueID** or **XUID** in the font dictionary, because there is no opportunity for registering the ID, and there is little to be gained from doing so in any event.

When you copy a font dictionary for the purpose of creating a modified font, you should *not* copy the **UniqueID**. As an exception to this general rule, it is acceptable (and preferable) to retain the original **UniqueID** if the only modified entries are **FontName**, **FontInfo**, **FontMatrix**, or **Encoding**, because those changes do not affect the characters' appearance or metrics.

5.8.1 UniqueID Numbers

The **UniqueID** entry in a font dictionary is an integer in the range 0 to 16777215 (which is $2^{24} - 1$). Each **FontType** has its own space of **UniqueID** values. Therefore, a Type 1 font and a Type 3 font could have the same **UniqueID** number and be safely used together without causing conflicts in the font cache.

The **UniqueID** numbers for Type 1 fonts are controlled. Adobe Systems maintains a registry of **UniqueID** numbers for Type 1 fonts. The numbers between 4000000 and 4999999 are reserved for private interchange in closed environments and cannot be registered.

5.8.2 Extended Unique ID Numbers

An **XUID** (*extended unique ID*) is an entry whose value is an array of integers. **XUID** arrays provide for distributed, hierarchical management of the space of unique ID numbers. A font is uniquely identified by the *entire* sequence of numbers in the array. **XUID**s are a Level 2 feature. They are ignored by Level 1 implementations.

The first element of an **XUID** array must be a *unique organization identifier*, assigned by the Adobe registry. The remaining elements—and the allowed length of **XUID** arrays starting with that organization ID—are controlled by the organization to which the organization ID is assigned. An organization can establish its own registry for managing the space of numbers in the second and subsequent elements of **XUID** arrays, which are interpreted relative to the organization ID.

The organization ID value 1000000 is reserved for private interchange in closed environments. **XUID** arrays starting with this number may be of any length.

This scheme also makes it possible to derive unique identifiers systematically when modifying existing fonts. This is not possible for **UniqueID** values since the space of numbers is too small. A program can replace an **XUID** array with a longer **XUID** array whose additional elements indicate exactly what modifications have been performed.

PostScript interpreters that recognize the **XUID** array ignore **UniqueID** whenever an **XUID** is present. For backward compatibility with the installed base of interpreters, font creator and font modifier software should continue to use and maintain appropriate **UniqueID** numbers for the foreseeable future.

5.9 Composite Fonts

This section describes how to build hierarchical *composite fonts* from base fonts. All fonts in the PostScript language are considered *base fonts*, except those with a **FontType** of 0. Base fonts contain individual character descriptions; composite fonts are combinations of base fonts. The ability to use composite fonts is supported by all Level 2 implementations and some Level 1 implementations that have the composite font extensions.

A composite font is a collection of base fonts organized hierarchically. The font at the top level of the hierarchy is the *root font*. Fonts at a lower level of the hierarchy are called *descendant fonts*. When the current font is composite, the **show** operator (and its variants) behaves differently than it does with base fonts. It uses a mapping algorithm that decodes **show** strings to select characters from descendant base fonts. This organization enables any given **show** string to select characters from any of the descendant fonts.

The composite font facility supports the use of very large character sets, such as those for the Japanese and Chinese languages. It also simplifies the organization of fonts that have complex encoding requirements. There are many uses of composite fonts that are not immediately apparent from the language specification. For more examples, see the document *Tutorial on Composite Fonts*, available from the Adobe Systems Developers' Association.

In addition to the required entries listed in Table 5.1 on page 266, composite font dictionaries can contain the entries listed in Table 5.5.

Table 5.5 *Additional entries specific to Type 0 (composite) fonts*

Key	Type	Semantics
FMapType	integer	(*Required*) Indicates which mapping algorithm to use when interpreting the sequence of bytes in a string. See Table 5.6 on page 287.
Encoding	array	(*Required*) Array of integers, each used as an index to extract a font dictionary from the **FDepVector**. Note that this is different from the use of **Encoding** in base fonts.
FDepVector	array	(*Required*) Array of font dictionaries that are the descendants of this composite font.
PrefEnc	array	(*Optional*) Array that is usually the same as the **Encoding** array that is most commonly used by the descendant fonts. If this entry is not initially present, **definefont** inserts one with a null value.
EscChar	integer	(*Optional*) Escape code value, used only when **FMapType** is 3 or 7. If this entry is not present but is needed, **definefont** inserts one with the value 255.
ShiftOut	integer	(*Optional; Level 2 only*) Shift code value, used only when **FMapType** is 8. If this entry is not present but is needed, **definefont** inserts one with the value 14.

| **ShiftIn** | integer | (*Optional; Level 2 only*) Shift code value, used only when **FMapType** is 8. If this entry is not present but is needed, **definefont** inserts one with the value 15. |
| **SubsVector** | string | (*Optional*) User-defined mapping algorithm, used only when **FMapType** is 6. |

5.9.1 Character Mapping

FMapType is an integer that indicates which mapping algorithm will be used to interpret the sequence of bytes in a **show** string. Instead of each byte selecting a character independently, as is done for base fonts, the **show** string encodes a more complex sequence of font and character selections. The mapping algorithm:

1. Decodes bytes from the **show** string to determine a font number and a character code.

2. Uses the font number as an index into the **Encoding** array of the composite font, obtaining an integer.

3. Uses that integer in turn as an index into the **FDepVector** array, selecting a descendant font.

4. Uses the character code to select a character from the descendant font, in whatever way is appropriate for that font.

Table 5.6 lists the mapping algorithms that the **FMapType** value can select. If the mapping of any string passed to a **show** operator is incomplete or if a font number or character code indexes beyond the end of an **FDepVector** or **Encoding** array, a **rangecheck** error results.

Table 5.6 *FMapType mapping algorithms*

Algorithm	*FMapType*	*Explanation*
8/8 mapping	2	Two bytes are extracted from the **show** string. The first byte is the font number and the second byte is the character code.
escape mapping	3	One byte is extracted from the **show** string. If it is equal to the value of the **EscChar** entry, the next byte is the font number, and subsequent bytes (until the next escape code) are character codes for that font. At the beginning of a **show** string, font 0 is selected. A font number equal to the escape code is treated specially; see section 5.9.3, "Nested Composite Fonts."
1/7 mapping	4	One byte is extracted from the **show** string. The most significant bit is the font number, and the remaining 7 bits are the character code.

9/7 mapping	5	Two bytes are extracted from the **show** string and combined to form a 16-bit number, high-order byte first. The most significant 9 bits are the font number, and the remaining 7 bits are the character code.
SubsVector mapping	6	One or more bytes are extracted from the **show** string and decoded according to information in the **SubsVector** entry of the font. The format of **SubsVector** is described below.
double escape mapping	7	(*Level 2 only*) This mapping is very similar to **FMapType** 3. However, when an escape code is immediately followed by an escape code, a third byte is extracted from the **show** string. The font number is the value of this byte plus 256.
shift mapping	8	(*Level 2 only*) This mapping provides exactly two descendant fonts. A byte is extracted from the **show** string. If it is the **ShiftIn** code, subsequent bytes are character codes for font 0. If it is the **ShiftOut** code, subsequent bytes are character codes for font 1. At the beginning of a **show** string, font 0 is selected.

EscChar, **ShiftIn**, and **ShiftOut** are integers that determine the escape and shift code values used with **FMapType** values 3, 7, and 8. If one of these entries is required but is not present, **definefont** inserts an entry with a default value as specified in Table 5.5 on page 286.

SubsVector is a string that controls the mapping algorithm for a composite font with an **FMapType** of 6. This mapping algorithm allows the space of character codes to be divided into ranges, where each range corresponds to one descendant font. The ranges can be of irregular sizes that are not necessarily powers of two.

The first byte of a **SubsVector** string specifies one fewer than the *code length*—the number of bytes to be extracted from the **show** string for each operation of the mapping algorithm. A value of 0 specifies a code length of one byte, 1 specifies two bytes, and so on. When a character code is longer than one byte, the bytes comprising it are interpreted high-order byte first. The code length cannot exceed the number of bytes representable in an integer (see Appendix B).

The remainder of the **SubsVector** string defines a sequence of ranges of consecutive code values. The first range is the one for font 0, the second range is the one for font 1, and so on. Each range is described by one or more bytes; the number of bytes is the same as the code length. The value contained in those bytes (interpreted high-order byte first) gives the *size* of the code range. There is an implicit code range at the end of the sequence that contains all remaining codes. This range should not be specified explicitly.

When using a **SubsVector**, the **show** operator interprets a character code extracted from the show string as follows:

1. Determine the code range that contains the character code. The position of the code range in the **SubsVector** sequence (counting from zero) is used as the index into the font's **Encoding** array, selecting a descendant font.

2. Subtract the base of the code range from the character code. The result is treated as a character code to select a character from the descendant font.

The following examples show how several of the other mapping algorithms could be described in terms of the **SubsVector** mapping. This is for illustrative purposes only. The other mapping algorithms should be used rather than the **SubsVector** mapping if they achieve the desired effect. The **SubsVector** strings are shown as hexadecimal string literals.

- 1/7 mapping: <00 80>
  The code length is one byte. There are two code ranges. The first one is explicitly of length 80 hex. It contains character codes 0 to 127 decimal. The second code range implicitly contains all remaining characters that can be coded in one byte—that is, character codes in the range 128 to 255.

- 9/7 mapping: <01 0080 0080 ... 0080>
  The code length is two bytes. There are up to 512 code ranges, each 80 hex (128 decimal) in size. The **SubsVector** string that describes all 512 code ranges would be 1023 bytes long. Remember that the last code range is specified implicitly.

- 8/8 mapping: <01 0100 0100 ... 0100>
  The code length is two bytes. There are up to 256 code ranges, each 100 hex (256 decimal) in size. The **SubsVector** string that describes all 256 code ranges would be 511 bytes long. The last code range is specified implicitly.

Note   *Escape and shift mappings cannot be described in terms of the* **SubsVector** *mapping.*

5.9.2   Other Dictionary Entries for Composite Fonts

FontMatrix plays the same role in a composite font as it does in a base font. When a character is shown, both the **FontMatrix** of the composite font and the **FontMatrix** of the descendant base font are concatenated to the CTM.

WMode is an integer with value 0 or 1, indicating which of two sets of character metrics will be used when characters from the base fonts are shown (see section 5.4, "Font Metric Information"). If it is omitted, writing mode 0 will be used. The writing mode of the root composite font overrides the writing modes of all its descendants. This allows a given base font to be used as part of many composite fonts, some of which use writing mode 0 and some of which use writing mode 1.

PrefEnc (preferred encoding) is an array that should be the same as the **Encoding** array of one or more of the descendant fonts. Characters from descendant fonts whose **Encoding** is the same as the **PrefEnc** of the parent will be processed more efficiently than characters from other descendant fonts. If this entry is not present, a null entry will be created by **definefont**.

A composite font dictionary should be large enough to have three additional entries—named **FID**, **MIDVector**, and **CurMID**—added to it by **definefont**. These entries serve internal purposes in the font machinery. In addition, a **PrefEnc** entry will be added if one is not already present, and escape and mapping fonts will have any required **EscChar**, **ShiftIn**, or **ShiftOut** entries added if not already present.

5.9.3   Nested Composite Fonts

The descendant fonts of a composite font may themselves be composite fonts, nested to a maximum depth of five levels. The mapping algorithms nest according to two sets of rules, depending on whether the composite fonts are modal or non-modal.

Fonts with **FMapType** 3, 7, or 8 are *modal* fonts, in that some byte codes select a descendant font, and then successive bytes of the **show** string are interpreted with respect to the selected font until a new descendant font is selected. Modal fonts follow these rules:

- The parent of an **FMapType** 3 font must be either **FMapType** 3 or 7. The **EscChar** of the root font overrides the **EscChar** of descendant escape-mapped fonts.

- Fonts with **FMapType** 7 and 8 may not be used as descendant fonts.

- Occurrence of an escape or shift code in the **show** string causes the mapping algorithm to ascend the font hierarchy from the currently-selected descendant font to the nearest parent modal font. If that font's **FMapType** is 8, the algorithm selects the new descendant according to the shift code. If the **FMapType** is 3 or 7, the algorithm extracts another byte from the **show** string. If the byte is not an escape code, the algorithm uses it as a font number to select a descendant of that font. But if the byte is an escape code and the **FMapType** is 3, the algorithm ascends to the parent of that font, extracts yet another byte from the **show** string, and repeats the selection process.

The other **FMapType** values (2, 4, 5, 6) are *non-modal,* in that their mapping algorithm restarts for each new character. Non-modal fonts follow these rules:

- The parent of a non-modal font may be any type of composite font, including a modal font.

- If the parent of a non-modal font is a modal font, the modal font's escape or shift code is recognized only when it appears as the *first* byte of a multi-byte mapping sequence for the non-modal font.

- If the descendant of a non-modal composite font is itself a non-modal composite font, the second part (character code) of the value extracted from the **show** string is reused as the first part of the descendant font's mapping algorithm.

The **FontMatrix** entries of nested composite fonts are treated in a non-obvious way. When a character is shown, the interpreter consults the **FontMatrix** entries of only the selected base font and the immediate parent of the base font. The immediate parent's **FontMatrix** contains the concatenation of the **FontMatrix** entries of all ancestor fonts. To achieve this, **definefont** concatenates the root font's **FontMatrix** to the **FontMatrix** entries of all descendant composite fonts, but not base fonts. Similarly, **makefont** and **scalefont** apply their transformations to all descendant composite fonts.

CHAPTER 6

Rendering

The PostScript language separates *graphics* (the specification of shapes and colors) from *rendering* (controlling a raster output device). Figure 4.5 and Figure 4.6 on pages 178 and 179 show this division. Chapter 4 also explains the facilities for describing the appearance of pages in a device independent way. This chapter explains the facilities for controlling how shapes and colors are rendered on the raster output device. Use of any of these facilities requires knowing the characteristics of the device. A PostScript language program that is intended to be device independent should not access any of the facilities described in this chapter.

Nearly all of the rendering facilities that are under program control have to do with the reproduction of color. The interpreter renders colors by a multiple-step process outlined below. Depending on the current color space and on the characteristics of the device, it is not always necessary to perform every step.

1. If a color has been specified in a CIE-based color space, as described in section 4.8, "Color Spaces," the interpreter must first transform it to one of the device color spaces (**DeviceRGB**, **DeviceCMYK**, or **DeviceGray**) appropriate for the raster output device. This transformation is controlled by a CIE-based *color rendering dictionary.*

2. If a color has been specified in a device color space that is inappropriate for the output device (for example, RGB color with a CMYK or gray-scale device), the interpreter invokes a *color conversion function.* A PostScript language program can also request explicit conversions between device color spaces.

3. The interpreter now maps the device color values through *transfer functions*, one for each component. The transfer functions compensate for peculiarities of the output device, such as non-linear gray-level response. This step is sometimes called *gamma correction.*

4. If the device cannot reproduce continuous tones, but only certain discrete colors, such as black and white pixels, the interpreter invokes a *halftone function*, which approximates the desired colors by means of patterns of pixels.

5. Finally, the interpreter performs *scan conversion* to paint the appropriate pixels of the raster output device with the requested colors.

Level 1 and Level 2 implementations of the PostScript language differ in the facilities they offer for rendering:

- CIE-based color spaces and CIE-based color rendering dictionaries are supported only in Level 2 implementations.

- Most Level 1 implementations support only a single transfer function controlled by the **settransfer** operator and a single halftone function controlled by the **setscreen** operator.

- Level 1 implementations with the color extensions support multiple transfer functions controlled by **setcolortransfer**, multiple halftone functions controlled by **setcolorscreen**, and various color conversion facilities. These operators provide separate control over rendering each of four color components. The Level 1 products containing this feature also support the **setcmykcolor** and **colorimage** operators.

- Level 2 implementations and the Display PostScript system also offer *halftone dictionaries*. A halftone dictionary is an object that can contain halftone screen thresholds, transfer functions, and many other rendering details. Halftone dictionaries are more general and more flexible than the Level 1 facilities, and they override those facilities when used. Of course, Level 2 implementations fully support the Level 1 facilities.

6.1 CIE-Based Color to Device Color

As discussed in section 4.8, "Color Spaces," the CIE-based color spaces are mathematically related to the CIE 1931 (XYZ)-space, which is based on a model of human color perception. To render CIE-based colors on a device, a PostScript interpreter must convert from the specified CIE-based color space to the device's native color space, taking into account the known properties of the device. The goal of this process is to produce output that accurately reproduces the requested CIE-based color values as perceived by a human observer. CIE-based color specification and rendering are supported only by Level 2 implementations.

The conversion from CIE-based color to device color is complex; the theory on which it is based is beyond the scope of this manual (see the bibliography). The algorithm has many parameters, including an optional, full three-dimensional color lookup table. The color fidelity of the output depends on these parameters being properly set, usually by a procedure that includes some form of calibration. Each product includes a default set of color rendering parameters that have been chosen to produce reasonable output based on the nominal characteristics of the device. The PostScript language does not prescribe procedures for calibrating the device or for computing a proper set of color rendering parameters.

Conversion from a CIE-based color value to a device color value requires two main operations:

1. Adjust the CIE-based color value according to a *CIE-based gamut mapping function*. A gamut is a subset of all possible colors in some color space. A page description has a *source gamut* consisting of all colors that it uses. A device has a *device gamut* which consists of all colors it can reproduce. This step transforms colors from the source gamut to the device gamut in a way that preserves color appearance and visual contrast.

2. Generate a corresponding device color value according to a *CIE-based color mapping function*. For a given CIE-based color value, this function computes a color value in the device's native color space.

The CIE-based gamut and color mapping functions are applied only to color values presented in a CIE-based color space. By definition, color values in device color spaces directly control the device color components.

The source gamut is specified by a page description when it selects a CIE-based color space by executing **setcolorspace**. This specification, which includes the values defined by the **WhitePoint** and **BlackPoint** entries of the parameter dictionary of **setcolorspace**, is device independent.

The device gamut, the gamut mapping function, and the color mapping function are described together by a *CIE-based color rendering dictionary*, which is a parameter of the graphics state that is set when the device is installed or recalibrated. Everything in this dictionary is device dependent. The **setcolorrendering** operator installs a color rendering dictionary in the graphics state; **currentcolorrendering** returns the current color rendering dictionary.

6.1.1 CIE-Based Color Rendering Dictionaries

The CIE-based gamut and color mapping functions, embodied by the color rendering dictionary, are defined in an extensible way. The PostScript language supports one standard type of color rendering dictionary, which works in all implementations. Some products support additional types of color rendering dictionaries that select other, possibly proprietary, gamut and color mapping methods. The set of available types and the meanings of specific color rendering dictionaries are product dependent. They are not described in this manual but in product documentation.

Most of the entries in a color rendering dictionary together define a composite color rendering function that transforms CIE-based color values to device color values by applying the gamut and color mapping functions. The output from this color rendering function is subject to further transformations—device color space conversion, transfer function, and halftoning. Device color space conversion is not normally needed, because a properly defined dictionary will produce output in the device's native color space.

Every color rendering dictionary must have a **ColorRenderingType** key whose value is an integer. The value specifies the architecture of the composite color rendering function as a whole. The remaining entries in the dictionary are interpreted according to this value.

6.1.2 Type 1 Color Rendering Dictionary

The type 1 color rendering dictionary is a standard part of the PostScript language. Some products support other types, and the default color rendering dictionary in any particular product may have a type other than 1.

The type 1 color rendering is based on the **CIEBasedABC** color space, which is a two-stage, non-linear transformation of the CIE 1931 (XYZ)-space. This space is called the *render color space*. Values in this space can be treated in one of two ways:

- Used directly as color values in the **DeviceRGB** or **DeviceGray** color space.

- Used to index a three-dimensional lookup table that in turn contains color values to be interpreted in the **DeviceRGB** or **DeviceCMYK** color space.

The first method usually works well with additive, linear color devices, which include many black and white and color displays. The second method is required for high-fidelity reproductions with most color printers, whose color rendition cannot be described by a simple formula.

Conceptually, conversion of a color value from a CIE-based color space to a device color space involves the following steps. In reality, the implementation does not perform these steps in sequence but in combination. Furthermore, there are important special cases in which the effects of two or more of the steps cancel out. The implementation detects these cases and omits the unnecessary transformations.

1. Transform the CIE-based color value from its original color space (**CIEBasedABC** or **CIEBasedA**) to the CIE 1931 (XYZ)-space. This transformation depends on various parameters of the color space.

2. Adjust the X, Y, and Z values to account for differences in the **WhitePoint** and **BlackPoint** of the source and the device. This transformation attempts to preserve color appearance and visual contrast, according to the **MatrixPQR** and **TransformPQR** entries of the color rendering dictionary. The diffuse white and black points of the source are given as the **WhitePoint** and **BlackPoint** parameters of the color space; the diffuse white and black points of the device are given by the **WhitePoint** and **BlackPoint** entries of the color rendering dictionary. If the corresponding **WhitePoint** and **BlackPoint** entries in the color space and color rendering dictionary are equal, this step reduces to the identity transformation.

3. Transform the color value from the CIE 1931 (XYZ)-space into the render color space according to the **MatrixLMN**, **EncodeLMN**, **MatrixABC**, and **EncodeABC** entries of the CIE-based color rendering dictionary, producing three components A, B, and C. (These have nothing to do with the A, B, and C components of color values in the source **CIEBasedABC** or **CIEBasedA** color spaces.)

4. If a **RenderTable** entry is present in the color rendering dictionary, use the A, B, and C components to index into this three-dimensional lookup table, yielding an interpolated color value. This value consists of three or four color components, depending on how the table is defined. Each of these components is transformed by a procedure to produce color components in device color space. If there are three components, they specify red, green and blue values according to

the **DeviceRGB** color space. If there are four components, they specify cyan, magenta, yellow, and black according to the **DeviceCMYK** color space.

If there is no **RenderTable** entry, use the A, B, and C components as the device color value directly. If the device's native color space is **DeviceGray**, the A component specifies the gray value and the B and C components are ignored. Otherwise, the A, B, and C components specify the red, green, and blue values, respectively, according to the **DeviceRGB** color space.

Table 6.1 describes the key-value pairs that a type 1 color rendering dictionary can contain and specifies the details of the transformations.

Table 6.1 *Entries in a type 1 CIE-based color rendering dictionary*

Key	Type	Semantics
ColorRenderingType	integer	(*Required*) Must be 1.
MatrixLMN	array	(*Optional*) Array of nine numbers $[L_X \ M_X \ N_X \ L_Y \ M_Y \ N_Y \ L_Z \ M_Z \ N_Z]$ that specify the linear interpretation of the X, Y, and Z components of the CIE 1931 (XYZ)-space with respect to an intermediate LMN representation. This is explained below. Default value: the identity matrix [1 0 0 0 1 0 0 0 1].
EncodeLMN	array	(*Optional*) Array of three PostScript language procedures $[E_L \ E_M \ E_N]$ that encode the L, M, and N components of the intermediate LMN representation. Default value: the array of identity procedures [{} {} {}].

Each of these procedures is called with an unencoded L, M, or N component on the operand stack and must return the corresponding encoded value. The result must be a monotonic function of the operand. Because these procedures are called at unpredictable times and in unpredictable environments, they must operate as pure functions without side effects.

The transformation defined by the **MatrixLMN** and **EncodeLMN** entries is:

$$L = E_L (X \times L_X + Y \times L_Y + Z \times L_Z)$$

$$M = E_M (X \times M_X + Y \times M_Y + Z \times M_Z)$$

$$N = E_N (X \times N_X + Y \times N_Y + Z \times N_Z)$$

In other words, the X, Y, and Z components of the CIE 1931 (XYZ)-space are treated as a three element vector and multiplied by **MatrixLMN** (a three by three matrix). The results are individually transformed by the **EncodeLMN** procedures to provide the L, M, and N components of the intermediate LMN representation.

RangeLMN	array	(*Optional*) Array of six numbers $[L_0 \ L_1 \ M_0 \ M_1 \ N_0 \ N_1]$ that specify the range of valid values for the L, M, and N components of the intermediate LMN representation—that is, $L_0 \leq L \leq L_1$, $M_0 \leq M \leq M_1$, and $N_0 \leq N \leq N_1$. Default value: [0 1 0 1 0 1].

MatrixABC   array   (*Optional*) Array of nine numbers $[A_L\ B_L\ C_L\ A_M\ B_M\ C_M\ A_N\ B_N\ C_N]$ that specify the linear interpretation of the encoded L, M, and N components of the intermediate LMN representation with respect to the render color space. This is explained below. Default value: the identity matrix $[1\ 0\ 0\ 0\ 1\ 0\ 0\ 0\ 1]$.

EncodeABC   array   (*Optional*) Array of three PostScript language procedures $[E_A\ E_B\ E_C]$ that encode the A, B, and C components of the color space. Default value: the array of identity procedures $[\{\}\ \{\}\ \{\}]$.

Each of these procedures is called with an unencoded A, B, or C component on the operand stack and must return the corresponding encoded value. The result must be a monotonic function of the operand. Because these procedures are called at unpredictable times and in unpredictable environments, they must operate as pure functions without side effects.

The transformation defined by the **MatrixABC** and **EncodeABC** entries is:

$$A = E_A\,(L \times A_L + M \times A_M + N \times A_N)$$

$$B = E_B\,(L \times B_L + M \times B_M + N \times B_N)$$

$$C = E_C\,(L \times C_L + M \times C_M + N \times C_N)$$

RangeABC   array   (*Optional*) Array of six numbers $[A_0\ A_1\ B_0\ B_1\ C_0\ C_1]$ that specify the range of valid values for the A, B, and C components—that is, $A_0 \leq A \leq A_1$, $B_0 \leq B \leq B_1$, and $C_0 \leq C \leq C_1$. If there is no **RenderTable** entry, these ranges must lie within the range 0 to 1, since the render color space maps directly onto a device color space. If a **RenderTable** entry is present, these ranges define the boundaries of the three-dimensional lookup table. Default value: $[0\ 1\ 0\ 1\ 0\ 1]$.

WhitePoint   array   (*Required*) Array of three numbers $[X_W\ Y_W\ Z_W]$ that specify the CIE 1931 (XYZ)-space tristimulus value of the device's diffuse white point. The numbers X_W and Z_W must be positive and Y_W must be equal to 1.

WhitePoint is assumed to represent the device's diffuse, achromatic highlight, and hence its value must correspond to the nearly lightest, achromatic color that the device can produce. A color somewhat darker that the absolutely lightest color may be used to avoid blocking of highlights and to provide some flexibility for rendering specular highlights.

BlackPoint   array   (*Optional*) Array of three numbers $[X_B\ Y_B\ Z_B]$ that specify the CIE 1931 (XYZ)-space tristimulus value of the device's diffuse black point. These numbers must be non-negative. Default value: $[0\ 0\ 0]$.

BlackPoint is assumed to represent the device's diffuse, achromatic shadow. Its value is defined by the nearly darkest, nearly achromatic color that the device can produce. A color somewhat lighter than the absolutely darkest color may be used to avoid blocking of shadows. A slightly chromatic color may be used to increase dynamic range in situations where the darkest color that the device can produce is slightly chromatic.

MatrixPQR	array	(*Optional*) Array of nine numbers $[P_X\ Q_X\ R_X\ P_Y\ Q_Y\ R_Y\ P_Z\ Q_Z\ R_Z]$ that specify the linear interpretation of the X, Y, and Z components of the CIE 1931 (XYZ)-space, respectively, with respect to an intermediate PQR representation. This is explained below. Default value: the identity matrix $[1\ 0\ 0\ 0\ 1\ 0\ 0\ 0\ 1]$.
RangePQR	array	(*Optional*) Array of six numbers $[P_0\ P_1\ Q_0\ Q_1\ R_0\ R_1]$ that specify the range of valid values for the P, Q, and R components of the intermediate PQR representation— that is, $P_0 \le P \le P_1$, $Q_0 \le Q \le Q_1$, and $R_0 \le R \le R_1$. Default value: $[0\ 1\ 0\ 1\ 0\ 1]$.
TransformPQR	array	(*Required*) Array of three PostScript language procedures $[T_P\ T_Q\ T_R]$ that transform the P, Q, and R components of the intermediate PQR representation in a way that accommodates for the differences between the source's and the device's diffuse white and black points while preserving color appearance and visual contrast.

Let X_{Ws}, Y_{Ws}, Z_{Ws} and X_{Bs}, Y_{Bs}, Z_{Bs} be the CIE 1931 (XYZ)-space tristimulus values of the source's diffuse white and black points, respectively. Let X_{Wd}, Y_{Wd}, Z_{Wd} and X_{Bd}, Y_{Bd}, Z_{Bd} be the CIE 1931 (XYZ)-space tristimulus values of the device's diffuse white and black points. Then the source and device tristimulus values X_s, Y_s, Z_s and X_d, Y_d, Z_d in the CIE 1931 (XYZ)-space, respectively, are related by the **MatrixPQR** and **TransformPQR** entries as follows:

$$P_s = X_s \times P_X + Y_s \times P_Y + Z_s \times P_Z$$
$$Q_s = X_s \times Q_X + Y_s \times Q_Y + Z_s \times Q_Z$$
$$R_s = X_s \times R_X + Y_s \times R_Y + Z_s \times R_Z$$

$$P_d = T_P(W_s, B_s, W_d, B_d, P_s)$$
$$Q_d = T_Q(W_s, B_s, W_d, B_d, Q_s)$$
$$R_d = T_R(W_s, B_s, W_d, B_d, R_s)$$

$$X_d = P_d \times X_P + Q_d \times X_Q + R_d \times X_R$$
$$Y_d = P_d \times Y_P + Q_d \times Y_Q + R_d \times Y_R$$
$$Z_d = P_d \times Z_P + Q_d \times Z_Q + R_d \times Z_R$$

where

$$W_s = [X_{Ws}\ Y_{Ws}\ Z_{Ws}\ P_{Ws}\ Q_{Ws}\ R_{Ws}]$$
$$B_s = [X_{Bs}\ Y_{Bs}\ Z_{Bs}\ P_{Bs}\ Q_{Bs}\ R_{Bs}]$$
$$W_d = [X_{Wd}\ Y_{Wd}\ Z_{Wd}\ P_{Wd}\ Q_{Wd}\ R_{Wd}]$$
$$B_d = [X_{Bd}\ Y_{Bd}\ Z_{Bd}\ P_{Bd}\ Q_{Bd}\ R_{Bd}]$$

$$P_{Ws} = X_{Ws} \times P_X + Y_{Ws} \times P_Y + Z_{Ws} \times P_Z$$
$$Q_{Ws} = X_{Ws} \times Q_X + Y_{Ws} \times Q_Y + Z_{Ws} \times Q_Z$$
$$R_{Ws} = X_{Ws} \times R_X + Y_{Ws} \times R_Y + Z_{Ws} \times R_Z$$

$$P_{Bs} = X_{Bs} \times P_X + Y_{Bs} \times P_Y + Z_{Bs} \times P_Z$$
$$Q_{Bs} = X_{Bs} \times Q_X + Y_{Bs} \times Q_Y + Z_{Bs} \times Q_Z$$
$$R_{Bs} = X_{Bs} \times R_X + Y_{Bs} \times R_Y + Z_{Bs} \times R_Z$$

$$P_{Wd} = X_{Wd} \times P_X + Y_{Wd} \times P_Y + Z_{Wd} \times P_Z$$
$$Q_{Wd} = X_{Wd} \times Q_X + Y_{Wd} \times Q_Y + Z_{Wd} \times Q_Z$$
$$R_{Wd} = X_{Wd} \times R_X + Y_{Wd} \times R_Y + Z_{Wd} \times R_Z$$

$$P_{Bd} = X_{Bd} \times P_X + Y_{Bd} \times P_Y + Z_{Bd} \times P_Z$$
$$Q_{Bd} = X_{Bd} \times Q_X + Y_{Bd} \times Q_Y + Z_{Bd} \times Q_Z$$
$$R_{Bd} = X_{Bd} \times R_X + Y_{Bd} \times R_Y + Z_{Bd} \times R_Z$$

$$\begin{bmatrix} X_P & Y_P & Z_P \\ X_Q & Y_Q & Z_Q \\ X_R & Y_R & Z_R \end{bmatrix} = \begin{bmatrix} P_X & Q_X & R_X \\ P_Y & Q_Y & R_Y \\ P_Z & Q_Z & R_Z \end{bmatrix}^{-1}$$

In other words, the X_s, Y_s, and Z_s components of the source color in CIE 1931 (XYZ)-space are treated as a three element vector and multiplied by **MatrixPQR** (a three by three matrix), yielding the P_s, Q_s, and R_s components of the source color with respect to the intermediate PQR representation. These components are individually transformed by the **TransformPQR** procedures, producing the P_d, Q_d, and R_d components of the corresponding device color. Each of the components is transformed separately; there is no interaction between components. Finally, the P_d, Q_d, and R_d components of the device color are treated as a three element vector and multiplied by the inverse of **MatrixPQR**. The results provide the X_d, Y_d, and Z_d components of the device color in the CIE 1931 (XYZ)-space.

The transformation embodied by the **TransformPQR** procedures usually consists of two conceptually separate processes. The first allows for the chromatic adaptation involved when the two diffuse white points differ. The second allows for the contrast adaptation involved when the dynamic ranges between the two sets of diffuse white and black points differ.

In addition to the appropriate P_s, Q_s, or R_s component, each of the **TransformPQR** procedures takes the additional four operands W_s, B_s, W_d, and B_d that specify the source's diffuse white and black points and the device's diffuse white and black points, respectively. Each of these operands is an array of six elements giving the white or black point twice: once in CIE 1931 (XYZ)-space and again in PQR space.

Each of these procedures is called with the four W_s, B_s, W_d, and B_d arrays and the appropriate P_s, Q_s, or R_s component on the operand stack (in that order) and must return the corresponding transformed P_d, Q_d, or R_d component. The result must be a monotonic function of the last operand. Because these procedures are called at unpredictable times and in unpredictable environments, they must operate as pure functions without side effects.

RenderTable   array   (Optional) Array of the form $[N_A \ N_B \ N_C \ table \ m \ T_1 \ T_2 \ ... \ T_m]$, which, if present, describes a three-dimensional lookup table that maps colors in render color space to colors in device color space via table look-up and interpolation. The table contains $N_A \times N_B \times N_C$ entries, each of which consists of m encoded color component values. The element m must be the integer 3 or 4; N_A, N_B, and N_C must be integers greater than 1. The entry at integer coordinates (a, b, c) in the table, where $0 \le a < N_A$, $0 \le b < N_B$, and $0 \le c < N_C$, contains the encoded device color value that corresponds to render color space components A, B, and C, where:

$$A = A_0 + a \times (A_1 - A_0) / (N_A - 1)$$
$$B = B_0 + b \times (B_1 - B_0) / (N_B - 1)$$
$$C = C_0 + c \times (C_1 - C_0) / (N_C - 1)$$

The values A_0, A_1, B_0, B_1, C_0, and C_1 are given in the **RangeABC** entry.

The element *table* must be an array of N_A strings, which define the contents of the lookup table. Each string must contain $m \times N_B \times N_C$ characters. Within the string at index a in the array, the m characters starting at position $m \times (b \times N_C + c)$ constitute the table entry at location (a, b, c). These characters are interpreted as encoded device color components e_1, e_2, ... e_m, which are integers in the range 0 to 255.

The elements T_1, T_2, ... T_m are PostScript language procedures that transform the interpolated, encoded components to device color component values. These transformations are:

$$d_1 = T_1 (e_1 / 255)$$
$$d_2 = T_2 (e_2 / 255)$$
$$...$$
$$d_m = T_m (e_m / 255)$$

In other words, the interpreter divides an encoded component by 255, producing a number in the range 0 to 1, and pushes it on the operand stack. It then calls the appropriate T procedure, which is expected to consume its operand and produce a result in the range 0 to 1. Because these procedures are called at unpredictable times and in unpredictable environments, they must operate as pure functions without side effects.

The values d_1, d_2, ... d_m constitute the final device color value. That is, if m is 3, then d_1, d_2, and d_3 are the red, green, and blue components; if m is 4, then d_1, d_2, d_3, and d_4 are the cyan, magenta, yellow, and black components.

6.2 Conversions Among Device Color Spaces

Each raster output device has a *native* device color space, which corresponds to one of the PostScript language color spaces **DeviceGray**, **DeviceRGB**, or **DeviceCMYK**. In other words, the device supports reproduction of colors according to a gray-scale (monochrome), red-green-blue, or cyan-magenta-yellow-black model. If the device supports continuous-tone output, reproduction occurs directly. Otherwise, it is accomplished by means of halftoning.

The PostScript interpreter knows the native color space and other output capabilities of the device. It can automatically convert color values as specified in a document to the appropriate color values for the native color space of the device. For example, if a PostScript language program specifies colors in the **DeviceRGB** color space, but the device supports gray scale, such as a monochrome display, or CMYK, such as a color printer, the interpreter performs the necessary conversions. If a program specifies colors in the device's native color space, no conversions are necessary.

A program can also request explicit conversions among device color spaces by executing the operators **currentgray**, **currentrgbcolor**, **currenthsbcolor**, or **currentcmykcolor**, which return color values according to specific color spaces. These operators are described in section 4.8.2, "Device Color Spaces." Conversions between **DeviceRGB** and **DeviceGray** are supported by all implementations. Conversions to and from **DeviceCMYK** are a Level 2 feature.

Note   *These operators can convert colors only among device color spaces, not to or from CIE-based or special color spaces.*

The conversions described here do not involve use of transfer functions or halftone functions. When colors are to be rendered on the output device, the transfer functions and halftone functions are applied at a later stage to the *output* of the color conversion operation. When colors are simply read back by a PostScript language program by executing one of the above-mentioned operators, the transfer functions and halftone functions are not applied at all.

The algorithms used to convert among device color spaces are very simple. As perceived by a human viewer, the conversions produce only crude approximations of the original colors. Device color conversions ordinarily are not performed when a program specifies colors in CIE-based color spaces; the CIE-based color rendering functions map directly to the device's native color space (see section 6.1, "CIE-Based Color to Device Color").

6.2.1 Conversion Between DeviceRGB and DeviceGray

Black, white, and intermediate shades of gray can be considered special cases of RGB color. A gray-scale value is described by a single number: 0 corresponds to black, 1 to white, and intermediate values to different gray levels.

A gray value is equivalent to an RGB value with all three components the same. In other words, the RGB color value equivalent to a specific gray value is simply:

$red = gray$
$green = gray$
$blue = gray$

The gray value for a given RGB value is computed according to the NTSC video standard. This standard determines how a color television signal is rendered on a black and white television.

$$gray = .3 \times red + .59 \times green + .11 \times blue$$

Colors specified according to the HSB (hue-saturation-brightness) model are equivalent to those specified in the RGB model, but expressed in a different coordinate system called the "hexcone" model. See the bibliography. Either form of specification produces colors in the **DeviceRGB** color space. HSB is not a color space in its own right.

6.2.2 Conversion Between DeviceCMYK and DeviceGray

Nominally, a gray value is the complement of the black component of CMYK. Therefore, the CMYK color value equivalent to a specific gray value is simply:

$cyan = 0.0$
$magenta = 0.0$
$yellow = 0.0$
$black = 1.0 - gray$

To obtain the gray value for a given CMYK value, one must take the contributions of all components into account.

$$gray = 1.0 - \min(1.0, .3 \times cyan + .59 \times magenta + .11 \times yellow + black)$$

The interactions between the black component and the other three are explained below.

6.2.3   Conversion from DeviceRGB to DeviceCMYK

Conversion of a color value from RGB to CMYK is a two-step process. The first step is described by the equations that express the relationship between red-green-blue and cyan-magenta-yellow. The second step is to use black generation and undercolor removal to generate a black component and alter the other components to produce a better approximation of the original color.

The subtractive color primaries *cyan*, *magenta*, and *yellow* are the complements of the additive primaries *red*, *green*, and *blue*. For example, a cyan ink subtracts the red component of white light. In theory, the conversion is very simple:

$$cyan = 1.0 - red$$
$$magenta = 1.0 - green$$
$$yellow = 1.0 - blue$$

For example, a color that is 0.2 red, 0.7 green, and 0.4 blue can also be expressed as $1.0 - 0.2 = 0.8$ cyan, $1.0 - 0.7 = 0.3$ magenta, and $1.0 - 0.4 = 0.6$ yellow.

Logically, only cyan, magenta, and yellow are needed to generate a printing color. An equal percentage of cyan, magenta, and yellow should create the equivalent percentage of black.

In reality, colored printing inks do not mix perfectly; such combinations often form dark brown shades instead. It is often desirable to substitute real black ink for the mixed-black portion of a color to obtain a truer color rendition on a printer. Most color printers support a black component (the K component of CMYK). Computing the quantity of this component requires some additional steps:

- *Black generation* calculates the amount of black to be used when trying to reproduce a particular color.

- *Undercolor removal* reduces the amount of cyan, magenta, and yellow components to compensate for the amount of black that was added by the black generation.

Flexibility in performing these functions is important for achieving good results under a variety of printing conditions. The PostScript language provides limited control over black generation and undercolor removal when converting from **DeviceRGB** to **DeviceCMYK** color spaces. Applications requiring finer control must specify colors in CIE-based color spaces and control conversion to CMYK by means of the CIE-based color rendering dictionary (see section 6.1, "CIE-Based Color to Device Color").

The complete conversion from RGB to CMYK is as follows, where BG (k) and UCR (k) are invocations of the black generation and undercolor removal functions, respectively:

$c = 1.0 - red$
$m = 1.0 - green$
$y = 1.0 - blue$
$k = \min (c, m, y)$

$cyan = \min (1.0, \max (0.0, c - UCR (k)))$
$magenta = \min (1.0, \max (0.0, m - UCR (k)))$
$yellow = \min (1.0, \max (0.0, y - UCR (k)))$
$black = \min (1.0, \max (0.0, BG(k)))$

The black generation and undercolor removal functions are defined as PostScript language procedures. The **setblackgeneration** and **setundercolorremoval** operators set these parameters in the graphics state. The interpreter calls these procedures when it needs to perform RGB to CMYK conversion. Each procedure is called with a single numeric operand and is expected to return a single numeric result. The procedures are called at unpredictable times, so they must operate as pure functions without side effects.

The operand of both procedures is k, the minimum of the intermediate c, m, and y values that have been computed by subtracting the original *red*, *green*, and *blue* values from 1. Nominally, k is the amount of black that can be removed from the cyan, magenta, and yellow components and be substituted as a separate black component.

The black generation function computes the black component as a function of the nominal k value. It can simply return its k operand or it can return a larger value for extra black, a smaller value for less black, or zero for no black at all.

The undercolor removal function computes the amount that is to be subtracted from each of the intermediate *c*, *m*, and *y* values to produce the final cyan, magenta, and yellow components. It can simply return its *k* operand or it can return zero (so no color is removed), some fraction of the black amount, or even a negative amount, thereby adding to the total amount of ink.

The component values that result from black generation and undercolor removal are expected to be in the range 0 to 1. If a value falls outside this range, the nearest valid value is substituted automatically, without error indication. This is indicated explicitly by invocations of *min* and *max* operations in the formulas given above.

The correct choice of black generation and undercolor removal functions depends on the characteristics of the output device—for example, how inks mix. Each device is configured with default values that are appropriate for that device.

6.2.4 Conversion from DeviceCMYK to DeviceRGB

Conversion of a color value from CMYK to RGB is a simple operation that does not involve the black generation or undercolor removal functions:

$red = 1.0 - \min (1.0, cyan + black)$
$green = 1.0 - \min (1.0, magenta + black)$
$blue = 1.0 - \min (1.0, yellow + black)$

In other words, the black component is simply added to each of the other components. Then those components are converted to their complementary colors by subtracting each of them from 1.

6.3 Transfer Functions

A transfer function adjusts the values of color components to compensate for non-linear response in an output device and in the human eye. Each component of a device color space—for example, the red component of the **DeviceRGB** color space—is intended to represent the perceived lightness or intensity of that component in proportion to the numeric value. Many devices do not behave this way; a transfer function can compensate for the device's actual behavior. This operation is sometimes called *gamma correction* (not to be confused with the *CIE-based gamut mapping function* performed as part of CIE-based color rendering).

In the sequence of steps for processing colors, the PostScript interpreter applies the transfer function *after* performing conversions between color spaces, if necessary, but *before* applying the halftone function, if necessary. A separate transfer function applies to each color component. There is no interaction between components.

Transfer functions operate in the *native* color space of the output device regardless of the color space in which colors were originally specified. For example, for a CMYK device, the transfer functions apply to the device's cyan, magenta, yellow, and black color components, even if the colors were originally specified in, say, the **DeviceRGB** or **CIEBasedABC** color space.

There are three ways to specify transfer functions:

- The **settransfer** operator establishes a single transfer function to be applied to all color components of the device. Most Level 1 implementations support only a single transfer function.

- The **setcolortransfer** operator establishes four separate transfer functions, one each for red, green, blue, and gray or their complements cyan, magenta, yellow, and black. An RGB device uses the first three; a monochrome device uses the gray transfer function only, and a CMYK device uses all four. **setcolortransfer** is supported in Level 2 and in certain Level 1 implementations, primarily those in color printers.

- The **sethalftone** operator can establish transfer functions as optional entries in *halftone dictionaries* (see section 6.4.3, "Halftone Dictionaries"). This is the only way to set transfer functions for separation color components—those that are not primary colors for the device. Transfer functions specified in halftone dictionaries override those specified by **settransfer** or **setcolortransfer**. Halftone dictionaries are supported by all Level 2 and Display PostScript implementations.

A transfer function is a PostScript language procedure that can be called with a number in the range 0.0 to 1.0 (inclusive) on the operand stack and must return a number in the same range. The procedure's operand is the value of a color component in the device's native color space, either specified directly or produced by conversion from some other color space. The procedure's result is the transformed value that is to be transmitted to the device (after halftoning, if necessary).

The operand and result of a transfer function are always interpreted as if the component were *additive*—red, green, blue, or gray. That is, larger numbers indicate lighter colors. If the component is *subtractive* (cyan, magenta, yellow, black, or a separation), the PostScript interpreter converts it to additive form by subtracting it from 1.0 before passing it to the transfer function. The result from the transfer function is always in additive form; it is passed on to the halftone function in this form.

The PostScript interpreter calls transfer functions at unpredictable times and in unpredictable environments. A transfer function procedure must behave as a pure function. It must not depend on variable data other than its operand, and it must not have side effects.

In addition to their intended use for gamma correction, transfer functions can be used to produce a variety of special, device-dependent effects. For example, on a monochrome device, the transfer function

{1 exch sub}

inverts the output colors, producing a negative rendition of the page. In general, this method does not work for color devices; inversion can be more complicated than merely inverting each of the components. Because the effects produced are device dependent, transfer functions should not be altered by a page description that is intended to be device independent.

When the current color space is **DeviceGray** and the output device's native color space is **DeviceCMYK**, the interpreter uses only the gray transfer function. The normal conversion from **DeviceGray** to **DeviceCMYK** produces 0 for the cyan, magenta, and yellow components. Those components are *not* passed through their respective transfer functions, but are rendered directly, producing output containing no colored inks. This special case applies *only* to colors specified in the **DeviceGray** color space. It exists for compatibility with existing applications that use **settransfer** to obtain special effects on monochrome devices.

6.4 Halftones

Halftoning is the process by which continuous-tone colors are approximated by a pattern of pixels that can achieve only a limited number of discrete colors. The most familiar case of this is rendering of gray tones with black and white pixels, as in a newspaper photograph.

If halftoning is required, it occurs after all color components have been transformed by the appropriate transfer function. The input to the halftone function consists of continuous-tone, gamma-corrected color components in the device's native color space. The output consists of pixels representing colors the device can reproduce.

Some devices can reproduce continuous-tone colors directly. For such devices, halftoning is not required. After gamma correction by the transfer functions, the color components are transmitted directly to the device.

The PostScript language provides a high degree of control over details of the halftoning process. For example, in color printing, one must specify independent halftone screens for each of three or four color separations. When rendering on low-resolution displays, one must have fine control over halftone patterns to achieve the best approximations of gray levels or colors, and to minimize visual artifacts.

Note   *Remember that everything pertaining to halftones is, by definition, device dependent. In general, when an application provides its own halftone specifications, it sacrifices portability. Associated with every device is a default halftone definition that is appropriate for most applications. Only relatively sophisticated applications need to define their own halftones to achieve special effects.*

All halftones are defined in *device space*, unaffected by the current transformation matrix. For correct results, a PostScript language program that defines a new halftone must know the resolution and orientation of device space. The best choice of halftone parameters often depends on specific physical properties of the output device—for example, pixel shape, overlap between pixels, and effects of electronic or mechanical noise.

6.4.1 How Halftones Are Defined

There are three ways to specify halftones:

- The **setscreen** operator establishes a single halftone screen that is to be applied to all color components of the device. The halftone screen can be specified in only one way: as frequency, angle, and spot function. Most Level 1 implementations support only a single halftone screen.

- The **setcolorscreen** operator establishes four separate halftone screens, one each for red, green, blue, and gray or their complements cyan, magenta, yellow, and black. An RGB device uses the first three, a monochrome device uses the gray screen only, and a CMYK device uses all four. **setcolorscreen** is supported in Level 2 and in certain Level 1 implementations, primarily those in color printers.

- The **sethalftone** operator installs a halftone dictionary, which can describe any of several types of halftones. The dictionary contains the parameters of the halftoning algorithm, either for all components together or for each component separately. It optionally contains other rendering controls, such as transfer functions.

sethalftone is the most general way to specify halftones. Any halftone that can be defined in the other two ways can also be defined as a halftone dictionary. However, halftone dictionaries are supported only in Level 2 and Display PostScript implementations, whereas **setscreen** (and sometimes **setcolorscreen**) is available in Level 1 implementations.

The **setscreen** operator specifies a halftone screen by three operands: *frequency*, *angle*, and *spot function*. These operands are interpreted the same as the **Frequency**, **Angle**, and **SpotFunction** entries in a type 1 halftone dictionary, described in section 6.4.4, "Spot Functions." This is the only form of halftone specification supported in most Level 1 implementations.

For compatibility between Level 1 and Level 2 implementations, the **setscreen**, **setcolorscreen**, **sethalftone**, **currentscreen**, **currentcolorscreen**, and **currenthalftone** operators interact in various ways to ensure reasonable behavior when a halftone that has been defined in one way is read out in a different way. The details of these interactions are given in the descriptions of the six operators.

6.4.2 How Halftone Screens Work

The halftone functions supported by the PostScript language are based on the use of a *halftone screen*. A screen is defined by conceptually laying a uniform rectangular grid of *halftone cells* over the device pixel array. Each pixel belongs to one cell of the grid; a halftone cell usually contains many device pixels. The screen grid is defined entirely in device space, unchanged by modifications to the current transformation matrix (CTM). This property is essential for ensuring that adjacent areas colored by halftones are properly stitched together without "seams."

For a black and white device, each cell of a screen can be made to approximate a shade of gray by painting some of the cell's pixels black and some white. Numerically, the gray level produced within a cell is the ratio of the cell's pixels that are white to the total number of pixels in that cell. If a cell contains n pixels, then it can render $n + 1$ different gray levels: all pixels black, one pixel white, two pixels white, ... $n - 1$ pixels white, all n pixels white. A desired gray value g in the range 0 to 1 is produced by making i pixels white, where $i = \mathrm{floor}(g \times n)$.

The foregoing description also applies to color output devices whose pixels consist of primary colors that are either completely on or completely off. Most color printers, but not color displays, work this way. Halftoning is applied to each color component independently, producing shades of that color.

Color components are presented to the halftoning machinery in *additive* form, regardless of whether they were originally specified in additive (RGB or gray) or subtractive (CMYK or tint) form. Larger values of a color component represent lighter colors—greater intensity in an additive device, such as a display, and less ink in a subtractive device, such as a printer. Transfer functions produce color values in additive form. See section 6.3, "Transfer Functions."

6.4.3 Halftone Dictionaries

A *halftone dictionary* is a dictionary object whose entries are parameters to the halftoning machinery. The graphics state includes a *current halftone dictionary,* which specifies the halftoning process to be used by the painting operators. The operator **currenthalftone** returns the current halftone dictionary. **sethalftone** establishes a different halftone dictionary as the current one. The halftone dictionary is a feature of Level 2 and Display PostScript implementations. In Level 1 implementations, the **setscreen** operator controls halftoning in a more limited way.

A halftone dictionary is a self-contained description of a halftoning process. Painting operations, such as **fill**, **stroke**, and **show**, consult the current halftone dictionary when they require information about the halftoning process. The interpreter consults the halftone dictionary at unpredictable times. It can cache the results internally for later use. For these reasons, once a halftone dictionary has been passed to **sethalftone**, its contents should be considered read only. Some of the entries in the dictionary are procedures that are called to compute the required information. Such procedures must compute results that depend only on information in the halftone dictionary, not on outside information—for example, the graphics state itself—and they must not have side effects.

Note   *This rules out certain techniques, such as the "pattern fill" example in the PostScript Language Tutorial and Cookbook, that depend on the spot function being executed at predictable times. Such techniques work for halftones defined by* **setscreen**, *but not for halftones defined by halftone dictionaries. See section 4.9, "Patterns," for recommended ways to create device-independent patterns.*

Every halftone dictionary must have a **HalftoneType** entry whose value is an integer. This specifies the major type of halftoning process. The remaining entries in the dictionary are interpreted according to the type. Table 6.2 lists the standard halftone types.

Table 6.2 *Types of halftone dictionaries*

Type	Semantics
1	Defines a single halftone screen by *frequency*, *angle*, and *spot function*. The **setscreen** operator, available in Level 1, also defines halftones this way, but it expects the parameters to be given as separate operands instead of being bundled into a halftone dictionary.
2	Defines four separate halftone screens, one for each primary color component. Each screen is given as a frequency, angle, and spot function.
3	Defines a single halftone screen directly by a *threshold array* at device resolution.
4	Defines four separate halftone screens, one for each primary color component. Each screen is given as a threshold array.
5	(*Level 2*) Defines an arbitrary number of halftone screens, one for each color component, including both primary and separation (spot color) components. The keys in this dictionary are names of color components. The values are halftone dictionaries (type 1 or 3), each of which describes the halftone screen for a single color component.

6.4.4 Spot Functions

A halftone dictionary whose **HalftoneType** is 1 defines a halftone screen according to a *frequency*, *angle*, and *spot function*. The **setscreen** operator, which is available in Level 1 implementations, defines a halftone screen given a *frequency*, *angle*, and *spot function* as operands. Whichever way it is defined, this type of halftone screen works as described below. The features that can be specified by optional entries in the halftone dictionary are not available for screens defined by **setscreen** or by **setcolorscreen**.

The halftone screen grid has a *frequency* (number of halftone cells per inch) and *angle* (orientation of the grid lines relative to the device coordinate system). The **sethalftone** or **setscreen** operator may make slight adjustments to the requested frequency and angle to ensure that the patterns of enclosed pixels remain constant as the screen cells are replicated over the entire page.

Figure 6.1 *Various halftoning effects*

| 150/inch at 45° round dot screen | 100/inch at 45° round dot screen | 50/inch at 45° round dot screen | 75/inch at 30° line screen |

As a cell's desired gray value varies from black to white, individual pixels in the cell change from black to white in a well-defined sequence. If a particular gray includes certain white pixels, lighter grays will include the same white pixels and some additional pixels. The order in which pixels change from black to white for increasing gray levels is specified by a *spot function*, which is defined by a PostScript language procedure. The spot function describes the order of pixel whitening in an indirect way that minimizes interactions with screen frequency and angle.

Consider a halftone cell to have its own coordinate system: The center of the square is the origin and the corners are at ±1 in x and y. In this system, each pixel in the cell is centered at x and y coordinates that are both in the range –1 to 1. For each pixel, the interpreter pushes the pixel's coordinates on the operand stack and calls the spot function procedure. The procedure must return a single number in the range –1 to 1 that defines the pixel's position in the ordering.

The values the spot function returns are not significant. All that matters is the *relative* spot function values for different pixels. As a cell's gray value varies from black to white, the first pixel whitened is the one whose spot function has the lowest value, the next pixel is the one with the next higher spot function value, and so on. If two pixels have the same spot function value, **setscreen** chooses their relative order arbitrarily.

There are relatively simple spot functions that define common halftone patterns. A spot function whose value is inversely related to the distance from the center of the cell produces a "dot screen" in which the black pixels are clustered within a circle whose area is inversely proportional to the gray level. An example of such a spot function is:

{180 mul cos exch 180 mul cos add 2 div}

A spot function whose value is the distance from a line through the center of the cell produces a "line screen" in which the white pixels grow away from that line. More complex patterns are occasionally useful.

Table 6.3 *Entries in a type 1 halftone dictionary*

Key	Type	Semantics
HalftoneType	integer	(*Required*) Must be 1.
Frequency	number	(*Required*) Screen frequency, measured in halftone cells per inch in device space.
Angle	number	(*Required*) Screen angle: Number of degrees by which the screen is to be rotated with respect to the device coordinate system.
SpotFunction	procedure	(*Required*) Procedure that defines the order in which device pixels within a screen cell are adjusted for different gray levels.
AccurateScreens	boolean	(*Optional; Level 2*) If present and the value is *true*, invokes a special halftone algorithm that is extremely precise, but computationally expensive.
ActualFrequency	number	(*Optional; Level 2*) If present, **sethalftone** replaces its value with the actual frequency that was achieved.
ActualAngle	number	(*Optional; Level 2*) If present, **sethalftone** replaces its value with the actual angle that was achieved.
TransferFunction	procedure	(*Optional; Level 2*) Overrides the transfer function specified by **settransfer** or **setcolortransfer**. Required in a type 1 halftone dictionary that is used as an element of a type 5 halftone dictionary for a non-primary color component.

A type 1 halftone dictionary can optionally contain the key **AccurateScreens**, with a boolean value. If the value is *true*, a highly precise halftoning algorithm is enabled; if it is *false* or if the **AccurateScreens** entry is not present, ordinary halftoning is used. Accurate halftoning achieves the requested screen angle and frequency with very high accuracy, whereas ordinary halftoning adjusts the angle and frequency so a single screen cell is quantized to device pixels. High accuracy is important mainly for making color separations on high-resolution devices. However, it may be computationally expensive and so is ordinarily disabled.

When **AccurateScreens** is *true*, **sethalftone** intentionally defers calling the spot function until the screen is needed by some operator (for example, **fill**) that renders marks on the current page. This means that the **sethalftone** operator itself executes quickly. The potentially high cost of building the screen is not incurred until the screen is used. This makes it convenient to obtain **ActualFrequency** and **ActualAngle** values for various candidate screens without incurring the cost of building them.

If the entries **ActualFrequency** and **ActualAngle** appear in the halftone dictionary, the **sethalftone** operator replaces their values with the actual frequency and angle that were achieved. The **Frequency** and **Angle** entries remain undisturbed; they reflect the values that were requested by the program.

In principle, the PostScript language permits defining screens with arbitrarily large cells—in other words, arbitrarily low frequencies. However, cells that are very large relative to device resolution or that are at unfavorable angles may exceed available memory. If this occurs, **setscreen** or **sethalftone** executes a **limitcheck** error. The **AccurateScreens** feature often requires very large amounts of memory to achieve highest accuracy. See Appendix C for information on system parameters affecting halftone screens.

6.4.5 Threshold Arrays

A halftone dictionary whose **HalftoneType** is 3 defines a halftone as an array of threshold values that directly control individual device pixels in a halftone cell. This provides a high degree of control over halftone rendering. Also, it permits halftone cells to be rectangular, whereas halftone cells defined by a spot function are always square. Both of these capabilities are important for low-resolution display devices.

A *threshold array* is much like a sampled image: It is a rectangular array of pixel values. However, it is defined entirely in device space, and the sample values always occupy 8 bits each. The pixel values nominally represent gray levels in the usual way, where 0 is black and 255 is white. The threshold array is replicated to tile the entire device space; each pixel of device space is mapped to a particular sample of the threshold array. On a bi-level device, where each pixel is either black or white, halftoning with a threshold array proceeds as follows:

- For each device pixel that is to be painted with some gray level, consult the corresponding pixel of the threshold array.

- If the desired gray level is less than the pixel value in the threshold array, paint the device pixel black; otherwise, paint it white. Gray values in the range 0 to 1 (inclusive) correspond to pixel values 0 to 255 in the threshold array.

Note   *A threshold value of 0 is treated as if it were 1; therefore, a gray value of 0 paints all pixels black, regardless of what is in the threshold array.*

This scheme easily generalizes to monochrome devices with multiple bits per pixel. For example, if there are 2 bits per pixel, then each pixel can directly represent one of four different gray levels: black, dark gray, light gray, and white, encoded as 0, 1, 2, and 3, respectively. For each device pixel that is to be painted with some in-between gray level, the algorithm consults the corresponding pixel of the threshold array to determine whether to use the next-lower or next-higher representable gray level. In this situation, the samples in the threshold array do not represent absolute gray values, but rather gradations between two adjacent representable gray levels.

A halftone defined in this way can also be used with color displays that have a limited number of values for each color component. The red, green, and blue values are simply treated independently as gray levels. The same threshold array applies to each color. (This technique also works for a screen defined as a spot function, since the interpreter uses the spot function to compute a threshold array internally.)

Table 6.4 *Entries in a type 3 halftone dictionary*

Key	Type	Semantics
HalftoneType	integer	(*Required*) Must be 3.
Width	integer	(*Required*) Width of threshold array, in pixels.
Height	integer	(*Required*) Height of threshold array, in pixels.

Thresholds	string	(*Required*) Threshold values. This string must be *width* × *height* characters long. The individual characters represent threshold values as described above. The order of pixels is the same as for a sampled image mapped directly onto device space, with the first sample at device coordinates (0, 0) and *x* coordinates changing faster than *y* coordinates.
TransferFunction	procedure	(*Optional; Level 2*) If present, overrides the transfer function specified by **settransfer** or **setcolortransfer**. Required in a type 3 halftone dictionary used as an element of a type 5 halftone dictionary for a non-primary color component.

6.4.6   HalftoneType 5 Dictionaries

Some devices, particularly color printers, require different halftones for each of the device's color components. Also, devices that can produce named separations may require individual halftones for each of those separations. The **HalftoneType** 5 dictionary allows specification of individual halftones for an arbitrary number of color components.

A type 5 halftone dictionary contains entries whose keys are separation or colorant names and whose values are halftone dictionaries. The keys are the separation names used as operands of the **setcolorspace** operator for the **Separation** color space (see section 4.8.4, "Special Color Spaces"). The values are type 1 or type 3 halftone dictionaries, each of which describes the halftone and transfer function for a single separation or colorant.

The primary colors are named **Red**, **Green**, and **Blue** in an RGB device; **Cyan**, **Magenta**, **Yellow**, and **Black** in a CMYK device; and **Gray** in a monochrome device. In a device that supports named separations, non-primary separations can have arbitrary names. The keys can be either names or strings, which are treated equivalently.

A type 5 halftone dictionary must also contain an entry whose key is **Default**. The value of this entry is the halftone dictionary to be used for any separation that does not have its own entry.

When a type 1 or type 3 halftone dictionary appears as the value of an entry in a type 5 halftone dictionary, it applies only to a single color component. This is in contrast to such a dictionary appearing as the main halftone dictionary (operand to **sethalftone**), which applies to all color components.

If non-primary separations are requested when the current halftone is defined by any means other than a type 5 halftone dictionary, the gray screen and transfer function are used for all such separations.

6.4.7 Other Types of Halftone Dictionaries

There are two additional standard halftone types. However, their use is not recommended because the same effects can be obtained using the type 5 halftone dictionary, described above. They are supported only for compatibility with existing Display PostScript applications.

The type 2 halftone dictionary is similar to type 1, but it defines four halftone screens—as frequency, angle, and spot function—instead of just one. Each primary color has its own screen. In place of a **Frequency** entry, the dictionary has entries named **RedFrequency**, **GreenFrequency**, **BlueFrequency**, and **GrayFrequency**. Likewise, in place of the **Angle** and **SpotFunction** entries, the dictionary has entries named **RedAngle**, **RedSpotFunction**, and so on. The optional entries of a type 1 halftone dictionary are not available in a type 2 halftone dictionary.

The type 4 halftone dictionary is similar to type 3, but it defines four halftone screens (as threshold arrays) instead of just one. **Width**, **Height**, and **Thresholds** are replicated for each color, just as in a type 2 halftone dictionary. Optional entries are not available.

There are many techniques for rendering halftones in addition to those supported as a standard part of the PostScript language. Some techniques work well only with certain types of output device technology, or they require special hardware to work efficiently.

Some products support special halftone techniques, in addition to the standard ones. The **HalftoneType** entry in the halftone dictionary selects the halftone technique to be used. It also determines how the other entries in the dictionary are to be interpreted. The set of available types and the meanings of specific types are product dependent. They are not described in this manual, but rather in product documentation.

Ordinarily, a page description should not define halftone dictionaries with non-standard types; doing so ties the page description to a specific product. Indeed, *any* use of halftone dictionaries in a page description compromises device independence.

In some products, a device's *default* halftone dictionary may have a non-standard type. This arises when a non-standard halftone technique is the one best suited to the device technology. A program that executes **currenthalftone** may obtain a halftone dictionary whose **HalftoneType** it doesn't recognize.

6.5 Scan Conversion Details

The final step of rendering is *scan conversion*. As discussed in section 2.2, "Scan Conversion," the PostScript interpreter executes a scan conversion algorithm to paint graphics, text, and images in the raster memory of the output device.

The specifics of the scan conversion algorithm are *not* defined as part of the PostScript language. Different implementations can perform scan conversion in different ways; techniques that are appropriate for one device may be inappropriate for another. Most scan conversion details are not under program control.

Still, it is useful to have a general understanding of how scan conversion works. When creating applications that are intended to drive computer displays, one must pay some attention to scan conversion details. At the low resolutions that are typical of displays, variations of even one pixel's width can have a noticeable effect on the appearance of painted shapes.

The following sections describe the scan conversion algorithms that are typical of Level 2 and Display PostScript implementations from Adobe, including the basic rules and the effects of using the automatic stroke adjustment feature. Once again, these details are *not* a standard part of the PostScript language.

6.5.1 Scan Conversion Rules

The following rules determine which device pixels a painting operation will affect. All references to coordinates and pixels are in device space. A "shape" is a path to be painted with the current color or with an image. Its coordinates are mapped into device space, but not rounded to device pixel boundaries. At this level, curves have been flattened to sequences of straight lines, and all "insideness" computations have been performed.

Pixel boundaries always fall on integer coordinates in device space. A pixel is a square region identified by the coordinates of its minimum x, minimum y corner. A pixel is a *half-open* region, meaning that it includes half of its boundary points. More precisely, for any point whose real number coordinate is (x, y), let $i = floor(x)$ and $j = floor(y)$. The pixel that contains this point is the one identified as (i, j). The region belonging to that pixel is defined to be the set of points (x', y') such that $i \leq x' < i + 1$ and $j \leq y' < j + 1$.

Like pixels, shapes to be painted by operators such as **fill** or **stroke** are also treated as half-open regions that include the boundaries along their "floor" sides, but not along their "ceiling" sides.

A shape is scan converted by painting any pixel whose square region intersects the shape, no matter how small the intersection is. This ensures that no shape ever disappears as a result of unfavorable placement relative to the device pixel grid, as might happen with other possible scan conversion rules. The area covered by painted pixels is always at least as large as the area of the original shape.

This scan conversion rule applies to both fill operations and to strokes with non-zero width. Zero-width strokes are done in a device-dependent manner that may include fewer pixels than this rule specifies.

The region of device space to be painted by the **image** operator is determined similarly to that of a filled shape, though not identically. The interpreter transforms the image source rectangle into device space and defines a half-open region, just as for fill operations. However, only those pixels whose *centers* lie within the region are painted. The position of the *center* of such a pixel—in other words, the point whose coordinate values have fractional parts of one-half—is mapped back into source space to determine how to color the pixel. There is no averaging over the pixel area; if the resolution of the source image is higher than that of device space, some source samples will not be used.

For clipping, the clip region consists of the set of pixels that would be included by a **fill**. A subsequent painting operation affects a region that is the intersection of the set of pixels defined by the clip region with the set of pixels for the region to be painted.

Scan conversion of character shapes is performed by a different algorithm than the one above. That font rendering algorithm uses hints in the character descriptions and techniques that are specialized to character rasterization.

6.5.2 Automatic Stroke Adjustment

When a stroke is drawn along a path, the scan conversion algorithm may produce lines of non-uniform thickness because of rasterization effects. In general, the line width and the coordinates of the endpoints, transformed into device space, are arbitrary real numbers not quantized to device pixels. A line of a given width can intersect with a different number of device pixels, depending on where it is positioned. Figure 6.2 shows this.

Figure 6.2 *Rasterization without stroke adjustment*

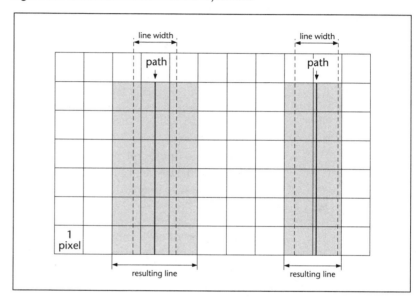

For best results, it is important to compensate for the rasterization effects to produce strokes of uniform thickness. This is especially important in low-resolution display applications. To meet this need, Level 2 and Display PostScript implementations provide an optional *stroke adjustment* feature. When stroke adjustment is enabled, the line width and the coordinates of a stroke are automatically adjusted as necessary to produce lines of uniform thickness. The thickness is as near as possible to the requested line width—no more than half a pixel different.

Note   *If stroke adjustment is enabled and the requested line width, transformed into device space, is less than half a pixel, the stroke is rendered as a single-pixel line. This is the thinnest line that can be rendered at device resolution. It is equivalent to the effect produced by setting the line width to zero (see section 6.5.1, "Scan Conversion Rules").*

Because automatic stroke adjustment can have a substantial effect on the appearance of lines, an application must be able to control whether or not the adjustment is to be performed. The operator **setstrokeadjust** alters a boolean value in the graphics state that determines if stroke adjustment will be performed during subsequent **stroke** and related operators.

CHAPTER 7

Display PostScript

This chapter introduces the concepts and PostScript language operators specific to display applications. Display PostScript system features are not part of Level 2.

The Display PostScript system provides application programs with a device-independent imaging model for displaying information on a screen. It is only a component of a complete application programming environment, consisting of:

- The PostScript interpreter.

- The Client Library, a C language interface to the basic facilities of the Display PostScript system.

- *pswrap*, a preprocessor that facilitates invoking arbitrary PostScript language programs from a C program.

- Window system support libraries, such as one for the X Window System™.

- Operating system, runtime library, and libraries of higher-level tools.

This chapter describes the PostScript language extensions that are supported by the interpreter in a Display PostScript system. Other components of the application programming environment are described in a separate document, the *Display PostScript System Reference Manual*. The language extensions include:

- *Multiple execution contexts*. The Display PostScript system can support the execution of multiple independent PostScript language programs at the same time.

- *User name encodings.* The Client Library can dynamically encode arbitrary name objects as small integers instead of as full text strings, resulting in improved efficiency.

- *Support for windowing systems.* These features extend the imaging model to deal with special display-specific requirements, including incremental update, hit detection, and halftone phase adjustment.

- *Bitmap font coordination.* The Display PostScript system provides support for hand-tuned screen resolution bitmap fonts to improve legibility of text.

7.1 Multiple Execution Contexts

The Display PostScript system can support multiple, concurrent execution contexts. Each context has an environment consisting of stacks, local and global VM, graphics state, and certain variables, such as VM allocation mode and array packing mode. Except for VM, a context's environment is entirely private to that context and is never visible to any other context. Under suitable conditions, a context's VM can be shared with other contexts.

7.1.1 Creating Contexts

Applications normally access the Display PostScript system through the *Client Library*, which includes procedures for creating, communicating with, and destroying PostScript execution contexts. The Client Library facilities are not part of the PostScript language definition; they are described in the *Display PostScript System Reference Manual*.

When an application creates a context, it chooses whether the context is to share VM with some other existing context. The choices are:

1. Local and global VM are completely private to the context.

2. Local VM is private to the context, but global VM is shared with some other context.

3. Local and global VM are shared with some other context.

The Client Library procedure that creates a context provides a means to specify how the new context's VM is to be set up and which other context's VM, if any, it is to share. A PostScript language program can also create a context by executing the **fork** operator, which always uses method 3.

Method 1 creates a context that is completely isolated from other contexts. The context has its own private **userdict**, **globaldict**, and other standard dictionaries, all of which have their standard initial contents. A context that is to operate as a "job server," supporting the encapsulated job model described in section 3.7.7, "Job Execution Environment," must be created by method 1, because the semantics of job encapsulation conflict with the semantics of shared VM.

Method 2 creates a context with its own private local VM but sharing the global VM of one or more other contexts. In other words, objects in local VM, such as **userdict**, are private to the context; objects in global VM, such as **globaldict** and **GlobalFontDirectory**, are shared with the other contexts. When one context modifies the value of a global object, the effect is immediately visible to the other contexts.

Method 3 creates a context that shares both the local VM and the global VM of one or more other contexts. When one context modifies the value of *any* object in VM, the effect is immediately visible to the other contexts.

7.1.2 Context Operators

For the context operators, a *context* is an integer that identifies a PostScript execution context. Each context has a unique identifier, whether it was created by calling a Client Library procedure or by executing the **fork** operator. This integer identifies the context during communication between the application and the Display PostScript system, and during execution of the **join** and **detach** operators. Identifiers for contexts that have terminated become invalid and are not reused during the lifetime of any currently active session. The **currentcontext** operator returns the identifier for the context that is executing.

The **fork** operator creates a new context that shares the local and global VM of the context that executes **fork**. One of the operands to **fork** is a procedure the new context is to execute. The remaining operands are used to initialize the new context's operand stack.

The **join** operator waits for a context that was previously created by **fork** to return from its top-level procedure. It then copies that context's operand stack to the caller's operand stack and destroys the context. If there is no need for the context to return results when it terminates, it can declare this by means of the **detach** operator.

A context can *suspend* its own execution by any of a variety of means: execute the **wait**, **monitor**, or **yield** operators (described below) or return from its top-level procedure to await a **join**. The context retains the state it had at the moment of suspension and can ordinarily be resumed from the point of suspension.

A context can *terminate* by executing the **quit** operator or as a result of an explicit termination request from the Client Library. Termination also occurs if an error occurs that is not caught by an explicit use of **stopped**. When a context terminates, its stacks are destroyed, its standard input and output files are closed, and its context identifier becomes invalid.

There is no hierarchical relationship among contexts. Termination of a context has no effect on other contexts that it may have created. An integer that identifies a context has the same meaning in every context; it may be referenced in a context different from the one that created it.

An **invalidcontext** error occurs if an invalid context identifier is presented to any of the context operators or if certain other improper conditions are detected. See section 7.1.4, "Programming Restrictions."

7.1.3 Context Synchronization

When multiple contexts share objects in a single VM, they require a way to synchronize their activities. To facilitate this, the language includes two special types of synchronization objects and several operators for manipulating them.

A *lock* is a semaphore for mutual exclusion. Cooperating contexts can use it to guard against concurrent access to data that they are sharing. A context acquires a lock before accessing the data and releases it afterward. During that time, other contexts are prevented from acquiring the lock—they cannot access the data when it is in a possibly inconsistent state. The association between a lock object and the data protected by the lock is entirely a matter of programming convention.

A *condition* is a binary semaphore that cooperating contexts can use to synchronize their activity. One or more contexts can wait on a condition—in other words, suspend execution for an arbitrary length of time until notified by another context that the condition has been satisfied. Once again, the association between the condition object and the event or state it represents is a matter of programming convention.

The objects *lock* and *condition* are distinct types of objects, created by the operators **lock** and **condition**, respectively. They are composite objects in the sense that their values occupy space in VM separate from the objects themselves. When a lock or condition object is stored in multiple places, all the instances share the same value. However, the values of locks and conditions can be accessed only by the synchronization operators.

Locks and conditions are ordinarily used together in a stylized way. The **monitor** operator acquires a lock (waiting if necessary), executes an arbitrary PostScript language procedure, then releases the lock. The **wait** operator is executed within a procedure invoked by **monitor**. It releases the lock, waits for the condition to be satisfied, and reacquires the lock. The **notify** operator indicates that a condition has been satisfied and resumes any contexts waiting on that condition.

The recommended style of use of **wait** and **notify** is based on the notion that a context first waits for a shared data structure to reach some desired state, then performs some computation based on that state, and finally alerts other contexts of any changes it has made to the data. A lock and a condition are used to implement this protocol. The lock protects against concurrent access to the data; the condition is used to notify other contexts that some potentially interesting change has occurred.

Note   *Locks and conditions are treated separately because one may want to have several conditions that represent different states of the same shared data.*

This protocol is illustrated by the following two program fragments, which are likely to be executed by different contexts.

Example 7.1

```
/lock1 lock def
/cond1 condition def

lock1 {
  {
    ... boolean expression testing monitored data ...
    {exit} {lock1 cond1 wait} ifelse
  } loop
  ... computation involving monitored data ...
} monitor
```

Example 7.2

```
lock1 {
  ... computation that changes monitored data ...
  cond1 notify
} monitor
```

Example 7.1 executes **monitor** to acquire the lock named lock1; it must do so to safely access the shared data associated with it. The program then checks whether the *boolean expression* has become *true*; it waits on the condition named cond1 (repeatedly, if necessary) until the expression evaluates to *true*. Now, while still holding the lock, it performs some *computation* based on this state of the shared data. It might alter the data in such a way that the *boolean expression* would evaluate *false*. Finally, it releases lock1 by leaving the procedure invoked by **monitor**.

Example 7.2 acquires lock1 and then performs some computation that alters the data in a way that might favorably affect the outcome of the *boolean expression*. It then notifies cond1 and releases lock1. If there is a context suspended at the **wait** in Example 7.1, it now resumes and gets another chance to evaluate the *boolean expression*. (If multiple contexts are waiting for cond1, the **notify** resumes all of them; however, only one context at a time gets to acquire lock1.)

Note that it is unsafe to assume that the state tested by the *boolean expression* is *true* immediately after resumption from a **wait**. Even if it was *true* at the moment of the **notify**, it might have become *false* due to intervening execution by some other context. Notifying cond1 does not certify that the value of the *boolean expression* is *true*, only that it might be *true*. Programs that conform to this protocol are immune from deadlocks due to "lost notifies" or malfunctions due to "extra notifies."

A program must not make any assumptions regarding context scheduling. In some environments, the PostScript interpreter switches control among contexts pre-emptively and at any time; therefore, program execution in different contexts may be interleaved arbitrarily. Pre-emption may occur within a single operator, such as one that causes a PostScript language procedure to be executed or that reads or writes a file. To ensure predictable behavior, contexts must use the synchronization primitives to control access to shared data.

In any environment that supports concurrent execution of independent threads of control, there is the possibility of deadlock. The most familiar form of deadlock occurs among two or more contexts when each waits for a notification from the other or each attempts to acquire a lock already held by the other. Another deadlock situation arises when all available communication buffers become filled with data for a context that is waiting for notification from some other context, but the other context cannot proceed because it has no way to communicate. Such deadlocks can be avoided only through careful system and application design.

The synchronization primitives can be used to synchronize access to shared data in either local or global VM. Of course, this requires prearrangement among all contexts involved; the lock and condition objects used for this purpose should be in the same VM as the data being shared.

7.1.4 Programming Restrictions

Each context has its own private pair of standard input and output files. That is, different contexts obtain different file objects as a result of executing **currentfile** or applying the **file** operator to the special device names %stdin and %stdout. A context must not attempt to make its standard input and output files available for use by other contexts. Doing so will cause unpredictable behavior.

The behavior of the **save** and **restore** operators varies according to how the executing context was created. In the case of an isolated context, created by method 1 as described in section 7.1.1, "Creating Contexts," the outermost **save** and **restore** apply to both global and local VM; nested **save** and **restore** apply only to local VM. This supports the encapsulated job model.

In the case of a context that can share VM with other contexts, created by method 2 or 3, **save** and **restore** always apply only to local VM, never to global VM. Additionally, when multiple contexts share local

VM (method 3), the semantics of **save** and **restore** become restricted. The operation performed by **restore** is logically to restore local VM to its state when **save** was executed. If one context does this, another context sharing the same local VM might observe the effect of the **restore** at some totally unpredictable time during its own execution. That is, its recent computations would be undone unexpectedly.

If any context executes **save**, all other contexts sharing the same local VM are suspended until the original context executes the matching **restore**. This ensures that the **restore** does not disrupt the activities of those other contexts. This restriction applies only to contexts sharing the same local VM. Contexts that have different local VMs proceed unhindered.

Note   *In contexts that can share VM,* **save** *and* **restore** *never affect global VM. Therefore, contexts with separate local VMs but shared global VM cannot interfere with each other by executing* **save** *and* **restore**.

There are some restrictions on the synchronization operators that a context may execute while it has an unmatched **save** pending. For example, attempting to acquire a lock that is already held by another context sharing the same local VM is not allowed because it would surely lead to deadlock. If a context terminates when it has an unmatched **save** pending, an automatic **restore** is executed, allowing other contexts to proceed.

As a practical matter, **save** and **restore** are not of much use when a local VM is shared among multiple contexts. Programs organized this way should avoid using **save** and **restore**. On the other hand, programs organized as one local VM per context can use **save** and **restore** without restriction. The semantics described above are designed to maintain compatibility with existing page descriptions and font programs.

7.2   Encoded User Names

Section 3.12, "Binary Encoding Details," discusses binary token and binary object sequence encodings. Both encodings provide optional ways to represent names as small integers instead of as full text strings. Such an integer is either a *system name index* or a *user name index*. Careful use of encoded names can result in substantial space savings and execution performance improvement.

As discussed in section 3.12.3, "Encoded System Names," a *name index* is a reference to an element of a name table already known to the PostScript interpreter. A *system name index* is an index into the system name table, which is built-in and has a standard value. Encoded system names are supported by all Level 2 implementations.

A *user name index* is an index into the user name table, whose contents may be defined by a PostScript language program using the **defineusername** operator. This provides efficient encodings of arbitrary names that are used frequently. However, there are various restrictions on user name encodings, making them suitable for use only with the Display PostScript system.

Note *Do not confuse encoded user names with user objects, described in section 3.7.6, "User Objects," and available in all Level 2 implementations.*

The user name index facility is intended for use only during interactive sessions, where the application generates PostScript language commands that are immediately consumed by the Display PostScript system. It should not be used in a PostScript language program that must stand by itself, such as one sent to a printer or written to a file for later use. *If a program contains user name index encodings, it cannot be composed with or embedded in other PostScript language programs, and it cannot easily be translated to the ASCII encoding.* The Client Library has an option to disable generation of user name encodings and produce plain text names always. This option may be invoked dynamically in an application program to produce a PostScript language program that is to be captured in a file or diverted to a printer.

As with everything else related to binary encodings, encoded names are intended for machine generation only. The *pswrap* and Client Library facilities are the preferred means for application programs to generate binary-encoded programs. Those facilities maintain the user name table automatically and can encode names using both the system and user name tables. An application should not attempt to alter the user name table itself, because that would interfere with the activity of the Client Library.

The meaning of a given user name index is local to a specific PostScript execution context—precisely, to a context's local VM. If several contexts share the same local VM, a user name index defined in one context may be used in another context. In this case, it is the application programmer's responsibility to synchronize execution of the contexts so definition and use occur in the correct order.

Entries placed in the user name table by **defineusername** accumulate during the lifetime of the context's local VM; they do not obey **save** and **restore**, and they cannot be removed or replaced. These restrictions are intentional: they permit the Client Library to manage user name definitions without understanding the semantics of the PostScript language program being generated.

If the scanner encounters a binary encoded system or user name index for which no name has been defined, it generates an **undefined** error. The name object produced is system*n* or user*n*. For example, if entry number 123 is missing from the user name table, the name object produced is user123.

7.3 Graphics and Window Systems

For each windowing system that uses the Display PostScript system for graphical output, there is a collection of operators for doing such things as specifying the window that is to be affected by subsequent painting operators, for scrolling the contents of the window, for obtaining input events (keystrokes and mouse clicks), and so on. These operators are *window system specific* because their syntax and semantics vary according to the properties and capabilities of the underlying window system. They are not documented in this manual, but in manuals for specific window systems or operating systems.

In addition to the window system specific operators, there are several operators that are window related but have a consistent meaning across *all* window systems. They fall into the following categories:

- *View clipping*, to control the areas affected by incremental updates.

- *Hit detection*, to associate cursor positions with displayed objects.

- *Halftone phase adjustment*, to compensate for the effect of scrolling.

- *Device information*, to obtain characteristics of the display device.

The Display PostScript system supports these features with all windowing systems.

7.3.1 View Clipping

Interactive applications frequently make incremental updates to the displayed image. Such updates arise from changes to the displayed graphical objects and from window system manipulations that cause formerly obscured objects to become visible. For efficiency's sake, it is desirable for the application to redraw only those graphical objects that are affected by the change. This function is assisted by operators that do *view clipping*.

One way to handle incremental updating is to define a path that encloses the changed areas of the display, then redraw only those graphical objects that are enclosed or partially enclosed within the path. To produce correct results, it is necessary to impose this path as a *clipping path* while redrawing. Otherwise, portions of objects that are redrawn might incorrectly obscure objects that are not redrawn.

This clipping could be accomplished by adjusting the clipping path in the graphics state in the normal way. However, this is not particularly convenient, because the program that imposes the clipping and the program that is executed to redraw objects on the display may have different ideas about what the clipping path should be. This problem becomes particularly acute given the ability to switch entire graphics states arbitrarily.

To alleviate this, the Display PostScript system provides another level of clipping, the *view clip*, that is entirely independent of the graphics state. Objects are rendered on the device only in areas that are enclosed by *both* the current clipping path and the current view clipping path.

The view clipping path is part of the PostScript execution context, not the graphics state. A context initially has no view clipping path (see **initviewclip** in Chapter 8). The operators that alter the view clipping path do not affect the clipping path in the graphics state or vice versa. The view clipping path is not affected by **gsave** and **grestore**. However, a **restore** will reinstate the view clipping path that was in effect at the time of the matching **save**. View clips do not nest; rather, a new view clipping path replaces the existing one.

Note   *View clipping is temporarily disabled when the current output device is a mask device, such as the one installed by **setcachedevice**.*

The following operators manipulate view clips:

- **viewclip** replaces the current view clipping path by a copy of the current path in the graphics state.

- **eoviewclip** is similar to **viewclip**, but it uses the even-odd rule instead of the non-zero winding number rule to determine the inside of the current path. See section 4.5.2, "Filling."

- **rectviewclip** replaces the current view clipping path by a rectangular path. See section 4.6.5, "Rectangles."

- **initviewclip** replaces the current view clipping path with one that encloses the entire imageable area of the output device.

- **viewclippath** replaces the current path by a copy of the current view clipping path.

7.3.2 Hit Detection

Interactive windowing systems usually have some system specific method of detecting the movement and clicking of pointing devices. Some means is required to associate this information with the position of graphical objects that are visible on the display. This operation is called *hit detection*.

The insideness testing operators, such as **infill** and **instroke**, can assist in hit detection. Those operators are a standard part of Level 2 implementations, not just of Display PostScript. They are described in section 4.5.3, "Insideness Testing." Having obtained the user space coordinates of some interesting point, a program can:

- Determine whether that point would be painted by filling or stroking some object defined by either the current path or a user path.

- Determine whether an *aperture* surrounding the point would intersect any painted area of the object. The aperture defines a "sensitive area," that can have various shapes such as a circle or a diamond.

If a window system specific extension provides a way for a PostScript language program to receive input events directly, the program itself can perform operations such as mouse tracking and hit detection. With some window systems, however, the application always receives input events. In that case, the application must either perform such computations itself or issue queries to the Display PostScript system. This decision involves a trade-off between performance and application complexity. One possible approach is for the application to perform hit detection itself for simple shapes, but to query for more complex shapes.

Some window systems report the coordinates of an input event in a window coordinate system that is translated from the PostScript interpreter's device space. The **wtranslation** operator returns the amount of this translation. A PostScript language program can shift the coordinates by this amount, then use **itransform** to transform them into user space for testing by means of the insideness testing operators.

7.3.3 Halftone Phase

Normally, the halftone screen tiles the device space starting at the device space origin. That is, the halftone grid is aligned such that the lower-left corner of the lower-left halftone cell is positioned at (0, 0) in device space, independent of the value of the current transformation matrix. This ensures that adjacent gray areas will be painted with halftones having the same phase, avoiding "seams" or other such artifacts.

On a display, the *phase relationship* between the halftone grid and device space must be more flexible. This need arises because most window systems provide a *scrolling* operation in which the existing contents of raster memory are copied from one place to another in device space. This operation can alter the phase of halftones that have already been scan converted. It is necessary to alter the phase of the halftone generation algorithm correspondingly so that newly painted halftones will align with the existing ones.

In the Display PostScript system, the graphics state includes a pair of *halftone phase* parameters, one for x and one for y. These integers define an offset from the device space origin to the halftone grid origin. Of course, the halftone grid does not actually have an origin, so the offset values are interpreted *modulo* the width and height of the halftone cell. They ensure that *some* halftone cell will have its lower-left corner at (x, y) in device space.

The intended use of the halftone phase operators **sethalftonephase** and **currenthalftonephase** is with window system operations that perform scrolling. If the application scrolls the displayed image by (dx, dy) pixels in device space, it should simply add dx and dy to the halftone phase parameters; it should not worry about computing them *modulo* the size of the halftone cell. This has the correct effect even if the displayed image is composed of several different halftone screens.

The halftone phase is defined to be part of the graphics state, not part of the device. This is because an application may subdivide device space into multiple regions that it scrolls independently. A recommended technique is to associate a separate gstate (graphics state) object with each such region. This object carries all the parameters required to paint within that region, including the halftone phase.

Altering the halftone phase also alters the placement of any patterns that were previously instantiated by **makepattern** (see section 4.9, "Patterns"). This ensures that in areas painted with the same pattern before and after the halftone phase adjustment, the pattern cells will align. The current halftone phase does not affect **makepattern** itself; rather, *changes* to the halftone phase affect the placement of *existing* patterns.

7.3.4 Device Information

A program may require information about certain properties of the raster output device, such as whether or not it supports color and how many distinguishable color or gray values it can reproduce. A PostScript language program that is a page description should not need such information; using it compromises device independence. However, an interactive application may need to vary its behavior according to the available display technology. For example, a computer aided design application may use stipple patterns on a binary black-and-white display, but separate colors on a color display.

The **deviceinfo** operator returns a dictionary whose entries describe static information about the device. (Dynamic information must be read from the graphics state or obtained through operators such as **wtranslation**.) Some of the entries in this dictionary have standard names that are described in Table 7.1; others may have meanings that are device dependent. Most entries are optional and are present *only* if they are relevant for that type of device.

Table 7.1 *Entries in the* **deviceinfo** *dictionary*

Key	Type	Semantics
Colors	integer	Number of independent color components:
		1 Black-and-white or gray scale only
		3 Red, green, and blue
		4 Red, green, blue, and gray or their complements: cyan, magenta, yellow, and black, as is typically used in printers.

GrayValues	integer	Number of different gray values that individual pixels can reproduce without halftoning. For example:
		2 Binary black-and-white device
		256 8 bits-per-pixel, gray-scale device.
RedValues	integer	Number of different red values that individual pixels can reproduce, independent of other colors.
GreenValues	integer	Number of different green values.
BlueValues	integer	Number of different blue values.
ColorValues	integer	Total number of different color values that each pixel can reproduce. If this entry is present and the entries for gray, red, green, and blue are absent, this means the color components cannot be varied independently, only in combination.

7.4 Bitmap Fonts

In display systems, the resolution of the device is typically quite low when compared with printers and typesetters. Resolutions in the range of 60 to 100 pixels per inch are common. When characters are produced algorithmically from outlines in typical sizes (10 to 12 points), the results are often not as legible as they must be for comfortable reading. The usual way to deal with this problem is to use *screen fonts* consisting of bitmap characters that have been tuned manually. The hand tuning increases legibility, although possibly at the expense of fidelity to the original character shapes.

The Display PostScript system includes the ability to take advantage of hand-tuned bitmap fonts when they are available. This facility is fully integrated with the font machinery. Its operation is almost totally invisible to a PostScript language program.

When a program sets text by executing an operator such as **show**, this is what happens internally:

1. The PostScript interpreter consults the font cache.

2. If the character is *not* there, the interpreter consults the current device, requesting it to provide a bitmap form of the character at the required size.

3. If the device can provide such a bitmap, it does so. The PostScript interpreter places the bitmap in the font cache for subsequent use.

4. If there is no such character, the interpreter executes the character description, placing the scan converted result in the font cache.

The mechanism by which bitmap characters are provided by a device is not part of the language and is entirely hidden from a PostScript language program. The conventions for locating and representing bitmap characters are environment dependent; they vary from one window system to another. Re-encoding a font preserves the association with bitmap characters. Most other modifications to a font dictionary destroy the association.

Bitmap fonts are typically provided in one orientation and a range of sizes from 10 to 24 points. Beyond 24 points, characters scan converted from outlines are perfectly acceptable. The PostScript interpreter can usually choose a bitmap character whose size is sufficiently close to the one requested and render it directly.

Associated with each hand-tuned bitmap is a *width*—a displacement from the origin of the character to the origin of the next character. This width is also hand-tuned for maximum legibility; it is an *integer* interpreted in device space. It is different from the width produced when the same character is scan converted from the font definition, because that width (the *scalable width*) is defined by a real number scaled according to the requested font size.

Note   *Hand-tuned bitmaps are carefully designed so the bitmap widths and scalable widths are as similar as possible when averaged over large amounts of text.*

To achieve fidelity between displays and printers when rendering characters, an application *must* use the scalable widths to position characters on the display. Unfortunately, this leads to uneven letter spacing due to the need to round character positions to device pixel boundaries. At display resolution, this unevenness is objectionable. On the other hand, using the integer bitmap widths to produce evenly spaced text on the display leads to incorrect results on the printer.

One solution is to use integer widths for spacing within a word, but to use scalable widths for word-positioning and word-wrapping. This provides correctness at the cost of maintaining *two* current points. Many word processing and page layout programs use the following technique when rendering text on the display:

• Set the characters according to their integer bitmap widths, but keep track of the accumulated difference between the bitmap widths and the true scalable widths.

- Adjust the spaces between words to compensate for the accumulated error. The most accurate way to do this is to compute the error for an entire line and then distribute the accumulated error among all the spaces in that line.

This technique allows minor variation between display and printer within a line but maintains fidelity on a line-by-line basis.

The Display PostScript system determines whether to use bitmap widths or scalable widths for a font by checking the **BitmapWidths** entry in the font dictionary. If this entry is present, it must have a boolean value: *true* indicates that bitmap widths are to be used if available; *false* indicates that scalable widths are to be used always. If the entry is not present or if the device does not provide bitmaps for this font, scalable widths are always used.

The hand-tuned bitmaps are ordinarily used at rotations that are multiples of 90 degrees (0, 90, 180, and 270) relative to device space. In all other cases, the scan converted outlines are used. There is usually a difference in appearance between the hand-tuned bitmaps and the scan converted outlines for a given character at a given size. If this difference is found to be objectionable, the application can request that transformed characters be produced by transforming the bitmaps instead of scan converting the transformed outlines.

Hand-tuned bitmaps are provided in a range of discrete sizes. When a size is requested that doesn't match the hand-tuned bitmap size exactly, but lies between two discrete sizes, one of the discrete sizes is used and its widths are scaled accordingly. An application can request that the bitmaps be scaled for these in-between sizes or that the scan converted outlines be used.

There are three entries that can be added to a font dictionary to control the behavior for each of three cases: **ExactSize**, **InBetweenSize**, and **TransformedChar**. Each entry's value is an integer code:

0   Use outlines.
1   Use the discrete size directly.
2   Transform the discrete size.

The entries are interpreted as follows:

- **ExactSize** determines what to do when there is an exact match between the size requested and a hand-tuned bitmap, the user coordinate system axes are perpendicular to each other, the scale is uniform in x and y, and the angle of rotation is a multiple of 90 degrees. (Default value: 1)

- **InBetweenSize** determines what to do when a size requested falls between discrete hand-tuned bitmap sizes under the same conditions as **ExactSize**. (Default value: 0)

- **TransformedChar** determines what to do for any size request when the transformation is other than the ones described for **ExactSize**. (Default value: 0)

Since font dictionaries are read-only, the usual way to change whether bitmap widths are used for a font and to control their behavior is to create a copy of the font dictionary, modify the copy, and execute a new **definefont**. Example 7.3 creates a copy of the Helvetica font and adds the **BitmapWidths** key.

Example 7.3

```
/Helvetica findfont
dup length 1 add dict begin
   {1 index /FID ne {def} {pop pop} ifelse} forall
   /BitmapWidths true def
   currentdict
end
/Helvetica-BitmapWidths exch definefont pop
```

CHAPTER 8

Operators

This chapter contains detailed information about all the standard operators in the PostScript language. It is divided into two parts.

First, there is a summary of the operators, organized into groups of related functions. The summary is intended to help locate the operators needed to perform specific tasks.

Second, there are detailed descriptions of all operators, organized alphabetically by operator name. Each operator description is presented in the following format:

operator   *operand₁ operand₂ ... operandₙ* **operator** *result₁ ... resultₘ*

Detailed explanation of the operator.

Example

> An example of the use of this operator.
> The symbol ⇒ designates the values left on the operand stack by the example.

Errors: **A list of errors that this operator might execute.**

See Also: **A list of related operators.**

At the head of an operator description, *operand₁* through *operandₙ* are the operands that the operator requires, with *operandₙ* being the topmost element on the operand stack. The operator pops these objects from the operand stack and consumes them. After executing, the operator leaves the objects *result₁* through *resultₘ* on the stack, with *resultₘ* being the topmost element.

Normally, the operand and result names suggest either their types or their uses. Table 8.1 summarizes names (other than basic type names) that appear commonly.

Table 8.1 *Operand and result types*

Name	Description
angle	Angle (in degrees)
any	Value of any type
bool	Boolean (*true* or *false*) value
context	Integer representing an execution context
dict	Dictionary object
font	Font dictionary
form	Form dictionary
halftone	Halftone dictionary
int	Integer number
matrix	Array of six numbers describing a transformation matrix
num	Number (integer or floating point)
numarray	Array of numbers
numstring	Encoded number string
pattern	Pattern dictionary
proc	Procedure (executable array or executable packed array)
real	Floating point (real) number
userpath	Array of path construction operators and their operands

Some operators are polymorphic: their operands may be any of several types. For example, the notation *file|proc|string* indicates an operand that is a file, procedure, or string.

The notation " ⊢" indicates the bottom of the stack. The notation "–" in the operand position indicates that the operator expects no operands, and a "–" in the result position indicates that the operator returns no results.

The documented effects on the operand stack and the possible errors are those produced directly by the operator itself. Many operators invoke arbitrary PostScript language procedures. Such procedures can have arbitrary effects that are not mentioned in the operator descriptions.

Note *In several descriptions of operators, the semantics of an operator are described as "being equivalent to" a PostScript language program using lower-level operators. Unless explicitly documented to the contrary, operator definitions are independent; redefining an operator name does not change the behavior of any other operator.*

The PostScript language consists of three distinct groups of operators: Level 1, Level 2, and Display PostScript operators. This chapter clearly identifies Level 2 and Display PostScript operators with the following icons:

LEVEL 2   Level 2 operator

DPS   Display PostScript operator

Level 1 operators are not identified with a specific icon. Note that some Level 2 operators are present in Level 1 implementations that contain various language extensions; see Appendix A for details.

8.1 Operator Summary

Operand Stack Manipulation Operators

any	**pop** –	discard top element
any$_1$ any$_2$	**exch** *any$_2$ any$_1$*	exchange top two elements
any	**dup** *any any*	duplicate top element
any$_1$ ... any$_n$ n	**copy** *any$_1$ ... any$_n$ any$_1$ ... any$_n$*	duplicate top *n* elements
any$_n$ ... any$_0$ n	**index** *any$_n$ ... any$_0$ any$_n$*	duplicate arbitrary element
a$_{n-1}$ ... a$_0$ n j	**roll** *a$_{(j-1)\,mod\,n}$ ... a$_0$ a$_{n-1}$ ... a$_{j\,mod\,n}$*	roll *n* elements up *j* times
⊢ *any$_1$ ... any$_n$*	**clear** ⊢	discard all elements
⊢ *any$_1$ ... any$_n$*	**count** ⊢ *any$_1$ ... any$_n$ n*	count elements on stack
–	**mark** *mark*	push mark on stack
mark obj$_1$ ... obj$_n$	**cleartomark** –	discard elements down through *mark*
mark obj$_1$ ... obj$_n$	**counttomark** *mark obj$_1$ ... obj$_n$ n*	count elements down to *mark*

Arithmetic and Math Operators

num$_1$ num$_2$	**add** *sum*	*num$_1$* plus *num$_2$*
num$_1$ num$_2$	**div** *quotient*	*num$_1$* divided by *num$_2$*
int$_1$ int$_2$	**idiv** *quotient*	integer divide
int$_1$ int$_2$	**mod** *remainder*	*int$_1$* mod *int$_2$*
num$_1$ num$_2$	**mul** *product*	*num$_1$* times *num$_2$*
num$_1$ num$_2$	**sub** *difference*	*num$_1$* minus *num$_2$*
num$_1$	**abs** *num$_2$*	absolute value of *num$_1$*
num$_1$	**neg** *num$_2$*	negative of *num$_1$*
num$_1$	**ceiling** *num$_2$*	ceiling of *num$_1$*
num$_1$	**floor** *num$_2$*	floor of *num$_1$*
num$_1$	**round** *num$_2$*	round *num$_1$* to nearest integer
num$_1$	**truncate** *num$_2$*	remove fractional part of *num$_1$*
num	**sqrt** *real*	square root of *num*
num den	**atan** *angle*	arctangent of *num*/*den* in degrees
angle	**cos** *real*	cosine of *angle* (degrees)
angle	**sin** *real*	sine of *angle* (degrees)
base exponent	**exp** *real*	raise *base* to *exponent* power
num	**ln** *real*	natural logarithm (base *e*)
num	**log** *real*	logarithm (base 10)
–	**rand** *int*	generate pseudo-random integer
int	**srand** –	set random number seed
–	**rrand** *int*	return random number seed

Array Operators

int	**array**	*array*	create array of length *int*
–	**[**	*mark*	start array construction
mark obj$_0$ ... obj$_{n-1}$	**]**	*array*	end array construction
array	**length**	*int*	number of elements in *array*
array index	**get**	*any*	get array element indexed by *index*
array index any	**put**	–	put *any* into *array* at *index*
array index count	**getinterval**	*subarray*	subarray of *array* starting at *index* for *count* elements
array$_1$ index array$_2$	**putinterval**	–	replace subarray of *array$_1$* starting at *index* by *array$_2$*
any$_0$ ... any$_{n-1}$ array	**astore**	*array*	pop elements from stack into *array*
array	**aload**	*a$_0$ ... a$_{n-1}$ array*	push all elements of *array* on stack
array$_1$ array$_2$	**copy**	*subarray$_2$*	copy elements of *array$_1$* to initial subarray of *array$_2$*
array proc	**forall**	–	execute *proc* for each element of *array*

Packed Array Operators

any$_0$ ... any$_{n-1}$ n	**packedarray**	*packedarray*	create packed array consisting of the specified *n* elements
–	**currentpacking**	*bool*	return array packing mode
bool	**setpacking**	–	set array packing mode for {...} syntax (*true* = packedarray)
packedarray	**length**	*int*	number of elements in *packedarray*
packedarray index	**get**	*any*	get *packedarray* element indexed by *index*
packedarray index count	**getinterval**	*subarray*	subarray of *packedarray* starting at *index* for *count* elements
packedarray	**aload**	*a$_0$ ... a$_{n-1}$ packedarray*	push all elements of *packedarray* on stack
packedarray$_1$ array$_2$	**copy**	*subarray$_2$*	copy elements of *packedarray$_1$* to initial subarray of *array$_2$*
packedarray proc	**forall**	–	execute *proc* for each element of *packedarray*

Dictionary Operators

int	**dict** *dict*	create dictionary with capacity for *int* elements
–	**<<** *mark*	start dictionary construction
mark key$_1$ value$_1$ ... key$_n$ value$_n$	**>>** *dict*	end dictionary construction
dict	**length** *int*	number of key-value pairs in *dict*
dict	**maxlength** *int*	current capacity of *dict*
dict	**begin** –	push *dict* on dictionary stack
–	**end** –	pop dictionary stack
key value	**def** –	associate *key* and *value* in current dictionary
key	**load** *value*	search dictionary stack for *key* and return associated *value*
key value	**store** –	replace topmost definition of *key*
dict key	**get** *any*	get value associated with *key* in *dict*
dict key value	**put** –	associate *key* with *value* in *dict*
dict key	**undef** –	remove *key* and its value from *dict*
dict key	**known** *bool*	test whether *key* is in *dict*
key	**where** *dict true* or *false*	find dictionary in which *key* is defined
dict$_1$ dict$_2$	**copy** *dict$_2$*	copy contents of *dict$_1$* to *dict$_2$*
dict proc	**forall** –	execute *proc* for each element of *dict*
–	**currentdict** *dict*	push current dictionary on operand stack
–	**errordict** *dict*	error handler dictionary
–	**$error** *dict*	error control and status dictionary
–	**systemdict** *dict*	system dictionary
–	**userdict** *dict*	writable dictionary in local VM
–	**globaldict** *dict*	writable dictionary in global VM
–	**statusdict** *dict*	product-dependent dictionary
–	**countdictstack** *int*	count elements on dictionary stack
array	**dictstack** *subarray*	copy dictionary stack into *array*
–	**cleardictstack** –	pop all non-permanent dictionaries off dictionary stack

String Operators

int	**string** *string*	create string of length *int*
string	**length** *int*	number of elements in *string*
string index	**get** *int*	get string element indexed by *index*
string index int	**put** –	put *int* into *string* at *index*
string index count	**getinterval** *substring*	substring of *string* starting at *index* for *count* elements
string$_1$ index string$_2$	**putinterval** –	replace substring of *string$_1$* starting at *index* by *string$_2$*
string$_1$ string$_2$	**copy** *substring$_2$*	copy elements of *string$_1$* to initial substring of *string$_2$*

string proc	**forall**	–	execute *proc* for each element of *string*
string seek	**anchorsearch**	*post match true* or *string false*	determine if *seek* is initial substring of *string*
string seek	**search**	*post match pre true* or *string false*	search for *seek* in *string*
string	**token**	*post token true* or *false*	read token from start of *string*

Relational, Boolean, and Bitwise Operators

any_1 any_2	**eq**	*bool*	test equal
any_1 any_2	**ne**	*bool*	test not equal
$num_1 \| str_1$ $num_2 \| str_2$	**ge**	*bool*	test greater or equal
$num_1 \| str_1$ $num_2 \| str_2$	**gt**	*bool*	test greater than
$num_1 \| str_1$ $num_2 \| str_2$	**le**	*bool*	test less or equal
$num_1 \| str_1$ $num_2 \| str_2$	**lt**	*bool*	test less than
$bool_1 \| int_1$ $bool_2 \| int_2$	**and**	$bool_3 \| int_3$	logical | bitwise and
$bool_1 \| int_1$	**not**	$bool_2 \| int_2$	logical | bitwise not
$bool_1 \| int_1$ $bool_2 \| int_2$	**or**	$bool_3 \| int_3$	logical | bitwise inclusive or
$bool_1 \| int_1$ $bool_2 \| int_2$	**xor**	$bool_3 \| int_3$	logical | bitwise exclusive or
–	**true**	*true*	push boolean value *true*
–	**false**	*false*	push boolean value *false*
int_1 *shift*	**bitshift**	int_2	bitwise shift of int_1 (positive is left)

Control Operators

any	**exec**	–	execute arbitrary object
bool proc	**if**		execute *proc* if *bool* is true
bool $proc_1$ $proc_2$	**ifelse**	–	execute $proc_1$ if *bool* is true, $proc_2$ if *bool* is false
init incr limit proc	**for**	–	execute *proc* with values from *init* by steps of *incr* to *limit*
int proc	**repeat**	–	execute *proc* *int* times
proc	**loop**	–	execute *proc* an indefinite number of times
–	**exit**	–	exit innermost active loop
–	**stop**	–	terminate **stopped** context
any	**stopped**	*bool*	establish context for catching **stop**
–	**countexecstack**	*int*	count elements on exec stack
array	**execstack**	*subarray*	copy exec stack into *array*
–	**quit**	–	terminate interpreter
–	**start**	–	executed at interpreter startup

Type, Attribute, and Conversion Operators

any	**type** *name*		return name identifying the type of *any*
any	**cvlit** *any*		make object be literal
any	**cvx** *any*		make object be executable
any	**xcheck** *bool*		test executable attribute
array|packedarray|file|string	**executeonly** *array|packedarray|file|string*		
			reduce access to execute-only
array|packedarray|dict|file|string	**noaccess** *array|packedarray|dict|file|string*		
			disallow any access
array|packedarray|dict|file|string	**readonly** *array|packedarray|dict|file|string*		
			reduce access to read-only
array|packedarray|dict|file|string	**rcheck** *bool*		test read access
array|packedarray|dict|file|string	**wcheck** *bool*		test write access
num|string	**cvi** *int*		convert to integer
string	**cvn** *name*		convert to name
num|string	**cvr** *real*		convert to real
num radix string	**cvrs** *substring*		convert to string with radix
any string	**cvs** *substring*		convert to string

File Operators

string$_1$ string$_2$	**file** *file*	open file identified by *string$_1$* with access *string$_2$*
src|tgt param$_1$ ... param$_n$ name	**filter** *file*	establish filtered file
file	**closefile** –	close *file*
file	**read** *int true*	read one character from *file*
	or *false*	
file int	**write** –	write one character to *file*
file string	**readhexstring** *substring bool*	read hex from *file* into *string*
file string	**writehexstring** –	write *string* to *file* as hex
file string	**readstring** *substring bool*	read string from *file*
file string	**writestring** –	write *string* to *file*
file string	**readline** *substring bool*	read line from *file* into *string*
file	**token** *token true*	read token from *file*
	or *false*	
file	**bytesavailable** *int*	number of bytes available to read
–	**flush** –	send buffered data to standard output file
file	**flushfile** –	send buffered data or read to EOF
file	**resetfile** –	discard buffered characters
file	**status** *bool*	return status of *file*
string	**status** *pages bytes referenced created true*	return information about named file
	or *false*	
string	**run** –	execute contents of named file
–	**currentfile** *file*	return file currently being executed
string	**deletefile** –	delete named file

string$_1$ *string*$_2$	**renamefile** –	rename file *string*$_1$ to *string*$_2$
template proc scratch	**filenameforall** –	execute *proc* for each file name matching *template*
file int	**setfileposition** –	set *file* to specified position
file	**fileposition** *int*	return current position in *file*
string	**print** –	write *string* to standard output file
any	**=** –	write text representation of *any* to standard output file
any	**==** –	write syntactic representation of *any* to standard output file
⊢ *any*$_1$ ... *any*$_n$	**stack** ⊢ *any*$_1$ ... *any*$_n$	print stack non-destructively using =
⊢ *any*$_1$ ... *any*$_n$	**pstack** ⊢ *any*$_1$ ... *any*$_n$	print stack non-destructively using ==
obj int	**printobject** –	write binary object to standard output file, using *int* as tag
file obj int	**writeobject** –	write binary object to *file*, using *int* as tag
int	**setobjectformat** –	set binary object format (0=disable, 1=IEEE high, 2=low, 3=native high, 4=low)
–	**currentobjectformat** *int*	return binary object format

Resource Operators

key instance category	**defineresource** *instance*	register named resource *instance* in *category*
key category	**undefineresource** –	remove resource registration
key category	**findresource** *instance*	return resource *instance* identified by *key* in *category*
key category	**resourcestatus** *status size true* or *false*	return *status* of resource instance
template proc scratch category	**resourceforall** –	enumerate resource instances in *category*

Virtual Memory Operators

–	**save** *save*	create VM snapshot
save	**restore** –	restore VM snapshot
bool	**setglobal** –	set VM allocation mode (*false* = local, *true* = global)
–	**currentglobal** *bool*	return current VM allocation mode
any	**gcheck** *bool*	*true* if *any* is simple or in global VM, *false* if in local VM
bool$_1$ *password*	**startjob** *bool*$_2$	start new job that will alter initial VM if *bool*$_1$ is *true*
index any	**defineuserobject** –	define user object associated with *index*
index	**execuserobject** –	execute user object associated with *index*
index	**undefineuserobject** –	remove user object associated with *index*
–	**UserObjects** *array*	current **UserObjects** array defined in **userdict**

Miscellaneous Operators

proc	**bind** *proc*	replace operator names in *proc* by operators
–	**null** *null*	push *null* on operand stack
–	**version** *string*	interpreter version
–	**realtime** *int*	return real time in milliseconds
–	**usertime** *int*	return execution time in milliseconds
–	**languagelevel** *int*	level of language features
–	**product** *string*	product name
–	**revision** *int*	product revision level
–	**serialnumber** *int*	machine serial number
–	**executive** –	invoke interactive executive
bool	**echo** –	turn on/off echoing
–	**prompt** –	executed when ready for interactive input

Graphics State Operators—Device Independent

–	**gsave** –	push graphics state
–	**grestore** –	pop graphics state
–	**grestoreall** –	pop to bottommost graphics state
–	**initgraphics** –	reset graphics state parameters
–	**gstate** *gstate*	create graphics state object
gstate	**setgstate** –	set graphics state from *gstate*
gstate	**currentgstate** *gstate*	copy current graphics state into *gstate*
num	**setlinewidth** –	set line width
–	**currentlinewidth** *num*	return current line width
int	**setlinecap** –	set shape of line ends for stroke (0 = butt, 1 = round, 2 = square)
–	**currentlinecap** *int*	return current line cap
int	**setlinejoin** –	set shape of corners for stroke (0 = miter, 1 = round, 2 = bevel)
–	**currentlinejoin** *int*	return current line join
num	**setmiterlimit** –	set miter length limit
–	**currentmiterlimit** *num*	return current miter limit
bool	**setstrokeadjust** –	set stroke adjust (*false* = disable, *true* = enable)
–	**currentstrokeadjust** *bool*	return current stroke adjust
array offset	**setdash** –	set dash pattern for stroking
–	**currentdash** *array offset*	return current dash pattern
array	**setcolorspace** –	set color space
–	**currentcolorspace** *array*	return current color space
comp₁ ... compₙ	**setcolor** –	set color components
–	**currentcolor** *comp₁ ... compₙ*	return current color components
num	**setgray** –	set color space to **DeviceGray** and color to specified gray value (0 = black, 1 = white)

–	**currentgray** *num*	return current color as gray value
hue sat brt	**sethsbcolor** –	set color space to **DeviceRGB** and color to specified hue, saturation, brightness
–	**currenthsbcolor** *hue sat brt*	return current color as hue, saturation, brightness
red green blue	**setrgbcolor** –	set color space to **DeviceRGB** and color to specified red, green, blue
–	**currentrgbcolor** *red green blue*	return current color as red, green, blue
:yan magenta yellow black	**setcmykcolor** –	set color space to **DeviceCMYK** and color to specified cyan, magenta, yellow, black
–	**currentcmykcolor** *cyan magenta yellow black*	
		return current color as cyan, magenta, yellow, black

Graphics State Operators—Device Dependent

dict	**sethalftone** –	set halftone dictionary
–	**currenthalftone** *dict*	return current halftone dictionary
frequency angle proc	**setscreen** –	set gray halftone screen
–	**currentscreen** *frequency angle proc*	
		return current gray halftone screen
redfreq redang redproc greenfreq greenang greenproc bluefreq blueang blueproc grayfreq grayang grayproc	**setcolorscreen** –	set all four halftone screens
–	**currentcolorscreen** *redfreq redang redproc greenfreq greenang greenproc bluefreq blueang blueproc grayfreq grayang grayproc*	
		return all four halftone screens
proc	**settransfer** –	set gray transfer function
–	**currenttransfer** *proc*	return current gray transfer function
redproc greenproc blueproc grayproc	**setcolortransfer** –	set all four transfer functions
–	**currentcolortransfer** *redproc greenproc blueproc grayproc*	
		return current transfer functions
proc	**setblackgeneration** –	set black generation function
–	**currentblackgeneration** *proc*	return current black generation function
proc	**setundercolorremoval** –	set undercolor removal function
–	**currentundercolorremoval** *proc*	return current undercolor removal function
dict	**setcolorrendering** –	set CIE based color rendering dictionary
–	**currentcolorrendering** *dict*	return current CIE based color rendering dictionary
num	**setflat** –	set flatness tolerance
–	**currentflat** *num*	return current flatness
bool	**setoverprint** –	set overprint parameter
–	**currentoverprint** *bool*	return current overprint parameter

Coordinate System and Matrix Operators

–	**matrix**	*matrix*	create identity matrix
–	**initmatrix**	–	set CTM to device default
matrix	**identmatrix**	*matrix*	fill *matrix* with identity transform
matrix	**defaultmatrix**	*matrix*	fill *matrix* with device default matrix
matrix	**currentmatrix**	*matrix*	fill *matrix* with CTM
matrix	**setmatrix**	–	replace CTM by *matrix*
t_x t_y	**translate**	–	translate user space by (t_x, t_y)
t_x t_y *matrix*	**translate**	*matrix*	define translation by (t_x, t_y)
s_x s_y	**scale**	–	scale user space by s_x and s_y
s_x s_y *matrix*	**scale**	*matrix*	define scaling by s_x and s_y
angle	**rotate**	–	rotate user space by *angle* degrees
angle matrix	**rotate**	*matrix*	define rotation by *angle* degrees
matrix	**concat**	–	replace CTM by *matrix* × CTM
*matrix*₁ *matrix*₂ *matrix*₃	**concatmatrix**	*matrix*₃	fill *matrix*₃ with *matrix*₁ × *matrix*₂
x *y*	**transform**	*x′ y′*	transform (*x, y*) by CTM
x *y* *matrix*	**transform**	*x′ y′*	transform (*x, y*) by *matrix*
dx *dy*	**dtransform**	*dx′ dy′*	transform distance (*dx, dy*) by CTM
dx *dy* *matrix*	**dtransform**	*dx′ dy′*	transform distance (*dx, dy*) by *matrix*
x′ y′	**itransform**	*x y*	inverse transform (*x′, y′*) by CTM
x′ y′ matrix	**itransform**	*x y*	inverse transform (*x′, y′*) by *matrix*
dx′ dy′	**idtransform**	*dx dy*	inverse transform distance (*dx′, dy′*) by CTM
dx′ dy′ matrix	**idtransform**	*dx dy*	inverse transform distance (*dx′, dy′*) by *matrix*
*matrix*₁ *matrix*₂	**invertmatrix**	*matrix*₂	fill *matrix*₂ with inverse of *matrix*₁

Path Construction Operators

–	**newpath**	–	initialize current path to be empty
–	**currentpoint**	*x y*	return current point coordinate
x y	**moveto**	–	set current point to (*x, y*)
dx dy	**rmoveto**	–	relative **moveto**
x y	**lineto**	–	append straight line to (*x, y*)
dx dy	**rlineto**	–	relative **lineto**
*x y r ang*₁ *ang*₂	**arc**	–	append counterclockwise arc
*x y r ang*₁ *ang*₂	**arcn**	–	append clockwise arc
x_1 y_1 x_2 y_2 *r*	**arct**	–	append tangent arc
x_1 y_1 x_2 y_2 *r*	**arcto**	xt_1 yt_1 xt_2 yt_2	append tangent arc
x_1 y_1 x_2 y_2 x_3 y_3	**curveto**	–	append Bézier cubic section
dx_1 dy_1 dx_2 dy_2 dx_3 dy_3	**rcurveto**	–	relative **curveto**
–	**closepath**	–	connect subpath back to its starting point
–	**flattenpath**	–	convert curves to sequences of straight lines
–	**reversepath**	–	reverse direction of current path
–	**strokepath**	–	compute outline of stroked path
userpath	**ustrokepath**	–	compute outline of stroked *userpath*

userpath matrix	**ustrokepath** –	compute outline of stroked _userpath_
string bool	**charpath** –	append character outline to current path
userpath	**uappend** –	interpret _userpath_ and append to current path
–	**clippath** –	set current path to clipping path
_ll_x ll_y ur_x ur_y_	**setbbox** –	set bounding box for current path
–	**pathbbox** ll_x ll_y ur_x ur_y	return bounding box of current path
move line curve close	**pathforall** –	enumerate current path
bool	**upath** _userpath_	create _userpath_ for current path; include **ucache** if _bool_ is _true_
–	**initclip** –	set clipping path to device default
–	**clip** –	clip using non-zero winding number rule
–	**eoclip** –	clip using even-odd inside rule
x y width height	**rectclip** –	clip with rectangular path
numarray|numstring	**rectclip** –	clip with rectangular paths
–	**ucache** –	declare that user path is to be cached

Painting Operators

–	**erasepage** –	paint current page white
–	**fill** –	fill current path with current color
–	**eofill** –	fill using even-odd rule
–	**stroke** –	draw line along current path
userpath	**ufill** –	interpret and fill _userpath_
userpath	**ueofill** –	fill _userpath_ using even-odd rule
userpath	**ustroke** –	interpret and stroke _userpath_
userpath matrix	**ustroke** –	interpret _userpath_, concatenate _matrix_, and stroke
x y width height	**rectfill** –	fill rectangular path
numarray|numstring	**rectfill** –	fill rectangular paths
x y width height	**rectstroke** –	stroke rectangular path
numarray|numstring	**rectstroke** –	stroke rectangular paths
dict	**image** –	paint any sampled image
width height bits/samp matrix datasrc	**image** –	paint monochrome sampled image
width height bits/comp matrix datasrc₀ ... datasrc_{n−1} multi ncomp	**colorimage** –	paint color sampled image
dict	**imagemask** –	paint current color through mask
width height polarity matrix datasrc	**imagemask** –	paint current color through mask

Insideness Testing Operators

x y	**infill**	*bool*		test whether point (*x, y*) would be painted by **fill**
userpath	**infill**	*bool*		test whether pixels in *userpath* would be painted by **fill**
x y	**ineofill**	*bool*		test whether point (*x, y*) would be painted by **eofill**
userpath	**ineofill**	*bool*		test whether pixels in *userpath* would be painted by **eofill**
x y userpath	**inufill**	*bool*		test whether point (*x, y*) would be painted by **ufill** of *userpath*
userpath₁ userpath₂	**inufill**	*bool*		test whether pixels in *userpath₁* would be painted by **inufill** of *userpath₂*
x y userpath	**inueofill**	*bool*		test whether point (*x, y*) would be painted by **ueofill** of *userpath*
userpath₁ userpath₂	**inueofill**	*bool*		test whether pixels in *userpath₁* would be painted by **ueofill** of *userpath₂*
x y	**instroke**	*bool*		test whether point (*x, y*) would be painted by **stroke**
x y userpath	**inustroke**	*bool*		test whether point (*x, y*) would be painted by **ustroke** of *userpath*
x y userpath matrix	**inustroke**	*bool*		test whether point (*x, y*) would be painted by **ustroke** of *userpath*
userpath₁ userpath₂	**inustroke**	*bool*		test whether pixels in *userpath₁* would be painted by **ustroke** of *userpath₂*
userpath₁ userpath₂ matrix	**inustroke**	*bool*		test whether pixels in *userpath₁* would be painted by **ustroke** of *userpath₂*

Form and Pattern Operators

pattern matrix	**makepattern**	*pattern'*	create pattern instance from prototype
comp₁ ... compₙ pattern	**setpattern**	–	install *pattern* as current color
form	**execform**	–	paint *form*

Device Setup and Output Operators

–	**showpage**	–	transmit and reset current page
–	**copypage**	–	transmit current page
dict	**setpagedevice**	–	install page-oriented output device
–	**currentpagedevice**	*dict*	return current page device parameters
–	**nulldevice**	–	install no-output device

Character and Font Operators

key font	**definefont** *font*	register *font* as a font dictionary
key	**undefinefont** –	remove font registration
key	**findfont** *font*	return font dictionary identified by *key*
font scale	**scalefont** *font'*	scale *font* by *scale* to produce new *font'*
font matrix	**makefont** *font'*	transform *font* by *matrix* to produce new *font'*
font	**setfont** –	set font dictionary in graphics state
–	**currentfont** *font*	return current font dictionary
–	**rootfont** *font*	return root composite font dictionary
key scale|matrix	**selectfont** –	set font dictionary given name and transform
string	**show** –	paint characters of *string* on page
a_x a_y *string*	**ashow** –	add (a_x, a_y) to width of each character while showing *string*
c_x c_y *char string*	**widthshow** –	add (c_x, c_y) to width of *char* while showing *string*
c_x c_y *char* a_x a_y *string*	**awidthshow** –	combine effects of **ashow** and **widthshow**
string numarray|numstring	**xshow** –	paint characters of *string* using *x* widths in *numarray|numstring*
string numarray|numstring	**xyshow** –	paint characters of *string* using *x* and *y* widths in *numarray|numstring*
string numarray|numstring	**yshow** –	paint characters of *string* using *y* widths in *numarray|numstring*
name	**glyphshow** –	paint character identified by *name*
string	**stringwidth** w_x w_y	width of *string* in current font
proc string	**cshow** –	invoke show mapping algorithm and call *proc*
proc string	**kshow** –	execute *proc* between characters shown from *string*
–	**FontDirectory** *dict*	dictionary of font dictionaries
–	**GlobalFontDirectory** *dict*	dictionary of font dictionaries in global VM
–	**StandardEncoding** *array*	Adobe standard font encoding vector
–	**ISOLatin1Encoding** *array*	international ISO Latin-1 font encoding vector
key	**findencoding** *array*	find encoding array
w_x w_y ll_x ll_y ur_x ur_y	**setcachedevice** –	declare cached character metrics
$w0_x$ $w0_y$ ll_x ll_y ur_x ur_y $w1_x$ $w1_y$ v_x v_y	**setcachedevice2** –	declare cached character metrics
w_x w_y	**setcharwidth** –	declare uncached character metrics

Interpreter Parameter Operators

dict	**setsystemparams** –		set system-wide interpreter parameters
–	**currentsystemparams** *dict*		return system-wide interpreter parameters
dict	**setuserparams** –		set per-context interpreter parameters
–	**currentuserparams** *dict*		return per-context interpreter parameters
string dict	**setdevparams** –		set parameters for input/output device
string	**currentdevparams** *dict*		return device parameters
int	**vmreclaim** –		control garbage collector
int	**setvmthreshold** –		control garbage collector
–	**vmstatus** *level used maximum*		report VM status
–	**cachestatus** *bsize bmax msize mmax csize cmax blimit*		
			return font cache status and parameters
num	**setcachelimit** –		set maximum bytes in cached character
mark size lower upper	**setcacheparams** –		change font cache parameters
–	**currentcacheparams** *mark size lower upper*		
			return current font cache parameters
mark blimit	**setucacheparams** –		set user path cache parameters
–	**ucachestatus** *mark bsize bmax rsize rmax blimit*		
			return user path cache status and parameters

Display PostScript Operators

–	**currentcontext** *context*		return current context identifier
mark obj$_1$ ... obj$_n$ proc	**fork** *context*		create context executing *proc* with obj$_1$ ... obj$_n$ as operands
context	**join** *mark obj$_1$ ... obj$_n$*		await context termination and return its results
context	**detach** –		enable context to terminate immediately when done
–	**lock** *lock*		create lock object
lock proc	**monitor** –		execute *proc* while holding *lock*
–	**condition** *condition*		create condition object
lock condition	**wait** –		release *lock*, wait for *condition*, reacquire *lock*
condition	**notify** –		resume contexts waiting for *condition*
–	**yield** –		suspend current context momentarily
index name	**defineusername** –		define encoded name index
–	**viewclip** –		set view clip from current path
–	**eoviewclip** –		set view clip using even-odd rule
x y width height	**rectviewclip** –		set rectangular view clipping path
numarray\numstring	**rectviewclip** –		set rectangular view clipping paths
–	**initviewclip** –		reset view clip
–	**viewclippath** –		set current path from view clip
–	**deviceinfo** *dict*		return dictionary containing information about current device

–	**wtranslation** *x y*	return translation from window origin to device space origin
x y	**sethalftonephase** –	set halftone phase
–	**currenthalftonephase** *x y*	return current halftone phase

Errors

configurationerror	**setpagedevice** request cannot be satisfied
dictfull	no more room in dictionary
dictstackoverflow	too many **begin**s
dictstackunderflow	too many **end**s
execstackoverflow	exec nesting too deep
handleerror	called to report error information
interrupt	external interrupt request (e.g., Control-C)
invalidaccess	attempt to violate access attribute
invalidcontext	improper use of context operation
invalidexit	**exit** not in loop
invalidfileaccess	unacceptable access string
invalidfont	invalid font name or dictionary
invalidid	invalid identifier for external object
invalidrestore	improper **restore**
ioerror	input/output error occurred
limitcheck	implementation limit exceeded
nocurrentpoint	current point is undefined
rangecheck	operand out of bounds
stackoverflow	operand stack overflow
stackunderflow	operand stack underflow
syntaxerror	PostScript language syntax error
timeout	time limit exceeded
typecheck	operand of wrong type
undefined	name not known
undefinedfilename	file not found
undefinedresource	resource instance not found
undefinedresult	over/underflow or meaningless result
unmatchedmark	expected mark not on stack
unregistered	internal error
VMerror	VM exhausted

8.2 Operator Details

[– [*mark*

pushes a mark object on the operand stack (see **mark**). The customary use of the [operator is to mark the beginning of an indefinitely long sequence of objects that will eventually be formed into a new array object by the] operator. See the discussion of the array syntax in section 3.2, "Syntax," and of array construction in section 3.6, "Overview of Basic Operators."

Errors: **stackoverflow**

See Also: **], mark, array, astore**

]   *mark obj$_0$ ... obj$_{n-1}$* **]** *array*

creates a new array of *n* elements, where *n* is the number of elements above the topmost mark on the operand stack; stores those elements into the array; and returns the array on the operand stack. The] operator stores the topmost object from the stack into element *n*–1 of *array* and the bottommost one (the one immediately above the mark) into element 0 of *array*. It removes all the array elements from the stack, as well as the mark object.

The array is allocated in local or global VM according to the current VM allocation mode. An **invalidaccess** error occurs if the array is in global VM and any of *obj$_0$* ... *obj$_{n-1}$* are in local VM. See section 3.7.2, "Local and Global VM."

Example

    [5 4 3] ⇒ % a 3-element array, with elements 5, 4, 3
    mark 5 4 3 counttomark array astore exch pop ⇒ [5 4 3]
    [1 2 add] ⇒ % a 1-element array, with element 3

The second line of the example has the same effect as the first, but uses lower-level array and stack manipulation primitives instead of [and].

In the last line of the example, note that the PostScript interpreter acts on all of the array elements as it encounters them (unlike its behavior with the {...} syntax for executable array construction) so the **add** operator is executed before the array is constructed.

Errors: **stackoverflow, unmatchedmark, VMerror**

See Also: **[, mark, array, astore**

<<   – << *mark*

pushes a mark object on the operand stack (same as **mark** and **[** operators).

Errors: **stackoverflow**

See Also: **>>, mark**

>>   *mark key₁ value₁ ... keyₙ valueₙ >> dict*

creates and returns a dictionary containing the specified key-value pairs. The operands are a mark followed by an even number of objects, which the operator uses alternately as keys and values to be inserted into the dictionary. The dictionary is allocated space for precisely the number of key-value pairs supplied.

The dictionary is allocated in local or global VM according to the current VM allocation mode. An **invalidaccess** error occurs if the dictionary is in global VM and any keys or values are in local VM. See section 3.7.2, "Local and Global VM." A **rangecheck** error occurs if there is an odd number of objects above the topmost mark on the stack.

>> is equivalent to:

```
counttomark 2 idiv dup dict begin
{def} repeat
pop currentdict
end
```

Example

```
<< /Duplex true /PageSize [612 792] /Collate false >>
setpagedevice
```

This example constructs a dictionary containing three key-value pairs, which it immediately passes to the **setpagedevice** operator.

Errors: **invalidaccess, rangecheck, unmatchedmark, VMerror**

See Also: **<<, mark, dict**

=   *any* = –

pops an object from the operand stack, produces a text representation of that object's value, and writes the result followed by a newline character to the standard output file. The text is that produced by the **cvs** operator; thus, = prints the value of a number, boolean, string, name, or operator object and prints --nostringval-- for an object of any other type.

The name = is not special. In PostScript language programs it must be delimited by white space or special characters the same as names composed of alphabetical characters. The value of = is not an operator, but rather a built-in procedure.

Errors: **stackunderflow**

See Also: **==, stack, cvs, print, flush**

==   *any* == –

pops an object from the operand stack, produces a text representation of that object followed by a newline character, and writes the result to the standard output file. == attempts to produce a result that resembles the PostScript syntax for creating the object. It precedes literal names by /, brackets strings with (...), and expands the values of arrays and packed arrays and brackets them with [...] or {...}. For an object with no printable representation, == produces the name of its type in the form -mark- or -dict-. For an operator object, it produces the operator's name in the form --add--.

The name == is not special. In PostScript language programs it must be delimited by white space or special characters the same as names composed of alphabetical characters. The value of == is not an operator, but rather a built-in procedure.

The == operator is intended for convenience in debugging. The details of how == formats its output are intentionally unspecified. A program requiring detailed control over output format should do its own formatting explicitly, using lower-level operators, such as **cvs**. Also, **printobject** and **writeobject** (Level 2 features) may be more suitable for generating machine-readable output.

Errors: **stackunderflow**

See Also: **=, print, pstack, flush**

$error – $error *dict*

pushes the dictionary object **$error** on the operand stack (see section 3.10, "Errors"). **$error** is not an operator; it is a name in **systemdict** associated with the dictionary object.

Errors: stackoverflow

See Also: errordict

abs   *num*$_1$ **abs** *num*$_2$

returns the absolute value of *num*$_1$. The type of the result is the same as the type of *num*$_1$ unless *num*$_1$ is the most negative integer, in which case the result is a real.

Example

> 4.5 abs $\Rightarrow$ 4.5
> –3 abs $\Rightarrow$ 3
> 0 abs $\Rightarrow$ 0

Errors: stackunderflow, typecheck

See Also: neg

add   *num*$_1$ *num*$_2$ **add** *sum*

returns the sum of *num*$_1$ and *num*$_2$. If both operands are integers and the result is within integer range, the result is an integer; otherwise, the result is a real.

Example

> 3 4 add $\Rightarrow$ 7
> 9.9 1.1 add $\Rightarrow$ 11.0

Errors: stackunderflow, typecheck, undefinedresult

See Also: div, mul, sub, idiv, mod

aload   *array* **aload** *array$_0$ ... array$_{n-1}$ array*
packedarray **aload** *packedarray$_0$ ... packedarray$_{n-1}$ packedarray*

successively pushes all *n* elements of *array* or *packedarray* on the operand stack (where *n* is the length of the operand), and finally pushes the operand itself.

Example

[23 (ab) –6] aload $\Rightarrow$ 23 (ab) –6 [23 (ab) –6]

Errors: **invalidaccess, stackoverflow, stackunderflow, typecheck**

See Also: **astore, get, getinterval**

anchorsearch   *string* *seek* **anchorsearch** *post match true*   *(if found)*
string false   *(if not found)*

determines if the string *seek* matches the initial substring of *string* (that is, *string* is at least as long as *seek* and the corresponding characters are equal). If it matches, **anchorsearch** splits *string* into two segments: *match,* the portion of *string* that matches *seek,* and *post,* the remainder of *string*; it then pushes the string objects *post* and *match* and the boolean *true*. If not, **anchorsearch** pushes the original *string* and the boolean *false*. **anchorsearch** is a special case of the **search** operator.

Example

(abbc) (ab) anchorsearch $\Rightarrow$ (bc) (ab) true
(abbc) (bb) anchorsearch $\Rightarrow$ (abbc) false
(abbc) (bc) anchorsearch $\Rightarrow$ (abbc) false
(abbc) (B) anchorsearch $\Rightarrow$ (abbc) false

Errors: **invalidaccess, stackoverflow, stackunderflow, typecheck**

See Also: **search, token**

and   *bool$_1$ bool$_2$* **and** *bool$_3$*
int$_1$ int$_2$ **and** *int$_3$*

If the operands are booleans, **and** returns their logical conjunction. If the operands are integers, **and** returns the bitwise *and* of their binary representations.

Example

true true and ⇒ true   % a complete truth table
true false and ⇒ false
false true and ⇒ false
false false and ⇒ false

99 1 and ⇒ 1
52 7 and ⇒ 4

Errors: **stackunderflow, typecheck**

See Also: or, xor, not, true, false

---

arc   *x y r* ang₁ ang₂ **arc** –

appends a counterclockwise arc of a circle to the current path, possibly preceded by a straight line segment. The arc has (x, y) as center, r as radius, ang_1 the angle of a vector from (x, y) of length r to the first endpoint of the arc, and ang_2 the angle of a vector from (x, y) of length r to the second endpoint of the arc.

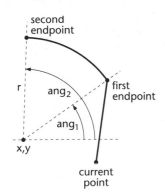

If there is a current point, the **arc** operator includes a straight line segment from the current point to the first endpoint of this arc and then adds the arc into the current path. If the current path is empty, the **arc** operator does not produce the initial straight line segment. In any event, the second endpoint of the arc becomes the new current point.

Angles are measured in degrees counterclockwise from the positive x-axis of the current user coordinate system. The curve produced is circular in user space. If user space is scaled non-uniformly (i.e., differently in x and y) **arc** will produce elliptical curves in device space.

The operators that produce arcs (**arc, arcn, arct,** and **arcto**) represent them internally as one or more Bézier cubic curves (see **curveto**) that approximate the required shape. This is done with sufficient accuracy that a faithful rendition of an arc is produced. However, a program that reads the constructed path using **pathforall** will encounter **curveto** segments where arcs were specified originally.

Example

   newpath 0 0 moveto 0 0 1 0 45 arc closepath

This constructs a 1-unit radius, 45-degree "pie slice."

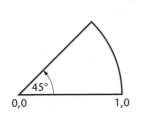

Errors: **limitcheck, stackunderflow, typecheck**

See Also: arcn, arct, arcto, curveto

arcn x y r ang_1 ang_2 **arcn** –

(arc negative) behaves like **arc**, but **arcn** builds its arc segment in a clockwise direction in user space.

Example

> newpath 0 0 2 0 90 arc 0 0 1 90 0 arcn closepath

This constructs a 2-unit radius, 1-unit wide, 90-degree "windshield wiper swath."

Errors: limitcheck, stackunderflow, typecheck

See Also: arc, arct, arcto, curveto

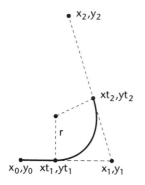

arct x_1 y_1 x_2 y_2 r **arct** –   LEVEL 2

appends an arc of a circle to the current path, possibly preceded by a straight line segment. The arc is defined by a radius r and two tangent lines. The tangent lines are those drawn from the current point, here called (x_0, y_0), to (x_1, y_1), and from (x_1, y_1) to (x_2, y_2). If the current point is undefined, **arct** executes the error **nocurrentpoint**.

The center of the arc is located within the inner angle between the tangent lines. It is the only point located at distance r in a direction perpendicular to both lines. The arc begins at the first tangent point (xt_1, yt_1) on the first tangent line, passes between its center and the point (x_1, y_1), and ends at the second tangent point (xt_2, yt_2) on the second tangent line.

Before constructing the arc, **arct** adds a straight line segment from the current point (x_0, y_0) to (xt_1, yt_1), unless those points are the same. In any event, (xt_2, yt_2) becomes the new current point.

The curve produced is circular in user space. If user space is scaled non-uniformly (i.e., differently in x and y) **arct** will produce elliptical curves in device space.

If the two tangent lines are collinear, (xt_1, yt_1) and (xt_2, yt_2) are identical. In this case, the joining arc has length zero and **arct** merely appends a straight line segment from (x_0, y_0) to (x_1, y_1).

Example

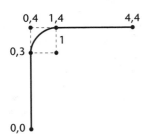

newpath 0 0 moveto
0 4 4 1 arct
4 4 lineto

This constructs a 4-unit wide, 4-unit high right angle with a 1-unit radius "rounded corner."

Errors: limitcheck, nocurrentpoint, stackunderflow, typecheck, undefinedresult

See Also: arc, arcn, arcto, curveto

arcto x_1 y_1 x_2 y_2 r **arcto** xt_1 yt_1 xt_2 yt_2

produces the same effect as **arct**. It also returns the two tangent point coordinates (xt_1, yt_1) and (xt_2, yt_2) in user space. **arcto** is not allowed as an element of a user path, whereas **arct** is allowed. See section 4.6, "User Paths."

Errors: limitcheck, nocurrentpoint, stackunderflow, typecheck, undefinedresult

See Also: arc, arcn, arct, curveto

array   *int* **array** *array*

creates an array of length *int*, each of whose elements is initialized with a null object, and pushes this array on the operand stack. The *int* operand must be a non-negative integer not greater than the maximum allowable array length (see Appendix B). The array is allocated in local or global VM according to the current VM allocation mode. See section 3.7.2, "Local and Global VM."

Example

3 array ⇒ [null null null]

Errors: limitcheck, rangecheck, stackunderflow, typecheck, VMerror

See Also: [,], aload, astore, packedarray

ashow $a_x\ a_y$ *string* **ashow** –

paints the characters of *string* in a manner similar to **show**. But while doing so, **ashow** adjusts the width of each character shown by adding a_x to the character's x width and a_y to its y width, thus modifying the spacing between characters. The numbers a_x and a_y are x and y displacements in the user coordinate system, not in the character coordinate system.

This operator enables a string of text to be fitted to a specific width by adjusting all the spaces between characters by a uniform amount. For a discussion about character widths, see section 5.4, "Font Metric Information."

Example

Normal spacing
W i d e   s p a c i n g

```
/Helvetica findfont 12 scalefont setfont
14 61 moveto (Normal spacing) show
14 47 moveto 4 0 (Wide spacing) ashow
```

Errors: invalidaccess, invalidfont, nocurrentpoint, stackunderflow, typecheck

See Also: show, awidthshow, cshow, kshow, widthshow, xshow, xyshow, yshow

astore $any_0\ ...\ any_{n-1}$ *array* **astore** *array*

stores the objects any_0 through any_{n-1} from the operand stack into *array,* where n is the length of *array.* The **astore** operator first removes the *array* operand from the stack and determines its length. It then removes that number of objects from the stack, storing the topmost one into element $n-1$ of *array* and the bottom-most one into element 0 of *array.* Finally, it pushes *array* back on the stack. Note that **astore** cannot be performed on packed arrays.

If the value of *array* is in global VM and any of $any_0\ ...\ any_{n-1}$ are composite objects whose values are in local VM, an **invalidaccess** error occurs. See section 3.7.2, "Local and Global VM."

Example

(a) (bcd) (ef) 3 array astore $\Rightarrow$ [(a) (bcd) (ef)]

This creates a three element array, stores the strings (a), (bcd), and (ef) into it as elements 0, 1, and 2, and leaves the array object on the operand stack.

Errors: invalidaccess, stackunderflow, typecheck

See Also: aload, put, putinterval

atan   *num den* **atan** *angle*

returns the angle (in degrees between 0 and 360) whose tangent is *num/den*. Either *num* or *den* may be zero, but not both. The signs of *num* and *den* determine the quadrant in which the result will lie: a positive *num* yields a result in the positive *y* plane, a positive *den* yields a result in the positive *x* plane. The result is a real.

Example

    0 1 atan ⇒ 0.0
    1 0 atan ⇒ 90.0
    –100 0 atan ⇒ 270.0
    4 4 atan ⇒ 45.0

Errors: stackunderflow, typecheck, undefinedresult

See Also: cos, sin

awidthshow c_x c_y *char* a_x a_y *string* **awidthshow** –

paints the characters of *string* in a manner similar to **show,** but combines the special effects of **ashow** and **widthshow. awidthshow** adjusts the width of each character shown by adding a_x to its *x* width and a_y to its *y* width, thus modifying the spacing between characters. Furthermore, **awidthshow** modifies the width of each occurrence of the character *char* by an additional amount *(c_x, c_y)*. The interpretation of *char* is as described for the **widthshow** operator.

This operator enables fitting a string of text to a specific width by adjusting all of the spaces between characters by a uniform amount, while independently controlling the width of some specific character, such as the space character. For a discussion about character widths, see section 5.4, "Font Metric Information."

Example

Normal spacing
Wide   spacing

    /Helvetica findfont 12 scalefont setfont
    30 60 moveto (Normal spacing) show
    30 46 moveto 6 0 8#040 .5 0 (Wide spacing) awidthshow

Errors: invalidaccess, invalidfont, nocurrentpoint, rangecheck, stackunderflow, typecheck

See Also: ashow, cshow, kshow, show, widthshow, xshow, xyshow, yshow

begin   *dict* **begin** –

pushes *dict* on the dictionary stack, making it the current dictionary and installing it as the first of the dictionaries consulted during implicit name lookup and by **def**, **load**, **store**, and **where**.

Errors: **dictstackoverflow, invalidaccess, stackunderflow, typecheck**

See Also: **end, countdictstack, dictstack**

bind   *proc* **bind** *proc*

replaces executable operator names in *proc* by their values. For each element of *proc* that is an executable name, **bind** looks up the name in the context of the current dictionary stack as if by **load**. If the name is found and its value is an operator object, **bind** replaces the name by the operator in *proc*. If the name is not found or its value is not an operator, **bind** does not make a change.

For each procedure object in *proc*, **bind** applies itself recursively to that procedure, makes the procedure read-only, and stores it back into *proc*. The **bind** operator applies to both arrays and packed arrays, but it treats their access attributes differently. It will ignore a read-only array; that is, it will neither bind elements of the array nor examine nested procedures. On the other hand, **bind** will operate on a packed array (which is always read-only), disregarding its access attribute. No error occurs in either case.

The effect of **bind** is that all operator names in *proc* and in procedures nested in *proc* to any depth become "tightly bound" to the operators themselves. During subsequent execution of *proc,* the interpreter encounters the operators themselves rather than the names of operators. See section 3.11, "Early Name Binding."

Errors: **typecheck**

See Also: **load**

bitshift int_1 *shift* **bitshift** int_2

shifts the binary representation of int_1 left by *shift* bits and returns the result. Bits shifted out are lost; bits shifted in are zero. If *shift* is negative, then a right shift by *–shift* bits is performed. This produces an arithmetically correct result only for positive values of int_1. Both int_1 and *shift* must be integers.

Example

   7 3 bitshift $\Rightarrow$ 56
   142 –3 bitshift $\Rightarrow$ 17

Errors: **stackunderflow, typecheck**

See Also: **and, or, xor, not**

bytesavailable   *file* **bytesavailable** *int*

returns the number of bytes that are immediately available for reading from *file* without waiting. The result is –1 if end-of-file has been encountered or if the number of bytes available cannot be determined for other reasons.

Errors: **ioerror, stackunderflow, typecheck**

See Also: **read, readhexstring, readline, readstring**

cachestatus   – **cachestatus** *bsize bmax msize mmax csize cmax blimit*

returns measurements of several aspects of the font cache (see section 5.5, "Font Cache"). **cachestatus** reports the current consumption and limit for each of three font cache resources: bytes of bitmap storage (*bsize* and *bmax*), font/matrix combinations (*msize* and *mmax*), and total number of cached characters (*csize* and *cmax*). It also reports the limit on the number of bytes occupied by a single cached character *(blimit)*. Characters whose bitmaps are larger than this are not cached.

Errors: **stackoverflow**

See Also: **setcachelimit, setsystemparams**

ceiling num_1 **ceiling** num_2

returns the least integer value greater than or equal to num_1. The type of the result is the same as the type of the operand.

Example

> 3.2 ceiling $\Rightarrow$ 4.0
> –4.8 ceiling $\Rightarrow$ –4.0
> 99 ceiling $\Rightarrow$ 99

Errors: stackunderflow, typecheck

See Also: floor, round, truncate, cvi

---

charpath   *string* *bool* **charpath** –

obtains the character path outlines that would result if *string* were shown at the current point using **show**. Instead of painting the path, however, **charpath** appends the path to the current path. This yields a result suitable for general filling, stroking, or clipping (see sections 4.4, "Path Construction," 4.5, "Painting," and 5.1, "Organization and Use of Fonts").

The *bool* operand determines what happens if the character path is designed to be stroked rather than filled or outlined. If *bool* is *false*, **charpath** simply appends the character path to the current path; the result is suitable only for stroking. If *bool* is *true*, **charpath** applies the **strokepath** operator to the character path; the result is suitable for filling or clipping, but not for stroking. **charpath** does not produce results for portions of a character defined as images or masks rather than as paths.

The outlines of some fonts are protected. (In Level 1 implementations, this applies to all fonts; in Level 2, only to certain special fonts and not to ordinary Type 1 or Type 3 fonts.) If the current font is protected, using **charpath** to obtain its outlines causes the **pathforall** and **upath** operators to be disabled for as long as those outlines remain in the current path.

Errors: limitcheck, nocurrentpoint, stackunderflow, typecheck

See Also: show, flattenpath, pathbbox, clip

clear   ⊢ *any*₁ ... *any*ₙ **clear**   ⊢

pops all objects from the operand stack and discards them.

Errors: (none)

See Also: **count, cleartomark, pop**

cleardictstack   – **cleardictstack** –

pops all dictionaries off the dictionary stack except for the permanent entries. In Level 1 implementations the permanent entries are **systemdict** and **userdict**; in Level 2 they are **systemdict**, **globaldict**, and **userdict**. (In Level 1 implementations, **cleardictstack** is a procedure defined in **userdict** instead of an operator defined in **systemdict**.)

Errors: (none)

See Also: **begin, end**

cleartomark   *mark* *obj*₁ ... *obj*ₙ **cleartomark** –

pops the operand stack repeatedly until it encounters a mark, which it also pops from the stack (*obj*₁ through *obj*ₙ are any objects other than marks).

Errors: **unmatchedmark**

See Also: **clear, mark, counttomark, pop**

clip   – clip –

intersects the inside of the current clipping path with the inside of the current path to produce a new, smaller current clipping path. The inside of the current path is determined by the normal PostScript non-zero winding number rule (see section 4.5, "Painting"), while the inside of the current clipping path is determined by whatever rule was used at the time that path was created.

In general, **clip** produces a new path whose inside (according to the non-zero winding number rule) consists of all areas that are inside both of the original paths. The way this new path is constructed (the order of its segments, whether it self-intersects, etc.) is not specified. **clip** treats an open subpath of the current path as though it were closed; it does not actually alter the path itself. It is permissible for the current path to be empty. The result of executing **clip** is always a non-empty clipping path, though it may enclose zero area.

There is no way to enlarge the current clipping path (other than by **initclip** or **initgraphics**) or to set a new clipping path without reference to the current one. The recommended way of using **clip** is to bracket the **clip** and the sequence of graphics to be clipped with **gsave** and **grestore**. The **grestore** will restore the clipping path that was in effect before the **gsave**. The **setgstate** operator can also be used to reset the clipping path to an earlier state.

Unlike **fill** and **stroke, clip** does not implicitly perform a **newpath** after it has finished using the current path. Any subsequent path construction operators will append to the current path unless **newpath** is executed explicitly. This can cause unexpected behavior.

Errors: **limitcheck**

See Also: **eoclip, clippath, initclip, rectclip**

clippath   – clippath –

sets the current path to one that describes the current clipping path. This operator is useful for determining the exact extent of the imaging area on the current output device.

If the current clipping path is the result of application of the **clip** or **eoclip** operator, the path set by **clippath** is generally suitable only for filling or clipping. It is not suitable for stroking because it may contain interior segments or disconnected subpaths produced by the clipping process.

Example

    clippath 1 setgray fill

This erases (fills with white) the interior of the current clipping path.

Errors: (none)

See Also: **clip, eoclip, initclip, rectclip**

closefile   *file* **closefile** –

closes *file*—in other words, breaks the association between the file object and the underlying file. For an output file, **closefile** first performs a **flushfile**. It may also take device-dependent actions, such as truncating a disk file to the current position or transmitting an end-of-file indication. See section 3.8, "File Input and Output."

Errors: **ioerror, stackunderflow, typecheck**

See Also: **file, filter, status**

closepath   – **closepath** –

closes the current subpath by appending a straight line segment connecting the current point to the subpath's starting point—generally, the point most recently specified by **moveto**. If the current subpath is already closed or the current path is empty, **closepath** does not do anything (see section 4.4, "Path Construction").

closepath terminates the current subpath. Appending another segment to the current path will begin a new subpath, even if it is drawn from the endpoint reached by the **closepath.**

Errors: **limitcheck**

See Also: **newpath, moveto, lineto**

colorimage   *width height bits/comp matrix*
datasrc$_0$ ... datasrc$_{n-1}$ multi ncomp **colorimage** –

paints a sampled image onto the current page. The description here only summarizes the **colorimage** operator. See section 4.10, "Images" for full details.

The sampled image is a rectangular array of *width* × *height* sample values. **colorimage** interprets the *width*, *height*, and *matrix* operands in the same way as does **image**.

Each image sample consists of 1, 3, or 4 color components, as specified by the *ncomp* operand. Each component consists of *bits/comp* bits (1, 2, 4, 8, or 12). All components are the same size.

If *ncomp* is 1, the samples have only one (gray) component; the operation of **colorimage** is equivalent to that of **image** using the first five operands. If *ncomp* is 3, the samples consist of red, green, and blue components. If *ncomp* is 4, the samples consist of cyan, magenta, yellow, and black components. The 1, 3, and 4 component values are interpreted according to the **DeviceGray**, **DeviceRGB**, and **DeviceCMYK** color spaces, respectively (see section 4.8, "Color Spaces"), regardless of the current color space.

The *multi* operand is a boolean that determines how **colorimage** is to obtain sample data from its data sources. If *multi* is *false*, there is a single data source, *datasrc$_0$*; **colorimage** obtains all components from that source, interleaved on a per-sample basis. If *multi* is *true*, there are *ncomp* data sources, *datasrc$_0$ ... datasrc$_{n-1}$*, one for each component. The data sources can be procedures, strings, or files, including filtered files. They must all be of the same type (see section 4.10.2, "Sample Data Representation").

Unlike **image** and **imagemask**, **colorimage** does not have an alternate form in which the parameters are bundled into a single image dictionary operand. In Level 2 implementations, given the appropriate image dictionary, the **image** operator can do anything that **colorimage** can do, and many other things. For example, **image** can interpret color samples in any color space, whereas **colorimage** is limited to the **DeviceGray**, **DeviceRGB**, and **DeviceCMYK** color spaces.

Execution of this operator is not permitted in certain circumstances; see section 4.8, "Color Spaces."

Errors: invalidaccess, ioerror, limitcheck, rangecheck, stackunderflow, typecheck, undefined, undefinedresult

See Also: image, imagemask

concat   *matrix* **concat** –

concatenates *matrix* with the current transformation matrix (CTM). Precisely, **concat** replaces the CTM by *matrix* × CTM (see section 4.3, "Coordinate Systems and Transformations"). The effect of this is to define a new user space whose coordinates are transformed into the former user space according to *matrix.*

Examples

> [72 0 0 72 0 0] concat
> 72 72 scale

The two examples have the same effect on the current transformation.

Errors: **rangecheck, stackunderflow, typecheck**

See Also: **concatmatrix, matrix, rotate, scale, setmatrix, translate**

concatmatrix   *matrix_1 matrix_2 matrix_3* **concatmatrix** *matrix_3*

replaces the value of *matrix_3* by the result of multiplying *matrix_1* × *matrix_2*, and pushes the modified *matrix_3* back on the operand stack. This operator does not affect the CTM.

Errors: **rangecheck, stackunderflow, typecheck**

See Also: **concat, matrix, rotate, scale, setmatrix, translate**

condition   – **condition** *condition*   DPS

creates a new condition object, unequal to any condition object already in existence, and pushes it on the operand stack. The condition initially has no contexts waiting on it (see section 7.1, "Multiple Execution Contexts"). Since a condition is a composite object, creating one consumes VM. The condition's value is allocated in local or global VM according to the current VM allocation mode.

Errors: **stackoverflow, VMerror**

See Also: **wait, notify**

configurationerror   *(error)*   **LEVEL 2**

occurs when **setpagedevice** or **setdevparams** has been executed with a request for a feature that either is not available in the interpreter implementation or is not currently available because of the state of the hardware. For **setpagedevice**, this error is generated only if the **PolicyDict** entry in a page device dictionary specifies that an error should be generated.

When a **configurationerror** is generated, a two-element array called **errorinfo** is placed in **$error**. This array contains the key and value of the request that could not be met. See section 3.10, "Errors."

See Also: setpagedevice, setdevparams

copy $any_1 \dots any_n$ n **copy** $any_1 \dots any_n$ $any_1 \dots any_n$

$array_1$ $array_2$ **copy** $subarray_2$
$dict_1$ $dict_2$ **copy** $dict_2$
$string_1$ $string_2$ **copy** $substring_2$
$packedarray_1$ $array_2$ **copy** $subarray_2$
$gstate_1$ $gstate_2$ **copy** $gstate_2$

performs two entirely different functions, depending on the type of the topmost operand.

In the first instance, where the top element on the operand stack is a non-negative integer *n*, **copy** pops *n* from the stack and duplicates the top *n* elements on the operand stack as shown above. This form of **copy** operates only on the objects themselves, not on the values of composite objects.

Example

1 2 3 2 copy $\Rightarrow$ 1 2 3 2 3
1 2 3 0 copy $\Rightarrow$ 1 2 3

In the other instances, **copy** copies all the elements of the first composite object into the second. The composite object operands must be of the same type, except that a packed array can be copied into an array. This form of **copy** copies the *value* of a composite object. This is quite different from **dup** and other operators that copy only the objects themselves (see section 3.3.1, "Simple and Composite Objects"). However, **copy** performs only one level of copying. It does not apply recursively to elements that are themselves composite objects; instead, the values of those elements become shared.

In the case of arrays or strings, the length of the second object must be at least as great as the first; **copy** returns the initial *subarray* or *substring* of the second operand into which the elements were copied. Any remaining elements of *array₂* or *string₂* are unaffected. **copy** cannot copy into packed arrays, because they are read-only, but it can copy packed arrays into ordinary arrays.

In the case of dictionaries, Level 1 implementations require that $dict_2$ have a **length** of zero and a **maxlength** at least as great as the length of $dict_1$. Level 2 implementations do not impose this restriction, since dictionaries can expand when necessary.

The attributes (literal or executable and access) of the result are normally the same as those of the second operand. However, in Level 1 implementations, the access attribute of $dict_2$ is copied from that of $dict_1$.

If the value of the destination object is in global VM and any of the elements copied from the source object are composite objects whose values are in local VM, an **invalidaccess** error occurs (see section 3.7.2, "Local and Global VM").

Example

    /a1 [1 2 3] def
    a1 dup length array copy ⇒ [1 2 3]

Errors: **invalidaccess, rangecheck, stackunderflow, stackoverflow, typecheck**

See Also: **dup, get, put, putinterval**

---

copypage   – copypage –

transmits one copy of the current page to the current output device without erasing the current page or changing the graphics state. This is in contrast to **showpage**, which performs the equivalent of an **erasepage** and an **initgraphics**. Aside from these differences, the behavior of **copypage** is identical to that of **showpage**.

copypage is intended primarily as a debugging aid or as a means of printing successive pages with incrementally accumulated contents. Routine use of **copypage** as a substitute for **showpage** may *severely* degrade the page throughput of some PostScript printers. To print multiple copies of the same page, use the **#copies** implicit parameter of **showpage** or the **NumCopies** parameter of **setpagedevice**.

Errors: (none)

See Also: **showpage, erasepage**

cos   *angle* **cos** *real*

returns the cosine of *angle,* which is interpreted as an angle in degrees. The result is a real.

Example

    0 cos $\Rightarrow$ 1.0
    90 cos $\Rightarrow$ 0.0

Errors: **stackunderflow, typecheck**

See Also: **atan, sin**

count $\vdash$ *any*$_1$ ... *any*$_n$ **count** $\vdash$ *any*$_1$ ... *any*$_n$ *n*

counts the number of items on the operand stack and pushes this count on the operand stack.

Example

    clear count $\Rightarrow$ 0
    clear 1 2 3 count $\Rightarrow$ 1 2 3 3

Errors: **stackoverflow**

See Also: **counttomark**

countdictstack   – **countdictstack** *int*

counts the number of dictionaries currently on the dictionary stack and pushes this count on the operand stack.

Errors: **stackoverflow**

See Also: **dictstack, begin, end**

countexecstack   – countexecstack *int*

counts the number of objects on the execution stack and pushes this count on the operand stack.

Errors: **stackoverflow**

See Also: **execstack**

counttomark   *mark obj*$_1$ ... *obj*$_n$ **counttomark** *mark obj*$_1$ ... *obj*$_n$ *n*

counts the number of objects on the operand stack starting with the top element and continuing down to but not including the first mark encountered. *obj*$_1$ through *obj*$_n$ are any objects other than marks.

Example

1 mark 2 3 counttomark ⇒ 1 mark 2 3 2
1 mark counttomark ⇒ 1 mark 0

Errors: **stackoverflow, unmatchedmark**

See Also: **mark, count**

cshow   *proc string* **cshow** –   LEVEL 2

invokes *proc* once for each operation of the font mapping algorithm (see section 5.9.1, "Character Mapping"). The value of **currentfont** during the execution of *proc* is the base font that the algorithm ultimately selects. When *proc* is invoked, the stack contains three values: the selected character's code (an integer) and the *x* and *y* components of the width vector for the character in the user coordinate system. **cshow** does not paint the character and does not change the current point, although *proc* may do so. When *proc* completes execution, the value of **currentfont** is restored.

cshow can be used to provide careful positioning of individual characters while taking advantage of the composite font mapping machinery of the interpreter. **cshow** is intended primarily for use with composite fonts (see section 5.9, "Composite Fonts"). However, it can also be used with a base font. The mapping algorithm for a base font simply selects consecutive characters from the string.

Errors: **invalidfont, invalidaccess, nocurrentpoint, rangecheck, stackunderflow, typecheck**

See Also: **show, ashow, awidthshow, kshow, widthshow, xshow, xyshow, yshow**

currentblackgeneration

– currentblackgeneration *proc*

LEVEL 2

returns the current black generation function in the graphics state.

Errors: stackoverflow

See Also: setblackgeneration

currentcacheparams

– currentcacheparams *mark size lower upper*

LEVEL 2

pushes a mark object followed by the current cache parameters on the operand stack. The number of cache parameters returned is variable (see **setcacheparams**).

Errors: stackoverflow

See Also: setcacheparams, setsystemparams, setuserparams

currentcmykcolor

– currentcmykcolor *cyan magenta yellow black*

LEVEL 2

returns the current color in the graphics state according to the cyan-magenta-yellow-black color space. If the current color space is **DeviceCMYK**, **currentcmykcolor** returns the color values most recently specified by **setcmykcolor** or **setcolor**. If the current color space is **DeviceRGB** or **DeviceGray**, **currentcmykcolor** converts the current color to CMYK according to the conventions described in section 6.2, "Conversions Among Device Color Spaces." For any other color space, **currentcmykcolor** returns 0.0 0.0 0.0 1.0.

Errors: stackoverflow

See Also: setcmykcolor

currentcolor

– currentcolor *comp$_1$ comp$_2$ ... comp$_m$*

LEVEL 2

returns the components, in the current color space, of the color specified by the current color parameters in the graphics state.

Errors: stackoverflow

See Also: setcolor, setcolorspace

currentcolorrendering   – **currentcolorrendering** *dict*

returns the value of the CIE based color rendering dictionary parameter in the graphics state.

Errors: **stackoverflow**

See Also: **setcolorrendering**

currentcolorscreen   – **currentcolorscreen** *redfreq redang redproc*
greenfreq greenang greenproc
bluefreq blueang blueproc
grayfreq grayang grayproc

If the current halftone screen was specified by **setcolorscreen**, **currentcolorscreen** returns all 12 current halftone screen parameters in the graphics state. If the current screen was specified by **setscreen**, **currentcolorscreen** returns the three screen parameters repeated four times. If the current screen was specified by **sethalftone**, **currentcolorscreen** returns 60, 0, and the halftone dictionary, repeated four times.

Errors: **stackoverflow**

See Also: **setcolorscreen, setscreen, sethalftone**

currentcolorspace   – **currentcolorspace** *array*

returns an array containing the identifying key and parameters of the color space in the graphics state. **currentcolorspace** always returns an array, even if the color space has no parameters and was selected by presenting just a name to **setcolorspace**.

Errors: **stackoverflow**

See Also: **setcolorspace, setcolor**

currentcolortransfer   – **currentcolortransfer** *redproc greenproc blueproc grayproc*   `LEVEL 2`

returns the current transfer functions in the graphics state for all four color components. If the current transfer functions were specified by **setcolortransfer**, **currentcolortransfer** returns those four operands. If **settransfer** was used, **currentcolortransfer** returns the single transfer function, repeated four times.

Errors: **stackoverflow**

See Also: **setcolortransfer, settransfer**

currentcontext   – **currentcontext** *context*   `DPS`

returns an integer that identifies the current execution context. See section 7.1, "Multiple Execution Contexts."

Errors: **stackoverflow**

See Also: **fork, join, detach**

currentdash   – **currentdash** *array offset*

returns the current dash array and offset in the graphics state.

Errors: **stackoverflow**

See Also: **setdash, stroke**

currentdevparams   *string* **currentdevparams** *dict*   `LEVEL 2`

returns a dictionary containing the keys and current values of all parameters for the device identified by *string*. The returned dictionary is merely a container for key-value pairs. Each execution of **currentdevparams** allocates and returns a new dictionary.

Errors: **stackoverflow, VMerror**

See Also: **setdevparams**

currentdict   – currentdict *dict*

pushes the current dictionary (the dictionary on top of the dictionary stack) on the operand stack. **currentdict** does not pop the dictionary stack; it just pushes a duplicate of its top element on the operand stack.

Errors: **stackoverflow**

See Also: **begin, dictstack**

currentfile   – currentfile *file*

returns the file object from which the PostScript interpreter is currently or was most recently reading program input. Precisely, **currentfile** returns the topmost file object on the execution stack. If there isn't one, it returns an invalid file object that doesn't correspond to any file. This never occurs during execution of ordinary user programs.

The file returned by **currentfile** is usually but not always the standard input file. An important exception occurs during interactive mode operation (see section 3.8.3, "Special Files"). In this case, the interpreter does not read directly from the standard input file; instead, it reads from a file representing an edited statement (each statement is represented by a different file).

The **currentfile** operator is useful for obtaining images or other data residing in the program file itself (see the example below). At any given time, this file is positioned at the end of the last PostScript language token read from the file by the interpreter. If that token was a number or a name immediately followed by a white space character, the file is positioned after the white space character (the first, if there are several). Otherwise it is positioned after the last character of the token.

Example

```
/str 100 string def
currentfile str readline
here is a line of text
pop /textline exch def
```

After execution of this example, the name /textline is associated with the string "here is a line of text".

Errors: **stackoverflow**

See Also: **exec, run**

currentflat   – **currentflat** *num*

returns the current value of the flatness parameter in the graphics state.

Errors: **stackoverflow**

See Also: **setflat, flattenpath, stroke, fill**

currentfont   – **currentfont** *font*

returns the current font dictionary in the graphics state. Normally, this is the font most recently established by **setfont** or **selectfont**. However, when executed inside a font's **BuildGlyph** or **BuildChar** procedure or a procedure invoked by **cshow**, **currentfont** returns the currently selected base font (descendant of a composite font).

Errors: **stackoverflow**

See Also: **rootfont, selectfont, setfont**

currentglobal   – **currentglobal** *bool*   LEVEL 2

returns the VM allocation mode currently in effect.

Errors: **stackoverflow**

See Also: **setglobal**

currentgray   – **currentgray** *num*

returns the gray value of the current color parameter in the graphics state. If the current color space is **DeviceGray**, **currentgray** returns the color value most recently specified to **setgray** or **setcolor**. If the current color space is **DeviceRGB** or **DeviceCMYK**, **currentgray** converts the current color to a gray value according to the conventions described in section 6.2, "Conversions Among Device Color Spaces." For any other color space, **currentgray** returns 0.0.

Errors: **stackoverflow**

See Also: **setgray, currentcolor, currentcolorspace, currenthsbcolor, currentrgbcolor**

currentgstate   *gstate* **currentgstate** *gstate*   LEVEL 2

replaces the value of the *gstate* object by a copy of the current graphics state and pushes *gstate* back on the operand stack. If *gstate* is in global VM (see section 3.7, "Memory Management"), **currentgstate** will generate an **invalidaccess** error if any of the composite objects in the current graphics state are in local VM. Such objects might include the current font, screen function, halftone dictionary, transfer function, or dash pattern. In general, allocating gstate objects in global VM is risky and should be avoided.

Errors: **invalidaccess, stackunderflow, typecheck**

See Also: **gstate, setgstate**

currenthalftone   – **currenthalftone** *halftone*   LEVEL 2

returns the current halftone dictionary in the graphics state. If the current halftone was defined by **setscreen** or **setcolorscreen** instead of by **sethalftone**, **currenthalftone** fabricates and returns a halftone dictionary (type 1 or 2) that contains the screen parameters.

Errors: **stackoverflow, VMerror**

See Also: **setscreen, setcolorscreen, sethalftone**

currenthalftonephase   – **currenthalftonephase** *x y*   DPS

returns the current values of the halftone phase parameters in the graphics state. If **sethalftonephase** has not been executed, zero is returned for both values.

Errors: **stackoverflow**

See Also: **sethalftonephase**

currenthsbcolor   – **currenthsbcolor** *hue saturation brightness*

returns the current color parameter in the graphics state according to the hue-saturation-brightness model. If the current color space is **DeviceRGB**, **currenthsbcolor** returns the color values most recently specified by **sethsbcolor**, **setrgbcolor**, or **setcolor**, converting them from RGB to HSB coordinates if necessary. If the current color space is **DeviceGray** or **DeviceCMYK**, **currenthsbcolor** first converts the current color to RGB according to the conventions described in section 6.2, "Conversions Among Device Color Spaces." For any other color space, **currenthsbcolor** returns 0.0 0.0 0.0.

Errors: stackoverflow

See Also: sethsbcolor, currentcolor, currentgray, currentrgbcolor

currentlinecap   – **currentlinecap** *int*

returns the current value of the line cap parameter in the graphics state.

Errors: stackoverflow

See Also: setlinecap, stroke, currentlinejoin

currentlinejoin   – **currentlinejoin** *int*

returns the current value of the line join parameter in the graphics state.

Errors: stackoverflow

See Also: setlinejoin, stroke, currentlinecap

currentlinewidth   – **currentlinewidth** *num*

returns the current value of the line width parameter in the graphics state.

Errors: stackoverflow

See Also: setlinewidth, stroke

currentmatrix   *matrix* **currentmatrix** *matrix*

replaces the value of *matrix* with the value of the current transformation matrix (CTM) in the graphics state, and pushes the modified matrix back on the operand stack (see section 4.3, "Coordinate Systems and Transformations").

Errors: **rangecheck, stackunderflow, typecheck**

See Also: **setmatrix, defaultmatrix, initmatrix, rotate, scale, translate**

currentmiterlimit   – **currentmiterlimit** *num*

returns the current value of the miter limit parameter in the graphics state.

Errors: **stackoverflow**

See Also: **setmiterlimit, stroke**

currentobjectformat   – **currentobjectformat** *int*   LEVEL 2

returns the object format parameter currently in effect.

Errors: **stackoverflow**

See Also: **setobjectformat**

currentoverprint   – **currentoverprint** *bool*   LEVEL 2

returns the value of the overprint parameter in the graphics state.

Errors: **stackoverflow**

See Also: **setoverprint**

currentpacking   – **currentpacking** *bool*   LEVEL 2

returns the array packing mode currently in effect.

Errors: **stackoverflow**

See Also: **setpacking, packedarray**

currentpagedevice   – **currentpagedevice** *dict*   LEVEL 2

returns a read-only dictionary that describes the page-oriented output device in the current graphics state. **currentpagedevice** creates a new dictionary if necessary. If the device in the current graphics state is not a page device, **currentpagedevice** returns an empty dictionary (length of 0). See section 4.11, "Device Setup."

Changes made to the hardware state of the output device since the last execution of **setpagedevice**, such as changing paper trays or switches, are not immediately reflected in this dictionary. If the current context is under the control of a job server (see section 3.7.7, "Job Execution Environment"), the server sets up a device that matches the hardware state before starting each job. At the beginning of each job, therefore, the dictionary **currentpagedevice** returns matches the current hardware state.

Errors: **stackoverflow, VMerror**

See Also: **setpagedevice**

currentpoint   – **currentpoint** *x y*

returns the *x* and *y* coordinates of the current point in the graphics state (i.e., the trailing endpoint of the current path). If the current point is undefined because the current path is empty, **currentpoint** executes the **nocurrentpoint** error.

The current point is reported in the user coordinate system. As discussed in section 4.4, "Path Construction," points entered into a path are immediately converted to device coordinates by the current transformation matrix (CTM); existing points are not changed by subsequent modifications to the CTM. **currentpoint** computes the user space coordinate that corresponds to the current point according to the current value of the CTM. If a current point is set and then the CTM is changed, **currentpoint** will report a different position in user space than it did before.

Errors: **nocurrentpoint, stackoverflow, undefinedresult**

See Also: **moveto, lineto, curveto, arc**

currentrgbcolor   – **currentrgbcolor** *red green blue*

returns the three components of the current color in the graphics state according to the red-green-blue color model. If the current color space is **DeviceRGB**, **currentrgbcolor** returns the color values most recently specified to **setrgbcolor** or **setcolor** (or transformed values specified to **sethsbcolor**). If the current color space is **DeviceGray** or **DeviceCMYK**, **currentrgbcolor** converts the current color to RGB according to the conventions described in section 6.2, "Conversions Among Device Color Spaces." For any other color space, **currentrgbcolor** returns 0.0 0.0 0.0.

Errors: stackoverflow

See Also: setrgbcolor, currentcolor, currentgray, currenthsbcolor

currentscreen   – **currentscreen** *frequency angle proc*
             – **currentscreen** *frequency angle halftone*

returns the current halftone screen parameters (*frequency, angle,* and *proc*) in the graphics state, assuming the current screen was established by **setscreen**. If **setcolorscreen** was executed, **currentscreen** returns the parameters for the gray screen. If **sethalftone** was executed, **currentscreen** returns the frequency, angle, and halftone dictionary. For type 1 halftone dictionaries, the *frequency* and *angle* values are extracted from the halftone dictionary. For all other types, **currentscreen** returns a frequency of 60 and an angle of 0.

Errors: stackoverflow

See Also: setcolorscreen, setscreen, sethalftone

currentshared   – **currentshared** *bool*   <u>LEVEL 2</u>

has the same semantics as **currentglobal**. This operator is defined for compatibility with existing Display PostScript applications.

Errors: stackoverflow

See Also: setglobal, setshared

currentstrokeadjust   – **currentstrokeadjust** *bool*   <u>LEVEL 2</u>

returns the current stroke adjust parameter in the graphics state.

Errors: stackoverflow

See Also: setstrokeadjust

currentsystemparams

– currentsystemparams *dict*

LEVEL 2

returns a dictionary containing the keys and current values of all system parameters that are defined in the implementation. The returned dictionary is merely a container for key-value pairs. Each execution of **currentsystemparams** allocates and returns a new dictionary. See Appendix C for information about specific system parameters.

Errors: stackoverflow, VMerror

See Also: setsystemparams

currenttransfer

– currenttransfer *proc*

returns the current transfer function in the graphics state, assuming that it was established by **settransfer**. If **setcolortransfer** was executed, **currenttransfer** returns the gray transfer function.

Errors: stackoverflow

See Also: settransfer, setcolortransfer

currentundercolorremoval

– currentundercolorremoval *proc*

LEVEL 2

returns the current undercolor removal function in the graphics state.

Errors: stackoverflow

See Also: setundercolorremoval

currentuserparams

– currentuserparams *dict*

LEVEL 2

returns a dictionary containing the keys and current values of all user parameters that are defined in the implementation. The returned dictionary is a container for key-value pairs. Each execution of **currentuserparams** allocates and returns a new dictionary. See Appendix C for more information about specific user parameters.

Errors: stackoverflow, VMerror

See Also: setuserparams

curveto x_1 y_1 x_2 y_2 x_3 y_3 **curveto** –

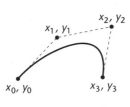

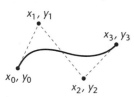

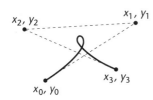

adds a Bézier cubic section to the current path between the current point, referred to here as (x_0, y_0), and the point (x_3, y_3), using (x_1, y_1) and (x_2, y_2) as the Bézier cubic control points. After constructing the curve, **curveto** makes (x_3, y_3) the new current point. If the current point is undefined because the current path is empty, **curveto** executes the error **nocurrentpoint**.

The four points define the shape of the curve geometrically. The curve starts at (x_0, y_0), it is tangent to the line from (x_0, y_0) to (x_1, y_1) at that point, and it leaves the point in that direction. The curve ends at (x_3, y_3), it is tangent to the line from (x_2, y_2) to (x_3, y_3) at that point, and it approaches the point from that direction. The lengths of the lines (x_0, y_0) to (x_1, y_1) and (x_2, y_2) to (x_3, y_3) represent, in a sense, the "velocity" of the path at the endpoints. The curve is always entirely enclosed by the convex quadrilateral defined by the four points.

The mathematical formulation of a Bézier cubic curve is derived from a pair of parametric cubic equations:

$$x(t) = a_x t^3 + b_x t^2 + c_x t + x_0$$
$$y(t) = a_y t^3 + b_y t^2 + c_y t + y_0$$

The cubic section produced by **curveto** is the path traced by $x(t)$ and $y(t)$ as t ranges from 0 to 1. The Bézier control points corresponding to this curve are:

$$x_1 = x_0 + c_x/3 \qquad\qquad y_1 = y_0 + c_y/3$$

$$x_2 = x_1 + (c_x + b_x)/3 \qquad y_2 = y_1 + (c_y + b_y)/3$$

$$x_3 = x_0 + c_x + b_x + a_x \qquad y_3 = y_0 + c_y + b_y + a_y$$

Errors: limitcheck, nocurrentpoint, stackunderflow, typecheck

See Also: lineto, moveto, arc, arcn, arct, arcto

cvi   *num* **cvi** *int*
       string **cvi** *int*

(convert to integer) takes an integer, real, or string object from the stack and produces an integer result. If the operand is an integer, **cvi** simply returns it. If the operand is a real, it truncates any fractional part (i.e., rounds it toward 0) and converts it to an integer. If the operand is a string, it interprets the characters of the string as a number according to the PostScript syntax rules. If that number is a real, **cvi** converts it to an integer. **cvi** executes a **rangecheck** error if a real is too large to convert to an integer. (See the **round, truncate, floor,** and **ceiling** operators, which remove fractional parts without performing type conversion.)

Example

> (3.3E1) cvi ⇒ 33
> –47.8 cvi ⇒ –47
> 520.9 cvi ⇒ 520

Errors: **invalidaccess, rangecheck, stackunderflow, syntaxerror, typecheck, undefinedresult**

See Also: **cvr, ceiling, floor, round, truncate**

cvlit   *any* **cvlit** *any*

(convert to literal) makes the object on the top of the operand stack have the literal instead of executable attribute.

Errors: **stackunderflow**

See Also: **cvx, xcheck**

cvn   *string* **cvn** *name*

(convert to name) converts the string operand to a name object that is lexically the same as the string. The name object is executable if the string was.

Example

> (abc) cvn ⇒ /abc
> (abc) cvx cvn ⇒ abc

Errors: **invalidaccess, limitcheck, stackunderflow, typecheck**

See Also: **cvs, type**

cvr   *num* **cvr** *real*
           string **cvr** *real*

(convert to real) takes an integer, real, or string object and produces a real result. If the operand is an integer, **cvr** converts it to a real. If the operand is a real, **cvr** simply returns it. If the operand is a string, it interprets the characters of the string as a number according to the PostScript syntax rules. If that number is an integer, **cvr** converts it to a real.

Errors: **invalidaccess, limitcheck, stackunderflow, syntaxerror, typecheck, undefinedresult**

See Also: **cvi**

cvrs   *num radix string* **cvrs** *substring*

(convert to string with radix) produces a text representation of the number *num* in the specified *radix,* stores the text into the supplied *string* (overwriting some initial portion of its value), and returns a string object designating the substring actually used. If *string* is too small to hold the result of the conversion, **cvrs** executes the error **rangecheck.**

If *radix* is 10, **cvrs** produces the same result as **cvs** when applied to either an integer or a real. That is, it produces a signed integer or real token that conforms to the PostScript language syntax for that number.

If *radix* is not 10, **cvrs** converts *num* to an integer, as if by **cvi.** Then it treats the machine representation of that integer as an unsigned positive integer and converts it to text form according to the specific radix. The resulting text is not necessarily a valid number. However, if it is immediately preceded by the same radix and #, the combination is a valid PostScript language token that represents the same number.

Example

```
/temp 12 string def
123 10 temp cvrs ⇒ (123)
–123 10 temp cvrs ⇒ (–123)
123.4 10 temp cvrs ⇒ (123.4)
123 16 temp cvrs ⇒ (7B)
–123 16 temp cvrs ⇒ (FFFFFF85)
123.4 16 temp cvrs ⇒ (7B)
```

Errors: **invalidaccess, rangecheck, stackunderflow, typecheck**

See Also: **cvs**

cvs   *any string* **cvs** *substring*

(convert to string) produces a text representation of an arbitrary object *any*, stores the text into the supplied *string* (overwriting some initial portion of its value), and returns a string object designating the substring actually used. If the *string* is too small to hold the result of conversion, **cvs** executes the error **rangecheck**.

If *any* is a number, **cvs** produces a string representation of that number. If *any* is a boolean, **cvs** produces either the string true or the string false. If *any* is a string, **cvs** copies its contents into *string*. If *any* is a name or an operator, **cvs** produces the text representation of that name or the operator's name. If *any* is any other type, **cvs** produces the text --nostringval--.

If *any* is a real number, the precise format of the result string is implementation dependent and not under program control. For example, the value 0.001 might be represented as 0.001 or as 1.0E-3.

Example

```
/str 20 string def
123  456 add str cvs ⇒ (579)
mark str cvs  ⇒ (--nostringval--)
```

Errors: **invalidaccess, rangecheck, stackunderflow, typecheck**

See Also: cvi, cvr, string, type

cvx   *any* **cvx** *any*

(convert to executable) makes the object on top of the operand stack have the executable instead of literal attribute.

Errors: **stackunderflow**

See Also: cvlit, xcheck

def   *key value* **def** –

associates *key* with *value* in the current dictionary—the one on the top of the dictionary stack (see section 3.4, "Stacks"). If *key* is already present in the current dictionary, **def** simply replaces its value. Otherwise, **def** creates a new entry for *key* and stores *value* with it.

If the current dictionary is in global VM and *value* is a composite object whose value is in local VM, an invalidaccess error occurs (see section 3.7.2, "Local and Global VM").

Example

```
/ncnt 1 def                % Define ncnt to be 1 in current dict
/ncnt ncnt 1 add def       % ncnt now has value 2
```

Errors: **dictfull, invalidaccess, limitcheck, stackunderflow, typecheck, VMerror**

See Also: **store, put**

defaultmatrix   *matrix* **defaultmatrix** *matrix*

replaces the value of *matrix* with the default transformation matrix for the current output device and pushes this modified matrix back on the operand stack.

Errors: **rangecheck, stackunderflow, typecheck**

See Also: **currentmatrix, initmatrix, setmatrix**

definefont   *key font* **definefont** *font*

registers *font* as a font dictionary associated with *key* (usually a name), as discussed in section 5.2, "Font Dictionaries." **definefont** first checks that *font* is a well-formed font dictionary—in other words, contains all required key-value pairs. It inserts an additional entry whose key is **FID** and whose value is an object of type fontID. The dictionary must be large enough to accommodate this additional entry. It makes the dictionary's access read-only. Finally, it associates *key* with *font* in the font directory.

In Level 2, it is permissible to associate a font dictionary with more than one key. If *font* has already been registered, **definefont** does not alter it in any way.

If *font* is a composite font (see section 5.9, "Composite Fonts"), **definefont** also inserts the entries **MIDVector** and **CurMID**, and adds entries **PrefEnc**, **EscChar**, **ShiftIn**, and **ShiftOut** if they are required and are not already present. All the descendant fonts must have been registered by **definefont** previously.

Subsequent invocation of **findfont** with *key* will return *font*. Font registration is subject to the normal semantics of VM (see section 3.7, "Memory Management"). In particular, the lifetime of the definition depends on the VM allocation mode at the time **definefont** is executed. A local definition can be undone by a subsequent **restore**.

definefont is actually a special case of **defineresource** operating on the **Font** category. For details, see **defineresource** and section 3.9, "Named Resources."

Errors: **limitcheck, rangecheck, dictfull, invalidfont, stackunderflow, typecheck, invalidaccess**

See Also: **makefont, scalefont, setfont, defineresource, FontDirectory, GlobalFontDirectory, setglobal**

defineresource   *key instance category* **defineresource** *instance*   LEVEL 2

associates a resource instance with a resource name in a specified category. *category* is a name object that identifies a resource category, such as **Font** (see section 3.9.2, "Resource Categories"). *key* is a name or string object that will be used to identify the resource instance. (Names and strings are interchangeable; other types of keys are permitted but are not recommended.) *instance* is the resource instance itself; its type must be appropriate to the resource category.

Before defining the resource instance, **defineresource** verifies that the instance object is the correct type. Depending on the resource category, it may also perform additional validation of the object and may have other side effects. Finally, it makes the object read-only if its access is not already restricted.

The lifetime of the definition depends on the VM allocation mode in effect at the time **defineresource** is executed. If local VM allocation is in effect (**currentglobal** returns *false*), the effect of **defineresource** is undone by the next non-nested **restore**. If global VM allocation is in effect (**currentglobal** returns *true*), the effect of **defineresource** persists until global VM is restored at the end of the job. If the current job is not encapsulated, the effect of a global **defineresource** persists indefinitely, and may be visible to other execution contexts.

Local and global definitions are maintained separately. If a new resource instance is defined with the same category and key as an existing one, the new definition overrides the old one. The precise effect depends on whether the old definition is local or global and whether the new definition (current VM allocation mode) is local or global. There are two main cases:

1. New definition is local—**defineresource** installs the new local definition, replacing an existing local definition if there is one. If there is an existing global definition, **defineresource** does not disturb it. However, the global definition is obscured by the local one. If the local definition is later removed, the global definition reappears.

2. New definition is global—**defineresource** first removes an existing local definition if there is one. It then installs the new global definition, replacing an existing global definition if there is one.

It is permissible to use **defineresource** multiple times to associate a given resource instance with more than one key.

If the category name is unknown, an **undefined** error occurs. If the instance is of the wrong type for the specified category, a **typecheck** error occurs. If the instance is in local VM but the current VM allocation mode is global, an **invalidaccess** error occurs. This is analogous to storing a local object into a global dictionary. Other errors can occur for specific categories. For example, when dealing with the **Font** category, **defineresource** can execute an **invalidfont** error.

Errors: invalidaccess, stackunderflow, typecheck, undefined

See Also: undefineresource, findresource, resourcestatus, resourceforall

defineusername   *index name* **defineusername** –   `DPS`

establishes an association between the non-negative integer *index* and the name object *name* in the user name table. Subsequently, the scanner will substitute *name* when it encounters any binary encoded name token or object that refers to the specified user name *index*. Because binary encoded names specify their own literal or executable attributes, it does not matter whether *name* is literal or executable. See section 7.2, "Encoded User Names."

The user name table is an adjunct to the current context's local VM (see section 7.1, "Multiple Execution Contexts"). The effect of adding an entry to the table is immediately visible to all contexts that share the same local VM. Additions to the table are not affected by **save** and **restore**. The association between *index* and *name* persists for the remaining lifetime of the local VM.

The specified *index* must previously be unused in the name table or must already be associated with the same *name*. Changing an existing association is not permitted (an **invalidaccess** error will occur). There may be an implementation limit on *index* values. Assigning index values sequentially starting at zero is strongly recommended.

Errors: **invalidaccess, limitcheck, rangecheck, stackunderflow, typecheck**

defineuserobject   *index any* **defineuserobject** –   `LEVEL 2`

establishes an association between the non-negative integer *index* and the object *any* in the **UserObjects** array. First, it creates a **UserObjects** array in **userdict** if one is not already present. It extends an existing **UserObjects** array if necessary. It then executes the equivalent of

    userdict /UserObjects get
    3 1 roll put

In other words, it simply stores *any* into the array at the position specified by *index*. See section 3.7.6, "User Objects."

If **defineuserobject** creates or extends the **UserObjects** array, it allocates the array in local VM, regardless of the current VM allocation mode.

The behavior of **defineuserobject** obeys normal PostScript language semantics in all respects. In particular, the modification to the **UserObjects** array and to **userdict,** if any, is immediately visible to all contexts that share the same local VM. It can be undone by a subsequent **restore** according to the usual VM rules. *index* values must be within the range permitted for arrays; a large *index* value may cause allocation of an array that would exhaust VM resources. Assigning *index* values sequentially starting at zero is strongly recommended.

Errors: limitcheck, rangecheck, stackunderflow, typecheck, VMerror

See Also: execuserobject, undefineuserobject, UserObjects

deletefile

filename **deletefile** – `LEVEL 2`

removes the specified file from its storage device. If no such file exists, an **undefinedfilename** error occurs. If the device does not allow this operation, an **invalidfileaccess** error occurs. If an environment dependent error is detected, an **ioerror** occurs. See section 3.8.2, "Named Files."

Errors: invalidfileaccess, ioerror, stackunderflow, typecheck, undefinedfilename

See Also: file, renamefile, status

detach

context **detach** – `DPS`

specifies that the execution context identified by the integer *context* is to terminate immediately when it finishes executing its top-level procedure, whereas ordinarily it would wait for a **join**. If the context is already waiting for a **join**, **detach** causes it to terminate immediately. See section 7.1, "Multiple Execution Contexts."

detach executes an **invalidcontext** error if *context* is not a valid context identifier or if the context has already been joined or detached. It is permissible for *context* to identify the current context.

Errors: invalidcontext, stackunderflow, typecheck

See Also: currentcontext, fork, join

deviceinfo   – deviceinfo *dict*

returns a read-only dictionary containing static information about the current device. The composition of this dictionary varies according to the properties of the device. Typical entries are given in the table in section 7.3, "Graphics and Window Systems." The information in the dictionary may not be meaningful for a page-oriented or other non-display device.

The use of **deviceinfo** after a **setcachedevice** operation within the scope of a **BuildChar** procedure is not permitted. An **undefined** error results.

Errors: **stackoverflow, undefined**

dict   *int* **dict** *dict*

creates an empty dictionary with an initial capacity of *int* elements and pushes the created dictionary object on the operand stack. *int* is expected to be a non-negative integer. The dictionary is allocated in local or global VM according to the VM allocation mode. See section 3.7.2, "Local and Global VM."

In Level 1 implementations, the resulting dictionary has a maximum capacity of *int* elements. Attempting to exceed that limit causes a **dictfull** error.

In Level 2 implementations, the *int* operand specifies only the initial capacity; the dictionary can grow beyond that capacity if necessary. The **dict** operator immediately consumes sufficient VM to hold *int* key-value pairs. If more than that number of entries are subsequently stored in the dictionary, additional VM is consumed at that time.

There is a cost associated with expanding a dictionary beyond its initial allocation. For efficiency reasons, a dictionary is expanded in chunks rather than one element at a time, so it may contain a substantial amount of unused space. If a program knows how large a dictionary it needs, it should create one of that size initially. On the other hand, if a program cannot predict how large the dictionary will eventually grow, it should choose a small initial allocation sufficient for its immediate needs. The built-in writable dictionaries (for example, **userdict**) follow the latter convention.

Errors: **limitcheck, stackunderflow, typecheck, VMerror**

See Also: **begin, end, length, maxlength**

402   Chapter 8: Operators

dictfull   *(error)*

occurs when **def, put,** or **store** attempts to define a new entry in a dictionary that is already full—in other words, whose **length** and **maxlength** are already equal. This can occur only in Level 1 implementations, where a dictionary has a fixed limit on the number of entries with distinct keys it can hold. This limit is established by the operand to the **dict** operator that creates the dictionary.

See Also: def, put, store, dict

dictstack   *array* **dictstack** *subarray*

stores all elements of the dictionary stack into *array* and returns an object describing the initial *n*-element subarray of *array*, where *n* is the current depth of the dictionary stack. **dictstack** copies the topmost dictionary into element *n*–1 of *array* and the bottommost one into element 0 of *array*. The dictionary stack itself is unchanged. If the length of *array* is less than the depth of the dictionary stack, **dictstack** executes a **rangecheck** error.

Errors: invalidaccess, rangecheck, stackunderflow, typecheck

See Also: countdictstack

dictstackoverflow   *(error)*

The dictionary stack has grown too large. Too many **begin** operators without corresponding **end** operators have pushed too many dictionaries on the dictionary stack. See Appendix B for the limit on the size of the dictionary stack.

Before invoking this error, the interpreter creates an array containing all elements of the dictionary stack stored as if by **dictstack**, pushes this array on the operand stack, and resets the dictionary stack to contain only the permanent entries.

See Also: begin, countdictstack, cleardictstack

dictstackunderflow   *(error)*

An attempt has been made to remove (**end**) the bottommost instance of **userdict** from the dictionary stack. This occurs if an **end** is executed for which there was no corresponding **begin**.

See Also: end

div num_1 num_2 **div** *quotient*

divides num_1 by num_2, producing a result that is always a real even if both operands are integers. Use **idiv** if an integer result is desired.

Example

>   3 2 div ⇒ 1.5
>   4 2 div ⇒ 2.0

Errors: stackunderflow, typecheck, undefinedresult

See Also: idiv, add, mul, sub, mod

dtransform   *dx dy* **dtransform** *dx′ dy′*
dx dy matrix **dtransform** *dx′ dy′*

With no *matrix* operand, **dtransform** (delta transform) transforms the distance vector (*dx, dy*) by the CTM to produce the corresponding distance vector (*dx′, dy′*) in device space. If the *matrix* operand is supplied, **dtransform** transforms the distance vector by *matrix* rather than by CTM.

A delta transformation is similar to a normal transformation (see section 4.3, "Coordinate Systems and Transformations"), but the translation components (t_x and t_y) of the transformation matrix are not used, making the distance vectors positionless in both user space and device space. This is useful for determining how distances map from user space to device space.

Errors: rangecheck, stackunderflow, typecheck

See Also: idtransform, transform, itransform

dup   *any* **dup** *any any*

duplicates the top element on the operand stack. Note that **dup** copies only the object. The value of a composite object is not copied but is shared. See section 3.3, "Data Types and Objects."

Errors: stackoverflow, stackunderflow

See Also: copy, index

echo   *bool* **echo** –

specifies whether the special files %lineedit and %statementedit are to copy characters from the standard input file to the standard output file. This affects only the behavior of **executive**; it does not apply to normal communication with the PostScript interpreter. **echo** is not defined in products that do not support **executive**. See section 2.4.4, "Using the Interpreter Interactively," and section 3.8.3, "Special Files."

Errors: **stackunderflow, typecheck**

See Also: **executive, file**

eexec   *file* **eexec** –
             string **eexec** –

causes the contents of *file* (open for reading) or *string* to be decrypted and then executed in a manner similar to the **exec** operator. The decryption operation does not cause the *file* or *string* to be modified.

eexec creates a new file object that serves as a decryption filter on the specified *file* or *string*. It pushes the new file object on the execution stack, making it the current file for the PostScript interpreter. Subsequently, each time the interpreter reads a character from this file, or a program reads explicitly from **currentfile**, the decryption filter reads one character from the original *file* or *string* and decrypts it.

The decryption filter file is closed automatically when the end of the original *file* or *string* is encountered. It may also be closed explicitly by **closefile**. If the file passed to **eexec** was **currentfile**, this resumes direct execution of that file with the decryption filter removed. The file may consist of encrypted text followed by unencrypted text if the last thing executed in the encrypted text is **currentfile closefile**.

Before beginning execution, **eexec** pushes **systemdict** on the dictionary stack. This ensures that the operators executed by the encrypted program have their standard meanings. When the decryption filter file is closed either explicitly or implicitly, the dictionary stack is popped. The program must be aware that it is being executed with **systemdict** as the current dictionary; in particular, any definitions that it makes must be into a specific dictionary rather than the current one, since **systemdict** is read-only.

The encrypted file may be represented in either binary or hex; the **eexec** operator can decrypt it without being told which type it is. The recommended representation is hex, because hex data can be transmitted through communication channels that are not completely transparent. Regardless of the representation of the encrypted file, the encryption and decryption processes are transparent. That is, an arbitrary binary file can be encrypted, transmitted as either binary or hex, and decrypted to yield the original information.

The encryption employed by **eexec** is intended primarily for use in Type 1 font programs. The book *Adobe Type 1 Font Format* contains a complete description of the encryption algorithm and recommended uses of **eexec**.

Errors: **dictstackoverflow, invalidaccess, invalidfileaccess, limitcheck, stackunderflow, typecheck**

See Also: **exec, filter**

end   – end –

pops the current dictionary off the dictionary stack, making the dictionary below it the current dictionary. If **end** tries to pop the bottommost instance of **userdict,** it executes the error **dictstackunderflow.**

Errors: **dictstackunderflow**

See Also: **begin, dictstack, countdictstack**

eoclip   – eoclip –

intersects the inside of the current clipping path with the inside of the current path to produce a new, smaller current clipping path. The inside of the current path is determined by the even-odd rule (see section 4.5, "Painting"), while the inside of the current clipping path is determined by whatever rule was used at the time that path was created.

Except for the choice of insideness rule, the behavior of **eoclip** is identical to that of **clip.**

Errors: **limitcheck**

See Also: **clip, clippath, initclip**

eofill   – eofill –

paints the inside of the current path with the current color, using the even-odd rule (see section 4.5, "Painting") to determine what points are inside. Except for the choice of insideness rule, the behavior of **eofill** is identical to that of **fill.**

Errors: limitcheck

See Also: fill, ineofill, ueofill

---

eoviewclip   – eoviewclip

is similar to **viewclip**, except that it uses the even-odd rule (see section 4.5, "Painting") to determine the inside of the current path.

Errors: limitcheck

See Also: viewclip

---

eq any_1 any_2 **eq** *bool*

pops two objects from the operand stack and pushes the boolean value *true* if they are equal, *false* if not. The definition of equality depends on the types of the objects being compared. Simple objects are equal if their types and values are the same. Strings are equal if their lengths and individual elements are equal. Other composite objects (arrays and dictionaries) are equal only if they share the same value. Separate values are considered unequal, even if all the components of those values are the same.

Some type conversions are performed by **eq**. Integers and reals can be compared freely: An integer and a real representing the same mathematical value are considered equal by **eq**. Strings and names can likewise be compared freely: A name defined by some sequence of characters is equal to a string whose elements are the same sequence of characters.

The literal/executable and access attributes of objects are not considered in comparisons between objects.

Example

```
4.0 4 eq ⇒ true              % A real and an integer may be equal
(abc) (abc) eq ⇒ true        % Strings with equal elements are equal
(abc) /abc eq ⇒ true         % A string and a name may be equal
[1 2 3] dup eq ⇒ true        % An array is equal to itself
[1 2 3] [1 2 3] eq ⇒ false   % Distinct array objects not equal
```

Errors: invalidaccess, stackunderflow

See Also: ne, le, lt, ge, gt

erasepage   – erasepage –

erases the entire current page by painting it with gray level 1, which is ordinarily white, but may be some other color if an atypical transfer function has been defined. The entire page is erased, regardless of the clip path currently in force. **erasepage** affects only the contents of raster memory. It does not modify the graphics state nor does it cause a page to be transmitted to the output device.

erasepage is executed automatically by **showpage** after imaging. There are few situations in which a PostScript language page description should execute **erasepage** explicitly, because the operator affects portions of the current page outside the current clip path. It is usually more appropriate to erase just the inside of the current clip path (see **clippath**). Then the page description can be embedded within another, composite page without undesirable effects.

Errors: (none)

See Also: showpage, clippath, fill

errordict   – errordict *dict*

pushes the dictionary object **errordict** on the operand stack (see section 3.10, "Errors"). **errordict** is not an operator; it is a name in **systemdict** associated with the dictionary object.

Errors: stackoverflow

See Also: $error

exch   *any$_1$ any$_2$* **exch** *any$_2$ any$_1$*

exchanges the top two elements on the operand stack.

Example

   1 2 exch $\Rightarrow$ 2 1

Errors: stackunderflow

See Also: dup, roll, index, pop

exec   *any* **exec** –

pushes the operand on the execution stack, executing it immediately. The effect of executing an object depends on the object's type and literal/executable attribute; this is discussed in detail in section 3.5, "Execution." In particular, executing a literal object will cause it only to be pushed back on the operand stack. Executing a procedure, however, will cause the procedure to be called.

Example

> (3 2 add) cvx exec ⇒ 5
> 3 2 /add exec ⇒ 3 2 /add
> 3 2 /add cvx exec ⇒ 5

In the first line, the string (3 2 add) is made executable and then executed. Executing a string causes its characters to be scanned and interpreted according to the PostScript language syntax rules.

In the second line, the literal objects 3, 2, and /add are pushed on the operand stack, then **exec** is applied to the **add**. Since the **add** is a literal name, executing it simply causes it to be pushed back on the operand stack. The **exec** in this case has no useful effect.

In the third line, the literal name /add on the top of the operand stack is made executable by **cvx**. Applying **exec** to this executable name causes it to be looked up and the **add** operation to be performed.

Errors: stackunderflow

See Also: xcheck, cvx, run

paints a form specified by a form dictionary constructed as described in section 4.7, "Forms." The graphical output produced by **execform** is defined by the form dictionary's **PaintProc** procedure.

If this is the first invocation of **execform** for *form*, **execform** first verifies that the dictionary contains the required entries. Then it adds an entry to the dictionary with the key **Implementation**, whose value is private to the implementation. Finally, it makes the dictionary read-only. (**execform** performs these alterations directly to the operand dictionary; it does not copy the dictionary.)

When **execform** needs to call the **PaintProc** procedure, it pushes the form dictionary on the operand stack, then executes the equivalent of

```
gsave                        % Operand stack: dict
dup /Matrix get concat
dup /BBox get aload pop       % Stack: dict llx lly urx ury
exch 3 index sub
exch 2 index sub              % Stack: dict llx lly width height
rectclip                      % Also does a newpath
dup /PaintProc get            % Stack: dict proc
exec                          % Execute PaintProc with dict on stack
grestore
```

The **PaintProc** procedure is expected to consume the dictionary operand and to execute a sequence of graphics operators to paint the form. The **PaintProc** must always produce the same output, given the same graphics state parameters, independent of the number of times it is called and independent, for example, of the contents of **userdict**. The PostScript language program should not expect any particular execution of **execform** to cause execution of the specified **PaintProc**.

The documented errors are those produced directly by **execform**. Obviously, the **PaintProc** can cause other errors.

Errors: limitcheck, rangecheck, stackunderflow, typecheck, undefined, VMerror

See Also: findresource

execstack   *array* **execstack** *subarray*

stores all elements of the execution stack into *array* and returns an object describing the initial *n*-element subarray of *array,* where *n* is the current depth of the execution stack. **execstack** copies the topmost object into element *n*–1 of *array* and the bottommost one into element 0 of *array*. The execution stack itself is unchanged. If the length of *array* is less than the depth of the execution stack, **execstack** executes a **rangecheck** error.

Errors: **invalidaccess, rangecheck, stackunderflow, typecheck**

See Also: **countexecstack, exec**

execstackoverflow   *(error)*

The execution stack has grown too large; procedure invocation is nested deeper than the PostScript interpreter permits. See Appendix B for the limit on the size of the execution stack.

See Also: **exec**

execuserobject   *index* **execuserobject** –   LEVEL 2

executes the object associated with the non-negative integer *index* in the **UserObjects** array. **execuserobject** is equivalent to:

    userdict /UserObjects get
    exch get exec

execuserobject's semantics are similar to those of **exec** or other explicit execution operators. That is, if the object is executable, it is executed; otherwise, it is pushed on the operand stack. See section 3.7.6, "User Objects."

If **UserObjects** is not defined in **userdict** because **defineuserobject** has never been executed, an **undefined** error occurs. If *index* is not a valid index for the existing **UserObjects** array, a **rangecheck** error occurs. If *index* is a valid index but **defineuserobject** has not been executed previously for that index, a null object is returned.

Errors: **invalidaccess, rangecheck, stackunderflow, typecheck, undefined**

See Also: **defineuserobject, undefineuserobject, UserObjects**

executeonly

array **executeonly** *array*
packedarray **executeonly** *packedarray*
file **executeonly** *file*
string **executeonly** *string*

reduces the access attribute of an array, packed array, file, or string object to execute-only (see section 3.3.2, "Attributes of Objects"). Access can only be reduced by these means, never increased. When an object is execute-only, its value cannot be read or modified explicitly by PostScript operators (an **invalidaccess** error will result), but it can still be executed by the PostScript interpreter—for example, by invoking it with **exec**.

executeonly affects the access attribute only of the object that it returns. If there are other composite objects that share the same value, their access attributes are unaffected.

Errors: **invalidaccess, stackunderflow, typecheck**

See Also: **rcheck, wcheck, xcheck, readonly, noaccess**

executive   – executive –

invokes the interactive executive, which facilitates direct user interaction with the PostScript interpreter. See section 2.4.4, "Using the Interpreter Interactively" for complete information.

executive uses the special %statementedit file to obtain commands from the user (see section 3.8.3, "Special Files"). The **echo** operator and the value of **prompt** also affect the behavior of **executive**.

executive is not necessarily defined in all products. It should not be considered a standard part of the PostScript language.

Errors: **undefined**

See Also: **prompt, echo, file**

exit   – exit –

terminates execution of the innermost, dynamically enclosing instance of a looping context without regard to lexical relationship. A looping context is a procedure invoked repeatedly by one of the following control operators:

cshow	**forall**	**pathforall**
filenameforall	**kshow**	**repeat**
for	**loop**	**resourceforall**

exit pops the execution stack down to the level of that operator. The interpreter then resumes execution at the next object in normal sequence after that operator.

exit does not affect the operand or dictionary stacks. Any objects pushed on those stacks during execution of the looping context remain after the context is exited.

If **exit** would escape from the context of a **run** or **stopped** operator, it executes the **invalidexit** error (still in the context of the **run** or **stopped**). If there is no enclosing looping context, the interpreter prints an error message and executes the built-in operator **quit**. This never occurs during execution of ordinary user programs, because they are enclosed by a **stopped** context.

Errors: **invalidexit**

See Also: **stop, stopped**

exp   *base exponent* **exp** *real*

raises *base* to the *exponent* power. The operands may be either integers or reals. If the exponent has a fractional part, the result is meaningful only if the base is non-negative. The result is always a real.

Example

9 0.5 exp $\Rightarrow$ 3.0
–9 –1 exp $\Rightarrow$ –0.111111

Errors: **stackunderflow, typecheck, undefinedresult**

See Also: **sqrt, ln, log, mul**

false   – **false** *false*

pushes a boolean object whose value is *false* on the operand stack. **false** is not an operator; it is a name in **systemdict** associated with the boolean value *false*.

Errors: **stackoverflow**

See Also: **true, and, or, not, xor**

file   *filename access* **file** *file*

creates a file object for the file identified by *filename*, accessing it as specified by *access*. Both operands are strings. Conventions for both file names and access specifications depend on the operating system environment in which the Post-Script interpreter is running. See section 3.8.2, "Named Files."

Once created and opened, the *file* object remains valid until the file is closed either explicitly (by executing **closefile**) or implicitly (by encountering end-of-file while reading or executing the file). A file is also closed by **restore** if the file object was created more recently than the **save** snapshot being restored, or is closed by garbage collection if the file object is no longer accessible. There is a limit on the number of files that can be open simultaneously. See Appendix B.

If the specified *filename* is malformed or if the file doesn't exist and *access* does not permit creating a new file, **file** executes an **undefinedfilename** error. If *access* is malformed or the requested access is not permitted by the device, an **invalidfileaccess** error occurs. If the number of files opened by the current context exceeds an implementation limit, a **limitcheck** error occurs. If an environment-dependent error is detected, an **ioerror** occurs.

Example

```
(%stdin) (r) file ⇒ % standard input file object
(myfile) (w) file ⇒ % output file object, writing to named file
```

Errors: **invalidfileaccess, ioerror, limitcheck, stackunderflow, typecheck, undefinedfilename**

See Also: **closefile, currentfile, filter, status**

filenameforall   *template proc scratch* **filenameforall** –

enumerates all files whose names match the specified *template* string. For each matching file, **filenameforall** copies the file's name into the supplied *scratch* string, pushes a string object designating the substring of *scratch* actually used, and calls *proc*. **filenameforall** does not return any results of its own, but *proc* may do so.

The details of template matching are device dependent, but the following convention is typical. All characters in the template are treated literally and are case sensitive, except the following special characters:

*   matches zero or more consecutive characters.

?   matches exactly one character.

\   causes the next character of the template to be treated literally, even if it is *, ?, or \.

If *template* does not begin with %, it is matched against device relative file names of all devices in the search order (see section 3.8.2, "Named Files"). When a match occurs, the file name passed to *proc* is likewise device relative—in other words, it does not have a %*device*% prefix.

If *template* does begin with %, it is matched against complete file names in the form %*device*%*file*. Template matching can be performed on the *device*, the *file*, or both parts of the name. When a match occurs, the file name passed to *proc* is likewise in the complete form %*device*%*file*.

The order of enumeration is unspecified and device dependent. There are no restrictions on what *proc* can do. However, if *proc* causes new files to be created, it is unspecified whether or not those files will be encountered later in the same enumeration. Likewise, the set of file names considered for template matching is device dependent.

Errors: **invalidaccess, ioerror, rangecheck, stackoverflow, stackunderflow, typecheck**

See also: **file, status**

fileposition   *file* **fileposition** *position*   LEVEL 2

returns the current position in an existing open file. The result is a non-negative integer interpreted as number of bytes from the beginning of the file. If the file object is not valid or the underlying file is not positionable, an **ioerror** occurs.

Errors: ioerror, stackunderflow, typecheck

See also: setfileposition, file

fill   – fill –

paints the area enclosed by the current path with the current color. Any previous contents of that area on the current page are obscured, so areas may be erased by filling with color set to white.

Before painting, **fill** implicitly closes any open subpaths of the current path. The inside of the current path is determined by the normal non-zero winding number rule (see section 4.5, "Painting").

fill implicitly performs a **newpath** after it has finished filling the current path. To preserve the current path across a **fill** operation, use the sequence:

    gsave fill grestore

Errors: limitcheck

See Also: clip, eofill, stroke, ufill

filter   *src|tgt param*$_1$ *... param*$_n$ *name* **filter** *file*   LEVEL 2

creates and returns a filtered *file*. Filters are described in section 3.8.4, "Filters," and section 3.13, "Filtered Files Details."

The *src|tgt* operand specifies the underlying data source or data target that the filter is to read or write. It can be a file, procedure, or string.

The *param*$_1$ *... param*$_n$ operands are additional parameters that control how the filter is to operate. The number and types of these operands depend on the filter name. Most filters require no additional parameters.

The *name* operand identifies the data transformation that the filter is to perform. The standard filter names are:

ASCIIHexEncode	ASCIIHexDecode
ASCII85Encode	ASCII85Decode
LZWEncode	LZWDecode
RunLengthEncode	RunLengthDecode
CCITTFaxEncode	CCITTFaxDecode
DCTEncode	DCTDecode
NullEncode	SubFileDecode

An encoding filter is an output (writable) file. A decoding filter is an input (readable) file. The *file* object returned by the filter can be used as an operand of normal file input and output operators, such as **read** and **write**. Reading from an input filtered file causes the filter to read from the underlying data source and transform the data. Similarly, writing to an output filtered file causes the filter to transform the data and write it to the underlying data target.

Errors: limitcheck, undefined, typecheck, rangecheck, stackunderflow, invalidaccess

See Also: file, closefile, resourceforall

findencoding   *key* **findencoding** *array*   `LEVEL 2`

obtains an encoding vector identified by the specified *key* and pushes it onto the operand stack. Encoding vectors are described in section 5.3, "Character Encoding."

findencoding is a special case of **findresource** applied to the **Encoding** category (see section 3.9, "Named Resources"). If the encoding array specified by *key* does not exist or cannot be found, **findencoding** executes the **undefinedresource** error.

Errors: stackunderflow, typecheck, undefinedresource

See Also: findresource, StandardEncoding, ISOLatin1Encoding

findfont   *key* **findfont** *font*

obtains a font dictionary identified by the specified *key* and pushes it on the operand stack (see section 5.1, "Organization and Use of Fonts"). *key* may be a key previously passed to **definefont**, in which case the font dictionary associated with *key* (in the font directory) is returned.

If *key* is not registered as a font in VM, **findfont** takes an action that varies according to the environment in which the PostScript interpreter is operating. In some environments, **findfont** may attempt to read a font definition from an external source, such as a file. In other environments, **findfont** substitutes a default font or executes the error **invalidfont**. **findfont** is a special case of **findresource** applied to the **Font** category. See section 3.9, "Named Resources."

findfont, like **findresource**, normally looks first for fonts defined in local VM, then for fonts defined in global VM. However, if the current VM allocation mode is global, **findfont** considers only fonts defined in global VM. If **findfont** needs to load a font into VM, it may use either local or global VM, depending on the font. Generally, Type 1 fonts are loaded into global VM; fonts of other types are loaded in to local VM. See section 3.9.2, "Resource Categories," for an explanation of the VM behavior of font definitions.

findfont is not an operator, but rather a built-in procedure. It may be redefined by a PostScript language program that requires different strategies for finding fonts.

Errors: **invalidfont, stackunderflow, typecheck**

See Also: **scalefont, makefont, setfont, selectfont, definefont, findresource, FontDirectory, GlobalFontDirectory**

findresource   *key category* **findresource** *instance*   `LEVEL 2`

attempts to obtain a named resource instance in a specified category. *category* is a name object that identifies a resource category, such as **Font** (see section 3.9.2, "Resource Categories"). *key* is a name or string object that identifies the resource instance. (Names and strings are interchangeable; other types of keys are permitted but are not recommended.) If it succeeds, **findresource** pushes the resource instance on the operand stack; this is an object whose type depends on the resource category.

findresource first attempts to obtain a resource instance that has previously been defined in VM by **defineresource**. If the current VM allocation mode is local, **findresource** considers local resource definitions first, then global definitions (see **defineresource**). However, if the current VM allocation mode is global, **findresource** considers only global resource definitions.

If the requested resource instance is not currently defined in VM, **findresource** attempts to obtain it from an external source. The way this is done is not specified by the PostScript language; it varies among different implementations and different resource categories. The effect of this action is to create an object in VM and execute **defineresource**. **findresource** then returns the newly created object. If *key* is not a name or string, **findresource** will not attempt to obtain an external resource.

When **findresource** loads an object into VM, it ordinarily attempts to use global VM, regardless of the current VM allocation mode. In other words, it sets the VM allocation mode to global (true setglobal) while loading the resource instance and executing **defineresource**. However, certain resource instances do not function correctly when loaded into global VM; **findresource** uses local VM instead. This always occurs for type 3 font definitions and for any resource instance whose definition includes an explicit false setglobal.

During its execution, **findresource** may remove the definitions of resource instances that were previously loaded into VM by **findresource**. The mechanisms and policies for this depend on the category and the implementation; reclamation of resources may occur at times other than during execution of **findresource**. However, resource definitions that were made by explicit execution of **defineresource** are never disturbed by automatic reclamation.

If the specified resource category does not exist, an **undefined** error occurs. If the category exists but there is no instance whose name is *key*, an **undefinedresource** error occurs.

Errors: stackunderflow, typecheck, undefined, undefinedresource

See Also: defineresource, resourcestatus, resourceforall, undefineresource

---

flattenpath   – flattenpath –

replaces the current path with an equivalent path that preserves all straight line segments, but has all **curveto** segments replaced by sequences of **lineto** (straight line) segments that approximate the curves. If the current path does not contain any **curveto** segments, **flattenpath** leaves it unchanged.

This "flattening" of curves to straight line segments is done automatically when a path is used to control painting (for example, by **stroke**, **fill**, or **clip**). Only rarely does a program need to flatten a path explicitly (see **pathbbox**). The accuracy of the approximation to the curve is controlled by the current flatness parameter in the graphics state (see **setflat**).

Errors: limitcheck

See Also: setflat, curveto, lineto, pathbbox

floor num_1 **floor** num_2

returns the greatest integer value less than or equal to num_1. The type of the result is the same as the type of the operand.

Example

    3.2 floor $\Rightarrow$ 3.0
    –4.8 floor $\Rightarrow$ –5.0
    99 floor $\Rightarrow$ 99

Errors: **stackunderflow, typecheck**

See Also: **ceiling, round, truncate, cvi**

flush   – **flush** –

causes any buffered characters for the standard output file to be delivered immediately. In general, a program requiring output to be sent immediately, such as during real-time, two-way interactions, should call **flush** after generating that output.

Errors: **ioerror**

See Also: **flushfile, print**

flushfile   *file* **flushfile** –

If *file* is an output file, **flushfile** causes any buffered characters for that file to be delivered immediately. In general, a program requiring output to be sent immediately, such as during real-time, two-way interactions, should call **flushfile** after generating that output.

If *file* is an input file, **flushfile** reads and discards data from *file* until the end-of-file indication is encountered. This is useful during error recovery, and the PostScript job server uses it for that purpose. **flushfile** does not close the file, unless it is a decoding filter file.

Errors: **ioerror, stackunderflow, typecheck**

See Also: **flush, read, write**

FontDirectory   – **FontDirectory** *dict*

pushes a dictionary of defined fonts on the operand stack. **FontDirectory** is not an operator; it is a name in **systemdict** associated with the dictionary object.

The **FontDirectory** dictionary associates font names with font dictionaries. **definefont** places entries in **FontDirectory**, and **findfont** looks there first. The dictionary is read-only; only **definefont** and **undefinefont** can change it.

Although **FontDirectory** contains all fonts that are currently defined in VM, it does not necessarily describe all the fonts available to a PostScript language program. This is because the **findfont** operator can sometimes obtain fonts from an external source and load them into VM dynamically. Consequently, examining **FontDirectory** is not a reliable method of inquiring about available fonts. The preferred method is to use the **resourcestatus** and **resourceforall** operators, which are Level 2 features, to inquire about the **Font** resource category. See section 3.9, "Named Resources."

In Level 2, when global VM allocation mode is in effect (see section 3.7.2, "Local and Global VM"), the name **FontDirectory** is temporarily rebound to the value of **GlobalFontDirectory**, which contains only those fonts that have been defined in global VM. This ensures the correct behavior of fonts that are defined in terms of other fonts.

Errors: stackoverflow

See Also: definefont, undefinefont, findfont, findresource, GlobalFontDirectory

for   *initial increment limit proc* **for** –

executes *proc* repeatedly, passing it a sequence of values from *initial* by steps of *increment* to *limit*. The **for** operator expects *initial*, *increment*, and *limit* to be numbers. It maintains a temporary internal variable, known as the *control variable*, which it first sets to *initial*. Then, before each repetition, it compares the control variable with the termination value *limit*. If *limit* has not been exceeded, it pushes the control variable on the operand stack, executes *proc*, and adds *increment* to the control variable.

The termination condition depends on whether *increment* is positive or negative. If *increment* is positive, **for** terminates when the control variable becomes greater than *limit*. If *increment* is negative, **for** terminates when the control variable becomes less than *limit*. If *initial* meets the termination condition, **for** does not execute *proc* at all. If *proc* executes the **exit** operator, **for** terminates prematurely.

Usually, *proc* will use the value on the operand stack for some purpose. However, if *proc* does not remove the value, it will remain there. Successive executions of *proc* will cause successive values of the control variable to accumulate on the operand stack.

Example

    0 1 1 4 {add} for ⇒ 10
    1 2 6 { } for ⇒ 1 3 5
    3 −.5 1 { } for ⇒ 3.0 2.5 2.0 1.5 1.0

In the first example, the value of the control variable is added to whatever is on the stack, so 1, 2, 3, and 4 are added in turn to a running sum whose initial value is 0. The second example has an empty procedure, so the successive values of the control variable are left on the stack. The last example counts backward from 3 to 1 by halves, leaving the successive values on the stack.

Beware of using reals instead of integers for any of the first three operands. Most real numbers are not represented exactly. This can cause an error to accumulate in the value of the control variable, with possibly surprising results. In particular, if the difference between *initial* and *limit* is a multiple of *increment*, as in the third line of the example, the control variable may not achieve the *limit* value.

Errors: **stackoverflow, stackunderflow, typecheck**

See Also: **repeat, loop, forall, exit**

forall

$$\begin{array}{r}\textit{array proc } \textbf{forall } -\\ \textit{packedarray proc } \textbf{forall } -\\ \textit{dict proc } \textbf{forall } -\\ \textit{string proc } \textbf{forall } -\end{array}$$

enumerates the elements of the first operand, executing the procedure *proc* for each element. If the first operand is an array, string, or packed array, **forall** pushes an element on the operand stack and executes *proc* for each element in the array, string, or packed array, beginning with the element whose index is 0 and continuing sequentially. The objects pushed on the operand stack are the array, packed array, or string elements. In the case of a string, these elements are integers in the range 0 to 255, *not* one-character strings.

If the first operand is a dictionary, **forall** pushes a key and a value on the operand stack and executes *proc* for each key-value pair in the dictionary. The order in which **forall** enumerates the entries in the dictionary is arbitrary. New entries put in the dictionary during execution of *proc* may or may not be included in the enumeration.

If the first operand is empty (i.e., has length 0), **forall** does not execute *proc* at all. If *proc* executes the **exit** operator, **forall** terminates prematurely.

Although **forall** does not leave any results on the operand stack when it is finished, the execution of *proc* may leave arbitrary results there. If *proc* does not remove each enumerated element from the operand stack, the elements will accumulate there.

Example

```
0 [13 29 3 –8 21] {add} forall ⇒ 58
/d 2 dict def
d /abc 123 put
d /xyz (test) put
d {} forall ⇒ /xyz (test) /abc 123
```

Errors: **invalidaccess, stackoverflow, stackunderflow, typecheck**

See Also: **for, repeat, loop, exit**

fork   *mark obj₁ ... objₙ proc* **fork** *context*

creates a new execution context using the same local and global VM as the current context. The new context begins execution concurrent with continued execution of the current context. Which context executes first is unpredictable. See section 7.1, "Multiple Execution Contexts."

The new context's environment is formed by copying the dictionary and graphics state stacks of the current context. The initial operand stack consists of *obj*₁ through *obj*ₙ, pushed in the same order (*obj*₁ through *obj*ₙ are objects of any type other than mark). **fork** consumes all operands down to and including the topmost mark. It then pushes an integer that uniquely identifies the new context. The forked context inherits its object format from the current context; other per-context parameters are initialized to default values.

When the new context begins execution, it executes the procedure *proc*. If *proc* runs to completion and returns, the context ordinarily will suspend until some other context executes a **join** on *context*. However, if the context has been detached, it will terminate immediately (see **join** and **detach**).

If *proc* executes a **stop** that causes the execution of *proc* to end prematurely, the context will terminate immediately. *proc* is effectively called as follows:

```
proc stopped {handleerror quit} if
% ...Wait for join or detach...
quit
```

In other words, if *proc* stops due to an error, the context invokes the error handler in the usual way to report the error. Then it terminates regardless of whether it has been detached.

It is illegal to execute **fork** if there has been any previous **save** not yet matched by a **restore**. Attempting to do so will cause an **invalidcontext** error.

Errors: invalidaccess, invalidcontext, limitcheck, stackunderflow, typecheck, unmatchedmark

See Also: join, detach, currentcontext

gcheck *any* **gcheck** *bool*

returns *true* if the operand is simple or if it is composite and its value resides in global VM. It returns *false* if the operand is composite and its value resides in local VM. In other words, **gcheck** returns *true* if one could legally store its operand as an element of another object in global VM. See section 3.7.2, "Local and Global VM."

Errors: **stackunderflow**

ge num_1 num_2 **ge** *bool*
$string_1$ $string_2$ **ge** *bool*

pops two objects from the operand stack and pushes the boolean value *true* if the first operand is greater than or equal to the second, *false* otherwise. If both operands are numbers, **ge** compares their mathematical values. If both operands are strings, **ge** compares them element by element, treating the elements as integers in the range 0 to 255, to determine whether the first string is lexically greater than or equal to the second. If the operands are of other types or one is a string and the other is a number, **ge** executes the **typecheck** error.

Example

```
4.2 4 ge ⇒ true
(abc)(d) ge ⇒ false
(aba)(ab) ge ⇒ true
(aba)(aba) ge ⇒ true
```

Errors: **Invalidaccess, stackunderflow, typecheck**

See Also: **gt, eq, ne, le, lt**

get

$$\text{array index } \textbf{get } any$$
$$\text{packedarray index } \textbf{get } any$$
$$\text{dict key } \textbf{get } any$$
$$\text{string index } \textbf{get } int$$

gets a single element from the value of an array, packed array, dictionary, or string.

If the first operand is an array, packed array, or string, **get** treats the second operand as an index and returns the element identified by the index, counting from zero. *index* must be in the range 0 to $n–1$, where n is the length of the array, packed array, or string. If it is outside this range, **get** will execute a **rangecheck** error.

If the first operand is a dictionary, **get** looks up the second operand as a key in the dictionary and returns the associated value. If the key is not present in the dictionary, **get** executes the **undefined** error.

Example

```
[31 41 59] 0 get ⇒ 31
[0 (a mixed-type array) [ ] {add 2 div}]
2 get ⇒ [ ]                              % An empty array

/mykey (myvalue) def
currentdict /mykey get ⇒ (myvalue)

(abc) 1 get ⇒ 98                         % Character code for "b"
(a) 0 get ⇒ 97
```

Errors: invalidaccess, rangecheck, stackunderflow, typecheck, undefined

See Also: put, getinterval

getinterval

$$\text{array index count } \textbf{getinterval } subarray$$
$$\text{packedarray index count } \textbf{getinterval } subarray$$
$$\text{string index count } \textbf{getinterval } substring$$

creates a new array, packed array, or string object whose value consists of some subsequence of the original array, packed array, or string. The subsequence consists of *count* elements starting at the specified *index* in the original object. The elements in the subsequence are shared between the original and new objects (see section 3.3.1, "Simple and Composite Objects").

The returned subarray or substring is an ordinary array, packed array, or string object whose length is *count* and whose elements are indexed starting at 0. The element at index 0 in *subarray* is the same as the element at index *index* in the original *array*.

getinterval requires *index* to be a valid index in the original object and *count* to be a non-negative integer such that *index + count* is not greater than the length of the original object.

Example

> [9 8 7 6 5] 1 3 getinterval ⇒ [8 7 6]
> (abcde) 1 3 getinterval ⇒ (bcd)
> (abcde) 0 0 getinterval ⇒ ()   % An empty string

Errors: **invalidaccess, rangecheck, stackunderflow, typecheck**

See Also: **get, putinterval**

---

globaldict   – **globaldict** *dict*   LEVEL 2

pushes the dictionary object **globaldict** on the operand stack (see section 3.7.5, "Standard and User-Defined Dictionaries"). **globaldict** is not an operator; it is a name in **systemdict** associated with the dictionary object.

Errors: **stackoverflow**

See Also: **systemdict, userdict**

GlobalFontDirectory   – **GlobalFontDirectory** *dict*   LEVEL 2

pushes a dictionary of defined fonts on the operand stack. Its contents are limited to those fonts that have been defined in global VM. See **FontDirectory** for a complete explanation. **GlobalFontDirectory** is not an operator; it is a name in **systemdict** associated with the dictionary object.

Errors: **stackoverflow**

See Also: **FontDirectory**

glyphshow   *name* **glyphshow** –

shows a single character, identified by *name*, from the current font. Unlike all other **show** variants, **glyphshow** bypasses the current font's **Encoding**. It can access any character in the font, whether or not that character's name is present in the font's encoding vector.

The behavior of **glyphshow** depends on the current font's **FontType**. For **FontType** 1, **glyphshow** looks up *name* in the font's **CharStrings** dictionary to obtain a character description to execute. If *name* is not present in the **CharStrings** dictionary, **glyphshow** substitutes the .notdef entry, which must be present in every Type 1 font.

For **FontType** 3, if the font dictionary contains a **BuildGlyph** procedure, **glyphshow** pushes the current font dictionary and *name* on the operand stack, then invokes **BuildGlyph** in the usual way (see section 5.7, "Type 3 Fonts"). If there is no **BuildGlyph** procedure, but only a **BuildChar** procedure, **glyphshow** searches the font's **Encoding** array for an occurrence of *name*. If it finds one, it pushes the font dictionary and the array index on the operand stack, then invokes **BuildChar** in the usual way. If *name* is not present in the encoding, **glyphshow** substitutes the name .notdef and repeats the search. If .notdef isn't present either, an **invalidfont** error occurs.

Like **show**, **glyphshow** can access characters that are already in the font cache. **glyphshow** does not always need to execute the character's description.

glyphshow operates only with base fonts. If the current font is composite (**FontType** 0), an **invalidfont** error occurs.

Errors: invalidaccess, invalidfont, nocurrentpoint, stackunderflow, typecheck

See Also: show

grestore   – grestore –

resets the current graphics state from the one on the top of the graphics state stack and pops the graphics state stack, restoring the graphics state in effect at the time of the matching **gsave**. This operator provides a simple way to undo complicated transformations and other graphics state modifications without having to re-establish all graphics state parameters individually.

If there is no matching **gsave** or if the most recent **gsave** preceded the most recent unmatched **save**, **grestore** does not pop the graphics state stack, although it does restore the graphics state from the top of the graphics state stack.

Errors: (none)

See Also: **gsave, grestoreall, setgstate**

grestoreall   – grestoreall –

repeatedly pops the graphics state stack until it encounters either the bottom-most graphics state or one that was saved by **save** as opposed to **gsave**, leaving that state on top of the graphics state stack. It then resets the current graphics state from that saved one.

Errors: (none)

See Also: **gsave, grestore, setgstate**

gsave   – gsave –

pushes a copy of the current graphics state on the graphics state stack. All elements of the graphics state are saved, including the CTM, current path, clip path, and identity of the raster output device, but not the contents of raster memory. The saved state may later be restored by a matching **grestore**. See section 4.2, "Graphics State."

The **save** operator implicitly performs a **gsave**, but restoring a graphics state saved by **save** is slightly different from restoring one saved by **gsave** (see the descriptions of **grestore** and **grestoreall**).

Note that, unlike **save**, **gsave** does not return a save object on the operand stack to represent the saved state. **gsave** and **grestore** work strictly in a stack-like fashion, except for the wholesale restoration performed by **restore** and **grestoreall**.

Errors: **limitcheck**

See Also: **grestore, grestoreall, restore, save, gstate, currentgstate**

gstate   – gstate *gstate*   LEVEL 2

creates a new gstate (graphics state) object and pushes it on the operand stack. Its initial value is a copy of the current graphics state.

This operator consumes VM; it is the only graphics state operator that does. The gstate is allocated in either local or global VM according to the current VM allocation mode (see section 3.7, "Memory Management").

If *gstate* is allocated in global VM, **gstate** will generate an **invalidaccess** error if any of the composite objects in the current graphics state are in local VM. Such objects might include the current font, screen function, halftone dictionary, transfer function, or dash pattern. In general, allocating gstate objects in global VM is risky and should be avoided.

Errors: **invalidaccess, stackoverflow, VMerror**

See Also: **currentgstate, setgstate**

gt   *num₁ num₂* **gt** *bool*
          string₁ string₂ **gt** *bool*

pops two objects from the operand stack and pushes the boolean value *true* if the first operand is greater than the second, *false* otherwise. If both operands are numbers, **gt** compares their mathematical values. If both operands are strings, **gt** compares them element by element, treating the elements as integers in the range 0 to 255, to determine whether the first string is lexically greater than the second. If the operands are of other types or one is a string and the other is a number, **gt** executes the **typecheck** error.

Errors: **invalidaccess, stackunderflow, typecheck**

See Also: **ge, eq, ne, le, lt**

handleerror   *(error)*

is looked up in **errordict** and executed to report error information saved by the default error handlers (see section 3.10, "Errors"). There is also a procedure named **handleerror** in **systemdict**; it merely calls the procedure in **errordict**.

identmatrix   *matrix* **identmatrix** *matrix*

replaces the value of *matrix* with the value of the identity matrix

[1.0 0.0 0.0 1.0 0.0 0.0]

and pushes this modified matrix back on the operand stack. The identity matrix transforms any coordinate to itself.

Errors: **rangecheck, stackunderflow, typecheck**

See Also: **matrix, currentmatrix, defaultmatrix, initmatrix**

idiv int_1 int_2 **idiv** *quotient*

divides int_1 by int_2 and returns the integer part of the quotient, with any fractional part discarded. Both operands of **idiv** must be integers and the result is an integer.

Example

3 2 idiv $\Rightarrow$ 1
4 2 idiv $\Rightarrow$ 2
–5 2 idiv $\Rightarrow$ –2

Errors: **stackunderflow, typecheck, undefinedresult**

See Also: **div, add, mul, sub, mod, cvi**

idtransform   *dx′ dy′* **idtransform** *dx dy*
              dx′ dy′ matrix **idtransform** *dx dy*

With no *matrix* operand, **idtransform** (inverse delta transform) transforms the device space distance vector (*dx′*, *dy′*) by the inverse of CTM to produce the corresponding distance vector (*dx*, *dy*) in user space. If the *matrix* operand is supplied, **idtransform** transforms the distance vector by the inverse of *matrix* rather than by the inverse of CTM.

A delta transformation is similar to a normal transformation (see section 4.3, "Coordinate Systems and Transformations"), but the translation components (t_x and t_y) of the transformation matrix are not used, making the distance vectors be positionless in both user space and device space. **idtransform** is the inverse of **dtransform**. It is useful for determining how distances map from device space to user space.

Errors: **rangecheck, stackunderflow, typecheck, undefinedresult**

See Also: **dtransform, transform, itransform**

if   *bool proc* **if** –

removes both operands from the stack, then executes *proc* if *bool* is *true*. The **if** operator pushes no results of its own on the operand stack, but the *proc* may do so (see section 3.5, "Execution").

Example

3 4 lt {(3 is less than 4)} if $\Rightarrow$ (3 is less than 4)

Errors: **stackunderflow, typecheck**

See Also: **ifelse**

ifelse   *bool proc$_1$ proc$_2$* **ifelse** –

removes all three operands from the stack, then executes *proc$_1$* if *bool* is *true* or *proc$_2$* if *bool* is *false*. The **ifelse** operator pushes no results of its own on the operand stack, but the procedure it executes may do so (see section 3.5, "Execution").

Example

4 3 lt {(TruePart)} {(FalsePart)} ifelse $\Rightarrow$ (FalsePart)   % Since 4 is not less than 3

Errors: **stackunderflow, typecheck**

See Also: **if**

image   *width height bits/sample matrix datasrc* **image** –
                                    dict **image** –

paints a sampled image onto the current page. The description here only summarizes the **image** operator. See section 4.10, "Images."

The sampled image is a rectangular array of *width* × *height* sample values, each of which consists of *bits/sample* bits of data (1, 2, 4, 8, or 12). The data is received as a sequence of characters—in other words, 8-bit integers in the range 0 to 255. If *bits/sample* is less than 8, sample values are packed left to right within a character (see section 4.10.2, "Sample Data Representation").

In the first form of **image**, the parameters are specified as separate operands. This is the only form Level 1 implementations support. **image** renders a monochrome image according to the **DeviceGray** color space, regardless of the current color space.

In the second form, the parameters are contained as key-value pairs in an image dictionary, which is specified as the single operand of **image**. This form is a Level 2 feature. **image** renders either a monochrome or color image according to the current color space parameter in the graphics state. The number of component values per source sample and the interpretations of those values depend on the current color space.

The image is considered to exist in its own coordinate system. The rectangular boundary of the image has its lower-left corner at (0, 0) and its upper-right corner at (*width*, *height*). The *matrix* operand specifies a transformation from user space to the image coordinate system.

In Level 1, *datasrc* must be a procedure. In Level 2, *datasrc* may be any data source (see section 3.13, "Filtered Files Details")—a procedure, string, or readable file object (including a filtered file).

If *datasrc* is a procedure, **image** executes *datasrc* repeatedly to obtain the actual image data. *datasrc* must return (on the operand stack) a string containing any number of additional characters of sample data. If *datasrc* returns a string of length zero, **image** will terminate execution prematurely. The sample values are assumed to be received in a fixed order: (0, 0) through (*width*–1, 0), then (0, 1) through (*width*–1, 1), and so on.

Execution of this operator is not permitted in certain circumstances; see section 4.8, "Color Spaces."

Errors: **limitcheck, invalidaccess, ioerror, rangecheck, stackunderflow, typecheck, undefinedresult, undefined**

See Also: **imagemask, colorimage**

imagemask   *width height polarity matrix datasrc* **imagemask** –
                                                dict **imagemask** –

is similar to the **image** operator. However, it treats the source image as a *mask* of 1-bit samples that are used to control where to apply paint with the current color and where not to apply any paint. See the description of the **image** operator and section 4.10, "Images."

In the first form of **imagemask**, the parameters are specified as separate operands. This is the only form Level 1 implementations support. In the second form, the parameters are contained as key-value pairs in an image dictionary. The second form is a Level 2 feature. The semantics of **imagemask** do not depend on which way the operands are specified.

imagemask uses the *width*, *height*, *matrix*, and *datasrc* operands in precisely the same way **image** uses them. The *polarity* operand is a boolean that determines the polarity of the mask. It controls the sense of the mask only; it has no effect on the color of the pixels that are painted. If *polarity* is *false*, portions of the image corresponding to source sample values of 0 are painted, while those corresponding to sample values of 1 are left unchanged. If *polarity* is *true*, sample values of 1 are painted and sample values of 0 are left unchanged.

In the second form of **imagemask**, the polarity is specified by means of the **Decode** entry in the image dictionary. **Decode** values of [0 1] and [1 0] correspond to polarity values of *false* and *true*, respectively.

In Level 1, *datasrc* must be a procedure. In Level 2, *datasrc* may be any data source (see section 3.13, "Filtered Files Details")—a procedure, string, or readable file object (including a filtered file).

imagemask is most useful for painting characters represented as bitmaps. Such bitmaps represent masks through which a color is to be transferred; the bitmaps themselves do not have a color (see section 4.10.6, "Masks").

Example

```
54 112 translate                    % Locate lower-left corner of square
120 120 scale                       % Scale 1 unit to 120 points
0 0 moveto 0 1 lineto               % Fill square with gray background
1 1 lineto 1 0 lineto closepath
.9 setgray fill
0 setgray                           % Paint mask black
24 23                               % Dimensions of source mask
true                                % Paint the 1 bits
[24 0 0 –23 0 23]                   % Map unit square to mask
{<003B00 002700 002480 0E4940 114920
14B220 3CB650 75FE88 17FF8C 175F14
1C07E2 3803C4 703182 F8EDFC B2BBC2
BB6F84 31BFC2 18EA3C 0E3E00 07FC00
03F800 1E1800 1FF800>}              % Mask data
imagemask
```

Errors: **stackunderflow, typecheck, undefinedresult, limitcheck, invalidaccess, ioerror**

See Also: **image, colorimage**

index any_n ... any_0 n **index** any_n ... any_0 any_n

removes the non-negative integer n from the operand stack, counts down to the nth element from the top of the stack, and pushes a copy of that element on the stack.

Example

(a)(b)(c)(d) 0 index $\Rightarrow$ (a)(b)(c)(d)(d)
(a)(b)(c)(d) 3 index $\Rightarrow$ (a)(b)(c)(d)(a)

Errors: **rangecheck, stackunderflow, typecheck**

See Also: **copy, dup, roll**

ineofill x y **ineofill** *bool*   <kbd>LEVEL 2</kbd>
            userpath **ineofill** *bool*

is similar to **infill**, but its "insideness" test is based on **eofill** instead of **fill**.

Errors: **invalidaccess, limitcheck, rangecheck, stackunderflow, typecheck**

See Also: **eofill, infill**

infill   *x y* **infill** *bool*
          userpath **infill** *bool*

> The first form returns *true* if the device pixel containing the point (*x, y*) in user space would be painted by a **fill** of the current path in the graphics state. Otherwise, it returns *false*.
>
> In the second form, the device pixels that would be painted by filling *userpath* become an "aperture." This form of the operator returns *true* if any of the pixels in the aperture would be painted by a **fill** of the current path in the graphics state. Otherwise, it returns *false*.
>
> Both forms of this operator ignore the current clipping path and current view clip; that is, they detect a "hit" anywhere within the current path, even if filling that path would not mark the current page due to clipping. They do not place any marks on the current page nor do they disturb the current path. The following program fragment takes the current clipping path into account:
>
>   gsave clippath *x y* infill grestore
>   *x y* infill and
>
> **Errors:**   **invalidaccess, limitcheck, rangecheck, stackunderflow, typecheck**
>
> **See Also:**   **fill, ineofill**

initclip   – initclip –

> replaces the current clip path parameter in the graphics state by the default clip path for the current output device. This path usually corresponds to the boundary of the maximum imageable area for the current output device. For a page-oriented output device, its dimensions are those established by the **setpagedevice** operator. For a display device, the clipping region established by **initclip** is not well defined. Display PostScript applications should not make the assumption that the clipping region corresponds to the window boundary (see **viewclippath**).
>
> There are few situations in which a PostScript language program should execute **initclip** explicitly. A page description that executes **initclip** usually produces incorrect results if it is embedded within another, composite page.
>
> **Errors:**   (none)
>
> **See Also:**   **clip, eoclip, clippath, initgraphics**

initgraphics   – initgraphics –

resets several values in the current graphics state to their default values:

> current transformation matrix (default for current device)
> current path (empty)
> current point (undefined)
> current clipping path (default for current device)
> current color space (**DeviceGray**)
> current color (black)
> current line width (one user space unit)
> current line cap style (butt end caps)
> current line join style (miter joins)
> current dash description (undashed, i.e., solid lines)
> current miter limit (10)

The **initgraphics** operator does not change the other graphics state parameters. These include the current output device, font, stroke adjust, and *all* device-dependent parameters. This operator affects only the graphics state, not the contents of raster memory or the output device.

initgraphics is equivalent to the PostScript language sequence:

```
initmatrix newpath initclip
1 setlinewidth 0 setlinecap 0 setlinejoin
[ ] 0 setdash 0 setgray 10 setmiterlimit
```

There are few situations in which a PostScript language program should execute **initgraphics** explicitly. A page description that executes **initgraphics** usually produces incorrect results if it is embedded within another, composite page. A program requiring information about its initial graphics state should read and save that state at the beginning of the program rather than assume that the default state prevailed initially.

Errors: (none)

See Also: grestoreall

initmatrix   – initmatrix –

sets the current transformation matrix (CTM) to the default matrix for the current output device. This matrix transforms the default user coordinate system to device space (see section 4.3, "Coordinate Systems and Transformations"). For a page-oriented device, the default matrix is initially established by the **setpagedevice** operator.

There are few situations in which a PostScript language program should execute **initmatrix** explicitly. A page description that executes **initmatrix** usually produces incorrect results if it is embedded within another, composite page.

Errors: (none)

See Also: defaultmatrix, currentmatrix, setmatrix

---

initviewclip   – initviewclip –   `DPS`

returns the context to its initial view clipping state, in which no view clipping path exists.

Errors: (none)

See Also: viewclip, viewclippath

---

instroke   *x y* **instroke** *bool*   `LEVEL 2`
userpath **instroke** *bool*

The first form returns *true* if the device pixel containing the point (*x*, *y*) in user space would be painted by a **stroke** of the current path in the graphics state. Otherwise, it returns *false*. It does not place any marks on the current page nor does it disturb the current path.

In the second form of the operator, the device pixels that would be painted by filling *userpath* become an "aperture." **instroke** returns *true* if any of the pixels in the aperture would be painted by a **stroke** of the current path in the graphics state. Otherwise, it returns *false*.

As with **infill**, this operator ignores the current clipping path and current view clip; that is, it detects a "hit" on any pixel that lies beneath a stroke drawn along the current path, even if stroking that path would not mark the current page due to clipping.

The shape against which the point (*x*, *y*) or the aperture, *userpath*, is tested is computed according to the current, stroke-related parameters in the graphics state: line width, line cap, line join, miter limit, dash pattern, and stroke adjust. If the current line width is zero, the set of pixels considered to be part of the stroke is device dependent.

Errors: invalidaccess, limitcheck, rangecheck, stackunderflow, typecheck

See Also: infill, inustroke, stroke

internaldict   *int* **internaldict** *dict*

pushes the internal dictionary object on the operand stack. The *int* operand *must* be the integer 1183615869. The internal dictionary is in local VM and is writable. It contains operators and other information whose purpose is internal to the PostScript interpreter. It should be referenced only in special circumstances, such as during construction of Type 1 font programs. (See the book *Adobe Type 1 Font Format* for specific information about constructing Type 1 fonts.) The contents of **internaldict** are undocumented and subject to change at any time.

This operator is not present in some PostScript interpreters.

Errors: **invalidaccess, stackunderflow, undefined**

interrupt   *(error)*

processes an external request to interrupt execution of a PostScript language program. When the interpreter receives an interrupt request, it executes **interrupt** as if it were an error—in other words, it looks up the name **interrupt** in **errordict**. Execution of **interrupt** is sandwiched between execution of two objects being interpreted in normal sequence.

Unlike most other errors, occurrence of an **interrupt** does not cause the object being executed to be pushed on the operand stack nor does it disturb the operand stack in any way.

The precise nature of an external interrupt request depends on the environment in which the PostScript interpreter is running. For example, in some environments, receipt of a control-C character from a serial communication channel gives rise to the **interrupt** error. This enables a user to explicitly abort a PostScript computation. The default definition of **interrupt** executes a **stop**.

inueofill   *x y userpath* **inueofill** *bool*   [LEVEL 2]
          userpath₁ userpath₂ **inueofill** *bool*

is similar to **inufill**, but its "insideness" test is based on **ueofill** instead of **ufill**.

Errors: **invalidaccess, limitcheck, rangecheck, stackunderflow, typecheck**

See Also: **inufill, eofill**

inufill   *x y userpath* **inufill** *bool*   LEVEL 2
              userpath₁ userpath₂ **inufill** *bool*

The first form returns *true* if the device pixel containing the point (*x, y*) in user space would be painted by a **ufill** of the specified *userpath* (see section 4.6, "User Paths"). Otherwise, it returns *false.*

In the second form, the device pixels that would be painted by filling *userpath₁* become an "aperture." **inufill** returns *true* if any of the pixels in the aperture would be painted by a **ufill** of *userpath₂*. Otherwise, it returns *false.*

This operator does not place any marks on the current page nor does it disturb the current path in the graphics state. Except for the manner in which the path is specified, **inufill** behaves the same as **infill**.

By itself, this operator is seemingly a trivial composition of several other operators:

```
gsave
newpath uappend
infill
grestore
```

However, when used with a user path that specifies **ucache**, **inufill** can access the user path cache, potentially resulting in improved performance.

Errors: **invalidaccess, limitcheck, rangecheck, stackunderflow, typecheck**

See also: **inueofill, infill, ufill**

inustroke

LEVEL 2

x y *userpath* **inustroke** *bool*
x y *userpath* *matrix* **inustroke** *bool*
userpath$_1$ *userpath*$_2$ **inustroke** *bool*
userpath$_1$ *userpath*$_2$ *matrix* **inustroke** *bool*

The first form returns *true* if the device pixel containing the point (x, y) in user space would be painted by a **ustroke** applied to the same operands (see section 4.6, "User Paths"). Otherwise it returns *false*.

In the second form, **inustroke** concatenates *matrix* to the CTM after interpreting the user paths, but before computing the stroke (see **ustroke** operator).

In the third and fourth forms, the device pixels that would be painted by filling *userpath*$_1$ become an "aperture." **inustroke** returns *true* if any of the pixels in the aperture would be painted by a **ustroke** of *userpath*$_2$. Otherwise it returns *false*.

This operator does not place any marks on the current page nor does it disturb the current path in the graphics state. Except for the manner in which the path is specified, **inustroke** behaves the same as **instroke**.

As with **inufill**, if *userpath* is already present in the user path cache, **inustroke** can take advantage of the cached information to optimize execution.

Errors: **invalidaccess, limitcheck, rangecheck, stackunderflow, typecheck**

See also: **stroke, ustroke, instroke**

invalidaccess *(error)*

An access violation has occurred. Principal causes of **invalidaccess** are:

- Accessing the value of a composite object in violation of its access attribute (for example, storing into a read-only array).

- Storing a composite object in local VM as an element of a composite object in global VM.

- Executing **pathforall** if the current path contains an outline for a protected font.

See Also: **rcheck, wcheck, gcheck, readonly, executeonly, noaccess**

invalidcontext *(error)*

indicates that an invalid use of the context synchronization facilities has been detected. Possible causes include:

- Presenting an invalid context identifier to **join** or **detach**.

- Executing **monitor** on a lock already held by the current context.

- Executing **wait** on a lock not held by the current context.

- Executing any of several synchronization operators when an unmatched **save** is pending if the result would be a deadlock.

The PostScript interpreter detects only the simplest types of deadlock. It is possible to encounter deadlocks for which no **invalidcontext** error is generated.

invalidexit *(error)*

An **exit** has been executed for which there is no dynamically enclosing looping context (for example, **for**, **loop**, **repeat**, or **pathforall**) or it has attempted to leave the context of a **run** or **stopped** operator.

invalidfileaccess *(error)*

The access string specification to the **file** operator is unacceptable or a file operation has been attempted (for example, **deletefile**) that is not permitted by the storage device. See section 3.8.2, "Named Files."

invalidfont *(error)*

Either the operand to **findfont** is not a valid font name or the operand to **makefont** or **setfont** is not a well-formed font dictionary. The **invalidfont** error may also be executed by other font operators upon discovering a font dictionary is malformed.

invalidid   *(error)*

indicates that an invalid identifier has been presented to a window system specific operator. In each integration of the Display PostScript system with a window system, there is a collection of window system specific operators. The operands of such operators are usually integers that identify windows and other objects that exist outside the PostScript language. This error occurs when the operand does not identify a valid object. It is generated only by window system specific operators and not by any standard operator.

invalidrestore   *(error)*

An improper **restore** has been attempted. One or more of the operand, dictionary, or execution stacks contains composite objects whose values were created more recently than the **save** whose context is being restored. Since **restore** would destroy those values, but the stacks are unaffected by **restore**, the outcome would be undefined and cannot be allowed.

See Also: **restore, save**

invertmatrix   *matrix*₁ *matrix*₂ **invertmatrix** *matrix*₂

replaces the value of *matrix*₂ with the result of inverting *matrix*₁ and pushes the modified *matrix*₂ back on the operand stack. The result of inverting a matrix is that if *matrix*₁ transforms a coordinate (x, y) to (x', y') then *matrix*₂ transforms (x', y') to (x, y). See section 4.3, "Coordinate Systems and Transformations."

Errors: **rangecheck, stackunderflow, typecheck, undefinedresult**

See Also: **itransform, idtransform**

ioerror   *(error)*

An exception other than end-of-file has occurred during execution of one of the file operators. The nature of the exception is environment dependent, but may include such events as parity or checksum errors, or broken network connections. Attempting to write to an input file or to a file that has been closed will also cause an **ioerror**. Occurrence of an **ioerror** does not cause the file to become closed unless it was already closed or the error occurs during **closefile**.

ISOLatin1Encoding   – ISOLatin1Encoding *array*   LEVEL 2

pushes the ISO Latin-1 encoding vector on the operand stack. This is a 256-element literal array object, indexed by character codes whose values are the character names for those codes. **ISOLatin1Encoding** is not an operator; it is a name in **systemdict** associated with the array object.

Roman text fonts produced by Adobe usually use the **StandardEncoding** encoding vector. However, they contain all the characters needed to support the use of **ISOLatin1Encoding**. A font can have its **Encoding** changed to **ISOLatin1Encoding** by means of the procedure shown in section 5.6.1, "Changing the Encoding Vector." The contents of **ISOLatin1Encoding** are documented in Appendix E.

Errors: stackoverflow

See Also: StandardEncoding, findencoding

itransform   *x′ y′* **itransform** *x y*
               x′ y′ matrix **itransform** *x y*

With no *matrix* operand, **itransform** (inverse transform) transforms the device space coordinate (*x′, y′*) by the inverse of CTM to produce the corresponding user space coordinate (*x, y*). If the *matrix* operand is supplied, **itransform** transforms (*x′, y′*) by the inverse of *matrix* rather than by the inverse of CTM.

Errors: rangecheck, stackunderflow, typecheck, undefinedresult

See Also: transform, dtransform, idtransform, invertmatrix

join   *context* **join** *mark obj₁ ... objₙ*

waits for the execution context identified by the integer *context* to finish executing its top-level procedure (the *proc* operand of **fork**). It then pushes a mark followed by the entire contents of that context's operand stack onto the current context's operand stack. Finally, it causes the other context to terminate.

The objects *obj₁* through *objₙ* are those left on the operand stack by the context that is terminating. Ordinarily, there should not be a mark among those objects, because its presence might cause confusion in the context that executes the **join**.

If *context* is not a valid context identifier, perhaps because the context has terminated prematurely due to executing **quit** or encountering an error, **join** executes an **invalidcontext** error. This also occurs if the context has already been joined or detached, if *context* identifies the current context, or if the context does not share the current context's local and global VM.

It is illegal to execute **join** if there has been any previous **save** not yet matched by a **restore**. Attempting to do so will cause an **invalidcontext** error.

Errors: **invalidcontext, stackunderflow, stackoverflow, typecheck**

See Also: fork, detach, currentcontext

known   *dict key* **known** *bool*

returns the boolean value *true* if there is an entry in the dictionary *dict* whose key is *key*. Otherwise, it returns *false*. *dict* does not have to be on the dictionary stack.

Example

```
/mydict 5 dict def
mydict /total 0 put
mydict /total known ⇒ true
mydict /badname known ⇒ false
```

Errors: invalidaccess, stackunderflow, typecheck

See Also: where, load, get

kshow   *proc string* **kshow** –

paints the characters of *string* in a manner similar to **show**, but allowing program intervention between characters. If the character codes in *string* are c_0, c_1, ... c_n, **kshow** proceeds as follows: First it shows c_0 at the current point, updating the current point by c_0's width. Then it pushes the character codes c_0 and c_1 on the operand stack (as integers) and executes *proc*. The *proc* may perform any actions it wishes; typically, it will modify the current point to affect the subsequent placement of c_1. **kshow** continues by showing c_1, pushing c_1 and c_2 on the stack, executing *proc*, and so on. It finishes by pushing c_{n-1} and c_n on the stack, executing *proc*, and finally showing c_n.

When *proc* is called for the first time, the graphics state (in particular, the CTM) is the same as it was at the time **kshow** was invoked, except that the current point has been updated by the width of c_0. Execution of *proc* is permitted to have any side effects, including changes to the graphics state. Such changes persist from one call of *proc* to the next and may affect graphical output for the remainder of **kshow**'s execution and afterward.

The name **kshow** is derived from "kern-show." To *kern* characters is to adjust the spacing between adjacent pairs of characters in order to achieve a visually pleasing result. The **kshow** operator enables user-defined kerning and other manipulations, because arbitrary computations can be performed between each pair of characters.

kshow can be applied only to base fonts. If the current font is composite, **kshow** issues an **invalidfont** error.

Errors: **invalidaccess, invalidfont, nocurrentpoint, stackunderflow, typecheck**

See Also: **show, ashow, awidthshow, widthshow, xshow, xyshow, yshow, cshow**

languagelevel   – **languagelevel** *int*   `LEVEL 2`

is an integer designating the PostScript language level supported by the Post-Script interpreter. If the value of **languagelevel** is 2, the PostScript interpreter supports all PostScript Level 2 language features. If the value of **languagelevel** is 1 or if **languagelevel** is not defined in **systemdict**, the PostScript interpreter does not support all PostScript Level 2 language features.

Errors: **stackoverflow, undefined**

See Also: **product, revision, serialnumber, version**

le num_1 num_2 **le** *bool*
            $string_1$ $string_2$ **le** *bool*

pops two objects from the operand stack and pushes the boolean value *true* if the first operand is less than or equal to the second, *false* otherwise. If both operands are numbers, **le** compares their mathematical values. If both operands are strings, **le** compares them element by element (treating the elements as integers in the range 0 to 255) to determine whether the first string is lexically less than or equal to the second. If the operands are of other types or one is a string and the other is a number, **le** executes the **typecheck** error.

Errors: **invalidaccess, stackunderflow, typecheck**

See Also: **lt, eq, ne, ge, gt**

length   *array* **length** *int*
            packedarray **length** *int*
                   dict **length** *int*
                 string **length** *int*
                   name **length** *int*

depends on the type of its operand. If the operand is an array, packed array, or string, **length** returns the number of elements in its value. If the operand is a dictionary, **length** returns the current number of key-value pairs it contains, as opposed to its maximum capacity, which is returned by **maxlength**. If the operand is a name object, the length is the number of characters in the text string that defines it.

Example

```
[1 2 4] length ⇒ 3
[ ] length ⇒ 0                          % An array of zero length
/ar 20 array def ar length ⇒ 20

/mydict 5 dict def
mydict length ⇒ 0
mydict /firstkey (firstvalue) put
mydict length ⇒ 1

(abc\n) length ⇒ 4                      % The "\n" is one character
() length ⇒ 0                           % No characters between ( and )
/foo length ⇒ 3
```

Errors: **invalidaccess, stackunderflow, typecheck**

See Also: **maxlength**

limitcheck   *(error)*

An implementation limit has been exceeded (for example, too many files have been opened simultaneously or a path has become too complex). Appendix B gives typical values for all such limits.

lineto   *x y* **lineto** –

appends a straight line segment to the current path (see section 4.4, "Path Construction"). The line extends from the current point to the point (*x, y*) in user space; (*x, y*) then becomes the current point. If the current point is undefined because the current path is empty, **lineto** executes the error **nocurrentpoint**.

Errors: **limitcheck, nocurrentpoint, stackunderflow, typecheck**

See Also: **rlineto, moveto, arc, curveto, closepath**

ln   *num* **ln** *real*

returns the natural logarithm (base *e*) of *num*. The result is a real.

Example

    10 ln ⇒ 2.30259
    100 ln ⇒ 4.60517

Errors: **rangecheck, stackunderflow, typecheck**

See Also: **log, exp**

load   *key* **load** *value*

searches for *key* in each dictionary on the dictionary stack, starting with the topmost (current) dictionary. If *key* is found in some dictionary, **load** pushes the associated value on the operand stack. If *key* is not found in any dictionary on the dictionary stack, **load** executes the error **undefined**.

load looks up *key* the same way the interpreter looks up executable names that it encounters during execution. However, **load** always pushes the associated value on the operand stack; it never executes that value.

Example

    /avg {add 2 div} def
    /avg load ⇒ {add 2 div}

Errors: **invalidaccess, stackunderflow, typecheck, undefined**

See Also: where, get, store

lock   – **lock** *lock*   `DPS`

creates a new lock object, unequal to any lock object already in existence, and pushes it on the operand stack. The state of the lock is initially free (see section 7.1, "Multiple Execution Contexts").

Since a lock is a composite object, creating one consumes VM. The lock's value is allocated in local or global VM according to the current VM allocation mode (see section 3.7.2, "Local and Global VM").

Errors: **stackoverflow, VMerror**

See Also: monitor, wait

log   *num* **log** *real*

returns the common logarithm (base 10) of *num*. The result is a real.

Example

    10 log ⇒ 1.0
    100 log ⇒ 2.0

Errors: **rangecheck, stackunderflow, typecheck**

See Also: ln, exp

loop   *proc* **loop** –

repeatedly executes *proc* until *proc* executes the **exit** operator, at which point interpretation resumes at the object next in sequence after the **loop**. Control also leaves *proc* if the **stop** operator is executed. If *proc* never executes **exit** or **stop**, an infinite loop results, which can be broken only via an external interrupt (see **interrupt**).

Errors: **stackunderflow, typecheck**

See Also: **for, repeat, forall, exit**

lt num_1 num_2 **lt** *bool*
      $string_1$ $string_2$ **lt** *bool*

pops two objects from the operand stack and pushes the boolean value *true* if the first operand is less than the second, *false* otherwise. If both operands are numbers, **lt** compares their mathematical values. If both operands are strings, **lt** compares them element by element (treating the elements as integers in the range 0 to 255) to determine whether the first string is lexically less than the second. If the operands are of other types or one is a string and the other is a number, **lt** executes the **typecheck** error.

Errors: **invalidaccess, stackunderflow, typecheck**

See Also: **le, eq, ne, ge, gt**

makefont   *font matrix* **makefont** *font'*

applies *matrix* to *font*, producing a new *font'* whose characters are transformed by *matrix* when they are shown. **makefont** first creates a copy of *font*. Then it replaces the new font's **FontMatrix** entry with the result of concatenating the existing **FontMatrix** with *matrix*. It inserts two additional entries, **OrigFont** and **ScaleMatrix**, whose purpose is internal to the implementation. Finally, it returns the result as *font'*.

The **makefont**, **scalefont**, and **selectfont** operators produce a font dictionary derived from an original font dictionary, but with the **FontMatrix** entry altered. The derived font dictionary is allocated in local or global VM according to whether the original font dictionary is in local or global VM. This is independent of the current VM allocation mode.

Normally, **makefont** copies only the font dictionary. Subsidiary objects, such as the **CharStrings** and **FontInfo** dictionaries, are shared with the original font. However, if *font* is a composite font, **makefont** also copies the font dictionaries of any descendant composite fonts. It does not copy descendant base fonts.

Showing characters from the transformed font produces the same results as showing from the original font after having transformed user space by the same matrix. **makefont** is essentially a convenience operator that permits the desired transformation to be encapsulated in the font description. The most common transformation is to scale a font by a uniform factor in both *x* and *y*. **scalefont** is a special case of the more general **makefont** and should be used for such uniform scaling. Another operator, **selectfont**, combines the effects of **findfont** and **makefont**.

The interpreter keeps track of font dictionaries recently created by **makefont**. Calling **makefont** multiple times with the same *font* and *matrix* will usually return the same *font'* rather than create a new one. However, it is usually more efficient for a PostScript language program to apply **makefont** only once for each font that it needs and to keep track of the resulting font dictionaries on its own.

See Chapter 5 for general information about fonts and section 4.3, "Coordinate Systems and Transformations," for a discussion of transformations.

Example

/Helvetica findfont [10 0 0 12 0 0] makefont setfont

This obtains the standard Helvetica font, which is defined with a one unit line height, and scales it by a factor of 10 in the *x* dimension and 12 in the *y* dimension. This produces a 12-unit high font (i.e., a 12-point font in default user space) whose characters are "condensed" in the *x* dimension by a ratio of 10/12.

Errors: **invalidfont, rangecheck, stackunderflow, typecheck, VMerror**

See Also: **scalefont, setfont, findfont, selectfont**

makepattern   *dict matrix* **makepattern** *pattern*

verifies that *dict* is a prototype pattern dictionary with all required key-value pairs (see section 4.9, "Patterns"). It then creates a copy of *dict* in local VM, adding an entry, with key **Implementation**, for use by the implementation. **makepattern** copies only the contents of *dict* itself, not the values of subsidiary composite objects, which are shared with the original dictionary.

makepattern saves a copy of the current graphics state, to be used later when the interpreter calls the **PaintProc** to render the pattern cell. It then modifies certain parameters in the *saved* graphics state, as follows:

- Concatenates *matrix* with the saved copy of the CTM.

- Adjusts the resulting matrix to ensure that the device space can be tiled properly with a pattern cell of the given size in accordance with the **TilingType**.

- Resets the path to empty.

- Replaces the clipping path by the pattern cell bounding box specified by the **BBox** entry in the pattern dictionary.

- Replaces the device by a special one the implementation provides.

Finally, **makepattern** makes the new dictionary read-only and pushes it on the operand stack. The resulting pattern dictionary is suitable for use as an operand of **setpattern** or as a "color value" in the **Pattern** color space.

Errors: **limitcheck, rangecheck, stackunderflow, typecheck, undefined, VMerror**

See Also: **setpattern, findresource**

mark   – mark *mark*

pushes a *mark* (an object whose type is mark, not the **mark** operator itself) on the operand stack. All marks are identical, and the operand stack may contain any number of them at once.

The primary use of marks is to indicate the stack position of the beginning of an indefinitely long list of operands being passed to an operator or procedure. The] operator (array construction) is the most common operator that works this way. It treats as operands all elements of the stack down to a mark that was pushed by the [operator ([is a synonym for **mark**). It is possible to define procedures that work similarly. Operators such as **counttomark** and **cleartomark** are useful within such procedures.

Errors: **stackoverflow**

See Also: **counttomark, cleartomark, pop**

matrix   – matrix *matrix*

creates a 6-element array object, fills it in with the values of an identity matrix [1.0 0.0 0.0 1.0 0.0 0.0] and pushes this array on the operand stack. The array is allocated in local or global VM according to the current VM allocation mode (see section 3.7.2, "Local and Global VM").

Example

    matrix ⇒ [1.0 0.0 0.0 1.0 0.0 0.0]
    6 array identmatrix ⇒ [1.0 0.0 0.0 1.0 0.0 0.0]

The two lines in the example yield identical results.

Errors: **stackoverflow, VMerror**

See Also: **currentmatrix, defaultmatrix, initmatrix, setmatrix, array**

maxlength   *dict* **maxlength** *int*

returns the capacity of *dict*—in other words, the maximum number of key-value pairs that *dict* can hold using the VM currently allocated to it. In Level 1 implementations, **maxlength** returns the length operand of the **dict** operator that created the dictionary; this is the dictionary's maximum capacity (exceeding it causes a **dictfull** error). In a Level 2 implementation, which permits a dictionary to grow beyond its initial capacity, **maxlength** returns its current capacity, a number at least as large as that returned by **length**.

Example

```
/mydict 5 dict def
mydict length ⇒ 0
mydict maxlength ⇒ 5
```

Errors: invalidaccess, stackunderflow, typecheck

See Also: length, dict

---

mod int_1 int_2 **mod** *remainder*

returns the remainder that results from dividing int_1 by int_2. The sign of the result is the same as the sign of the dividend int_1. Both operands must be integers. The result is an integer.

Example

```
5 3 mod ⇒ 2
5 2 mod ⇒ 1
–5 3 mod ⇒ –2
```

The last line of the example demonstrates that **mod** is a *remainder* operation rather than a true *modulo* operation.

Errors: stackunderflow, typecheck, undefinedresult

See Also: idiv, div

---

monitor   *lock* *proc* **monitor** –   DPS

acquires *lock*, first waiting if necessary for it to become free, then executes *proc*, and finally releases *lock* again. The release of *lock* occurs whether *proc* runs to completion or terminates prematurely for any reason. See section 7.1, "Multiple Execution Contexts."

If *lock* is already held by the current context, **monitor** executes an **invalidcontext** error without disturbing the lock. If the current context has previously executed a **save** not yet matched by a **restore** and *lock* is already held by another context sharing the same local VM as the current context, an **invalidcontext** error results. These restrictions prevent the most straightforward cases of a context deadlocking with itself.

Errors: invalidcontext, stackunderflow, typecheck

See Also: lock, fork, wait

moveto   *x y* **moveto** –

starts a new subpath of the current path. **moveto** sets the current point in the graphics state to the user space coordinate (*x*, *y*) without adding any line segments to the current path.

If the previous path operation in the current path was also a **moveto** or **rmoveto**, that point is deleted from the current path and the new **moveto** point replaces it.

Errors: limitcheck, stackunderflow, typecheck

See Also: rmoveto, lineto, curveto, arc, closepath

mul   *num₁ num₂* **mul** *product*

returns the product of *num₁* and *num₂*. If both operands are integers and the result is within integer range, the result is an integer. Otherwise, the result is a real.

Errors: stackunderflow, typecheck, undefinedresult

See Also: div, idiv, add, sub, mod

ne   *any₁ any₂* **ne** *bool*

pops two objects from the operand stack and pushes the boolean value *false* if they are equal, *true* if not. What it means for objects to be equal is presented in the description of the **eq** operator.

Errors: invalidaccess, stackunderflow

See Also: eq, ge, gt, le, lt

neg   *num₁* **neg** *num₂*

returns the negative of *num₁*. The type of the result is the same as the type of *num₁*, unless *num₁* is the most negative integer, in which case the result is a real.

Example

    4.5 neg ⇒ –4.5
    –3 neg ⇒ 3

Errors: stackunderflow, typecheck

See Also: abs

---

newpath   – newpath –

initializes the current path to be empty, causing the current point to become undefined.

Errors: (none)

See Also: closepath, stroke, fill

---

noaccess
$$\begin{array}{rcl}
\textit{array} & \textbf{noaccess} & \textit{array} \\
\textit{packedarray} & \textbf{noaccess} & \textit{packedarray} \\
\textit{dict} & \textbf{noaccess} & \textit{dict} \\
\textit{file} & \textbf{noaccess} & \textit{file} \\
\textit{string} & \textbf{noaccess} & \textit{string}
\end{array}$$

reduces the access attribute of an array, packed array, dictionary, file, or string object to none (see section 3.3.2, "Attributes of Objects"). The value of a no-access object cannot be executed or accessed directly by PostScript operators. No-access objects are of no use to PostScript language programs, but serve certain internal purposes that are not documented in this manual.

For an array, packed array, file, or string, **noaccess** affects the access attribute only of the object that it returns. If there are other objects that share the same value, their access attributes are unaffected. However, in the case of a dictionary, **noaccess** affects the *value* of the object, so all dictionary objects sharing the same dictionary are affected.

Errors: invalidaccess, stackunderflow, typecheck

See Also: rcheck, wcheck, xcheck, readonly, executeonly

---

nocurrentpoint   *(error)*

The current path is empty, and thus there is no current point, but an operator requiring a current point has been executed (for example, **lineto**, **curveto**, **currentpoint**, **show**). The most common cause of this error is neglecting to perform an initial **moveto**.

See Also: moveto

not $bool_1$ **not** $bool_2$
int_1 **not** int_2

If the operand is a boolean, **not** returns its logical negation. If the operand is an integer, **not** returns the bitwise complement (one's complement) of its binary representation.

Example

true not $\Rightarrow$ false   % A complete truth table
false not $\Rightarrow$ true

52 not $\Rightarrow$ –53

Errors: **stackunderflow, typecheck**

See Also: **and, or, xor, if**

notify   *condition* **notify** –   DPS

resumes execution of all contexts, if any, that are suspended in a **wait** for *condition*. See section 7.1, "Multiple Execution Contexts."

Ordinarily, **notify** should be invoked only within the execution of a **monitor** that references the same *lock* used in the **wait** for *condition*. This ensures that notifications cannot be lost due to a race between a context executing **notify** and one executing **wait**. However, this recommendation is not enforced by the language.

Errors: **stackunderflow, typecheck**

See Also: **wait, monitor, condition**

null   – **null** *null*

pushes a literal null object on the operand stack. **null** is not an operator; it is a name in **systemdict** associated with the null object.

Errors: **stackoverflow**

nulldevice – **nulldevice** –

installs the "null device" as the current output device. The null device corresponds to no physical output device and has no raster memory associated with it. Marks placed on the current page by painting operators (for example, **show** or **stroke**) are discarded; output operators (**showpage** and **copypage**) do nothing. However, in all other respects the null device behaves like a real raster output device: the graphics operators have their normal side-effects on the graphics state, the character operators invoke the font machinery, and so on.

nulldevice sets the default transformation matrix to be the identity transform [1.0 0.0 0.0 1.0 0.0 0.0]. A PostScript language program may change this to any other matrix (using **setmatrix**) if it desires to simulate the device coordinate system of some real device. **nulldevice** also establishes the clipping path as a degenerate path consisting of a single point at the origin.

The null device is useful for exercising the PostScript interpreter's graphics and font machinery for such purposes as operating on paths, computing bounding boxes for graphical shapes, and performing coordinate transformations using CTM without generating output. Such manipulations should be bracketed by **gsave** and **grestore** so the former device can be reinstated and the other side effects of **nulldevice** undone.

Errors: (none)

See Also: **setpagedevice**

or $bool_1$ $bool_2$ **or** $bool_3$
            int_1 int_2 **or** int_3

If the operands are booleans, **or** returns their logical disjunction. If the operands are integers, **or** returns the bitwise "inclusive or" of their binary representations.

Example

    true true or $\Rightarrow$ true   % A complete truth table
    true false or $\Rightarrow$ true
    false true or $\Rightarrow$ true
    false false or $\Rightarrow$ false

    17 5 or $\Rightarrow$ 21

Errors: **stackunderflow, typecheck**

See Also: **and, not, xor**

packedarray $any_0 \ldots any_{n-1}$ n **packedarray** *packedarray*   LEVEL 2

creates a packed array object of length n containing the objects any_0 through any_{n-1} as elements. **packedarray** first removes the non-negative integer n from the operand stack. It then removes that number of objects from the operand stack, creates a packed array containing those objects as elements, and finally pushes the resulting packed array object on the operand stack.

The resulting object has a type of packedarraytype, a literal attribute, and read-only access. In all other respects, its behavior is identical to that of an ordinary array object.

The packed array is allocated in local or global VM according to the current VM allocation mode. An **invalidaccess** error occurs if the packed array is in global VM and any of $any_0 \ldots any_{n-1}$ are in local VM (see section 3.7.2, "Local and Global VM").

Errors: **invalidaccess, rangecheck, stackunderflow, typecheck, VMerror**

See Also: **aload**

pathbbox   – **pathbbox** ll_x ll_y ur_x ur_y

returns the bounding box of the current path in the current user coordinate system. The results are four real numbers: lower-left x, lower-left y, upper-right x, and upper-right y. These coordinates describe a rectangle, oriented with its sides parallel to the x and y axes in user space, that completely encloses all elements of the path. If the current path is empty, **pathbbox** executes the error **nocurrentpoint**.

pathbbox first computes the bounding box of the current path in *device* space. It then transforms these coordinates to user space by the inverse of CTM and computes the bounding box of the resulting figure in user space. If the user coordinate system is rotated (other than by multiples of 90 degrees) or skewed, **pathbbox** may return a bounding box that is larger than expected.

If the path includes curve segments, the bounding box encloses the control points of the curves as well as the curves themselves. To obtain a bounding box that fits the path more tightly, one should first "flatten" the curve segments by executing **flattenpath**.

In Level 2 implementations of the PostScript language, if the current path ends with a **moveto**, the bounding box does not necessarily include it, unless the **moveto** is the only element of the path. If an explicit bounding box has been established by **setbbox**, **pathbbox** returns a result derived from that bounding box, not from the actual path.

Errors: nocurrentpoint, stackoverflow

See Also: flattenpath, clippath, charpath, setbbox

pathforall   *move line curve close* **pathforall** –

removes four operands from the stack, all of which must be procedures. **pathforall** then enumerates the current path in order, executing one of the four procedures for each element in the path. The four basic kinds of elements in a path are **moveto**, **lineto**, **curveto**, and **closepath**. The relative variants **rmoveto**, **rlineto**, and **rcurveto** are converted to the corresponding absolute forms; **arc**, **arcn**, and **arcto** are converted to sequences of **curveto**. For each element in the path, **pathforall** pushes the element's coordinates on the operand stack and executes one of the four procedures as follows:

moveto	push *x y*; execute *move*
lineto	push *x y*; execute *line*
curveto	push $x_1\, y_1\, x_2\, y_2\, x_3\, y_3$; execute *curve*
closepath	execute *close*

The operands passed to the procedures are coordinates in user space. **pathforall** transforms them from device space to user space using the inverse of the CTM. Ordinarily, these coordinates will be the same as the ones originally entered by **moveto**, **lineto**, and so forth. However, if the CTM has been changed since the path was constructed, the coordinates reported by **pathforall** will be different from those originally entered.

Among other uses, **pathforall** enables a path constructed in one user coordinate system to be read out in another user coordinate system.

pathforall enumerates the current path existing at the time it begins execution. If any of the procedures change the current path, such changes do not alter the behavior of **pathforall**.

If **charpath** was used to construct any portion of the current path from a font whose outlines are protected, **pathforall** is not allowed. Its execution will produce an **invalidaccess** error (see **charpath**).

Errors: invalidaccess, stackoverflow, stackunderflow, typecheck

See Also: moveto, lineto, curveto, closepath, charpath

pop   *any* **pop** –

removes the top element from the operand stack and discards it.

Example

1 2 3 pop ⇒ 1 2
1 2 3 pop pop ⇒ 1

Errors: **stackunderflow**

See Also: **clear, dup**

print   *string* **print** –

writes the characters of *string* to the standard output file (see section 3.8, "File Input and Output"). The **print** operator provides the simplest means to send text to an application or an interactive user. Note that **print** is a *file* operator that has nothing to do with painting character shapes on the current page (see **show**) or with sending the current page to a raster output device (see **showpage**).

Errors: **invalidaccess, ioerror, stackunderflow, typecheck**

See Also: **write, flush, =, ==, printobject**

printobject   *obj tag* **printobject** –

writes a binary object sequence to the standard output file; see section 3.12.6, "Structured Output." The binary object sequence contains a top-level array whose length is one; its single element is an encoding of *obj*. If *obj* is composite, the binary object sequence also includes subsidiary array and string values for the components of *obj*. The *tag* operand, which must be an integer in the range 0 to 255, is used to tag the top-level object; it appears as the second byte of the object's representation. Tag values 0 through 249 are available for general use; tag values 250 through 255 are reserved for special purposes, such as reporting errors.

The binary object sequence uses the number representation established by the most recent execution of **setobjectformat**. The token type given as the first byte of the binary object sequence reflects the number representation that was used. If the object format parameter has been set to zero, **printobject** executes an **undefined** error.

The object *obj* and its components must be of type null, integer, real, name, boolean, string, array, or mark (see section 3.12, "Binary Encoding Details"). Appearance of an object of any other type, including packed array, will result in a **typecheck** error. If arrays are nested too deeply or are cyclical, a **limitcheck** error occurs.

printobject always encodes a name object as a reference to a text name in the string value portion of the binary object sequence, never as a system or user name index.

As is the case for all operators that write to files, the output produced by **printobject** may accumulate in a buffer instead of being transmitted immediately. To ensure immediate transmission, a **flush** is required. This is particularly important in situations where the output produced by **printobject** is the response to a query from the application.

Errors: invalidaccess, ioerror, limitcheck, rangecheck, stackunderflow, typecheck, undefined

See Also: print, setobjectformat, writeobject

product   – **product** *string*   LEVEL 2

is a read-only string object that is the name of the product in which the Post-Script interpreter is running. The value of this string is typically a manufacturer defined trademark; it has no direct connection with specific features of the Post-Script language.

Errors: **stackoverflow**

See Also: **languagelevel, revision, serialnumber, version**

prompt   – **prompt** –

is a procedure executed by **executive** whenever it is ready for the user to enter a new statement. The standard definition of **prompt** is "(PS>) print flush" and is defined in **systemdict**; it can be overridden by defining **prompt** in **userdict** or some other dictionary higher on the dictionary stack. **prompt** is not defined in products that do not support **executive**. See section 2.4.4, "Using the Interpreter Interactively."

Errors: (none)

See Also: **executive**

pstack   ⊢   *any₁ ... anyₙ* **pstack** ⊢   *any₁ ... anyₙ*

writes text representations of every object on the stack to the standard output file, but leaves the stack unchanged. **pstack** applies the **==** operator to each element of the stack, starting with the topmost element. See the **==** operator for a description of its effects.

Errors: (none)

See Also: **stack, =, ==**

put   *array index any* **put** –
       dict key any **put** –
      string index int **put** –

replaces a single element of the value of an array, dictionary, or string.

If the first operand is an array or string, **put** treats the second operand as an index and stores the third operand at the position identified by the index, counting from zero. *index* must be in the range 0 to *n*–1, where *n* is the length of the array or string. If it is outside this range, **put** will execute a **rangecheck** error.

If the first operand is a dictionary, **put** uses the second operand as a key and the third operand as a value, and it stores this key-value pair into *dict*. If *key* is already present as a key in *dict*, **put** simply replaces its value by *any*. Otherwise, **put** creates a new entry for *key* and associates *any* with it. In Level 1 implementations, if *dict* is already full, **put** executes the error **dictfull**.

If the value of *array* or *dict* is in global VM and *any* is a composite object whose value is in local VM, an **invalidaccess** error occurs (see section 3.7.2, "Local and Global VM").

Example

```
/ar [5 17 3 8] def
ar 2 (abcd) put
ar ⇒ [5 17 (abcd) 8]

/d 5 dict def
d /abc 123 put
d {} forall ⇒ /abc 123

/st (abc) def
st 0 65 put                    % 65 is ASCII code for character "A"
st ⇒ (Abc)
```

Errors: **dictfull, invalidaccess, rangecheck, stackunderflow, typecheck**

See Also: **get, putinterval**

putinterval $array_1$ $index$ $array_2$ **putinterval** –
$array_1$ $index$ $packedarray_2$ **putinterval** –
$string_1$ $index$ $string_2$ **putinterval** –

replaces a subsequence of the elements of the first operand by the entire contents of the third operand. The subsequence that is replaced begins at the specified *index* in the first operand; its length is the same as the length of the third
operand.

The objects are copied from the third operand to the first, as if by a sequence of
individual **get**s and **put**s. In the case of arrays, if the copied elements are themselves composite objects, the values of those objects are shared between $array_2$
and $array_1$ (see section 3.3.1, "Simple and Composite Objects").

putinterval requires *index* to be a valid index in $array_1$ or $string_1$ such that *index*
plus the length of $array_2$ or $string_2$ is not greater than the length of $array_1$ or
$string_1$.

If the value of $array_1$ is in global VM and any of the elements copied from $array_2$
or $packedarray_2$ are composite objects whose values are in local VM, an
invalidaccess error occurs (see section 3.7.2, "Local and Global VM").

Example

```
/ar [5 8 2 7 3] def
ar 1 [(a) (b) (c)] putinterval
ar ⇒ [5 (a) (b) (c) 3]

/st (abc) def
st 1 (de) putinterval
st ⇒ (ade)
```

Errors: **invalidaccess, rangecheck, stackunderflow, typecheck**

See Also: **getinterval, put**

quit   – quit –

terminates operation of the interpreter. The precise action of **quit** depends on the environment in which the PostScript interpreter is running. It may give control to an operating system command interpreter, halt or restart the machine, and so on.

In an interpreter that supports multiple execution contexts (see section 7.1, "Multiple Execution Contexts"), the **quit** operator causes termination of the current context only. Termination is immediate, even if the context was created by **fork** in the expectation of a subsequent **join**.

In a context that is under the control of a job server (see section 3.7.7, "Job Execution Environment"), the definition of the **quit** operator in **systemdict** is masked by another definition of **quit** in **userdict**, which usually is searched before **systemdict**. The default definition of **quit** in **userdict** is the same as **stop**, which terminates the current job, but not the interpreter as a whole. The **quit** operator in **systemdict** can be executed only by an unencapsulated job; in an encapsulated job, it causes an **invalidaccess** error.

Errors: **invalidaccess**

See Also: **stop, start**

rand   – **rand** *int*

returns a random integer in the range 0 to $2^{31} - 1$, produced by a pseudo-random number generator. The random number generator's state can be reset by **srand** and interrogated by **rrand**.

Errors: **stackoverflow**

See Also: **srand, rrand**

rangecheck   *(error)*

A numeric operand's value is outside the range expected by an operator—for example, an array or string index is out of bounds, or a negative number appears where a non-negative number is required. **rangecheck** can also occur if a matrix operand does not contain exactly six elements.

rcheck

> *array* **rcheck** *bool*
> *packedarray* **rcheck** *bool*
> *dict* **rcheck** *bool*
> *file* **rcheck** *bool*
> *string* **rcheck** *bool*

tests whether the operand's access permits its value to be read explicitly by PostScript operators. **rcheck** returns *true* if the operand's access is unlimited or read-only, *false* otherwise.

Errors: stackunderflow, typecheck

See Also: executeonly, noaccess, readonly, wcheck

rcurveto

> dx_1 dy_1 dx_2 dy_2 dx_3 dy_3 **rcurveto** –

(relative **curveto**) adds a Bézier cubic section to the current path in the same manner as **curveto**. However, the three number pairs are interpreted as displacements relative to the current point (x_0, y_0) rather than as absolute coordinates. That is, **rcurveto** constructs a curve from (x_0, y_0) to (x_0+dx_3, y_0+dy_3), using (x_0+dx_1, y_0+dy_1) and (x_0+dx_2, y_0+dy_2) as Bézier control points. See the description of **curveto** for complete information.

Errors: limitcheck, nocurrentpoint, stackunderflow, typecheck, undefinedresult

See Also: curveto, rlineto, rmoveto

read

> *file* **read** *int true*   *(if not end-of-file)*
>   *false*   *(if end-of-file)*

reads the next character from the input file *file*, pushes it on the stack as an integer, and pushes *true* as an indication of success. If an end-of-file indication is encountered before a character has been read, **read** closes the file and returns *false*. If some other error indication is encountered (for example, parity or checksum error), **read** executes **ioerror**.

Errors: invalidaccess, ioerror, stackoverflow, stackunderflow, typecheck

See Also: readhexstring, readline, readstring, bytesavailable

readhexstring   *file string* **readhexstring** *substring bool*

reads characters from *file*, expecting to encounter a sequence of hexadecimal digits 0 through 9 and A through F (or a through f). **readhexstring** interprets each successive pair of digits as a two-digit hexadecimal number representing an integer value in the range 0 to 255. It then stores these values into successive elements of *string* starting at index 0 until either the entire string has been filled or an end-of-file indication is encountered in *file*. Finally, **readhexstring** returns the substring of *string* that was filled and a boolean indicating the outcome (*true* normally, *false* if end-of-file was encountered before the string was filled).

readhexstring ignores any characters that are not valid hexadecimal digits, so the data in *file* may be interspersed with spaces, newlines, etc., without changing the interpretation of the data.

See section 3.8.4, "Filters," for more information about ASCII-encoded, binary data representations and how to deal with them.

Errors: **invalidaccess, ioerror, rangecheck, stackunderflow, typecheck**

See Also: **read, readline, readstring, filter**

readline   *file string* **readline** *substring bool*

reads a line of characters (terminated by a newline character) from *file* and stores them into successive elements of *string*. **readline** then returns the substring of *string* that was filled and a boolean indicating the outcome (*true* normally, *false* if end-of-file was encountered before a newline character was read).

A "line of characters" is a sequential string of ASCII characters, including space, tab, and non-printing "control" characters. A line terminates with a *newline*—a carriage return character, a line-feed character, or both. See section 3.2, "Syntax," and section 3.8, "File Input and Output."

The terminating newline character is not stored into *string* or included at the end of the returned *substring*. If **readline** completely fills *string* before encountering a newline character, it executes the error **rangecheck**.

Errors: **invalidaccess, ioerror, rangecheck, stackunderflow, typecheck**

See Also: **read, readhexstring, readonly**

readonly

> *array* **readonly** *array*
> *packedarray* **readonly** *packedarray*
> *dict* **readonly** *dict*
> *file* **readonly** *file*
> *string* **readonly** *string*

reduces the access attribute of an array, packed array, dictionary, file, or string object to read-only (see section 3.3.2, "Attributes of Objects"). Access can only be reduced this way, never increased. When an object is read-only, its value cannot be modified by PostScript operators (an **invalidaccess** error will result), but it can still be read by operators or executed by the PostScript interpreter.

For an array, packed array, file, or string, **readonly** affects the access attribute only of the object that it returns. If there are other objects that share the same value, their access attributes are unaffected. However, in the case of a dictionary, **readonly** affects the *value* of the object, so all dictionary objects sharing the same dictionary are affected.

Errors: invalidaccess, stackunderflow, typecheck

See Also: executeonly, noaccess, rcheck, wcheck

readstring

> *file string* **readstring** *substring bool*

reads characters from *file* and stores them into successive elements of *string* until either the entire string has been filled or an end-of-file indication is encountered in *file*. **readstring** then returns the substring of *string* that was filled and a boolean indicating the outcome (*true* normally, *false* if end-of-file was encountered before the string was filled).

All character codes are treated the same—as integers in the range 0 to 255. There are no special characters (in particular, the newline character is not treated specially). However, the communication channel may usurp certain control characters; see section 3.8, "File Input and Output."

Errors: invalidaccess, ioerror, rangecheck, stackunderflow, typecheck

See Also: read, readhexstring, readline

realtime   – **realtime** *int*

returns the value of a clock that counts in real time, independent of the execution of the PostScript interpreter. The clock's starting value is arbitrary; it has no defined meaning in terms of calendar time. The unit of time represented by the **realtime** value is one millisecond. However, the rate at which it changes is implementation dependent. As the time value becomes greater than the largest integer allowed in a particular implementation, it "wraps" to the smallest (most negative) integer.

Errors: **stackoverflow**

See Also: **usertime**

rectclip   *x y width height* **rectclip** –   LEVEL 2
                 numarray **rectclip** –
                 numstring **rectclip** –

intersects the inside of the current clipping path with a rectangular path the operands describe. In the first form, the operands are four numbers that describe a single rectangle. In the other two forms, the operand is an array or an encoded number string that describes an arbitrary number of rectangles (see section 3.12.5, "Encoded Number Strings," and section 4.6.5, "Rectangles"). After computing the new clipping path, **rectclip** resets the current path to empty, as if by **newpath**.

In the first form, assuming *width* and *height* are positive, **rectclip** is equivalent to:

```
newpath
x y moveto
width 0 rlineto
0 height rlineto
width neg 0 rlineto
closepath
clip
newpath
```

Note that if the second or third form is used to specify multiple rectangles, the rectangles are treated together as a single path and used for a single **clip** operation. The "inside" of this combined path is the union of all the rectangular subpaths, because the paths are all drawn in the same direction and the non-zero winding number rule is used.

Errors: **limitcheck, stackunderflow, typecheck**

See Also: **clip, rectfill, rectstroke**

rectfill   *x y width height* **rectfill** –
                 numarray **rectfill** –
                 numstring **rectfill** –

fills a path consisting of one or more rectangles the operands describe. In the first form, the operands are four numbers that describe a single rectangle. In the other two forms, the operand is an array or an encoded number string that describes an arbitrary number of rectangles (see section 3.12.5, "Encoded Number Strings," and section 4.6.5, "Rectangles"). **rectfill** neither reads nor alters the current path in the graphics state.

In the first form, assuming *width* and *height* are positive, **rectfill** is equivalent to:

```
gsave
newpath
x y moveto
width 0 rlineto
0 height rlineto
width neg 0 rlineto
closepath
fill
grestore
```

Errors: **limitcheck, stackunderflow, typecheck**

See Also: **fill, rectclip, rectstroke**

rectstroke
x y width height **rectstroke** –
x y width height matrix **rectstroke** –
numarray **rectstroke** –
numarray matrix **rectstroke** –
numstring **rectstroke** –
numstring matrix **rectstroke** –

strokes a path consisting of one or more rectangles the operands describe. In the first two forms, the operands are four numbers that describe a single rectangle. In the remaining forms, the operand is an array or an encoded number string that describes an arbitrary number of rectangles (see section 3.12.5, "Encoded Number Strings," and section 4.6.5, "Rectangles"). **rectstroke** neither reads nor alters the current path in the graphics state.

If the *matrix* operand is present, **rectstroke** concatenates *matrix* to the CTM after defining the path, but before stroking it. The *matrix* applies to the line width and dash pattern, if any, but not to the path itself.

In the first two forms, assuming *width* and *height* are positive, **rectstroke** is equivalent to:

```
gsave
newpath
x y moveto
width 0 rlineto
0 height rlineto
width neg 0 rlineto
closepath
matrix concat                    % If matrix operand is supplied
stroke
grestore
```

Errors: limitcheck, rangecheck, stackunderflow, typecheck

See Also: stroke, rectclip, rectfill

rectviewclip   *x y width height* **rectviewclip** –   DPS
                                 numarray **rectviewclip** –
                                 numstring **rectviewclip** –

replaces the current view clip with a rectangular path the operands describe. In the first form, the operands are four numbers that describe a single rectangle. In the other two forms, the operand is an array or an encoded number string that describes an arbitrary number of rectangles (see section 3.12.5, "Encoded Number Strings," section 7.3.1, "View Clipping," and section 4.6.5, "Rectangles"). After computing the new view clipping path, **rectviewclip** resets the current path to empty, as if by **newpath**.

Except for the manner in which the path is defined, **rectviewclip** behaves the same as **viewclip**.

Note that if the second or third form is used to specify multiple rectangles, the rectangles are treated together as a single path and used for a single **viewclip** operation. The "inside" of this combined path is the union of all the rectangular subpaths, because the paths are all drawn in the same direction and the non-zero winding number rule is used.

Errors: **limitcheck, stackunderflow, typecheck**

See Also: **rectclip, viewclip**

renamefile   *old new* **renamefile** – LEVEL 2

changes the name of a file from *old* to *new*, where *old* and *new* are strings that specify file names on the same storage device. If no such file exists, an **undefinedfilename** error occurs. If the device does not allow this operation, an **invalidfileaccess** error occurs. If an environment-dependent error is detected, an **ioerror** occurs. Whether or not an error occurs if a file named *new* already exists is environment dependent. See section 3.8.2, "Named Files."

Errors: **invalidfileaccess, ioerror, stackunderflow, typecheck, undefinedfilename**

See Also: **file, deletefile, status**

repeat   *int proc* **repeat** –

executes *proc int* times, where *int* is a non-negative integer. The **repeat** operator removes both operands from the stack before executing *proc* for the first time. If *proc* executes the **exit** operator, **repeat** terminates prematurely. **repeat** leaves no results of its own on the stack, but *proc* may do so.

Example

```
4 {(abc)} repeat ⇒ (abc)(abc)(abc)(abc)
1 2 3 4 3 {pop} repeat ⇒ 1                % Pops 3 values (down to the 1)
4 {} repeat ⇒                             % Does nothing four times
mark 0 {(won't happen)} repeat ⇒ mark
```

In the last example, a zero repeat count meant that the procedure is not executed at all, hence the mark is still topmost on the stack.

Errors: **rangecheck, stackunderflow, typecheck**

See Also: **for, loop, forall, exit**

476   Chapter 8: Operators

resetfile *file* **resetfile** –

discards buffered characters belonging to a file object. For an input file, **resetfile** discards any characters that have been received from the source, but not yet consumed. For an output file, it discards any characters that have been written to the file, but not yet delivered to their destination.

resetfile may have other side effects that depend on the properties of the underlying file. For example, it may restart communication via a channel that was blocked waiting for buffer space to become available. **resetfile** never waits for characters to be received or transmitted.

Errors: **stackunderflow, typecheck**

See Also: **file, closefile, flushfile**

enumerates the names of all instances of a specified resource category or a subset selected by *template*. *category* is a name object that identifies a resource category, such as **Font** (see section 3.9.2, "Resource Categories"). *template* is a string object to be matched against names of resource instances. For each matching name, **resourceforall** copies the name into the supplied *scratch* string, pushes a string object that is the substring of *scratch* that was actually used, and calls *proc*. **resourceforall** does not return any results of its own, but *proc* may do so.

The *template* is matched against the names of resource instances, treating them as if they were strings. Within the template, all characters are treated literally and are case sensitive, with the exception of the following:

*   matches zero or more consecutive characters.

?   matches exactly one character.

\   causes the next character of the template to be treated literally, even if it is *, ?, or \.

Note that the scratch string is reused during every call to *proc*. If *proc* wishes to save the string that is passed to it, it must make a copy or use **cvn** to convert the string to a name. Use of strings instead of names allows **resourceforall** to function without creating new name objects, which would consume VM needlessly during a large enumeration. It is prudent to provide a scratch string at least as long as the implementation limit for names (see Appendix B).

It is possible for a resource instance to have a key which is not a name or string. Such a key matches only the template (*). In this case, **resourceforall** passes the key directly to *proc* instead of copying it into the *scratch* string. This case can arise only for a resource instance defined in VM by a previous **defineresource**; the keys for external resource instances are always names or strings.

Like **resourcestatus**, but unlike **findresource**, **resourceforall** never loads a resource instance into VM.

resourceforall enumerates the resource instances in order of status (the status value returned by **resourcestatus**); that is, it enumerates groups in this order:

1. Instances defined in VM by an explicit **defineresource**; not subject to automatic removal.

2. Instances defined in VM by a previous execution of **findresource**; subject to automatic removal.

3. Instances not currently defined in VM, but available from external storage.

Within each group, the order of enumeration is unpredictable. It is unrelated to order of definition or to whether the definition is local or global. A given resource instance is enumerated only once, even if it exists in more than one group. If *proc* adds or removes resource instances, those instances may or may not appear later in the same enumeration.

Like **resourcestatus**, **resourceforall** considers both local and global definitions if the current VM allocation mode is local, but only global definitions if the current VM allocation mode is global (see **resourcestatus** and **defineresource**).

If the specified resource category does not exist, an **undefined** error occurs. However, no error occurs if there are no instances whose names match the template. Of course, the *proc* that is called can generate errors of its own.

Errors: invalidaccess, stackoverflow, stackunderflow, typecheck, undefined

See Also: defineresource, undefineresource, findresource, resourcestatus

resourcestatus   *key category* **resourcestatus** *status size true*   *(if resource exists)*   LEVEL 2
                                                false   *(if not)*

returns status information about a named resource instance. *category* is a name object that identifies a resource category, such as **Font** (see section 3.9.2, "Resource Categories"). *key* is a name or string object that identifies the resource instance. (Names and strings are interchangeable; keys of other types are permitted but are not recommended.)

If the named resource instance exists, either defined in VM or available from some external source, **resourcestatus** returns two integers and the value *true*; otherwise, it returns *false*. Unlike **findresource**, **resourcestatus** never loads a resource instance into VM.

status is an integer with the following meanings:

0   Defined in VM by an explicit **defineresource**; not subject to automatic removal.

1   Defined in VM by a previous execution of **findresource**; subject to automatic removal.

2   Not currently defined in VM, but available from external storage.

size is an integer giving the estimated VM consumption of the resource instance in bytes. This information may not be available for certain resources; if the size is unknown, –1 is returned. Usually, **resourcestatus** can obtain the size of a status 1 or 2 resource (derived from the %%VMusage comment in the resource file), but it has no general way to determine the size of a status 0 resource. See section 3.9.4, "Resources as Files," for an explanation of how the size is determined. A size value of 0 is returned for implicit resources, whose instances do not occupy VM.

If the current VM allocation mode is local, **resourcestatus** considers both local and global resource definitions, in that order (see **defineresource**). However, if the current VM allocation mode is global, only global resource definitions are visible to **resourcestatus**. Resource instances in external storage are visible without out regard to the current VM allocation mode.

If the specified resource category does not exist, an **undefined** error occurs.

Errors: **stackoverflow, stackunderflow, typecheck, undefined**

See Also: **defineresource, undefineresource, findresource, resourceforall**

restore   *save* **restore** –

resets the virtual memory (VM) to the state represented by the supplied *save* object—in other words, the state at the time the corresponding **save** was executed. See section 3.7, "Memory Management," for a description of the VM and the effects of **save** and **restore**.

If the current execution context supports job encapsulation and if *save* represents the outermost saved VM state for this context, then objects in both local and global VM revert to their saved state. If the current context does not support job encapsulation or if *save* is not the outermost saved VM state for this context, then only objects in local VM revert to their saved state; objects in global VM are undisturbed. Job encapsulation is described in section 3.7.7, "Job Execution Environment." Its relationship to multiple contexts is described in section 7.1, "Multiple Execution Contexts."

restore can reset the VM to the state represented by any save object that is still valid, not necessarily the one produced by the most recent **save**. After restoring the VM, **restore** invalidates its *save* operand along with any other save objects created more recently than that one. That is, a VM snapshot can be used only once; to restore the same environment repeatedly, it is necessary to do a new **save** each time.

restore does not alter the contents of the operand, dictionary, or execution stack, except to pop its *save* operand. If any of these stacks contains composite objects whose values reside in local VM and are newer than the snapshot being restored, **restore** executes the **invalidrestore** error. This restriction applies to save objects and, in Level 1 implementations, to name objects.

restore does alter the graphics state stack: It performs the equivalent of a **grestoreall** and then removes the graphics state created by **save** from the graphics state stack. **restore** also resets several per-context parameters to their state at the time of **save**. These include:

- Array packing mode (see **setpacking**).

- VM allocation mode (see **setglobal**).

- Object output format (see **setobjectformat**).

- View clipping path (see **viewclip**).

- All user interpreter parameters (see **setuserparams**).

Errors: **invalidrestore, stackunderflow, typecheck**

See Also: **save, grestoreall, vmstatus, startjob**

reversepath   – **reversepath** –

replaces the current path with an equivalent one whose segments are defined in the reverse order. Precisely, **reversepath** reverses the directions and order of segments within each subpath of the current path. However, it does not alter the order of the subpaths in the path with respect to each other.

Errors: **limitcheck**

revision   – **revision** *int*   LEVEL 2

is an integer designating the current revision level of the product in which the PostScript interpreter is running. Each product has its own numbering system for revisions, independent of those of any other product. This is distinct from the value of **version** in **systemdict**, which is the revision level of the PostScript interpreter, without regard to the product in which it is running.

Errors: **stackoverflow**

See Also: **languagelevel, product, serialnumber, version**

rlineto   *dx dy* **rlineto** –

(relative **lineto**) appends a straight line segment to the current path in the same manner as **lineto**. However, the number pair is interpreted as a displacement relative to the current point (x, y) rather than as an absolute coordinate. That is, **rlineto** constructs a line from (x, y) to $(x + dx, y + dy)$ and makes $(x + dx, y + dy)$ the new current point. If the current point is undefined because the current path is empty, **rlineto** executes the error **nocurrentpoint**.

Errors: **limitcheck, nocurrentpoint, stackunderflow, typecheck**

See Also: **lineto, rmoveto, rcurveto**

rmoveto   *dx dy* **rmoveto** –

(relative **moveto**) starts a new subpath of the current path in the same manner as **moveto**. However, the number pair is interpreted as a displacement relative to the current point (x, y) rather than as an absolute coordinate. That is, **rmoveto** makes $(x + dx, y + dy)$ the new current point, without connecting it to the previous point. If the current point is undefined because the current path is empty, **rmoveto** executes the error **nocurrentpoint**.

Errors: **limitcheck, nocurrentpoint, stackunderflow, typecheck**

See Also: **moveto, rlineto, rcurveto**

roll $any_{n-1} \ldots any_0 \; n \; j$ **roll** $any_{(j-1) \bmod n} \cdots any_0 \; any_{n-1} \cdots any_{j \bmod n}$

performs a circular shift of the objects any_{n-1} through any_0 on the operand stack by the amount j. Positive j indicates upward motion on the stack, whereas negative j indicates downward motion.

n must be a non-negative integer and j must be an integer. **roll** first removes these operands from the stack; there must be at least n additional elements. **roll** then performs a circular shift of these n elements by j positions.

If j is positive, each shift consists of removing an element from the top of the stack and inserting it between element $n - 1$ and element n of the stack, moving all intervening elements one level higher on the stack. If j is negative, each shift consists of removing element $n - 1$ of the stack and pushing it on the top of the stack, moving all intervening elements one level lower on the stack.

Example

(a)(b)(c) 3 –1 roll $\Rightarrow$ (b)(c)(a)
(a)(b)(c) 3 1 roll $\Rightarrow$ (c)(a)(b)
(a)(b)(c) 3 0 roll $\Rightarrow$ (a)(b)(c)

Errors: **rangecheck, stackunderflow, typecheck**

See Also: **exch, index, copy, pop**

rootfont   – rootfont *font*   LEVEL 2

returns the font that has been selected most recently by **setfont** or **selectfont**. Normally, **rootfont** returns the same result as **currentfont**. If the current font is a composite font and **rootfont** is invoked from a descendant font's **BuildGlyph** or **BuildChar** procedure or from **cshow**, **rootfont** returns the root composite font, whereas **currentfont** would return the currently selected base font.

Errors: **stackoverflow**

See Also: **setfont, selectfont, currentfont**

rotate   *angle* **rotate** –
          angle matrix **rotate** *matrix*

With no *matrix* operand, **rotate** builds a temporary matrix

$$R = \begin{bmatrix} \cos\theta & \sin\theta & 0 \\ -\sin\theta & \cos\theta & 0 \\ 0 & 0 & 1 \end{bmatrix}$$

where θ is the operand *angle* in degrees, and concatenates this matrix with the current transformation matrix (CTM). Precisely, **rotate** replaces the CTM by $R \times$ CTM. The effect of this is to rotate the user coordinate system axes about their origin by *angle* degrees (positive is counterclockwise) with respect to their former orientation. The position of the user coordinate origin and the sizes of the *x* and *y* units are unchanged.

If the *matrix* operand is supplied, **rotate** replaces the value of *matrix* by R and pushes the modified *matrix* back on the operand stack (see section 4.3.3, "Matrix Representation and Manipulation," for a discussion of how matrices are represented as arrays). In this case, **rotate** does not affect the CTM.

Errors: **rangecheck, stackunderflow, typecheck**

See Also: **scale, translate, concat**

round num_1 **round** num_2

returns the integer value nearest to num_1. If num_1 is equally close to its two nearest integers, **round** returns the greater of the two. The type of the result is the same as the type of the operand.

Example

3.2 round $\Rightarrow$ 3.0
6.5 round $\Rightarrow$ 7.0
–4.8 round $\Rightarrow$ –5.0
–6.5 round $\Rightarrow$ –6.0
99 round $\Rightarrow$ 99

Errors: **stackunderflow, typecheck**

See Also: **ceiling, floor, truncate, cvi**

rrand   – **rrand** *int*

returns an integer representing the current state of the random number generator used by **rand**. This may later be presented as an operand to **srand** to reset the random number generator to the current position in the sequence of numbers produced.

Errors: **stackoverflow**

See Also: **rand, srand**

run   *string* **run** –

    executes the contents of the file identified by *string*—in other words, interprets the characters in that file as a PostScript language program. When **run** encounters end-of-file or terminates for some other reason (for example, **stop**), it closes the file.

    run is essentially a convenience operator for the sequence

        (r) file cvx exec

    except for its behavior upon abnormal termination. Also, the context of a **run** cannot be left by executing **exit**; an attempt to do so produces the error **invalidexit**. The **run** operator leaves no results on the operand stack, but the program executed by **run** may alter the stacks arbitrarily.

    Errors: **ioerror, limitcheck, stackunderflow, typecheck, undefinedfilename**

    See Also: **exec, file**

save   – **save** *save*

    creates a snapshot of the current state of the virtual memory (VM) and returns a *save* object representing that snapshot. Subsequently, this save object may be presented to **restore** to reset the VM to this snapshot. See section 3.7, "Memory Management," for a description of the VM and of the effects of **save** and **restore**. See the **restore** operator for a detailed description of what is saved in the snapshot.

    save also saves the current graphics state by pushing a copy of it on the graphics state stack in a manner similar to **gsave**. This saved graphics state is restored by **restore** and **grestoreall**.

    Example

        /saveobj save def
        ...arbitrary computation...
        saveobj restore   % Restore saved VM state

    Errors: **limitcheck, stackoverflow**

    See Also: **restore, gsave, grestoreall, vmstatus**

scale s_x s_y **scale** –
          s_x s_y *matrix* **scale** *matrix*

With no *matrix* operand, **scale** builds a temporary matrix

$$S = \begin{bmatrix} s_x & 0 & 0 \\ 0 & s_y & 0 \\ 0 & 0 & 1 \end{bmatrix}$$

and concatenates this matrix with the current transformation matrix (CTM). Precisely, **scale** replaces the CTM by $S \times$ CTM. The effect of this is to make the *x* and *y* units in the user coordinate system the size of s_x and s_y units in the former user coordinate system. The position of the user coordinate origin and the orientation of the axes are unchanged.

If the *matrix* operand is supplied, **scale** replaces the value of *matrix* by S and pushes the modified *matrix* back on the operand stack (see section 4.3, "Coordinate Systems and Transformations," for a discussion of how matrices are represented as arrays). In this case, **scale** does not affect the CTM.

Errors: rangecheck, stackunderflow, typecheck

See Also: rotate, translate, concat

scalefont   *font scale* **scalefont** *font'*

applies the scale factor *scale* to *font*, producing a new *font'* whose characters are scaled by *scale* (in both *x* and *y*) when they are shown. **scalefont** first creates a copy of *font*, then replaces the new font's **FontMatrix** entry with the result of scaling the existing **FontMatrix** by *scale*. It inserts two additional entries, **OrigFont** and **ScaleMatrix**, whose purpose is internal to the implementation. Finally, it returns the result as *font'*.

Showing characters from the transformed font produces the same results as showing from the original font after having scaled user space by the factor *scale* in both *x* and *y* by means of the **scale** operator. **scalefont** is essentially a convenience operator that enables the desired scale factor to be encapsulated in the font description. Another operator, **makefont**, performs more general transformations than simple scaling. See the description of **makefont** for more information on how the transformed font is derived. **selectfont** combines the effects of **findfont** and **scalefont**.

The interpreter keeps track of font dictionaries recently created by **scalefont**. Calling **scalefont** multiple times with the same *font* and *scale* will usually return the same *font'* rather than create a new one each time. However, it is usually more efficient for a PostScript language program to apply **scalefont** only once for each font that it needs and to keep track of the resulting font dictionaries on its own.

See Chapter 5 for general information about fonts and section 4.3, "Coordinate Systems and Transformations."

The **makefont**, **scalefont**, and **selectfont** operators produce a font dictionary derived from an original font dictionary, but with the **FontMatrix** entry altered. The derived font dictionary is allocated in local or global VM according to whether the original font dictionary is in local or global VM. This is independent of the current VM allocation mode.

Example

>   /Helvetica findfont 12 scalefont setfont

This obtains the standard Helvetica font, which is defined with a 1-unit line height, and scales it by a factor of 12 in both *x* and *y* dimensions. This produces a 12-unit high font (i.e., a 12-point font in default user space) whose characters have the same proportions as those in the original font.

Errors: invalidfont, stackunderflow, typecheck, undefined

See Also: makefont, setfont, findfont, selectfont

scheck   *any* **scheck** *bool*

has the same semantics as **gcheck**. This operator is defined for compatibility with existing Display PostScript applications.

Errors: **stackunderflow**

See Also: **gcheck**

search   *string seek* **search** *post match pre true*   *(if found)*
                              string false   *(if not found)*

looks for the first occurrence of the string *seek* within *string* and returns results of this search on the operand stack. The topmost result is a boolean that indicates if the search succeeded.

If **search** finds a subsequence of *string* whose elements are equal to the elements of *seek*, it splits *string* into three segments: *pre*, the portion of *string* preceding the match; *match*, the portion of *string* that matches *seek*; and *post*, the remainder of *string*. It then pushes the string objects *post*, *match*, and *pre* on the operand stack, followed by the boolean *true*. All three of these strings are substrings sharing intervals of the value of the original *string*.

If **search** does not find a match, it pushes the original *string* and the boolean *false*.

Example

    (abbc) (ab) search → (bc) (ab) () true
    (abbc) (bb) search ⇒ (c) (bb) (a) true
    (abbc) (bc) search ⇒ () (bc) (ab) true
    (abbc) (B) search ⇒ (abbc) false

Errors: **invalidaccess, stackoverflow, stackunderflow, typecheck**

See Also: **anchorsearch, token**

selectfont

key scale **selectfont** –
key matrix **selectfont** –

obtains a font whose name is *key*, transforms it according to *scale* or *matrix*, and establishes it as the current font dictionary in the graphics state. **selectfont** is equivalent to one of the following, according to whether the second operand is a number or a matrix:

key findfont *scale* scalefont setfont
key findfont *matrix* makefont setfont

If the font named by *key* is already defined in VM, **selectfont** obtains the font dictionary directly and does not execute **findfont**. However, if the font is not defined, **selectfont** invokes **findfont** in the normal way. In the latter case, it actually executes the name object findfont, so it uses the current definition of that name in the environment of the dictionary stack. On the other hand, redefining **exch**, **scalefont**, **makefont**, or **setfont** would not alter the behavior of **selectfont**.

selectfont can give rise to any of the errors possible for the component operations, including arbitrary errors from a user-defined **findfont** procedure.

Example

    /Helvetica 10 selectfont
    /Helvetica findfont 10 scalefont setfont

The two lines of the example have the same effect, but the first one is almost always more efficient.

The **makefont**, **scalefont**, and **selectfont** operators produce a font dictionary derived from an original font dictionary, but with the **FontMatrix** entry altered. The derived font dictionary is allocated in local or global VM according to whether the original font dictionary is in local or global VM. This is independent of the current VM allocation mode.

Errors: invalidfont, rangecheck, stackunderflow, typecheck

See Also: findfont, makefont, scalefont, setfont

serialnumber

– **serialnumber** *int*

returns an integer that purports to represent the specific machine on which the PostScript interpreter is running. The precise significance of this number (including any claim of its uniqueness) is product dependent.

Errors: stackoverflow

See Also: languagelevel, product, revision, version

setbbox ll_x ll_y ur_x ur_y **setbbox** –

establishes a bounding box for the current path, within which the coordinates of all subsequent path construction operators must fall. The bounding box is defined by two pairs of coordinates in user space: ll_x and ll_y specify the lower-left corner, ur_x and ur_y the upper-right corner. It is a rectangle oriented with the user space coordinate system axes.

The bounding box remains in effect for the lifetime of the current path—that is, until the next **newpath** or operator that resets the path implicitly. Any attempt to append a path element with a coordinate lying outside the bounding box will give rise to a **rangecheck** error.

Note that arcs are converted to sequences of **curveto** operations. The coordinates computed as control points for those **curveto**s must also fall within the bounding box. This means that the figure of the arc must be entirely enclosed by the bounding box. On the other hand, the bounds checking applies only to the path itself, not to the result of rendering the path. For example, stroking the path may place marks outside the bounding box. This does not cause an error.

Although the **setbbox** operator can be used when defining any path, its main use is in defining a user path, where it is mandatory. That is, a user path procedure passed to one of the user path rendering operators, such as **ufill**, must begin with a **setbbox** optionally preceded by a **ucache**. The bounding box information passed to **setbbox** enables the user path rendering operator to optimize execution. See section 4.6, "User Paths."

If **setbbox** appears more than once during definition of a path, the path's effective bounding box is successively enlarged to enclose the union of all specified bounding boxes. This is not legal in a user path definition. However, this case might arise if **uappend** is executed multiple times in building up a single current path by concatenating several user paths.

If **setbbox** has established a bounding box, execution of **pathbbox** returns a result derived from that bounding box instead of one derived from the actual path. The upper-right coordinate values must be greater than or equal to the lower-left values. Otherwise, a **rangecheck** error will occur.

Errors: rangecheck, stackunderflow, typecheck

See Also: pathbbox

setblackgeneration   *proc* **setblackgeneration** –   LEVEL 2

sets the black generation function parameter in the graphics state. The *proc* operand must be a procedure that can be called with a number in the range 0.0 to 1.0 (inclusive) on the operand stack and that returns a number in the same range.

This procedure computes the value of the black component during conversion from **DeviceRGB** color space to **DeviceCMYK**. For additional information, see section 6.2.3, "Conversion from DeviceRGB to DeviceCMYK."

setblackgeneration sets a graphics state parameter whose effect is device dependent. It should not be used in a page description that is intended to be device independent.

Execution of this operator is not permitted in certain circumstances; see section 4.8, "Color Spaces."

Errors: **stackunderflow, typecheck, undefined**

See Also: **setundercolorremoval**

setcachedevice w_x w_y ll_x ll_y ur_x ur_y **setcachedevice** –

passes width and bounding box information to the PostScript interpreter's font machinery. **setcachedevice** may be executed only within the context of the **BuildGlyph** or **BuildChar** procedure for a type 3 font. See section 5.7, "Type 3 Fonts." **BuildGlyph** or **BuildChar** must invoke **setcachedevice**, **setcachedevice2**, or **setcharwidth** *before* executing graphics operators to define and paint the character. **setcachedevice** requests the font machinery to transfer the results of those operators both into the font cache, if possible, and onto the current page.

The operands to **setcachedevice** are all numbers interpreted in the *character* coordinate system (see section 5.4, "Font Metric Information"). w_x and w_y comprise the basic width vector for this character—in other words, the normal position of the origin of the next character relative to origin of this one.

ll_x and ll_y are the coordinates of the lower-left corner and ur_x and ur_y are the coordinates of the upper-right corner of the character bounding box. The character bounding box is the smallest rectangle, oriented with the character coordinate system axes, that completely encloses all marks placed on the page as a result of executing the character's description. For a character defined as a path, this may be determined by means of the **pathbbox** operator. The font machinery needs this information to make decisions about clipping and caching. The declared bounding box must be correct—in other words, sufficiently large to enclose the entire character. If any marks fall outside this bounding box, they will be clipped off and not moved to the current page.

setcachedevice installs identical sets of metrics for writing modes 0 and 1, while **setcachedevice2** installs separate metrics.

After execution of **setcachedevice** and until the termination of the **BuildGlyph** or **BuildChar** procedure, execution of color setting operators or **image** is not allowed; see section 4.8, "Color Spaces." Note that use of the **imagemask** operator is permitted.

Errors: stackunderflow, typecheck, undefined

See Also: setcachedevice2, setcharwidth, setcachelimit, cachestatus

---

setcachedevice2 w_{0x} w_{0y} ll_x ll_y ur_x ur_y w_{1x} w_{1y} v_x v_y **setcachedevice2** – $\boxed{\text{LEVEL 2}}$

passes two sets of character metrics to the font machinery. w_{0x} and w_{0y} are the distances from the current point to the new current point when showing text in writing mode 0. ll_x,ll_y and ur_x,ur_y are the distances from origin 0 to the lower-left and upper-right corners of the character bounding box. w_{1x}, w_{1y} are the distances from the current point to the new current point when showing text in writing mode 1. v_x and v_y are the distances from origin 0 to origin 1. See section 5.4, "Font Metric Information."

Aside from its interpretation of the operands, **setcachedevice2** works the same as **setcachedevice** in all respects.

After execution of **setcachedevice2** and until the termination of the **BuildGlyph** or **BuildChar** procedure, execution of color setting operators or **image** is not allowed; see section 4.8, "Color Spaces." Note that use of the **imagemask** operator is permitted.

Errors: stackunderflow, typecheck, undefined

See Also: setcachedevice, setcharwidth, setcachelimit, cachestatus

setcachelimit   *int* **setcachelimit** –

establishes the maximum number of bytes the pixel array of a single cached character may occupy. Any character larger than this (according to the character bounding box information passed to **setcachedevice**) is not saved in the font cache. Instead, its description is executed every time the character is encountered.

setcachelimit affects the decision whether to place new characters in the font cache; it does not disturb any characters already in the cache. Making the limit larger allows larger characters to be cached, but may decrease the total number of different characters that can be held in the cache simultaneously. Changing this parameter is appropriate only in very unusual situations.

The maximum limit for *int* is implementation dependent, representing the total available size of the font cache (see **cachestatus**). As a practical matter, *int* should not be larger than a small fraction of the total font cache size.

Modifications to the cache limit parameter obey **save** and **restore**. In a Display PostScript system, which supports multiple contexts, this parameter is maintained separately for each context.

The parameter set by **setcachelimit** is the same as the **MaxFontItem** user parameter set by **setuserparams** (see Appendix C).

Errors: limitcheck, rangecheck, stackunderflow, typecheck

See Also: cachestatus, setuserparams

setcacheparams   *mark size lower upper* **setcacheparams** –

sets cache parameters as specified by the integer objects above the topmost mark on the stack, then removes all operands and the mark object as if by **cleartomark.**

The number of cache parameters is variable. In future versions of the PostScript interpreter, there may be more than three cache parameters defined. If more operands are supplied to **setcacheparams** than are needed, the topmost ones are used and the remainder ignored. If fewer are supplied than are needed, **setcacheparams** implicitly inserts default values between the mark and the first supplied operand.

The *upper* operand specifies the maximum number of bytes the pixel array of a single cached character may occupy, as determined from the information presented by the **setcachedevice** operator. This is the same parameter set by **setcachelimit.**

The *lower* operand specifies the threshold at which characters may be stored in compressed form rather than as full pixel arrays. If a character's pixel array requires more than *lower* bytes to represent, it may be compressed in the cache and reconstituted from the compressed representation each time it is needed. Some devices do not support compression of characters.

Setting *lower* to zero forces all characters to be compressed, permitting more characters to be stored in the cache, but increasing the work required to print them. Setting *lower* to a value greater than or equal to *upper* disables compression altogether.

The *size* operand specifies the new size of the font cache in bytes (the *bmax* value returned by **cachestatus**). If *size* is not specified, the font cache size is unchanged. If *size* lies outside the range of font cache sizes permitted by the implementation, the nearest permissible size is substituted with no error indication. Reducing the font cache size can cause some existing cached characters to be discarded, increasing execution time when those characters are next shown.

The parameters set by **setcacheparams** are the same as the **MaxFontCache** system parameter and the **MinFontCompress** and **MaxFontItem** user parameters, set by **setsystemparams** and **setuserparams**, respectively (see Appendix C).

Errors: rangecheck, typecheck, unmatchedmark

See Also: currentcacheparams, setcachelimit, setsystemparams, setuserparams

setcharwidth w_x w_y **setcharwidth** –

is similar to **setcachedevice**, but it passes only width information to the Post-Script interpreter's font machinery and it declares that the character being defined is not to be placed in the font cache.

setcharwidth is useful, for example, in defining characters that incorporate two or more specific opaque colors, such as opaque black and opaque white. This is unusual. Most characters have no inherent color, but are painted with the current color within the character's outline, leaving the area outside unpainted (transparent).

Another use of **setcharwidth** is in defining characters that intentionally change their behavior based on the environment in which they execute. Such characters must not be cached, because that would subvert the intended variable behavior.

Errors: stackunderflow, typecheck, undefined

See Also: setcachedevice, setcachedevice2

setcmykcolor   *cyan magenta yellow black* **setcmykcolor** –   `LEVEL 2`

sets the color space to **DeviceCMYK**, then sets the current color parameter in the graphics state to a color described by the parameters *cyan*, *magenta*, *yellow*, and *black*, each of which must be a number in the range 0.0 to 1.0. This establishes the color subsequently used to paint shapes, such as lines, areas, and characters on the current page (see section 4.8.2, "Device Color Spaces"). Color values set by **setcmykcolor** are not affected by the black generation and undercolor removal operations.

setcmykcolor does not give an error for a value outside the range 0 to 1. It substitutes the nearest legal value.

Execution of this operator is not permitted in certain circumstances; see section 4.8, "Color Spaces."

Errors: stackunderflow, typecheck, undefined

See Also: setcolorspace, setcolor, currentcmykcolor

setcolor   *comp₁ comp₂ ... compₙ* **setcolor** –

sets the current color parameter in the graphics state to that described by the color components $comp_1$, $comp_2$ ..., $comp_n$ in the current color space (see section 4.8, "Color Spaces").

The number of color components and the valid range of color component values depends on the current color space. If the wrong number of components is specified, an error will occur, such as **stackunderflow** or **typecheck**. If a component value is outside the valid range, the nearest valid value will be substituted without error indication.

The initial value of the color parameter varies by color space. It is initialized by the **setcolorspace** operator.

Execution of this operator is not permitted in certain circumstances; see section 4.8, "Color Spaces."

Errors: stackunderflow, typecheck, undefined

See Also: currentcolor, setcolorspace

setcolorrendering   *dict* **setcolorrendering** –   LEVEL 2

establishes *dict* as the current CIE based color rendering dictionary in the graphics state. The default color rendering dictionary is device dependent (see section 6.1, "CIE Based Color to Device Color"). **setcolorrendering** sets a graphics state parameter whose effect is device dependent. It should not be used in a page description that is intended to be device independent.

Execution of this operator is not permitted in certain circumstances; see section 4.8, "Color Spaces."

Errors: stackunderflow, typecheck, limitcheck, rangecheck, undefined

See Also: currentcolorrendering

setcolorscreen   *redfreq redang redproc greenfreq greenang greenproc*   LEVEL 2
 bluefreq blueang blueproc grayfreq grayang grayproc **setcolorscreen** –

sets the halftone parameter in the graphics state. **setcolorscreen** specifies halftone screen definitions for all four primary color components of the output device: red, green, blue, and gray or their complements: cyan, magenta, yellow, and black. For each component, **setcolorscreen** expects frequency, angle, and spot function operands, which it interprets the same as **setscreen** (see section 6.4, "Halftones").

setcolorscreen sets a graphics state parameter whose effect is device dependent. It should not be used in a page description that is intended to be device independent.

Example

```
% 50 line dot screen with 75 degree cyan, 15 degree magenta
% 0 degree yellow, and 45 degree black angled screens,
% which are commonly used for color printing
/sfreq 50 def                          % 50 halftone cells per inch
/sproc {dup mul exch dup mul add 1 exch sub} def
                                       % Dot-screen spot function
sfreq 75 /sproc load                   % 75 degree red (cyan) screen
sfreq 15 /sproc load                   % 15 degree green (magenta) screen
sfreq 0 /sproc load                    % 0 degree blue (yellow) screen
sfreq 45 /sproc load                   % 45 degree gray (black) screen
setcolorscreen
```

Execution of this operator is not permitted in certain circumstances; see section 4.8, "Color Spaces."

Errors: **limitcheck, rangecheck, stackunderflow, typecheck**

See Also: **currentcolorscreen, setscreen, sethalftone**

setcolorspace   *array* **setcolorspace** –   LEVEL 2
 name **setcolorspace** –

The first form sets the color space parameter in the graphics state to that described by the specified array. The array must be in the form

  [*key param$_1$ ... param$_n$*]

where *key* is a name that identifies the color space family and the parameters *param$_1$ ... param$_n$* further describe the space as a whole.

The second form specifies a color space by giving just its name. This is allowed only for those color spaces that require no parameters, namely **DeviceGray**, **DeviceRGB**, **DeviceCMYK**, and **Pattern**. Specifying a color space by name is equivalent to specifying it by an array containing just that name.

The **setcolorspace** operator also sets the current color parameter in the graphics state to its initial value, which depends on the color space. Execution of this operator is not permitted in certain circumstances; see section 4.8, "Color Spaces."

The details of the color space parameters, the definitions of the components of a specific color in the space, and initial values of those components vary from one color space to another. They are described in section 4.8, "Color Spaces." The initial value of the color space parameter is /DeviceGray.

Errors: stackunderflow, typecheck, rangecheck, undefined

See Also: currentcolorspace, setcolor

---

setcolortransfer   *redproc greenproc blueproc grayproc* **setcolortransfer** –   LEVEL 2

sets the transfer function parameter in the graphics state. **setcolortransfer** specifies transfer functions for all four primary color components of the output device: red, green, blue, and gray or their complements: cyan, magenta, yellow, and black. Each operand must be a PostScript language procedure that may be called with a number in the range 0.0 to 1.0 (inclusive) on the operand stack and that will return a number in the same range.

These procedures adjust the values of device color components (see section 6.3, "Transfer Functions"). Only those transfer functions corresponding to color components supported by a device will have an effect on that device's output. For example, *redproc*, *greenproc*, and *blueproc* will have no effect on a black-and-white device, while *grayproc* will have no effect on an RGB device.

setcolortransfer sets a graphics state parameter whose effect is device dependent. It should not be used in a page description that is intended to be device independent.

Execution of this operator is not permitted in certain circumstances; see section 4.8, "Color Spaces."

Errors: stackunderflow, typecheck, undefined

See Also: currentcolortransfer, settransfer

setdash   *array offset* **setdash** –

sets the dash pattern parameter in the graphics state, controlling the dash pattern used during subsequent executions of the **stroke** operator and operators based on **stroke**, such as **rectstroke** and **ustroke**. If *array* is empty (i.e., its length is zero), **stroke** produces a normal, unbroken line. If *array* is not empty, **stroke** produces dashed lines whose pattern is given by the elements of *array*, all of which must be non-negative numbers and not all zero.

stroke interprets the elements of *array* in sequence as distances along the path, measured in user space. These distances alternately specify the length of a dash and the length of a gap between dashes. **stroke** uses the contents of *array* cyclically. When it reaches the end of the array, it starts again at the beginning.

Dashed lines wrap around curves and corners just as normal strokes do. The ends of each dash are treated with the current line cap; corners within a dash are treated with the current line join. **stroke** does not take any measures to coordinate the dash pattern with features of the path. It simply dispenses dashes along the path as specified by *array*.

The *offset* operand may be thought of as the "phase" of the dash pattern relative to the start of the path. It is interpreted as a distance into the dash pattern (measured in user space) at which the pattern should be started. Before beginning to stroke a path, **stroke** cycles through the elements of *array*, adding up distances and alternating dashes and gaps as usual, but without generating any output. When it has travelled the *offset* distance into the dash pattern, it starts stroking the path from its beginning, using the dash pattern from the point that has been reached.

Each subpath of a path is treated independently—in other words, the dash pattern is restarted and *offset* applied to it at the beginning of each subpath.

Example

	[ ] 0 setdash	% Turn dashing off: solid lines
	[3] 0 setdash	% 3-unit on, 3-unit off, ...
	[2] 1 setdash	% 1 on, 2 off, 2 on, 2 off, ...
	[2 1] 0 setdash	% 2 on, 1 off, 2 on, 1 off, ...
	[3 5] 6 setdash	% 2 off, 3 on, 5 off, 3 on, 5 off, ...
	[2 3] 11 setdash	% 1 on, 3 off, 2 on, 3 off, 2 on, ...

Errors: **limitcheck, stackunderflow, typecheck**

See Also: currentdash, stroke

setdevparams   *string dict* **setdevparams** –   LEVEL 2

attempts to set one or more parameters for the device identified by *string* according to keys and new values contained in the *dict* operand. The *string* identifies a storage or I/O device (see section 3.8.2, "Named Files"). The dictionary is a container for key-value pairs; **setdevparams** reads the information from the dictionary but does not retain the dictionary itself. Device parameters whose keys are not mentioned in *dict* are left unchanged.

Each parameter is identified by a key, which is always a name object. The value is usually (but not necessarily) an integer. The names of I/O devices and the names and semantics of their parameters are product-dependent. They are not documented in this manual, but rather in product-specific documentation.

Permission to alter device parameters is controlled by a password. The dictionary must contain an entry named **Password** whose value is the system parameter password (a string or integer). If the password is incorrect, **setdevparams** executes an **invalidaccess** error and does not alter any parameters.

Some device parameters can be set permanently in non-volatile storage that survives restarts of the PostScript interpreter. This capability is implementation dependent. No error occurs if parameters cannot be stored permanently. For more details on device parameters, see Appendix C.

Various errors are possible. Details of error behavior are product dependent, but the following behavior is typical:

- If a parameter name is not known to the implementation, an **undefined** error occurs.

- If a parameter value is of the wrong type, a **typecheck** error occurs.

- If a parameter value is unreasonable—for instance, a negative integer for a parameter that must be positive—a **rangecheck** error occurs.

- If a parameter value is reasonable but cannot be achieved by the implementation, either the nearest achievable value is substituted or a **configurationerror** occurs, depending on the device and the parameter.

Errors: **configurationerror, invalidaccess, rangecheck, stackunderflow, typecheck**

See Also: **currentdevparams, setsystemparams, setuserparams**

setfileposition   *file position* **setfileposition** –

repositions an existing open file to a new *position* so the next read or write operation will commence at that position. The *position* operand is a non-negative integer interpreted as number of bytes from the beginning of the file. For an output file, **setfileposition** first performs an implicit **flushfile** (see section 3.8, "File Input and Output").

The result of positioning beyond end-of-file for both reading and writing depends on the behavior of the underlying file system. Typically, positioning beyond the existing end-of-file will lengthen the file if it is open for writing and the file's access permits. The storage appended to the file has unspecified contents. If lengthening the file is not permitted, an **ioerror** occurs. Possible causes of an **ioerror** are: the file object is not valid, the underlying file is not positionable, the specified position is invalid for the file, or a device-dependent error condition is detected.

Errors: **ioerror, rangecheck, stackunderflow, typecheck, undefinedfilename**

See Also: **fileposition, file**

setflat   *num* **setflat** –

sets the flatness parameter in the graphics state to *num*, which must be a positive number. This controls the accuracy with which curved path segments are to be rendered on the raster output device by operators such as **stroke**, **fill**, and **clip**. Those operators render curves by approximating them with a series of straight line segments. "Flatness" is an informal term for the error tolerance of this approximation; it is the maximum distance of any point of the approximation from the corresponding point on the true curve, measured in output device pixels.

'flatness' error tolerance

The accompanying illustration is only for emphasis. If the flatness parameter is large enough to cause visible straight line segments to appear, the result is unpredictable. The purpose of **setflat** is to control the accuracy of curve rendering, *not* to draw inscribed polygons.

The choice of flatness value is a trade-off between accuracy and execution efficiency. Very small values (less than 1 device pixel) produce very accurate curves at high cost, because enormous numbers of tiny line segments must be produced. Larger values produce cruder approximations with substantially less computation. A default value of the flatness parameter is established by the device setup routine for each raster output device. This value is based on characteristics of that device and is the one suitable for most applications.

The acceptable range of values for *num* is 0.2 to 100. Values outside this range are forced into range without error indication.

setflat sets a graphics state parameter whose effect is device dependent. It should not be used in a page description that is intended to be device independent.

Errors: **stackunderflow, typecheck**

See Also: **currentflat, flattenpath, stroke, fill**

setfont   *font* **setfont** –

establishes the font dictionary parameter in the graphics state. This specifies the font to be used by subsequent character operators, such as **show** and **stringwidth**. *font* must be a valid font dictionary previously returned by **findfont**, **scalefont**, or **makefont**. See section 5.1, "Organization and Use of Fonts."

Example

```
/Helvetica findfont        % Obtain prototype Helvetica font
10 scalefont               % Scale it to 10-unit size
setfont                    % Establish it as current font
```

Errors: **invalidfont, stackunderflow, typecheck**

See Also: **currentfont, scalefont, makefont, findfont, selectfont**

setglobal   *bool* **setglobal** –   LEVEL 2

sets the VM allocation mode: *true* denotes global, *false* denotes local. This controls the VM region in which the values of new composite objects are to be allocated. It applies to objects created implicitly by the scanner and to those created explicitly by PostScript operators. The semantics of local and global VM are described in section 3.7, "Memory Management."

Modifications to the VM allocation mode are subject to **save** and **restore**. In a Display PostScript system, which supports multiple execution contexts, the VM allocation mode is maintained separately for each context.

The standard error handlers in **errordict** execute false setglobal, reverting to local VM allocation mode if an error occurs.

Errors: **stackunderflow, typecheck**

See Also: **currentglobal**

setgray   *num* **setgray** −

sets the color space to **DeviceGray**, then sets the current color parameter in the graphics state to a gray shade corresponding to *num*. This must be a number between 0 and 1, with 0 corresponding to black, 1 corresponding to white, and intermediate values corresponding to intermediate shades of gray. **setgray** establishes the color subsequently used to paint shapes, such as lines, areas, and characters, on the current page. See section 4.8.2, "Device Color Spaces," for more information on gray-scale values.

setgray does not give a **rangecheck** error for a value outside the range 0 to 1; it substitutes the nearest legal value.

Execution of this operator is not permitted in certain circumstances; see section 4.8, "Color Spaces."

Errors: **stackunderflow, typecheck, undefined**

See Also: **currentgray, setcolorspace, setcolor**

setgstate   *gstate* **setgstate** −   LEVEL 2

replaces the current graphics state by the value of the *gstate* object. This is a copying operation, so subsequent modifications to the value of *gstate* will not affect the current graphics state or vice versa. Note that this is a wholesale replacement of all components of the graphics state; in particular, the current clipping path is replaced by the value in *gstate*, not intersected with it (see section 4.2, "Graphics State").

Errors: **invalidaccess, stackunderflow, typecheck**

See Also: **gstate, currentgstate, gsave, grestore**

sethalftone *halftone* **sethalftone** –

establishes *halftone* as the halftone parameter in the graphics state. This must be a dictionary constructed according to the rules in section 6.4.3, "Halftone Dictionaries." Once established, the halftone dictionary should be treated as read-only. If the halftone dictionary's **HalftoneType** value is out of bounds or is not supported by the PostScript interpreter, a **rangecheck** error occurs. If a required entry is missing or its value is of the wrong type, a **typecheck** error occurs.

sethalftone sets a graphics state parameter whose effect is device dependent. It should not be used in a page description that is intended to be device independent.

Errors: limitcheck, rangecheck, stackunderflow, typecheck

See Also: currenthalftone, setscreen, setcolorscreen

sethalftonephase *x y* **sethalftonephase** –

sets the halftone phase parameters in the graphics state. *x* and *y* are integers specifying the new halftone phase, interpreted in device space. See section 7.3.3, "Halftone Phase."

sethalftonephase sets a graphics state parameter whose effect is device dependent. It should not be used in a page description that is intended to be device independent.

Errors: stackunderflow, typecheck

See Also: currenthalftonephase

sethsbcolor   *hue saturation brightness* **sethsbcolor** –

sets the color space to **DeviceRGB**, then sets the current color parameter in the graphics state to a color described by the parameters *hue*, *saturation*, and *brightness*, each of which must be a number in the range 0 to 1. This establishes the color subsequently used to paint shapes, such as lines, areas, and characters on the current page. See section 4.8, "Color Spaces," for an explanation of these color parameters.

Note that the color value entered by **sethsbcolor** is immediately converted into the RGB model and used with the **DeviceRGB** color space. HSB is not a color space in its own right, merely a means for entering RGB color values in a different coordinate system.

sethsbcolor does not give a **rangecheck** error for a value outside the range 0 to 1; it substitutes the nearest legal value.

Execution of this operator is not permitted in certain circumstances; see section 4.8, "Color Spaces."

Errors: **stackunderflow, typecheck, undefined**

See Also: **currenthsbcolor, setrgbcolor, setcolorspace, setcolor**

---

setlinecap   *int* **setlinecap** –

sets the line cap parameter in the graphics state to *int*, which must be one of the integers 0, 1, or 2. This establishes the shape to be put at the ends of open subpaths painted by the **stroke** operator (see section 4.5, "Painting"). The integers select the following shapes:

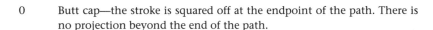

0   Butt cap—the stroke is squared off at the endpoint of the path. There is no projection beyond the end of the path.

1   Round cap—a semicircular arc with diameter equal to the line width is drawn around the endpoint and filled in.

2   Projecting square cap—the stroke continues beyond the endpoint of the path for a distance equal to half the line width and is squared off.

Errors: **rangecheck, stackunderflow, typecheck**

See Also: **currentlinecap, setlinejoin, stroke**

setlinejoin   *int* **setlinejoin** –

sets the line join parameter in the graphics state to *int*, which must be one of the integers 0, 1, or 2. This establishes the shape to be put at corners in paths painted by the **stroke** operator (see section 4.5, "Painting"). The integers select the following shapes:

0   Miter join—the outer edges of the strokes for the two segments are extended until they meet at an angle, as in a picture frame. If the segments meet at too sharp an angle, a bevel join is used instead. This is controlled by the miter limit parameter established by **setmiterlimit**.

1   Round join—a circular arc with diameter equal to the line width is drawn around the point where the segments meet and is filled in, producing a rounded corner. **stroke** draws a full circle at this point. If path segments shorter than one-half the line width meet at sharp angles, an unintentional "wrong side" of this circle may appear.

2   Bevel join—the meeting path segments are finished with butt end caps (see **setlinecap**); then the resulting notch beyond the ends of the segments is filled with a triangle.

Join styles are significant only at points where consecutive segments of a path connect at an angle. Segments that meet or intersect fortuitously receive no special treatment. Curved lines are actually rendered as sequences of straight line segments, and the current line join is applied to the "corners" between those segments. However, for typical values of the flatness parameter (see **setflat**), the corners are so shallow that the difference between join styles is not visible.

Errors: **rangecheck, stackunderflow, typecheck**

See Also: **currentlinejoin, setlinecap, stroke, setmiterlimit**

setlinewidth   *num* **setlinewidth** –

sets the line width parameter in the graphics state to *num*. This controls the thickness of lines rendered by subsequent execution of the **stroke** operator. **stroke** paints all points whose perpendicular distance from the current path in user space is less than or equal to one-half the absolute value of *num*. The effect produced in device space depends on the current transformation matrix (CTM) in effect at the time of the **stroke**. If the CTM specifies scaling by different factors in the *x* and *y* dimensions, the thickness of stroked lines in device space will vary according to their orientation.

A line width of zero is acceptable: It is interpreted as the thinnest line that can be rendered at device resolution—in other words, one device pixel wide. Some devices cannot reproduce one-pixel lines, and on high-resolution devices, such lines are nearly invisible. Since the results of rendering such "zero-width" lines are device dependent, their use is not recommended.

The actual line width achieved by **stroke** can differ from the requested width by as much as two device pixels, depending on the positions of lines with respect to the pixel grid. One can enable automatic stroke adjustment (by **setstrokeadjust**) to assure uniform line width.

Errors: stackunderflow, typecheck

See Also: currentlinewidth, stroke, setstrokeadjust

setmatrix   *matrix* **setmatrix** –

replaces the current transformation matrix (CTM) in the graphics state by the value of *matrix*. This establishes an arbitrary transformation from user space to device space without reference to the former CTM. Except in device setup procedures, use of **setmatrix** should be very rare. PostScript language programs should ordinarily *modify* the CTM (by use of the **translate**, **scale**, **rotate**, and **concat** operators) rather than replace it.

Errors: rangecheck, stackunderflow, typecheck

See Also: currentmatrix, defaultmatrix, initmatrix, rotate, scale, translate, concat

setmiterlimit   *num* **setmiterlimit** –

sets the miter limit parameter in the graphics state to *num*, which must be a number greater than or equal to 1. The miter limit controls the **stroke** operator's treatment of corners when miter joins have been specified (see **setlinejoin**). When path segments connect at a sharp angle, a miter join results in a spike that extends well beyond the connection point. The purpose of the miter limit is to cut off such spikes when they become objectionably long.

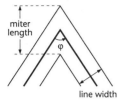

At any given corner, the *miter length* is the distance from the point at which the inner edges of the stroke intersect to the point at which the outside edges of the strokes intersect—in other words, the diagonal length of the miter. This distance increases as the angle between the segments decreases. If the ratio of the miter length to the line width exceeds the miter limit parameter, **stroke** treats the corner with a bevel join instead of a miter join.

The ratio of miter length to line width is directly related to the angle φ between the segments in user space by the formula:

$$\frac{\text{miter length}}{\text{line width}} = \frac{1}{\sin\left(\dfrac{\varphi}{2}\right)}$$

Examples of miter limit values are: 1.415 cuts off miters (converts them to bevels) at angles less than 90 degrees, 2.0 cuts off miters at angles less than 60 degrees, and 10.0 cuts off miters at angles less than 11 degrees. The default value of the miter limit is 10. Setting the miter limit to 1 cuts off miters at all angles so that bevels are always produced even when miters are specified.

Errors: ranqecheck, stackunderflow, typecheck

See Also: currentmiterlimit, stroke, setlinejoin

int **setobjectformat** –   LEVEL 2

establishes the number representation to be used in binary object sequences written by subsequent execution of **printobject** and **writeobject**. Output produced by those operators will have a token type that identifies the representation used. The *int* operand is one of the following (see section 3.12, "Binary Encoding Details"):

0   Disable binary encodings (see below).

1   High-order byte first, IEEE standard real format.

2   Low-order byte first, IEEE standard real format.

3   High-order byte first, native real format.

4   Low-order byte first, native real format.

Note that any of the latter four values specifies the number representation only for output. Incoming binary encoded numbers use a representation that is specified as part of each token (in the initial token type character).

The value 0 disables all binary encodings for both input and output. That is, the PostScript language scanner treats all incoming characters as part of the ASCII encoding, even if a token starts with a character code in the range 128 to 159. The **printobject** and **writeobject** operators are disabled; executing them will cause an **undefined** error. This mode is provided for compatibility with certain existing PostScript language programs.

The initial value of this parameter is implementation dependent. A program must execute **setobjectformat** to generate output with a predictable number representation.

Modifications to the object format parameter obey **save** and **restore**. In a Display PostScript system, which supports multiple contexts, this parameter is maintained seperately for each context.

Errors: **rangecheck, stackunderflow, typecheck**

See Also: **currentobjectformat, printobject, writeobject**

setoverprint   *bool* **setoverprint** –   LEVEL 2

sets the overprint parameter in the graphics state. This rendering parameter is used when the device is producing separations. It specifies whether painting on one separation causes the corresponding areas of other separations to be erased (*false*) or left unchanged (*true*). See section 4.8.4, "Special Color Spaces."

setoverprint sets a graphics state parameter whose effect is device dependent. It should not be used in a program that is intended to be device independent.

Errors: **stackunderflow, typecheck**

See Also: **currentoverprint, setcolorspace**

setpacking   *bool* **setpacking** –   LEVEL 2

sets the array packing mode to the specified boolean value. This determines the type of executable arrays subsequently created by the PostScript language scanner. The value *true* selects packed arrays; *false* selects ordinary arrays.

The packing mode affects only the creation of procedures by the scanner when it encounters program text bracketed by { and } during interpretation of an executable file or string object, or during execution of the **token** operator. It does not affect the creation of literal arrays by the [and] operators or by the **array** operator.

Modifications to the array packing mode parameter obey **save** and **restore**. In a Display PostScript system, which supports multiple contexts, this parameter is maintained seperately for each context.

Example

```
systemdict /setpacking known
{/savepacking currentpacking def
  true setpacking
} if
...Arbitrary procedure definitions...
systemdict /setpacking known {savepacking setpacking} if
```

This illustrates how to use packed arrays in a way that is compatible with Level 1 and Level 2 interpreters. If the packed array facility is available, the procedures represented by "arbitrary procedure definitions" are defined as packed arrays; otherwise, they are defined as ordinary arrays. This example is careful to preserve the array packing mode in effect before its execution.

Errors: **stackunderflow, typecheck**

See Also: **currentpacking, packedarray**

dict **setpagedevice** –

installs a new raster output device in the graphics state based on a combination of the information in the current device and the information found in the dictionary operand. The dictionary is a container for communicating requests as property-value pairs, which are logically passed by value and copied by the **setpagedevice** machinery into internal storage. The interpretation of those parameters is described in section 4.11, "Device Setup."

Calls to **setpagedevice** are cumulative: information established in a previous call to **setpagedevice** will persist unless overridden explicitly in a subsequent call. Therefore, there are no required keys in any particular call. This behavior applies not only to the top-level dictionary, but recursively to the sub-dictionaries **Policies**, **InputAttributes**, and **OutputAttributes**.

The result of executing **setpagedevice** is to instantiate a device, perform the equivalent of **initgraphics** and **erasepage**, and install the device as an implicit part of the graphics state. The effects of **setpagedevice** are subject to **save** and **restore, gsave** and **grestore**, and **setgstate**.

setpagedevice can be used by system administrators to establish a default state of the device by executing it as part of an unencapsulated job (see section 3.7.7, "Job Execution Environment"). This default state persists until the next restart of the PostScript interpreter. Some PostScript interpreter implementations store some of the device values in persistent storage when **setpagedevice** is executed as part of an unencapsulated job, making those parameters persist through interpreter restart.

setpagedevice reinitializes everything in the graphics state, including parameters not affected by **initgraphics**. Device-dependent rendering parameters, such as halftone, transfer functions, flatness, and color rendering, are reset to built-in default values or to ones provided in the **Install** procedure of the page device dictionary.

When the device in the current graphics state is not a page device, such as after **nulldevice** has been executed, or when an interactive display device is active, **setpagedevice** creates a new device from scratch before merging in the parameters from *dict*. The properties of that device are specific to each implementation.

Errors: **configurationerror, typecheck, rangecheck, stackunderflow, limitcheck, invalidaccess**

See Also: **currentpagedevice, nulldevice, gsave, grestore**

setpattern

pattern **setpattern** –
comp$_1$ ... *comp*$_n$ *pattern* **setpattern** –

establishes the specified pattern as the current color in the graphics state. Subsequent painting operations (except **image** and **colorimage**) use the pattern to tile the areas of the page that are to be painted. The *pattern* operand is a pattern dictionary constructed as specified in the section 4.9, "Patterns," and instantiated by **makepattern**. **setpattern** is a convenience operator that sets the current color space to **Pattern**, then sets the current "color" to a specific pattern.

Normally, **setpattern** establishes a **Pattern** color space whose underlying color space parameter is the color space in effect prior to execution of **setpattern**. However, if the current color space is already a **Pattern** color space, **setpattern** leaves it unchanged.

setpattern then invokes **setcolor** with the operands given to **setpattern**. The behavior depends on the **PaintType** entry of the pattern dictionary:

- If *pattern* defines a colored pattern (**PaintType** is 1), the color of the pattern is part of the pattern itself; there are no underlying color components. Therefore, the *comp*$_1$ ... *comp*$_n$ operands of **setpattern** should not be specified.

- If *pattern* defines an uncolored pattern (**PaintType** is 2), the pattern itself has no color; the color must be specified separately by the operands *comp*$_1$ ... *comp*$_n$, interpreted as components of the underlying color space of the **Pattern** color space. If the **Pattern** color space does not have an underlying color space parameter, a **rangecheck** error occurs.

setpattern is equivalent to:

```
currentcolorspace 0 get /Pattern ne
  { [/Pattern currentcolorspace] setcolorspace} if
setcolor
```

Execution of this operator is not permitted in certain circumstances; see section 4.8, "Color Spaces."

Errors: **rangecheck, stackunderflow, typecheck, undefined**

See Also: **findresource, makepattern, setcolor, setcolorspace**

setrgbcolor   *red green blue* **setrgbcolor** –

sets the color space to **DeviceRGB**, then sets the current color parameter in the graphics state to a color described by the parameters *red*, *green*, and *blue*, each of which must be a number in the range 0 to 1. This establishes the color subsequently used to paint shapes, such as lines, areas, and characters, on the current page. See section 4.8, "Color Spaces," for an explanation of these color parameters.

setrgbcolor does not give a **rangecheck** for a value outside the range 0 to 1; it substitutes the nearest legal value.

Execution of this operator is not permitted in certain circumstances; see section 4.8, "Color Spaces."

Errors: **stackunderflow, typecheck, undefined**

See Also: **currentrgbcolor, setgray, sethsbcolor, setcolorspace, setcolor**

setscreen   *frequency angle proc* **setscreen** –
frequency angle halftone **setscreen** –

sets the halftone parameter in the graphics state. The *frequency* operand is a number that specifies the screen frequency, measured in halftone cells per inch in device space. The *angle* operand specifies the number of degrees by which the halftone screen is to be rotated with respect to the device coordinate system. The *proc* operand is a PostScript procedure defining the spot function, which determines the order in which pixels within a halftone cell are whitened to produce any desired shade of gray. See section 6.4, "Halftones," for complete information about halftone screens.

A **rangecheck** occurs if *proc* returns a result outside the range –1 to 1. A **limitcheck** occurs if the size of the screen cell exceeds implementation limits.

setscreen sets the screens for all four color components (red, green, blue, and gray) to the same value. **setcolorscreen** sets the screens individually. If the topmost operand is a halftone dictionary instead of a procedure, **setscreen** performs the equivalent of **sethalftone** with the following exceptions. If the halftone dictionary is of type 1, the *frequency* and *angle* operands will be copied into the halftone dictionary overriding the values of the dictionary's **Frequency** and **Angle** keys. If the dictionary is read-only, **setscreen** makes a copy of it before copying the values. If the halftone dictionary is a type other than 1, the *frequency* and *angle* operands are ignored.

setscreen sets a graphics state parameter whose effect is device dependent. It should not be used in a page description that is intended to be device independent. Execution of this operator is not permitted in certain circumstances; see section 4.8, "Color Spaces."

Errors: limitcheck, rangecheck, stackunderflow, typecheck

See Also: currentscreen, sethalftone

setshared   *bool* **setshared** –   LEVEL 2

has the same semantics as **setglobal**. This operator is defined for compatibility with existing Display PostScript applications.

Errors: stackunderflow, typecheck

See Also: setglobal

setstrokeadjust   *bool* **setstrokeadjust** –   LEVEL 2

sets the stroke adjust parameter in the graphics state to *bool*. If *bool* is *true*, automatic stroke adjustment will be performed during subsequent execution of **stroke** and related operators, including **strokepath** (see section 6.5, "Scan Conversion Details"). If *bool* is *false*, stroke adjustment will not be performed.

The initial value of the stroke adjustment parameter is device dependent; typically it is *true* for displays and *false* for printers. It is set to *false* when a font's **BuildChar** or **BuildGlyph** procedure is called, but the procedure can change it. It is not altered by **initgraphics**.

Errors: stackunderflow, typecheck

See Also: currentstrokeadjust, stroke

setsystemparams *dict* **setsystemparams** –

attempts to set one or more system parameters whose keys and new values are contained in the *dict* operand. The dictionary is merely a container for key-value pairs; **setsystemparams** reads the information from the dictionary, but does not retain the dictionary itself. System parameters whose keys are not mentioned in *dict* are left unchanged.

Each parameter is identified by a key, which is always a name object. The value is usually (but not necessarily) an integer. If the named system parameter does not exist in the implementation, it is ignored. If the specified value is the correct type, but is not achievable by the implementation, the nearest achievable value is substituted without error indication.

The names of system parameters and details of their semantics are given in Appendix C. Some user parameters have default values that can be specified as system parameters with the same names.

Permission to alter system parameters is controlled by a password. The dictionary must contain an entry named **Password** whose value is the system parameter password (a string or integer). If the password is incorrect, **setsystemparams** executes an **invalidaccess** error and does not alter any parameters.

Some system parameters can be set permanently in non-volatile storage that survives restarts of the PostScript interpreter. This capability is implementation dependent. No error occurs if parameters cannot be stored permanently.

Example

```
<< /MaxFontCache 500000
   /MaxFontItem 7500
   /Password (xxxx)
>> setsystemparams
```

This attempts to set the **MaxFontCache** system parameter to 500000 and to set the default value of the **MaxFontItem** user parameter to 7500.

Errors: **invalidaccess, stackunderflow, typecheck**

See Also: **currentsystemparams, setuserparams, setdevparams**

settransfer *proc* **settransfer** –

sets the transfer function parameter in the graphics state. The *proc* operand must be a procedure that can be called with a number in the range 0 to 1 (inclusive) on the operand stack and will return a number in the same range. This procedure adjusts the values of the gray color component. See section 6.3, "Transfer Functions," for a complete explanation.

settransfer actually sets the transfer functions for all four color components (red, green, blue, and gray) to the same value. **setcolortransfer** sets the transfer functions individually.

settransfer sets a graphics state parameter whose effect is device dependent. It should not be used in a page description that is intended to be device independent.

Execution of this operator is not permitted in certain circumstances; see section 4.8, "Color Spaces."

Errors: stackunderflow, typecheck

See Also: currenttransfer, setcolortransfer, sethalftone

---

setucacheparams   *mark blimit* **setucacheparams** –   LEVEL 2

sets user path cache parameters as specified by the integer objects above the topmost mark on the stack, then removes all operands and the mark object as if by **cleartomark**. The number of cache parameters is variable and may increase in future versions of the PostScript interpreter. If more operands are supplied to **setucacheparams** than are needed, the topmost ones are used and the remainder ignored. If too few are supplied, **setucacheparams** implicitly inserts default values between the mark and the first supplied operand.

blimit specifies the maximum number of bytes that can be occupied by the reduced representation of a single path in the user path cache. Any reduced path larger than this is not saved in the cache. Changing *blimit* does not disturb any paths that are already in the cache. A *blimit* value that is too large is automatically reduced to the maximum permissible value without error indication.

Modifications to the cache limit parameter obey **save** and **restore**. In a Display PostScript system, which supports multiple contexts, this parameter is maintained separately for each context.

The parameter that **setucacheparams** sets is the same as the **MaxUPathItem** user parameter set by **setuserparams** (see Appendix C).

Errors: rangecheck, typecheck, unmatchedmark

See Also: ucachestatus, setuserparams

setundercolorremoval   *proc* **setundercolorremoval** –

sets the undercolor removal function parameter in the graphics state. The *proc* operand must be a procedure that may be called with a number in the range 0.0 to 1.0 (inclusive) on the operand stack and that will return a number in the range –1.0 (to *increase* the color components) to +1.0 (to *decrease* the color components).

This procedure computes the amount to subtract from the cyan, magenta, and yellow components during conversion of color values from **DeviceRGB** color space to **DeviceCMYK**. See section 6.2.3, "Conversion from DeviceRGB to DeviceCMYK."

setundercolorremoval sets a graphics state parameter whose effect is device dependent. It should not be used in a page description that is intended to be device independent.

Execution of this operator is not permitted in certain circumstances; see section 4.8, "Color Spaces."

Errors: **stackunderflow, typecheck, undefined**

See Also: **currentundercolorremoval, setblackgeneration**

setuserparams   *dict* **setuserparams** –   LEVEL 2

attempts to set one or more user parameters whose keys and new values are contained in the *dict* operand. The dictionary is merely a container for key-value pairs; **setuserparams** reads the information from the dictionary, but does not retain the dictionary itself. User parameters whose keys are not mentioned in *dict* are left unchanged.

Each parameter is identified by a key, which is always a name object. The value is usually (but not necessarily) an integer. If the named user parameter does not exist in the implementation, it is ignored. If the specified value is the correct type, but is not achievable by the implementation, the nearest achievable value is substituted without error indication.

The names of user parameters and details of their semantics are given in Appendix C. Some user parameters have default values that are system parameters with the same names. These defaults can be set by **setsystemparams**.

User parameters, unlike system parameters, can be set without supplying a password. Alterations to user parameters are subject to **save** and **restore**. In a Display PostScript system, which supports multiple execution contexts, user parameters are maintained separately for each context.

Example

> << /MaxFontItem 7500 >> setuserparams

This attempts to set the **MaxFontItem** user parameter to 7500.

Errors: **invalidaccess, stackunderflow, typecheck**

See Also: **currentuserparams, setsystemparams, setdevparams**

---

setvmthreshold *int* **setvmthreshold** – `LEVEL 2`

sets the allocation threshold used to trigger garbage collections. If the specified value is less than the implementation-dependent minimum value, the threshold is set to that minimum value. If the specified value is greater than the implementation-dependent maximum value, the threshold is set to that maximum value. If the value specified is –1, then the threshold is set to the implementation-dependent default value. All other negative values result in a **rangecheck** error.

Modifications to the allocation threshhold parameter obey **save** and **restore**. In a Display PostScript system, which supports multiple contexts, this parameter is maintained seperately for each context.

The parameter specified by **setvmthreshold** is the same as the **VMThreshold** user parameter set by **setuserparams** (see Appendix C).

Errors: **rangecheck**

See Also: **setuserparams**

---

shareddict – **shareddict** *dict* `LEVEL 2`

is the same dictionary as **globaldict**. The name **shareddict** is defined for compatibility with existing Display PostScript applications.

Errors: **stackoverflow**

See Also: **globaldict**

SharedFontDirectory   – **SharedFontDirectory** *dict*

is the same dictionary as **GlobalFontDirectory**. The name **SharedFontDirectory** is defined for compatibility with existing Display PostScript applications.

Errors: **stackoverflow**

See Also: **GlobalFontDirectory**

show   *string* **show** –

paints the characters identified by the elements of *string* on the current page starting at the current point, using the font face, size, and orientation specified by the most recent **setfont** or **selectfont**. The spacing from each character of the string to the next is determined by the character's width, which is an (x, y) displacement that is part of the character's definition. When it is finished, **show** adjusts the current point in the graphics state by the sum of the widths of all the characters shown. **show** requires that the current point initially be defined (for example, by a **moveto**); otherwise, it executes the error **nocurrentpoint**.

If a character code would index beyond the end of the font's **Encoding**, or the character mapping algorithm goes out of bounds in other ways, a **rangecheck** error occurs.

See Chapter 5 for complete information about the definition, manipulation, and rendition of fonts.

Errors: **invalidaccess, invalidfont, nocurrentpoint, rangecheck, stackunderflow, typecheck**

See Also: **ashow, awidthshow, widthshow, kshow, cshow, xshow, yshow, xyshow, charpath, moveto, setfont**

showpage   – **showpage** –

transmits the current page to the raster output device, causing any marks painted on the current page to appear. **showpage** then executes the equivalent of **erasepage** (usually) and **initgraphics** (always) in preparation for composing the next page.

If the device is a page device that was installed by **setpagedevice** (a Level 2 feature), the detailed behavior of **showpage** is determined by parameters of the device dictionary (see section 4.11, "Device Setup").

The main actions are as follows:

1. **showpage** executes the **EndPage** procedure in the device dictionary. It passes two operands to **EndPage**, a page count and a reason indicator, which are described in section 4.11.6, "BeginPage and EndPage." The **EndPage** procedure is expected to return a boolean result. The default **EndPage** procedure always returns *true*.

2. If the result from **EndPage** is *true*, **showpage** transmits the page to the output device and executes the equivalent of **erasepage**. If the result is *false*, **showpage** does not transmit the page or execute an **erasepage**.

3. **showpage** executes the equivalent of **initgraphics**.

4. **showpage** executes the **BeginPage** procedure in the device dictionary, passing it a page-count operand.

For a device that produces physical output, such as printed paper, **showpage** optionally produces multiple copies of each page as part of transmitting it to the output device (step 2, above). The number of copies is specified in one of two ways. If the device dictionary contains a **NumCopies** entry whose value is a non-negative integer, that is the number of copies. Otherwise, **showpage** looks up the value of **#copies** in the environment of the dictionary stack. The default value of **#copies** is 1, defined in **userdict**. The **#copies** method for specifying number of copies is available in Level 1 implementations.

The behavior of **showpage** is further modified by the **Collate**, **Duplex**, and perhaps other entries in the device dictionary.

Whether or not the device is a page device, the precise manner in which the current page is transmitted is device dependent. For certain devices, such as displays, no action is required because the current page is visible while it is being composed.

Example

```
/#copies 5 def
showpage
```

This prints five copies of the current page, then erases the current page and initializes the graphics state.

Errors: (none)

See Also: copypage, erasepage, setpagedevice

sin   *angle* **sin** *real*

returns the sine of *angle*, which is interpreted as an angle in degrees. The result is a real.

    Errors: **stackunderflow, typecheck**

    See Also: **cos, atan**

sqrt   *num* **sqrt** *real*

returns the square root of *num*, which must be a non-negative number. The result is a real.

    Errors: **rangecheck, stackunderflow, typecheck**

    See Also: **exp**

srand   *int* **srand** –

initializes the random number generator with the seed *int*, which may be any integer value. Executing **srand** with a particular value causes subsequent invocations of **rand** to generate a reproducible sequence of results.

    Errors: **stackunderflow, typecheck**

    See Also: **rand, rrand**

stack   ⊢ any_1 ... any_n **stack** ⊢ any_1 ... any_n

writes text representations of every object on the stack to the standard output file, but leaves the stack unchanged. **stack** applies the = operator to each element of the stack, starting with the topmost element. See the = operator for a description of its effects.

    Errors: (none)

    See Also: **pstack, =, ==, count**

stackoverflow   *(error)*

The operand stack has grown too large. Too many objects have been pushed on the stack and not popped off. See Appendix B for the limit on the size of the operand stack.

Before invoking this error, the interpreter creates an array containing all elements of the operand stack (stored as if by **astore**), resets the operand stack to empty, and pushes the array on the operand stack.

stackunderflow   *(error)*

An attempt has been made to remove an object from the operand stack when it is empty. This usually occurs because some operator did not have all of its required operands on the stack.

StandardEncoding   – **StandardEncoding** *array*

pushes the standard encoding vector on the operand stack. This is a 256-element literal array object, indexed by character codes, whose values are the character names for those codes. See section 5.3, "Character Encoding," for an explanation of encoding vectors. **StandardEncoding** is not an operator; it is a name in **systemdict** associated with the array object.

StandardEncoding is the Adobe standard encoding vector used by most Roman text fonts, but not by special fonts, such as Symbol. A new Roman text font having no unusual encoding requirements should specify its **Encoding** entry to be the value of **StandardEncoding** rather than define its own private array. The contents of the standard encoding vector are tabulated in Appendix E.

Errors: **stackoverflow**

See Also: **ISOLatin1Encoding, findencoding**

start   – **start** –

is executed by the PostScript interpreter when it starts up. After setting up the VM (restoring it from a file, if appropriate), the interpreter executes the name **start** in the context of the default dictionary stack (**systemdict, globaldict,** and **userdict**). The procedure associated with the name **start** is expected to provide whatever top-level control is required—for example, for receiving page descriptions, interacting with a user, or recovering from errors. The precise definition of **start** depends on the environment in which the PostScript interpreter is operating. It is not of any interest to ordinary PostScript language programs and the effect of executing it explicitly is undefined.

Errors: (none)

See Also: **quit**

---

startjob   *bool password* **startjob** *bool*   LEVEL 2

conditionally starts a new job whose execution may alter the initial VM for subsequent jobs. The *bool* operand specifies whether the new job's side effects are to be persistent. The semantics of job execution are described in section 3.7.7, "Job Execution Environment."

The behavior of **startjob** depends on whether all three of the following conditions are true:

- The current execution context supports job encapsulation—in other words, is under the control of a job server.

- The *password* is correct—in other words, matches the **StartJobPassword** system parameter.

- The current level of **save** nesting is not any deeper than it was at the time the current job started.

If all three conditions are satisfied, **startjob** performs the following actions:

1. Ends the current job—in other words, resets the stacks and, if the current job was encapsulated, executes a **restore**.

2. Begins a new job. If the *bool* operand is *true*, the usual **save** at the beginning of the job is omitted, enabling the new job to make persistent alterations to the initial VM. If the *bool* operand is *false*, the usual **save** is performed, encapsulating the new job.

3. Returns *true* on the operand stack.

If any of the three conditions is not satisfied, **startjob** pushes *false* on the operand stack. It has no other effect.

The *password* is a string that authorizes switching between encapsulated and unencapsulated jobs. If *password* is an integer, it is first converted to a string, as if by **cvs**. It is compared to the **StartJobPassword** system parameter, which is established by means of the **setsystemparams** operator (see Appendix C).

Errors: invalidaccess, stackunderflow, typecheck

See Also: exitserver, setsystemparams, save, restore

status   *file* **status** *bool*
              string **status** *pages bytes referenced created true*   (if found)
                         false   (if not found)

If the operand is a file object, **status** returns *true* if it is still valid (i.e., is associated with an open file), *false* otherwise.

If the operand is a string, **status** treats it as a file name according to the conventions described in section 3.8.2, "Named Files." If there is a file by that name, **status** pushes four integers of status information followed by the value *true*; otherwise, it pushes *false*. The four integer values are:

pages   Storage space occupied by the file, in implementation dependent units.

hytes   Length of file in characters.

referenced   Date and time when the file was last referenced for reading or writing. The interpretation of the value is according to the conventions of the underlying operating system. The only assumption that a program can make is that larger values indicate later times.

created   Date and time when the information in the file was created.

Errors: invalidaccess, stackoverflow, stackunderflow, typecheck

See Also: file, closefile, filenameforall

statusdict   – **statusdict** *dict*

pushes a product-dependent dictionary on the operand stack. **statusdict** is not an operator; it is a name associated with the dictionary in **systemdict**. The **statusdict** dictionary is in local VM and is writable.

statusdict contains product-dependent operators and other data whose names and values vary from product to product, and sometimes from one version of a product to another. Information in **statusdict** is associated with unique features of a product that cannot be accessed in any standard way. The contents of **statusdict** are not documented here, but in product-specific documentation.

In Level 1 implementations, **statusdict** includes operators to select print-engine features, to set communication parameters, and to control other aspects of the interpreter's operating environment. In Level 2, most of these functions have been subsumed by standard operators, such as **setpagedevice**, **setdevparams**, and **setsystemparams**.

statusdict is not necessarily defined in all products. Any reference to **statusdict** in a PostScript language program impairs the portability of that program.

Errors: **stackoverflow, undefined**

stop   – **stop** –

terminates execution of the innermost, dynamically enclosing instance of a **stopped** context, without regard to lexical relationship. A **stopped** context is a procedure or other executable object invoked by the **stopped** operator. **stop** pops the execution stack down to the level of the **stopped** operator. The interpreter then pushes the boolean *true* on the operand stack and resumes execution at the next object in normal sequence after the **stopped**. It thus appears that **stopped** returned the value *true*, whereas it normally returns *false*.

stop does not affect the operand or dictionary stacks. Any objects pushed on those stacks during the execution of the **stopped** context remain after the context is terminated.

If **stop** is executed when there is no enclosing **stopped** context, the interpreter prints an error message and executes the built-in operator **quit**. This never occurs during execution of ordinary user programs.

Errors: (none)

See Also: **stopped, exit**

stopped   *any* **stopped** *bool*

executes *any*, which is typically, but not necessarily, a procedure, executable file, or executable string object. If *any* runs to completion normally, **stopped** returns *false* on the operand stack. If *any* terminates prematurely as a result of executing **stop**, **stopped** returns *true* on the operand stack. Regardless of the outcome, the interpreter resumes execution at the next object in normal sequence after **stopped**.

This mechanism provides an effective way for a PostScript language program to "catch" errors or other premature terminations, retain control, and perhaps perform its own error recovery. See section 3.10, "Errors."

Example

        { ... } stopped {handleerror} if

If execution of the procedure {...} causes an error, the default error-reporting procedure is invoked (by **handleerror**). In any event, normal execution continues at the token following the **if**.

Errors: **stackunderflow**

See Also: **stop**

store   *key value* **store** –

searches for *key* in each dictionary on the dictionary stack, starting with the topmost (current) dictionary. If *key* is found in some dictionary, **store** replaces its value by the *value* operand. If *key* is not found in any dictionary on the dictionary stack, **store** creates a new entry with *key* and *value* in the current dictionary.

If the chosen dictionary is in global VM and *value* is a composite object whose value is in local VM, an **invalidaccess** error occurs (see section 3.7.2, "Local and Global VM").

Example

        /abc 123 store
        /abc where {} {currentdict} ifelse /abc 123 put

The two lines of the example have the same effect.

Errors: **dictfull, invalidaccess, limitcheck, stackunderflow**

See Also: **def, put, where, load**

string   *int* **string** *string*

creates a string of length *int*, each of whose elements is initialized with the integer 0, and pushes this string on the operand stack. The *int* operand must be a non-negative integer not greater than the maximum allowable string length (see Appendix B). The string is allocated in local or global VM according to the current VM allocation mode; see section 3.7.2, "Local and Global VM."

Errors: **limitcheck, rangecheck, stackunderflow, typecheck, VMerror**

See Also: **length, type**

stringwidth   *string* **stringwidth** w_x w_y

calculates the change in the current point that would occur if *string* were given as the operand to **show** with the current font. w_x and w_y are computed by adding together the width vectors of all the individual characters in *string* and converting the result to user space. They form a distance vector in *x* and *y* describing the width of the entire string in user space. See section 5.4, "Font Metric Information," for a discussion about character widths.

To obtain the character widths, **stringwidth** may execute the descriptions of one or more of the characters in the current font and may cause the results to be placed in the font cache. However, **stringwidth** prevents the graphics operators that are executed from painting anything into the current page.

Note that the "width" of a string is defined as movement of the current point. It has nothing to do with the dimensions of the character outlines (see **charpath** and **pathbbox**).

Errors: **invalidaccess, invalidfont, rangecheck, stackunderflow, typecheck**

See Also: **show, setfont**

stroke   – **stroke** –

paints a line following the current path and using the current color. This line is centered on the path, has sides parallel to the path segments, and has a width (thickness) given by the current line width parameter in the graphics state (see **setlinewidth**). **stroke** paints the joints between connected path segments with the current line join (see **setlinejoin**) and the ends of open subpaths with the current line cap (see **setlinecap**). The line is either solid or broken according to the dash pattern established by **setdash**. Uniform stroke width can be assured by enabling automatic stroke adjustment (see **setstrokeadjust**).

The parameters in the graphics state controlling line rendition (line width, line join, and so on) are consulted at the time **stroke** is executed. Their values during the time the path is being constructed are irrelevant.

A degenerate subpath is a subpath consisting of a single point closed path or two or more points at the same coordinates. If a subpath is degenerate, **stroke** paints it only if round line caps have been specified, producing a filled circle centered at that point. If butt or projecting square line caps have been specified, **stroke** produces no output, because the orientation of the caps would be indeterminate. If a subpath consists of a single point non-closed path, no output is produced.

stroke implicitly performs a **newpath** after it has finished painting the current path. To preserve the current path across a **stroke** operation, use the sequence

gsave stroke grestore

Errors: **limitcheck**

See Also: **setlinewidth, setlinejoin, setmiterlimit, setlinecap, setdash, setstrokeadjust, ustroke**

strokepath   – *strokepath* –

replaces the current path with one enclosing the shape that would result if the **stroke** operator were applied to the current path. The path resulting from **strokepath** is suitable as the implicit operand to **fill**, **clip**, or **pathbbox**. In general, this path is not suitable for **stroke**, as it may contain interior segments or disconnected subpaths produced by **strokepath**'s stroke to outline conversion process.

Errors: **limitcheck**

See Also: **fill, clip, stroke, pathbbox, charpath**

sub num_1 num_2 **sub** *difference*

returns the result of subtracting num_2 from num_1. If both operands are integers and the result is within integer range, the result is an integer. Otherwise, the result is a real.

Errors: **stackunderflow, typecheck, undefinedresult**

See Also: **add, div, mul, idiv, mod**

syntaxerror *(error)*

The scanner has encountered program text that does not conform to the Post-Script language syntax rules (see section 3.2, "Syntax"). This can occur either during interpretation of an executable file or string object, or during explicit invocation of the **token** operator.

Because the syntax of the PostScript language is simple, the set of possible causes for a **syntaxerror** is very small:

- An opening string or procedure bracket, (, <, <~, or {, is not matched by a corresponding closing bracket before the end of the file or string being interpreted.

- A closing string or procedure bracket,), >, ~>, or }, appears for which there is no previous matching opening bracket.

- A character other than a hexadecimal digit or white space character appears within a hexadecimal string literal bracketed by <...>.

- An encoding violation occurs in an ASCII base-85 string literal bracketed by <~...~>.

- A binary token or binary object sequence has incorrect structure (see section 3.12, "Binary Encoding Details").

Erroneous tokens, such as malformed numbers, do not produce a **syntaxerror**; such tokens are instead treated as name objects (often producing an **undefined** error when executed). Tokens that exceed implementation limits, such as names that are too long or numbers whose values are too large, produce a **limitcheck** (see Appendix B).

systemdict   – systemdict *dict*

pushes the dictionary object **systemdict** on the operand stack (see section 3.7.5, "Standard and User-Defined Dictionaries"). **systemdict** is not an operator; it is a name in **systemdict** associated with the dictionary object.

Errors: **stackoverflow**

See Also: **errordict, globaldict, userdict**

timeout   *(error)*

A time limit has been exceeded; that is, a PostScript language program has executed for too long or has waited too long for some external event to occur.

Execution of **timeout** is sandwiched between execution of two objects being interpreted in normal sequence. Unlike most other errors, occurrence of a **timeout** does not cause the object being executed to be pushed on the operand stack nor does it disturb the operand stack in any way.

The PostScript language does not define any standard causes for **timeout** errors. However, a PostScript interpreter running in a particular environment may provide a set of timeout facilities appropriate for that environment.

token

file **token**	*any true*		*(if found)*
	false		*(if not found)*
string **token**	*post any true*		*(if found)*
	false		*(if not found)*

reads characters from *file* or *string*, interpreting them according to the PostScript language syntax rules (see section 3.2, "Syntax"), until it has scanned and constructed an entire object.

In the *file* case, **token** normally pushes the scanned object followed by *true*. If **token** reaches end-of-file before encountering any characters besides white space, it closes *file* and returns *false*.

In the *string* case, **token** normally pushes *post* (the substring of *string* beyond the portion consumed by **token**), the scanned object, and *true*. If **token** reaches the end of *string* before encountering any characters besides white space, it simply returns *false*.

In either case, the *any* result is an ordinary object. It may be simple—an integer, real, or name—or composite—a string bracketed by (...) or a procedure bracketed by {...}. The object returned by **token** is the same as the object that would be encountered by the interpreter if the *file* or *string* were executed directly. However, **token** scans just a single object and it always pushes that object on the operand stack rather than executing it.

token consumes all characters of the token and sometimes the terminating character as well. If the token is a name or a number followed by a white-space character, **token** consumes the white-space character (only the first one if there are several). If the token is terminated by a special character that is part of the token—one of), >,], or }—**token** consumes that character, but no following ones. If the token is terminated by a special character that is part of the next token—one of /, (, <, [, or {—**token** does not consume that character, but leaves it in the input sequence. If the token is a binary token or a binary object sequence, **token** consumes no additional characters.

Example

```
(15(St1) {1 2 add}) token ⇒ ((St1) {1 2 add}) 15 true
((St1) {1 2 add}) token ⇒ ( {1 2 add}) (St1) true
( {1 2 add}) token ⇒ () {1 2 add} true
() token ⇒ false
```

Errors: invalidaccess, ioerror, limitcheck, stackoverflow, stackunderflow, syntaxerror, typecheck, undefinedresult, VMerror

See Also: search, anchorsearch, read

transform   *x y* **transform** *x′ y′*
                 x y matrix **transform** *x′ y′*

With no *matrix* operand, **transform** transforms the user space coordinate (*x*, *y*) by CTM to produce the corresponding device space coordinate (*x′*, *y′*). If the *matrix* operand is supplied, **transform** transforms (*x*, *y*) by *matrix* rather than by CTM.

Errors: rangecheck, stackunderflow, typecheck

See Also: itransform, dtransform, idtransform

translate t_x t_y **translate** –
                 t_x t_y *matrix* **translate** *matrix*

With no *matrix* operand, **translate** builds a temporary matrix

$$T = \begin{bmatrix} 1 & 0 & 0 \\ 0 & 1 & 0 \\ t_x & t_y & 1 \end{bmatrix}$$

and concatenates this matrix with the current transformation matrix (CTM). Precisely, **translate** replaces the CTM by $T \times$ CTM. The effect of this is to move the origin of the user coordinate system by t_x units in the *x* direction and t_y units in the *y* direction relative to the former user coordinate system. The sizes of the *x* and *y* units and the orientation of the axes are unchanged.

If the *matrix* operand is supplied, **translate** replaces the value of *matrix* by *T* and pushes the modified matrix back on the operand stack (see section 4.3, "Coordinate Systems and Transformations," for a discussion of how matrices are represented as arrays). In this case, **translate** does not affect the CTM.

Errors: rangecheck, stackunderflow, typecheck

See Also: rotate, scale, concat, setmatrix

true   – **true** *true*

pushes a boolean object whose value is *true* on the operand stack. **true** is not an operator; it is a name in **systemdict** associated with the boolean value *true*.

Errors: stackoverflow

See Also: false, and, or, not, xor

truncate num_1 **truncate** num_2

truncates num_1 toward zero by removing its fractional part. The type of the result is the same as the type of the operand.

Example

3.2 truncate $\Rightarrow$ 3.0
−4.8 truncate $\Rightarrow$ −4.0
99 truncate $\Rightarrow$ 99

Errors: **stackunderflow, typecheck**

See Also: **ceiling, floor, round, cvi**

type   *any* **type** *name*

returns a name object that identifies the type of the object *any*. The possible names that **type** can return are as follows:

arraytype	marktype
booleantype	nametype
conditiontype	nulltype
dicttype	operatortype
filetype	packedarraytype
fonttype	realtype
gstatetype	savetype
integertype	stringtype
locktype	

The name fonttype identifies an object of type *fontID*. It has nothing to do with a font dictionary, which is identified by dicttype the same as any other dictionary.

The returned name has the executable attribute. This makes it convenient to perform type-dependent processing of an object simply by executing the name returned by **type** in the context of a dictionary that defines all the type names to have procedure values (this is how == works).

The set of types is subject to enlargement in future revisions of the language. A program that examines the types of arbitrary objects should be prepared to behave reasonably if **type** returns a name that is not in this list.

Errors: **stackunderflow**

typecheck   *(error)*

Some operand's type is different from what an operator expects. This is probably the most frequent error encountered. It is often the result of faulty stack manipulation, such as operands supplied in the wrong order or procedures leaving results on the stack when they are not supposed to.

Certain operators require dictionaries or other composite objects as operands, constructed according to specific rules (for example, pattern dictionaries or user paths). A **typecheck** error can occur if the contents of such objects are of incorrect type or are otherwise malformed.

uappend   *userpath* **uappend** –   `LEVEL 2`

interprets a user path definition and appends the result to the current path in the graphics state. If *userpath* is an ordinary user path (in other words, an array or packed array whose length is at least 5), **uappend** is equivalent to:

```
systemdict begin        % Ensure standard operator meanings
cvx exec                % Interpret userpath
end
```

If *userpath* is an encoded user path, **uappend** interprets it and performs the encoded operations. It does not matter whether the *userpath* object is literal or executable; see section 4.6, "User Paths."

Note that **uappend** uses the standard definitions of all operator names mentioned in the user path, unaffected by any name redefinition that may have occurred.

A **ucache** appearing in *userpath* may or may not have an effect, depending on the environment in which **uappend** is executed. If the current path is initially empty and no path construction operators are executed after **uappend**, a subsequent painting operator *may* access the user path cache. Otherwise, it definitely will not. This is particularly useful in the case of **clip** and **viewclip**.

uappend performs a temporary adjustment to the current transformation matrix as part of its execution. This adjustment consists of rounding the t_x and t_y components of the CTM to the nearest integer values. The reason for this is discussed in section 4.6.4, "User Path Operators."

Errors: **invalidaccess, limitcheck, rangecheck, stackunderflow, typecheck**

See Also: **upath, ucache**

notifies the PostScript interpreter that the enclosing user path is to be retained in the cache if it is not already there. If present, this operator must appear as the first element of a user path definition (before the mandatory **setbbox**); see section 4.6.3, "User Path Cache."

The **ucache** operator has no effect of its own when executed; if executed outside a user path definition, it does nothing. It is useful only with a user path painting operator, such as **ufill** or **ustroke,** that takes the user path as an operand. If the user path is not already in the cache, the painting operator performs the path construction operations specified in the user path and places the results (referred to as the *reduced path*) in the cache. If the user path is already present in the cache, the painting operator does not interpret the user path, but rather obtains the reduced path from the cache.

Errors: (none)

See Also: **uappend, upath**

ucachestatus   – **ucachestatus** *mark bsize bmax rsize rmax blimit*

reports the current consumption and limit for two user path cache resources: bytes of reduced path storage (*bsize* and *bmax*) and total number of cached reduced paths (*rsize* and *rmax*). It also reports the limit on the number of bytes occupied by a single reduced path (*blimit*)—reduced paths that are larger than this are not cached. All **ucachestatus** results except *blimit* are for information only. A PostScript language program can change *blimit* (see **setucacheparams**).

The number of values pushed on the operand stack is variable. Future versions of the PostScript interpreter may push additional values between *mark* and *bsize*. The purpose of the *mark* is to delimit the values returned by **ucachestatus**. This enables a program to determine how many values were returned (by **counttomark**) and to discard any unused ones (by **cleartomark**).

The *bsize, bmax,* and *blimit* parameters reported by **ucachestatus** are the same as the **CurUPathCache** and **MaxUPathCache** system parameters and **MaxUPathItem** user parameter reported by **currentsystemparams** and **currentuserparams,** respectively.

Errors: **stackoverflow**

See Also: **setucacheparams, setsystemparams, setuserparams**

ueofill   *userpath* **ueofill** –   `LEVEL 2`

is similar to **ufill**, but does **eofill** instead of **fill**.

Errors: **invalidaccess, limitcheck, rangecheck, stackunderflow, typecheck**

See Also: **eofill, ufill**

ufill   *userpath* **ufill** –   `LEVEL 2`

interprets a user path definition and fills the resulting path as if by **fill**. The entire operation is effectively enclosed by **gsave** and **grestore**, so **ufill** has no lasting effect on the graphics state; see section 4.6, "User Paths." **ufill** is equivalent to:

    gsave newpath uappend fill grestore

Errors: **invalidaccess, limitcheck, rangecheck, stackunderflow, typecheck**

See Also: **fill, uappend, ueofill**

undef   *dict key* **undef** –   `LEVEL 2`

removes *key* and its associated value from the dictionary *dict*. *dict* does not need to be on the dictionary stack. No error occurs if *key* is not present in *dict*.

If the value of *dict* is in local VM, the effect of **undef** can be undone by a subsequent **restore**. That is, if *key* was present in *dict* at the time of the matching **save**, **restore** will reinstate *key* and its former value. But if *dict* is in global VM, the effect of **undef** is permanent.

Errors: **invalidaccess, stackunderflow, typecheck**

See Also: **def, put, undefinefont**

undefined   *(error)*

A name used as a dictionary key in some context cannot be found. This occurs if a name is looked up explicitly in a specified dictionary (**get**) or in the current dictionary stack (**load**) and is not found. It also occurs if an executable name is encountered by the interpreter and is not found in any dictionary on the dictionary stack.

A few PostScript operators are disabled in certain contexts—for example, it is illegal to execute **image**, or operators that specify colors or set color-related parameters in the graphics state, after a **setcachedevice** or **setcachedevice2** in a **BuildChar** or **BuildGlyph** procedure. Attempting to execute such disabled operators results in an **undefined** error.

See Also: **known, where, load, exec, get**

undefinedfilename   *(error)*

A file identified by a name string operand of **file**, **run**, **deletefile**, or **renamefile** cannot be found or cannot be opened. The **undefinedfilename** error also occurs if the special file %statementedit or %lineedit is opened when the standard input file has reached end-of-file.

undefinedresource   *(error)*   `LEVEL 2`

A named resource instance sought by **findresource** cannot be found; that is, no such instance exists either in VM or in external storage. This error arises only in the case of **findresource** with a defined resource category. If the category itself is not defined, resource operators execute the **undefined** error.

See Also: **findresource**

undefinedresult   *(error)*

A numeric computation would produce a meaningless result or one that cannot be represented as a number. Possible causes include numeric overflow or underflow, division by zero, or inverse transformation of a non-invertible matrix. A large number of graphics and font operators can generate an **undefinedresult** error if the CTM is not invertible (scaled by zero, for instance). See Appendix B for the limits of the values representable as integers and reals.

undefinefont   *key* **undefinefont** –   LEVEL 2

removes *key* and its associated value (a font dictionary) from the font directory, reversing the effect of a previous **definefont**. **undefinefont** is a special case of the **undefineresource** operator applied to the **Font** category. For details, see **undefineresource** and section 3.9, "Named Resources."

Errors: **stackunderflow, typecheck**

See Also: **definefont, undefineresource**

undefineresource   *key category* **undefineresource** –   LEVEL 2

removes the named resource instance identified by *key* from the specified *category*. This undoes the effect of a previous **defineresource**. If no such resource instance exists in VM, **undefineresource** does nothing; no error occurs. However, the resource category must exist, or else an **undefined** error occurs.

Local and global resource definitions are maintained separately; the precise effect of **undefineresource** depends on the current VM allocation mode:

1. Local—**undefineresource** removes a local definition if there is one. If there is a global definition with the same key, **undefineresource** does not disturb it; the global definition, formerly obscured by the local one, now reappears.

2. Global—**undefineresource** removes a local definition, a global definition, or both.

Depending on the resource category, **undefineresource** may have other side effects (see section 3.9.2, "Resource Categories"). However, it does not alter the resource instance in any way. If the instance is still accessible (say, stored directly in some dictionary or defined as a resource under another name), it can still be used in whatever ways are appropriate. The object becomes a candidate for garbage collection only if it is no longer accessible.

The effect of **undefineresource** is subject to normal VM semantics. In particular, removal of a local resource instance can be undone by a subsequent non-nested **restore**. In this case, the resource instance is not a candidate for garbage collection.

undefineresource removes the resource instance definition from VM only. If the resource instance also exists in external storage, it can still be found by **findresource**, **resourcestatus**, and **resourceforall**.

Errors: **stackunderflow, typecheck, undefined**

See Also: **defineresource, findresource, resourcestatus, resourceforall**

undefineuserobject   *index* **undefineuserobject** –   LEVEL 2

breaks the association between the non-negative integer *index* and an object established by some previous execution of **defineuserobject**. It does so simply by replacing the specified **UserObjects** array element by the null object. This is equivalent to:

```
userdict /UserObjects get
exch null put
```

undefineuserobject does not take any other actions such as shrinking the **UserObjects** array. If *index* is not a valid index for the existing **UserObjects** array, a **rangecheck** error occurs. See section 3.7.6, "User Objects."

There is no need to execute **undefineuserobject** prior to executing a **defineuserobject** that reuses the same index. The purpose of **undefineuserobject** is to eliminate references to objects that are no longer needed. This may enable the garbage collector to reclaim such objects.

Errors: rangecheck, stackunderflow, typecheck

See Also: defineuserobject, UserObjects

unmatchedmark   *(error)*

A mark object is sought on the operand stack by the **]**, **>>**, **cleartomark**, **counttomark**, **fork**, **setcacheparams**, or **setucacheparams** operator, but none is present.

unregistered   *(error)*

An operator object has been executed for which the interpreter has no built-in action. This represents an internal malfunction in the PostScript interpreter and should not occur.

upath   *bool* **upath** *userpath*

creates a new user path object that is equivalent to the current path in the graphics state. **upath** creates a new executable array object of the appropriate length and fills it with the operands and operators needed to describe the current path. **upath** produces only an ordinary user path array, not an encoded user path. It does not disturb the current path in the graphics state.

The *bool* operand specifies whether the resulting user path is to include **ucache** as its first element.

Since the current path's coordinates are maintained in device space, **upath** transforms them to user space using the inverse of the CTM while constructing the user path. Applying **uappend** to the resulting user path will reproduce the same current path in the graphics state, but only if the same CTM is in effect at that time.

upath is equivalent to:

```
[
exch {/ucache cvx} if
pathbbox /setbbox cvx
{/moveto cvx} {/lineto cvx} {/curveto cvx} {/closepath cvx} pathforall
] cvx
```

If **charpath** was used to construct any portion of the current path from a font whose outlines are protected, **upath** is not allowed. Its execution will produce an **invalidaccess** error (see **charpath**).

Errors: **invalidaccess, stackoverflow, typecheck, VMerror**

See Also: **uappend, ucache, pathforall**

userdict   – **userdict** *dict*

pushes the dictionary object **userdict** on the operand stack (see section 3.7.5, "Standard and User-Defined Dictionaries"). **userdict** is not an operator; it is a name in **systemdict** associated with the dictionary object.

Errors: **stackoverflow**

See Also: **systemdict, globaldict, errordict**

UserObjects   – **UserObjects** *array*   LEVEL 2

returns the current **UserObjects** array defined in **userdict**. **UserObjects** is not an operator; it is simply a name associated with an array in **userdict**. This array is created and managed by the operators **defineuserobject**, **undefineuserobject**, and **execuserobject**. It defines a mapping from small integers (used as array indices) to arbitrary objects (the elements of the array). See section 3.7.6, "User Objects."

The **UserObjects** entry in **userdict** is present only if **defineuserobject** has been executed at least once by the current execution context or a context that shares the same local VM. The length of the array depends on the index operands of all previous executions of **defineuserobject**.

Note that **defineuserobject**, **undefineuserobject**, and **execuserobject** operate on the value of **UserObjects** in **userdict**, without regard to the dictionaries currently on the dictionary stack. Defining **UserObjects** in some other dictionary on the dictionary stack changes the value returned by executing the name object **UserObjects**, but does not alter the behavior of the user object operators.

Although **UserObjects** is an ordinary array object, it should be manipulated only by the user object operators. Improper direct alteration of **UserObjects** can subsequently cause the user object operators to malfunction.

Errors: **stackoverflow, undefined**

See Also: **defineuserobject, undefineuserobject, execuserobject**

usertime   – **usertime** *int*

returns the value of a clock that increments by 1 for every millisecond of execution by the PostScript interpreter. The value has no defined meaning in terms of calendar time or time of day; its only use is interval timing. The accuracy and stability of the clock depends on the environment in which the PostScript interpreter is running. As the time value becomes greater than the largest integer allowed in the implementation, it wraps to the smallest (most negative) integer.

In a Display PostScript system that supports multiple execution contexts, the value returned by **usertime** reports execution time on behalf of the current context only. A context that executes **usertime** can subsequently execute with reduced efficiency, because in order to perform user time accounting, the PostScript interpreter must perform an operating system call whenever it switches control to and from that context. Therefore, one should not execute **usertime** gratuitously.

Errors: **stackoverflow**

See Also: **realtime**

ustroke
userpath **ustroke** –
userpath matrix **ustroke** –

interprets a user path definition and strokes the resulting path as if by **stroke**. The entire operation is effectively enclosed by **gsave** and **grestore**, so **ustroke** has no lasting effect on the graphics state (see section 4.6, "User Paths").

In the first form (with no *matrix* operand), **ustroke** is equivalent to:

```
gsave newpath uappend stroke grestore
```

In the second form, **ustroke** concatenates *matrix* to the CTM after interpreting *userpath*, but before executing **stroke**. The matrix applies to the line width and the dash pattern, if any, but not to the path itself. This form of **ustroke** is equivalent to:

```
gsave
newpath
exch uappend          % Interpret userpath
concat                % Concat matrix to CTM
stroke
grestore
```

The main use of the second form of **ustroke** is to compensate for variations in line width and dash pattern that occur if the CTM has been scaled by different amounts in *x* and *y*. This is accomplished by defining *matrix* to be the inverse of the unequal scaling transformation.

Errors: **invalidaccess, limitcheck, rangecheck, stackunderflow, typecheck**

See Also: **stroke, uappend**

ustrokepath

userpath **ustrokepath** –
userpath matrix **ustrokepath** –

replaces the current path with one enclosing the shape that would result if the **ustroke** operator were applied to the same operands. The path resulting from **ustrokepath** is suitable as the implicit operand to a subsequent **fill**, **clip**, or **pathbbox**. In general, this path is not suitable for **stroke**, as it may contain interior segments or disconnected subpaths produced by **ustrokepath**'s stroke to outline conversion process.

In the first form, **ustrokepath** is equivalent to:

    newpath uappend strokepath

In the second form, **ustrokepath** is equivalent to:

    newpath
    exch uappend   % Interpret *userpath*
    matrix currentmatrix   % Save CTM
    exch concat   % Concat *matrix* to CTM
    strokepath   % Compute outline of stroke
    setmatrix   % Restore original CTM

Errors: **invalidaccess, limitcheck, rangecheck, stackunderflow, typecheck**

See Also: **ustroke, strokepath**

version

– **version** *string*

returns a string that identifies the version of the PostScript interpreter being used. This identification does not include information about the language features or the hardware or operating system environment in which the PostScript interpreter is running.

Errors: **stackoverflow**

See Also: **languagelevel, product, revision, serialnumber**

viewclip

– **viewclip** –

replaces the current view clipping path by a copy of the current path in the graphics state; see section 7.3.1, "View Clipping." The inside of the current path is determined by the normal non-zero winding number rule. **viewclip** implicitly closes any open subpaths of the view clipping path. After setting the view clip, **viewclip** resets the current path to empty, as if by **newpath**.

viewclip is similar to **clip** in that it causes subsequent painting operations to affect only those areas of the current page that lie inside the new view clipping path. However, it differs from **clip** in three important respects:

- The view clipping path is independent of the current clipping path, which is unaffected. A subsequent **clippath** returns the current clipping path, uninfluenced by the additional clipping imposed by the view clip.

- **viewclip** entirely replaces the current view clipping path, whereas **clip** computes the intersection of the current and new clipping paths.

- **viewclip** performs an implicit **newpath** at the end of its execution, whereas **clip** leaves the current path unchanged.

The view clipping path is independent of the graphics state; it is maintained separately for each execution context. Modifications to the view clipping path obey **save** and **restore**.

The view clipping path can be described by a user path (see section 4.4, "Path Construction"). This is accomplished by:

    newpath *userpath* uappend viewclip

If *userpath* specifies **ucache**, this operation may take advantage of information in the user path cache.

Errors: **limitcheck**

See Also: **initviewclip, viewclippath, clip**

viewclippath   – viewclippath –   `DPS`

replaces the current path by a copy of the current view clipping path. If no view clipping path exists, it replaces the current path by one that exactly corresponds to the bounding rectangle of the imageable area of the output device.

Example

    initviewclip viewclippath pathbbox

If the current device is a window device, this returns the bounding box of the window.

Errors: (none)

See Also: **viewclip, initviewclip, clippath**

VMerror   *(error)*

An error has occurred in the virtual memory (VM) machinery. The most likely problems are:

- An attempt to create a new composite object (string, array, dictionary, or packed array) would exhaust VM resources. Either the program's requirements exceed available capacity or, more likely, the program has failed to use the **save/restore** facility appropriately (see section 3.7, "Memory Management").

- The interpreter has attempted to perform an operation that should be impossible due to access restrictions (for example, store into **systemdict**, which is read-only). This represents an internal error in the interpreter.

The default handler for this error, unlike those for all other errors, does not snapshot the stacks.

vmreclaim   *int* **vmreclaim** –   LEVEL 2

controls the garbage collection machinery as specified by *int*:

-2   Disable automatic collection in both local and global VM.

-1   Disable automatic collection in local VM.

0   Enable automatic collection.

1   Perform immediate collection in local VM.

2   Perform immediate collection in local and global VM. This can take a long time, because it must consult the local VMs of all execution contexts.

Garbage collection causes the memory occupied by the values of inaccessible objects to be reclaimed and made available for reuse. It does not have any effects that are visible to the PostScript language program. There is normally no need to execute the **vmreclaim** operator, because garbage collection is invoked automatically when necessary. However, there are a few situations in which this operator may be useful:

- In an interactive application that is temporarily idle, the idle time can be put to good use by invoking an immediate garbage collection. This defers the need to perform an automatic collection subsequently. In a context that is under the control of a job server, described in section 3.7.7, "Job Execution Environment," garbage collection is invoked automatically between jobs.

- When monitoring the VM consumption of a program, one must invoke garbage collection before executing **vmstatus** to obtain meaningful results.

- When measuring the execution time of a program, one must disable automatic garbage collection to obtain repeatable results.

The negative values that disable garbage collection apply only to the current execution context; that is, they do not prevent collection from occurring during execution of other contexts. Note that disabling garbage collection for too long may eventually cause a program to run out of memory and fail with a **VMerror**.

Executing **vmreclaim** with an operand of 0, –1, or –2 has the same effect as setting the **VMReclaim** user parameter to the same value by means of **setuserparams** (see Appendix C).

Errors: rangecheck, stackunderflow, typecheck

See Also: setvmthreshold, setuserparams

vmstatus   – vmstatus *level used maximum*

returns three integers describing the state of the PostScript interpreter's virtual memory (VM). *level* is the current depth of **save** nesting—in other words, the number of **save**s that haven't been matched by a **restore**. *used* and *maximum* measure VM resources in units of 8-bit bytes; *used* is the number of bytes currently in use and *maximum* is the maximum available capacity.

VM consumption is monitored separately for local and global VM. The *used* and *maximum* values apply to either local or global VM according to the current VM allocation mode (see **setglobal**).

The *used* value is meaningful only immediately after a garbage collection has taken place (see **vmreclaim**). At other times, it may be too large because it includes memory occupied by objects that have become inaccessible, but have not yet been reclaimed.

The *maximum* value is an estimate of the maximum size to which the current VM (local or global) could grow, assuming that all other uses of available memory remain constant. Because that assumption is never valid in practice, there is some uncertainty about the *maximum* value. Also, in some environments (workstations, for instance), the PostScript interpreter can obtain more memory from the operating system. In this case, memory is essentially inexhaustible and the *maximum* value is meaningless—it is an extremely large number.

Errors: stackoverflow

See Also: setuserparams

releases *lock*, waits for *condition* to be notified by some other execution context, and finally reacquires *lock*. The *lock* must originally have been acquired by the current context, which means that **wait** can be invoked only within the execution of a **monitor** that references the same *lock* (see section 7.1, "Multiple Execution Contexts").

If *lock* is initially held by some other context or is not held by any context, **wait** executes an **invalidcontext** error. On the other hand, during the wait for *condition*, the *lock* can be acquired by some other context. After *condition* is notified, **wait** will wait an arbitrary length of time to reacquire *lock*.

If the current context has previously executed a **save** not yet matched by a **restore**, **wait** executes **invalidcontext** unless both **lock** and **condition** are in global VM. The latter case is permitted under the assumption that the **wait** is synchronizing with some context whose local VM is different from that of the current context.

Errors:　invalidcontext, stackunderflow, typecheck

See Also:　condition, lock, monitor, notify

wcheck

array	**wcheck**	*bool*
packedarray	**wcheck**	*false*
dict	**wcheck**	*bool*
file	**wcheck**	*bool*
string	**wcheck**	*bool*

tests whether the operand's access permits its value to be written explicitly by PostScript operators. **wcheck** returns *true* if the operand's access is unlimited, *false* otherwise.

Errors:　stackunderflow, typecheck

See Also:　rcheck, readonly, executeonly, noaccess

where   *key* **where** *dict true*   *(if found)*
              false   *(if not found)*

determines which dictionary on the dictionary stack, if any, contains an entry whose key is *key*. **where** searches for *key* in each dictionary on the dictionary stack, starting with the topmost (current) dictionary. If *key* is found in some dictionary, **where** returns that dictionary object and the boolean *true*. If *key* is not found in any dictionary on the dictionary stack, **where** simply returns *false*.

Errors: **invalidaccess, stackoverflow, stackunderflow, typecheck**

See Also: **known, load, get**

widthshow c_x c_y *char string* **widthshow** –

paints the characters of *string* in a manner similar to **show**. But while doing so, **widthshow** adjusts the width of each occurrence of the character *char* by adding c_x to its *x* width and c_y to its *y* width, thus modifying the spacing between it and the next character. *char* is an integer used as a character code. This operator enables fitting a string of text to a specific width by adjusting the width of all occurrences of some specific character, such as the space character.

For a base font, *char* is simply an integer in the range 0 to 255 compared to successive elements of *string*. For a composite font, *char* is compared to an integer computed from the font mapping algorithm. The font number, *f*, and character code, *c*, that are selected by the font mapping algorithm are combined into a single integer according to the **FMapType** of the immediate parent of the selected base font. For **FMapType** values of 4 and 5, the integer value is $(f \times 128) + c$; for all other **FMapType** values, it is $(f \times 256) + c$. See section 5.9.1, "Character Mapping."

Example

Normal spacing
Wide   word   spacing

```
/Helvetica findfont 12 scalefont setfont
14 60 moveto (Normal spacing) show
14 46 moveto 6 0 8#040 (Wide word spacing) widthshow
```

Errors: **invalidaccess, invalidfont, nocurrentpoint, stackunderflow, typecheck, rangecheck**

See Also: **show, ashow, awidthshow, kshow, xshow, yshow, xyshow, stringwidth**

write   *file int* **write** –

appends a single character to the output file *file*. The *int* operand should be an integer in the range 0 to 255 representing a character code (values outside this range are reduced modulo 256). If *file* is not a valid output file or some error is encountered, **write** executes **ioerror**.

As is the case for all operators that write to files, the output produced by **write** may accumulate in a buffer instead of being transmitted immediately. To ensure immediate transmission, a **flushfile** is required.

Errors: **invalidaccess, ioerror, stackunderflow, typecheck**

See Also: **read, writehexstring, writestring, file**

writehexstring   *file string* **writehexstring** –

writes all of the characters of *string* to *file* as hexadecimal digits. For each element of *string* (an integer in the range 0 to 255), **writehexstring** appends a two-digit hexadecimal number composed of the characters 0 through 9 and a through f.

(%stdout)(w) file (abz) writehexstring

writes the six characters 61627a to the standard output file.

See section 3.8.4, "Filters," for more information about ASCII-encoded, binary data representation and how to deal with them.

As is the case for all operators that write to files, the output produced by **writehexstring** may accumulate in a buffer instead of being transmitted immediately. To ensure immediate transmission, a **flushfile** is required.

Errors: **invalidaccess, ioerror, stackunderflow, typecheck**

See Also: **readhexstring, write, writestring, file, filter**

writeobject　　*file obj tag* **writeobject** –　　　　　　　　　　　　　　　　　　　　`LEVEL 2`

writes a binary object sequence to *file*. Except for taking an explicit *file* operand, **writeobject** is identical to **printobject** in all respects.

As is the case for all operators that write to files, the output produced by **writeobject** may accumulate in a buffer instead of being transmitted immediately. To ensure immediate transmission, a **flushfile** is required.

Errors:　　**invalidaccess, ioerror, limitcheck, rangecheck, stackunderflow, typecheck, undefined**

See Also:　**printobject, setobjectformat**

writestring　　*file string* **writestring** –

writes the characters of *string* to the output file *file*. **writestring** does not append a newline character or interpret the value of *string*, which can contain arbitrary binary data. However, the communication channel may usurp certain control characters or impose other restrictions; see section 3.8, "File Input and Output."

As is the case for all operators that write to files, the output produced by **writestring** may accumulate in a buffer instead of being transmitted immediately. To ensure immediate transmission, a **flushfile** is required.

Errors:　　**invalidaccess, ioerror, stackunderflow, typecheck**

See Also:　**readstring, write, writehexstring, file, filter**

wtranslation　　– **wtranslation** *x y*　　　　　　　　　　　　　　　　　　　　　`DPS`

returns the translation from the window origin to the PostScript interpreter's device space origin; see section 7.3, "Graphics and Window Systems." The integers *x* and *y* are the amounts that need to be added to a window system coordinate to produce the device space coordinate for the same position. That coordinate may in turn be transformed to user space by the **itransform** operator.

Window system and device space coordinates always correspond in resolution and orientation; they differ only in the positions of their origins. The translation from one origin to the other may change as windows are moved and resized. The precise behavior is window system specific.

Errors:　　**stackoverflow**

xcheck   *any* **xcheck** *bool*

tests whether the operand has the executable or literal attribute, returning *true* if it is executable or *false* if it is literal. This has nothing to do with the object's access attribute—for example, execute-only. See section 3.3.2, "Attributes of Objects."

Errors: **stackunderflow**

See Also: **cvx, cvlit**

xor $bool_1$ $bool_2$ **xor** $bool_3$
int_1 int_2 **xor** int_3

If the operands are booleans, **xor** pushes their logical "exclusive or." If the operands are integers, **xor** pushes the bitwise "exclusive or" of their binary representations.

> true true xor $\Rightarrow$ false   % A complete truth table
> true false xor $\Rightarrow$ true
> false true xor $\Rightarrow$ true
> false false xor $\Rightarrow$ false
>
> 7 3 xor $\Rightarrow$ 4
> 12 3 xor $\Rightarrow$ 15

Errors: **stackunderflow, typecheck**

See Also: **or, and, not**

xshow   *string numarray* **xshow** –   LEVEL 2
string numstring **xshow** –

is similar to **xyshow**. However, for each character shown, **xshow** extracts only one number from *numarray* or *numstring*. It uses that number as the *x* displacement and the value zero as the *y* displacement. In all other respects, **xshow** behaves the same as **xyshow**.

Errors: **invalidaccess, invalidfont, nocurrentpoint, rangecheck, stackunderflow, typecheck**

See Also: **xyshow, show**

xyshow

string numarray **xyshow** –
string numstring **xyshow** –

LEVEL 2

paints successive characters of *string* in a manner similar to **show**. After painting each character, it extracts two successive numbers from the array *numarray* or the encoded number string *numstring*. These two numbers, interpreted in user space, determine the position of the origin of the next character relative to the origin of the character just shown. The first number is the *x* displacement and the second number is the *y* displacement. In other words, the two numbers override the character's normal width.

If *numarray* or *numstring* is exhausted before all the characters of *string* have been shown, a **rangecheck** error will occur. See section 5.1.4, "Character Positioning," for further information about **xyshow**. See section 3.12.5, "Encoded Number Strings," for an explanation of the *numstring* operand.

Errors: **invalidaccess, invalidfont, nocurrentpoint, rangecheck, stackunderflow, typecheck**

See Also: **xshow, yshow, show**

---

yield   – **yield** –

DPS

suspends the current execution context until all other contexts have had a chance to execute; see section 7.1, "Multiple Execution Contexts." This should not be used as a synchronization primitive, because there is no way to predict how much execution the other contexts will be able to accomplish. The purpose of **yield** is to break up long-running computations that might lock out other contexts.

Errors: (none)

---

yshow   *string numarray* **yshow** –
string numstring **yshow** –

LEVEL 2

is similar to **xyshow**. However, for each character shown, **yshow** extracts only one number from *numarray* or *numstring*. It uses that number as the *y* displacement and the value zero as the *x* displacement. In all other respects, it behaves the same as **xyshow**.

Errors: **invalidaccess, invalidfont, nocurrentpoint, rangecheck, stackunderflow, typecheck**

See Also: **xyshow, show**

Changes to Language and Implementation

Since its introduction in 1985, the PostScript language has undergone a number of changes. Also, Adobe implementations of the PostScript interpreter have changed. This appendix summarizes these changes.

A.1 Language Extensions

The PostScript language has been extended several times to meet the needs of new imaging technologies and system environments. These extensions include functionality for CMYK color specification, composite fonts, file system support, and the Display PostScript system. All of the extensions have been consolidated and many new features have been added to create PostScript Level 2. The following sections list the PostScript language operators introduced by each of these extensions and, when possible, indicate which implementations support them.

A.1.1 PostScript Level 2 Operators

The following Level 2 operators, along with the Level 1 operators documented in the original *PostScript Language Reference Manual*, are present in all Level 2 implementations of the PostScript language:

<<	currentcolorspace
>>	currentcolortransfer
arct	currentdevparams
colorimage	currentglobal
cshow	currentgstate
currentblackgeneration	currenthalftone
currentcacheparams	currentobjectformat
currentcmykcolor	currentoverprint
currentcolor	currentpacking
currentcolorrendering	currentpagedevice
currentcolorscreen	currentshared

currentstrokeadjust
currentsystemparams
currentundercolorremoval
currentuserparams
defineresource
defineuserobject
deletefile
execform
execuserobject
filenameforall
fileposition
filter
findencoding
findresource
gcheck
globaldict
GlobalFontDirectory
glyphshow
gstate
ineofill
infill
instroke
inueofill
inufill
inustroke
ISOLatin1Encoding
languagelevel
makepattern
packedarray
printobject
product
realtime
rectclip
rectfill
rectstroke
renamefile
resourceforall
resourcestatus
revision
rootfont
scheck
selectfont
serialnumber
setbbox
setblackgeneration
setcachedevice2

setcacheparams
setcmykcolor
setcolor
setcolorrendering
setcolorscreen
setcolorspace
setcolortransfer
setdevparams
setfileposition
setglobal
setgstate
sethalftone
setobjectformat
setoverprint
setpacking
setpagedevice
setpattern
setshared
setstrokeadjust
setsystemparams
setucacheparams
setundercolorremoval
setuserparams
setvmthreshold
shareddict
SharedFontDirectory
startjob
uappend
ucache
ucachestatus
ueofill
ufill
undef
undefinefont
undefineresource
undefineuserobject
upath
UserObjects
ustroke
ustrokepath
vmreclaim
writeobject
xshow
xyshow
yshow

A.1.2 Display PostScript Operators

The following operators are present only in implementations of the Display PostScript system:

condition	lock
currentcontext	monitor
currenthalftonephase	notify
defineusername	rectviewclip
detach	sethalftonephase
deviceinfo	viewclip
eoviewclip	viewclippath
fork	wait
initviewclip	wtranslation
join	yield

A.1.3 Display PostScript Extensions

The following operators are from the PostScript language extensions for the Display PostScript system. These operators, along with the Level 1 operators, are present in all Display PostScript system implementations. Nearly all of them have been incorporated into the Level 2 operator set; the only exceptions are the operators listed in section A.1.2, "Display PostScript Operators."

arct	instroke
condition	inueofill
currentcontext	inufill
currentgstate	inustroke
currenthalftone	join
currenthalftonephase	lock
currentobjectformat	monitor
currentshared	notify
currentstrokeadjust	printobject
defineusername	rectclip
defineuserobject	rectfill
detach	rectstroke
deviceinfo	rectviewclip
eoviewclip	scheck
execuserobject	selectfont
fork	setbbox
gstate	setgstate
ineofill	sethalftone
infill	sethalftonephase
initviewclip	setobjectformat

setshared
setstrokeadjust
setucacheparams
setvmthreshold
shareddict
SharedFontDirectory
uappend
ucache
ucachestatus
ueofill
ufill
undef
undefinefont
undefineuserobject

upath
UserObjects
ustroke
ustrokepath
viewclip
viewclippath
vmreclaim
wait
writeobject
wtranslation
xshow
xyshow
yield
yshow

A.1.4   CMYK Color Extensions

The following Level 2 operators are from the PostScript language color extensions. They are present in certain Level 1 products, principally color printers, and in all implementations of the Display PostScript system.

colorimage
currentblackgeneration
currentcmykcolor
currentcolorscreen
currentcolortransfer
currentundercolorremoval

setblackgeneration
setcmykcolor
setcolorscreen
setcolortransfer
setundercolorremoval

A.1.5   Composite Font Extensions

The following Level 2 operators are from the PostScript language composite font extensions. They are present in certain Level 1 printer products and Display PostScript system implementations.

cshow
findencoding
rootfont
setcachedevice2

A.1.6　File System Operators

The following Level 2 operators are present in those Level 1 printer products that have disks or cartridges and in all implementations of the Display PostScript system:

deletefile
filenameforall
fileposition
renamefile
setfileposition

A.1.7　Version 25.0 Language Additions

The following Level 2 features and operators are present in all Level 1 implementations version 25.0 and greater:

// syntax for immediately evaluated names
packedarray object type

currentcacheparams
currentpacking
packedarray
setcacheparams
setpacking

A.1.8　Miscellaneous Language Additions

The following Level 2 operators are present in some Level 1 products that are not identifiable by specific versions or functions. (When **product** and **revision** are not present in **systemdict**, they are present in **statusdict** instead.)

ISOLatin1Encoding
product
realtime
revision
serialnumber

A.2 Language Changes Affecting Existing Operators

This section summarizes significant changes to the Level 1 operators documented in the original *PostScript Language Reference Manual*. All changes are upward-compatible. For Level 2, many existing operators have been extended to provide new functionality, to interact properly with other new language features, or to eliminate former restrictions on their use.

This list is not exhaustive. Many of these changes have appeared as part of extensions introduced prior to Level 2. For complete information, consult the individual operator descriptions in Chapter 8.

The dictionary stack has three permanent entries instead of two. The additional dictionary is **globaldict**, lying between **systemdict** and **userdict**.

Several of the basic polymorphic operators, such as **length**, **get**, **put**, **getinterval**, and **putinterval**, can deal with the newly introduced packed array object type.

The **$error** dictionary contains some additional entries to control error handling.

banddevice, **framedevice**, and **renderbands** no longer exist. These device-dependent setup operators were defined only in some implementations and were never appropriate for use by a page description.

charpath no longer protects the character outlines of most fonts. **pathforall** is permitted after **charpath** for normally constructed Type 1 and Type 3 fonts.

copy, when applied to dictionaries, leaves the destination dictionary's access unchanged instead of copying it from the source dictionary.

currentscreen can return a halftone dictionary if the current halftone was specified by **sethalftone** instead of **setscreen**. **setscreen** permits its operand to be a halftone dictionary.

definefont, **findfont**, and other font-related operators have been extended in various ways to support composite fonts, font dictionaries in local or global VM, accessing characters by name (**glyphshow**, **BuildGlyph**), and extended unique IDs (**XUID**s). Fonts are now treated as a special category of a general facility for named resources; **definefont** is a special case of **defineresource**.

The **dictfull** error is no longer possible. The operand to **dict** now specifies only the initial capacity; dictionaries expand their capacity automatically when necessary. **maxlength** returns a dictionary's current capacity.

The syntax of name and access string operands to **file** has been expanded.

fill, **stroke**, **show**, and all other operators that paint with the current color can make use of the new color spaces. These color spaces allow CIE-based color specification, color mapping, separations, and painting with a repeating pattern.

image and **imagemask** can accept their parameters in the form of an image dictionary. This single-operand form of **image** can handle monochrome or color image data according to any color space and can invoke various image processing options. Additionally, the data source for an image can be a file or string as well as a procedure.

makefont and **scalefont** allocate the derived font dictionary in local or global VM according to whether the original font dictionary was in local or global VM.

save and **restore** do not affect the values of objects in global VM except when executed at the outermost level in an encapsulated job.

setcacheparams takes an optional size operand.

setgray, **setrgbcolor**, and **sethsbcolor** set the current color space to **DeviceGray**, **DeviceRGB**, and **DeviceRGB**, respectively.

show and related operators decode their string operand in a special way if the current font is composite.

The behavior of **showpage** and **copypage** can be substantially altered by specifying optional parameters to **setpagedevice**.

status accepts a string operand and returns status information for a named file.

stroke optionally performs adjustments to ensure uniform line width.

A.3 Implementation and Documentation Changes

This section describes major changes, other than introduction of new language features, that have appeared in implementations of the Post-Script language from Adobe Systems. All such changes are included in Level 2 implementations. Many of them are included in some Level 1 implementations as well; when possible, those implementations are identified by specific version numbers (value returned by the **version** operator). There are two classes of changes:

- Correction of serious bugs. Only those bugs that have a significant impact on programming are listed here.

- Intentional changes to the language specification. In some cases, the original specification was incorrect, incomplete, or subject to misinterpretation. Only significant changes are described here; minor changes, such as corrections to operators' error lists, are omitted.

Level 1 and Level 2 implementations of the PostScript language scanner differ in several minor ways.

- If the source of text is a string instead of a file, an occurrence of a string literal enclosed in (...) is treated specially in Level 1. The scanner returns a substring of the original string instead of allocating a new string, and it does not recognize \ escape sequences within the string literal. In Level 2, the scanner operates in a consistent way for all sources of text.

- Occurrences of \ outside string literals are sometimes treated as self-delimiting special characters in Level 1. They are regular characters in Level 2.

- Tokens that are syntactically legal numbers but exceed implementation limits are treated as name objects in Level 1 but generate a **limitcheck** in Level 2.

The convention for uniform handling of end-of-line, described in section 3.8.1, "Basic File Operators," was introduced in version 40.0. In earlier versions, the sequence CR LF is treated as two end-of-line characters, and the **readline** operator recognizes only LF as its end-of-line terminator.

Implementations prior to version 38.0 perform conversions between the RGB and HSB color models incorrectly.

Implementations prior to version 38.0 have a bug which causes names longer than about 40 characters to be garbled.

In version 23.0, applying **bind** to a read-only procedure can cause an **invalidaccess** error. This is most likely to occur as a result of applying **bind** to the same procedure twice.

In Level 1 implementations, **charpath** correctly updates the current point by the width of the string, but it doesn't actually append a **moveto** element to the current path.

cleardictstack, present in all of Adobe's PostScript implementations, is now documented.

In all implementations, **cvrs** behaves as documented in this manual; the former specification was incorrect.

eexec, present in all of Adobe's PostScript implementations, is now documented.

executive, present in most of Adobe's PostScript implementations, is now documented.

In version 23.0, **idiv** permits real operands, though this behavior isn't documented. Later implementations permit only integer operands.

In implementations prior to version 47.0, execution of **imagemask** when an inverted transfer function is in effect produces incorrect output. The polarity of the mask is inverted instead of the polarity of the data.

In Level 1 implementations, the conditions that give rise to an **invalidrestore** error are more restrictive than they should be. If a program executes **put** followed by **get** of some composite object and leaves the resulting object on the stack during **restore**, an **invalidrestore** error occurs, even if the object's value existed prior to the corresponding **save**.

In most Level 1 implementations, executing **exit** within the procedure given to **kshow** causes a malfunction.

The **length** operator permits its operand to be a name object. This isn't mentioned in the original specification of **length**, but it has always been implemented this way. Additionally, version 23.0 permits simple operands and returns 1; later implementations do not permit this.

In Level 1 implementations, the **pathbbox** operator computes a bounding box that encloses all points in the current path. In Level 2, if the path ends with a **moveto**, the trailing endpoint is not included in the computation.

In Level 1 implementations, the definitions of **prompt**, **pstack**, and **start** are in **userdict** instead of **systemdict**.

statusdict and **internaldict** are now documented, but most of their contents remain implementation-dependent.

In implementations prior to version 41.0, each execution of **strokepath** causes a small amount of path storage to be permanently lost. This makes **strokepath** essentially useless in those implementations.

Implementation Limits

The PostScript language does not restrict the sizes or quantities of things described in the language, such as numbers, arrays, stacks, paths, and so on. However, a PostScript interpreter running on a particular processor in a particular operating environment does have such limits. The interpreter cannot execute PostScript language programs that exceed these limits. If it attempts to perform some operation that would exceed one of the limits, it executes the error **limitcheck** (or **VMerror** if it exhausts virtual memory resources).

All limits are sufficiently large that most PostScript language page descriptions should never come close to exceeding any of them, because the PostScript interpreter has been designed to handle very complex page descriptions. On the other hand, a program that is not a page description might encounter some of these limits because the interpreter has not been designed with unlimited general programming in mind. There is no formal distinction in the PostScript language between a page description and a general program. However, a Post-Script interpreter residing in a printer is deliberately optimized for its intended use: to produce raster output according to a fully specified graphical description generated by some external application program.

Occurrence of a **limitcheck** error during execution of a page description is often an indication of an error in the PostScript language program, such as unbounded recursion on one of the stacks. Occurrence of a **VMerror** is often an indication that the program is not using **save** and **restore** properly.

B.1 Typical Limits

This section describes limits that are typical of PostScript interpreter implementations from Adobe Systems. These limits fall into two main classes:

- *Architectural limits.* The hardware on which the PostScript interpreter executes imposes certain constraints. For example, an integer is usually represented in 32 bits, limiting the range of integers that are allowed. Additionally, the design of the software imposes other constraints, such as a limit of 65535 elements in an array or string.

- *Memory limits.* The amount of memory available to the PostScript interpreter limits the number of memory-consuming objects that the interpreter can hold simultaneously. Memory management is discussed below.

Table B.1 describes the architectural limits for most PostScript interpreters running on 32-bit machines. These limits are likely to remain constant across a wide variety of implementations.

Table B.1 *Architectural limits*

Quantity	Limit	Explanation
integer	2147483647	Largest integer value. This value is $2^{31} - 1$ and its representation is 16#7FFFFFFF. In most situations, an integer that would exceed this limit is converted into a real automatically.
	−2147483648	Smallest integer value. It is -2^{31} and its representation is 16#80000000.
real	$\pm 10^{38}$	Largest and smallest real values (approximately).
	$\pm 10^{-38}$	Non-zero real values closest to zero (approximately). Values closer than these are converted to zero automatically.
	8	Significant decimal digits of precision (approximately).
array	65535	Maximum length of an array, in elements.
dictionary	65535	Maximum capacity of a dictionary, in key-value pairs.
string	65535	Maximum length of a string, in characters.
name	127	Maximum length of a name, in characters.
filename	100	Maximum length of a file name, including the %device% prefix.
save level	15	Maximum number of active **save**s that have not yet been matched by a corresponding **restore**.
gsave level	31	Maximum number of active **gsave**s. Each **save** also performs a **gsave** implicitly.

Memory limits cannot be characterized so precisely, because the amount of available memory and the ways in which it is allocated vary from one product to another. Nevertheless, it's useful to give some general information about memory limits that a complex page description is likely to encounter.

The PostScript interpreter requires memory for a variety of purposes, including:

- VM for the values of composite objects.

- Stacks and other objects visible to a PostScript language program.

- Paths in the graphics state.

- Frame buffer or other internal representation of the raster memory for the current page.

- Font cache, user path cache, form cache, pattern cache, and other internal data structures that save the results of expensive computations in order to avoid redundant work.

Level 1 and Level 2 implementations have somewhat different conventions for dividing available memory among these uses. In Level 1, there is usually a static allocation for each purpose—so much memory for stacks, so much for paths, and so on. If a PostScript language program exceeds these static allocations, a **limitcheck** error occurs. Installing more memory in a Level 1 product, if possible at all, usually increases the limit on available VM but seldom affects any of the other limits.

In Level 2 implementations, the allocation of memory is much more flexible. Memory is automatically reallocated from one use to another when necessary. When more memory is needed for a particular purpose, it can be taken away from memory allocated for other purposes if that memory is currently unused or if its use is non-essential (a cache, for instance). Installing more memory in a Level 2 product causes most implementation limits to increase.

Of course, the added flexibility in Level 2 implementations results in a decrease in predictability. If a PostScript language program consumes an unusually large amount of memory for a particular purpose, it may decrease other implementation limits so that they become *less* than the corresponding limits in a Level 1 implementation.

In general, it is unwise for applications to generate page descriptions that operate near the implementation limits for resources. Such page descriptions cannot reasonably be included as components of larger page descriptions, because the combined resource requirements might exceed implementation limits.

Table B.2 gives memory limits that are typical of Level 1 implementations. These are the smallest limits that are likely to be encountered in any product. Many products have larger limits for some resources. Level 2 implementations have no fixed limits. However, a program can establish certain artificial limits by means described in Appendix C.

Table B.2 *Typical memory limits in Level 1*

Quantity	Limit	Explanation
userdict	200	Capacity of **userdict**. Note that **userdict** starts out with a few things already defined in it.
FontDirectory	100	Capacity of **FontDirectory**, determining the maximum number of fonts that may be defined simultaneously.
operand stack	500	Maximum depth of the operand stack—number of elements that may be pushed on and not yet popped off. This also defines a limit on the number of elements contained in all unfinished procedure definitions being processed by the PostScript language scanner, since the scanner uses the operand stack to accumulate them.
dictionary stack	20	Maximum depth of the dictionary stack.
execution stack	250	Maximum depth of the execution stack. Each procedure, file, or string whose execution has been suspended occupies one element of this stack. Also, control operators, such as **for**, **repeat**, and **stopped,** push a few additional elements on the stack to control their execution.
interpreter level	10	Maximum number of recursive invocations of the PostScript interpreter. Graphics operators that call PostScript language procedures, such as **pathforall**, **show**, and **image**, invoke the interpreter recursively.
path	1500	Maximum number of points specified in all active path descriptions, including the current path, clip path, and paths saved by **save** and **gsave**.
dash	11	Maximum number of elements in a dash pattern—the maximum length of the array operand of the **setdash** operator.
VM	240000	Maximum size of virtual memory in bytes. Typically, this limit is influenced by the size of the imageable area for the current page, which requires memory in proportion to its area. Thus, installing a larger size page reduces the VM limit. The current and maximum size of the VM are reported by the **vmstatus** operator.

| file | 6 | Maximum number of open files, including the standard input and output files. This limit is substantially larger in implementations that support named files. |
| image | 3300 | Maximum width of an image's source data in samples per scan line. (Most implementations have a larger limit, but it varies from product to product.) |

There are other implementation limits on uses of memory that are not directly under the control of a PostScript language program and are difficult to quantify. For example:

- Rendering extremely complex paths requires a substantial amount of memory, particularly when the **clip** operator is executed.

- Halftone screens occupy an amount of memory that depends on screen angle, frequency, and device resolution. Screens saved by **gsave** may occupy additional memory.

- High-resolution devices, such as typesetters, represent the current page as a display list on disk instead of as a full pixel array in memory. If disk space is exhausted, a **limitcheck** occurs.

B.2 Virtual Memory Use

It is impossible to predict accurately how much VM a program will consume, but it is possible to make a rough estimate. VM is occupied primarily by the values of composite objects. Simple objects do not consume VM, nor do composite objects that share the values of other objects. Some typical memory requirements are as follows:

- Array values are created and VM consumed when a program executes the **array**,], and **matrix** operators. An array value occupies 8 bytes per element.

- When the PostScript language scanner encounters a procedure delimited by {...}, it creates either an array or a packed array, according to the current packing mode (see **setpacking**). An array value occupies 8 bytes per element. A packed array value occupies 1 to 9 bytes per element depending on each element's type and value; a typical average is 2.5 bytes per element.

- String values are created and VM consumed when a program executes the **string** operator and when the scanner encounters string literals delimited by (...), <...>, and <~...~>. A string value occupies 1 byte per element.

- Dictionary values are created by the **dict** and >> operators and by certain other operators that return collections of parameters as dictionaries. VM consumption is based on the dictionary's capacity (its **maxlength**), regardless of how full it currently is. A dictionary value occupies about 20 bytes per key-value pair.

- Name objects consume VM at the time the scanner first encounters each distinct name. Computed names (generated by **cvn**, for instance) consume VM on their first use as names. Repeated occurrences of a particular name require no additional storage. Each distinct name occupies about 40 bytes plus the length of the name in characters.

- The **save/restore** machinery consumes VM in proportion to the magnitude of the changes that must be undone by **restore**, but independently of the total size of VM. **restore** reclaims all local VM resources consumed since the corresponding **save**.

- Loading a Type 1 font program typically consumes 20,000 to 30,000 bytes of VM, depending on the size of the character set and the complexity of the characters. VM consumption of a font remains essentially constant, regardless of the number of ways in which its characters are scaled, rotated, or otherwise transformed.

APPENDIX C

Interpreter Parameters

The facilities described in this section are available only in Level 2 implementations, with the exception of a few special-purpose operators that are explicitly described as Level 1 operators.

There are various parameters to control the operation and behavior of the PostScript interpreter. Most of these parameters have to do with allocation of memory and other resources for specific purposes. For example, there are parameters to control the maximum amount of memory to be used for VM, font cache, and halftone screens. Some input/output and storage devices have parameters that control the behavior of each device individually.

A product is initially configured with interpreter parameter values that are appropriate for most applications. However, with suitable authorization, a PostScript language program can alter the interpreter parameters to favor certain applications or to adapt the product to special requirements.

The interpreter parameters are divided into three categories:

- User parameters can be altered at will, within reasonable limits, by any PostScript language program without special authorization. The **setuserparams** and **currentuserparams** operators manipulate user parameters. Alterations to user parameters are subject to **save** and **restore**.

- System parameters can be altered only by a program that presents a valid password. The **setsystemparams** and **currentsystemparams** operators manipulate system parameters. Alterations to system parameters have a permanent, system-wide effect, which may persist through restarts of the PostScript interpreter.

- Device parameters are similar to system parameters, but they apply to individual input/output or storage devices. The **setdevparams** and **currentdevparams** operators manipulate device parameters.

The operators that manipulate interpreter parameters are described in Chapter 8; the semantics of the individual parameters are described below. The operators are a standard feature of Level 2 implementations. However, the set of interpreter parameters that exist in any given product is implementation dependent. The parameters described in this section are typical of current PostScript products from Adobe. Not all products support all parameters; some products may support additional parameters. The set of parameters a given product supports is subject to change.

Most of the user parameters establish temporary policies on matters such as whether to insert new items into caches. It is reasonable for a user or a spooler program acting on the user's behalf to alter user parameters when submitting jobs with unusual requirements.

The system parameters, on the other hand, permanently alter the overall configuration of the product. A user application should never attempt to alter system or device parameters. Only system management software should do that.

C.1 Defined User and System Parameters

Each user or system parameter is identified by a *key*, which is always a name object. The value of a parameter is usually—but not necessarily—an integer. The following tables summarize the user and system parameters that are commonly defined. These parameters are described in more detail in section C.3, "Parameter Details."

Table C.1 *User parameters*

Key	Value	Semantics
MaxFontItem	integer	Maximum bytes occupied by the pixel array of a single character in the font cache.
MinFontCompress	integer	Threshold at which a cached character is stored in compressed form instead of as a full pixel array.
MaxUPathItem	integer	Maximum bytes occupied by a single cached user path.
MaxFormItem	integer	Maximum bytes occupied by a single cached form.
MaxPatternItem	integer	Maximum bytes occupied by a single cached pattern.
MaxScreenItem	integer	Maximum bytes occupied by a single halftone screen.

MaxOpStack	integer	Maximum elements in operand stack.
MaxDictStack	integer	Maximum elements in dictionary stack.
MaxExecStack	integer	Maximum elements in execution stack.
MaxLocalVM	integer	Maximum bytes occupied by values in local VM.
VMReclaim	integer	0 enables automatic garbage collection. −1 disables it for local VM. −2 disables it for both local and global VM.
VMThreshold	integer	Frequency of automatic garbage collection, which is triggered whenever this many bytes have been allocated since the previous collection.

Table C.2 *System parameters*

Key	Value	Semantics
SystemParamsPassword	string	(*Write-only*) Password authorizing use of the **setsystemparams** and **setdevparams** operators.
StartJobPassword	string	(*Write-only*) Password authorizing use of the **startjob** operator.
BuildTime	integer	(*Read-only*) Time stamp identifying a specific build of the PostScript interpreter.
ByteOrder	boolean	(*Read-only*) Native (preferred) order of multiple-byte numbers in binary encoded tokens: *false* indicates high-order byte first; *true* indicates low-order byte first.
RealFormat	string	(*Read-only*) Native (preferred) representation for real numbers in binary encoded tokens. This is either IEEE or the name of some specific machine architecture. The interpreter will always accept IEEE-format reals, but it may process native-format reals more efficiently (see section 3.12.4, "Number Representations").
MaxFontCache	integer	Maximum bytes occupied by the font cache.
CurFontCache	integer	(*Read-only*) Bytes currently occupied by the font cache.
MaxOutlineCache	integer	Maximum bytes occupied by cached character outlines (**CharStrings**) for fonts whose definitions are kept on disk instead of in VM.
CurOutlineCache	integer	(*Read-only*) Bytes currently occupied by **CharStrings**.
MaxUPathCache	integer	Maximum bytes occupied by the user path cache.
CurUPathCache	integer	(*Read-only*) Bytes currently occupied by the user path cache.
MaxFormCache	integer	Maximum bytes occupied by the form cache.
CurFormCache	integer	(*Read-only*) Bytes currently occupied by the form cache.
MaxPatternCache	integer	Maximum bytes occupied by the pattern cache.
CurPatternCache	integer	(*Read-only*) Bytes currently occupied by the pattern cache.
MaxScreenStorage	integer	Maximum bytes occupied by all active halftone screens, including ones created by **setscreen** and saved by **gsave**.
CurScreenStorage	integer	(*Read-only*) Bytes currently occupied by all active halftone screens.

| MaxDisplayList | integer | Maximum bytes occupied by display lists, excluding those held in caches. |
| CurDisplayList | integer | (*Read-only*) Bytes currently occupied by display lists. |

A program alters user or system parameters by executing the **setuserparams** or **setsystemparams** operator, passing it a dictionary containing the names and new values of the parameters that are to be changed. The dictionary may contain additional information; in particular, there can be an entry named **Password**, described below.

C.2 General Properties of User and System Parameters

The detailed semantics of user and system parameters are implementation dependent. For example, limits on the sizes of caches are specified in bytes. The effects of such limits depend on how cached items are represented internally. Still, there are some guidelines that apply to interpreter parameters generally.

The **setuserparams** operator sets user parameters; **currentuserparams** reads their current values. Alterations to user parameters are subject to **save** and **restore**—that is, **restore** resets all user parameters to their values at the time of the most recent **save**. In a Display PostScript system, which supports multiple execution contexts, user parameters are maintained separately for each context.

Usually, altering user parameters by **setuserparams** does not affect the behavior of PostScript language programs, only their performance. For example, increasing the **MinFontCompress** parameter allows larger characters to be stored as full pixel arrays. This increases the speed at which those characters can be shown, but at the cost of using font cache storage less efficiently.

In a few cases, however, user parameters affect implementation limits. For example, the **MaxScreenItem** parameter imposes an implementation limit on the size of a halftone screen. These implementation limits are noted in the descriptions in section C.3, "Parameter Details."

In general, reducing the limit on the size of an individual cached item will not disturb any items that are already in the cache, even if they are larger than the new limit.

User parameters have default values that are implementation dependent. In some implementations, these default values are system parameters that can be altered with **setsystemparams**. The default value of a particular user parameter is a system parameter with the same name.

The **setsystemparams** operator sets system parameters; **currentsystemparams** reads their current values. Permission to alter system parameters is controlled by a password. The dictionary passed to **setsystemparams** must contain an entry named **Password** whose value is equal to the system parameter password (a string or integer). If the password is incorrect or absent, the operation will not be allowed.

Some system parameters can be set permanently—that is, in non-volatile storage that survives restarts of the PostScript interpreter. This capability is implementation dependent. No error occurs if parameters cannot be stored permanently. In some implementations, permanent parameter changes do not take effect until the *next* restart of the PostScript interpreter.

In general, the cache size parameters (for example, **MaxFontCache**) are simply limits. They do not represent memory dedicated to a specific use. Caches compete with each other for available memory. The main purpose of the limits is to prevent excessive memory from being devoted to one use, to the exclusion of other uses. Under some circumstances, memory in use by a cache may be unavailable for satisfying the needs of a PostScript language program—for instance, to allocate new objects in VM or to enlarge a stack.

Usually, reducing the size of a cache causes cached items to be discarded to make current consumption less than the new maximum. Sometimes, for implementation reasons, this operation must be deferred. Consequently, the current consumption for a cache may exceed the maximum temporarily.

Certain system parameters are read-only—that is, they are returned by **currentsystemparams**, but attempting to change one by **setsystemparams** has no effect. The read-only parameters report information such as current memory consumption. Certain other parameters, namely **SystemParamsPassword** and **StartJobPassword**, are write-only. They can be set by **setsystemparams**, but are not returned by **currentsystemparams**.

C.3 Parameter Details

The following sections explain each parameter.

C.3.1 Passwords

The password that controls changing system parameters is itself a system parameter, **SystemParamsPassword**, which can be changed by **setsystemparams**. There is another password, **StartJobPassword**, that controls the ability to execute the **startjob** operator to alter initial VM (see section 3.7.7, "Job Execution Environment"). These two passwords are separate so the system manager can be permissive about granting access to **startjob** without compromising control over **setsystemparams**.

A password is a string object subject to an implementation limit on its length (see Appendix B). If an integer appears where a password is expected, the integer is automatically converted to a string, as if by **cvs**. All characters of a password are significant, and password comparison is case-sensitive.

If a password is set to the empty (zero-length) string, password checking is disabled. If **SystemParamsPassword** has been set to the empty string, then **setsystemparams** is always allowed, regardless of the value of **Password** passed to it. Similarly, if **StartJobPassword** has been set to the empty string, then **startjob** is always allowed. When a PostScript interpreter is initially installed, both passwords are empty strings.

To change **SystemParamsPassword**, execute:

```
<<
/Password (oldpassword)
/SystemParamsPassword (newpassword)
>> setsystemparams
```

C.3.2 Font Cache

Two user parameters specify policies for inserting new items into the font cache. These parameters, **MaxFontItem** and **MinFontCompress**, control the behavior of the **setcachedevice** operator.

If a cached character would be larger than the **MaxFontItem** parameter, as determined from the bounding box passed to **setcachedevice**, the character will not be cached; otherwise, it will be (space permitting). If a character that is cached would be larger than the **MinFontCompress** parameter, it is stored in a space-efficient compressed representation. If it is smaller, it is stored in a time-efficient, full-pixel-array representation. Compressed characters consume much less space in the font cache than do full pixel arrays (by factors of up to 40), but require more computation to reconstitute when they are needed. The **MinFontCompress** parameter controls the trade-off between time and space.

There are three convenience operators that control the same font cache parameters: **setcachelimit**, **setcacheparams**, and **currentcacheparams**. **setcachelimit** exists in all Level 1 implementations; **setcacheparams** and **currentcacheparams** exist in most, but not all. The Level 1 **cachestatus** operator returns some implementation-dependent information in addition to what is available from **currentsystemparams**.

The **MaxFontCache** system parameter specifies an overall limit on the size of the font cache, including both the device pixel arrays themselves and other overhead, such as cached metrics.

C.3.3 Other Caches

User paths, forms, and patterns all use caches that are controlled in similar ways.

The user parameters **MaxUPathItem**, **MaxFormItem**, and **MaxPatternItem** specify limits on the sizes of individual items to be inserted into the respective caches. The system parameters **MaxUPathCache**, **MaxFormCache**, and **MaxPatternCache** specify overall limits on the sizes of the caches.

Two convenience operators, **setucacheparams** and **ucachestatus**, also deal with the user path cache parameters. These operators exist for compatibility with some existing Display PostScript applications.

C.3.4 Halftone Screens

Storage for halftone screens is managed somewhat differently than storage for caches. The halftone machinery must have enough storage to hold an expanded internal representation of the screen in use. It can use any excess storage to hold a cache of screens that are not in use.

The **MaxScreenItem** user parameter specifies the maximum number of bytes a single halftone screen can occupy. This is not a simple function of the size of a halftone cell; it is influenced by frequency, angle, device resolution, and quantization of raster memory. The **MaxScreenItem** parameter imposes an implementation limit on the size of screens that can be used.

Use of the **AccurateScreens** feature of halftone dictionaries substantially increases the storage requirement for a screen. Highest accuracy is achieved only when sufficient memory is available. As a rule of thumb, **MaxScreenItem** should be at least $R \times D \times 5$, where R is the device resolution in pixels per inch and D is the diagonal length of the imageable area of device space in inches.

The **MaxScreenStorage** system parameter specifies an overall limit on the amount of storage for all active screens. A screen is active if it is the current screen or if it was created by **setscreen** and has been saved on the graphics state stack or in a gstate object. A screen created by **sethalftone** is active only if it is the current screen.

C.3.5 VM and Stacks

The **MaxLocalVM** user parameter imposes a limit on the total amount of local VM in use. Attempting to create a new composite object in local VM will fail (with a **VMerror**) if the VM would exceed its limit. There is no corresponding limit for global VM. The method for sharing global VM among multiple execution contexts does not provide a way to attribute VM consumption to a particular context.

Three other user parameters, **MaxOpStack**, **MaxDictStack**, and **MaxExecStack**, impose limits on the number of elements that can be pushed onto the operand, dictionary, and execution stacks, respectively. Attempting to exceed one of these limits will result in a **stackoverflow**, **dictstackoverflow**, or **execstackoverflow**, respectively.

Normally, there are no limits on VM or stack allocation; that is, the default values of these user parameters are extremely large numbers. VM and stacks can grow without limit, subject only to the total amount of memory that exists in the machine on which the PostScript interpreter is running. As VM and stack consumption increases, less memory is available for the font cache and other uses. This can degrade performance. The main use of the VM and stack limit parameters is to test the behavior of applications in limited memory.

Two user parameters, **VMReclaim** and **VMThreshold**, control the behavior of the garbage collector. Normally, garbage collection is triggered periodically and automatically to reclaim inaccessible objects in VM. It is sometimes useful to disable garbage collection temporarily—say, in order to obtain repeatable timing measurements.

Like all user parameters, the VM and stack parameters are maintained separately for each context in a Display PostScript system. In particular, if VM is shared among multiple contexts, the effects of a particular context's VM parameters apply only while that context is executing.

The **vmstatus**, **vmreclaim**, and **setvmthreshold** operators manipulate some of the VM parameters. **vmreclaim** can also be used to trigger immediate garbage collection.

C.4 Device Parameters

Each PostScript interpreter supports a collection of input/output and storage devices, such as communication channels, disks, and cartridges. The standard file operators, described in section 3.8, "File Input and Output," access these devices as files. Some devices have device-dependent parameters. The **setdevparams** and **currentdevparams** operators access these parameters.

A device is identified by a string of the form %*device*, or %*device*%, which is a prefix of the %*device*%*file* syntax for named files in storage devices (see section 3.8.2, "Named Files"). The available devices can be enumerated by invoking the **resourceforall** operator for the **IODevice** category (see section 3.9, "Named Resources").

setdevparams is very similar to **setsystemparams**; the same restrictions apply. The names and values of parameters for specific devices are device and product dependent. They are not documented in this manual, but in product-specific documentation.

APPENDIX D

Compatibility Strategies

As discussed in section 1.2, "Evolution of the PostScript Language," the PostScript language has undergone several significant extensions in order to adapt to new technology and to incorporate new functionality and flexibility. While the PostScript language is designed to be a universal standard for device-independent page description, the reality is that there are different PostScript language implementations that have different sets of features. This appendix presents guidelines for taking advantage of language extensions while maintaining compatibility with all PostScript interpreters.

D.1 The Level Approach

PostScript implementations are organized into *levels*, of which two have been defined.

- Level 1 interpreters implement all Level 1 features. Those features are documented in the first edition of the *PostScript Language Reference Manual*. In the present manual (second edition), Level 1 consists of all features except the ones designated Level 2 or Display PostScript features.

- Level 2 interpreters implement all Level 1 and Level 2 features. The Level 2 features include CMYK color extensions, composite font extensions, most of the Display PostScript extensions (to the extent to which they apply to all raster devices), and many new features.

Level 2 is upwardly compatible with Level 1. Applications that work with Level 1 interpreters, using language features as documented in the first *PostScript Language Reference Manual*, will also work with Level 2 interpreters.

Level 2, however, is not backwardly compatible with Level 1. PostScript language programs that use Level 2 operators and features do not automatically work on Level 1 interpreters. For applications to take advantage of Level 2 features while remaining compatible with Level 1 interpreters, one or more of the strategies described in section D.3, "Compatibility Techniques," must be adopted.

In addition to the two standard language levels, there are several language extensions. An *extension* is a collection of language features that are not a standard part of the language level (Level 1 or Level 2) supported by an implementation. For example, if a Level 1 implementation includes the CMYK color features, those features are an extension, since CMYK color is not part of Level 1. On the other hand, *all* Level 2 implementations include CMYK color features, since CMYK color is part of Level 2.

Extensions exist because the PostScript language must evolve to support new technologies and new applications. When an extension is introduced, it is based on an existing language level. Extensions that prove to be of general utility are candidates for inclusion in the next higher standard language level. Many Level 2 features originated as extensions to Level 1. Appendix A describes how these extensions are organized.

The advantages of the level approach are clear. Organizing features into a small number of levels simplifies the choices that application software developers must make. In contrast, organizing them as independent extensions implemented in arbitrary combinations leads to an exponential increase in choices. An application using features at a given level is guaranteed to work with PostScript interpreter implementations at that level and higher. PostScript Level 2 is a well-defined standard of functionality for software developers to support.

Although the level approach simplifies application programming, it's sometimes necessary for applications to depend on specific extensions for functional reasons. The following sections emphasize techniques for Level 1 and Level 2 compatibility, but many of them are applicable when dealing with extensions as well.

D.2 When To Provide Compatibility

An application must know what PostScript language operators are available to it. Essentially, there are two different scenarios:

- The application is outputting to a specific PostScript interpreter, in which case it knows what the target interpreter is.

- The application is printing through a spooler or saving to a file, in which case it does not know what the target interpreter is.

In the first case, the application can generate the PostScript language program appropriate for the target interpreter. The application simply needs to determine whether the interpreter is a Level 1 or Level 2 implementation *before* generating the PostScript language page description. There are two ways to do this:

- Consult a PPD file.

- Query the interpreter directly.

A *PostScript printer description* (PPD) file is a text file that can be read by an application to obtain information about a specific printer product. In the PPD file, the *LanguageLevel entry specifies the PostScript language level the product supports. (If the entry is absent, the product supports Level 1.) For information on PPD files, refer to the *PostScript Printer Description Files Specification* available from the Adobe Systems Developers' Association.

If there is a bi-directional communication channel between the application driver and the PostScript interpreter, the driver can determine the interpreter's capabilities by sending it a query job. The following program queries the interpreter's implementation level:

```
%!PS-Adobe-3.0 Query
%%?BeginQuery: Level
/languagelevel where
  {pop languagelevel}
  {1}
ifelse = flush
%%?EndQuery: 1
```

This query job returns a text line consisting of a single integer number: the implementation level of the interpreter. Section G.8, "Query Conventions," presents guidelines for constructing query jobs.

Checking for the existence of language extensions that are not part of a particular level is very similar. For example, some Level 1 implementations have the CMYK color extension. If the application wants to use the CMYK color operators, it needs to find out whether the target interpreter supports them. This, too, can be tested either by consulting the product's PPD file or by sending a query job to the interpreter. For example:

```
%!PS-Adobe-3.0 Query
%%?BeginQuery: Color
/setcmykcolor where
  {pop true}
  {false}
ifelse = flush
%%?EndQuery: false
```

This returns either true or false, indicating whether the **setcmykcolor** operator is available.

If an application is producing output not targeted to a particular interpreter, the strategy is entirely different. The application has three options:

1. Generate a Level 1-only page description. The resulting program uses only Level 1 features and can be sent to any interpreter.

2. Generate a Level 2-only page description. The resulting program uses both Level 1 and Level 2 features and will execute correctly only when sent to a Level 2 interpreter implementation.

3. Generate a page description that utilizes Level 2 features but provides for Level 1 compatibility. The resulting program can be sent to any interpreter.

Option 1 is the simplest method for producing fully portable output. It is entirely adequate for many applications. However, it sacrifices any improvements in performance or programming convenience available through use of Level 2 features.

Option 2 allows the application to take advantage of Level 2 features, but at the cost of incompatibility with a Level 1 interpreter. This approach makes the most sense when an application *must* use Level 2 features to perform functions that are simply unavailable in Level 1, such as device-independent CIE-based color specification. Especially in this case, the application should include the appropriate document structuring comments (see Appendix G), so a print manager or spooler can know that it must direct the page description to a Level 2 interpreter.

Option 3 is the most desirable, because the resulting page description is portable yet takes advantage of Level 2 features when they are available. The idea behind this strategy is for the application to provide PostScript language emulations of the Level 2 features the page description actually uses. When the program is executed, it determines whether the interpreter supports the features and installs the emulations only if necessary (see section D.4, "Installing Emulations"). This strategy may not be the simplest or most efficient, but it takes best advantage of the features available in different interpreters.

D.3 Compatibility Techniques

It is not possible to emulate every Level 2 feature in terms of Level 1 operators, but many features can be at least partially emulated. For example, the *array* form of the user path operators can be emulated easily, but the *encoded user path* form can be emulated only with great difficulty and probably with unacceptable cost in performance. The application must determine an appropriate trade-off between the benefit of using a feature and the cost of providing emulation for that feature.

The following sections outline three main compatibility techniques: complete emulation, partial emulation, and emulation in the application driver.

D.3.1 Complete Emulation

Some Level 2 features are sufficiently simple that they can be completely emulated in terms of Level 1 features. For instance, the Level 2 operator **selectfont** is defined as:

> *key scale* **selectfont**
> *key matrix* **selectfont**

selectfont obtains a font whose name is *key*, transforms it according to *scale* or *matrix*, and establishes it as the current font dictionary in the graphics state. This is equivalent to executing **findfont**, **scalefont** (or **makefont**), and **setfont**. But **selectfont** is more than just a convenience operator: Its implementation is more efficient as well. Using **selectfont** can significantly improve the performance of programs that switch fonts frequently.

The **selectfont** operator can be completely emulated in terms of Level 1 features as follows:

```
/selectfont {
    exch findfont exch
    dup type /arraytype eq {makefont}{scalefont} ifelse setfont
} bind def
```

A program can then invoke this emulation if the **selectfont** operator is unavailable. Section D.4, "Installing Emulations," describes the recommended method for accomplishing this.

Note that this emulation of **selectfont** does not have the performance gain that the *real* **selectfont** operator has. It is possible to write a PostScript language emulation of **selectfont** that caches scaled font dictionaries, although this is tricky and probably not worthwhile.

D.3.2 Partial Emulation

Not all forms of certain operators can be emulated efficiently. For example, the **rectfill** operator is defined as follows:

$$x \; y \; width \; height \; \textbf{rectfill}$$
$$numarray \; \textbf{rectfill}$$
$$numstring \; \textbf{rectfill}$$

It is straightforward to emulate the first form of **rectfill**, and, with a little more work, the *numarray* form as well. However, it is difficult to efficiently emulate the *numstring* form in terms of Level 1 features. For this reason, Adobe recommends that applications avoid using the *numstring* form when compatibility with Level 1 interpreters is required.

Note that an application can choose to emulate only the form of an operator it actually uses. This eliminates unnecessary overhead in the emulation procedure.

Example D.1 defines a procedure named *RF that is a partial emulation of the **rectfill** operator.

Example D.1

```
/BuildRectPath {
  dup type dup /integertype eq exch /realtype eq or { %ifelse
    4 –2 roll moveto                    % Operands are: x y width height
    dup 0 exch rlineto exch 0 rlineto neg 0 exch rlineto closepath
  }{ %else
    dup length 4 sub 0 exch 4 exch      % Operand is: numarray
    { %for
      1 index exch 4 getinterval aload pop
      BuildRectPath
    } for
    pop
  } ifelse
} bind def

/*RF {
  gsave newpath BuildRectPath fill grestore
} bind def
```

The reason for naming this emulation *RF and not rectfill is explained in section D.4, "Installing Emulations."

This emulation, in addition to omitting the *numstring* case altogether, doesn't emulate the *numarray* case precisely. **rectfill** draws all rectangles counterclockwise in user space, whereas *RF draws a rectangle clockwise if its height or width is negative. This affects the "insideness" computation if the rectangles overlap.

D.3.3   Emulation in the Driver

When emulation of a Level 2 feature is found to be too costly, the alternative is not to use that feature at all but to redesign the application's PostScript driver to obtain the same effect in a more efficient way. This often requires the application to do more work, such as keeping track of information that a Level 2 interpreter would maintain automatically.

For example, instead of using **selectfont**, a driver can keep track of scaled font dictionaries it has referenced recently. When it detects that a given font dictionary is needed multiple times, it can generate Post-Script language commands to save the dictionary on first use and refer to the saved dictionary on later uses. This achieves approximately the same performance benefits as using **selectfont**, but at the cost of additional complexity in the driver.

Adobe has developed a prototype driver implementing this strategy. This software is available in C language source form from the Adobe Systems Developers' Association.

D.4   Installing Emulations

When defining a PostScript language emulation of some operator, it is important *not* to give the emulation the same name as the *real* operator unless it is a complete emulation. This is because another page description included in the same job (an encapsulated file, for instance) may require a particular form of an operator that is not emulated; when it encounters the emulation, an error results. Note that in Example D.1 on page 587, the emulation of **rectfill** is not complete and is not named rectfill.

Emulation of operators should be done conditionally, based on whether the operator already exists. For example, it does not make sense to define a procedure named selectfont if the real **selectfont** operator already exists. Conditional emulation can be performed in one of two ways:

- Use the **languagelevel** operator to determine whether to install emulations of all required Level 2 operators as a group.

- Use the **where** operator to determine whether to install emulations of Level 2 operators individually. This is appropriate for those operators that are available as extensions to Level 1 in some products (see Appendix A).

Example D.2 uses the first method to provide conditional emulation of the Level 2 **selectfont** and **rectfill** operators. This example makes use of the *RF procedure defined in Example D.1 on page 587.

Example D.2

```
/*SF {                              % Complete selectfont emulation
  exch findfont exch
  dup type /arraytype eq {makefont}{scalefont} ifelse setfont
} bind def

/languagelevel where               % Determine language level
  {pop languagelevel} {1} ifelse    % of implementation
2 lt { % ifelse
  /SF /*SF load def                 % Level 1 interpreter present, so
  /RF /*RF load def                 % use emulations defined above
```

```
} { % else
  /SF /selectfont load def        % Level 2 interpreter present, so
  /RF /rectfill load def          % use existing operators
} ifelse
```

The examples together define procedures named *SF and *RF to emulate
selectfont and **rectfill**, respectively. Then, based on the results of the
languagelevel operator, Example D.2 binds either the emulations or the
real Level 2 operators to short names—SF and RF—that can be used later
in the page description.

This approach has three noteworthy features.

- An existing operator will always be used in preference to an
  emulation.

- An emulation is never given the same name as an operator. Thus,
  embedded programs will not be fooled into believing that an operator is defined when it isn't.

- The script of the page description can invoke operations using short
  names, such as SF and RF, without regard for whether those operations are performed by operators or by emulations.

Although testing for desired PostScript language operators with the
where operator is appropriate, testing for application-defined procedures this way is not. This can lead to trouble in the future if an operator of the same name happens to come into existence. The correct way
to test for application-defined procedures is to look them up in the
application's own dictionary with the **known** operator rather than
using the **where** operator.

Standard Character Sets and Encoding Vectors

This appendix describes the characters sets and encoding vectors of font programs found in a typical PostScript printer or Display PostScript system. While there is not a standard set of fonts that is required by the PostScript language, most PostScript products include software for 13 standard fonts from the Times*, Helvetica*, Courier, and Symbol families. Samples of the complete character sets for these fonts appear in the following sections.

The appendix then documents the entire character set for Adobe's standard text fonts, expert fonts, and the Symbol font. For each character set, every character is shown along with its full name and octal character code (unencoded characters are indicated by —). This is followed by detailed tables of the encoding vectors normally associated with a font program using that character set. These encoding vectors include **StandardEncoding**, **ISOLatin1Encoding**, Expert, ExpertSubset and Symbol.

The **StandardEncoding** and **ISOLatin1Encoding** encoding vectors are names in **systemdict** associated with their encoding array objects. The Expert, ExpertSubset, and Symbol encoding vectors are defined in the font program itself. The ExpertSubset encoding vector is used by some Adobe font programs, such as AGaramondExpert-Bold, that do not contain the entire expert character set. For more information on encoding vectors, see section 5.3, "Character Encoding."

E.1 Times Family

In 1931 *The Times* of London commissioned Monotype corporation, under the direction of Stanley Morison, to design a newspaper typeface. Times New Roman® was the result. The Linotype version shown here is called Times Roman. It continues to be popular for both newspaper and business applications, such as reports and correspondence.

Times-Roman

A B C D E F G H I J K L M N O P Q R S T U V W X Y Z
a b c d e f g h i j k l m n o p q r s t u v w x y z & 0 1 2 3 4 5 6 7 8 9
Æ Á Â Ä À Å Ã Ç Ð É Ê Ë È Í Î Ï Ì Ł Ñ Œ Ó Ô Ö Ò Õ Ø Š Þ Ú
Û Ü Ù Ÿ Ý Ž æ á â ä à å ã ç é ê ë è ð fi fl í î ï ì ı µ ł ñ œ ó ô ö ò õ ø š þ ß
ú û ü ù ÿ ý ž £ ¥ ƒ $ ¢ ¤ ™ © ® @ ª º † ‡ § ¶ * ! ¡ ? ¿ . , ; : ' ' " " , „ … ' "
‹ › « » ( ) [ ] { } | / \ - – — _ . , ´ ^ ¨ ` ˚ ˜ ¯ ˘ ˙ ˝ •
% ‰ ¼ ¾ ½ = − + × ~ < ± > ÷ ¬ ° ^ / . ¦ ¹ ² ³

Times-Italic

A B C D E F G H I J K L M N O P Q R S T U V W X Y Z
a b c d e f g h i j k l m n o p q r s t u v w x y z & 0 1 2 3 4 5 6 7 8 9
Æ Á Â Ä À Å Ã Ç Ð É Ê Ë È Í Î Ï Ì Ł Ñ Œ Ó Ô Ö Ò Õ Ø Š Þ Ú
Û Ü Ù Ÿ Ý Ž æ á â ä à å ã ç é ê ë è ð fi fl í î ï ì ı µ ł ñ œ ó ô ö ò õ ø š þ ß
*ú û ü ù ÿ ý ž £ ¥ ƒ $ ¢ ¤ ™ © ® @ ª º † ‡ § ¶ * ! ¡ ? ¿ . , ; : ' ' " " , „ … ' "*
‹ › « » ( ) [ ] { } | / \ - – — _ . , ´ ^ ¨ ` ˚ ˜ ¯ ˘ ˙ ˝ •
 # % ‰ ¼ ¾ ½ = − + × ~ < ± > ÷ ¬ ° ^ / . ¦ ¹ ² ³

Times-Bold

A B C D E F G H I J K L M N O P Q R S T U V W X Y Z
a b c d e f g h i j k l m n o p q r s t u v w x y z & 0 1 2 3 4 5 6 7 8 9
Æ Á Â Ä À Å Ã Ç Ð É Ê Ë È Í Î Ï Ì Ł Ñ Œ Ó Ô Ö Ò Õ Ø Š Þ Ú
Û Ü Ù Ÿ Ý Ž æ á â ä à å ã ç é ê ë è ð fi fl í î ï ì ı µ ł ñ œ ó ô ö ò õ ø š þ ß
ú û ü ù ÿ ý ž £ ¥ ƒ $ ¢ ¤ ™ © ® @ ª º † ‡ § ¶ * ! ¡ ? ¿ . , ; : ' ' " " , „ … ' "
‹ › « » ( ) [ ] { } | / \ - – — _ . , ´ ^ ¨ ` ˚ ˜ ¯ ˘ ˙ ˝ •
 # % ‰ ¼ ¾ ½ = − + × ~ < ± > ÷ ¬ ° ^ / . ¦ ¹ ² ³

Times-BoldItalic

A B C D E F G H I J K L M N O P Q R S T U V W X Y Z
a b c d e f g h i j k l m n o p q r s t u v w x y z & 0 1 2 3 4 5 6 7 8 9
Æ Á Â Ä À Å Ã Ç Ð É Ê Ë È Í Î Ï Ì Ł Ñ Œ Ó Ô Ö Ò Õ Ø Š Þ Ú
Û Ü Ù Ÿ Ý Ž æ á â ä à å ã ç é ê ë è ð fi fl í î ï ì ı µ ł ñ œ ó ô ö ò õ ø š þ ß
ú û ü ù ÿ ý ž £ ¥ ƒ $ ¢ ¤ ™ © ® @ ª º † ‡ § ¶ * ! ¡ ? ¿ . , ; : ' ' " " , „ … ' "
‹ › « » ( ) [ ] { } | / \ - – — _ . , ´ ^ ¨ ` ˚ ˜ ¯ ˘ ˙ ˝ •
 # % ‰ ¼ ¾ ½ = − + × ~ < ± > ÷ ¬ ° ^ / . ¦ ¹ ² ³

E.2 Helvetica Family

One of the most popular typefaces of all time, Helvetica was designed by Max Miedinger in 1957 for the Hass foundry in Switzerland. The name is derived from *Helvetia*, the Swiss name for Switzerland. Helvetica's range of styles allows a variety of uses, including headlines, packaging, posters, and short text blocks, such as captions.

Helvetica

ABCDEFGHIJKLMNOPQRSTUVWXYZ
abcdefghijklmnopqrstuvwxyz&0123456789
ÆÁÂÄÀÅÃÇÐÉÊËÈÍÎÏÌŁÑŒÓÔÖÒÕØŠÞÚ
ÛÜÙŸÝŽæáâäàåãçéêëèðfiflíîïìµłñœóôöòõøšþß
úûüùÿýž£¥ƒ$¢¤™©®@ªº†‡§¶*!¡?¿.,;:''""‚„…'"
‹›«»()[]{}|/\--—_¸˛´ˆˋˉ˚˜¯˘˙ˇ•
#%‰¼¾½=−+×~<±>÷¬°∧/·¦¹²³

Helvetica-Oblique

ABCDEFGHIJKLMNOPQRSTUVWXYZ
abcdefghijklmnopqrstuvwxyz&0123456789
ÆÁÂÄÀÅÃÇÐÉÊËÈÍÎÏÌŁÑŒÓÔÖÒÕØŠÞÚ
ÛÜÙŸÝŽæáâäàåãçéêëèðfiflíîïìµłñœóôöòõøšþß
úûüùÿýž£¥ƒ$¢¤™©®@ªº†‡§¶*!¡?¿.,;:''""‚„…'"
‹›«»()[]{}|/\--—_¸˛´ˆˋˉ˚˜¯˘˙ˇ•
#%‰¼¾½=−+×~<±>÷¬°∧/·¦¹²³

Helvetica-Bold

ABCDEFGHIJKLMNOPQRSTUVWXYZ
abcdefghijklmnopqrstuvwxyz&0123456789
ÆÁÂÄÀÅÃÇÐÉÊËÈÍÎÏÌŁÑŒÓÔÖÒÕØŠÞÚ
ÛÜÙŸÝŽæáâäàåãçéêëèðfiflíîïìµłñœóôöòõøšþß
úûüùÿýž£¥ƒ$¢¤™©®@ªº†‡§¶*!¡?¿.,;:''""‚„…'"
‹›«»()[]{}|/\--—_¸˛´ˆˋˉ˚˜¯˘˙ˇ•
#%‰¼¾½=−+×~<±>÷¬°∧/·¦¹²³

Helvetica-BoldOblique

ABCDEFGHIJKLMNOPQRSTUVWXYZ
abcdefghijklmnopqrstuvwxyz&0123456789
ÆÁÂÄÀÅÃÇÐÉÊËÈÍÎÏÌŁÑŒÓÔÖÒÕØŠÞÚ
ÛÜÙŸÝŽæáâäàåãçéêëèðfiflíîïìµłñœóôöòõøšþß
úûüùÿýž£¥ƒ$¢¤™©®@ªº†‡§¶*!¡?¿.,;:''""‚„…'"
‹›«»()[]{}|/\--—_¸˛´ˆˋˉ˚˜¯˘˙ˇ•
#%‰¼¾½=−+×~<±>÷¬°∧/·¦¹²³

E.3 Courier Family

Courier was originally designed as a typewriter face for IBM in 1952 by Howard Kettler. Courier is a monospaced, or fixed-pitch, font suitable for use in tabular material, program listings, or word processing.

Courier

A B C D E F G H I J K L M N O P Q R S T U V W X Y Z
a b c d e f g h i j k l m n o p q r s t u v w x y z & 0 1 2 3 4 5 6 7 8 9
Æ Á Â Ä À Å Ã Ç Ð É Ê Ë È Í Î Ï Ì Ł Ñ Œ Ó Ô Ö Ò Õ Š Þ Ú
Û Ü Ù Ÿ Ý Ž æ á â ä à å ã ç é ê ë è ð fi fl í î ï ì ı µ ł ñ œ ó ô ö ò õ ø š þ ß
ú û ü ù ÿ ý ž £ ¥ ƒ $ ¢ ¤ ™ © ® @ ª º † ‡ § ¶ * ! ¡ ? ¿ . , ; : ' ' " " , „ … ' "
< > « » ( ) [ ] { } | / \ - – — _ . , ´ ^ ¨ ` ˚ ~ ¯ ˘ ˙ ˇ ˝ •
‰ ‱ ¼ ¾ ½ = – + × ~ < ± > ÷ ¬ º ^ / . ¦ ¹ ² ³

Courier-Oblique

A B C D E F G H I J K L M N O P Q R S T U V W X Y Z
a b c d e f g h i j k l m n o p q r s t u v w x y z & 0 1 2 3 4 5 6 7 8 9
Æ Á Â Ä À Å Ã Ç Ð É Ê Ë È Í Î Ï Ì Ł Ñ Œ Ó Ô Ö Ò Õ Š Þ Ú
Û Ü Ù Ÿ Ý Ž æ á â ä à å ã ç é ê ë è ð fi fl í î ï ì ı µ ł ñ œ ó ô ö ò õ ø š þ ß
*ú û ü ù ÿ ý ž £ ¥ ƒ $ ¢ ¤ ™ © ® @ ª º † ‡ § ¶ * ! ¡ ? ¿ . , ; : ' ' " " , „ … ' '*
< > « » ( ) [ ] { } | / \ - – — _ . , ´ ^ ¨ ` ˚ ~ ¯ ˘ ˙ ˇ ˝ •
 # ‰ ‱ ¼ ¾ ½ = – + × ~ < ± > ÷ ¬ º ^ / . ¦ ¹ ² ³

Courier-Bold

A B C D E F G H I J K L M N O P Q R S T U V W X Y Z
a b c d e f g h i j k l m n o p q r s t u v w x y z & 0 1 2 3 4 5 6 7 8 9
Æ Á Â Ä À Å Ã Ç Ð É Ê Ë È Í Î Ï Ì Ł Ñ Œ Ó Ô Ö Ò Õ Š Þ Ú
Û Ü Ù Ÿ Ý Ž æ á â ä à å ã ç é ê ë è ð fi fl í î ï ì ı µ ł ñ œ ó ô ö ò õ ø š þ ß
ú û ü ù ÿ ý ž £ ¥ ƒ $ ¢ ¤ ™ © ® @ ª º † ‡ § ¶ * ! ¡ ? ¿ . , ; : ' ' " " , „ … ' "
< > « » ( ) [ ] { } | / \ - – — _ . , ´ ^ ¨ ` ˚ ~ ¯ ˘ ˙ ˇ ˝ •
 # % ‰ ¼ ¾ ½ = – + × ~ < ± > ÷ ¬ º ^ / . ¦ ¹ ² ³

Courier-BoldOblique

A B C D E F G H I J K L M N O P Q R S T U V W X Y Z
a b c d e f g h i j k l m n o p q r s t u v w x y z & 0 1 2 3 4 5 6 7 8 9
Æ Á Â Ä À Å Ã Ç Ð É Ê Ë È Í Î Ï Ì Ł Ñ Œ Ó Ô Ö Ò Õ Š Þ Ú
Û Ü Ù Ÿ Ý Ž æ á â ä à å ã ç é ê ë è ð fi fl í î ï ì ı µ ł ñ œ ó ô ö ò õ ø š þ ß
ú û ü ù ÿ ý ž £ ¥ ƒ $ ¢ ¤ ™ © ® @ ª º † ‡ § ¶ * ! ¡ ? ¿ . , ; : ' ' " " , „ … ' '
< > « » ( ) [ ] { } | / \ - – — _ . , ´ ^ ¨ ` ˚ ~ ¯ ˘ ˙ ˇ ˝ •
 # % ‰ ¼ ¾ ½ = – + × ~ < ± > ÷ ¬ º ^ / . ¦ ¹ ² ³

E.4 Symbol

αβχδεφγηικλμνοπθρστυϖξψζφϖϑς ∫⌠{⎰}⎱[⌈⌉](⎛)
ΑΒΧΔΕΦΓΗΙΚΛΜΝΟΠΘΡΣΤΥΩΞΨΖΥ │{}│││││
=≠≡≈≅<>≤≥∧∨∴−+±×÷¬•· ⌡⌡⌊⌋⎝

∀∃ƒ∂∍∩∪⊃⊂⊇⊆⊄∈∉∅⊗⊕∞∝
↔←—→↑↓⇔⇐⇒⇑⇓°′″⌟ℵℑℜ℘
...⟨◊®©™®©™∑∏⟩∠⊥∇♣♦♥♠
!#%∗&0123456789.,;:_~│∣∕√ ⎺

Sample Uses

$$\varepsilon = \min_{x>0} (x \mid (1 + x) \neq 1)$$

$$w\,(\xi' - \xi'') = \sum_{i=1}^{m} |\,C_i \cap \{\,\xi'\,\}\,| \cdot |\,C_i \cap \{\,\xi''\,\}\,| \ \text{ if } \ \xi', \xi'' \in L \text{ and } \xi' \neq \xi''$$

$$\bigcup_{i=1}^{n} Z_i\,(t) \subseteq M$$

$$Z_i\,(t) \cap Z_j\,(t) = \emptyset \quad (i \neq j)$$

proposition	true if and only if
$(\forall u)\ s\ (p)$	$S \cap T'_p = \emptyset$
$(\exists u)\ s\ (p)$	$S \cap T_p \neq \emptyset$
$(\forall u)\ s\ (\sim p)$	$S \cap T_p = \emptyset$
$(\exists u)\ s\ (\sim p)$	$S \cap T'_p \neq \emptyset$
$\sim((\forall u)\ s\ (p))$	$S \cap T'_p \neq \emptyset$
$\sim((\exists u)\ s\ (p))$	$S \cap T_p = \emptyset$

$$kp^{k/2}\,t^{-1}I_k\,(at) \Leftrightarrow \left| \frac{s + \sqrt{s^2 - 4\lambda\mu}}{2\lambda} \right|^{-k}$$

E.5 Standard Roman Character Set

Char	Name	Code (octal) Std	ISO	Char	Name	Code (octal) Std	ISO	Char	Name	Code (octal) Std	ISO
A	A	101	101	Ø	Oslash	351	330	|	bar	174	174
Æ	AE	341	306	Õ	Otilde	—	325	{	braceleft	173	173
Á	Aacute	—	301	P	P	120	120	}	braceright	175	175
Â	Acircumflex	—	302	Q	Q	121	121	[	bracketleft	133	133
Ä	Adieresis	—	304	R	R	122	122	]	bracketright	135	135
À	Agrave	—	300	S	S	123	123	˘	breve	306	226
Å	Aring	—	305	Š	Scaron	—	—	¦	brokenbar	—	246
Ã	Atilde	—	303	T	T	124	124	•	bullet	267	—
B	B	102	102	Þ	Thorn	—	336	c	c	143	143
C	C	103	103	U	U	125	125	ˇ	caron	317	237
Ç	Ccedilla	—	307	Ú	Uacute	—	332	ç	ccedilla	—	347
D	D	104	104	Û	Ucircumflex	—	333	¸	cedilla	313	270
E	E	105	105	Ü	Udieresis	—	334	¢	cent	242	242
É	Eacute	—	311	Ù	Ugrave	—	331	ˆ	circumflex	303	223
Ê	Ecircumflex	—	312	V	V	126	126	:	colon	072	072
Ë	Edieresis	—	313	W	W	127	127	,	comma	054	054
È	Egrave	—	310	X	X	130	130	©	copyright	—	251
Ð	Eth	—	320	Y	Y	131	131	¤	currency	250	244
F	F	106	106	Ý	Yacute	—	335	d	d	144	144
G	G	107	107	Ÿ	Ydieresis	—	—	†	dagger	262	—
H	H	110	110	Z	Z	132	132	‡	daggerdbl	263	—
I	I	111	111	Ž	Zcaron	—	—	°	degree	—	260
Í	Iacute	—	315	a	a	141	141	¨	dieresis	310	250
Î	Icircumflex	—	316	á	aacute	—	341	÷	divide	—	367
Ï	Idieresis	—	317	â	acircumflex	—	342	$	dollar	044	044
Ì	Igrave	—	314	´	acute	302	222	˙	dotaccent	307	227
J	J	112	112	´	acute	302	264	ı	dotlessi	365	220
K	K	113	113	ä	adieresis	—	344	e	e	145	145
L	L	114	114	æ	ae	361	346	é	eacute	—	351
Ł	Lslash	350	—	à	agrave	—	340	ê	ecircumflex	—	352
M	M	115	115	&	ampersand	046	046	ë	edieresis	—	353
N	N	116	116	å	aring	—	345	è	egrave	—	350
Ñ	Ntilde	—	321	^	asciicircum	136	136	8	eight	070	070
O	O	117	117	~	asciitilde	176	176	…	ellipsis	274	—
Œ	OE	352	—	*	asterisk	052	052	—	emdash	320	—
Ó	Oacute	—	323	@	at	100	100	–	endash	261	—
Ô	Ocircumflex	—	324	ã	atilde	—	343	=	equal	075	075
Ö	Odieresis	—	326	b	b	142	142	ð	eth	—	360
Ò	Ograve	—	322	\	backslash	134	134	!	exclam	041	041

Char	Name	Code (octal) Std	ISO	Char	Name	Code (octal) Std	ISO	Char	Name	Code (octal) Std	ISO
¡	exclamdown	241	241	o	o	157	157	s	s	163	163
f	f	146	146	ó	oacute	—	363	š	scaron	—	—
fi	fi	256	—	ô	ocircumflex	—	364	§	section	247	247
5	five	065	065	ö	odieresis	—	366	;	semicolon	073	073
fl	fl	257	—	œ	oe	372	—	7	seven	067	067
ƒ	florin	246	—	˛	ogonek	316	236	6	six	066	066
4	four	064	064	ò	ograve	—	362	/	slash	057	057
⁄	fraction	244	—	1	one	061	061		space	040	040
g	g	147	147	½	onehalf	—	275	£	sterling	243	243
ß	germandbls	373	337	¼	onequarter	—	274	t	t	164	164
`	grave	301	221	¹	onesuperior	—	271	þ	thorn	—	376
>	greater	076	076	ª	ordfeminine	343	252	3	three	063	063
«	guillemotleft	253	253	º	ordmasculine	353	272	¾	threequarters	—	276
»	guillemotright	273	273	ø	oslash	371	370	³	threesuperior	—	263
‹	guilsinglleft	254	—	õ	otilde	—	365	˜	tilde	304	224
›	guilsinglright	255	—	p	p	160	160	™	trademark	—	—
h	h	150	150	¶	paragraph	266	266	2	two	062	062
˝	hungarumlaut	315	235	(	parenleft	050	050	²	twosuperior	—	262
-	hyphen	055	255	)	parenright	051	051	u	u	165	165
i	i	151	151	%	percent	045	045	ú	uacute	—	372
í	iacute	—	355	.	period	056	056	û	ucircumflex	—	373
î	icircumflex	—	356	·	periodcentered	264	267	ü	udieresis	—	374
ï	idieresis	—	357	‰	perthousand	275	—	ù	ugrave	—	371
ì	igrave	—	354	+	plus	053	053	_	underscore	137	137
j	j	152	152	±	plusminus	—	261	v	v	166	166
k	k	153	153	q	q	161	161	w	w	167	167
l	l	154	154	?	question	077	077	x	x	170	170
<	less	074	074	¿	questiondown	277	277	y	y	171	171
¬	logicalnot	—	254	"	quotedbl	042	042	ý	yacute	—	375
ł	lslash	370	—	„	quotedblbase	271	—	ÿ	ydieresis	—	377
m	m	155	155	"	quotedblleft	252	—	¥	yen	245	245
¯	macron	305	257	"	quotedblright	272	—	z	z	172	172
–	minus	—	055	'	quoteleft	140	140	ž	zcaron	—	—
µ	mu	—	265	'	quoteright	047	047	0	zero	060	060
×	multiply	—	327	‚	quotesinglbase	270	—				
n	n	156	156	'	quotesingle	251	—				
9	nine	071	071	r	r	162	162				
ñ	ntilde	—	361	®	registered	—	256				
#	numbersign	043	043	°	ring	312	232				

E.6 StandardEncoding Encoding Vector

octal	0	1	2	3	4	5	6	7
\00x								
\01x								
\02x								
\03x								
\04x		!	"	#	$	%	&	'
\05x	(	)	*	+	,	-	.	/
\06x	0	1	2	3	4	5	6	7
\07x	8	9	:	;	<	=	>	?
\10x	@	A	B	C	D	E	F	G
\11x	H	I	J	K	L	M	N	O
\12x	P	Q	R	S	T	U	V	W
\13x	X	Y	Z	[	\	]	^	_
\14x	'	a	b	c	d	e	f	g
\15x	h	i	j	k	l	m	n	o
\16x	p	q	r	s	t	u	v	w
\17x	x	y	z	{	|	}	~	
\20x								
\21x								
\22x								
\23x								
\24x		¡	¢	£	/	¥	f	§
\25x	¤	'	"	«	‹	›	fi	fl
\26x		–	†	‡	·		¶	•
\27x	‚	„	"	»	…	‰		¿
\30x		`	´	^	~	¯	˘	˙
\31x	¨		°	¸		˝	˛	ˇ
\32x	—							
\33x								
\34x		Æ		ª				
\35x	Ł	Ø	Œ	º				
\36x		æ				ı		
\37x	ł	ø	œ	ß				

E.7 ISOLatin1Encoding Encoding Vector

octal	0	1	2	3	4	5	6	7
\00x								
\01x								
\02x								
\03x								
\04x		!	"	#	$	%	&	'
\05x	(	)	*	+	,	−	.	/
\06x	0	1	2	3	4	5	6	7
\07x	8	9	:	;	<	=	>	?
\10x	@	A	B	C	D	E	F	G
\11x	H	I	J	K	L	M	N	O
\12x	P	Q	R	S	T	U	V	W
\13x	X	Y	Z	[	\	]	^	_
\14x	`	a	b	c	d	e	f	g
\15x	h	i	j	k	l	m	n	o
\16x	p	q	r	s	t	u	v	w
\17x	x	y	z	{	|	}	~	
\20x								
\21x								
\22x	1	`	´	^	~	¯	˘	˙
\23x	¨		°	˛		˝	˚	ˇ
\24x		¡	¢	£	¤	¥	¦	§
\25x	¨	©	ª	«	¬	-	®	¯
\26x	°	±	²	³	´	µ	¶	·
\27x	¸	¹	º	»	¼	½	¾	¿
\30x	À	Á	Â	Ã	Ä	Å	Æ	Ç
\31x	È	É	Ê	Ë	Ì	Í	Î	Ï
\32x	Ð	Ñ	Ò	Ó	Ô	Õ	Ö	×
\33x	Ø	Ù	Ú	Û	Ü	Ý	Þ	ß
\34x	à	á	â	ã	ä	å	æ	ç
\35x	è	é	ê	ë	ì	í	î	ï
\36x	ð	ñ	ò	ó	ô	õ	ö	÷
\37x	ø	ù	ú	û	ü	ý	þ	ÿ

E.8 Expert Character Set

Char	Name	Code	Char	Name	Code	Char	Name	Code
Æ	AEsmall	346	¯	Macronsmall	257	¢	centoldstyle	242
Á	Aacutesmall	341	M	Msmall	155	¢	centsuperior	103
Â	Acircumflexsmall	342	N	Nsmall	156	:	colon	072
´	Acutesmall	047	Ñ	Ntildesmall	361	₡	colonmonetary	173
Ä	Adieresissmall	344	Œ	OEsmall	367	,	comma	054
À	Agravesmall	340	Ó	Oacutesmall	363	,	commainferior	337
Å	Aringsmall	345	Ô	Ocircumflexsmall	364	'	commasuperior	074
A	Asmall	141	Ö	Odieresissmall	366	$	dollarinferior	335
Ã	Atildesmall	343	˛	Ogoneksmall	266	$	dollaroldstyle	044
˘	Brevesmall	251	Ò	Ogravesmall	362	$	dollarsuperior	045
B	Bsmall	142	Ø	Oslashsmall	370	d	dsuperior	104
ˇ	Caronsmall	252	O	Osmall	157	8	eightinferior	332
Ç	Ccedillasmall	347	Õ	Otildesmall	365	8	eightoldstyle	070
¸	Cedillasmall	270	P	Psmall	160	8	eightsuperior	320
ˆ	Circumflexsmall	136	Q	Qsmall	161	e	esuperior	105
C	Csmall	143	°	Ringsmall	267	i	exclamdownsmall	241
¨	Dieresissmall	250	R	Rsmall	162	!	exclamsmall	041
˙	Dotaccentsmall	254	Š	Scaronsmall	246	ff	ff	126
D	Dsmall	144	S	Ssmall	163	ffi	ffi	131
É	Eacutesmall	351	Þ	Thornsmall	376	ffl	ffl	132
Ê	Ecircumflexsmall	352	˜	Tildesmall	176	fi	fi	127
Ë	Edieresissmall	353	T	Tsmall	164	–	figuredash	262
È	Egravesmall	350	Ú	Uacutesmall	372	⅝	fiveeighths	302
E	Esmall	145	Û	Ucircumflexsmall	373	5	fiveinferior	327
Ð	Ethsmall	360	Ü	Udieresissmall	374	5	fiveoldstyle	065
F	Fsmall	146	Ù	Ugravesmall	371	5	fivesuperior	315
`	Gravesmall	140	U	Usmall	165	fl	fl	130
G	Gsmall	147	V	Vsmall	166	4	fourinferior	326
H	Hsmall	150	W	Wsmall	167	4	fouroldstyle	064
˝	Hungarumlautsmall	042	X	Xsmall	170	4	foursuperior	314
Í	Iacutesmall	355	Ý	Yacutesmall	375	/	fraction	057
Î	Icircumflexsmall	356	Ÿ	Ydieresissmall	377	-	hyphen	055
Ï	Idieresissmall	357	Y	Ysmall	171	-	hypheninferior	263
Ì	Igravesmall	354	Ž	Zcaronsmall	247	ˉ	hyphensuperior	137
I	Ismall	151	Z	Zsmall	172	i	isuperior	111
J	Jsmall	152	&	ampersandsmall	046	l	lsuperior	114
K	Ksmall	153	a	asuperior	101	m	msuperior	115
Ł	Lslashsmall	243	b	bsuperior	102	9	nineinferior	333
L	Lsmall	154	¢	centinferior	334	9	nineoldstyle	071

Char	Name	Code	Char	Name	Code	Char	Name	Code
9	ninesuperior	321	.	period	056	s	ssuperior	123
n	nsuperior	116	.	periodinferior	336	⅜	threeeighths	301
.	onedotenleader	053	·	periodsuperior	076	3	threeinferior	325
⅛	oneeighth	300	¿	questiondownsmall	277	3	threeoldstyle	063
1	onefitted	174	?	questionsmall	077	¾	threequarters	276
½	onehalf	275	r	rsuperior	122	—	threequartersemdash	075
1	oneinferior	323	Rp	rupiah	175	3	threesuperior	313
I	oneoldstyle	061	;	semicolon	073	t	tsuperior	124
¼	onequarter	274	⅞	seveneighths	303	..	twodotenleader	052
1	onesuperior	311	7	seveninferior	331	2	twoinferior	324
⅓	onethird	304	7	sevenoldstyle	067	2	twooldstyle	062
o	osuperior	117	7	sevensuperior	317	2	twosuperior	312
(	parenleftinferior	133	6	sixinferior	330	⅔	twothirds	305
(	parenleftsuperior	050	6	sixoldstyle	066	0	zeroinferior	322
)	parenrightinferior	135	6	sixsuperior	316	0	zerooldstyle	060
)	parenrightsuperior	051		space	040	0	zerosuperior	310

E.9　Expert Encoding Vector

octal	0	1	2	3	4	5	6	7
\00x								
\01x								
\02x								
\03x								
\04x		!	″		$	$	&	'
\05x	(	)	..	.	,	-	.	/
\06x	o	I	2	3	4	5	6	7
\07x	8	9	:	;	'	—	.	?
\10x		a	b	¢	d	e		
\11x		i			l	m	n	o
\12x			r	s	t		ff	fi
\13x	fl	ffi	ffl	(		)	^	-
\14x	`	A	B	C	D	E	F	G
\15x	H	I	J	K	L	M	N	O
\16x	P	Q	R	S	T	U	V	W
\17x	X	Y	Z	₡	1	Rp	˘	
\20x								
\21x								
\22x								
\23x								
\24x		¡	¢	Ł			Š	Ž
\25x	¨	˘	ˇ		·			-
\26x			–	-			‛	°
\27x	‚				¼	½	¾	¿
\30x	⅛	⅜	⅝	⅞	⅓	⅔		
\31x	0	1	2	3	4	5	6	7
\32x	8	9	0	1	2	3	4	5
\33x	6	7	8	9	¢	$	.	,
\34x	À	Á	Â	Ã	Ä	Å	Æ	Ç
\35x	È	É	Ê	Ë	Ì	Í	Î	Ï
\36x	Đ	Ñ	Ò	Ó	Ô	Õ	Ö	Œ
\37x	Ø	Ù	Ú	Û	Ü	Ý	Þ	Ÿ

E.10 ExpertSubset Encoding Vector

octal	0	1	2	3	4	5	6	7
\00x								
\01x								
\02x								
\03x								
\04x					$	$		
\05x	(	)	..	.	,	-	.	/
\06x	0	1	2	3	4	5	6	7
\07x	8	9	:	;	'	—	.	
\10x		a	b	c	d	e		
\11x		i			l	m	n	o
\12x			r	s	t		ff	fi
\13x	fl	ffi	ffl	(		)		-
\14x								
\15x								
\16x								
\17x				₵	1	Rp		
\20x								
\21x								
\22x								
\23x								
\24x			¢					
\25x								
\26x			—	-				
\27x					¼	½	¾	
\30x	⅛	⅜	⅝	⅞	⅓	⅔		
\31x	0	1	2	3	4	5	6	7
\32x	8	9	0	1	2	3	4	5
\33x	6	7	8	9	¢	$	.	,
\34x								
\35x								
\36x								
\37x								

E.11   Symbol Character Set

Char	Name	Code	Char	Name	Code	Char	Name	Code
A	Alpha	101	⇑	arrowdblup	335	δ	delta	144
B	Beta	102	↓	arrowdown	257	♦	diamond	250
X	Chi	103	—	arrowhorizex	276	÷	divide	270
Δ	Delta	104	←	arrowleft	254	·	dotmath	327
E	Epsilon	105	→	arrowright	256	8	eight	070
H	Eta	110	↑	arrowup	255	∈	element	316
Γ	Gamma	107			arrowvertex	275	…	ellipsis	274
ℑ	Ifraktur	301	*	asteriskmath	052	∅	emptyset	306
I	Iota	111	|	bar	174	ε	epsilon	145
K	Kappa	113	β	beta	142	=	equal	075
Λ	Lambda	114	{	braceleft	173	≡	equivalence	272
M	Mu	115	}	braceright	175	η	eta	150
N	Nu	116	⎧	bracelefttp	354	!	exclam	041
Ω	Omega	127	⎨	braceleftmid	355	∃	existential	044
O	Omicron	117	⎩	braceleftbt	356	5	five	065
Φ	Phi	106	⎫	bracerighttp	374	ƒ	florin	246
Π	Pi	120	⎬	bracerightmid	375	4	four	064
Ψ	Psi	131	⎭	bracerightbt	376	⁄	fraction	244
ℜ	Rfraktur	302	|	braceex	357	γ	gamma	147
P	Rho	122	[	bracketleft	133	∇	gradient	321
Σ	Sigma	123	]	bracketright	135	>	greater	076
T	Tau	124	⎡	bracketlefttp	351	≥	greaterequal	263
Θ	Theta	121	⎢	bracketleftex	352	♥	heart	251
Y	Upsilon	125	⎣	bracketleftbt	353	∞	infinity	245
ϒ	Upsilon1	241	⎤	bracketrighttp	371	∫	integral	362
Ξ	Xi	130	⎥	bracketrightex	372	⌠	integraltp	363
Z	Zeta	132	⎦	bracketrightbt	373	⎮	integralex	364
ℵ	aleph	300	•	bullet	267	⌡	integralbt	365
α	alpha	141	↵	carriagereturn	277	∩	intersection	307
&	ampersand	046	χ	chi	143	ι	iota	151
∠	angle	320	⊗	circlemultiply	304	κ	kappa	153
⟨	angleleft	341	⊕	circleplus	305	λ	lambda	154
⟩	angleright	361	♣	club	247	<	less	074
≈	approxequal	273	:	colon	072	≤	lessequal	243
↔	arrowboth	253	,	comma	054	∧	logicaland	331
⇔	arrowdblboth	333	≅	congruent	100	¬	logicalnot	330
⇓	arrowdbldown	337	©	copyrightsans	343	∨	logicalor	332
⇐	arrowdblleft	334	©	copyrightserif	323	◊	lozenge	340
⇒	arrowdblright	336	°	degree	260	−	minus	055

Char	Name	Code	Char	Name	Code	Char	Name	Code
′	minute	242	⊥	perpendicular	136	~	similar	176
μ	mu	155	φ	phi	146	6	six	066
×	multiply	264	φ	phi1	152	/	slash	057
9	nine	071	π	pi	160		space	040
∉	notelement	317	+	plus	053	♠	spade	252
≠	notequal	271	±	plusminus	261	϶	suchthat	047
⊄	notsubset	313	∏	product	325	Σ	summation	345
ν	nu	156	⊂	propersubset	314	τ	tau	164
#	numbersign	043	⊃	propersuperset	311	∴	therefore	134
ω	omega	167	∝	proportional	265	θ	theta	161
ϖ	omega1	166	ψ	psi	171	ϑ	theta1	112
o	omicron	157	?	question	077	3	three	063
1	one	061	√	radical	326	™	trademarksans	344
(	parenleft	050	‾	radicalex	140	™	trademarkserif	324
)	parenright	051	⊆	reflexsubset	315	2	two	062
⌈	parenlefttp	346	⊇	reflexsuperset	312	_	underscore	137
⎜	parenleftex	347	®	registersans	342	∪	union	310
⌊	parenleftbt	350	®	registerserif	322	∀	universal	042
⌉	parenrighttp	366	ρ	rho	162	υ	upsilon	165
⎟	parenrightex	367	″	second	262	℘	weierstrass	303
⌋	parenrightbt	370	;	semicolon	073	ξ	xi	170
∂	partialdiff	266	7	seven	067	0	zero	060
%	percent	045	σ	sigma	163	ζ	zeta	172
.	period	056	ς	sigma1	126			

E.12 Symbol Encoding Vector

octal	0	1	2	3	4	5	6	7
\00x								
\01x								
\02x								
\03x								
\04x		!	∀	#	∃	%	&	϶
\05x	(	)	*	+	,	−	.	/
\06x	0	1	2	3	4	5	6	7
\07x	8	9	:	;	<	=	>	?
\10x	≅	A	B	Χ	Δ	E	Φ	Γ
\11x	H	I	ϑ	K	Λ	M	N	O
\12x	Π	Θ	P	Σ	T	Y	ς	Ω
\13x	Ξ	Ψ	Z	[	∴	]	⊥	_
\14x	‾	α	β	χ	δ	ε	φ	γ
\15x	η	ι	φ	κ	λ	μ	ν	o
\16x	π	θ	ρ	σ	τ	υ	ϖ	ω
\17x	ξ	ψ	ζ	{	|	}	~	
\20x								
\21x								
\22x								
\23x								
\24x		ϒ	′	≤	/	∞	f	♣
\25x	♦	♥	♠	↔	←	↑	→	↓
\26x	°	±	″	≥	×	∝	∂	•
\27x	÷	≠	≡	≈	…	|	—	↵
\30x	ℵ	ℑ	ℜ	℘	⊗	⊕	∅	∩
\31x	∪	⊃	⊇	⊄	⊂	⊆	∈	∉
\32x	∠	∇	®	©	™	∏	√	·
\33x	¬	∧	∨	⇔	⇐	⇑	⇒	⇓
\34x	◊	⟨	®	©	™	Σ	⌠	|
\35x	⎮	⌈	⎮	⌊	⌈	{	⎮	|
\36x		⟩	∫	⌠	|	⌡	⟩	|
\37x	⎮	⌉	|	⌋	⌉	}	⎮	

System Name Encodings

Index	Name	Index	Name
0	abs	31	currentfile
1	add	32	currentfont
2	aload	33	currentgray
3	anchorsearch	34	currentgstate
4	and	35	currenthsbcolor
5	arc	36	currentlinecap
6	arcn	37	currentlinejoin
7	arct	38	currentlinewidth
8	arcto	39	currentmatrix
9	array	40	currentpoint
10	ashow	41	currentrgbcolor
11	astore	42	currentshared
12	awidthshow	43	curveto
13	begin	44	cvi
14	bind	45	cvlit
15	bitshift	46	cvn
16	ceiling	47	cvr
17	charpath	48	cvrs
18	clear	49	cvs
19	cleartomark	50	cvx
20	clip	51	def
21	clippath	52	defineusername
22	closepath	53	dict
23	concat	54	div
24	concatmatrix	55	dtransform
25	copy	56	dup
26	count	57	end
27	counttomark	58	eoclip
28	currentcmykcolor	59	eofill
29	currentdash	60	eoviewclip
30	currentdict	61	eq

62	exch	106	mod	150	setgray
63	exec	107	moveto	151	setgstate
64	exit	108	mul	152	sethsbcolor
65	file	109	ne	153	setlinecap
66	fill	110	neg	154	setlinejoin
67	findfont	111	newpath	155	setlinewidth
68	flattenpath	112	not	156	setmatrix
69	floor	113	null	157	setrgbcolor
70	flush	114	or	158	setshared
71	flushfile	115	pathbbox	159	shareddict
72	for	116	pathforall	160	show
73	forall	117	pop	161	showpage
74	ge	118	print	162	stop
75	get	119	printobject	163	stopped
76	getinterval	120	put	164	store
77	grestore	121	putinterval	165	string
78	gsave	122	rcurveto	166	stringwidth
79	gstate	123	read	167	stroke
80	gt	124	readhexstring	168	strokepath
81	identmatrix	125	readline	169	sub
82	idiv	126	readstring	170	systemdict
83	idtransform	127	rectclip	171	token
84	if	128	rectfill	172	transform
85	ifelse	129	rectstroke	173	translate
86	image	130	rectviewclip	174	truncate
87	imagemask	131	repeat	175	type
88	index	132	restore	176	uappend
89	ineofill	133	rlineto	177	ucache
90	infill	134	rmoveto	178	ueofill
91	initviewclip	135	roll	179	ufill
92	inueofill	136	rotate	180	undef
93	inufill	137	round	181	upath
94	invertmatrix	138	save	182	userdict
95	itransform	139	scale	183	ustroke
96	known	140	scalefont	184	viewclip
97	le	141	search	185	viewclippath
98	length	142	selectfont	186	where
99	lineto	143	setbbox	187	widthshow
100	load	144	setcachedevice	188	write
101	loop	145	setcachedevice2	189	writehexstring
102	lt	146	setcharwidth	190	writeobject
103	makefont	147	setcmykcolor	191	writestring
104	matrix	148	setdash	192	wtranslation
105	maxlength	149	setfont	193	xor

194	xshow	268	condition	312	inustroke
195	xyshow	269	copypage	313	join
196	yshow	270	cos	314	kshow
197	FontDirectory	271	countdictstack	315	ln
198	SharedFontDirectory	272	countexecstack	316	lock
199	Courier	273	cshow	317	log
200	Courier-Bold	274	currentblackgeneration	318	mark
201	Courier-BoldOblique	275	currentcacheparams	319	monitor
202	Courier-Oblique	276	currentcolorscreen	320	noaccess
203	Helvetica	277	currentcolortransfer	321	notify
204	Helvetica-Bold	278	currentcontext	322	nulldevice
205	Helvetica-BoldOblique	279	currentflat	323	packedarray
206	Helvetica-Oblique	280	currenthalftone	324	quit
207	Symbol	281	currenthalftonephase	325	rand
208	Times-Bold	282	currentmiterlimit	326	rcheck
209	Times-BoldItalic	283	currentobjectformat	327	readonly
210	Times-Italic	284	currentpacking	328	realtime
211	Times-Roman	285	currentscreen	329	renamefile
212	execuserobject	286	currentstrokeadjust	330	renderbands
213	currentcolor	287	currenttransfer	331	resetfile
214	currentcolorspace	288	currentundercolorremoval	332	reversepath
215	currentglobal	289	defaultmatrix	333	rootfont
216	execform	290	definefont	334	rrand
217	filter	291	deletefile	335	run
218	findresource	292	detach	336	scheck
219	globaldict	293	deviceinfo	337	setblackgeneration
220	makepattern	294	dictstack	338	setcachelimit
221	setcolor	295	echo	339	setcacheparams
222	setcolorspace	296	erasepage	340	setcolorscreen
223	setglobal	297	errordict	341	setcolortransfer
224	setpagedevice	298	execstack	342	setfileposition
225	setpattern	299	executeonly	343	setflat
256	=	300	exp	344	sethalftone
257	==	301	false	345	sethalftonephase
258	ISOLatin1Encoding	302	filenameforall	346	setmiterlimit
259	StandardEncoding	303	fileposition	347	setobjectformat
260	[	304	fork	348	setpacking
261	]	305	framedevice	349	setscreen
262	atan	306	grestoreall	350	setstrokeadjust
263	banddevice	307	handleerror	351	settransfer
264	bytesavailable	308	initclip	352	setucacheparams
265	cachestatus	309	initgraphics	353	setundercolorremoval
266	closefile	310	initmatrix	354	sin
267	colorimage	311	instroke	355	sqrt

356	srand	400	Y	444	resourceforall
357	stack	401	Z	445	resourcestatus
358	status	402	a	446	revision
359	statusdict	403	b	447	serialnumber
360	true	404	c	448	setcolorrendering
361	ucachestatus	405	d	449	setdevparams
362	undefinefont	406	e	450	setoverprint
363	usertime	407	f	451	setsystemparams
364	ustrokepath	408	g	452	setuserparams
365	version	409	h	453	startjob
366	vmreclaim	410	i	454	undefineresource
367	vmstatus	411	j	455	GlobalFontDirectory
368	wait	412	k	456	ASCII85Decode
369	wcheck	413	l	457	ASCII85Encode
370	xcheck	414	m	458	ASCIIHexDecode
371	yield	415	n	459	ASCIIHexEncode
372	defineuserobject	416	o	460	CCITTFaxDecode
373	undefineuserobject	417	p	461	CCITTFaxEncode
374	UserObjects	418	q	462	DCTDecode
375	cleardictstack	419	r	463	DCTEncode
376	A	420	s	464	LZWDecode
377	B	421	t	465	LZWEncode
378	C	422	u	466	NullEncode
379	D	423	v	467	RunLengthDecode
380	E	424	w	468	RunLengthEncode
381	F	425	x	469	SubFileDecode
382	G	426	y	470	CIEBasedA
383	H	427	z	471	CIEBasedABC
384	I	428	setvmthreshold	472	DeviceCMYK
385	J	429	<<	473	DeviceGray
386	K	430	>>	474	DeviceRGB
387	L	431	currentcolorrendering	475	Indexed
388	M	432	currentdevparams	476	Pattern
389	N	433	currentoverprint	477	Separation
390	O	434	currentpagedevice		
391	P	435	currentsystemparams		
392	Q	436	currentuserparams		
393	R	437	defineresource		
394	S	438	findencoding		
395	T	439	gcheck		
396	U	440	glyphshow		
397	V	441	languagelevel		
398	W	442	product		
399	X	443	pstack		

Document Structuring Conventions—Version 3.0

As discussed in Chapter 3, the PostScript language standard does not specify the overall structure of a PostScript language program. Any sequence of tokens conforming to the syntax and semantics of the PostScript language is a valid program that may be presented to a PostScript interpreter for execution.

For a PostScript language program that is a page description (in other words, a description of a printable document), it is often advantageous to impose an overall program structure.

A page description can be organized as a prolog and a script, as discussed in section 2.4.2, "Program Structure." The prolog contains application-dependent definitions. The script describes the particular desired results in terms of those definitions. The prolog is written by a programmer, stored in a place accessible to an application program, and incorporated as a standard preface to each page description created by the application. The script is usually generated automatically by an application program.

Beyond this simple convention, this appendix defines a standard set of document structuring conventions (DSC). Use of the document structuring conventions not only helps assure that a document is device independent, it allows PostScript language programs to communicate their document structure and printing requirements to *document managers* in a way that does not affect the PostScript language page description.

A document manager can be thought of as an application that manipulates the PostScript language document based on the document structuring conventions found in it. In essence, a document manager accepts one or more PostScript language programs as input, transforms them in some way, and produces a PostScript language program as output. Examples of document managers include print spoolers, font and other resource servers, post-processors, utility programs, and toolkits.

If a PostScript language document properly communicates its structure and requirements to a document manager, it can receive certain *printing services*. A document manager can offer different types of services to a document. If the document in question does not conform to the DSC, some or all of these services may be denied to it.

Specially formatted PostScript language comments communicate the document structure to the document manager. Within any PostScript language document, any occurrence of the character % *not* inside a PostScript language string introduces a *comment*. The comment consists of all characters between the % and the next newline, including regular, special, space, and tab characters. The scanner ignores comments, treating each one as if it were a single white-space character. DSC comments, which are legal PostScript language comments, do not affect the destination interpreter in any manner.

DSC comments are specified by two percent characters (%%) as the first characters on a line (no leading white space). These characters are immediately followed by a unique keyword describing that particular comment—again, no white space. The keyword always starts with a capital letter and is almost always mixed-case. For example:

```
%%BoundingBox: 0 0 612 792
%%Pages: 45
%%BeginSetup
```

Note that some keywords end with a colon (considered to be part of the keyword), which signifies that the keyword is further qualified by options or arguments. There should be one space character between the ending colon of a keyword and its subsequent arguments.

The PostScript language was designed to be inherently device independent. However, there are specific physical features that an output device may have that certain PostScript operators activate (in Level 1 implementations many of these operators are found in **statusdict**). Examples of device-dependent operators are **legal**, **letter**, and **setsoftwareiomode**. Use of these operators can render a document *device dependent*; that is, the document images properly on one type of device and not on others.

Use of DSC comments such as %%BeginFeature:, %%EndFeature (note that the colon is part of the first comment and that this comment pair is often referred to as %%Begin(End)Feature) and %%IncludeFeature: can help reduce device dependency if a document manager is available to recognize these comments and act upon them.

The DSC are designed to work with *PostScript printer description* (PPD) files, which provide the PostScript language extensions for specific printer features in a regular parsable format. PPD files include information about printer-specific features, and include information about the fonts built into the ROM of each printer. The DSC work in tandem with PPD files to provide a way to specify and invoke these printer features in a *device-independent* manner. For more information about PPD files, see the *PostScript Printer Description Files Specification* available from the Adobe Systems Developers' Association.

Note   *Even though the DSC comments are a layer of communication beyond the PostScript language and do not affect the final output, their use is considered to be good PostScript language programming style.*

G.1 Using the Document Structuring Conventions

Ideally, a document composition system should be able to compose a document regardless of available resources—for example, font availability and paper sizes. It should be able to rely on the document management system at printing time to determine the availability of the resources and give the user reasonable alternatives if those resources are not available.

Realistically, an operating environment may or may not provide a document management system. Consequently, the DSC contain some redundancy. There are two philosophically distinct ways a resource or printer-specific feature might be specified:

- The document composition system *trusts* its environment to handle the resource and feature requirements appropriately, and merely specifies what its particular requirements are.

- The document composer may not know what the network environment holds or even that one exists, and *includes* the necessary resources and printer-specific PostScript language instructions within the document. In creating such a document, the document composer delimits these included resources or instructions in such a way that a document manager can recognize and manipulate them.

It is up to the software developer to determine which of these methods is appropriate for a given environment. In some cases, both may be used.

These two methods are mirrored in the DSC comments:

- Many DSC comments provide %%Begin and %%End constructs for identifying resources and printer-specific elements of a document. The document then prints regardless of whether a document manager is present or not.

- Many of the requirement conventions provide a mechanism to specify a need for some resource or printer-specific feature through the use of %%Include comments, and leave the inclusion of the resource or invocation of the feature to the document manager. This is an example of complete network cooperation, where a document can forestall some printing decisions and pass them to the next layer of document management. In general, this latter approach is the preferred one.

G.2   Document Manager Services

A document manager can provide a wide variety of services. The types of services are grouped into five management categories: spool, resource, error, print, and page management. The DSC help facilitate these services. A document that conforms to this specification can expect to receive any of these services, if available; one that does not conform may not receive any service. Listed below are some of the services that belong to each of these categories.

G.2.1   Spool Management

Spooling management services are the most basic services that a document manager can perform. A category of DSC comments known as general conventions—specifically the header comments—provide information concerning the document's creator, title, pages, and routing information.

Spooling

The basic function of spool management is to deliver the document to the specified printer or display. The document manager should establish queues for each device to handle print job traffic in an effective manner, giving many users access to one device. In addition, the document manager should notify the user of device status (busy/idle, jammed, out of paper, waiting) and queue status (held, waiting, printing). More advanced document managers can offer job priorities and delayed-time printing.

Banner and Trailer Pages

As a part of spool management, a document manager can add a banner or trailer page to the beginning or end, respectively, of each print job to separate the output in the printer bin. The document manager can parse information from the DSC comments to produce a proper banner that includes the title, creator, creation date, the number of pages, and routing information of the document.

Print Logging

If a document manager tracks the number of pages, the type of media used, and the job requirements for each document, the document manager can produce a comprehensive report on a regular basis detailing paper and printer usage. This can help a systems administrator plan paper purchases and estimate printing costs. Individual reports for users can serve as a way to bill internally for printing.

G.2.2 Resource Management

Resource management services deal with the inclusion, caching, and manipulation of resources, such as fonts, forms, files, patterns, and documents. A category of DSC comments, known as requirement conventions, enables a document manager to properly identify instances in the document when resources are either needed or supplied.

Resource Inclusion

Frequently used resources, such as company logos, copyright notices, special fonts, and standard forms, can take up vast amounts of storage space if they are duplicated in a large number of documents. The DSC support special %%Include comments so a document manager can include a resource at print time, saving disk space.

Supplied resources can be cached in a resource library for later use. For example, a document manager that identifies a frequently used logo while processing a page description subsequently stores the logo in a resource library. The document manager then prints the document normally. When future %%IncludeResource: comments are found in succeeding documents, the document manager retrieves the PostScript language program for the logo from the resource library. The program is inserted into the document at the position indicated by the DSC comment before the document is sent to the printer.

Resource Downloading

Another valuable service that a document manager can provide is automatically downloading frequently used resources to specific printers so those resources are available instantly. Transmission and print time of documents can be greatly reduced by using this service.

For example, the document manager judges that the Stone-Serif font program is a frequently used resource. It downloads the font program from the resource library to the printer. Later, the document manager receives a document that requests the Stone-Serif font program. The document manager knows this resource is already available in the printer and sends the document to the printer without modification. Note that the resource can be downloaded persistently into VM or onto a hard disk if the printer has one. For Level 2 interpreters, resources are found automatically by the **findresource** operator.

Resource Optimization

An intelligent document manager can alter the position of included resources within a document to optimize memory and/or resource usage. For example, if an encapsulated PostScript (EPS) file is included several times in a document, the document manager can move duplicate *procedure set definitions* (procsets) to the top of the document to reduce transmission time. If a document manager performs dynamic resource positioning, it must maintain the relative order of the resources to preserve any interdependencies among them.

G.2.3 Error Management

A document manager can provide advanced error reporting and recovery services. By downloading a special error handler to the printer, the document manager can detect failed print jobs and isolate error-producing lines of PostScript language instructions. It can send this information, a descriptive error message, and suggestions for solution back to the user.

There may be other instances where a document manager can recover from certain types of errors. Resource substitution services can be offered to the user. For example, if your document requests the Stone-Serif font program and this font program is not available on the printer or in the resource library, a document manager could select a similar font for substitution.

G.2.4 Print Management

Good print management ensures that the requested printer can fulfill the requirements of a particular document. This is a superset of the spool management spooling function, which is concerned with delivering the print job to the printer regardless of the consequences. By understanding the capabilities of a device and the requirements of a document, a document manager can provide a wide variety of print management services.

Printer Rerouting

A document manager can reroute documents based on printer availability. Heavily loaded printers can have their print jobs off-loaded to different printers in the network. The document manager can also inform a user if a printer is busy and suggest an idle printer for use as a backup.

If a specified printer cannot meet the requirements of a document (if for example, the document requests duplex printing and the printer does not support this feature), the document manager can suggest alternate printers.

For example, a user realizes that a document to be printed on a monochrome printer contains a color page. The user informs the document manager that the document should be rerouted to the color printer. Any printer-specific portions are detected by the document manager via the %%Begin(End)Feature: comments. The document manager consults the appropriate PostScript printer description (PPD) file, the printer-specific portion is replaced in the document, and the document is rerouted to the appropriate queue.

Feature Inclusion

This service is similar in concept to resource inclusion. Instead of using PostScript language instructions that activate certain features of a target printer, an application can use the %%IncludeFeature: comment to specify that a fragment of feature instructions should be included in the document at a specific point. A document manager can recognize such a request, consult the PPD file for the target printer, look for the specified feature, and insert the code into the document before sending it to the printer.

Parallel Printing

Parallel printing, another possible feature of a document manager, is especially useful for large documents or rush orders. Basically, the document manager splits the document based on the %%Page: comment, sending different pieces of the document to different printers simultaneously. The document is printed in parallel.

For example, a user requests that the first 100 pages of a document be printed in parallel on five separate printers. The document manager splits the document into five sections of 20 pages each, replicating the original prolog and document setup for each section. Also, a banner page is specified for each section to identify the pages being printed.

Page Breakout

Color and high-resolution printing are often expensive propositions. It does not make sense to send an entire document to a color printer if the document contains only one color illustration. When the appropriate comments are used, document managers can detect color illustrations and detailed drawings that need to be printed on high resolution printers, and split them from the original document. The document manager sends these pages separately to a high-resolution or color printer, while sending the rest of the document to lower-cost monochrome printers.

G.2.5   Page Management

Page management deals with organizing and reorganizing individual pages in the document. A category of comments known as *page comments* facilitate these services. See section G.4.5, "Convention Categories," for a thorough description of page-level comments.

Page Reversal

Some printers place output in the tray face-up, some face-down. This small distinction can be a nuisance to users who have to reshuffle output into the correct order. Documents that come out of the printer into a face-up tray should be printed last page first; conversely, documents that end up face-down should be printed first page first. A document manager can reorder pages within the document based on the %%Page: comment to produce either of these effects.

n-Up Printing

n-up, thumbnail, and signature printing all fall under this category. This enables the user to produce a document that has multiple *virtual* pages on fewer *physical* pages. This is especially useful when proofing documents, and requires less paper.

For example, suppose a user wants a proof of the first four pages of a document (two copies, because the user's manager is also interested). Two-up printing is specified, where two virtual pages are mapped onto one physical sheet. The document manager adds PostScript language instructions (usually to the document setup section) that will implement this service.

Range Printing

Range printing is useful when documents need not be printed in their entirety. A document manager can isolate the desired pages from the document (using the %%Page: comment and preserving the prolog and document setup) before sending the new document to the printer. In the previous example, the user may want only the first four pages of the document. The document manager determines where the first four pages of the document reside and discards the rest.

Collated Printing

When using the **#copies** or **setpagedevice** features to specify multiple copies, on some printers the pages of the document emerge uncollated (1-1-1-2-2-2-3-3-3). Using the same mechanics as those for range printing, a document manager can print a group of pages multiple times and obtain collated output (1-2-3-1-2-3-1-2-3), saving the user the frustration of hand collating the document.

Underlays

Underlays are text and graphic elements, such as draft and confidential notices, headers, and images, that a document manager can add to a document so they appear on every page. By adding PostScript language instructions to the document setup, each page of the document renders the underlay before drawing the page itself.

G.3   DSC Conformance

The PostScript interpreter does not distinguish between PostScript language page descriptions that do or do not conform to the DSC. However, the structural information communicated through DSC comments is of considerable importance to document managers that operate on PostScript page descriptions as data. Because document managers cannot usually interpret the PostScript language directly, they must rely on the DSC comments to properly manipulate the document. It is necessary to distinguish between those documents that conform to the DSC and those that do not.

Note   *In previous versions of the DSC, there were references to partially conforming documents. This term has caused some confusion and its use has been discontinued. A document either conforms to the conventions or it does not.*

G.3.1   Conforming Documents

A *conforming* document can expect to receive the maximum amount of services from any document manager. A conforming document is recognized by the header comment %!PS-Adobe-3.0 and is optionally followed by keywords indicating the type of document. Please see the description of this comment in section G.5, "General Conventions," for more details about optional keywords.

A fully conforming document is one that adheres to the following rules regarding syntax and semantics, document structure, and the compliance constraints. It is also strongly suggested that documents support certain printing services.

Syntax and Semantics

If a comment is to be used within a document, it must follow the syntactical and semantic rules laid out in this specification for that comment.

Consider the following *incorrect* example:

%%BoundingBox 43.22 50.45 100.60 143.49

This comment is incorrect on two counts. First, there is a colon missing from the %%BoundingBox: comment. Abbreviations for comments are not acceptable. Second, floating point arguments are used instead of the integer arguments this comment requires.

Document Structure

The document structure rules described in section G.4, "Document Structure Rules," must be followed. The following comments delineate the structure of the document. If there is a section of a document that corresponds to a particular comment, that comment *must* be used to identify that section of the document.

```
%!PS-Adobe-3.0
%%Pages:
%%EndComments
%%BeginProlog
%%EndProlog
%%BeginSetup
%%EndSetup
%%Page:
%%BeginPageSetup
%%EndPageSetup
%%PageTrailer
%%Trailer
%%EOF
```

For example, if there are distinct independent pages in a document, the %%Page: comment must be used at the beginning of each page to identify those pages.

Where sections of the structure are not applicable, those sections and their associated comments need not appear in the document. For example, if a document setup is not performed inside a particular document, the %%BeginSetup and %%EndSetup comments are unnecessary. Figure G.1 illustrates the structure of a conforming PostScript language document.

Figure G.1 *Structure of a conforming PostScript language document*

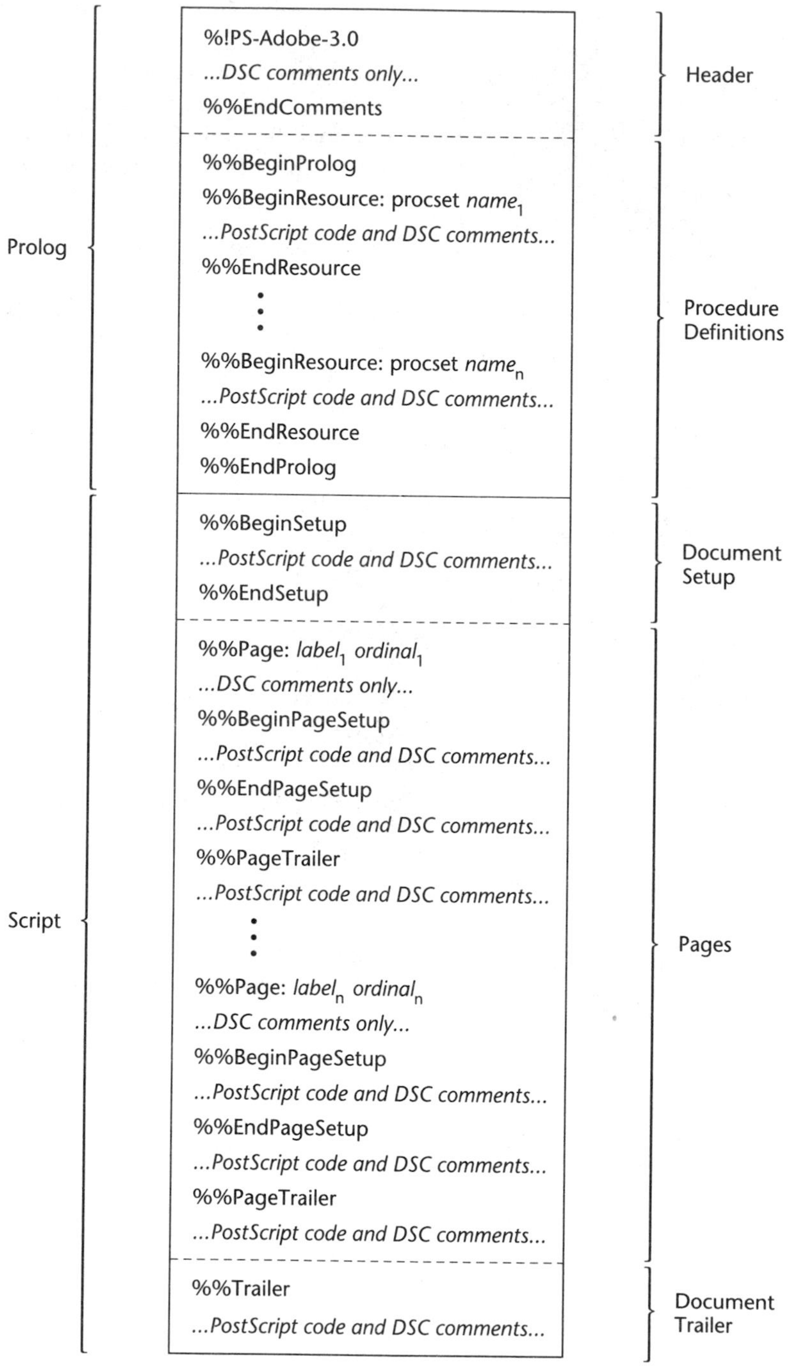

Prolog	**Header** %!PS-Adobe-3.0 *...DSC comments only...* %%EndComments
	Procedure Definitions %%BeginProlog %%BeginResource: procset $name_1$ *...PostScript code and DSC comments...* %%EndResource • • • %%BeginResource: procset $name_n$ *...PostScript code and DSC comments...* %%EndResource %%EndProlog
Script	**Document Setup** %%BeginSetup *...PostScript code and DSC comments...* %%EndSetup
	Pages %%Page: $label_1$ $ordinal_1$ *...DSC comments only...* %%BeginPageSetup *...PostScript code and DSC comments...* %%EndPageSetup *...PostScript code and DSC comments...* %%PageTrailer *...PostScript code and DSC comments...* • • • %%Page: $label_n$ $ordinal_n$ *...DSC comments only...* %%BeginPageSetup *...PostScript code and DSC comments...* %%EndPageSetup *...PostScript code and DSC comments...* %%PageTrailer *...PostScript code and DSC comments...*
	Document Trailer %%Trailer *...PostScript code and DSC comments...*

Compliance Constraints

The compliance constraints described in section G.4.3, "Constraints," including the proper use of restricted operators, *must* be adhered to.

Printing Services

There are document manager printing services (such as those described in section G.2, "Document Manager Services") that can be easily supported and add value to an application. Although it is not a requirement of a conforming document, it is *strongly suggested* that applications support these services by using the comments listed below. Note that 20 comments will ensure support of all services.

Spool Management
(Spooling, Banner and Trailer Pages, and Print Logging)

%%Creator:	%%PageMedia:
%%CreationDate:	%%PageRequirements:
%%DocumentMedia:	%%Requirements:
%%DocumentPrinterRequired:	%%Routing:
%%For:	%%Title:

Resource Management
(Resource Inclusion, Downloading, and Optimization)

%%DocumentNeededResources:	%%IncludeResource:
%%DocumentSuppliedResources:	%%Begin(End)Resource:
%%PageResources:	

Error Management
(Error Reporting and Recovery)

%%Extensions:	%%ProofMode:
%%LanguageLevel:	

Printer Management
(Printer Rerouting, Feature Inclusion, Parallel Printing, Color Breakout)

%%Begin(End)Feature:	%%IncludeFeature:
%%Begin(End)Resource:	%%IncludeResource:
%%DocumentMedia:	%%LanguageLevel:
%%DocumentNeededResources:	%%PageMedia:
%%DocumentPrinterRequired:	%%PageRequirements:
%%DocumentSuppliedResources:	%%PageResources:
%%Extensions:	%%Requirements:

Page Management
(Page Reversal, N-up Printing, Range Printing, Collation, Underlays)

%%Pages:	%%Page:
%%EndComments	%%Begin(End)PageSetup
%%Begin(End)Setup	%%PageTrailer
%%Begin(End)Prolog	%%Trailer

G.3.2   Non-Conforming Documents

A *non-conforming* document most likely will not receive any services from a document manager, may not be able to be included into another document, and may not be portable. In some cases, this may be appropriate; a PostScript language program may require an organization that is incompatible with the DSC. This is especially true of very sophisticated page descriptions composed directly by a programmer.

However, for page descriptions that applications generate automatically, adherence to the structuring conventions is strongly recommended, simple to achieve, and essential in achieving a transparent corporate printing network.

A non-conforming document is recognized by the %! header comment. Under *no* circumstances should a non-conforming document use the %!PS-Adobe-3.0 header comment.

G.4   Document Structure Rules

One of the most important levels of document structuring in the PostScript language is the distinction between the *document prolog* and the *document script*. The *prolog* is typically a set of procedure definitions appropriate for the set of operations a document composition system needs, and the *script* is the software-generated program that represents a particular document.

A *conforming* PostScript language document description must have a clearly defined prolog and script separated by the %%EndProlog comment.

G.4.1   Prolog

The prolog consists of a header section, an optional defaults subsection, and the prolog proper, sometimes known as the procedures section.

The *header section* consists of DSC comments only and describes the environment that is necessary for the document to be output properly. The end of the header section is denoted by the %%EndComments comment (see the note on header comments in section G.4.5, "Convention Categories").

The *defaults section* is an optional section that is used to save space in the document and as an aid to the document manager. The beginning of this section is denoted by the %%BeginDefaults comment. Only DSC page comments should appear in the defaults section. Information on the page-level comments that are applicable and examples of their use can be found in section G.5.2, "General Body Comments" under the definition of %%Begin(End)Defaults. The end of the defaults section is indicated by the %%EndDefaults comment.

The beginning of the *procedures section* is indicated by the %%BeginProlog comment. This section is a series of procedure set (procset) definitions; each procset is enclosed between a %%BeginResource: procset and %%EndResource pair. Procsets are groups of definitions and routines appropriate for different imaging requirements.

The prolog has the following restrictions:

- Executing the prolog should define procsets only. For example, these procsets can consist of abbreviations, generic routines for drawing graphics objects, and routines for managing text and images.

- A document-producing application should almost always use the same prolog for all of its documents, or at least the prolog should be drawn from a pool of common procedure sets. The prolog should always be constructed in a way that it can be removed from the document and downloaded only once into the printer. All subsequent documents that are downloaded with this prolog stripped out should still execute correctly.

- No output can be produced while executing the prolog, no changes can be made to the graphics state, and no marks should be made on the page.

G.4.2   Script

The document *script* consists of three sections: a document setup section, page sections, and a document trailer.

- The *document setup* section is denoted by the %%Begin(End)Setup comments. The document setup should consist of procedure calls for invoking media selections (for example, setting page size), running initialization routines for procsets, downloading a font or other resource, or setting some aspect of the graphics state. This section should appear after the %%EndProlog comment, but before the first %%Page: comment.

- The *pages* section of the script consists of 1 to *n* pages, each of which should be *functionally independent* of the other pages. This means that each page should be able to execute in any order and may be physically rearranged, resulting in an identical document as long as the information within it is the same, but with the physical pages ordered differently. A typical example of this page reordering occurs during a page-reversal operation performed by a document manager.

  The start of each page is denoted by the %%Page: comment and can also contain a %%Begin(End)PageSetup section (analogous to the document setup section on a page level), and an optional %%PageTrailer section (similar to the document trailer). In any event, each page will contain between the setup and the trailer sections the PostScript language program necessary to mark that page.

- The *document trailer* section is indicated by the %%Trailer comment. PostScript language instructions in the trailer consists of calls to termination routines of procedures and post-processing or cleanup instructions. In addition, any header comments that were deferred using the (atend) notation will be found here. See section G.4.6, "Comment Syntax Reference," for a detailed description of (atend).

There are generally few restrictions on the script. It can have definitions like the prolog and it can also modify the graphics environment, draw marks on the page, issue **showpage**, and so on. There are some PostScript language operators that should be avoided or at least used with extreme caution. A thorough discussion of these operators can be found in Appendix I.

The end of a document should be signified by the %%EOF comment.

G.4.3   Constraints

There are several constraints on the use of PostScript language operators in a conforming document. These constraints are detailed below and are not only applicable to documents that conform to the DSC. Even a *non-conforming* document is much more portable across different PostScript interpreters if it observes these constraints.

Page Independence

Pages should not have *any* inter-dependencies. Each page may rely on certain PostScript language operations defined in the document prolog or in the document setup section, but it is not acceptable to have any graphics state set in one page of a document on which another page in the same document relies on. It is also risky to reimpose or rely on a state defined in the document setup section; the graphics state should only be added to or modified, not reimposed. See Appendix I for more details on proper preservation of the graphics state with operators like **settransfer**.

Page independence enables a document manager to rearrange the document's pages physically without affecting the execution of the document description. Other benefits of page independence include the ability to print different pages in parallel on more than one printer and to print ranges of pages. Also, PostScript language previewers need page independence to enable viewing the pages of a document in arbitrary order.

For the most part, page independence can be achieved by placing a **save-restore** pair around each page, as shown below:

```
%!PS-Adobe-3.0
...Header comments, prolog definitions, document setup...
%%Page: cover 1
%%BeginPageSetup
/pgsave save def
...PostScript language instructions to perform page setup...
%%EndPageSetup
...PostScript language instructions to mark page 1...
pgsave restore
showpage
...Rest of the document...
%%EOF
```

The **save-restore** pair will also reclaim any non-global VM used during the page marking (for example, text strings).

Note *If pages must have interdependencies, the %%PageOrder: Special comment should be used. This ensures that a document manager will not attempt to reorder the pages.*

Line Length

To provide compatibility with a large body of existing application and document manager software, a conforming PostScript language document description *does not* have lines exceeding 255 characters, excluding line-termination characters. The intent is to be able to read lines into a 255-character buffer without overflow (Pascal strings are a common example of this sort of buffer).

The PostScript interpreter imposes no constraints as to where line breaks occur, even in string bodies and hexadecimal bitmap representations. This level of conformance should not pose a problem for software development. Any document structuring comment that needs to be continued on another line to avoid violating this guideline should use the %%+ notation to indicate that a comment line is being continued (see %%+ in section G.5.2, "General Body Comments").

Line Endings

Lines *must* be terminated with one of the following combinations of characters: CR, LF, or CR LF. CR is the carriage-return character and LF is the line-feed character (decimal ASCII 13 and 10, respectively).

Use of showpage

To reduce the amount of VM used at any point, it is common practice to delimit PostScript language instructions used for a particular page with a **save-restore** pair. See the page-independence constraint for an example of **save-restore** use.

If the **showpage** operator is used in combination with **save** and **restore**, the **showpage** should occur *after* the page-level **restore** operation. The motivation for this is to redefine the **showpage** operator so it has side effects in the printer VM, such as maintaining page counts for printing *n*-up copies on one sheet of paper. If **showpage** is executed within the confines of a page-level **save-restore**, attempts to redefine **showpage** to perform extra operations will not work as intended. This also applies to the **BeginPage** and **EndPage** parameters of the **setpagedevice** dictionary. The above discussion also applies to **gsave-grestore** pairs.

Document Copies

In a conforming document, the number of copies *must* be modified in the document setup section of the document (see %%BeginSetup and %%EndSetup). Changing the number of copies within a single page automatically breaks the page independence constraint. Also, using the **copypage** operator is not recommended because doing so inhibits page independence. If multiple copies of a document are desired, use the **#copies** key or the **setpagedevice** operator.

In Level 1 implementations, the **#copies** key can be modified to produce multiple copies of a document as follows:

```
%!PS-Adobe-3.0
%%Pages: 23
%%Requirements: numcopies(3) collate
%%EndComments
...Prolog with procset definitions...
%%EndProlog
%%BeginSetup
/#copies 3 def
%%EndSetup
...Rest of the Document (23 virtual pages)...
%%EOF
```

In Level 2 implementations, the number of copies of a document can be set using the **setpagedevice** operator as follows:

```
<< /NumCopies 3 >> setpagedevice
```

The %%Pages: comment should not be modified if the number of copies is set, as it represents the number of unique virtual pages in the document. However, the %%Requirements: comment should have its numcopies option modified, and the collate option set, if applicable.

Restricted Operators

There are several PostScript language operators intended for system-level jobs that are not appropriate in the context of a page description program. Also, there are operators that impose conditions on the graphics state directly instead of modifying or concatenating to the existing graphics state. However, improper use of these operators may cause a document manager to process a document incorrectly. The risks of using these operators involve either rendering a document device dependent or unnecessarily inhibiting constructive post-processing of document files for different printing needs—for example, embedding one PostScript language document within another.

In addition to all operators in **statusdict** and the operators in **userdict** for establishing an imageable area, the following operators should be used carefully, or not at all, in a PostScript language page description:

banddevice	framedevice	quit	setpagedevice
clear	grestoreall	renderbands	setscreen
cleardictstack	initclip	setglobal	setshared
copypage	initgraphics	setgstate	settransfer
erasepage	initmatrix	sethalftone	startjob
exitserver	nulldevice	setmatrix	undefinefont

For more specific information on the proper use of these operators in various situations, see Appendix I.

There are certain operators specific to the Display PostScript system that are not part of the Level 1 and Level 2 implementations. These operators are for display systems only and *must not* be used in a document. This is a much more stringent restriction than the above list of restricted operators, which may be used with extreme care. For a complete list see section A.1.2, "Display PostScript Operators."

G.4.4 Parsing Rules

Here are a few explicit rules that can help a document manager parse the DSC comments:

- In the interest of forward compatibility, any comments that are not recognized by the parser should be ignored. Backward compatibility is sometimes difficult, and it may be helpful to develop an "upgrading parser" that will read in documents conforming to older versions of the DSC and write out DSC version 3.0 conforming documents.

- Many comments have a colon separating the comment keyword from its arguments. This colon is not present in all comment keywords (for example, %%EndProlog) and should be considered part of the keyword for parsing purposes. It is *not* an optional character.

- Comments with arguments (like %%Page:) should have a space separating the colon from the first argument. Due to existing software, this space must be considered optional.

- "White space" characters within comments may be either spaces or tabs (decimal ASCII 32 and 9, respectively).

- Comment keywords are case-sensitive, as are all of the arguments following a comment keyword.

- The character set for comment keywords is limited to printable ASCII characters. The keywords only contain alphabetic characters and the :, !, and ? characters. The arguments may include any character valid in the PostScript language character set, especially where procedure names, font names, and strings are represented. See the definition of the *<text>* elementary type for the use of the \ escape mechanism.

- When looking for the %%Trailer comment (or any (atend) comments), allow for nested documents. Observe %%BeginDocument: and %%EndDocument comments as well as %%BeginData: and %%EndData.

- In the case of multiple header comments, the *first* comment encountered is considered to be the truth. In the case of multiple *trailer* comments (those comments that were deferred using the (atend) convention), the last comment encountered is considered to be the truth. For example, if there are two %%Requirements: comments in the header of a document, use the first one encountered.

- Header comments can be terminated explicitly by an instance of %%EndComments, or implicitly by any line that does not begin with %*X*, where *X* is any printable character except space, tab, or newline.

- The order of some comments in the document is significant, but in a section of the document they may appear in any order. For example, in the header section, %%DocumentResources:, %%Title:, and %%Creator: may appear in any order.

- Lines must never exceed 255 characters, and line endings should follow the line ending restrictions set forth in section G.4.3, "Constraints."

- If a document manager supports resource or feature inclusion, at print time it should replace %%Include comments with the resource or feature requested. This resource or feature code should be encapsulated in %%Begin and %%End comments upon inclusion. If a document manager performs resource library extraction, any resources that are removed, including their associated %%Begin and %%End comments, should be replaced by equivalent %%Include comments.

G.4.5 Convention Categories

The DSC comments are roughly divided into the following five categories of conventions:

- General conventions

- Requirement conventions

- Color separation conventions

- Query conventions

- Open structuring conventions

- Special conventions

Typically, some subsets of the general, requirement, and color separation conventions are used consistently in a particular printing environment. The DSC have been designed with maximum flexibility in mind and with a minimum amount of interdependency between conventions. For example, one may use only general conventions in an environment where the presence of a document manager may not be guaranteed, or may use the requirement conventions on a highly spooled network.

General conventions delimit the various structural components of a PostScript language page description, including its prolog, script, and trailer, and where the page breaks fall, if there are any. The general convention comments include document and page setup information, and they provide a markup convention for noting the beginning and end of particular pieces of the page description that might need to be identified for further use.

Requirement conventions are comments that suggest document manager action. These comments can be used to specify resources the document supplies or needs. Document managers may make decisions based on resource frequency (those that are frequently used) and load resources permanently into the printer, download them before the job, or store them on a printer's hard disk, thus reducing transmission time.

Other requirement comments invoke or delimit printer-specific features and requirements, such as paper colors and weights, collating order, and stapling. The document manager can replace printer-specific Post-Script language fragments based on these comments when rerouting a print job to another printer, by using information in the PostScript printer description (PPD) file for that printer.

Color separation conventions are used to complement the color extensions to the PostScript language. Comments typically identify PostScript language color separation segments in a page, note custom color ratios (RGB or CMYK), and list document and page level color use.

Query conventions delimit parts of a PostScript language program that query the current state or characteristics of a printer, including the availability of resources (for example, fonts, files, procsets), VM, and any printer-specific features and enhancements. The type of program that uses this set of conventions is usually interactive—that is, one that expects a response from the printer. This implies that document managers should be able to send query jobs to a printer, and route an answer back to the application that issued the query. Query conventions should only be used in %!PS-Adobe-3.0 Query jobs.

Open structuring conventions are user-defined conventions. Section G.9, "Open Structuring Conventions," provides guidelines for creating these vendor-specific comments.

Special conventions include those comments that do not fall into the above categories.

The general, requirement, and color separation conventions can be further broken down into three classes: header comments, body comments, and page comments.

Header Comments

Header comments appear first in a document file, before any of the executable PostScript language instructions and before the procedure definitions. They may be thought of as a table of contents. In order to simplify a document manager's job in parsing these header comments, there are two rules that apply:

- If there is more than one instance of a header comment in a document file, *the first one encountered takes precedence.* This simplifies nesting documents within one another without having to remove the header comments.

- *Header comments must be contiguous.* That is, if a document manager comes across a line that does not begin with %, the document manager may quit parsing for header comments. The comments may also be ended *explicitly* with the %%EndComments convention.

All instances of lines beginning with %! *after the first instance* are ignored by document managers, although to avoid confusion, this notation should not appear twice within the block of header comments (see %%BeginDocument: and %%EndDocument for examples of embedded documents).

Body Comments

Body comments may appear anywhere in a document, except the header section. They are designed to provide structural information about the organization of the document file and should match any related information provided in the header comments section. They generally consist of %%Begin and %%End constructs to delimit specific components of the document file, such as procsets, fonts, or emulation code, and %%Include comments that request the document manager to take action when encountering the comment, such as including a document, resource, or printer-specific fragment of code.

Page Comments

Page comments are page-level structure comments. They should not span across page boundaries (see the exception below). That is, a page comment applies only to the page in which it appears. The beginning of a page should be noted by the %%Page: comment. The other page comments are similar to their corresponding header comments (for example, %%BoundingBox: vs. %%PageBoundingBox:), except for %%Begin or %%End comments that are more similar to body comments in use (e.g., %%Begin(End)Setup vs. %%Begin(End)PageSetup).

Note   *Some page comments that are similar to header comments can be used in the defaults section of the file to denote default requirements or media for all pages. See the %%Begin(End)Defaults comments for a more detailed explanation.*

G.4.6   Comment Syntax Reference

Before describing the DSC comments, it is prudent to specify the syntax with which they are documented. This section introduces a syntax known as Backus-Naur form (BNF) that helps eliminate syntactical ambiguities and helps comprehend the comment definitions. A brief explanation of the BNF operators is given in Table G.1. The following section discusses elementary types, which are used to specify the keywords and options of the DSC comments.

Table G.1 *Explanation of BNF operators*

BNF Operator	Explanation
<token>	This indicates a token item. This item may comprise other tokens or it may be an elementary type (see below).
::=	Literally means "is defined as."
[*expression*]	This indicates that the expression inside the brackets is optional.
{ *expression* }	The braces are used to group expressions or tokens into single expressions. It is often used to denote parsing order (it turns the expression inside the braces into a single token).
<token> ...	The ellipsis indicates that one or more instances of *<token>* can be specified.
I	The I character literally means "or" and delimits alternative expressions.

Elementary Types

An *elementary* or *base* type is a terminating expression. That is, it does not reference any other tokens and is considered to be a base on which other expressions are built. For the sake of clarity, these base types are defined here in simple English, without the exhaustive dissection that BNF normally requires.

(atend)

Some of the header and page comments can be deferred until the end of the file (that is, to the %%Trailer section) or to the end of a page (that is, the %%PageTrailer section). This is for the benefit of application programs that generate page descriptions on-the-fly. Such applications might not have the necessary information about fonts, page count, and so on at the beginning of generating a page description, but have them at the end. If a particular comment is to be deferred, it must be listed in the header section with an (atend) for its argument list. A comment with the same keyword and its appropriate arguments *must* appear in the %%Trailer or %%PageTrailer sections of the document.

The following comments support the (atend) convention:

%%BoundingBox:	%%DocumentSuppliedProcSets:
%%DocumentCustomColors:	%%DocumentSuppliedResources:
%%DocumentFiles:	%%Orientation:
%%DocumentFonts:	%%Pages:
%%DocumentNeededFiles:	%%PageBoundingBox:
%%DocumentNeededFonts:	%%PageCustomColors:
%%DocumentNeededProcSets:	%%PageFiles:
%%DocumentNeededResources:	%%PageFonts:
%%DocumentProcSets:	%%PageOrder:
%%DocumentProcessColors:	%%PageOrientation:
%%DocumentSuppliedFiles:	%%PageProcessColors:
%%DocumentSuppliedFonts:	%%PageResources:

Note   *Page-level comments specified in the defaults section of the document cannot use the* (atend) *syntax to defer definition of their arguments.* (atend) *can only be used in the header section and within individual pages.*

In Example G.1, the bounding box information is deferred until the end of the document:

Example G.1

```
%!PS-Adobe-3.0
...Document header comments...
%%BoundingBox: (atend)
%%EndComments
...Rest of the document...
%%Trailer
%%BoundingBox: 0 0 157 233
...Document clean up...
%%EOF
```

<filename>

A *filename* is similar to the *<text>* elementary type in that it can comprise any printable character. It is usually very operating system specific. The following example comment lists four different files:

```
%%DocumentNeededResources: file /usr/smith/myfile.epsf
%%+ file (Corporate Logo \042large size\042) (This is (yet) another file)
%%+ file C:\LIB\LOGO.EPS
```

Note that the backslash escape mechanism is only supported inside parentheses. It can also be very convenient to list files on separate lines using the continuation comment %%+.

<fontname>

A *fontname* is a variation of the simple text string (see <*text*>). Because font names cannot include blanks, font names are considered to be delimited by blanks. In addition, the \ escape mechanism is not supported. The following example comment uses five font names:

```
%%DocumentNeededResources: font Times-Roman Palatino-Bold
%%+ font Helvetica Helvetica-Bold NewCenturySchoolbook-Italic
```

The font name does not start with a slash character (/) as it does in the PostScript language when you are specifying the font name as a literal.

<formname>

A *formname* is the PostScript language object name of the form as used by the **defineresource** operator. It is a simple text string as defined by the <*text*> elementary type.

<int>

An *integer* is a non-fractional number that may be signed or unsigned. There are practical limitations for an integer's maximum and minimum values (see Appendix B).

<procname> ::= <name> <version> <revision>
    <name> ::= <text>
    <version> ::= <real>
    <revision> ::= <uint>

A *procname* token describes a procedure set (procset), which is a block of PostScript language definitions. A procset is labeled by a text string describing its contents and a version number. A procset *version* may undergo several revisions, which is indicated by the *revision* number. Procset names should be descriptive and meaningful. It is also suggested that the corporate name and application name be used as part of the procset name to reduce conflicts, as in this example:

```
(MyCorp MyApp - Graphic Objects) 1.1 0
Adobe-Illustrator-Prolog 2.0 1
```

The *name*, *version*, and *revision* fields should uniquely identify the procset. If a version numbering scheme is not used, these fields should still be filled with a dummy value of 0.

The *revision* field should be taken to be upwardly compatible with procsets of the same *version* number. That is, if myprocs 1.0 0 is requested, then myprocs 1.0 2 should be compatible, although the converse (backward compatibility) is not necessarily true. If the *revision* field is not present, a procset may be substituted as long as the *version* numbers are equal. Different versions of a procset may not be upwardly compatible and should not be substituted.

<patternname>

A *patternname* is the PostScript language object name of the pattern as used by the **defineresource** operator. It is a simple text string as defined by the *<text>* elementary type.

<real>

A *real* number is a fractional number that may be signed or unsigned. There are practical limitations on the maximum size of a real (see Appendix B). Real numbers may or may not include a decimal point, and exponentiation using either an 'E' or an 'e' is allowed. For example,

    -.002 34.5 -3.62 123.6e10 1E-5 -1. 0.0

are all valid real numbers.

<resource> ::= font *<fontname>* | file *<filename>* |
    procset *<procname>* | pattern *<patternname>* |
    form *<formname>* | encoding *<vectorname>*
<resources> ::= font *<fontname>* ... | file *<filename>* ... |
    procset *<procname>* ... | pattern *<patternname>* ... |
    form *<formname>* ... | encoding *<vectorname>* ...

A *resource* is a PostScript object, referenced by name, that may or may not be available to the system at any given time. Times-Roman is the name of a commonly available resource. The name of the resource should be the same as the name of the PostScript object—in other words, the same name used when using the **defineresource** operator.

Note   *Although files are not resources in the PostScript language sense, they can be thought of as a resource when document managers are dealing with them.*

<text>

A *text string* comprises any printable characters and is usually considered to be delimited by blanks. If blanks or special characters are desired inside the text string, the entire string should be enclosed in parentheses. Document managers parsing text strings should be prepared to handle multiple parentheses. Special characters can be denoted using the PostScript language string \ escape mechanism.

The following are examples of valid DSC text strings:

```
Thisisatextstring
(This is a text string with spaces)
(This is a text string (with parentheses))
(This is a special character \262 using the \\ mechanism)
```

It is a good idea to enclose numbers that should be treated as text strings in parentheses to avoid confusion. For example, use (1040) instead of 1040.

The sequence () denotes an empty string.

Note that a text string must obey the 255 character line limit as set forth in section G.3, "DSC Conformance."

<textline>

This is a modified version of the *<text>* elementary type. If the first character encountered is a left parenthesis, it is equivalent to a *<text>* string. If not, the token is considered to be the rest of the characters on the line until end of line is reached (some combination of the CR and LF characters).

<uint>

An *unsigned integer* is a non-fractional number that has no sign. There are practical limitations for an unsigned integer's maximum value, but as a default it should be able to range between 0 and twice the largest integer value given in Appendix B.

<vectorname>

A *vectorname* denotes the name of a particular encoding vector and is also a simple text string. It should have the same name as the encoding vector the PostScript language program uses. Examples of encoding vector names are **StandardEncoding** and **ISOLatin1Encoding**.

G.5 General Conventions

The general conventions are the most basic of all the comments. They impart general information, such as the bounding box, language level, extension usage, orientation, title of the document, and other basics. There are comments that are used to impart structural information (end of header, setup, page breaks, page setup, page trailer, trailer) that are the keys to abiding by the document structure rules of G.3, "DSC Conformance." Other general comments are used to identify special sections of the document, including binary and emulation data, bitmap previews, and page level objects.

G.5.1 General Header Comments

%!PS-Adobe-3.0 *<keyword>*
<keyword> ::= EPSF-3.0 | Query | ExitServer | Resource-*<restype>*
<restype> ::= Font | File | ProcSet | Pattern | Form | Encoding

This comment differs from the previous %!PS-Adobe-2.1 comment only in version number. It indicates that the PostScript language page description fully conforms to the DSC version 3.0. This comment must occur as the *first* line of the PostScript language file.

There are four *keywords* that may follow the %!PS-Adobe-3.0 comment on the same line. They flag the entire print job as a particular type of job so document managers may immediately switch to some appropriate processing mode. The following job types are recognized:

- EPSF—The file is an *Encapsulated PostScript file*, which is primarily a PostScript language file that produces an illustration. The EPS format is designed to facilitate including these illustrations in other documents. The exact format of an EPS file is described in Appendix H.

- Query—The entire job consists of PostScript language queries to a printer from which replies are expected. A systems administrator or document manager is likely to create a query job. See section G.12.4, "Query Conventions."

- ExitServer—This flags a job that executes the **exitserver** or **startjob** operator to allow the contents of the job to persist within the printer until it is powered off. Some document managers require this command to handle these special jobs effectively. See the discussion of **exitserver** under %%Begin(End)ExitServer.

- Resource—As a generalization of the idea of Level 2 resources, files that are strictly resource definitions (fonts, procsets, files, patterns, forms) should start with this comment and keyword. For example, a procset resource should start with the %!PS-Adobe-3.0 Resource-ProcSet comment.

Fonts are resources, as well, but most fonts use one of two different header comments: %!PS-AdobeFont-1.0 and %!FontType1-1.0. In the future, fonts conforming to this specification should use the %!PS-Adobe-3.0 Resource-Font comment.

Note *Document composition programs should not use these keywords when producing a document intended for printing or display. Instead, they should use only the %!PS-Adobe-3.0 comment. Illustration applications may use the EPSF-3.0 keyword.*

%%BoundingBox: { *<llx>* *<lly>* *<urx>* *<ury>* } | **(atend)**

    <llx> ::= *<int>*   (Lower left x coordinate)
    <lly> ::= *<int>*   (Lower left y coordinate)
    <urx> ::= *<int>*   (Upper right x coordinate)
    <ury> ::= *<int>*   (Upper right y coordinate)

This comment specifies the bounding box that encloses all marks painted on all pages of a document. That is, it must be a "high water mark" in all directions for marks made on any page. The four arguments correspond to the lower left (*llx, lly*) and upper right corners (*urx, ury*) of the bounding box in the *default user coordinate system* (PostScript units). See also the %%PageBoundingBox: comment.

Figure G.2 *Determining the document bounding box*

Page 1 bounding box   *Page 2 bounding box*   *Page 3 bounding box*   *Document bounding box*

%%Copyright: *<textline>*

This comment details any copyright information associated with the document or resource.

%%Creator: *<textline>*

This comment indicates the document creator, usually the name of the document composition software.

%%CreationDate: *<textline>*

This comment indicates the date and time the document was created. Neither the date nor time need be in any standard format. This comment is meant to be used purely for informational purposes, such as printing on banner pages.

%%DocumentData: **Clean7Bit | Clean8Bit | Binary**

This header comment specifies the type of data, usually located between %%Begin(End)Data: comments, that appear in the document. It applies only to data that are part of the document itself, not bytes that are added by communications software—for example, an EOF character marking the end of a job, or XON/XOFF characters for flow control. This comment warns a print manager, such as a spooler, to avoid communications channels that reserve the byte codes used in the document. A prime example of this is a serial channel, which reserves byte codes like 0x04 for end of job and 0x14 for status request.

There are three ranges of byte codes defined:

- Clean7Bit—The page description consists of only byte codes 0x1B to 0x7E (ESC to '~'), 0x0A (LF), 0x0D (CR), and 0x09 (TAB). Whenever 0x0A and/or 0x0D appear, they are used as end-of-line characters. Whenever 0x09 appears, it is used as a tab character (i.e. whitespace).

- Clean8Bit—The same as Clean7Bit, but the document may also contain byte codes 0x80-0xFF.

- Binary—Any byte codes from 0x00-0xFF may appear in the document.

The header section of the document (up to %%EndComments) must always consist of Clean7bit byte codes so it is universally readable. If the application declares the document to be Clean7Bit or Clean8Bit, it is responsible for transforming any byte codes that fall outside the acceptable range back into the acceptable range. Byte codes within character strings may be escaped—for example, a 0x05 may be written (\005).

Documents with Clean7Bit data may be transmitted to a PostScript interpreter over a serial line with 7 data bits. Documents with Clean8Bit data may be transmitted to a PostScript interpreter over a serial line with 8 data bits. Documents with Binary data cannot be transmitted over a serial line because they may use byte codes reserved by the communications protocol. However, they may be transmitted via a transparent protocol, such as LocalTalk.

%%Emulation: *<mode>* ...

<mode> ::= diablo630 | fx100 | lj2000 | hpgl | impress | hplj | ti855

This comment indicates that the document contains an invocation of the stated emulator. This allows a document manager to route the document to a printer that supports the correct type of emulation. See %%Begin(End)Emulation: for more details.

%%EndComments (no keywords)

This comment indicates an explicit end to the header comments of the document. Because header comments are contiguous, any line that does not begin with %X where X is any printable character except space, tab, or newline implicitly denotes the end of the header section.

```
%!PS-Adobe-3.0
%%Title: (Example of Header Comment Termination)
...More header comments...
%%DocumentResources: font Sonata
%GBDNodeName: smith@atlas.com
% This line implicitly denotes the end of the header section.
```

%%Extensions: *<extension>* ...

<extension> ::= DPS | CMYK | Composite | FileSystem

This comment indicates that in order to print properly, the document requires a PostScript Level 1 interpreter that supports the listed PostScript language extensions. The document manager can use this information to determine whether a printer can print the document or to select possible printers for rerouting the document. A list of operator sets specific to each extension is in Appendix A.

- DPS—The document contains operators defined in the PostScript language extensions for the Display PostScript system. Most of these operators are available in Level 2 implementations. See Appendix A for a list of operators that are present only in Display PostScript implementations.

- CMYK—The document uses operators defined in the PostScript language color extensions. Note that this is different from the %%Requirements: color comment, in that it specifies that the PostScript interpreter must be able to understand the CMYK color operators. It does not specify that the printer must be capable of producing color output.

- Composite—The document uses operators defined in the PostScript language composite font extensions.

- FileSystem—This keyword should be used if the document performs file system commands. Note that certain file operators are already available under the basic implementation of the PostScript language. See Appendix A for a list of those operators that are specifically part of the file system extensions to Level 1 implementations.

The %%Extensions: comment must be used if there are operators in the document specific to a particular extension of the PostScript language. However, documents that provide conditional Level 1 emulation do not need to use this comment. Also, if the document uses Level 2 operators, use the %%LanguageLevel: comment instead.

%%For: *<textline>*

This comment indicates the person and possibly the company name for whom the document is being printed. It is frequently the "user name" of the individual who composed the document, as determined by the document composition software. This can be used for banner pages or for routing the document after printing.

%%LanguageLevel: *<uint>*

This comment indicates that the document contains PostScript language operators particular to a certain level of implementation of the PostScript language. Currently, only Level 1 and Level 2 are defined.

This comment *must* be used if there are operators in the document specific to an implementation of the PostScript language above Level 1. However, documents that provide conditional Level 1 emulation (for example, Level 1 emulation of the Level 2 operators used) need not use this comment. See Appendix D for emulation and compatibility strategies.

Level 2 operators are essentially a superset of the DPS, CMYK, Composite, and FileSystem language extensions. If a language level of 2 is specified, the individual extensions need not be specified. That is, use of both the %%LanguageLevel: and %%Extensions: comments is not necessary; one or the other is sufficient. See the %%Extensions: comment.

Note   *To enable a document to be output to as many interpreters as possible, a document composition application should determine the minimum set of extensions needed for the document to print correctly. It is poor practice to use the* %%LanguageLevel: *comment when an* %%Extensions: *comment would have been able to encompass all of the operators used in the document.*

%%Orientation: **{ *<orientation>* ... } | (atend)**
<orientation> ::= Portrait | Landscape

This comment indicates the orientation of the pages in the document. It can be used by previewing applications and post-processors to determine how to orient the viewing window. A *portrait* orientation indicates that the longest edge of the paper is parallel to the vertical (y) axis. A *landscape* orientation indicates that the longest edge of the paper is parallel to the horizontal (x) axis. If more than one orientation applies to the document, an individual page should specify its orientation by using the %%PageOrientation: comment.

%%Pages: ***<numpages>* | (atend)**
<numpages> ::= *<uint>*   (Total number of pages)

This comment defines the number of *virtual* pages that a document will image. This may be different from the number of *physical* pages the printer prints (the **#copies** key or **setpagedevice** operator and other document manager features may reduce or increase the physical number of pages). If the document produces *no* pages (for instance, if it represents an included illustration that does not use **showpage**), the page count should be 0. See also the %%Page: comment.

In previous specifications, it was valid to include an optional *page order* number after the number of pages. Its use is now discouraged because of problems with the (atend) syntax (one might know the page order before one knows the number of pages). Please use the %%PageOrder: comment to indicate page order.

%%PageOrder: *<order>* | (atend)
                <order> ::= Ascend | Descend | Special

The %%PageOrder: comment is intended to help document managers determine the order of pages in the document file, which in turn enables a document manager optionally to reorder the pages. This comment can have three page orders:

- Ascend—The pages are in ascending order—for example, 1-2-3-4-5.

- Descend—The pages of the document are in descending order—for example, 5-4-3-2-1.

- Special—Indicates that the document is in a *special* order—for example, signature order.

The distinction between a page order of Special and no page order at all is that in the absence of the %%PageOrder comment, any assumption can be made about the page order, and the document manager permits any reordering of the page. However, if the page order comment is Special, the pages must be left intact in the order given.

%%Routing: *<textline>*

This comment provides information about how to route a document back to its owner after printing. At the discretion of the system administrator, it may contain information about mail addresses or office locations.

%%Title: *<textline>*

This comment provides a text title for the document that is useful for printing banner pages and for routing or recognizing documents.

%%Version: *<version> <revision>*
<version> ::= <real>
<revision> ::= <uint>

This comment can be used to note the version and revision number of a document or resource. A document manager may wish to provide version control services, or allow substitution of compatible versions/ revisions of a resource or document. Please see the *<procname>* elementary type for a more thorough discussion of version and revisions.

G.5.2   General Body Comments

%%+   (no keywords)

Any document structuring comment that must be continued on another line to avoid violating the 255-character line length constraint must use the %%+ notation to indicate that a comment line is being continued. This notation may be used after any of the document comment conventions, but may only be necessary in those comments that provide a large list of names, such as %%DocumentResources:. Here is an example of its use:

```
%%DocumentResources: font Palatino-Roman Palatino-Bold
%%+ font Palatino-Italic Palatino-BoldItalic Courier
%%+ font Optima LubalinGraph-DemiOblique
```

See section G.3, "DSC Conformance," for more information about line length and restrictions.

%%BeginBinary: *<bytecount>*
<bytecount> ::= <uint>

%%EndBinary   (no keywords)

These comments are used in a manner similar to the %%Begin(End)- Data: comments. The %%Begin(End)Binary: comments are designed to allow a document manager to effectively ignore any binary data these comments encapsulate.

To read data directly from the input stream in the PostScript language (using **currentfile**, for instance), it is necessary to invoke a procedure followed immediately by the data to be read. If the data is embedded in the %%Begin(End)Binary: construct, those comments are effectively *part of the data*, which typically is not desired. To avoid this problem, the procedure invocation should fall *inside* the comments, even though it is not binary, and the *bytecount* should reflect this so it can be skipped correctly. In the case of a byte count, allow for carriage returns, if any.

Note   *This comment has been included for backward compatibility only and may be discontinued in future versions of the DSC; use the more specific %%Begin(End)Data: comments instead.*

%%BeginData: *<numberof>*[*<type>* [*<bytesorlines>*]]
<numberof> ::= *<uint>*   (Lines or physical bytes)
<type> ::= Hex | Binary | ASCII   (Type of data)
<bytesorlines> ::= Bytes | Lines   (Read in bytes or lines)

%%EndData   (no keywords)

These comments are designed to provide information about embedded bodies of data. When a PostScript language document file is being parsed, encountering raw data can tremendously complicate the parsing process. Encapsulating data within these comments can allow a document manager to ignore the enclosed data, and speed the parsing process. If the *type* argument is missing, binary data is assumed. If the *bytesorlines* argument is missing, *numberof* should be considered to indicate bytes of data.

Note that *<numberof>* indicates the bytes of *physical* data, which vary from the bytes of *virtual* data in some cases. With hex, each byte of *virtual* data is represented by two ASCII characters (two bytes of *physical* data). Although the PostScript interpreter ignores white space in hex data, these count toward the byte count.

For example,

    FD 10 2A 05

is 11 bytes of *physical* data (8 bytes hex, 3 spaces) and 4 binary bytes of *virtual* data.

Remember that binary data is especially sensitive to different print environments because it is an 8-bit representation. This can be very important to the document manager if a print network has a channel that is 7 bit serial, for example. See also the %%DocumentData: comment.

To read data directly from the input stream (using **currentfile**, for instance), it is necessary to invoke a procedure followed *immediately* by the data to be read. If the data is embedded in the %%Begin(End)Data: construct, then those comments are effectively *part of the data,* which is typically not desirable. To avoid this problem, the procedure invocation should fall *inside* the comments, even though it is not binary, and the byte or line counts should reflect this so it can be skipped correctly. In the case of a byte count, allow for end-of-line characters, if any.

Note   *Document managers should ensure that the entire* %%BeginData: *comment line is read before acting on the byte count.*

In the example below, there are 135174 bytes of hex data, but the %%BeginData: and %%EndData comments encompass the call to the **image** operator. The resulting byte count includes 6 additional bytes, for the string "image" plus the newline character.

```
/picstr 256 string def
25 140 translate
132 132 scale
256 256 8 [256 0 0 -256 0 256] { currentfile picstr readhexstring pop }
%%BeginData: 135174 Hex Bytes
image
4c47494b3187c237d237b137438374ab
213769876c8976985a5c987675875756
...Additional 135102 bytes of hex...
%%EndData
```

Instead of keeping track of byte counts, it is probably easier to keep track of *lines* of data. In the following example, the line count is increased by one to account for the "image" string:

```
/picstr 256 string def
25 140 translate
132 132 scale
256 256 8 [256 0 0 -256 0 256] { currentfile picstr readhexstring pop }
%%BeginData: 4097 Hex Lines
image
4c47494b3187c237d237b137438374ab
213769876c8976985a5c987675875756
...Additional 4094 lines of hex...
%%EndData
```

With binary data, it is unlikely that the concept of lines would be used, because binary data is usually considered one whole stream.

%%BeginDefaults (no keywords)
%%EndDefaults (no keywords)

These comments identify the start and end of the *defaults* section of the document. These comments can only occur after the header section (%%EndComments), after the EPSI preview (%%Begin(End)Preview), if there is one, but before the prolog (%%BeginProlog) definitions.

Some page level comments that are similar to header comments can be used in this defaults section of the file to denote default requirements, resources, or media for all pages. This saves space in large documents (page-level values do not need to be repeated for every page) and can give the document manager some hints on how it might optimize resource usage in the file. The only comments that can be used this way are the following:

> %%PageBoundingBox:
> %%PageCustomColors:
> %%PageMedia:
> %%PageOrientation:
> %%PageProcessColors:
> %%PageRequirements:
> %%PageResources:

For example, if the %%PageOrientation: Portrait comment were used in the defaults section, it would indicate that the default orientation for all pages is portrait. When page-level comments are used this way they are known as *page defaults*. Page comments used in a page override any page defaults in effect. In reference to the previous example, if a particular page of the document were to have a landscape orientation, it would place a %%PageOrientation: Landscape comment after the %%Page: comment to override the default portrait orientation.

Example G.2 illustrates the page default concept.

Example G.2

```
%!PS-Adobe-3.0
%%Title: (Example of page defaults)
%%DocumentNeededResources: font Palatino-Roman Helvetica
%%DocumentMedia: BuffLetter 612 792 75 buff ( )
%%+ BlueLetter 612 792 244 blue (CorpLogo)
%%EndComments
%%BeginDefaults
%%PageResources: font Palatino-Roman
%%PageMedia: BuffLetter
%%EndDefaults
```

```
%%BeginProlog
...Prolog definitions...
%%EndProlog
%%BeginSetup
...PostScript language instructions to set the default paper size, weights, and color...
%%EndSetup
%%Page: Cover 1
%%PageMedia: BlueLetter
%%BeginPageSetup
...PostScript language instructions to set the blue corporate logo cover paper...
%%EndPageSetup
...Rest of page 1...
%Page: ii 2
%%PageResources: font Palatino-Roman Helvetica
...Rest of page 2...
%%Page: iii 3
...Rest of the document...
%%EOF
```

In this example, the font resource Palatino-Roman is specified in the defaults section as a page resource. This indicates that Palatino-Roman is a page default and will most likely be used on every page. Also, the media BuffLetter is specified as the page default. Buff-colored, 20-lb, 8.5" x 11" paper will be used for most pages.

Page 1 uses a special blue cover paper and overrides the page default (buff paper) by putting a %%PageMedia: comment in the page definition. Page 2 uses buff paper and therefore doesn't have to put the %%PageMedia: comment in its page definition. However, it does use the Helvetica font in addition to the Palatino-Roman font. The page default of Palatino-Roman is overridden by the %%PageResources: comment in the page definition.

Note   *In some instances it may be superfluous to use these page defaults. If only one type of orientation, media type, etc. is used in the entire document, the header comment alone is sufficient to indicate the default for the document. Page defaults should only be used if there is more than one bounding box, custom color, medium, orientation, process color, requirement, or resource used.*

%%BeginEmulation:	*\<mode\>*
	\<mode\> ::= diablo630	fx100	lj2000	hpgl	hplj	impress	ti855
%%EndEmulation	(no keyword)

The %%BeginEmulation: comment signifies that the input data following the comment contains some printer language other than PostScript. The first line after the %%BeginEmulation comment should be the PostScript language instructions to invoke the emulator. This code is in the PPD file for the printer. Note that the invocation of the emulator is restricted to one line.

This comment enables a document manager to route the document or piece of the document to an appropriate printer. The %%EndEmulation comment should be preceded by the code to switch back to PostScript mode on printers that support this type of switching (again, limit this code to one line). Alternatively, the %%EndEmulation comment may be omitted, in which case the end-of-file switches the printer back into PostScript mode. The following example illustrates the first approach:

```
%!PS-Adobe-3.0
%%Title: (Example of emulator comments)
%%Emulation: hplj
%%EndComments
...Prolog definitions and document setup...
%%BeginEmulation: hplj
3 setsoftwareiomode                   % Invoke hplj emulation
...Emulator data...
1B 7F 30                              % Switch back to PostScript
%%EndEmulation
...Remainder of document...
```

Note   *When including emulator data, this may break the page independence constraint for a conforming PostScript language file, because there is no way to signify page boundaries. Care should be taken when invoking specialized features of the document manager, such as n-up printing. The document may not be printed as expected.*

%%BeginPreview: *<width> <height> <depth> <lines>*

<width> ::= <uint>	(Width of the preview in pixels)
<height> ::= <uint>	(Height of the preview in pixels)
<depth> ::= <uint>	(Number of bits of data per pixel)
<lines> ::= <uint>	(Number of lines in the preview)

%%EndPreview   (no keywords)

These comments bracket the preview section of an EPS file in interchange format (EPSI). The EPSI format is preferred over other platform-dependent previews (for example, Apple Macintosh and IBM PC) when transferring EPS files between heterogenous platforms. The *width* and *height* fields provide the number of image samples (pixels) for the preview. The *depth* field indicates how many bits of data are used to establish one sample pixel of the preview (typical values are 1, 2, 4, or 8). The *lines* field indicates how many lines of hexadecimal data are contained in the preview, so that an application disinterested in the preview can easily skip it.

The preview consists of a bitmap image of the file, as it would be rendered on the page by the printer or PostScript language previewer. Applications that use the EPSI file can use the preview image for on-screen display. Each line of hexadecimal data should begin with a single percent sign. This makes the entire preview section a PostScript language comment so the file can be sent directly to a printer without modification. See section H.6, "Device-Independent Screen Preview."

The EPSI preview should be placed after the %%EndComments in the document file, but before the defaults section (%%Begin(End)Defaults), if there is one, and before the prolog (%%BeginProlog) definitions.

Note   *Preview comments can be used only in documents that comply with the EPS file format. See Appendix H for more details, including platform-specific versions of the preview (Apple Macintosh and IBM PC platforms).*

%%BeginProlog   (no keywords)

%%EndProlog   (no keywords)

These comments delimit the beginning and ending of the prolog in the document. The prolog must consist only of procset definitions. The %%EndProlog comment is widely used and parsed for, and must be included in all documents that have a distinct prolog and script.

Breaking a document into a prolog and a script is conceptually important, although not all document descriptions fall neatly into this model. If your document represents free form PostScript language fragments that might entirely be considered a *script*, you should still include the %%EndProlog comment, even though there may be nothing in the prolog part of the file. This effectively makes the entire document a script.

See section G.3.1, "Conforming Documents," and G.4, "Document Structure Rules," for more information on the contents of the document prolog.

%%BeginSetup   (no keywords)

%%EndSetup   (no keywords)

These comments delimit the part of the document that does device setup for a particular printer or document. There may be instructions for setting page size, invoking manual feed, establishing a scale factor (or "landscape" mode), downloading a font, or other document-level setup. Expect to see liberal use of the **setpagedevice** operator and **statusdict** operators between these two comments. There may also be some general initialization instructions, such as setting some aspects of the graphics state. This code should be limited to setting those items of the graphics state, such as the current font, transfer function, or halftone screen, that will not be affected by **initgraphics** or **erasepage** (**showpage** performs these two operations implicitly). Special care must be taken to ensure that the document setup code modifies the current graphics state and does not replace it. See Appendix I for more information about how to properly modify the graphics state.

If present, these comments appear after the %%EndProlog comment, but before the first %%Page: comment. In other words, these comments are not part of the prolog. They should be in the first part of the script before any pages are specified.

G.5.3   General Page Comments

Some of the following general page comments that specify the bounding box or orientation may appear in the defaults section or in a particular page. If these comments appear in the defaults section of the document file between %%BeginDefaults and %%EndDefaults, they are in effect for the entire print job. If they are found in the page-level comments for a page, they should be in effect only for that page. See %%Begin(End)Defaults for more details on page defaults.

%%BeginObject:	*<name>* [*<code>*]

<name> ::= *<text>*   (Name of object)
<code> ::= *<text>*   (Processing code)

%%EndObject   (no keywords)

These comments delimit individual graphic elements of a page. In a context where it is desirable to be able to recognize individual page elements, this comment provides a mechanism to label and recognize them at the PostScript language level. Labelling is especially useful when a document printing system can print selected objects in a document or on a page.

For instance, the *code* field of this comment can be used to represent *proofing levels* for a document. For example, the printing manager may be requested to "print only those objects with proofing levels less than 4." This can save printing time when proofing various elements of a document. It can also be useful in systems that allow PostScript language program segments to be parsed and re-edited into convenient groupings and categorizations of graphic page elements. In a document production system or in an application that is highly object-oriented, use of this comment is strongly recommended.

The user must specify to the application what things constitute an object and what the proofing level of each object will be.

%%BeginPageSetup   (no keywords)

%%EndPageSetup   (no keywords)

These comments are analogous to the %%BeginSetup: and %%EndSetup comments, except that %%BeginPageSetup: and %%EndPageSetup appear in the body of a document right after a %%Page: comment. They delimit areas that set manual feed, establish margins, set orientation, download fonts or other resources for the page, invoke particular paper colors, and so on. This is the proper place to set up the graphics state for the page. It should be assumed that an **initgraphics** and an **erasepage** (i.e. **showpage**) have been performed prior to this page. Take special care to ensure that the code in the page setup *modifies* the current graphics state rather than replaces it. See Appendix I for more information about how to properly modify the graphics state.

%%Page:	*<label> <ordinal>*	
	<label> ::= *<text>*	(Page name)
	<ordinal> ::= *<uint>*	(Page position)

This comment marks the beginning of the PostScript language instructions that describe a particular page. %%Page: requires two arguments: a *page label* and a *sequential page number*. The label may be anything, but the ordinal page number must reflect the position of that page in the body of the PostScript language file and must start with 1, not 0. In the following example, the name of the third page of the document is 1:

```
%!PS-Adobe-3.0
...Document prolog and setup...
%%Page: cover 1
...Rest of the cover page...
%%Page: ii 2
...Rest of the ii page...
%%Page: 1 3
...Rest of the first page...
%%Page: 2 4
...Rest of the second page...
%%EOF
```

A document manager should be able to *rearrange* the contents of the print file into a different order based on the %%Page: comment (or the pages may be printed in parallel, if desired). The %%PageOrder: Special comment can be used to inform a document manager that page reordering *should not* take place.

%%PageBoundingBox:	{ *<llx> <lly> <urx> <ury>* } | **(atend)**	
	<llx> ::= *<int>*	(Lower-left x coordinate)
	<lly> ::= *<int>*	(Lower-left y coordinate)
	<urx> ::= *<int>*	(Upper-right x coordinate)
	<ury> ::= *<int>*	(Upper-right y coordinate)

This comment specifies the bounding box that encloses all the marks painted on a particular page (this is *not* the bounding box of the whole document—see the %%BoundingBox: comment). *llx, lly* and *urx, ury* are the coordinates of the lower-left and upper-right corners of the bounding box in the *default user coordinate system* (PostScript units). This comment can pertain to an individual page or a document, depending on the location of the comment. For example, the comment may be in the page itself or in the document defaults section.

%%PageOrientation: **Portrait | Landscape**

This comment indicates the orientation of the page and can be used by preview applications and post-processors to determine how to orient the viewing window. This comment can pertain to an individual page or a document, depending on the location of the comment. For example, the comment may be in the page itself or in the document defaults section. See %%Orientation: for a description of the various orientations. See %%Begin(End)Defaults for use of this comment as a page default.

G.5.4   General Trailer Comments

Some trailer comments are special and work with other comments that support the (atend) notation. In addition, trailer comments delimit sections of PostScript language instructions that deal with cleanup and other housekeeping. This cleanup can affect a particular page or the document as a whole.

%%PageTrailer   (no keywords)

This comment marks the end of a page. Any page comments that may have been deferred by the (atend) convention should follow the %%PageTrailer comment.

%%Trailer   (no keywords)

This comment must only occur once at the end of the document *script*. Any post-processing or cleanup should be contained in the *trailer* of the document, which is anything that follows the %%Trailer comment. Any of the document-level structure comments that were *deferred* by using the (atend) convention must be mentioned in the trailer of the document after the %%Trailer comment.

When entire documents are embedded in another document file, there may be more than one %%Trailer comment as a result. To avoid ambiguity, embedded documents must be delimited by the %%Begin-Document: and %%EndDocument comments.

%%EOF (no keywords)

This comment signifies the end of the document. When the document manager sees this comment, it issues an end-of-file signal to the Post-Script interpreter. This is done so system-dependent file endings, such as Control-D and end-of-file packets, do not confuse the PostScript interpreter.

G.6 Requirement Conventions

The requirement conventions are comments that suggest document manager action. Some of these comments list the resources needed or supplied by the document, delimit those resources if they are supplied, and specify the insertion point for those resources if they are needed. Other comments deal with printer-specific features (listing requirements, delimiting portions of and indicating insertion points for printer specific code) and are used in tandem with the **setpagedevice** operators or **statusdict** operators, as well as the PostScript printer description (PPD) files.

Note *Use of the* %%Include *or* %%Operator *comments in an environment that does not have a document manager can result in the document being processed incorrectly.*

G.6.1 Requirement Header Comments

%%DocumentMedia: *<medianame> <attributes>*
<medianame> ::= <text>   (Tag name of the media)
<attributes> ::= <width> <height> <weight> <color> <type>
<width> ::= <real>   (Width in PostScript units)
<height> ::= <real>   (Height in PostScript units)
<weight> ::= <real>   (Weight in g/m^2)
<color> ::= <text>   (Paper color)
<type> ::= <text>   (Type of pre-printed form)

This comment indicates all types of paper media (paper sizes, weight, color) this document requires. If any of the attributes are not applicable to a particular printing situation, zeroes must be substituted for numeric parameters and null strings must be substituted for text parameters. Each different medium that is needed should be listed in its approximate order of *descending* quantity used.

```
%%DocumentMedia: Plain 612 792 75 white ( )
%%+ BlueCL 612 792 244 blue CorpLogo
%%+ Tax 612 792 75 ( ) (1040)
```

The preceding example indicates that the following media are needed for this job:

- 8.5" x 11", 20 lb. paper (Bond lbs $\times$ 3.76 = g/m^2).

- Cover pages in blue 8.5" x 11", 65 lb. paper preprinted with the corporate logo.

- Preprinted IRS 1040 tax forms.

Note that the *type* attribute refers to preprinted forms only, and does *not* refer to the PostScript language concept of form objects as resources. The following keywords for the *type* name are defined for general use:

19HoleCerlox	ColorTransparency	CustLetterHead	Tabs
3Hole	CorpLetterHead	DeptLetterHead	Transparency
2Hole	CorpLogo	Labels	UserLetterHead

The related %%PageMedia: comment explicitly calls for the medium that each page requires by referring to its *medianame*.

%%DocumentNeededResources: *<resources>*

This comment provides a list of resources the document needs—that is, resources *not* contained in the document file. This comment is intended to help a document manager decide whether further parsing of the document file is necessary to provide these needed resources. There must be at least one corresponding instance of the %%IncludeResource: comment for each resource this comment lists.

The application that produces the print file must not make any assumptions about which resources are resident in the output device; it must list all resources the document needs. Even if it is a resource, such as the Times-Roman font program, that exists in nearly all implementations, it must appear here. A resource must not be listed if it is not used anywhere in the document.

As a general rule, different types of resources should be listed on separate lines using the %%+ comment, as illustrated in the following example:

```
%%DocumentNeededResources: font Times-Roman Helvetica StoneSerif
%%+ font Adobe-Garamond Palatino-Roman
%%+ file /usr/lib/PostScript/logo.ps
%%+ procset Adobe_Illustrator_abbrev 1.0 0
%%+ pattern hatch bubbles
%%+ form (corporate order form)
%%+ encoding JIS
```

%%DocumentSuppliedResources: *<resources>*

The %%DocumentSuppliedResources: comment contains extra information for document managers designed to store and reuse the resources, and provides helpful directories of the resources contained in the print file. This comment lists all resources that have been *provided* in the document print file. There is a %%BeginResource: and %%EndResource pair for each resource in this list. It is assumed that all resources on the %%DocumentSuppliedResources: list are mutually exclusive of those resources found on the %%DocumentNeededResources: list.

%%DocumentPrinterRequired: *<print> <prod>* [*<vers>* [*<rev>*]]

<print> ::= *<text>*	(Printer name and print zone)
<prod> ::= *<text>*	(Product string or nickname)
<vers> ::= *<real>*	(Version number)
<rev> ::= *<uint>*	(Revision number)

This comment indicates that the PostScript language instructions in the document are intended for a particular printer, which is identified by its network printer name, nickname, or product string. The printer can optionally be identified by its version and revision strings, as defined by the printer's PPD file or as returned by the **product**, **version**, and **revision** operators.

%%DocumentPrinterRequired: can be used to request a particular printer in a highly networked environment where that printer may be more convenient or to override document manager defaults and prevent rerouting of the document. It can also be used if the PostScript language file itself contains printer-specific elements. This last case should rarely be necessary, as most documents requiring particular features of a PostScript printer can provide requirement conventions indicating a need for that feature, rather than require a particular printer. Then, if other printers are available that have the necessary features, the document may still be printed as desired. The following example unconditionally routes the document to a printer called SEVILLE in the network's "Sys_Marketing" zone:

%%DocumentPrinterRequired: (SEVILLE@Sys_Marketing) ( )

If the nickname of the printer is used (this is often necessary to differentiate among different models of printers), the version/revision numbers that are part of the nickname should be ignored.

For example, the product name for a series of printers may be (SpeedyLaser). There are several models of SpeedyLaser printers, the SL300, SL600, and SL1200. The nicknames of these printers are (SL300 Version 47.2), (SL600 Version 48.1), and (SL1200 Version 49.4). To specify the need for a SL600 printer, the nickname (excluding the version number) should be used. For example:

%%DocumentPrinterRequired: ( ) (SL600)

The version and revision numbers in this comment should be used infrequently.

%%DocumentNeededFiles: **{ *<filename>* ... } I (atend)**

The comment %%DocumentNeededFiles: lists the files a document description needs. Each file mentioned in this list appears later in the document as the argument of an %%IncludeFile: comment. It is assumed that files on the %%DocumentNeededFiles: list do not include those appearing on the %%DocumentSuppliedFiles: file list.

Note   *This comment is provided for backward compatibility and may be discontinued in later versions of the DSC. Use the more general comment* %%DocumentNeededResources: *instead.*

%%DocumentSuppliedFiles: **{ *<filename>* ... } I (atend)**

The comment %%DocumentSuppliedFiles: lists the files in a document description. Each file mentioned in this list appears later in the document in the context of a %%BeginFile: and %%EndFile: comment construct. It is assumed that files on the %%DocumentSuppliedFiles: list do not include those appearing on the %%DocumentNeededFiles: file list.

Note   *This comment is provided for backward compatibility and may be discontinued in later versions of the DSC. Use the more general comment* %%DocumentSuppliedResources: *instead.*

%%DocumentFonts: { <*fontname*> ... } | (atend)

This comment indicates that the print job uses all fonts listed. In particular, there is at least one invocation of the **findfont** or **findresource** operator for each of the font names listed. The application producing the print file should not make any assumptions about which fonts are resident in the printer (for example, Times-Roman). Note that the list of font names for %%DocumentFonts: should be the union of the %%DocumentNeededFonts: and %%DocumentSuppliedFonts: font lists. If the list of font names exceeds the 255 characters-per-line limit, the %%+ comment should be used to extend the line.

Note   *This comment is provided for backward compatibility and may be discontinued in later versions of the DSC. Use the more general comments* %%DocumentNeededResources: *and*   %%DocumentSuppliedResources: *instead.*

%%DocumentNeededFonts: { <*fontname*> ... } | (atend)

This comment provides a list of fonts the document *requires* and are *not* contained in the document file. It is assumed that fonts on the %%DocumentNeededFonts: list do not appear on the %%Document-SuppliedFonts: font list. It is also assumed that there is at least one corresponding instance of the %%IncludeFont: comment for each font listed in this section.

Note   *This comment is provided for backward compatibility and may be discontinued in later versions of the DSC. Use the more general comment* %%DocumentNeededResources: *instead.*

%%DocumentSuppliedFonts: { <*fontname*> ... } | (atend)

This comment provides a list of font files that have been provided in the document print file as downloaded fonts. It is assumed that fonts on the %%DocumentSuppliedFonts: list do not appear on the %%DocumentNeededFonts: font list. There is at least one corresponding %%BeginFont: and %%EndFont pair in the document description for each of the listed font names.

Note   *This comment is provided for backward compatibility and may be discontinued in later versions of the DSC. Use the more general comment* %%DocumentSuppliedResources: *instead.*

%%DocumentProcSets: { *<procname>* ... } | (atend)

This comment provides a list of *all* procsets referenced in the document. Its use is similar to the %%DocumentFonts: comment. The list of procsets for %%DocumentProcSets: should be the union of the %%DocumentNeededProcSets: and %%DocumentSuppliedProcSets: procset lists. If the list of procset names exceeds the 255 characters-per-line limit, the %%+ comment should be used to extend the line.

Note   *This comment is provided for backward compatibility and may be discontinued in later versions of the DSC. Use the more general* %%DocumentNeededResources: *and* %%DocumentSuppliedResources: *comments instead.*

%%DocumentNeededProcSets: { *<procname>* ... } | (atend)

This comment indicates that the document needs the listed procsets. It is assumed that procsets on the %%DocumentNeededProcSets: list do not appear on the %%DocumentSuppliedProcSets: procset list. This comment is used whenever any %%IncludeProcSet: comments appear in the file.

Note   *This comment is provided for backward compatibility and may be discontinued in later versions of the DSC. Use the more general comment* %%DocumentNeededResources: *instead.*

%%DocumentSuppliedProcSets: { *<procname>* ... } | (atend)

This comment indicates that the document contains the listed procsets. It is assumed that procsets in the %%DocumentSuppliedProcSets: list do not include those appearing on the %%DocumentNeededProcSets: procset list. This comment is used whenever any %%BeginProcSet and %%EndProcSet comments appear within the document.

Note   *This comment is provided for backward compatibility and may be discontinued in later versions of the DSC. Use the more general comment* %%DocumentSuppliedResources: *instead.*

%%OperatorIntervention: [*<password>*]
<password> ::= *<textline>*

This comment causes the document manager to block a print job in the print queue until the printer operator releases the print job for printing. The comment may contain an optional *password* that the print operator must supply to release the job. This allows the printing of sensitive documents to be delayed until the intended recipient is present at the printer to pick up the document.

%%OperatorMessage: *<textline>*

If the output device has an appropriate user interface, the %%OperatorMessage: comment provides a message that the document manager can display on the console before printing the job. This comment must only appear in the header of the file.

%%ProofMode: *<mode>*
<mode> ::= TrustMe | Substitute | NotifyMe

This comment provides information about the level of accuracy that is required for printing. It is intended to provide guidance to the document manager for appropriate tactics to use when error conditions arise or when resource and feature shortages are encountered.

The three modes may be thought of as instructions to the document manager. If the document manager detects a resource or feature shortage, such as a missing font or unavailable paper size, it should take action based on these proof modes:

- TrustMe—Indicates the document manager should *not* take special action. The intent is that the document formatting programs or the user knows more than the document manager. For example, fonts may be available on a network font server that the document manager does not know about.

  Even with a comment like %%IncludeResource:, if the %%ProofMode is TrustMe, the printing manager should proceed even if a resource cannot be found. The assumption is that the document can compensate for the resource not being included.

- Substitute—Indicates the printing manager should do the best it can to supply missing resources with alternatives. This may mean substituting fonts, scaling pages (or tiling) when paper sizes are not available, and so on. This is the default proofing level and should be used if the *mode* is missing from the comment or if the comment is missing from the document.

- NotifyMe—Indicates the document should not be printed if there are any mismatches or resource shortages noted by the printing manager. For example, when printing on an expensive color printer, if the correct font is not available, the user probably does *not* want a default font. The document manager, if it cancels the print job, should notify the user in some system-specific manner.

These modes are intended for the printing manager to consider *before* it prints the file, based on its own knowledge and queries of available fonts, paper sizes, and other resources. If the file is printed, and an error occurs, that is a separate issue.

%%Requirements: *<requirement>* [(*<style>* ...)] ...
        <requirement> ::= collate | color | duplex | faceup | fax | fold | jog |
                          manualfeed | numcopies | punch | resolution | rollfed |
                          staple
    <style> ::= *<text>*

This comment describes document requirements, such as duplex printing, hole punching, collating, or other physical document processing needs. These requirements may be activated by the document using **statusdict** operators or **setpagedevice**, or they may be requested using the %%IncludeFeature: comment.

The *requirement* parameter should correspond to a specific printer feature. The optional *style* parameter can be used to further describe the specifics of the processing. For example, the punch requirement has a style to indicate that a printer capable of 19 Hole Cerlox punching is required: punch(19). If more than one style of requirement is necessary, the styles can be listed in the enclosing parentheses (separated by commas) for that requirement. For example, if both positional stapling (staple in the lower right hand corner) and staple orientation (staple at 45 degrees) is desired, the requirement is: staple(*position,orient*). This informs the document manager that the printer printing this document must be equipped with a stapler that can position *and* orient the staple.

The %%Requirements: comment can be used to determine if the printer the user selects can meet the document's requirements. If it cannot, the document should be rerouted to a printer that can, otherwise the document is not processed as expected. It is the document manager's responsibility to determine if the printer can fulfill the requirements and if the operator and/or application should be notified of any incapability. See also the %%ProofMode: comment for actions to take when there are no printers available that satisfy the requirements.

Note   *The* %%Requirements: *comment is informational only; it does not suggest that the document manager actuate these requirements—that is, turn them on. The PostScript language instructions in the document activate these features.*

The following keywords for the *requirement* parameter are defined:

- collate—Indicates that the document contains code that will instruct the printer to produce collated copies (for example, 1-2-3-1-2-3-1-2-3), rather than uncollated copies (for example, 1-1-1-2-2-2-3-3-3). If collate is not specified, then non-collation of the document should be assumed, except if the duplex, fold, jog, or staple requirements are specified (they imply collation by definition). This requirement should be used in conjunction with the numcopies requirement.

- color—Indicates that the printer must be able to print in color. If this option is not specified, monochrome printing is assumed to be sufficient.

- color(separation)—Indicates that the printer must be able to perform internal color separation. If this style modifier is not specified, composite color output is assumed to be sufficient.

- duplex—Indicates that the document issues commands such that pages are printed on both sides of the paper. Any printer intended to print such a document properly must be capable of producing duplex output.

- duplex(tumble)—Indicates a style of duplex printing in which the logical top of the back side is rotated 180 degrees from the logical top of the front side. A wall calendar is an example of a document that is typically tumble duplexed.

- faceup—Indicates that output pages are stacked face-up. If this requirement is not specified, then the selected printer need not be capable of stacking pages face-up.

- fax—Indicates that the document contains segments of PostScript code pertaining to fax devices and should be sent to a fax-capable printer.

- fold—Indicates that the document requests that the printer fold the resulting output. Typical style modifiers to this requirement would be letter, z-fold, doublegate, leftgate, rightgate, and saddle. These are illustrated in Figure G.3.

- jog—Indicates that jobs or multiple replications of the same document are offset-stacked from one another in the output tray. The document manager must ensure that the selected printer has the ability to offset stack job output.

- manualfeed—Indicates that the document requests that paper be fed in from the manual feed slot. If this requirement is not specified, the selected printer need not have a manual feed slot.

- numcopies(<*uint*>)—Indicates that the document instructs the printer to produce <*uint*> number of copies of the output. If this requirement is not specified, a default of numcopies(1) should be assumed.

- punch—Indicates that the document specifies commands concerning hole punching. If punch is not specified, the printer need not be capable of punching.

- punch(<*uint*>)—Indicates that the document contains PostScript language instructions that cause the output to be punched with <*uint*> number of holes. Typical values are 3-, 5-, and 19-hole (Cerlox) punching. If there is no *style* modifier to the punch requirement, 3-hole punching should be assumed to be acceptable.

- resolution(*x, y*)—Indicates that the printer is set to a particular resolution in the *x* and *y* directions. The printer manager must provide a printer that can print in that resolution. If this requirement is not specified, any printer resolution is acceptable.

- rollfed—Indicates that the document issues commands specific to roll-fed devices, such as where and when to cut the paper, how far to advance the paper, and so on. If this requirement is not specified, the printer need not support roll-fed paper.

- staple—Indicates that PostScript language commands in the document cause the output to be stapled. If staple is not specified as a requirement, the printer need not support stapling.

- staple([*position*],[*orient*])—Indicates a staple position and a staple orientation. A stapler may be able to position staples on a page in several different locations. If the print job needs a printer stapler that performs positioning, this should be indicated by the style keyword *position*. If staple orientation is needed (for example, 0, 45, 90, or 135 degrees), the *orient* style should be included with the staple requirement. If no style modifiers are given, then simple stapling is assumed to be sufficient (top left-hand corner).

Figure G.3 *Various fold options*

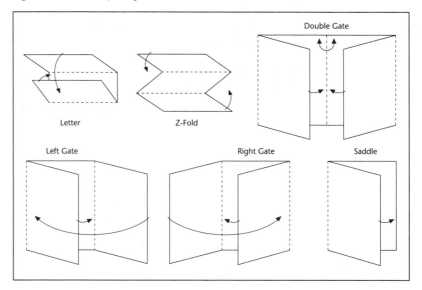

The order of the arguments to the %%Requirements: comment is significant and implies the order in which the operations occur in the Post-Script language code.

Example G.3 shows the proper use of the %%Requirements: comment and the associated %%Begin(End)Feature: comments. Three copies of this document will be printed duplex; the copies will be offset in the output tray from one another.

Example G.3

```
%!PS-Adobe-3.0
%%Title: (Example of requirements)
%%LanguageLevel: 2
%%Requirements: duplex numcopies(3) jog
%%EndComments
%%BeginProlog
...Various prolog definitions...
%%EndProlog
%%BeginSetup
% For Level 1 this could have been a series of statusdict operators
%%BeginFeature: *Duplex True
<< /Duplex true >> setpagedevice
%%EndFeature
/#copies 3 def
%%BeginFeature: *Jog 3
<< /Jog 3 >> setpagedevice
%%EndFeature
%%EndSetup
...Rest of the document...
%%EOF
```

Note that in this instance, calls to **setpagedevice** are separated for each feature. This enables a document manager to re-route the document to a Level 1 printer. If output is going to a Level 2 printer only, the following could have been used:

```
<< /Duplex true  /NumCopies true  /Jog 3 >> setpagedevice
```

Because Level 2 feature activation is device independent, the %%Begin(End)Feature: comments are unnecessary if the document is confined to Level 2 interpreters. The %%Requirements: and the %%LanguageLevel: comments are still necessary, however.

Note   *This comment lists all of the requirements for a particular job; individual pages may use some of the requirements in different combinations. To specify what the page requirements are for a particular page or for the whole document (page defaults), see the* %%PageRequirements: *comment.*

%%VMlocation: **global | local**

This comment is to inform resource users if a resource can be loaded into global or local VM. For all resource categories other than a font, the operator **findresource** unconditionally executes **true setglobal** before executing the file that defines the resource. This means a resource is loaded into global VM unless **false setglobal** appears in the resource definition.

The creator of a resource must determine if the resource works correctly in global VM. If it does, the resource must not execute **setglobal**. The resource may wish to include the %%VMlocation: global comment. The resource is loaded into global VM by **findresource**, but will be loaded into current VM under the control of a document manager if it is explicitly downloaded.

If the resource does not work in global VM or if the creator of the resource does not know if the resource will work reliably in global VM, the resource must use the %%VMlocation: local comment and the following PostScript language fragment:

```
currentglobal
false setglobal
...Definition of the resource, including defineresource...
setglobal
```

%%VMusage: *<max> <min>*

<max> ::= *<uint>*	(Maximum VM used by resource)
<min> ::= *<uint>*	(Minimum VM used by resource)

The document manager can use the information supplied by this comment to determine if the PostScript language interpreter has enough VM storage to handle this particular resource. This comment should be used only in static resource files, such as fonts, procsets, files, forms, and patterns, which are all resources that rarely change and should not generally be used in page descriptions.

max indicates the amount of VM storage this resource consumes if it is the first resource of its type to be downloaded. *min* indicates the minimum amount of VM this resource needs. The numbers may not be equal because some resources, such as fonts, can share VM storage in some versions of the PostScript interpreter. In synthetic fonts, for example, the **charstrings** of the font may be shared.

These numbers are not determined in the resource. Rather, they are determined by the resource creator when the resource (for example, a font) is initially programmed. The numbers are placed in the resource as static entities in this comment. To achieve accurate results when determining the *usage* values, make sure there are no dependencies on other resources or conditions.

The VM a resource uses can be found by issuing the **vmstatus** command before and after downloading a resource, and then again after downloading the same resource a second time. The difference between the first and second numbers (before and after the first downloading) yields the *max* value; the difference between the second and third (after the second download) yields the *min* value. The following example illustrates how to obtain the *max* and *min* values for a resource:

```
vmstatus pop /vmstart exch def pop
...The resource goes here...
vmstatus pop dup vmstart sub (Max: ) print == flush
/vmstart exch def pop
...The resource goes here...
vmstatus pop vmstart sub (Min: ) print == flush pop
```

Note   *To obtain accurate memory usage values, it is important to turn off the garbage collection mechanism in Level 2.*

G.6.2   Requirement Body Comments

Some of the comments listed in this section, if used, must have a corresponding comment in the header of the document. For example, if the %%IncludeResource: comment is used, there must be a %%DocumentNeededResources: comment in the header of the document.

Table G.2 *Body and header comment usage*

Body Comment Used	Corresponding Header Comment
%%Begin(End)Document:	%%DocumentSuppliedResources: file
%%IncludeDocument:	%%DocumentNeededResources: file
%%Begin(End)Resource:	%%DocumentSuppliedResources:
%%IncludeResource:	%%DocumentNeededResources:
%%Begin(End)File:	%%DocumentSuppliedResources: file
%%IncludeFile:	%%DocumentNeededResources: file
%%Begin(End)Font:	%%DocumentSuppliedResources: font

%%IncludeFont:	%%DocumentNeededResources: font
%%Begin(End)ProcSet:	%%DocumentSuppliedResources: procset
%%IncludeProcSet:	%%DocumentNeededResources: procset
%%Begin(End)Feature:	%%Requirements: or %%DocumentMedia:
%%IncludeFeature:	%%Requirements: or %%DocumentMedia

%%Begin and %%End comments indicate that the PostScript language instructions enclosed by these comments is a resource, feature, or document. An intelligent document manager may save resources for future use by creating a resource library on the host system. The document manager may replace printer-specific feature instructions when rerouting the document to a different printer, or may ignore duplicate DSC comments in an included document. The proper use of these comments facilitates this intelligent document handling.

%%Include comments indicate that the named resource, feature, or document (for example, font, procset, file, paper attribute, EPS file, and so on) should be included in the document at the point where the comment is encountered. The document manager fulfills these requirements so there is an inherent risk in using these comments in a document. If there is no document manager in your system environment, the document may not print correctly. As the DSC become more prevalent and strictly adhered to, there will be more document manager products available to take advantage of these %%Include comments.

%%BeginDocument:	*<name>* [*<version>* [*<type>*]]
	<name> ::= *<text>* (Document name)
	<version> ::= *<real>* (Document version)
	<type> ::= *<text>* (Document type)
%%EndDocument	(no keywords)

These comments delimit an *entire conforming document* that is imported as part of another PostScript language document or print job. The *name* of the document is usually environment-specific; it can be an operating system file name or a key to a document database. The *version* and *type* fields are optional and, if used, should provide extra information for recognizing specific documents (an example of usage is a version control system).

The %%BeginDocument: comment is necessary to allow multiple occurrences of the %!PS-Adobe-3.0, %%EndProlog, %%Trailer, and %%EOF comments in the body of a document. Any document file that is embedded within another document file *must* be surrounded by these comments.

Note   *All feature and resource requirements of an included (child) document should be inherited by the including (parent) document. For example, if a child document needs the StoneSerif font resource, this must be reflected in the %%DocumentNeededResources: comment of the parent. This is necessary so document managers can examine the top level header of any document and know all resources and features that are required.*

%%IncludeDocument: *<name>* [*<version>* [*<revision>*]]

<name> ::= *<text>*   (Document name)
<version> ::= *<real>*   (Version of the document)
<revision> ::= *<int>*   (Revision of version)

This comment is much like the %%IncludeResource: file comment except that it specifies that the included file is a *conforming document description* rather than a small portion of stand-alone PostScript language code. This means that, in all probability, the document contains at least one instance of **showpage**, and the included document should be wrapped with a **save** and **restore**. In particular, illustrations and EPSF files that have no effect other than to make marks on a page are perfectly suited for the %%IncludeDocument: convention.

When a document file is printed, usually a certain amount of PostScript language code is added to the file. Such code may deal with font downloading issues, paper sizes, or other aspects of printing once a printer has been selected for the document. At that stage, the printing manager must remove the %%IncludeDocument: comment and embed the requested document (along with all the structuring conventions that may fall within that file) between %%BeginDocument: and %%EndDocument comments.

%%BeginFeature:	*\<featuretype\>* [*\<option\>*]
	\<featuretype\> ::= *\<text\>* (PPD feature name)
	\<option\> ::= *\<text\>* (Feature option)
%%EndFeature	(no keywords)

The %%BeginFeature and %%EndFeature comments delimit any PostScript language fragments that invoke a printer-specific feature on a printer. The *featuretype* corresponds to one of the keywords in the PostScript printer description (PPD) file, and the *featuretype option* sequence must be exactly as it is found in the PPD file so it cooperates effectively with these conventions.

A document manager may choose to replace the enclosed PostScript language code with the proper sequence of instructions if the document is sent to a different printer than originally intended. In a sense, this is the opposite of the %%IncludeFeature: comment, which indicates that the document manager must invoke the specified printer feature at that position in the print file. The next two examples set up an imageable region for a job. Example G.4 uses the Level 1 **statusdict** method of selecting page size. Example G.5 uses the new Level 2 **setpagedevice** operator.

Example G.4

```
%%BeginFeature: *PageSize Legal
legal
%%EndFeature
```

Example G.5

```
%%BeginFeature: *PageSize Legal
 << /PageSize [612 1004] >> setpagedevice
%%EndFeature
```

%%IncludeFeature:	*\<featuretype\>* [*\<option\>*]
	\<featuretype\> ::= *\<text\>* (Name of desired feature)
	\<option\> ::= *\<text\>* (Feature option)

This comment specifies the need for a particular printer feature, as described in the PostScript printer description (PPD) file. Its use specifies a *requirement* a document manager must fulfill before printing (see also the discussion under %%BeginFeature). The document file may make the assumption that the %%IncludeFeature line in the file is replaced by the appropriate PostScript language fragment from the appropriate PPD file, and that the execution of the file may be contextually dependent upon this replacement. This offers a very powerful way of making a document behave differently on different printers in a device-independent manner. See the *PostScript Printer Description Files Specification* for more information about PPD files.

%%BeginFile: *<filename>*

%%EndFile   (no keywords)

The enclosed segment is a fragment of PostScript language code or some other type of resource that does not fall within any of the other resource categories. The file-server component of a document manager may extract a copy of this file for later use by the %%IncludeFile: or %%IncludeResource: file comments. The file name will usually correspond to the original disk file name on the host system.

Note   *This comment is provided for backward compatibility and may be discontinued in later versions of the DSC. Use the more general* %%Begin(End)Resource: *comments instead.*

%%IncludeFile: *<filename>*

Indicates that the document manager must insert the specified file at the current position in the document. The file name specified also must appear in the %%DocumentNeededResources: file or the %%DocumentNeededFiles: list.

Note   *This comment is provided for backward compatibility and may be discontinued in later versions of the DSC. Use the more general* %%IncludeResource: *comment instead.*

%%BeginFont: *<fontname>* [*<printername>*]
<printername> ::= *<text>*

%%EndFont   (no keywords)

These comments delimit a downloaded font. The font-server component of a document manager may remove the font from the print file (for instance, if the font is already resident on the chosen printer) or it may simply keep a copy of it for later use by the %%IncludeFont: or %%IncludeResource: font comments. The *fontname* field must be the valid PostScript language name of the font as used by the **definefont** operator, and the optional *printername* field may contain the network name of the printer, in an environment where fonts may be tied to particular printers.

Note   *This comment is provided for backward compatibility and may be discontinued in later versions of the DSC. Use the more general* %%Begin(End)Resource: *comments instead.*

%%IncludeFont: *<fontname>*

Indicates that the document manager must include the specified font at the current position in the document. The *fontname* specified should be the correct PostScript language name for the font (without the leading slash). Due to the presence of multiple **save/restore** contexts, a document manager may have to supply a specific font more than once in one document, and should do so whenever this comment is encountered.

Note   *This comment is provided for backward compatibility and may be discontinued in later versions of the DSC. Use the more general* %%IncludeResource: *comment instead.*

%%BeginProcSet: *<procname>*

%%EndProcSet   (no keywords)

The PostScript language instructions enclosed by the %%BeginProcSet: and %%EndProcSet comments typically represents some subset of the document prolog. The prolog may be broken down into many subpackages, or procedure sets (procsets), which may define groups of routines appropriate for different imaging requirements. These individual procsets are identified by name, version, and revision numbers for reference by a document management system. A document manager may choose to extract these procsets from the print file to manage them separately for a whole family of documents. An entire document prolog may be an instance of a procset, in that it is a body of procedure definitions used by a document description file. (See the %%DocumentProcSets:, %%IncludeProcSet:, and %%IncludeResource: *procset* comments). The *name*, *version*, and *revision* fields should uniquely identify the procset. The *name* may consist of a disk file name or it may use a PostScript language name under which the prolog is stored in the printer. See the %%?Begin(End)ProcSetQuery: and the %%?Begin(End)ResourceQuery: *procset* comment, which one may use to query the printer or document manager for the prolog name and version fields.

A document manager may assume that the document prolog consists of everything from the beginning of the print file through the %%EndProlog comment, which may encompass several instances of the %Begin(End)ProcSet: comments.

Note   *This comment is provided for backward compatibility and may be discontinued in later versions of the DSC. Use the more general* %%Begin(End)Resource: *comments instead.*

%%IncludeProcSet: *<procname>*

This is a special case of the more general %%IncludeResource: file comment. It requires that a PostScript language procset with the given name, version, and revision be inserted into the document at the current position. If a version-numbering scheme is not used, these fields should still be filled with a "dummy" value, such as 0. See the %%Begin(End)Resource: and %DocumentNeededResources: comments.

Note   *This comment is provided for backward compatibility and may be discontinued in later versions of the DSC. Use the more general* %%IncludeResource: *comment instead.*

%%BeginResource: *<resource>* [*<max>* *<min>*]

<max> ::= *<uint>*   (Maximum VM used by resource)

<min> ::= *<uint>*   (Minimum VM used by resource)

%%EndResource   (no keywords)

These comments delimit a resource that is defined by PostScript language code directly in the document file—for example, downloadable fonts. The resource-management component of the document manager may remove the resource from the print file and replace it with an %%IncludeResource comment (for instance, if the chosen printer already has the resource resident) or it may simply keep a copy of it for later use by the %%IncludeResource: comment. The resource name specified should also appear in the %%DocumentSuppliedResources: list.

The optional *usage* parameters should be supplied if the %%VMusage: comment is not provided in the resource. A document manager can use these numbers to determine if a particular resource will fit inside the printer VM. If it cannot, the document manager may move the resource within the print file, juggling resources until the file can fit, or it may reroute the print file to a printer with more VM. See the %%VMusage: comment for details on how to obtain these numbers for a resource.

Font note—These comments delimit a font that is being downloaded. The font server component of a document manager may remove the font from the print file (for instance, if the chosen printer already has the font resident) or it may simply keep a copy of it for later use by the %%IncludeResource: comment.

File note—The enclosed segment is a fragment of PostScript language code or some other item that does not fall within the other resource categories. The file-server component of the document manager may extract a copy of this file for later use by the %%IncludeResource: comment. The file name will usually correspond to the original disk file name on the host system.

Procset note—The PostScript language code enclosed by these comments typically represents some subset of the document prolog. The prolog may be broken down into many procedure sets, which may define groups of routines appropriate for different imaging requirements. These individual procsets are identified by a *name*, *version*, and optional *revision* numbers for reference by a print management system. A document manager may choose to extract these procsets from a print file to manage them separately for a whole family of documents. An entire document prolog may be an instance of a procset, in that it is a body of procedure definitions used by a document description file.

%%IncludeResource: *<resource>*

Indicates that the document manager must include the named resource at this point in the document. The resource name specified also must appear in the %%DocumentNeededResources: list. It is up to the application creating the document to manage memory for resources that employ this comment (using **save/restore** pairs). Although the font example below is specific to fonts, memory management and resource optimization are also applicable to forms, patterns, and other memory-intensive resources.

Font note—In the case of commonly available fonts, it is highly likely that the font server or document manager would ignore the inclusion request, because the fonts would already be available on the printer. However, the %%IncludeResource: font comment must still be included so that if a standard font is not available it can be supplied (there are printers that do not have the 13 standard fonts that are resident in most of Adobe's PostScript implementations). %%IncludeResource: font comments of this nature should be placed in the document setup section.

Due to the presence of multiple **save/restore** contexts, a font server may have to supply a specific font more than once within a single document, and should do so whenever this comment is encountered. Depending on the memory available in the target printer, a document manager may optimize font usage by moving the inclusion of fonts within the document. A frequently used font could be downloaded during the document setup, thus making it available for use by any page. A font that is used on one or two particular pages, could be downloaded during the page setups for each of the individual pages. A special font that is used for one or two paragraphs on one page only would not be moved.

In Example G.6, four different fonts (ITC Stone®, Palatino*, Carta®, and Sonata®) are downloaded. The memory management scheme used by the application that generated this code assumes that up to three fonts may be downloaded at any one point in time. Note the use of multiple %%IncludeResource: font comments for the same font when a **save-restore** pair "undefines" previously included fonts.

Example G.6

```
%!PS-Adobe-3.0
%%Title: (Example of memory management)
%%DocumentNeededResources: font Helvetica Helvetica-Bold
%%+ font StoneSerif Palatino-Roman Carta Sonata
%%EndComments
%%BeginDefaults
%%PageResources: font Helvetica Helvetica-Bold StoneSerif
%%EndDefaults
%%BeginProlog
...Document prolog...
%%EndProlog
%%BeginSetup
% Include the common fonts found in most implementations
%%IncludeResource: font Helvetica
%%IncludeResource: font Helvetica-Bold
...Rest of the set up...
%%EndSetup
%%Page: 1 1
%%PageResources: font Helvetica Helvetica-Bold
%%+ font StoneSerif Palatino-Roman Carta Sonata
%%BeginPageSetup
/pagelevel save def
%%EndPageSetup
...Text that uses common fonts like Helvetica...
/fontlevel save def
%%IncludeResource: font StoneSerif
...Text that uses the StoneSerif font and/or common fonts...
```

```
%%IncludeResource: font Palatino-Roman
...Text that uses Palatino-Roman, StoneSerif and/or common fonts...
%%IncludeResource: font Carta
...Text that uses the Carta, Palatino-Roman, StoneSerif, and/or common fonts...
fontlevel restore % Ran out of room for new fonts
/fontlevel save def
%%IncludeResource: font StoneSerif
%%IncludeResource: font Palatino-Roman
%%IncludeResource: font Sonata
...Text that uses the Sonata, Palatino-Roman, StoneSerif, and/or common fonts...
fontlevel restore % Need to switch fonts
/fontlevel save def
%%IncludeResource: font StoneSerif
%%IncludeResource: font Carta
...Text that uses the Carta, StoneSerif, and/or common fonts...
pagelevel restore
showpage
%%Page: 2 2
%%PageResources: font StoneSerif Palatino-Roman
...Rest of the document...
%%EOF
```

At print time, the document manager decides there is enough memory available in the VM of the target device to hold four fonts at any one point in time and decides to optimize the document. The Helvetica and Helvetica-Bold inclusions are ignored because these fonts are available on the printer. The page level comment %%PageResources: font StoneSerif is recognized in the defaults section, indicating that the font StoneSerif is likely to be used on every page. The document manager moves the inclusion of this font to the end of the document setup and ignores all subsequent inclusion requests for StoneSerif.

The document manager also realizes that the Palatino-Roman font is only used on pages 1 and 2. This font is downloaded at the end of the page setup for each page. The Carta and Sonata fonts are used on page 1 only. However, the Carta font is downloaded twice due to the three-font memory management scheme used by the application. The document manager also moves the downloading of the Carta font to the end of the page setup. The Sonata font is used only once and is downloaded at the %%IncludeResource: font comment. Example G.7 shows the resulting file:

Example G.7

```
%!PS-Adobe-3.0
%%Title: (Optimized file)
%%DocumentNeededResources: font Helvetica Helvetica-Bold
%%DocumentSuppliedResources: font StoneSerif Palatino-Roman Carta Sonata
```

```
%%EndComments
%%BeginDefaults
%%PageResources: font Helvetica Helvetica-Bold StoneSerif
%%EndDefaults
%%BeginProlog
...Document prolog...
%%EndProlog
%%BeginSetup
% Include the common fonts found in most implementations
%%IncludeResource: font Helvetica
%%IncludeResource: font Helvetica-Bold
%%BeginResource: font StoneSerif
...StoneSerif font is downloaded here...
%%EndResource
...Rest of the set up...
%%EndSetup
%%Page: 1 1
%%PageResources: font Helvetica Helvetica-Bold
%%+ font StoneSerif Palatino-Roman Carta Sonata
%%BeginPageSetup
/pagelevel save def
%%BeginResource: font Palatino-Roman
...Palatino-Roman font is downloaded here...
%%EndResource
%%BeginResource: font Carta
...Carta font is downloaded here...
%%EndResource
%%EndPageSetup
...Text that uses common fonts like Helvetica...
/fontlevel save def
...Text that uses the StoneSerif font and/or common fonts...
...Text that uses Palatino-Roman, StoneSerif and/or common fonts...
...Text that uses the Carta, Palatino-Roman, StoneSerif, and/or common fonts...
fontlevel restore                        % Ran out of room for new fonts
/fontlevel save def
%%BeginResource: font Sonata
...Sonata font is downloaded here...
%%EndResource
...Text that uses the Sonata, Palatino-Roman, StoneSerif, and/or common fonts...
fontlevel restore                        % Need to switch fonts again
/fontlevel save def
...Text that uses the Carta, StoneSerif, and/or common fonts...
pagelevel restore
showpage
%%Page: 2 2
%%PageResources: font StoneSerif Palatino-Roman
%%BeginPageSetup
/pagelevel save def
%%BeginResource: font Palatino-Roman
```

...Palatino-Roman font is downloaded again here...
%%EndResource
...Rest of the document...
%%EOF

Procset note—The %%IncludeResource: procset comment must appear in the document prolog only. Procsets do not generally have to worry about **save/restore** pairs as in the above example. In the case of procsets, the document manager may replace the desired procset with an upwardly compatible version of the desired procset (a newer version). See section G.4.6, "Comment Syntax," for more details on compatible procsets. In addition, the document manager may optimize procset inclusion by replacing a procset that occurs multiple times with a single copy at the top level of a document. Example G.8 shows the use of the %%IncludeResource: procset comment:

Example G.8

```
%!PS-Adobe-3.0
%%Creator: Adobe Illustrator 88(TM) 1.9.3
%%For: (Joe Smith) (Adobe Systems Incorporated)
%%Title: (Example.art)
%%CreationDate: (2/08/90) (8:30 am)
%%DocumentNeededResources: procset Adobe_packedarray 0 0
%%+ procset Adobe_cmykcolor 0 0 Adobe_cshow 0 0 Adobe_customcolor 0 0
%%+ procset Adobe_Illustrator881 0 0
%%+ font StoneSerif
%%EndComments
%%BeginProlog
%%IncludeResource: procset Adobe_packedarray 0 0
%%IncludeResource: procset Adobe_cmykcolor 0 0
%%IncludeResource: procset Adobe_cshow 0 0
%%IncludeResource: procset Adobe_customcolor 0 0
%%IncludeResource: procset Adobe_Illustrator881 0 0
%%EndProlog
...Rest of the document...
%%EOF
```

G.6.3   Requirement Page Comments

Some of the following comments that request particular page media, requirements, or resources may appear in the defaults section or in a particular page. If these comments fall within the defaults section of the document file (%%BeginDefaults to %%EndDefaults), they may be construed to be in effect for the entire print job. If they are found within the page-level comments for a page, they should only be in effect for that page. See %%Begin(End)Defaults for more details on page defaults.

%%PageFonts: { <*fontname*> ... } | (atend)

Indicates the names of all fonts used on the current page. The notation (atend) is permissible. In that case, the list of fonts must be provided after the %%PageTrailer comment. Also see the %%DocumentFonts: comment.

Note   *This comment is provided for backward compatibility and may be discontinued in later versions of the DSC. Use the more general* %%PageResources: *comment instead.*

%%PageFiles: { <*filename*> ... } | (atend)

Indicates the names of all files used on the current page. This should be used only if file inclusion is required of the document manager—that is, if there are subsequent instances of the %%IncludeFile: comment on that particular page. See also %%DocumentNeededFiles: and %%DocumentSuppliedFiles: comments.

Note   *This comment is provided for backward compatibility and may be discontinued in later versions of the DSC. Use the more general* %%PageResources: *comment instead.*

%%PageMedia: <*medianame*>

<*medianame*> ::= <*text*>   (Name of desired paper media)

Indicates that the paper attributes denoted by *medianame* are invoked on this page. The *medianame* is specified by the %%DocumentMedia: comment at the beginning of the document. This comment can pertain to either a page or a document depending on the position of the comment (for example, either in the page itself or in the defaults section). See also the %%DocumentMedia: and %%Begin(End)Defaults comments.

In Example G.9, a one-hundred page report is printed on regular white and heavy yellow paper. Ninety-nine of the pages use the white paper so the %%PageMedia: comment is found in the defaults section, denoting that the default media for this document is white paper. The white paper is set using the **setpagedevice** operator in the document setup. The cover page is the only page to use the yellow paper, and states so via the %%PageMedia: comment that appears after the first %%Page: comment. Note the use of the **currentpagedevice** operator to facilitate the restoration of the white-paper device after the cover page.

Example G.9

```
%!PS-Adobe-3.0
%%Title: (Example of %%PageMedia: as a page default)
%%DocumentMedia: Regular 612 792 75 white ( )
%%+ Cover 612 792 244 yellow DeptLetterHead
%%Pages: 100
%%LanguageLevel: 2
%%EndComments
%%BeginDefaults
%%PageMedia: Regular
%%EndDefaults
%%BeginProlog
...Prolog definitions...
%%EndProlog
%%BeginSetup
<<                                          % Attribute tray numbers to
  /InputAttributes <<                       % the particular media
    0 << /PageSize [612 792] /MediaWeight 75 /MediaColor (white) >>
    1 << /PageSize [612 792] /MediaWeight 244
        /MediaColor (yellow) /MediaType (DeptLetterHead) >>
  >>
>> setpagedevice

<< /MediaColor (white) >> setpagedevice     % Set the white paper to be the
%%EndSetup                                  % default for the document
%%Page: Cover 1
%%PageMedia: Cover
%%BeginPageSetup
/olddevice currentpagedevice def
<< /MediaColor (yellow) >> setpagedevice     % Set up the yellow paper
/pagelevel save def                          % for this page
%%EndPageSetup
...Mark the cover page...
pagelevel restore
showpage
%%PageTrailer
olddevice setpagedevice                      % Restore the white paper
%%Page: 1 2
...Rest of the document...                   % No %%PageMedia:
%%EOF                                        % comment, white letter paper
                                             % is the default
```

%%PageRequirements:	*<requirement>* [(*<style>*)] ...
	<requirement> ::= collate I color I duplex I faceup I fax I fold I jog I manualfeed I numcopies I punch I resolution I rollfed I staple
	<style> ::= *<text>*

This is the page-level invocation of a combination of the options listed in the %%Requirements: comment. It takes precedence over any document requirements set during the document setup. This comment can pertain to a page or a document depending on the position of the comment (either in the page itself or in the defaults section). See the %%Requirements: and %%Begin(End)Defaults comments.

%%PageResources:	{ *<resource>* ... } I (atend)

This comment indicates the names and values of all resources that are needed or supplied on the present page (procsets are an exception; they need not be listed). This comment can pertain to an individual page or a document, depending on the location of the comment. For example, the comment may be in the page itself or in the document defaults section. See the %%DocumentSuppliedResources:, %%DocumentNeededResources:, and %%Begin(End)Defaults comments.

G.7 Color Separation Conventions

Level 2 implementations and Level 1 implementations that contain the CMYK color extensions to the PostScript language provide more complete color functionality than the RGB color model in Level 1. There are corresponding color separation comments that programs producing PostScript language documents with color operators should use. Color separation applications can use these comments as an aid in proper color determination and to identify process color specific portions of PostScript language code. These comments can also be used to enable applications to communicate spot color usage.

Note   *These comments do not address the use of CIE based and special color spaces. Expect future versions of the DSC to do so.*

G.7.1   Color Header Comments

%%CMYKCustomColor: *\<cya> \<mag> \<yel> \<blk> \<colorname>*

\<cya> :: = *\<real>*	(Cyan percentage)
\<mag> ::= *\<real>*	(Magenta percentage)
\<yel> ::= *\<real>*	(Yellow percentage)
\<blk> ::= *\<real>*	(Black percentage)
\<colorname> ::= *\<text>*	(Custom color name)

This comment provides an *approximation* of the custom color specified by *colorname*. The four components of cyan, magenta, yellow, and black must be specified as numbers from 0 to 1 representing the percentage of that process color. The numbers are similar to the arguments to the **setcmykcolor** operator. The *colorname* follows the same custom color naming conventions as the %%DocumentCustomColors: comment.

%%DocumentCustomColors: { *\<colorname>* ... } | (atend)

\<colorname> ::= *\<text>*	(Custom color name)

This comment indicates the use of custom colors in a document. An application arbitrarily names these colors, and their CMYK or RGB approximations are provided through the %%CMYKCustomColor: or %%RGBCustomColor: comments in the body of the document. Normally, the *colorname* specified can be any arbitrary string except Cyan, Magenta, Yellow, or Black. If imaging to a specific process layer is desired, these names may be used.

%%DocumentProcessColors: { *\<color>* ... } | (atend)

\<color> ::= Cyan | Magenta | Yellow | Black

This comment marks the use of process colors in the document. Process colors are defined to be Cyan, Magenta, Yellow, and Black. This comment is used primarily when producing color separations. See also %%PageProcessColors:.

%%RGBCustomColor:	<red> <green> <blue> <colorname>	
	<red> ::= <real>	(Red percentage)
	<green> ::= <real>	(Green percentage)
	<blue> ::= <real>	(Blue percentage)
	<colorname> ::= <text>	(Custom color name)

This comment provides an *approximation* of the custom color specified by *colorname*. The three components of red, green, and blue must be specified as numbers from 0 to 1 representing the percentage of that process color. The numbers are similar to the arguments to the **setrgbcolor** operator. The *colorname* follows the same custom color naming conventions as the %%DocumentCustomColors: comment.

G.7.2 Color Body Comments

%%BeginCustomColor:	<colorname>	
	<colorname> ::= <text>	(Custom color name)
%%EndCustomColor	(no keywords)	

These comments specify that the PostScript language code fragment enclosed within should be interpreted only when rendering the separation identified by *colorname*. The *colorname* here is any text string except Cyan, Magenta, Yellow, and Black (see the exception in %%DocumentCustomColors:). During color separation, the code between these comments must only be downloaded during the appropriate pass for that custom color. Intelligent printing managers can save considerable time by omitting code within these bracketing comments during any other separations. The document composition software must be extremely careful to correctly control overprinting and knockouts if these comments are employed, because the enclosed code may or may not be executed.

Note   *In the absence of a document manager that understands these comments, the document will print incorrectly. These comments should be used only if the environment supports such a document manager.*

%%BeginProcessColor:	*<color>*
	<color> ::= Cyan | Magenta | Yellow | Black
%%EndProcessColor	(no keywords)

These comments specify that the PostScript language code fragment enclosed within should be interpreted only when rendering the separation identified by *color*. During color separation, the code between these comments must be downloaded only during the appropriate pass for that process color. Intelligent printing managers can save considerable time by omitting code within these bracketing comments on the other three separations. The document composition software must be extremely careful to correctly control overprinting and knockouts if these comments are employed, because the code may or may not be executed.

Note *In the absence of a document manager that understands these comments, the document will print incorrectly. These comments should only be used if the environment supports such a document manager.*

G.7.3 Color Page Comments

| %%PageCustomColors: | { *<colorname>* ... } \| (atend) |
| | *<colorname>* ::= *<text>*   (Custom color name) |

This comment indicates the use of custom colors in the page. An application arbitrarily names these colors, and their CMYK or RGB approximations are provided through the %%CMYKCustomColor: or %%RGBCustomColor: comments in the body of the document. See the %%DocumentCustomColors: comment.

| %%PageProcessColors: | { *<color>* ... } \| (atend) |
| | *<color>* ::= Cyan \| Magenta \| Yellow \| Black |

This comment marks the use of process colors in the page. Process colors are defined as Cyan, Magenta, Yellow, and Black. See the %%DocumentProcessColors: comment.

G.8 Query Conventions

A *query* is any PostScript language program segment that generates and returns information back to the host computer across the communications channel *before* a document can be formatted for printing. This might result from the execution of any of the **=, ==, print** or **pstack** operators, for instance. In particular, this definition covers information that is expected back from the PostScript printer for decision-making purposes. Such decision-making might include the generation of font lists or inquiries about the availability of resources, printer features, or the like.

All query conventions consist of a *begin* and *end* construct, with the keywords reflecting the type of query. For all of them, the %%?EndQuery comment should include a field for a *default* value, which document managers must return if they cannot understand or do not support query comments. The value of the default is entirely application dependent, and an application can use it to determine specific information about the spooling environment, if any, and to take appropriate default action.

G.8.1 Responsibilities

A document manager that expects to be able to interpret and correctly spool documents conforming to DSC version 3.0 must, at a minimum, perform certain tasks in response to these query conventions. In general, it must recognize the queries, remove them from the print stream, and send some reply back to the host. If a document manager cannot interpret the query, it must return the value provided as the argument to the %%?EndQuery comment.

A query can be recognized by the sequence %%?Begin followed by any number of characters (up to the 255 maximum per line, by convention) through the end-of-line indication (the % is decimal ASCII 37, and the ? is decimal ASCII 63). The end of the query is delimited by the sequence %%?End followed by some keywords, and optionally followed by a colon (: decimal ASCII 58) and the default response to the query (any text through end-of-line). A document manager should try to recognize the full query keyword, such as %%?BeginResourceQuery:, if it can, but it is obligated at least to respond to any validly formed query.

If a more intelligent query handling interface is desired, the document manager must recognize which printer the application is printing to (the %%DocumentPrinterRequired: comment may be helpful in this case). By using the PPD file for that particular printer, the known printer network configuration, and the printer status, the document manager should be able to answer the query.

G.8.2   Query Comments

%!PS-Adobe-3.0 Query   (no keywords)

A PostScript language query must be sent as a separate job to the printer to be fully spoolable. This means that an *end-of-file* indication must be sent immediately after the query job. A query job must always begin with the %!PS-Adobe-3.0 Query convention, which further qualifies the file as being a special case of a version 3.0 conforming PostScript language file. A query job contains only query comments, and need not contain any of the other standard structuring conventions. A document manager must be prepared to extract query information from any print file that begins with this comment convention. A document manager must fully parse a query job file until the EOF indication is reached.

Note   *It is permissible to include more than one query in a print job, but it is not permissible to include queries within the body of a regular print job. It cannot be guaranteed that a document manager can properly handle a print job with embedded queries.*

%%?BeginFeatureQuery: *<featuretype>* [*<option>*]
<featuretype> ::= *<text>*   (Requested feature)
<option> ::= *<text>*   (Feature option)

%%?EndFeatureQuery: *<default>*
<default> ::= *<text>*   (Default response)

This query provides information that describes the state of some specified, printer-specific feature as defined by the PostScript printer description (PPD) file. The *featuretype* field identifies the keyword as found in the PPD file. The standard response varies with the feature and is defined by the printer's PPD file. In general, the value of the *<featuretype>* or the value of *<option>* associated with the feature should be returned. In the example that follows, the PPD file keywords True or False are returned:

```
%%?BeginFeatureQuery: *InputSlot manualfeed
 statusdict /manualfeed known {
   statusdict /manualfeed get { (True) }{ (False) } ifelse
 }{
    (None)
 } ifelse = flush
%%?EndFeatureQuery: Unknown
```

%%?BeginFileQuery: *<filename>*

%%?EndFileQuery: *<default>*
                          <default> ::= *<text>*   (Default response)

The PostScript language code between these comments causes the printer to respond with information describing the availability of the specified file. This presumes the existence of a file system that is available to the PostScript interpreter, which is not the case on all implementations. The standard response consists of a line containing the file name, a colon, and either Yes or No, indicating whether the file is present.

Note   *This comment is provided for backward compatibility and may be discontinued in later versions of the DSC. Use the more general* %%?Begin(End)ResourceQuery: *comments instead.*

%%?BeginFontListQuery   (no keywords)

%%?EndFontListQuery: *<default>*
                             <default> ::= *<text>*   (Default response)

Provides a PostScript language sequence to return a list of all available fonts. It should consult the **FontDirectory** dictionary and any mass storage devices available to the interpreter. The list need not be in any particular order, but each name should be returned separated by a slash / character. This is normally the way the PostScript == operator returns a font name. All white space characters should be ignored. The end of the font list must be indicated by a trailing * (asterisk) sign on a line by itself (decimal ASCII 42).

Note   *This comment is provided for backward compatibility and may be discontinued in later versions of the DSC. Use the more general* %%?Begin(End)ResourceListQuery: *comments instead.*

%%?BeginFontQuery: *<fontname>* ...

%%?EndFontQuery: *<default>*
                          <default> ::= *<text>*   (Default response)

This comment provides a PostScript language query that should be combined with a particular list of font names being sought. It looks for any number of names on the stack and prints a list of values depending on whether the font is known to the PostScript interpreter. The font names must be provided on the operand stack by the document manager. This is done by simply sending the names, with leading slash / characters, before sending the query itself.

To prevent the document manager from having to keep track of the precise order in which the values are returned and to guard against errors from dropped information, the syntax of the returned value /FontName: Yes or /FontName: No. Each font in the list is returned this way. The slashes delimit the individually returned font names, although newlines should be expected (and ignored) between them. A final * (asterisk) character follows the returned values.

Note *This comment is provided for backward compatibility and may be discontinued in later versions of the DSC. Use the more general* %%?Begin(End)ResourceQuery: *comments instead.*

%%?BeginPrinterQuery (no keywords)

%%?EndPrinterQuery: *<default>*

<default> ::= *<text>*   (Default response)

This comment delimits PostScript language code that returns information describing the printer's *product name, version,* and *revision* numbers. The standard response consists of the printer's product name, version, and revision strings, each of which must be followed by a newline character, which must match the information in the printer's printer description file. This comment may also be used to identify the presence of a spooler, if necessary. In the following example the default response as represented in the %%?EndPrinterQuery: line is the word spooler, which would be returned by spooling software that *did not* have a specific printer type attached to it.

```
%%?BeginPrinterQuery
statusdict begin
revision == version == productname == flush
end
%%?EndPrinterQuery: spooler
```

%%?BeginProcSetQuery: *<procname>*

%%?EndProcSetQuery: *<default>*
<default> ::= *<text>*   (Default response)

These comments delimit a procset query. The combination of the *name,* *version,* and *revision* fields must uniquely identify the procset. The standard response to this query consists of a line containing any of the values 0, 1, 2 where a value of 0 means the procset is *missing*, a value of 1 means the procset is *present and OK*, and a value of 2 indicates the procset is present but is an incompatible version. Note that methods for procset queries are procset specific.

```
%%?BeginProcSetQuery: adobe_distill 1.1 1
/adobe_distill_dict where {
begin mark VERSION (1.) anchorsearch {(1)}{(2)} ifelse cleartomark
end
}{
(0)
} ifelse print flush
%%?EndProcSetQuery: unknown
```

Note   *This comment is provided for backward compatibility and may be discontinued in later versions of the DSC. Use the more general* %%?Begin(End)ResourceQuery: *comments instead.*

%%?BeginQuery: *<identifier>*
<identifier> ::= *<text>*   (Query identifier)

%%?EndQuery: *<default>*
<default> ::= *<text>*   (Default response)

These comments are for very general purposes and may serve any function that the rest of the query conventions, which are very specific, do not adequately cover. To understand and intelligently respond to a query, a document manager must semantically understand the query. Therefore, specific keywords, such as %%?BeginPrinterQuery, are used. When the generic %%?BeginQuery comment is encountered, a spooler may be forced to return the default value. The comment is included primarily for large installations that must implement specific additional queries not covered here, and which will likely implement the document composition software and the document manager software.

%%?BeginResourceListQuery: font | file | procset | pattern | form | encoding

%%EndResourceListQuery: *<text>*

These comments delimit a segment of PostScript language code that returns a list of all available resources. The arguments specify which type of resources to return. The code that these comments delimit should consult local VM, global VM, and any mass storage devices available to compile a complete list of resources. The resulting list need not be in any particular order, but the syntax of the returned values is the *resource type* followed by the *resource name*. The end of the resource list must be indicated by a trailing * (asterisk) on a line by itself.

Note that font names must be returned with a slash / character in front of each font name.

Note   *The use of this type of query is discouraged because it can be time consuming for interpreters with many accessible resources (for example, a printer with a hard disk attached). It is far better to query for individual resources by using the %%?Begin(End)ResourceQuery: comment.*

%%?BeginResourceQuery: *<resource>...*

%%?EndResourceQuery: *<default>*
<default> ::= *<text>*   (Default response)

The PostScript language code between these comments causes the printer to respond with information describing the availability of the specified resources. This code looks for any number of resource names on the stack, and prints a list of values depending on whether the resource is known to the PostScript interpreter.

The document manager could also process this query by using information known about the print network and current printer status. To reduce the overhead involved in keeping track of the precise order in which values are returned, and to guard against errors from dropped information, the syntax of the returned value is the *resource type* and *name* followed by a colon, a space and then a yes or a no. The end of the list should be denoted by a *.

Note   *It is recommended that a separate resource query be used for each type of resource.*

A file resource query presumes that a file system is available to the Post-Script interpreter. This is not the case in all implementations. Example G.10 shows a typical font resource query:

Example G.10

```
%!PS-Adobe-3.0 Query
%%Title: (Resource query for specified fonts)
%%?BeginResourceQuery: font Times-Roman Adobe-Garamond StoneSerif
/Times-Roman
/Adobe-Garamond
/StoneSerif
%%BeginFeature: *?FontQuery
save 4 dict begin /sv exch def
/str (fonts/                    ) def
/st2 128 string def
{
  count 0 gt {
    dup st2 cvs (Font /) print print
    dup FontDirectory exch known
    { pop (: Yes) }
    { str exch st2 cvs
      dup length /len exch def
      6 exch putinterval str 0 len 6 add getinterval mark exch
      { } st2 filenameforall counttomark
      0 gt {? cleartomark (: Yes) }{ cleartomark (: No) }ifelse
    } ifelse = flush
  }{ exit } ifelse
} bind loop
(*) = flush
sv end restore
%%EndFeature
%%?EndResourceQuery:  Unknown
%%EOF
```

The output from this sample program could be:

```
Font /StoneSerif: Yes
Font /Adobe-Garamond: No
Font /Times-Roman: No
*
```

%%?BeginVMStatus	(no keywords)
%%?EndVMStatus:	*<default>*
	<default> ::= *<text>* (Default response)

This comment delimits PostScript language instructions that return the state of the PostScript interpreter's VM. The standard response consists of a line containing the results of the PostScript language **vmstatus** operator as shown in Example G.11:

Example G.11

```
%!PS-Adobe-3.0 Query
%%Title: (VM status query)
%%?BeginVMStatus
vmstatus
(Maximum: ) print =
(Used: ) print =
(Save Level: ) print = flush
%%?EndVMStatus: Unknown
%%EOF
```

G.9 Open Structuring Conventions

There is an open extension mechanism for the DSC comments. Its purpose is to enable other vendors to extend the functionality of the DSC without having to rely on Adobe to amend the official specification.

Vendors may need or want to embed extra information in a file beyond the comments that Adobe has already specified. To facilitate this and to minimize conflicts and difficulties for the vendor, Adobe maintains a registry of comment prefixes that are allocated to vendors, and these comments may be used in any way that is meaningful to those vendors. You may contact the registry at the following address:

Adobe Systems Incorporated
DSC Coordinator
1585 Charleston Road
P.O. Box 7900
Mountain View, CA 94039-7900
(415) 961-4400

G.9.1 The Extension Mechanism

All existing Adobe-specified comments in the DSC begin with the same prefix, except one. Here is a quick summary of the syntax of existing comments:

The first line of a PostScript language file must, by convention, begin with the characters %! (percent and exclamation, often referred to as "percent-bang"). If the file is a conforming file, meaning that it conforms to the DSC version 3.0, then it is further qualified with **PS-Adobe-3.0**. This may be optionally continued by some special keywords, such as EPSF or ExitServer, to identify the entire file as a special instance. The first line of a PostScript language file may look something like this:

```
%!PS-Adobe-3.0 EPSF 3.0
```

This is the only Adobe-defined comment that does *not* begin with two percent signs.

All remaining structuring conventions, in their various forms, are represented as comments beginning with *two* percent signs (%%) as the first characters on the line.

The extension mechanism for the open structuring conventions is to use one percent character followed immediately by a *vendor-specific* prefix of up to five characters. Beyond those five characters the vendor who has registered the prefix is responsible for the comments. The comment is terminated at the end of the line.

Open structuring conventions may be used much like the existing DSC and have similar syntax and philosophy. Here are some examples of *fictitious* comments from made-up company prefixes:

```
%GCRImageName: myimage.ps
%BCASpoolerName: local_spool 1.0
%BCACoverStock: 10129
%BCADocumentOrigin: (New York Office)
```

Restrictions

Adobe does not specify where in the document open structuring convention comments can appear. However, the comments must not conflict in any way with the regular parsing of document structuring conventions, and their specification and use is otherwise truly open.

If these vendor-specific comments interact in some meaningful way with the DSC, this interaction should be clearly specified by the creator of the comments, and the description should specify the version number of the DSC with which they interact.

The new comments, however implemented, should still follow the conforming files restrictions discussed in section G.3, "DSC Conformance."

Parsing Rules

Although the exact syntax of the vendor-specific comments is up to the vendor, we strongly recommend adhering to the existing conventions and parsing rules to simplify the task of writing parsing software.

Note   *The syntax and parsing rules for vendor-specific comments are up to the vendor, and you should contact the vendor for details. The rules and details supplied in this document are guidelines and suggestions that are recommended, but are not enforced by Adobe.*

G.10   Special Structuring Conventions

There are two comments that do not readily fall into the other comment categories. They are listed below, along with a description of when they should be used.

%%BeginExitServer: *<password>*
<password> ::= *<text>*

%%EndExitServer   (no keywords)

These comments delimit the PostScript language sequence that causes the rest of the file to be executed as an unencapsulated job (see section 3.7.7, "Job Execution Environment"). This convention is used to flag any code that sets up or executes the **exitserver** or **startjob** operators, so a document manager can recognize and remove this sequence if necessary. The %%Begin(End)ExitServer comments may be used with the %%EOF requirement convention to pinpoint where the document manager should send an end-of-file indication. See the %!PS-Adobe-3.0 comment. PostScript language jobs that use **exitserver** or **startjob** should be specially flagged with the %!PS-Adobe-3.0 ExitServer notation. An example of appropriate use is shown in the following example:

```
%!PS-Adobe-3.0 ExitServer
%%Title: (Example of exitserver usage)
%%EndComments
```

```
%%BeginExitServer: 000000
serverdict begin 000000 exitserver
%%EndExitServer
...PostScript language instructions to perform persistent changes...
%%EOF
```

G.11 Changes Since Earlier Versions

The following section details changes made to the DSC specification since version 1.0 (Appendix C in the first edition of the *PostScript Language Manual*). These changes are important to document managers that may wish to allow backward compatibility with previous versions of this specification.

G.11.1 Changes Since Version 1.0

In DSC version 1.0, there were several comment conventions that were required to minimally conform to that version of the specification. These comments were:

```
%%DocumentFonts:
%%EndProlog
%%Page:
%%Trailer
```

As of version 2.1, there no longer are any *required* comments. All comments are optional in the sense that they may not be appropriate in a given situation. The only rule is to make sure to use them correctly.

The following comments were added as of version 2.1:

```
%%Begin(End)Binary:
%%Begin(End)CustomColor:
%%Begin(End)Document:
%%Begin(End)ExitServer:
%%Begin(End)Feature:
%%Begin(End)File:
%%Begin(End)Font:
%%Begin(End)Object:
%%Begin(End)PageSetup:
%%Begin(End)PaperSize:
%%Begin(End)ProcessColor:
%%Begin(End)ProcSet
%%Begin(End)Setup
```

%%CMYKCustomColor:
%%DocumentCustomColors:
%%DocumentNeededFiles:
%%DocumentNeededFonts:
%%DocumentNeededProcSets:
%%DocumentPaperColors:
%%DocumentPaperSizes:
%%DocumentPaperForms:
%%DocumentPaperWeights:
%%DocumentPrinterRequired:
%%DocumentProcSets:
%%DocumentProcessColors:
%%DocumentSuppliedFiles:
%%DocumentSuppliedFonts:
%%DocumentSuppliedProcSets:
%%ExecuteFile:
%%IncludeFile:
%%IncludeFont:
%%IncludeProcSet:
%%EOF
%%Feature:
%%PageBoundingBox:
%%PageCustomColors:
%%PageFonts:
%%PageFiles:
%%PageProcessColors:
%%PageTrailer
%%PaperColor:
%%PaperForm:
%%PaperSize:
%%PaperWeight:
%%ProofMode:
%%Requirements:
%%RGBCustomColor:
%%Routing:
%%?Begin(End)FeatureQuery:
%%?Begin(End)FileQuery:
%%?Begin(End)FontQuery:
%%?Begin(End)FontListQuery:
%%?Begin(End)ProcSetQuery:
%%?Begin(End)PrinterQuery:
%%?Begin(End)Query:
%%?Begin(End)VMStatus:

The following comment was discontinued in version 2.1 and should be ignored by document managers:

%%ChangeFont:

G.11.2 Changes Since Version 2.1

The DSC version 3.0 specification has been reorganized as a whole to better present the concepts. The first half of the specification is a how-to guide and discusses why the comments should be used. The second half is a reference, detailing the comments.

The introduction introduces the concepts of a document manager and how a document manager might use the comments.

A new section talks about the various services a document can receive from a document manager. These services can be obtained through proper use of the DSC comments. Services include spooling, banner and trailer pages, print logging, resource inclusion, resource download-ing, resource optimization, error reporting and recovery, printer rerout-ing, feature inclusion, parallel printing, color breakout, page reversal, n-up printing, range printing, collated printing, and overlays. See section G.2, "Document Manager Services."

The section detailing DSC conformance has been expanded and is more precise. A document either conforms or does not conform to this speci-fication. See section G.3, "DSC Conformance."

A new section describing proper document structure was added. In par-ticular, the placement of various comments in the document is dis-cussed as are restrictions on the prolog and script. See section G.4, "Document Structure Rules."

A section detailing the breakdown of conventions into different catego-ries was added, as well as detailed explanations of header, body and page comment types. The comments are arranged in the reference sec-tion of the document according to these categories. See section G.4.5, "Convention Categories."

The syntax of the DSC comments was qualified in Backus-Naur form (BNF) to avoid ambiguities. A new section of the document talks about BNF and defines some elementary types. See section G.4.6, "Comment Syntax Reference."

The open structuring conventions are new as of this version. They define an extensible mechanism for defining vendor-specific comments. See section G.9, "Open Structuring Conventions."

New Comments For Version 3.0

The following comments were added as of version 3.0:

```
%%Begin(End)Data:
%%Begin(End)Defaults
%%Begin(End)Emulation:
%%Begin(End)Preview:
%%BeginProlog
%%Begin(End)Resource:
%%Copyright:
%%DocumentData:
%%DocumentMedia:
%%DocumentNeededResources:
%%DocumentSuppliedResources:
%%Emulation:
%%Extensions:
%%IncludeDocument:
%%IncludeFeature:
%%IncludeResource:
%%LanguageLevel:
%%OperatorIntervention:
%%OperatorMessage:
%%Orientation:
%%PageMedia:
%%PageOrder:
%%PageOrientation:
%%PageRequirements:
%%PageResources:
%%Version
%%VMlocation:
%%VMusage:
%%?Begin(End)ResourceQuery:
%%?Begin(End)ResourceListQuery:
```

There are three justifications for the addition of the %%BeginProlog comment. Previously, the beginning of the prolog section of the document was implicitly declared after the %%EndComments comment. This was confusing in the case of EPSI files that needed to insert the EPSI preview after the comments and before the prolog, which was defined as the first %%BeginProcSet: comment. In addition, there may be instances when a document does not need formal procset definitions, but needs a prolog. Finally, in the interest of language purity, a corresponding %%Begin comment is necessary for each %%End comment. Expect to see this pairing of comments in future revisions of the DSC.

Changes to Existing Comments

%!PS-Adobe-3.0
In addition to changing the version number from 2.1 to 3.0, the new EPSF version number was added, as well as a general format keyword for resources.

%%Pages:
The optional *pageorder* number at the end of the comment is no longer recommended (-1 indicated descending order, 0 indicated special order, and 1 indicated ascending order). There have been cases of conflicts between pre-knowledge of page orders and page numbers; in other words, an application may not know the number of pages, and wishes to defer this comment to the end of the document, but it may already know the page order. Previewers and other document managers gain an advantage if they know the page order as soon as possible. If page order must be specified, it is recommended that it be done using the %%PageOrder: comment.

%%Begin(End)Binary:
There has been some confusion with this comment. Both hex and 8-bit binary data has been seen between these comments. There also have been some cases in which the byte count argument to this comment has been used to specify the number of lines of data. A new comment, %%Begin(End)Data:, has been introduced to deal with these ambiguities. The new comment may also be extended in future versions of the DSC to deal with compression and other filters, so a document manager can handle special filtering on Level 1 implementations.

%%Requirements:
The idea of option *styles* is introduced. These styles modify the requirement option in some manner. For example, punch(3) indicates that the printer needs to support 3 hole punching. Similarly, duplex(tumble) indicates that the printer must be able to perform tumble duplexing.

New options include manualfeed, numcopies, collate, jog, faceup, resolution, rollfed, fax, and punch. They reflect the additional functionality added by the Level 2 **setpagedevice** operator.

Deleted options include simplex, punch3, punch5. The simplex option is redundant because if duplex is not specified as a requirement, simplex is implied. The punch3 and punch5 options have been superceded by the idea of style modifiers (see above).

%%Begin(End)Document:
There has been a note added to this comment indicating that feature and resource requirements of an included document should be inherited by the including document.

%%ExecuteFile:
This comment has been renamed %%IncludeDocument to better reflect its meaning.

%%Feature:
This comment has been renamed %%IncludeFeature: to more clearly express its dependence on the document manager.

Discontinued Comments For Version 3.0

%%BeginPaperSize:
%%EndPaperSize
The comments %%BeginFeature: and %%EndFeature should be substituted.

%%DocumentPaperColors:
%%DocumentPaperForms:
%%DocumentPaperSizes:
%%DocumentPaperWeights:
These comments have been replaced by the single %%DocumentMedia: comment. This new comment addresses two shortcomings of DSC version 2.1. First, the new comment provides the linkage among the various parameters describing an output medium. Second, a generalized portable methodology for describing paper is provided.

For document managers concerned with backward compatibility, the following comments

```
%%DocumentPaperColors: white buff pink
%%DocumentPaperForms: Plain Plain CorpLetterHead
%%DocumentPaperSizes: letter letter legal
%%DocumentPaperWeights: 20 65 20
```

can be converted to

```
%%DocumentMedia: Wplain 612 792 75 white
%%+ Bplain 612 792 244 buff
%%+ CLHpink 612 1008 75 pink CorpLetterHead
```

Note that in version 2.1 there was no explicit link among the listed arguments and the other comments. The document manager will have to use a best-guess method of conversion or ignore these comments entirely.

```
%%PaperColor:
%%PaperForm:
%%PaperSize:
%%PaperWeight:
```
The individual paper-request comments are now replaced with the single %%PageMedia: comment.

Document managers trying to maintain backward compatibility should match the %%DocumentMedia: comment with its old counterparts (see above). %%PageMedia: will use the names of the different media specified in %%DocumentMedia: to specify changes in media. The paper comments for forms, colors, and weights should be replaced with the corresponding %%PageMedia: comment.

G.12　DSC Version 3.0 Summary

The following summary lists the comments that comprise version 3.0 of the document structuring conventions.

Note　*Some comments in this document may be discontinued in future versions of the DSC and are not found in this list. However, they are in the body of the document for backward compatibility with existing applications and document managers. Their use is discouraged; they will eventually be omitted from the specification.*

G.12.1　General Conventions

General Header Comments

```
%!PS-Adobe-3.0
%%BoundingBox:
%%Creator:
%%CreationDate:
%%DocumentData:
%%DocumentPrinterRequired:
%%Emulation:
%%EndComments
%%Extensions:
%%For:
%%Version:
%%Copyright:
%%LanguageLevel:
%%OperatorIntervention:
%%OperatorMessage:
%%Orientation:
%%Pages:
%%Routing:
%%Title:
```

General Body Comments

```
%%+
%%Begin(End)Data:
%%Begin(End)Defaults
%%Begin(End)Emulation:
%%Begin(End)ExitServer:
%%Begin(End)Preview:
%%Begin(End)Prolog
%%Begin(End)Setup
```

General Page Comments

%%Begin(End)Object:
%%Begin(End)PageSetup:
%%Page:
%%PageBoundingBox:
%%PageOrientation:

General Trailer Comments

%%PageTrailer
%%Trailer
%%EOF

G.12.2   Requirement Conventions

Requirement Header Comments

%%DocumentMedia:
%%DocumentNeededResources:
%%DocumentSuppliedResources:
%%Requirements:
%%ProofMode:
%%VMlocation:
%%VMusage:

Requirement Body Comments

%%Begin(End)Document:
%%Begin(End)Feature:
%%Begin(End)Resource:
%%EOF
%%IncludeDocument:
%%IncludeFeature:
%%IncludeResource:

Requirement Page Comments

%%PageMedia:
%%PageRequirements:
%%PageResources:

G.12.3 Color Separation Conventions

Color Header Comments

%%CMYKCustomColor:
%%DocumentCustomColors:
%%DocumentProcessColors:
%%RGBCustomColor:

Color Body Comments

%%Begin(End)CustomColor:
%%Begin(End)ProcessColor:

Color Page Comments

%%PageCustomColors
%%PageProcessColors

G.12.4 Query Conventions

%!PS-Adobe-3.0 Query
%%?Begin(End)FeatureQuery:
%%?Begin(End)PrinterQuery:
%%?Begin(End)Query:
%%?Begin(End)ResourceQuery:
%%?Begin(End)ResourceListQuery:
%%?Begin(End)VMStatus:

Encapsulated PostScript File Format—Version 3.0

The encapsulated PostScript file (EPSF) format is a standard format for importing and exporting PostScript language files among applications in a variety of heterogeneous environments. This appendix details the format and contains specific information about the Macintosh® and MS-DOS® environments. The EPSF format is based on and conforms to the document structuring conventions (DSC) detailed in Appendix G. Proper use of the document structuring conventions is required when creating a PostScript language file that conforms to the EPSF format.

The main topics of this appendix include creating encapsulated Post-Script (EPS) files, importing EPS files into other PostScript language files, and optional screen preview images for EPS files. Finally, a detailed example illustrates the concepts presented throughout this appendix.

H.1 Introduction

An encapsulated PostScript file is a PostScript language program describing the appearance of a single page. Typically, the purpose of the EPS file is to be included, or "encapsulated," in another PostScript language page description. The EPS file can contain any combination of text, graphics, and images, and it is the same as any other PostScript language page description with only a few restrictions. Figure H.1 conceptually shows how an EPS file can be included in another PostScript document.

Figure H.1 *Document with an imported EPS file*

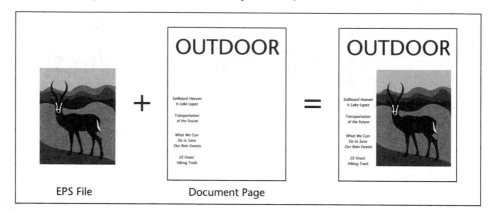

EPS File   Document Page

Applications that create conforming EPS files must follow the guidelines in section H.2, "Guidelines for Creating EPS Files." There are two required DSC comments, some conditionally required comments, and several programming guidelines to ensure that the EPS file can be reliably imported into an arbitrary PostScript language page description without causing any side effects. An example of a side effect is erasing the page of the importing document or terminating the print job.

Applications that import EPS files must follow the guidelines in section H.3, "Guidelines for Importing EPS Files." An application importing an EPS file must parse the EPS file for DSC comments and extract at least the bounding box and resource dependencies of the EPS file. The application should also read and display the screen preview, if present. If there is no screen preview provided in the EPS file, the application must provide an alternate representation and allow the user to place and transform the preview on the screen. The application must then convert the user's manipulations into the appropriate transformation to the PostScript coordinate system before sending the document to the printer. The application must also preserve its stacks, current dictionary, and graphics state before the imported EPS file is executed.

Note that EPS files are a *final-form* representation. They cannot be edited when imported into a document. However, the imported EPS file as a whole may be manipulated to some extent, including transformations such as translation, rotation, scaling, and clipping.

The device-independent nature of the PostScript language makes it an excellent interchange format. However, it normally requires a PostScript language interpreter to preview an EPS file on screen. Display PostScript systems allow EPS files to be dynamically interpreted, insuring the highest-quality, on-screen preview regardless of scale, rotation, or monitor type. For other environments where the Display PostScript system is not available, the EPS file format allows for an optional screen preview image.

The format of this preview representation varies from system to system. It is typically a Macintosh PICT resource, a TIFF file, or a device-independent hex bitmap. If the EPS file does not provide a preview image, the application that includes the EPS file must provide a representation of the preview, such as a gray box that represents the extent of the EPS file. The end user can use the screen preview to position and size the EPS file in the document.

To support encapsulated PostScript files effectively, some cooperation is required among the applications that *produce* EPS files and those that *use* EPS files. Typically, EPS files are used by importing (or including) them in other documents.

All DSC comments in an EPS file communicate information. How an application uses this information is up to the programmer of the including application. When importing an EPS file, do not reduce the amount of information in the EPS file by improperly removing or altering DSC comments. In general, the comments indicate what resources and language extensions are used, and where they are used in the EPS file. Encapsulated PostScript files are final-form print files that do not know anything about the printer on which they will be imaged. If they have specific resource needs, such as fonts, these needs must be carefully preserved and addressed.

Any application that generates PostScript language programs is potentially both a *consumer* and a *producer* of encapsulated PostScript files. It is probably best not to think that an application is at either end of the chain. If an application imports an EPS file, it is responsible for reading and understanding any of the resource needs of the imported EPS file. These needs must be reflected in the resource usage comments of the composite document the including application creates. For example, if an imported EPS file uses Lithos™, but the rest of the document is set in Times-Roman, then by importing the EPS file, the document now also uses the Lithos font. This fact must be reflected in the composite document's outermost %%DocumentNeededFonts: comment. This concept holds true for the %%DocumentNeededResources:, %%LanguageLevel: and %%Extensions: comments as well.

H.2 Guidelines for Creating EPS Files

To be considered a conforming EPSF version 3.0 file, a file must follow the rules set forth in this appendix, be a *single* page document that fully conforms to the DSC version 3.0 or later (described in Appendix G), and include two required DSC header comments.

H.2.1 Required DSC Header Comments

The two required DSC Header comments are

```
%!PS-Adobe-3.0 EPSF-3.0
%%BoundingBox: llx lly urx ury
```

The first required DSC header comment informs the including application that the file conforms to version 3.0 of the EPSF format as described in this appendix. This is the version comment.

The second required DSC header comment provides information about the size of the EPS file and must be present so the including application can transform and clip the EPS file properly. This is the bounding box comment.

The four arguments of the bounding box comment correspond to the lower-left (*llx, lly*) and upper-right (*urx, ury*) corners of the bounding box. They are expressed in the default PostScript coordinate system. For an EPS file, the bounding box is the smallest rectangle that encloses all the marks painted on the *single* page of the EPS file. Graphics state information, such as the current line width and line join parameters, must be considered when calculating the bounding box. Example H.1 shows a minimally conforming EPS file that draws a square with a line width of 10 units.

Example H.1

```
%!PS-Adobe-3.0 EPSF-3.0
%%BoundingBox: 5 5 105 105
10 setlinewidth
10 10 moveto
0 90 rlineto 90 0 rlineto 0 -90 rlineto closepath
stroke
```

The marks painted by Example H.1, and how they are positioned with respect to the PostScript coordinate system, are illustrated in Figure H.2. If the line width were not considered when calculating the bounding box, the bounding box would be incorrectly positioned by five units on each side of the square, causing the application to incorrectly place and clip the imported EPS file. The bounding box specified for this example is correct.

Figure H.2 *Calculating the correct bounding box*

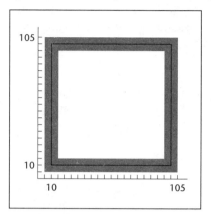

Regardless of the coordinate system in which an application operates, there is a convenient way to estimate the bounding box: Print the page, then use a point ruler to measure from the lower-left corner of the paper to the lower-left corner of the image. Then measure to the upper-right corner, also using the lower-left corner of the paper as the origin. These two measurements give the bounding box and do not depend on any computation.

H.2.2 Conditionally Required Comments

There are several optional DSC comments that may be conditionally required for a conforming EPS file. These comments must appear in an EPS file if certain features are present—for example, comments to bracket the preview section or to state that a certain language version or language extensions must be present in the interpreter.

The %%Begin(End)Preview comments must bracket the preview section of an EPS file if the preview is represented in the encapsulated Post-Script interchange (EPSI) format. See section H.6, "Device-Independent Screen Preview," for details and an example of EPSI.

The %%Extensions: comment is required if the EPS file requires a Post-Script language interpreter that supports particular PostScript language extensions to print properly. For example, the EPS file may contain

CMYK language extension operators and must be sent to a printer that can handle those operators. In such a case, the EPS file must contain either the %%Extensions: CMYK or the %%LanguageLevel: 2 comment.

The %%LanguageLevel: comment is required if the EPS file uses Level 2 features without providing conditional emulation. With this information, the including application can alert the user and avoid any errors that would be generated if the file were sent to a Level 1 printer.

If the EPS file uses language extensions or Level 2 features, and it provides complete emulation of the features in terms of Level 1 operators, the %%Extensions: and %%LanguageLevel: comments are not necessary. See Appendix D for compatibility and emulation strategies.

If the EPS file requires any fonts, files, forms, patterns, procsets (procedure sets), or any other resources, the appropriate DSC comment must appear in the header comments section of the file. See Appendix G.

H.2.3   Recommended Comments

An application or spooler may optionally use the general header comments %%Creator:, %%Title:, and %%CreationDate: to provide information about a document. These header comments are strongly recommended for EPS files.

H.2.4   Illegal and Restricted Operators

There are some PostScript language operators plus **statusdict** and **userdict** operators that are intended for system-level jobs or page descriptions that are not appropriate in an EPS file. In addition to all operators in **statusdict** and the operators in **userdict** for establishing an imageable area, the following operators must not be used in an EPS file:

banddevice	**exitserver**	**initmatrix**	**setshared**
clear	**framedevice**	**quit**	**startjob**
cleardictstack	**grestoreall**	**renderbands**	
copypage	**initclip**	**setglobal**	
erasepage	**initgraphics**	**setpagedevice**	

If used properly, the following operators are allowed in an EPS file. However, use of any of these must comply with the rules in Appendix I. Improper use can cause unpredictable results.

nulldevice	**sethalftone**	**setscreen**	**undefinefont**
setgstate	**setmatrix**	**settransfer**	

H.2.5 Stacks and Dictionaries

The PostScript interpreter's operand and dictionary stacks *must* be left in the state they were in before the EPS file was executed. The EPS file must not leave objects on either of these two stacks as a result of its execution. All operators placed on the operand stack must be used or removed from the stack with the **pop** operator.

It is strongly recommended that an EPS file make all of it definitions in its own dictionary. This means an EPS file should create its own dictionary or dictionaries instead of writing into the importing application's current dictionary. In Level 1 interpreters, the dictionary the importing application uses may not have room for the EPS file definitions. Also, to avoid the possibility of an **invalidrestore** error, make sure the EPS file's dictionary is removed from the dictionary stack using the PostScript language operator **end** when the EPS file has finished using it. Every dictionary that the EPS file places on the dictionary stack with a **begin** operator must be removed from the dictionary stack by the EPS file with a corresponding **end** operator.

Note   *Do not use the **clear** or **cleardictstack** operators to clear the stacks in an EPS file. These wholesale cleanup operators not only clear the EPS file's operands and dictionaries from the stacks, they may clear other objects as well.*

The PostScript dictionary lookup mechanism searches the dictionaries that are on the dictionary stack. Bypassing the dictionary lookup mechanism for system-level names is *illegal* in an EPS file. *Do not use the following type of code:*

```
/S systemdict /showpage get def          % Illegal EPS code
```

It may cause incorrect results in the including application's PostScript output by overriding the application's redefinitions.

H.2.6 Graphics State

An application importing an EPS file may transform the PostScript coordinate system or alter some other aspect of the graphics state so it is no longer in its default state. This allows the application to change the appearance of the EPS file, typically by resizing, clipping, or rotating the illustration. If the EPS file makes assumptions about the graphics state, such as the current clipping path, or explicitly sets something it shouldn't, such as the transformation matrix (see section H.2.4, "Illegal and Restricted Operators"), the results may not be what were expected.

In preparation for including an EPS file, the graphics state must be set by the including application as follows: current color to black, line caps to square butt end, line joins to mitered, line width to 1, dash pattern to solid, miter limit to 10, and current path to an empty path. Also, if printing to a Level 2 interpreter, overprint and stroke adjust should be set to *false*. An EPS file can assume that this is the default state. It is the responsibility of the application importing the EPS file to make sure that the graphics state is correctly set.

H.2.7 Initializing Variables

It is common for PostScript language programs to use short names, such as x, for variables or procedures. Name-conflict problems can occur if an EPS file does not initialize its variables *before* defining its procedures—in particular, before binding them. In the following example, the variable x is not initialized before being used in the procedure proc1. Because the value of x in the enclosing program happens to be an operator, **bind** causes the name x to be replaced by the operator **lineto** in proc1. This causes a **stackunderflow** error upon execution.

```
%!PS-Adobe-3.0
...Document prolog of including application...
/x /lineto load def                    % Application defines x to be lineto
...More of document prolog and setup...
%%BeginDocument: GRAPHIC.EPS
...Document prolog and setup for EPS file...
/proc1 {                               % Enter deferred execution mode
  /x exch def
  x 4 moveto
  } bind def                           % x associated with lineto after bind
4 proc1                                % Execute proc1 and cause error
...Rest of EPS file...
%%EndDocument
...Rest of including application document...
```

In the following example, the EPS file *correctly* initializes the variable x before defining the procedure proc1:

```
%!PS-Adobe-3.0
...Document prolog of including application...
/x /lineto load def                 % Application defines x to be lineto
...More of document prolog and setup...
%%BeginDocument: GRAPHIC.EPS
...Document prolog and setup for EPS file...
/x 0 def                            % Initialize variables before defining procs
/proc1 {
  /x exch def
  x 4 moveto
} bind def
4 proc1                             % Execute Proc1
...Rest of EPS file...
%%EndDocument
...Rest of including application document...
```

H.2.8   Ensuring Portability

Although using outside resources, such as fonts, patterns, files, and procsets, is allowed in an EPS file, the most portable files are those that are self-contained and do not rely on outside resources. For example, if an EPS file requires an encoding other than the default encoding for a font, then the EPS file should perform the re-encoding.

EPS files must never rely on procedures that are defined in application- or driver-provided prologs, such as procedures defined in the Apple LaserPrep file. Such definitions might or might not be present, depending on the actions of the enclosing program or previous jobs.

Because EPS files should be portable across heterogenous environments, 7-bit ASCII is the recommended format for data in EPS files. Although binary data is allowed, use caution when producing data that is expected to be portable. The use of binary data may make it impossible to print on some printers across some communication channels. Binary data that has special meaning, such as "flow control" or "marking the end of a file," can cause file transmission problems in certain communications environments. For example, the control-D character is used as an end-of-file indicator in serial and parallel communications channels. Because this character terminates the job in serial and parallel environments, it is not prudent to produce an EPS file with this character in it.

See Appendix D for guidelines about how to take advantage of language extensions and Level 2 features while maintaining compatibility with Level 1 PostScript interpreters.

H.2.9 Miscellaneous Constraints

EPS files must not have lines of ASCII text that exceed 255 characters, excluding line-termination characters.

Lines must be terminated with one of the following combinations of characters: CR, LF, CR LF, or LF CR.

CR is the carriage return character and LF is the line feed character (decimal ASCII 13 and 10, respectively).

H.3 Guidelines for Importing EPS Files

This section contains guidelines that should be followed when creating an application that imports EPS files. The first part discusses displaying an EPS file; the second covers producing the PostScript language code for the printer.

This section contains several PostScript language code fragments. A complete code example that implements all of these segments is in section H.7, "EPS Example."

H.3.1 Displaying an EPS File

There are several techniques for including an EPS file in a document. The following scenario is typical:

1. When the user imports an EPS file, the application prompts the user to select the EPS file to be imported.

2. The application opens the selected file and parses it for useful information. If either of the two required header comments is missing, the application should alert the user that the file is not a conforming EPS file and abort the import.

   The DSC elementary type (atend) may be used to defer bounding box data to the end of the EPS file. This means an application may need to parse through the %%Trailer comments to obtain the bounding box data.

3. If the version and bounding box comments are found, the application should prompt the user to place the EPS file. It should then display the screen preview. If no preview is provided with the EPS file, the application must provide a representation of the EPS file.

If the application must create its own representation, a gray box matching the extent of the bounding box with some information in it suffices. The information should at least include the title of the EPS file. This can be obtained from the DSC header comment: %%Title:. Other information, such as %%Creator: and %%CreationDate:, may also be displayed.

The bounding box comment can be used to help determine scaling factors and the proportions of the illustration. The including application should enable the user to specify a "placement box" to display the screen preview or the application-supplied representation of the screen preview if there is not a preview present in the EPS file.

The bounding box can be used to calculate a ratio that the application can use if the user wants to maintain original proportions while specifying a placement box. Alternately, the application may display the preview full size, and then allow the user to size and place the graphic as desired. Regardless of the method used to display the preview initially, the user should have the option of maintaining the original proportions supplied by the bounding box or distorting the proportions of the EPS graphic.

H.3.2 Producing a Composite PostScript Language Program

The following guidelines must be considered when producing a composite PostScript language program that includes an imported EPS file.

Use save and restore

An application should encapsulate the imported EPS file in a **save/restore** construct. This allows all VM the EPS file uses to be recovered and the graphics state to be restored.

Redefine showpage

The **showpage** operator is permitted in EPS files because it is present in so many PostScript language files. Therefore, it is reasonable for an EPS file to use the **showpage** operator, although it is not necessary if the EPS file will only be imported into another document. The application importing the EPS file is responsible for redefining **showpage**. **showpage** may be redefined using the following code segment:

```
/showpage { } def
```

Prepare the Graphics State

In preparation for including an EPS file, the including application must set the graphics state as follows: current color to black, line caps to square butt end, line joins to mitered, line width to 1, dash pattern to solid, miter limit to 10, and the current path should be set to an empty path. This state can be explicitly set using the following code segment:

```
0 setgray 0 setlinecap 1 setlinewidth
0 setlinejoin 10 setmiterlimit [ ] 0 setdash newpath
```

Also, if printing directly to a Level 2 printer, the overprint and stroke adjust graphics state parameters must be set to *false*. This can be done by conditionally using the following code segment:

```
false setoverprint false setstrokeadjust
```

Note   *If the application knows that any given parameter of the current graphics state is already in its default state, there is no need to execute the related PostScript language code to reset that parameter.*

Push userdict

It is recommended that an application importing an EPS file use the **begin** operator to push a copy of **userdict** on top of the dictionary stack. Ideally, the imported EPS file should create its own dictionary, but if it does not, and if the application's dictionary does not have enough room for the EPS file's definitions, a **dictfull** error may result when the EPS file makes its definitions. After execution of the EPS file, the application should remove the copy of **userdict** from the dictionary stack by executing the **end** operator.

Clear the Operand Stack

The application importing the EPS file must leave an empty operand stack for the EPS file. It is reasonable for the EPS file to expect that the entire operand stack be available for its own use. If the entire operand stack is needed and is not available, a **stackoverflow** error may occur. Also, if the operand stack is empty, an EPS file that inappropriately executes **clear** will not cause any problems.

Protect the Stacks

An EPS file should leave the operand and dictionary stacks as they were before the EPS file was executed. However, this may not always be the case. So before including the EPS file, the importing application should be sure to count the number of objects on the dictionary and operand stacks. Then, after executing the EPS file, it should make sure the stacks contain the same number of objects as they did before the EPS file was executed. The following code segment shows how to obtain the count of objects on the dictionary and operand stacks:

```
/Dict_Count countdictstack def
/Op_Count count def
```

Bracket EPS File with Comments

The included EPS file must be bracketed by the %%Begin(End)-Document: comments as described in Appendix G.

Handle Special Requirements

If either the %%LanguageLevel: comment or the %%Extensions: comment is present in the header comments section of the EPS file, then at print time the application printing the composite file is responsible for assuring that the printer can handle the specified language extensions. If the application determines that the printer does not have the necessary language features to print the document properly, or if the application cannot determine extension availability, the user should be notified and prompted for the appropriate action. Also, if an application has imported an EPS file that requires extensions, the application's output is now dependent on the *same* extensions. This must be reflected in the document's header comment section.

If any %%DocumentNeededResources: or %%DocumentNeededFonts: comments are present in the header comments section of the EPS file, before printing the document the application must be sure the resources are available. If any of the resource requirements cannot be handled, the user must be notified and prompted for an appropriate action. Such an action may involve having the user locate the resource or allowing the user or document manager to reroute the print job to a printer that has the required resources. Also, if an application has included an EPS file that requires these comments, the application's output is now dependent on the same resources. This must be reflected in the document's header comment section.

Default Coordinate System Transformation

Before including the EPS file in its page description, the importing application must transform the PostScript coordinate system according to the final user placement of the EPS file. The order of the transformation sequence must be:

1. Translate the origin to the new user-chosen origin.

2. Rotate, if the user has rotated the EPS file.

3. Scale, if the user has changed the size.

4. Translate the lower-left corner of the EPS file's bounding box to the user-chosen origin.

Details on transforming the PostScript coordinate system are below. The first example is a simple case in which the user coordinate system matches the default PostScript coordinate system. The second example is a general case transformation from application space to the default PostScript coordinate system.

Figure H.3 shows an EPS file and its bounding box superimposed on a target page. The EPS file is shown as it would be drawn if the EPS file were printed without first transforming the PostScript coordinate system. The placement box in the upper-right corner of the page shows where the user chose to place the EPS file.

Figure H.3 *EPS file and placement box*

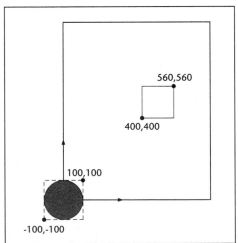

Figure H.4 contains three diagrams that show the steps necessary to properly translate and scale the PostScript coordinate system to achieve the user-chosen placement on the page.

Figure H.4 *Transforming the EPS file*

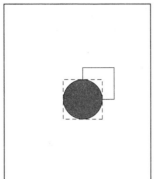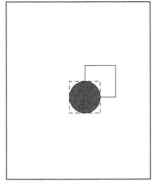

Translate to new origin   *Scale to fit placement box*   *Translate to final position*

Assuming that the bounding box found in the header of the EPS file is %%BoundingBox: -100 -100 100 100, the following PostScript language code fragment properly places the EPS file on the printed page:

```
400 400 translate        % Translate to new origin
.8 .8 scale              % Scale to fit "placement box"
100 100 translate        % –llx –lly translate
```

This transformation code must be inserted into the PostScript stream *ahead* of the EPS code being sent to the printer.

Figures H.3 and H.4 and the corresponding PostScript code fragment assume that the application coordinate system matches the default PostScript coordinate system. The following section discusses a more general coordinate system transformation.

General Coordinate System Transformation

Typically, an application transforms the PostScript coordinate system so the native drawing units of the application space can be used as the operands to the PostScript language operators defining the page. Consider Figure H.5, which represents an arbitrary application coordinate system and a placement box for an EPS file.

Figure H.5 *Application coordinate system plus placement box*

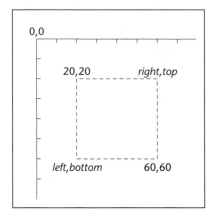

To transform the PostScript coordinate system to match the application coordinate system in Figure H.5, an application could execute the following code fragment:

```
0 792 translate
1 −1 scale
```

This assumes that each unit of application space is equal to one PostScript unit. If one unit in application space were equal to five PostScript units, then the transformation might look like this:

```
0 792 translate
5 −5 scale
```

Assuming that the coordinate system has already been properly translated and scaled from the PostScript coordinate system to the application coordinate system as above, then the following steps can be used to place the EPS file in the user-chosen box:

1. *left bottom* **translate**

2. *((right − left)/(urx − llx)) (top − bottom)/(ury − lly)* **scale**

3. *− (llx) − (lly)* **translate**

where *bottom*, *left*, *top*, and *right* are coordinates of the placement box in application space, and *llx*, *lly*, *urx*, and *ury* are bounding box parameters the EPS file supplies.

As a final example, assume that the PostScript coordinate system has already been transformed to match the application coordinate system, the EPS file bounding box is %%BoundingBox: 20 20 100 100, and the user-chosen placement box is the box shown in Figure H.5 on page 724. Using the formula and steps above, the transformation before executing the included EPS file would be as follows:

```
20 60 translate
.5 −.5 scale
−20 −20 translate
```

Set Up a Clipping Path

The importing application should set up a clipping path around the imported EPS file. This can be accomplished by setting a clipping path that corresponds to the bounding box of the imported EPS file after making the PostScript coordinate system transformations or by allowing the user to optionally supply an arbitrary clipping path for special effects.

Discard the Screen Preview

If an EPS file includes a screen preview in EPSI format, the importing application should discard the preview before sending the document to a printer. Although the EPSI preview is represented by PostScript comments and will not pose a problem when included in the PostScript language file sent to the printer, it takes extra time to transmit the preview.

If the preview in the EPS file is in Macintosh PICT format, do not include the PICT resource in the PostScript language file sent to the printer.

If the preview is in TIFF format or in Microsoft® Windows™ Metafile format, take care to extract the PostScript language code that is to be sent to the printer. See section H.5.2, "Windows Metafile or TIFF," for details.

If the EPS file does not include a screen preview, the entire EPS file can be included in the PostScript language file sent to the printer.

Maintain EPSF Version 2.0 Compatibility

The EPSF version 3.0 requires that an EPS file leave the operand and dictionary stacks as they were before the EPSF was executed. However, this was not explicitly stated in earlier versions of the EPSF format. Therefore, before including the EPS file, be sure to count the number of objects on the dictionary and operand stacks. After executing the EPS file, make sure the stacks contain the same number of objects they did before the EPS file was executed.

Preparation for Including an EPS File

Example H.2 shows procedure BeginEPSF, which an application might use to prepare to include an EPS file in its print stream. Execute the BeginEPSF procedure before the EPS file.

Example H.2

```
/BeginEPSF { %def
  /b4_Inc_state save def            % Save state for cleanup
  /dict_count countdictstack def    % Count objects on dict stack
  /op_count count 1 sub def         % Count objects on operand stack
  userdict begin                    % Push userdict on dict stack
  /showpage { } def                 % Redefine showpage, { } = null proc
  0 setgray 0 setlinecap            % Prepare graphics state
  1 setlinewidth 0 setlinejoin
  10 setmiterlimit [ ] 0 setdash newpath
  /languagelevel where              % If level not equal to 1 then
  {pop languagelevel                % set strokeadjust and
  1 ne                              % overprint to their defaults.
    {false setstrokeadjust false setoverprint
    } if
  } if
} bind def
```

Example H.3 shows procedure EndEPSF, which illustrates how to restore the PostScript state to the way it was before inclusion and execution of the EPS file. Execute the EndEPSF procedure after the EPS file.

Example H.3

```
/EndEPSF { %def
  count op_count sub {pop} repeat        % Clean up stacks
  countdictstack dict_count sub {end} repeat
  b4_Inc_state restore
} bind def
```

Example H.4 illustrates use of the BeginEPSF and EndEPSF procedures.

Example H.4

```
BeginEPSF                        % Prepare for the included EPS file
left bottom translate            % Place the EPS file
angle rotate
Xscale Yscale scale
-llx -lly translate
...Set up a clipping path...
%%BeginDocument: MyEPSFile
...Included EPS file here...
%%EndDocument
EndEPSF                          % Restore state, and cleanup stacks
```

H.4   File Types and Naming

EPS files have become a standard format for importing and exporting PostScript language files among applications in a variety of heterogenous environments. This section contains specific information about file types and naming conventions in a variety of environments.

H.4.1   Apple Macintosh File System

The Macintosh file type for application-created PostScript language files is EPSF. Files of type TEXT are also allowed so users can create EPS files with standard text editors. However, the DSC must still be strictly followed. A file of type EPSF should contain a PICT resource in the resource fork of the file containing a screen preview image of the EPS file. The file name may follow any naming convention as long as the file type is EPSF. If the file type is TEXT, the extensions .epsf, and .epsi should be used for EPS files with Macintosh-specific and device-independent preview images, respectively. See sections H.5, "Device-Specific Screen Preview," and H.6, "Device-Independent Screen Preview."

H.4.2   MS-DOS and PC-DOS File System

The recommended file extension is .EPS. For EPS files that provide an EPSI preview, the recommended extension is .EPI. Because the name and extension may be user-supplied, it is recommended that the application provide a default extension of .EPS or, if the file includes an EPSI preview, the application can provide .EPI as the default extension.

H.4.3　Other File Systems

Although naming is file-system dependent, in general the extension .epsf is the preferred way to name an EPS file. Likewise, .epsi is the preferred extension for the interchange format. In systems where lower-case letters are not recognized or are not significant, all upper-case letters can be used.

H.5　Device-Specific Screen Preview

The EPS file usually has a graphic screen preview so it can be transformed and displayed on a computer screen to aid in page composition before printing. Depending on the capabilities of the importing application, the user may position, scale, clip, or rotate this screen representation of the EPS file. The composing software should keep track of these transformations and reflect them in the PostScript language code that is ultimately sent to the printer.

The exact format of this screen representation is machine-specific. That is, each computing environment may have its own preferred preview image format, which is typically the appropriate screen representation for that environment. Also, a device-independent screen representation called EPSI is specified in section H.6, "Device-Independent Screen Preview." It is recommended that all applications support this format.

H.5.1　Apple Macintosh PICT Resource

A QuickDraw™ representation of the EPS file can be created and stored as a PICT resource in the resource fork of the EPS file. It must be given resource number 256. If the PICT exists, the importing application may use it for screen display. If the *picframe* is transformed to PostScript language coordinates, it should agree with the %%BoundingBox: comment.

Given the size limitations on PICT images, the *picframe* and bounding box may not always agree. If there is a discrepancy, the %%BoundingBox: must always be taken as the "truth," because it accurately describes the area the EPS file will image.

H.5.2 Windows Metafile or TIFF

Either a Microsoft Windows Metafile or a TIFF (tag image file format) section can be included as the screen representation of an EPS file.

The EPS file has a binary header added to the beginning that provides a sort of table of contents to the file. This is necessary because there is not a second "fork" in the file system as there is in the Macintosh file system.

Note   *It is always permissible to have a pure ASCII PostScript language file as an EPS file in the DOS environment.*

The importing application must check the first 4 bytes of the EPS file. If they match the header as shown in Table H.1, the binary header should be expected. If the first two match %!, it should be taken to be an ASCII PostScript language file.

Table H.1   *DOS EPS Binary File Header*

Bytes	Description
0–3	Must be hex C5D0D3C6 (byte 0=C5).
4–7	Byte position in file for start of PostScript language code section.
8–11	Byte length of PostScript language section.
12–15	Byte position in file for start of Metafile screen representation.
16–19	Byte length of Metafile section (*PSize*).
20–23	Byte position of TIFF representation.
24–27	Byte length of TIFF section.
28–29	Checksum of header (XOR of bytes 0–27). If Checksum is FFFF then ignore it.

It is assumed that either the Metafile or the TIFF position and length fields are zero. That is, only one or the other of these two formats is included in the EPS file.

The Metafile must follow the guidelines the Windows specification sets forth. It should not set the *viewport* or *mapping mode*, and it should set the *window origin* and *extent*. The application including the EPS file should scale the picture to fit within the %%BoundingBox: comment specified in the EPS file.

H.6   Device-Independent Screen Preview

This screen preview format is designed to allow EPS files to be used as an interchange format among widely varied systems. The preview section of the file is a bitmap represented as ASCII hexadecimal to be simple and easily transportable. This format is called encapsulated PostScript interchange format, or EPSI.

An EPSI file is truly portable and requires no special code for decompressing or otherwise understanding the bitmap portion, other than the ability to understand hexadecimal notation.

The %%BeginPreview: *width height depth lines* and %%EndPreview comments bracket the preview section of an EPSI file. The *width* and *height* fields provide the number of image samples (pixels) for the preview. The *depth* field provides the number of bits of data used to establish one sample pixel of the preview—typical values are 1, 2, 4, 8. An image that is 100 pixels wide will always have 100 in the *width* field, although the number of bytes of hexadecimal needed to build that line will vary if *depth* varies. The *lines* field tells how many lines of hexadecimal are contained in the preview, so an application that does not care may easily skip them. All arguments are integers.

The bit order of the preview image data is the same as the bit order used by the **image** operator. That is, the preview image is considered to exist in its own coordinate system. The rectangular boundary of the preview image has its lower-left corner at (0,0) and its upper-right corner at (*width, height*). The byte order is fixed and should be (0,0) through (*width* − 1), then (0,1) through (*width* − 1,1), etc.

H.6.1   Guidelines for EPSI Files

The following guidelines are to clarify a few basic assumptions about the EPSI format, which is intended to be extremely simple because its purpose is for interchange. No system should have to do much work to decipher EPSI files. The format is accordingly kept simple and option free.

- The preview section must appear after the header comment section, but before the document prologue definitions. That is, it should immediately follow the %%EndComments: line in the EPS file.

- In the preview section, 0 is white and 1 is black. Arbitrary transfer functions and "flipping" black and white are not supported. Note that in the PostScript language, 0 and 1 have the opposite meaning (0 is black and 1 is white) for the **setgray** operator.

- The preview image can be of any resolution. The size of the image is determined solely by its bounding box, and the preview data should be scaled to fit that rectangle. Thus, the *width* and *height* parameters from the image are *not* its measured dimensions, but rather describe the amount of data supplied for the preview. Only the bounding rectangle describes the dimensions.

- The hexadecimal lines must never exceed 255 bytes in length. In cases where the preview is very wide, the lines must be broken. The line breaks can be made at any even number of hex digits, because the dimensions of the finished preview are established by the *width*, *height*, and *depth* values.

- All non-hexadecimal characters must be ignored when collecting the data for the preview, including tabs, spaces, newlines, percent characters, and other stray ASCII characters. This is analogous to the **readhexstring** operator.

- Each line of hexadecimal begins with a percent character (%). This makes the entire preview section a PostScript language comment to be ignored by the PostScript interpreter. The file can be printed without modification.

- Although the EPSI hex preview can be sent to the printer, to shorten transmission time it is recommended that the preview image be stripped out of the document before transmitting the file to the printer.

- The data for each scan line of the image must be a multiple of 8 bits long. If necessary, pad the end of the scan line data with 0's.

Example H.5 is a sample EPSI format file. Remember there are 8 bits to a byte, and that it requires 2 hexadecimal digits to represent one binary byte. Therefore, the 80-pixel width of the image requires 20 bytes of hexadecimal data, which is $(80 / 8) \times 2$. The PostScript language segment simply draws a box, as can be seen in the last few lines.

Example H.5

```
%!PS-Adobe-3.0 EPSF-3.0
%%BoundingBox: 0 0 80 24
%%Pages: 0
%%Creator: John Smith
%%CreationDate: November 9, 1990
%%EndComments
%%BeginPreview: 80 24 1 24
%FFFFFFFFFFFFFFFFFFFF
%FFFFFFFFFFFFFFFFFFFF
%FFFFFFFFFFFFFFFFFFFF
%FFFFFFFFFFFFFFFFFFFF
%FFFFFFFFFFFFFFFFFFFF
%FFFFFFFFFFFFFFFFFFFF
%FFFFFFFFFFFFFFFFFFFF
%FFFFFFFFFFFFFFFFFFFF
%FF0000000000000000FF
%FF0000000000000000FF
%FF0000000000000000FF
%FF0000000000000000FF
%FF0000000000000000FF
%FF0000000000000000FF
%FF0000000000000000FF
%FF0000000000000000FF
%FFFFFFFFFFFFFFFFFFFF
%FFFFFFFFFFFFFFFFFFFF
%FFFFFFFFFFFFFFFFFFFF
%FFFFFFFFFFFFFFFFFFFF
%FFFFFFFFFFFFFFFFFFFF
%FFFFFFFFFFFFFFFFFFFF
%FFFFFFFFFFFFFFFFFFFF
%FFFFFFFFFFFFFFFFFFFF
%%EndPreview
%%EndProlog
%%Page: "one" 1
4 4 moveto 72 0 rlineto 0 16 rlineto -72 0 rlineto closepath
8 setlinewidth stroke
%%EOF
```

H.7 EPS Example

The following example illustrates the proper use of DSC comments in a typical page description that an application might produce when including an EPS file. For an EPS file that is represented as

```
%!PS-Adobe-3.0 EPSF-3.0
%%BoundingBox: 4 4 608 407
%%Title: (ARTWORK.EPS)
%%CreationDate: (10/17/89) (5:04 PM)
%%EndComments
...PostScript code for illustration..
showpage
%%EOF
```

the including document's page description, including the imported EPS file, would be represented as

```
%!PS-Adobe-3.0
%%BoundingBox: 0 0 612 792
%%Creator: SomeApplication
%%Title: (Smith.Text)
%%CreationDate:  11/9/89 (19:58)
%%Pages: 1
%%DocumentFonts: Times-Roman Times-Italic
%%DocumentNeededFonts: Times-Roman Times-Italic
%%EndComments

%%BeginProlog
/ms {moveto show} bind def
/s /show load def
/SF { %/FontIndex FontSize /FontName SF --
    findfont exch scalefont dup setfont def
} bind def
/sf /setfont load def
/rect { % llx lly w h                      % Used to create a clipping path
    4 2 roll moveto
    1 index 0 rlineto
    0 exch rlineto
    neg 0 rlineto
    closepath
} bind def
```

```
/BeginEPSF { %def                              % Prepare for EPS file
  /b4_Inc_state save def% Save state for cleanup
  /dict_count countdictstack def
  /op_count count 1 sub def                    % Count objects on op stack
  userdict begin                               % Make userdict current dict
  /showpage { } def                            % Redefine showpage to be null
  0 setgray 0 setlinecap
  1 setlinewidth 0 setlinejoin
  10 setmiterlimit [ ] 0 setdash newpath
  /languagelevel where                         % If level not equal to 1 then
    {pop languagelevel                         % set strokeadjust and
    1 ne                                       % overprint to their defaults
    {false setstrokeadjust false setoverprint
    } if
  } if
}bind def
/EndEPSF { %def
  count op_count sub {pop} repeat
  countdictstack dict_count sub {end}  repeat  % Clean up dict stack
  b4_Inc_state restore
} bind def
%%EndProlog

%%BeginSetup
%%IncludeFont: Times-Roman
%%IncludeFont: Times-Italic
%%EndSetup
%%Page: 1 1
%%BeginPageSetup
/pgsave save def
%%EndPageSetup
/F1 40 /Times-Roman  SF
...Set some text with F1...
/F2 40 /Times-Italic SF
...Set some text with F2...
F1 sf
...Set some more text with F1...
F2 sf
...Set some more text with F2...
BeginEPSF
65.2 10 translate                             % Position the EPS file
.80 .80 scale                                 % Scale to desired size
-4 -4 translate                               % Move to lower left of the EPS
4 4 604 403 rect                              % Set up clipping path
clip newpath                                  % Set the clipping path
```

```
%%BeginDocument: ARTWORK.EPS
%!PS-Adobe-3.0 EPSF-3.0
%%BoundingBox:  4 4  608 407
%%Title:  (ARTWORK.EPS)
%%CreationDate:  (10/17/90) (5:04 PM)
%%EndComments
...PostScript code for illustration..
showpage
%%EOF
%%EndDocument

EndEPSF                              % Restore state, cleanup stacks
pgsave restore
showpage
%%EOF
```

H.8   Changes Since Version 2.0

Detailed DSC comment descriptions have been left out of this specification. When developing an application that will support EPS files, the
DSC version 3.0 (see Appendix G) should be used with this specification.

The following conditionally required DSC comments were added to
this specification as of version 3.0:

```
%%Extensions:
%%LanguageLevel:
%%DocumentNeededResources:
%%IncludeResource:
%%Begin(End)Document:
```

H.8.1   Changes Relevant to Applications Producing EPS Files

To help avoid ambiguities, section H.2, "Guidelines for Creating EPS
Files," has been added. This new section has several guidelines for producing EPS files. Following these guidelines will help ensure that an EPS
file can be reliably included in documents without causing any annoy-
ing side effects. Also, these new rules allow applications to easily determine if an EPS file is compatible with version 3.0 of the EPS file format.
The following is an overview of the new guidelines:

- %%Begin(End)Preview: comments must bracket an EPSI preview.

- There is a list of illegal operators that must not be used in an EPS file.

- There is a list of restricted operators. If these operators are used in an EPS file, they must be used in accordance with the guidelines presented in Appendix I.

- The operand and dictionary stacks must be returned to the state that they were in before the EPS file was executed.

- It is strongly recommended that an EPS file make its definitions in its own dictionary or dictionaries.

- An EPS file must not rely on procedures defined outside of the server loop, such as procedures defined in the LaserPrep file.

H.8.2 Changes Relevant to Applications Importing EPS Files

To help clarify the responsibilities of an application including an EPS file, section H.3, "Guidelines for Importing EPS Files," specifies the following new rules:

- The including application must define **showpage** as null.

- The application must prepare the graphics state for the EPS file.

- The application must give the EPS file a clear operand stack.

- The application must surround the included EPS file by the %%Begin(End)Document: comments.

Guidelines for Specific Operators

If not properly used, some PostScript language operators can cause unintended side effects, render a document device dependent, or inhibit post-processing of a document. There are two basic situations where these guidelines apply: regular page descriptions and encapsulated PostScript files.

Regular page descriptions are PostScript language programs produced by a document composition program—for example, a word processor or page-layout program. Typically, the PostScript language program produces several pages, uses a number of fonts and other resources, and activates some printer-specific features such as paper trays or other physical requirements. A regular page description does not normally query the printer, perform calibration functions, cause VM to be permanently modified, or produce color separations.

PostScript language programs that have the notation %!PS Adobe-3.0 as the first line of the file are considered to be regular page descriptions that conform to the document structuring conventions (DSC) version 3.0. See Appendix G for more information about DSC conformance and conventions.

An encapsulated PostScript (EPS) file is a PostScript language program describing a single page that is typically imported by other applications. EPS files must be device independent and must not invoke printer specific operators. EPS files follow specific guidelines and have a particular structure that is further described in Appendix H.

Table I.1 summarizes the use of specific operators in either a regular page description or an EPS file. "No" indicates that the operator should not be used. Alternate suggestions, if any, are listed individually under each operator. "Careful" indicates that the operator can be used, but certain restrictions apply. These restrictions are listed individually under each operator.

Table I.1 *Guidelines summary*

Operator	Regular page description	EPS file
banddevice	No	No
clear	Careful	No
cleardictstack	No	No
copypage	No	No
erasepage	Careful	No
exitserver	No	No
framedevice	No	No
grestoreall	No	No
initclip	Careful	No
initgraphics	Careful	No
initmatrix	Careful	No
nulldevice	Careful	Careful
quit	No	No
renderbands	No	No
setglobal	Careful	No
setgstate	Careful	Careful
sethalftone	Careful	Careful
setmatrix	Careful	Careful
setpagedevice	Careful	No
setscreen	Careful	Careful
setshared	Careful	No
settransfer	Careful	Careful
startjob	No	No
undefinefont	Careful	Careful
statusdict *operators*	Careful	No
userdict *imageable area operators*	Careful	No

banddevice	Obsolete Level 1 device-setup operator. It should never be used in a page description.

clear Disrupts nesting of included documents and EPS files. Instead of using **clear**, it is recommended that the application keep track of which items have been placed on the operand stack and clean up the stack intelligently. If it is necessary to perform the equivalent of a **clear**, a count of the objects on the operand stack can be saved at the beginning of the document:

```
count /numstack exch def
```

When it is time to remove all objects the document has left on the operand stack, the following code should be executed:

```
count numstack sub {pop} repeat
```

cleardictstack Disrupts nesting of included documents and layering of document prologs. Instead of using **cleardictstack**, it is recommended that the application keep track of which dictionaries have been used and clean up the stack intelligently. If it is necessary to perform the equivalent of a **cleardictstack**, a count of the dictionaries present on the stack can be saved at the beginning of the document:

```
/numdict countdictstack def
```

When it is time to remove all dictionaries the document has left on the dictionary stack, the following code should be executed:

```
countdictstack numdict sub {end} repeat
```

copypage Disrupts operations that depend on page independence. **copypage** is primarily used for debugging and should not appear in a page description. For multiple copies of a document, use the **#copies** convention or the **NumCopies** parameter of the **setpagedevice** operator. The **copypage** operator should not be used to simulate forms functionality; use the **execform** operator (see section 4.7, "Forms").

erasepage Disrupts nesting of included documents. Normally, it is unnecessary to erase the page explicitly; a program can assume that the page is already erased. However, if necessary, the interior of the current clipping path can be erased by the following:

```
gsave
clippath
1 setgray fill
grestore
```

exitserver Should be used only by PostScript language programs that perform system administration functions, such as downloading a font program as part of an unencapsulated job to alter initial VM. While executing an unencapsulated job, VM is not protected. Also, VM resources the program consumes remain in use until the printer is power-cycled. If you use **exitserver**, use the %!PS-Adobe-3.0 ExitServer comment (see Appendix G).

framedevice Obsolete Level 1 device-setup operator. It should never be used in a page description.

grestoreall Discards any graphics state previously established by the document and disrupts nesting of included documents. Instead of **grestoreall**, use the **gsave** and **grestore** operators in properly balanced pairs.

initclip Disrupts nesting of included documents. If the current clipping path in the document must be changed, surround any calls to clipping operators with a **save-restore** or **gsave-grestore** pair.

initgraphics Disrupts nesting of included documents. If a document requires its graphics state to be initialized, the graphics state should be set explicitly using operators such as **setgray** and **setlinewidth**, surrounded by a **save-restore** or **gsave-grestore** pair.

initmatrix Disrupts nesting of included documents. If a document requires its CTM to be initialized, modify the current CTM (see **concat**), surrounded by a **save-restore** or **gsave-grestore** pair, so the current CTM is preserved.

nulldevice Installs the "null device" as the current output device. This device produces no physical output, but behaves like a normal device—in other words, the current point is moved, the font machinery is invoked, and so on. If used carefully, it can be helpful when performing color separations, where knock-out control and overprinting are needed. A **gsave-grestore** or **save-restore** pair around this operator is recommended.

quit Terminates the operation of the interpreter; the document will not be printed. Do not use this operator in a page description.

renderbands Obsolete Level 1 device-setup operator. It should never be used in a page description.

setglobal Disrupts page independence and nesting of included documents. In global VM allocation mode, the values of new composite objects are allocated in global VM. Creation and modification of global objects are unaffected by the **save-restore** operators.

setgstate Disrupts page independence and nesting of included documents. Proper use of **setgstate** involves resetting a previously obtained graphics state from the **currentgstate** operator. To assure page independence, the use of **setgstate** must not impose a graphics state defined in another page in the document. That is, it should impose a graphics state that is local to that page only. The following example illustrates a proper use of **setgstate**:

```
/oldstate gstate def
306 392 translate 135 rotate 5 5 scale
10 setlinewidth
...Draw objects in the transformed coordinate system...
oldstate setgstate
...Draw more objects in the original coordinate system...
```

To obtain a similar effect as the one produced above by **setgstate**, it is recommended that a **save-restore** or a **gsave-grestore** pair be used instead.

sethalftone Should not normally appear in a page description; it can cause problems if a post-processor attempts to perform color separations. However, it is appropriate for a systems administrator to use **sethalftone** to establish default screening values for the device.The use of **sethalftone** in a page description is device dependent; the results will vary from device to device.

Do not use **sethalftone** to create patterns; the resulting patterns will vary depending on the resolution of the output device. Also, patterns defined by the **sethalftone** operator cannot be color separated and will only appear on devices that support halftoning. Patterns should be created with the **setpattern** operator or by defining them as characters in a special font.

setmatrix	Should be used with a matrix that was previously obtained using the **currentmatrix** operator or its equivalent. It can be used for drawing objects such as ovals:

```
matrix currentmatrix
rx ry scale
0 0 1 0 360 arc
setmatrix
stroke
```

	This example ensures that the oval is drawn with an even stroke. However, do not use this operator to perform such operations as flipping the coordinate axes. Instead, use the **concat** operator and concatenate to the current transformation matrix. Ordinarily, PostScript programs should modify the CTM (by using the **translate**, **scale**, **rotate**, and **concat** operators) rather than replacing it.
setpagedevice	Can be used to set printer-specific features in a device independent way. **setpagedevice** establishes a new device, implicitly performing the equivalent of an **initgraphics** and an **erasepage**. **setpagedevice** must not be used inside an EPS file, as it will erase the entire page in which the EPS file is included. However, in a document page description it is often useful to use this operator in the document or page setup sections. Documents wanting Level 2 emulation services for Level 1 printers from a document manager should enclose the call to **setpagedevice** with %%Begin(End)Feature: comments (see section G.6.2, "Requirement Body Comments").
	The use of **setpagedevice** at the page level may disrupt any document manager services, such as n-up printing, that rely on this page count or rely on the current page being in a different state than the default. When using **setpagedevice** at the page level, save the current page device and re-establish it at the end of the page.
setscreen	Should not normally appear in a page description; it can cause problems if a post-processor attempts to perform color separations. However, it is appropriate for a systems administrator to use **setscreen** to establish default screening values for the device.The use of **setscreen** in a page description is device dependent; the results will vary from device to device.
	Do not use **setscreen** to create patterns; the resulting patterns will vary depending on the resolution of the output device. Also, patterns defined by the **setscreen** operator cannot be color separated and will

only appear on devices that support halftoning. Patterns should be created with the **setpattern** operator or by defining them as characters in a special font.

setshared Disrupts page independence and nesting of included documents. In global VM allocation mode, the values of new composite objects are allocated in global VM. Creation and modification of global objects are unaffected by the **save-restore** operators.

settransfer Output device colors can be precisely tuned using **settransfer** and wholesale replacement of the current transfer function can remove any calibration already in place. Instead, *modify* the current transfer function. In the following example, a negative transfer function is concatenated to the current transfer function:

[{1 exch sub} /exec load currenttransfer /exec load] cvx settransfer

Even when performed this way, the effect is device dependent.

startjob Should be used only by PostScript language programs that perform system administration functions, such as downloading a font program as part of an unencapsulated job to alter initial VM. While executing an unencapsulated job, VM is not protected. Also, VM resources the program consumes remain in use until the printer is power-cycled. If you use **startjob**, use the %!PS-Adobe-3.0 ExitServer comment (see Appendix G).

undefinefont Improper use of **undefinefont** can disrupt document manager processing of the document. For example, if the document manager were to perform resource optimization on the document and move the font within the document file, the **undefinefont** operator could cause that font to be unavailable for portions of the document. Instead, it is recommended that you use a **save-restore** pair around the font definition.

statusdict operators There are operators defined in the **statusdict** dictionary that are likely to be highly device dependent—that is, some interpreters will have these operators defined and others will not. These operators must not be used in EPS files. Examples of these operators include, but are not limited to: **setsccbatch**, **duplexmode**, **setpapertray**, **tumble**, and **setmargins**. Documents wanting to promote device independence and receive printer rerouting services from a document manager must enclose the calls to these operators with %%Begin(End)Feature: comments (see section G.6.2, "Requirement Body Comments").

userdict operators　　There are operators defined in the **userdict** dictionary that cause an imageable region to be defined. Examples of these operators include, but are not limited to: **a4**, **a4small**, **b5**, **ledger**, **legal**, **letter**, **lettersmall**, and **note**. These operators perform the equivalent of an **initgraphics** and an **erasepage**. These operators must not be used in an EPS file, as they will erase the entire page that includes the EPS file. However, in a document page description, they are valid in the document setup and page setup sections. The use of these operators is device dependent— some interpreters will have these operators defined and others will not. Documents wanting to promote device independence and receive printer rerouting services from a document manager must enclose the calls to these operators with %%Begin(End)Feature: comments (see section G.6.2, "Requirement Body Comments").

Bibliography

Adobe Systems Incorporated, *PostScript Language Tutorial and Cookbook*, Addison-Wesley, 1985. ISBN 0-201-10179-3. Emphasizes examples to illustrate the many capabilities of the PostScript language.

Adobe Systems Incorporated, *PostScript Language Program Design*, Addison-Wesley, 1988. ISBN 0-201-14396-8. For programmers interested in the effective and efficient design of PostScript language programs and printer drivers.

Adobe Systems Incorporated, *The Display PostScript System Reference Manual*, Adobe Systems Incorporated, 1990. Supplementary documentation for programmers writing applications that utilize the Display PostScript system for on-screen text and graphics imaging.

Adobe Systems Incorporated, *Adobe Type 1 Font Format*, Addison-Wesley, 1990. ISBN 0-201-57044-0. Explains the internal organization of a PostScript language Type 1 font program.

Aldus Corporation, *Tag Image File Format Specification*, Revision 5.0, 1988. Aldus Corporation, 411 First Avenue South, Suite 200, Seattle, WA 98104. This is the so-called TIFF standard. Several PostScript language filters use encoding schemes similar to ones included in TIFF. Also, the optional screen preview portion of an EPS file can be in TIFF format.

CCITT, *Blue Book*, volume VII.3, 1988. ISBN 92-61-03611-2. Recommendations T.4 and T.6 are the CCITT standards for Group 3 and Group 4 facsimile encoding. One place from which this document may be purchased is: Global Engineering Documents, P.O. Box 19539, Irvine, CA 92713.

Foley, J. and A. van Dam, *Fundamentals of Interactive Computer Graphics*, Addison-Wesley, 1982. ISBN 0-201-14468-9. Covers many graphics topics including a thorough treatment of the mathematics of Bézier cubics.

Foley, J. et al., *Computer Graphics: Principles and Practice*, Addison-Wesley, 1990. ISBN 0-201-12110-7.

Hunt, R., *The Reproduction of Colour in Photography, Printing, and Television*, Fountain Press, 1987. ISBN 0-85242-356-X. A comprehensive general reference on color reproduction; includes an introduction to the CIE system.

IEEE, *Standard 754-1985 for Binary Floating-Point Arithmetic*, Institute of Electrical and Electronic Engineers, Inc., 1985. IEEE, 345 East 47th Street, New York, NY 10017.

Joint Photographic Experts Group (JPEG), "Revision 8 of the JPEG Technical Specification," ISO/IEC JTC1/SC2/WG8, CCITT SGVIII, August 14, 1990. Defines a set of still picture gray-scale and color image data compression algorithms.

Newman, W. and R. Sproull, *Principles of Interactive Computer Graphics*, McGraw-Hill, 1979. ISBN 0-07-046338-7. A wide range of topics; the chapters on two-dimensional transformations and raster graphics are especially relevant to PostScript.

Smith, A., "Color Gamut Transform Pairs," *Computer Graphics* (ACM SIGGRAPH), Volume 12, number 3, August 1978. Explanation of color conversions between RGB, HSB, and gray levels. In this article, HSB is referred as hue-saturation-value, with conversions performed according to the "hexcone" model.

Wyszecki, G. and W. Styles, *Color Science: Concepts and Methods, Quantitative Data and Formulae*, John Wiley and Sons, 1982. ISBN 0-471-02106-7. A detailed reference on color theory.

Wallace, G., "Overview of the JPEG (ISO/CCITT) Still Image Compression Standard," presented at the 1990 SPIE/SPSE Symposium on Electronic Imaging Science & Technologies, February, 1990, Santa Clara, CA.

Warnock, J. and D. Wyatt, "A Device Independent Graphics Imaging Model for Use with Raster Devices," *Computer Graphics* (ACM SIGGRAPH), Volume 16, Number 3, July 1982. Technical background for the imaging model used in the PostScript language.

Index

Symbol 595
  character set 604–605
  encoding vector 606
synchronization
  context 328–331
syntax 25–33
syntaxerror 530
system name encodings 115–116,
  607–610
system name indexes 109, 115, 332–333
system parameters 516, 571–579
systemdict 41, 63–64, **531**
  dictionary stack and 44
  operators and 42
SystemParamsPassword 573, 575, 576
  changing 576

T

tab character 26
tag image file format (TIFF)
  EPS files and 729
  LZW filters and 132
targets
  data 81, 122–125
terminating context execution 328
text setting
  basic 258–260
threshold arrays 316–318
Thresholds
  type 3 halftone dictionary and 318
  type 4 halftone dictionary and 319
thumbnail printing. *See n-up printing*
TIFF. *See tag image file format*
tiling 200
TilingType
  pattern dictionary and 202
timeout 531
  error initiation and 99
Times 592
%%Title: 646
token 53, 72, **532**
token type character 106
token(s) 26
  binary 106–111
  string 109
%%Trailer 657
  parsing and 631
trailer pages 615
TranScript 19
transfer functions 149, 293, 307–309,
  516–517
TransferFunction
  type 1 halftone dictionary and 315

type 3 halftone dictionary and 318
transform 533
TransformPQR 297, 300–301
transformation matrix 152
transformations 150–157
  coordinate system 722–725
TransformedChar 341–342
transforming CIE-based color to device
  color 294–302
translate 151–152, 156, **533**
  image mapping and 218
  user path cache and 170
true 54, **533**
truncate 51, **534**
Tumble 235–236
type 55, **534**
  mark objects and 43
Type 0 fonts 265–266, 285–291
  dictionary entries specific to 286
Type 1 fonts 265–268
  dictionary entries specific to 267–268
Type 3 fonts 265–267, 278–283
type operators 55, 350
typecheck 535
  user paths and 166

U

uappend 171, **535**
  encoded number strings and 119
ucache 164, **536**
  user path cache and 169
ucachestatus 536, 577
ueofill 170, **537**
  encoded number strings and 119
ufill 164–165, 170, **537**
  encoded number strings and 119
  garbage collection and 62
uncolored patterns 208–210
Uncompressed
  CCITT fax filters and 135
undef 53, **537**
  garbage collection and 62–63
undefined 538
undefinedfilename 538
undefinedresource 538
undefinedresult 538
undefinefont 539
  font dictionaries and 265
  guidelines for 743
UndefineResource
  category implementation dictionary
  and 94
undefineresource 86, **539**

resource categories and 89
undefineuserobject 66, **540**
undercolor removal 305, 518
  graphics state and 149
underlays 620
UnderlinePosition 268
UnderlineThickness 268
unencapsulated job 69–70
UniqueID 267, 284–285
  *See also **XUID***
unlimited access 36
unmatchedmark 540
unregistered 540
upath 171, **541**
user name indexes 109, 115, 332–334
user names
  encoded 332–334
UserObjects 66, **542**
user objects 66–67
user parameters 518–519, 571–579
user path cache 169–170, 517
user path operators 170–171
user paths 164–172
  cache parameters 517, 572–574, 577
  constructing 165–167
  encoded 167–169, 171
  garbage collection and 62
user space 150–152
  default 151
user-defined dictionaries 63–66
user-defined fonts 265
userdict 41, 63–64, **541**
  creating contexts and 327
  dictionary stack and 44
  EPS files and 720
  typical limits in Level 1 568
userdict operators
  guidelines for 744
usertime 542
ustroke 170, **543**
  encoded number strings and 119
ustrokepath 171, **544**

V

value, defined 40
variable-pitch fonts, defined 264
variables
  initializing 716–717
%%Version: 647
version 268, **544**
view clipping 334–336
viewclip 336, **544**
viewclippath 336, **545**

virtual memory (VM) 56–57
    altering initial 69–71
    global 58–59
    local 58–59
    typical limits in Level 1 for 568–569
    usage 569–570
    user parameters and 578–579
virtual memory operators 351
VM allocation mode 58
VMerror 546
    implementation limits and 565
%%VMlocation: 670
VMReclaim 573, 579
vmreclaim 546–547, 579
vmstatus 547, 579
VMThreshold 573, 579
%%VMusage: 670–671
VSamples
    DCTEncode dictionary and 139

W

wait 328–330, **548**
wcheck 55, **548**
Weight 268–269
where 53, **549**
    conditional emulation and 589
    operator objects and 42
WhitePoint 188–190, 192, 297, 299
    gamut mapping and 295
white space characters 26–27
    names and 30
Width
    image dictionary and 219
    type 3 halftone dictionary and 317
    type 4 halftone dictionary and 319
widthshow 549
    character positioning and 264
wildcard file names. *See **filenameforall***
window devices 231
window systems
    graphics and 334–339
Windows Metafile
    EPS files and 729
WMode 266, 273
    composite fonts and 290
write 72, **550**
    end-of-line translation and 74
    filtered files and 81
writehexstring 72, **550**
writeobject 551
writestring 72, **551**
    end-of-line translation and 74
    filtered files and 81
wtranslation 337, **551**

X

xcheck 55, **552**
xor 54, **552**
xshow **552**
    character positioning and 264
    encoded number strings and 119
XStep
    pattern dictionary and 203
XUID 267, 284–285
    form dictionary and 174
    pattern dictionary and 202
    *See also **UniqueID***
xyshow **553**
    character positioning and 264
    encoded number strings and 119

Y Z

Yellow
    Separation color space and 198
    type 5 halftone dictionary and 318
yield 328, **553**
yshow **553**
    character positioning and 264
    encoded number strings and 119
YStep
    pattern dictionary and 203
YUV to RGB conversion 139–140

Colophon

This book was produced on Sun-3™, Macintosh, and NeXT™ computers using FrameMaker®, Adobe Illustrator®, and other application software packages that support the PostScript language and Type 1 fonts. Proof copies were printed on a DEC PrintServer 20 PostScript laser printer. Camera-ready film masters were produced on a high-resolution PostScript imagesetter.

The type used is from the ITC Stone family. Heads are set in ITC Stone Sans Semibold and the body text is set in 9 on 12 point ITC Stone Serif, ITC Stone Serif Italic, and ITC Stone Sans Semibold.

Authors—Ed Taft, Jeff Walden

Key Contributors—Rob Babcock, Doug Brotz, Matt Foley, Linda Gass, Ron Gentile, Peter Hibbard, Jim King, Ken Lent, Deborah MacKay, Carl Orthlieb, Paul Rovner, Mike Schuster, Scott Seltz, Andy Shore, John Warnock

Editing—Jeff Walden, Paul Engstrom

Index—Ira Kleinberg

Illustrations—Carl Yoshihara, Wendy Bell, Dayna Porterfield

Book and Cover Design—Nancy Winters

Book Production—Lisa Kelly, Minette Norman, Dayna Porterfield

Reviewers—Ken Anderson, Rob Babcock, Ned Batchelder, Perry Caro, Holly Cochran, David Gelphman, Deborah MacKay, Jim Sandman, Norin Saxe, Lydia Stang, Ed Taft, and numerous others at Adobe Systems and elsewhere.

Publication Management—Eve Lynes, Joan Delfino

Project Management—Rob Babcock